CONTENTS OF THE EDITION

Americans on Fiction, 1776–1900

1776–1900

Volume 2

AMERICANS ON FICTION, 1776–1900

Volume 2

Edited by

Peter Rawlings

MUNDUS
INTELLECTUALIS

LONDON
PICKERING & CHATTO
2002

Published by Pickering & Chatto (Publishers) Limited
21 Bloomsbury Way, London, WC1A 2TH

2252 Ridge Road, Brookfield, Vermont 05036, USA

www.pickeringchatto.com

All rights reserved.
No part of this publication may be reproduced,
stored in a retrieval system, or transmitted in any form or by any means,
electronic, mechanical, photocopying, recording, or otherwise
without prior permission of the publisher.

Copyright © Pickering & Chatto (Publishers) Limited 2002

BRITISH LIBRARY CATALOGUING IN PUBLICATION DATA

Americans on fiction
  1.   American fiction - 19th century – History and criticism
  2.   European fiction - 19th century – History and criticism
  3.   Criticism - United States
  I. Rawlings, Peter
  813.3'09

ISBN 1851967559

LIBRARY OF CONGRESS CATALOGING-IN-PUBLICATION DATA

Americans on fiction, 1776–1900/ edited by Peter Rawlings.
    p. cm
  ISBN 1-85196-755-9 (set : alk paper)
  1. American Fiction--History and criticism. 2. Fiction--History and criticism--Theory, etc. I.
Rawlings, Peter

PR371 .A55 2002
  813.009–dc21

2001045931

This publication is printed on acid-free paper that conforms to
the American National Standard for Permanence of Paper in Printed Library Materials.

Typeset by
Peter Rawlings

Printed and bound in Great Britain by
Antony Rowe Ltd., Chippenham

CONTENTS

INTRODUCTION:
THE GREAT AMERICAN NOVEL

"The Civil War," as Henry James was one of the first to observe in his book on *Hawthorne* (1879), "marks an era in the history of the American Mind."

> It introduced into the national consciousness a certain sense of proportion and relation, of the world being a more complicated place than it had hitherto seemed, the future more treacherous, success more difficult.

There is no doubt that forebodings and anticipations of war, and senses of its consequences during and after the period 1861-1865, inform much of the material in this volume. Since F. O. Matthiessen's *American Renaissance: Art and Expression in the Age of Emerson and Whitman* (1941) and before, the mid-nineteenth century has been regarded as the period when American literature came to maturity. It saw the advent and development of Matthiessen's pivotal writers (all male): Poe, Emerson, Thoreau, Hawthorne, Melville, and Whitman. Matthiessen's sense of American literary history, however, subordinates or ignores many earlier authors, such as Charles Brockden Brown or Catharine Maria Sedgwick, some of whom figure in the first volume of this edition. It also overlooks the extent to which an atmosphere of war, and the events precipitating it, was crucial to the development of a southern and southwestern literary consciousness.

In "An Inquiry into the Present State of Southern Literature" (No. 13), an anonymous contributor to the *Southern Literary Messenger* returns to the question of American literary independence which had beset writers since 1776. The terms of the polemic have changed, however, as the issue is refracted through a southern lens and related to the institution of slavery. Here, the South, vaunting its peculiarity and distinctiveness (conditions continuously sought in some quarters by American literature at large) contests the literary supremacy of New England and the East in ways analogous to earlier and persisting conflicts between America and England:

> There has been no question so often asked, and so variously answered of late years as this, "shall the South have a literature of her own?" It is one of vital importance to her social and political interests, a question on which hangs the integrity of her peculiar institutions, and on which is based the preservation of her social and political independence.

The "object" of the "literature which the South has adopted as her own," it is argued, is "to aim a blow at the existence of the very social fabric which supports it" (98); for this writer, "Massachusetts," five years after Harriet Beecher Stowe's *Uncle*

Tom's Cabin began to make its almost inestimable impact, is the "nursery of poisonous literature" (p. 99).

Similarly, in the same organ, "W. R. A." (No. 16) pleads for the "establishment of a Southern literature, standing secure and independent on its own pedestal," and "lighting up the threshold of its temple with the refulgent beams of its self-illumination" (p. 112). The South recognizes "African Slavery" as "a great social, moral and political blessing," and

> as literature has been the most powerful weapon which the enemies of African slavery have used in their attacks, so, also, to literature must we look for the maintenance of our position, and our justification before the world. (p. 113)

"With the great moral force of literature," the "unholy citadel erected by slander, fanaticism, and malignity" can be "overturned"; but the widespread emphasis on Harriet Beecher Stowe and her literary emasculation of the South, makes her and the cultural hegemony of the North the principal targets in an arena that has empowered both the novel and, to an extent, women writers of it:

> The success of *Uncle Tom's Cabin*, is an evidence of the manner in which our enemies are employing literature for our overthrow. Is that effusion, in which a woman, instigated by the devil, sows the seed of future strife between the two sections of her country, likely to be the last? No. The literary workshops of the North are even now resounding with the noisy and fanatical labours of those who, with Mrs. Stowe as their model, are forging calumnies, and hammering falsehood into the semblance of truth. Southern men, learn that the arms with which they assail you are the best for your defence. (p. 114)

Such acrimonies were far from confined to the South of course. A contributor to *Putnam's Monthly Magazine*, in 1857 (No. 18), devotes a good deal of his energy to impugning the South's potential for producing any kind of literature given its prevailing illiteracy and general cultural barbarism. *Uncle Tom's Cabin* is declared "the first proper novel in American literature," and one that "strikes" a "key-note that will not cease" (p. 140).

No limits were imposed on the degree of incontinence deployed at the rhetorical level against Mrs. Stowe. George Frederick Holmes tackles her *Facts for the People* (No. 9) despite professing little "predilection for the disgusting office of castigating such offences here, and rebuking the incendiary publication of a woman" once "an obscure Yankee school-mistress," and now "eaten up with fanaticism, festering with the malignant virus of abolitionism" (p. 66). The gender inflections are intense in southern assaults on Stowe as fears surface about the increasing ability of women to leave the quarantined area of domestic fiction and convert the pen into a sword. "Are scenes of license and impurity," enquires the writer, "and ideas of loathsome depravity and habitual prostitution to be made the cherished topics of the female pen, and the familiar staple of domestic consideration or promiscuous conversation? (p.68). John S. Hart's *Female Prose Writers of America*, which appeared in 1857 (Nos. 19-22)—and where attention is drawn to the "unprecedented success" of *Uncle Tom's Cabin*, with sales that "exceeded a million copies" in less than nine months—is evidence not of the arrival of women writers of course, but of their ascendance and re-evaluation (p. 147).

William Dean Howells observed, in his review (No. 31) of John W. De Forest's *Miss Ravenel's Conversion from Secession to Loyalty* (one of the few Civil War novels to have much posterity), that:

> Our war has not only left us the burden of a tremendous national debt, but has laid upon our literature a charge under which it has hitherto staggered very lamely. Every author who deals in fiction feels it to be his duty to contribute towards the payment of the accumulated interest in the events of the war, by relating his work to them.

"The heroes of young-lady writers in the magazines," he goes on, "have been everywhere fighting the late campaigns over, again, as young ladies would have fought them" (p. 249), whereas De Forest "is the first to treat the war really and artistically." Henry James, who also reviewed *Miss Ravenel's Conversion* (No. 32), though less positively, numbered three Civil War stories among his first in the late 1860's and used them, in line with the strategy of Howells's review, to attack what he saw as the feminine proclivities of the genre, and to undermine the writing of women. Neither man—unlike Poe, given his pieces on Catharine Maria Sedgwick and Caroline M. Kirkland, or John S. Hart—would have been out of sympathy with views expressed by Orestes A. Brownson (No. 29), towards the end of the war, in "Literature, Love, and Marriage." "We have any quantity of fictitious literature," avers Brownson, "fictitious in all senses of the term, produced chiefly by women, and therefore weak, sentimental, preventing instead of aiding high national culture" (p.220). James's praise for George Eliot's "masculine intellect," in his review of *Middlemarch* (No. 39), becomes more comprehensible in this context. John Weiss, writing in 1862 (No. 26), had higher expectations for the literary consequences of the war; although in surveying two-thousand years of warfare and its relation to literature, his main project was that of locating the Civil War in a heroic historical paradigm. "War," he believed should be "the last resort of truly noble and popular ideas," but once upon a nation, it "quickens the germs of Art, Beauty and Knowledge": "the pen, thus tempered to a sword, becomes a pen again, but flows with more iron than before" (p. 192).

John W. De Forest own major contribution to nineteenth-century letters was the phrase "great American novel" in an article with that title (No. 36) published in 1868. De Forest's focus is on the question of whether America is now ready to produce such a novel, hitherto "seldom attempted," a "picture of the ordinary emotions and manners of American existence." Moving into a mode of retrospective inventory that was to intensify as Americans developed a sense of their fiction's backward reach, De Forest concludes that Washington Irving was "too cautious to make the trial"; Cooper, on the other hand, "devoted himself to Indians, of whom he knew next to nothing, and to backwoodsman and sailors, whom he idealized" (p. 275). "There come to us from the deserts of the past" names that seem to sound like "Paulding," "Brown," Kennedy"—and we catch nothing further. These are ghosts, and they wrote about ghosts, and the ghosts have vanished utterly.

As for William Gilmore Simms, "another of these shadowy mediums, still living if we are not misinformed," the "best and the worst thing to be said is this—that he is nearly as good as Cooper, and deserves fame nearly as much" (p. 275). An anonymous contributor to the *International Magazine* (No. 2), who regarded Cooper as "both the Horace Vernet and the Claude Lorraine of novelists," would certainly have contested De Forest's relegation of these writers to the realms of the quaint and the rebarbative (p. 2). De Forest continues his campaign, however, with Hawthorne. In a perception that takes us back to views expressed by James Russell Lowell at the end of Volume 1 (pp. xix-xx, 380-394), De Forest writes of Nathaniel Hawthorne that "he staggered under the load of the American novel"; his "romances" are "full of acute spiritual analysis, of the light of other worlds, but also characterized by only a vague consciousness of this life." Hawthorne's romances, like those of his predecessors, are tried at the bar of De Forest's sense of the canons of realism, for which he is an initiating avatar (in theory, rather than in practice):

> Such personages as Hawthorne creates belong to the wide realm of art rather than to our nationality. They are probably natives of the furthest mountains of Cathay or of the moon as of the United States of America. They are what Yankees might come to be who should shut themselves up to meditate in old manses.

"They have no sympathy with this eager and laborious people," declares De Forest, which takes so many newspapers,"

> builds so many railroads, does the most business on a given capital, wages the biggest war in proportion to its population, believes in the physically impossible and does some of it. Hawthorne's characters cannot talk. Certainly not in the style of this western world; rather in the language of men who never expressed themselves but on paper, and paper in dreams. (p. 276)

After berating Hawthorne for filling his fiction with "New Englanders," and "of the queerest," De Forest offers *Uncle Tom's Cabin* as "the nearest approach to the desired phenomenon" of the "great American novel." Notwithstanding its "faulty plot," where a "black man is painted whiter than the angels," it "was a picture of American life, drawn with a few strong and passionate strokes, not filled in thoroughly, but still a portrait"; but in its successor, *Dred*, Stowe "shrank" once more "into her native shell of New England" (p. 276). De Forest proceeds, in one of the first canons of American fiction, to survey the fiction of James Russell Lowell, Oliver Wendell Holmes, and others, dismissing them all, in general, as "New England novels" or "localisms." Like many commentators on the causes of what they saw as America's negligible fiction, and with his own comparative failure as a novelist no doubt in mind, De Forest allocates at least some of the blame to the absence of an international copyright agreement, and to the ease with which foreign (mostly English) literature can be imported and sold more cheaply than American. But "so much for the artist," he continues, "now for the sitter":

Ask a portrait-painter if he can make a good likeness of a baby, and he will tell you that the features are not sufficiently marked nor the expression sufficiently personal. Is there not the same difficulty in limning this continental infant of American society, who is changing every year not only in physical attributes, but in the characteristics of the soul? (pp. 279-280)

"Well, what are our immediate chances for a 'great American novel?'" he asks, finally:

We fear that the wonder will not soon be wrought unless more talent can be enlisted in the work, and we are sure that this sufficient talent can hardly be obtained without the encouragement of an international copy right. And, even then, is it time? (p. 280)

At least two writers, Thomas Sergeant Perry (No. 38) and Henry T. Tuckerman (No. 5), have quite different views on American novels and Hawthorne, respectively, from those held by John W. De Forest.

The "outcry for the 'Great American Novel,'" insists Perry, so far from being of any assistance to our fellow-countryman who is trying to win fame by writing fiction," has "rather stood in his way by setting up before him a false aim for his art, and by giving the reader a defective standard by which to judge his art." What matters for Perry is precisely that element of Hawthorne's romances that De Forest thought quaint, irrelevant, and un-American:

There is an American nature, but then there is a human nature underlying it, and to that the novel must be true before anything else. That is what is of importance; it is that alone which makes the novel great, which causes it to be read in all times and in all countries. (p. 291)

What Perry fears, and what he identifies in a range of novels he considers, is "the simple rehearsal of the barrenest external phenomena of life and nature in this country" (pp. 291-292). Taking aim more directly at De Forest, Perry illustrates his point by arguing that "in his writings we find a great deal that is American, but not so much that goes to the making of a really great novel" (p. 293); the "idealizing novelist will be the real novelist," for "all truth does not lie in facts" (p. 300).

Henry T. Tuckerman finds himself able to take Hawthorne more on his own terms than can De Forest, and his elegant and precise account of the salient features of his style, written in the very year of *The Scarlet Letter's* publication (1851), anticipates the approach of much subsequent Hawthorne criticism. Hawthorne's "appeal is to consciousness," he "shadows forth," "hints," "makes signs," and "whispers" (p. 37). Hawthorne, far from confining himself to barren external phenomena, is a "prose-poet" bringing together "scattered beauties." Tuckerman—in an age of dawning realism (the word "realism," in relation to art, is very much an innovation of the 1850's), and as a sign of the greater abstraction of much American critical writing after 1850—makes a significant distinction between "melodramatic" and "meditative" narrative literature:

the former is in a great degree mechanical, and deals chiefly with incidents and adventure; a few types of character, and approved scenic material and what are called effective situations, make up the story; the other species, on the contrary, is modelled on no external pattern, but seems evolved from the author's mind.

With the latter, "we feel the glow of individual consciousness even in the most technical description." This division, as it mutates into anguished debates about the competing merits of "realism" and "idealism," "realism" and "naturalism," moral and immoral fiction and, for many, the question of whether technically self-conscious writers who produce analytical novels are, by default, pernicious, is to dominate discussion of American fiction henceforth. Within its interstices, "consciousness" (a concept hardly in retreat now in the realms of fiction)—in particular, disputes about the extent to which the novel can, does, or should, be seen as a vehicle for its presentation and registration—is to have an interminable career. Henry James and William Dean Howells, *bêtes noires* to be in the rancorous discussions ahead, are adumbrated in the bifurcation in American writing that Tuckerman begins to make. There is a contrast, he believes, between that "glow, vivacity and rapidity of action," as a function of the "restless temperament and enterprising life of the nation," favoured by American critics at large, and quieter styles that yet "may envelop the rarest energy of thought and depth of insight as well as earnestness of feeling." In a memorable phrase, Tuckerman suggests that proposed in Hawthorne "is not external but moral excitement," and that this is one of his most "felicitous merits" (p. 45). Ten years later, E. P. Whipple's essay on Hawthorne (No. 24), with its carping over "sombre . . . stories lacking in vigor" (p. 161), indicates just how discerning Tuckerman's essay is. It took nearly twenty years for a piece of a similar calibre to appear, Eugene Benson's "Poe and Hawthorne" (No. 35). "Poe and Hawthorne," Benson announces at the outset of his essay, "are two brilliant exceptions in American literature." If greatness lies in the exceptional, however, then the "great American novel" debate had been meaningless from the beginning. The most humorous attack on the exceptional in this volume, and a sign, if one were needed, that novelists neglecting moral imperatives as conventionally conceived are in for trouble, is the review of Melville's *Pierre* (No. 10).

This volume concludes with two essays by George Parsons Lathrop (Nos. 41 & 42), and one by Thomas Sergeant Perry on Ivan Turgenev (No. 43). The approach of Lathrop and Perry to formal aspects of novel construction, and the vocabulary and concepts they employ, have continued, like Tuckerman's, to exercise a powerful grip on contemporary novel criticism, albeit through the conduit of Henry James. For Lathrop, the quality of fiction is no longer separable from its technical elements; and narrowly moral, or didactic, concerns are certainly best left on one side during such evaluations. But in a line that stretches back to Tuckerman, and on to James, the New Critics, Lionel Trilling and beyond, Lathrop's preoccupation is with effective representations of consciousness, a preoccupation involving, in wider senses, immense moral dimensions. For these critics and novelists, the concern with American fiction is parochial in the extreme: what matters is the art and science of novel writing, and whether the novelist or critic is capable of giving an account of her or himself. On the evidence of the essays of Tuckerman, Henry James, Lathrop,

Perry, Howells, and others, however, this, paradoxically, is the terrain of great American fiction and its legacy.

Lathrop, in a position taken up ten years later by James in "The Art of Fiction" (1884), laments the failure of "criticism" to keep "pace with the novel"; missing, in the plethora of magazine scribble on fiction, is the "strong, central light of systematic meditation" (p. 314). The literary history that he goes on to sketch in "Growth of the Novel" situates drama and the theatre at the forefront of the novel's generic antecedents. In this respect, Lathrop can be seen as anticipating a good many of James's mature views on the organizing possibilities of the "centre of consciousness"; indeed, James might well have taken much of the narrative theory for which he is credited, involving a shifting and ambivalent advocating of restricted points-of-view and an attenuation of the narrative voice, directly from Lathrop's essays. The early currency of some of these ideas, however, if not the terms that Lathrop develops and James's subsequent adoptions of them, is evident from James's own assessment of *Middlemarch* (No. 39); his view being that the novel is close to *Romola*, technically, which "sins by excess of analysis; there is too much description and too little drama" (p. 301). Similarly, "philosophical parentheses" and the "interspersed epigram," Lathrop believed, fastened "a clog on the dramatic movement" of stories. The novelist "may fulfill to some extent the functions of a chorus; but he should be very cautious in the fulfilment" (p. 340). Fielding's "garrulous chatting . . . withheld from him the possibility of grouping his keen observations firmly about some centre of steady and assimilative thought" (p. 381). For a "dramatic effect," there had to be a "resolute act of self-renunciation" on the part of the author rather than a visible intervention between "readers and the characters" (p. 319). George Eliot, in *Middlemarch*, tells the reader too much, thus stifling the imagination: "all that can be said about the characters *is* said; but, after all, the result is not so good as if something had been withheld, for our imagination to reach after" (p.320). Pertinent, too, is Perry's assessment of Turgenev's *Rudin* (No. 43)

> Then, too, we ought to observe the life-like way in which the novel is written; we are never granted any side views of the hero which are denied the people in the story; we are deceived or put on guard just as they are; we have to study him just as they do; hence it is that a novel barren of incident, and in a way so clumsily put together, succeeds so well in interesting the reader, who finds his curiosity aroused and his sagacity baffled in a way that is not over-common about the heroes of fiction. (p. 357)

Unlike many post-Jamesian critics, problematically attempting to anchor themselves in James's "Prefaces" to the "New York Edition" of his novels and tales (1907-1909), Lathrop was careful in his assessment of the question of narrative intrusion. His assumptions were organicist in that, for instance, he celebrated the "vital and speaking form which we call the novel" (p. 330). But in anticipating Wayne C. Booth and others, he also proposed that the "retiring attitude of the story-mover does not imply total invisibility . . . but only inofficiousness" (p. 381).

It is clear at the end of this volume, then, that whereas some critics by 1875 still held adamantly to the view that the salvation of American fiction would be in the

evolution of a novel form, however distant the prospect, that could map the minutiae of life in the New World in a distinctive idiom, others regarded this as an irrele-
vance in a world where the coordinates of such questions, like it or not, were being
determined by European, even Parisian, preoccupations with the theory and practice of novel composition. Increasingly, however, especially in the approaches of
Lathrop and others, the signs were that American interventions in such theories,
rather than the Mississippi Valley, or wherever, would be the site of its own identity
in transnational realms of fiction.

NOTE ON THE TEXTS

With few exceptions, the texts made available here have been reproduced in their entirety; any excisions are clearly signalled in the end-notes. In the interests of consistent and uncluttered presentation, spelling has occasionally been modernized and the titles of longer texts italicized. Although the content is identical with that of the first publication of each item, no attempt has been made to reproduce the original layout, and any illustrations have been omitted. Footnotes original to each item have been included as footnotes.

Editorial interventions appear in square brackets, and explanatory notes (and a statement about their function) are listed at the end of each volume. The purpose of any head-notes is to supply information about the writer that may be helpful to the non-specialist reader. Such information only appears once; there is an alphabetical list of contributors for all three volumes at the end of Volume 3 to help readers navigate the head-notes. The aim of the introductions is to highlight some of the material, by no means all, and to suggest ways in which it might be thematized and placed in context. The combined index (at the end of Volume 3) contains the names and titles of every person and text cited or discussed.

1

THE EVENING BOOK

Anonymous

A review of Caroline M. Kirkland's *The Evening Book; or, Fireside Talk on Morals and Manners, with Sketches of Western Life. American Whig Review* (1851).

These sketches and essays of Mrs. Kirkland will add much to a reputation already high. Her style, always rich and sparkling, shines here with remarkable brilliancy. A shrewd observer of characters and manners, this lady has the rare faculty of combining wit and wisdom, and thus, whilst amusing, instructing and refining us. She is, besides, one of the most characteristically national of our writers. Her first work is unrivaled in its delineations of Western life and character. In this she confesses to "an ambition to make a peculiarly American book"; "not that I think American views of manners and morals should be partial or narrow, but because the foreign literature, which furnishes most of the reading of our young people, seems to me likely to inspire them with un-American ideas of society, and even of duty; and it becomes, therefore, especially desirable to refer sometimes to ancient and universal standards—those whose excellence is beyond dispute, though portions of the world have departed from their influence, led away by the incorrect notions of life which prevail in old and corrupt communities."

Mr. Scribner has presented the work in a holiday dress illustrated by beautiful plates from the burin of Burt, on splendid paper, and in elegant type.[1] It will be a great favorite as a present and will, as designed, brighten many a fireside in the coming winter evenings.

JAMES FENIMORE COOPER

Anonymous

International Magazine (1851). In its original form, a daguerreotype of James Fenimore Cooper precedes the article.

The readers of the *International* have in the above engraving from a daguerreotype by Brady, the best portrait ever published of an illustrious countryman of ours, who, as a novelist, take him all in all, is entitled to precedence of every other now living. "With what amazing power," exclaims Balzac in the *Revue de Paris,* "has he painted nature! how all his pages glow with creative fire! Who is there writing English among our contemporaries, if not of him, of whom it can be said that he has a genius of the first order?" And the *Edinburgh Review* says, "The empire of the sea has been conceded to him by acclamation"; that, "in the lonely desert or untrodden prairie, among the savage Indians or scarcely less savage settlers, all equally acknowledge his dominion. Within this circle none dares walk but he." And Christopher North, in the *Noctes*: "He writes like a hero."[2] And beyond the limits of his own country, everywhere, the great critics assign him a place among the foremost of the illustrious authors of the age. In each of the departments of romantic fiction in which he has written, he has had troops of imitators and in not one of them an equal. Writing not from books, but from nature, his descriptions, incidents, and characters, are as fresh as the fields of his triumphs. His Harvey Birch, Leather Stocking, Long Tom Coffin, and other heroes, rise before the mind, each in his clearly defined and peculiar lineaments, as striking original *creations*, as actual persons.[3] His infinitely varied descriptions of the oceans, ships gliding like beings of the air upon its surface, vast solitary wilderness, and indeed all his delineations of nature, are instinct with the breath of poetry; he is both the Horace Vernet and the Claude Lorraine of novelists; and through all his works are sentiments of genuine courtesy and honor, and an unobtrusive and therefore more powerful assertion of natural rights and dignity.[4]

William Cooper, the emigrant ancestor of James Fenimore Cooper, arrived in this country in 1679, and settled at Burlington, New Jersey.[5] He immediately took an active part in public affairs, and his name appears in the list of members of the Colonial Legislature for 1681. In 1687, or subsequent to the establishment of Penn at Philadelphia, he obtained a grant of land opposite the new city, extending several miles along the margin of the Delaware and tributary stream which has since borne the name of Cooper's Creek. The branch of the family to which the novelist belongs removed more than a century since into Pennsylvania, in which state his father was born. He married early, and while a young man established himself at a hamlet in Burlington county, New Jersey, which continues to be known by his name, and afterward in the city of Burlington. Having become possessed of extensive tracts of land on the border of Otsego Lake, in central New York, he began the settlement of his estate there in the autumn of 1785, and in the following spring, erected the first house in Cooperstown. From this time until 1799, Judge Cooper resided alternately at Cooperstown and Burlington, keeping up an establishment at both places. James Fenimore Cooper was born at Burlington on the nineteenth of September, 1789, and in the succeeding year was carried to the new home of his family, of which he is now proprietor.

Judge Cooper being a member of the Congress, which then held its sessions in Philadelphia, his family remained much of the time at Burlington, where our author, when but six years of age, commenced under a private tutor of some eminence his classical education. In 1800 he became an intimate of the family of Rev. Thomas Ellison, Rector of St. Peter's in Albany, who had fitted for the university three of his elder brothers, and on the death of that accomplished teacher was sent to New Haven, where he completed his preparatory studies. He entered Yale College at the beginning of the second term of 1802. Among his classmates were John A. Collier, Judge Cushman, and the late Justice Sutherland of New York, Judge Bissel of Connecticut, Colonel James Gadsden of Florida, and several others who afterwards became eminent in various professions.[6] John C. Calhoun was at the time a resident graduate, and Judge William Jay of Bedford, who had been his room mate at Albany, entered the class below him.[7] The late James A. Hillhouse originally entered the same class with Mr. Cooper; there was very little difference in their ages, both having been in the same month and both being much too young to be thrown into the arena of college life.[8] Hillhouse was judiciously withdrawn for this reason until the succeeding year, leaving Cooper the youngest student at the college; he, however, maintained a respectable position, and in the ancient languages particularly had no superior in his class.

In 1805 he quitted the college, and obtaining a midshipman's warrant, entered the navy. His frank, generous, and daring nature made him a favourite, and admirably fitted him for the service, in which he would unquestionably have obtained the highest honors had he not finally made choice of the ease and quite of the life of a private gentleman. After six years afloat—six years not unprofitably passed, since they gave him that knowledge of maritime affairs which enabled him subsequently, almost without an effort to place himself at the head of all the writers who in any period have attempted the description of the sea—he resigned his office, and on the first day of January, 1811, was married to Miss De Lancey, a sister of the present Bishop of the Diocese of Western New York, and a descendant of one of the oldest and most influential families in America.

Before removing to Cooperstown he resided a short time in Westchester, New York, and here he commenced his career as an author. His first book was *Precaution*. It was undertaken under circumstances purely accidental, and published under great disadvantages. Its success was moderate, though far from contemptible. It is a ludicrous evidence of the value of critical opinion in this country, that *Precaution* was thought to discover so much knowledge of *English* society, as to raise a question whether its alleged author could have written it. More reputation of this sort of knowledge accrued to Mr. Cooper from *Precaution* than from his subsequent real work on England. It was republished in London, and passed for an English novel.

The Spy followed. No one will dispute the success of *The Spy*. It was almost immediately republished in all parts of Europe. The novelty of an American book of this character probably contributed to its great circulation. It is worthy of remark that all our leading periodicals looked coldly upon it; though the country did not. The *North American Review*—ever unwilling to do justice to Mr. Cooper—had a very ill-natured notice of it, professing to place the *New England Tale* far above it![9] In spite of such shallow criticism, however, the book was universally popular. It was decidedly the best American romance then written by an American; not without faults, indeed, but with a fair plot, clearly and strongly drawn characters, and exhibiting great boldness and originality of conception. Its success was perhaps decisive of Mr. Cooper's career, and it gave an extraordinary impulse to literature in the country. More than anything that had before occurred, it roused the people from their feeling of intellectual dependence. The popularity of *The Spy* has been so universal, that there is scarcely a written language into which it is not translated. In 1847 it appeared in *Persian* at Ispalan.

In 1823 appeared *The Pioneers*. This book has passages of masterly description, and is as fresh as a landscape from another world; but it seems to me that it has always had a reputation partly factitious. It is the poorest of the Leather Stocking tales, nor was its success either marked or spontaneous. Still, it was very well received, though it was thought to be a proof that the author was written out. With this book commenced the absurdity of saying Mr. Cooper introduced family traits and family history into his novels. How little of truth there is in this supposition Mr. Cooper has explained in his revised edition, published the present year.

The Pilot succeeded. The success of *The Pilot* was at first a little doubtful in this country; but England gave it a reputation which it still maintains. It is due to Boston to say that its popularity in the United States was first manifested there. I say *due* to Boston, not from considerations of merit in the book, but because for some reason, praise for Mr. Cooper, from New England, has been so rare. The *North America Review* took credit to itself for magnanimity in saying some of his works had been rendered into French, when they were a part of every literature of Europe. America, it is often said, has no original literature. Where can the model of *The Pilot* be found? I know of nothing which could have suggested it but the following fact, which was related to me in a conversation with Mr. Cooper. *The Pirate* had been published a short time before.[10] Talking with the late Charles Wilkes, of New-York—a man of taste and judgment—our author heard extolled the universal knowledge of Scott, and the sea portions of *The Pirate* cited as a proof. He laughed at the idea, as most seamen would, and the discussion ended by his promising to write a sea story which could be read by landsmen, while seamen should feel its truth. *The Pilot* was the fruit of that conversation. It is one of the most remarkable novels of the time, and everywhere obtained instant and high applause.

Lionel Lincoln followed.[11] This was a second attempt to embody history in an American work of fiction. It failed, and perhaps justly; yet it contains one of the nicest delineations of character in Mr. Cooper's works. I know of no instance in which the distinction between a maniac and an idiot is so admirably drawn; the setting was bad, however, and the picture was not examined.

In 1826 came *The Last of the Mohicans*. This book succeeded from the first, and all over Christendom. It has strong parts and weak parts, but it was purely original, and originality always occupies the ground. In this respect it is like *The Pilot*.

After the publication of *The Last of the Mohicans*, Mr. Cooper went to Europe, where his reputation was already well established as one of the greatest writers of romantic fiction which our age, more prolific in men of genius than any other, had produced. The first of his works after he left his native country was *The Prairie*.[12] Its success everywhere was decided and immediate. By the French and English critics it has been deemed the best of his stories of Indian life. It has one leading fault, however, that of introducing any character superior to the family of the squatter. Of this fault Mr. Cooper was himself aware before he finished the work; but as he wrote and printed simultaneously, it was not easy to correct it. In this book, notwithstanding, Natty Bumppo is quite up to his mark, and is surpassed only in *The Pathfinder*. The reputation of *The Prairie*, like that of *The Pioneers*, is in a large degree owing to the opinions of the reviews; it is always a fault in a book that appeals to human sympathies that it fails with the multitude. In what relates to taste, the multitude is of no great authority; but in all that is connected with feeling, they are the highest; and for this simple reason, that as man becomes sophisticated he deviates from nature, the only true source of all our sympathies. Our feelings are doubtless improved by refinement, and vice versa; but their roots are struck in the human heart, and what fails to touch the heart, in these particulars, fails, while that which does touch it, succeeds. The perfection of this sort of writing is that which pleases equally the head and the heart.

The Red Rover followed *The Prairie*. Its success surpassed that of any of its predecessors. It was written and printed in Paris, and all in a few 3 months. Its merits and its reception prove the accuracy of those gentlemen who allege that "Mr.

Cooper never wrote a successful book after he left the United States." It is certainly a stronger work than *The Pilot*, though not without considerable faults.

The *Wept of Wish-Ton-Wish* was the next novel.[13] The author I believe regards this and *Lionel Lincoln* as the poorest of his works. It met with no great success.

The *Water Witch* succeeded, but is inferior to any of the other nautical tales. It was the first attempt by Mr. Cooper—the first by any author—to lay the scene of a tale of witchcraft on the coast of America. It has more imagination than many other of Mr. Cooper's works, but the blending of the real with the ideal was in some parts a little incongruous. The *Water Witch* was written in Italy and first printed in Germany.

Of all Americans who ever visited Europe, Mr. Cooper contributed most to our country's good reputation. His high character made him everywhere welcome; there was no circle, however aristocratic or distinguished, in which, if he appeared in it, he was not observed of all observers; and he had the somewhat singular merit of *never forgetting that he was an American*. Halleck, in his admirable poem of "Red Jacket," says well of him:

> Cooper, whose name is with his country's woven,
>   First in her fields, her pioneer of mind,
> *A wanderer now on other lands, has proven*
>   *His love for the young land he left behind.*[14]

After having been in Europe about two years he published his *Notions of the Americans*, in which he "endeavored to repel some of the hostile opinions of the other hemisphere, and to turn the tables on those who at that time most derided and calumniated us." It contained some unimportant errors, from having been written at a distance from necessary documentary materials, but was altogether as just as it was eloquent in vindication of our institutions, manners, and history. It shows how warm was his patriotism; how fondly, while receiving from strangers an homage withheld from him at home, he remembered the scenes of his first trials and triumphs, and how ready he was to sacrifice personal popularity and profit in defence of his country.

He was not only the first to defend and to praise America, but the first to whom appeals were made for information in regard to her by statesmen who felt an interest in our destiny. Following the revolution of the Three Days, in Paris, a fierce controversy took place between the absolutists, the republicans, and the constitutionalists. Among the subjects introduced in the Chambers was the comparative cheapness of our system of government; the absolutists asserting that the people of the United States paid more direct and indirect taxes than the French. La Fayette appealed to Mr. Cooper, who entered the arena, and though, from his peculiar position, at a heavy pecuniary loss, and the danger of incurring yet greater misfortunes, by a masterly *exposé* silenced at once the popular falsehoods.[15] So in all places, circumstances, and times, he was the "American in Europe," as jealous of his country's reputation as his own.

Immediately after, he published *The Bravo*, the success of which was very great: probably equal to that of *The Red Rover*. It is one of the best, if not the very best of the works Mr. Cooper had then written. Although he selected a foreign scene on this occasion, no one of his works is more American in its essential character. It was designed not only to extend the democratical principle abroad, but to confirm his countrymen in the opinion that nations "cannot be governed by an irresponsible minority without involving a train of nearly intolerable abuses." It gave aristocracy some hits, which aristocracy gave back again. The best notice which appeared of it was in the famous Paris gazette entitled *Figaro*, before *Figaro* was brought out by the French government. The change from the biting wit which characterized this peri- odical to the grave sentiment of such an article, was really touching, and added an indescribable grace to the remarks.

The Heidenmauer followed.[16] It is impossible for me to understand this book who has not some acquaintance with the scenes and habits described. It was not very successful.

The Headsman of Berne did much better.[17] It is inferior to *The Bravo,* though not so clashing to aristocracy. It met with very respectable success. It was the last of Mr. Cooper's novels written in Europe, and for some years the last of a political charac- ter.

The first work which Mr. Cooper published after his return to the United States was *A Letter to his Countrymen*. They had yielded him but a hesitating applause until his praise came back from Europe, and when the tone of foreign criticism was changed by acts and opinions of his which should have landed the whole American press for his defence, he was assailed here in articles which either echoed the tone or were actual translations of attacks upon him by foreigners. The custom peculiar to this country of "quoting the opinions of foreign nations by way of helping to make up its own estimate of the degree of merit which belongs to its public men" is treated in this letter with caustic and just severity, and shown to be "destructive of those sentiments of self-respect and of that manliness and independence of thought, that are necessary to render a people great or a nation respectable." The controlling influence of foreign ideas over our literature, fashions, and even politics, are illustrated by the manner in which he was himself treated, and by what he con- siders the English doctrines which have been broached in the speeches of many of our statesmen. It is a frank and honest book, which was unnecessary as a vindica- tion of Mr. Cooper, but was called for by the existence of the abuse against which it was chiefly directed, though it seems have had little effect upon it. Of the political opinions it contains I have no more to say than that I do not believe in their cor- rectness.

It was followed by *The Monikins*, a political satire, which was a failure.

The next publications of Mr. Cooper were his *Gleanings in Europe. Sketches in Swit- zerland,* first and second series, each in two volumes, appeared in 1836, and none of his works contain more striking and vivid descriptions of nature, or more agreeable views of characters and manners. It was followed by similar works on France, Italy, and England. All of these were well received, notwithstanding an independence of tone which is rarely popular, and some absurdities, as, for example, the imputations on the American Federalists in the *Sketches in Switzerland*. The book on England excited most attention and was reviewed in that country with as much asperity as if its own travellers were proverbially not the most shameless libellers that ever abused the hospitality of nations.[18] Altogether the ten volumes which comprise this series may be set down as the most intelligent and philosophical books of travels which have been written by our countrymen.

The American Democrat, or Hints on the Social and Civil Relations of the United States of America, was published in 1835. The design is stated to be, "to make a commence-ment toward a more just discrimination between truth and prejudice." It is essen-tially a good book on the virtues and vices of American character.

For a considerable time Mr. Cooper had entertained an intention of writing *The History of the Navy of the United States*, and his early experiences, his studies, his asso-ciations, and above all the peculiar felicity of his style when treating of nautical af-fairs, warranted the expectation that his work would be a solid and brilliant contri-bution to our historical literature. It appeared in two octavo volumes in 1839, and reached a second edition in 1840, and a third in 1846. The public had no reason to be disappointed; great diligence had been used in the collection of materials; every subject connected with the origin and growth of our national marine had been care-fully investigated, and the result was presented in the most attractive and authentic form. Yet a warm controversy soon arose respecting Mr. Cooper's account of the battle of Lake Erie, and in pamphlets, reviews, and newspapers, attempts were made to show that he had done injustice to the American commander in that ac-tion. The multitude rarely undertake particular investigations; and the attacks upon Mr. Cooper, conducted with a virulence for which it would be difficult to find any cause in the History, assuming the form of vindications of a brave and popular de-ceased officer, produced an impression so deep and so general that he was com-pelled to defend the obnoxious passages, which he did triumphantly in a small vol-ume entitled *The Battle of Lake Erie, or Answers to Messrs. Burgess, Duer, and Mackenize*, published in 1843, and in his notes to the last edition of his *Naval History*. Those who read the whole controversy will perceive that Mr. Cooper was guided by the authorities most entitled to a consideration of an historian, and that in his answers he has demonstrated the correctness of his statements and opinions; and they will perhaps be astonished that he in the first place gave so little cause for dissatisfac-tion on the part of the friends of Commodore Perry.[19] Besides the Naval History and the essays to which it gave rise, Mr. Cooper has published, in two volumes, *The Lives of the American Naval Officers*,* a work of the highest merit in its department, every life being written with conciseness yet fullness, and with great care in regard

---

* The first and second editions appeared in Philadelphia, and the third in Cooperstown. It was reprinted in 1830 in London, Paris, and Brussels; and an abridgement of it, by the author, has been largely introduced into common schools.

to facts; and in the *Democratic Review* has published an unanswerable reply to the attacks upon the American marine by James and other British historians.[20]

The first novel published by Mr. Cooper after his return to the United States was *Homeward Bound.*[21] The two generic characters of the book, however truly they may represent individuals, have no resemblance to classes. There may be Captain Trucks, and there certainly are Steadfast Dodges, but the officers of the American merchant service are in no manner or degree inferior to Europeans of the same pursuits and grade; and with all the abuses of the freedom of the press here, our newspapers are not worse than those of Great Britain in the qualities for which Mr. Cooper arraigns them. The opinions expressed of New-York society in *Home as Found* are identical with those in *Notions of the Americans*, a work almost as much abused for its praise of this country as was *Home as Found* for its censure, and most men of refinement and large observation seem disposed to admit their correctness. This is no doubt the cause of the feeling it excited, for a *nation* never gets in a passion at misrepresentation. It is a miserable country that cannot look down a falsehood, even from a native.

The next novel was *The Pathfinder*. It is a common opinion that this work deserves success more than any Mr. Cooper has written. I have heard Mr. Cooper say that in his own judgment the claim lay between *The Pathfinder* and *The Deerslayer*, but for myself I confess a preference for the sea novels.[22] Leather Stocking appears to more advantage in *The Pathfinder* than in any other book, and in *Deerslayer* next. In *The Pathfinder* we have him presented in the character of a lover, and brought in contact with such characters as he associates with in no other stages of his varied history, though they are hardly less favorites with the author. The scene of the novel being the great fresh water seas of the interior, sailors, Indians, and hunters, are so grouped together, that every kind of novel-writing in which he has been most successful is combined in one complete fiction, one striking exhibition of his best powers. Had it been written by some unknown author, probably the country would have hailed him as much superior to Mr. Cooper.

Mercedes of Castile, a Romance of the Days of Columbus, came next. It may be set down as a failure. The necessity of following facts that had become familiar, and which had so lately possessed the novelty of fiction, was too much for any writer.

The Deerslayer was written after *Mercedes* and *The Pathfinder*, and was very successful. Hetty Hunter is perhaps the best female character Mr. Cooper has drawn, though her sister is generally preferred. *The Deerslayer* was the last written of the "Leather Stocking Tales," having come out in 1841, nineteen years after the appearance of *The Pioneers* in 1822. Arranged according to the order of events, *The Deerslayer* should be the first of this remarkable series, followed by *The Last of the Mohicans, The Pathfinder, The Pioneers*, and *The Prairie*.

The Two Admirals followed *The Deerslayer*.[23] This book in some respects stands at the head of the nautical tales. Its fault is dealing with too important events to be thrown so deep into fiction; but this is a fault that may be pardoned in a romance. Mr. Cooper has written nothing in description, whether of sea or land, that surpasses either of the battle scenes of this work; especially that part of the first where the French ship is captured. *The Two Admirals* appeared at an unfortunate time, but it was nevertheless successful.

Wing-and-Wing, or, Le Feu Follet, was published in 1842.[24] The interest depends chiefly upon the manoeuvres by which a French privateer escapes capture by an English frigate. Some of its scenes are among Mr. Cooper's best, but altogether it is inferior to several of his nautical novels.

Wyandotté, or the Hutted Knoll, in its general features resembles *The Pathfinder* and *The Deerslayer*.[25] The female characters are admirable, and but for the opinion, believed by some, from its frequent repetition, that Mr. Cooper is incapable of depicting a woman, Maud Meredith would be regarded as among the very first class of such portraitures.

Next came the *Autobiography of a Pocket Handkerchief*, in one volume.[26] It is a story of fashionable life in New-York, in some respects peculiar among Mr. Cooper's works, and was decidedly successful. It appeared originally in a monthly magazine, and was the first of his novels printed in this manner.

Ned Myers, in one volume, which followed in the same year, is a genuine biography, though it was commonly regarded as a fiction.[27]

In the beginning of 1844 Mr. Cooper published *Ashore and Afloat*, and a few months afterward *Miles Wallingford*, a sequel to that tale.[28] They have the remarkable minuteness yet boldness of description, and dramatic skill of narration, which render the impressions he produces so deep and lasting. They were as widely read as any of his recent productions.

The extraordinary state of things which for several years has disgraced a part of the state of New-York, where, with unblushing effrontery, the tenants of several large proprietors have refused to pay rents, and claimed, without a shadow of right, to be absolute possessors of the soil, gave just occasion of alarm to the intelligent friends of our institutions; and this alarm increased, when it was observed that the ruffianism of the "anti-renters," as they are styled, was looked upon by many persons of respectable social positions with undisguised approval.[29] Mr. Cooper addressed himself to the exposure and correction of the evil, in a series of novels, purporting to be edited from the manuscripts of a family named Littlepage; and in the preface to the first of these, entitled *Satanstoe, a Tale of the Colony*, published in 1845, announces his intention of treating it with the utmost freedom, and declares his opinion, that the "existence of true liberty among us, the perpetuity of our institutions, and the safety of public morals, are all dependent on putting down, wholly, absolutely, and unqualifiedly, the false and dishonest theories and statements that have been advanced in connection with this subject." *Satanstoe* presents a vivid picture of the early condition of colonial New-York. The time is from 1737 to the close of the memorable campaign in which the British were so signally defeated at Ticonderoga. *Chainbearer*, the second of the series, tracing the family history through the Revolution, also appeared in 1845, and the last, *The Red Skins*, a story of the present day, in 1846.[30] "This book," says the author, in his preface, "closes the series of the Littlepage manuscripts, which have been given to the world as containing a fair account of the comparative sacrifices of time, money, and labor, made respectively by the landlord the tenants, on a New-York estate, together with the manner in which usages and opinions are changing among us, and the causes of these changes." These books, in which the most important practical truths are stated, illustrated and enforced, in a manner equally familiar and powerful, were received by the educated and right-minded with a degree of favor that showed the soundness of the common mind beyond the crime-infected districts, and their influence will add to the evidences of the value of the novel as a means of upholding principles in art, literature, morals, and politics.

The Crater, or Vulcan's Peak, followed in 1847. It is a story of the Pacific, embracing some of Mr. Cooper's finest sea pictures, but altogether is not so interesting as the average of his nautical tales.

Oak Openings, or the Bee-Hunter, came next.[31] It has the merits characteristic of his Indian novels, masterly scene-painting, and decided individuality in the persons introduced.

Jack Tier, or the Florida Reef, appeared in 1848, and is one of the best of the sea stories. The chief character is a woman, deserted by a half smuggler, half buccaneer, whom she joins in the disguise of a sailor, and accompanies undiscovered during a cruise. In vividness of painting and dramatic interest it has rank with the *Red Rover* and *The Pilot*.

The Sea Lions, or the Lost Sealers, was published in 1849. It deals to some extent in metaphysics, and its characters are for the most part of humble conditions. It has more of domestic life than any of the other nautical pieces.

In the spring of 1850 came out *The Ways of the Hour*, the last of this long series of more than thirty novels, and like the Littlepage MSS, it was devoted to the illustration of social and political evils, having for its main subject the constitution and office of juries.[32] In other works Mr. Cooper appears as a conservative; in this as a destructive. The book is ingenious and able, but has not been very successful.

In 1850 Mr. Cooper came out for the first time as a dramatic writer, in a comedy performed at Burton's theatre in New-York.[33] A want of practice in writing for the stage prevented a perfect adaptation of his piece for this purpose, but it was conceded to be remarkable for wit and satirical humor. He has now in press a work illustrative of the social history and condition of New-York, which will be published during the summer by Mr. Putnam, who from time to time is giving to the public the previous works of Mr. Cooper, with his final revisions, and such notes and introductions as are necessary for the new generation of readers.[34] The Leather Stocking Tales, constituting one of the great works to be ranked hereafter with the chief masterpieces of prose fiction in the literature of the world, are among the volumes now printed.

It cannot be denied that Mr. Cooper is personally unpopular, and the fact is suggestive of one of the chief evils in our social condition. In a previous number of this magazine we have asserted the ability and eminently honorable character of a large class of American journals. The spirit of another class, also in many instances conducted with ability, is altogether bad and base; jealous, detracting, suspicious, "delighting to deprave";[35] betraying a familiarity with low standards in mind and morals, and a consciousness habituated to interested views and sordid motives; degrading every thing that wears the appearance of greatness, sometimes by plain denial and insolent contempt, and sometimes by wretched innuendo and mingled lie and sophistry; effectually dissipating all the romance of character, and all the enthusiasm of life; hating dignity having no sympathies with goodness, insensible to the very existence of honor as a spring of human conduct; treating patriotism and disinterestedness with an elaborate sneer, and receiving the suggestions of duty with a horselaugh. There is a difference not easily to be mistaken between the lessening of men which is occasioned by the loftiness of the platform whence the observation is made, and that which is produced by the malignant envy of the observer; between the gloomy judicial ferocity of a Pope or a Tacitus, and the villain levity which revels in the contemplation of imputed faults, or that fiendishness of feeling which gloats and howls over the ruins of reputations which itself has stabbed.[36]

For a few years after Mr. Cooper's return from Europe, he was repeatedly urged by his friends to put a stop to the libels of newspapers by an appeal to the law; but he declined. He perhaps supposed that the common sense of the people would sooner or later discover and right the wrong that was done to him by those who, without the slightest justification, invaded the sacredest privacies of his life for subjects of public observation. He finally decided, at the end of five years after his return, to appeal to the tribunals, in every case in which anything not by himself submitted to public criticism, in his works, should be offensively treated, within the limits of the state of New-York. Some twenty suits were brought by him, and his course was amply vindicated by unanimous verdicts in his behalf. But the very conduct to which the press had compelled him was made cause of ungenerous prejudices. He has never objected to the widest latitude or extremest severity in criticisms of his writings, but simply contended that the author should be let alone. With him, individually, the public had nothing to do. In the case of a public officer, slanders may be lived down, but a literary man, in his retirement, has no such means of vindication; his only appeal is to the laws, and if they afford no protection in such cases, the name of law is contemptible.

I enter here upon no discussion of the character of the late Commander Slidell Mackenzie, but observe simply that no one can read Mr. Cooper's volume upon the battle of Lake Erie and retain a very profound respect for that person's sagacity or sincerity. The proprietors of the copyright of Mr. Cooper's abridged *Naval History* offered it, without his knowledge, to John C. Spencer, then Secretary of the State of New-York, for the school libraries of which that officer had the selection.[37] Mr. Spencer replied with peculiar brevity that he would have nothing to do with such a partisan performance, but soon after directed the purchase of Commander Mackenzie's *Life of Commodore Perry*,[38] which was entirely and avowedly partisan, while Mr. Cooper's book was rigidly impartial. Commander Mackenzie returned the favor by hanging the Secretary's son.[39] A circumstance connected with this event illustrates what we have said of obtaining justice from the newspapers. A month before Commander Mackenzie's return to New-York in the *Somers*, Mr. Cooper sent to me, for publication in a magazine of which I was editor, an examination of certain statements in the *Life of Perry*; but after it was in type, hearing of the terrible mistake which Mackenzie had made, he chose to suffer a continuation of injustice rather than strike a fallen enemy, and so directed the suppression of his criticism. Nevertheless, as the statements in the *Life of Perry* very materially affected his own reputation, in the following year, when the natural excitement against Mackenzie had nearly subsided, he gave his answer to the press, and was immediately accused in a "leading journal of the country" of having in its preparation devoted himself, from the date of that person's misfortune, to his injury. The reader supposes, of course, that the slander was contradicted as generally as it had been circulated, and that justice was done to the forbearance and delicacy with which Mr. Cooper had acted in the matter; but to this day, neither the journal in which he was assailed, nor one in a hundred of those which repeated the falsehood, has stated these facts. Here is another instance: The late William L. Stone agreed with Mr. Cooper to submit a certain matter of libel for amicable arbitration, agreeing, in the event of a decision against him, to pay Mr. Cooper two hundred dollars toward the expenses he must incur in attending to it.[40] The affair attracted much attention. Before an ordinary court Mr. Cooper should have received ten thousand dollars; but he accepted the verdict agreed upon, the referees deciding without hesitation that he had been grossly wronged by the publication of which he had complained. After the death of Mr. Stone one of the principal papers of the city stated that his widow was poor, and had appealed to Mr. Cooper's generosity for the remission of a fine, which could be of no importance to a gentleman of his liberal fortune, but had been answered with a rude refusal. The statement was entirely and in all respects false, and it was indignantly contradicted upon the authority of President Wayland, the brother of Mrs. Stone; but the editors who gave it currency have never retracted it, and it yet swells the tide of miserable defamation which makes up the bad reputations of so many of the purest of men.[41] Numerous other instances might be quoted to show not only the injustice with which Mr. Cooper has been treated, but the addiction of the press to libel, and its unwillingness to atone for wrongs it has itself inflicted.

It used to be the custom of the *North American Review* to speak of Mr. Cooper's works as "translated into French," as if thus giving the highest existing evidence of their popularity, while there was not a language in Europe into which they did not all, after the publication of *The Red Rover*, appear almost as soon as they were printed in London. He has been the chosen companion of the prince and the peasant, on the borders of the Volga, the Danube, and the Guadalquivir; by the Indus and the Ganges, the Paraguay and the Amazon; where the name even of Washington was never spoken, and our country is known only as the borne of Cooper. The world has living no other writer whose fame is so universal.

Mr. Cooper has the faculty of giving to his pictures an astonishing reality. They are not mere transcripts of nature, though as such they would possess extraordinary merit, but actual creations, embodying the very spirit of intelligent and genial experience and observation. His Indians, notwithstanding all that has been written to the contrary, are no more inferior in fidelity than they are in poetical interest to those of his most successful imitators or rivals. His hunters and trappers have the same vividness and freshness, and in the whole realm of fiction there is nothing more actual, harmonious, and sustained. They evince not only the first order of inventive power, but a profoundly philosophical study of the influences of situation upon human character. He treads the deck with the conscious pride of home and dominion: the aspects of the sea and sky, the terrors of the tornado, the excitement of the chase, the tumult of battle, fire, and wreck, are presented by him with a freedom and breadth of outline, a glow and strength of coloring and contrast, and a distinctness and truth of general and particular conception, that place him far in advance of all the other artists who have attempted with pen or pencil to paint the ocean. The same vigorous originality is stamped upon his nautical characters. The sailors of Smollett are as different in every respect as those of Eugène Sue and Marryat are inferior.[42] He goes on board his ship with his own creations, disdaining all society and assistance but that with which he is thus surrounded. Long Tom Coffin, Tom Tiller, Trysail, Bob Yarn, the boisterous Nightingale, the mutinous Nighthead, the fierce but honest Boltrope, and others who crowd upon our memories, as familiar as if we had ourselves been afloat with them, attest the triumph of this self-reliance. Amid when, as if to rebuke the charge of envy that he owed his successes to the novelty of his scenes and persons, he entered upon fields which for centuries had been illustrated by the first geniuses of Europe, his abounding power and inspiration were vindicated by that series of political novels ending with *The Bravo*, which have the same supremacy in their class that is held by *The Pilot* and *The Red Rover* among stories of the sea. It has been urged that his leading characters are essentially alike, having no difference but that which results from situation. But this opinion will not bear investigation. It evidently arose from the habit of clothing his heroes alike with an intense individuality, which under all circumstances sustains the sympathy they at first awaken, without the aid of those accessories to which artists of less power are compelled to resort. Very few authors have added more than one original and striking character to the world of imagination; none has added more than Cooper; and his are all as distinct and actual as the personages that stalk before us on the stage of history.

To be American, without falling into Americanism, is the true task that is set before the native artist in literature, the accomplishment of which awaits the reward of the best approval in these times, and the promise of an enduring name. Some of our authors, fascinated very excusably with the faultless models of another age, have declined this condition, and have given us Spectators and Tattlers with false dates, and developed a style of composition of which the very merits imply an anachronism in the proportion of excellence.[43] Others have understood the result to be attained better than the means of arriving at it. They have not considered the difference between those peculiarities in our society, manners, tempers, and tastes, which are genuine and characteristic, and those which are merely defects and errors upon the English system; they have acquired the force and gayety of liberty, but not the dignity of independence, and are only provincial, when they hoped to be national. Mr. Cooper has been more happy than any other writer in reconciling these repugnant qualities, and displaying the features, character, and tone of a great rational style in letters, which, original and unimitative, is yet in harmony with the ancient models.

3

THE MORAL AND ARTISTIC IN PROSE FICTION

Anonymous

American Whig Review (1851).

The popular novel of modern times is perhaps too well known to need a definition. Still it may be proper, in reference to the acquisition of just standards, to throw out some general considerations in regard to this peculiar structure in art. The history of the novel is a very simple one. In general respects it is that of the drama; one of the happy modes by which ingenuity contrives to beguile ignorance to knowledge. Its beginnings are to be found amongst the first dawnings of the human intellect. The child himself is a *raconteur*.[44] He begins the exercise of his thought by taking his constructive faculty for its assistance, in the ambitious desire to provoke the wonder and admiration of his young and less endowed companions. He invents facts and situations, and accumulates events in proper order and becoming relation, so as to form a history. And in this exercise he becomes an artist. The continuance of the practice results in a greater or smaller degree of perfection, more or less modified by the surrounding influences of society and proper models.

Even in childhood, however, the faculty is an extraordinary one. It betrays talents which are by no means shared by many. Not one child in the hundred possesses the endowment, or certainly to no great extent. They may possess large faculties of thought and of expression. They may give forth elaborate sentiments and show proofs of ingenious speculation, accompanied by eloquent utterance. They may be poets even, without possessing the faculty of weaving together, in intricate relation and with due dependency, such scenes and events in life, indicated by the interposition of moral agents, as distinguish the labors of the composer in prose fiction. For this they strive vainly; and many strive, who, highly endowed in seemingly kindred departments of art, yet fail utterly to take the first step in the constructing of prose fiction.

Not so with him who is "to the manner born."[45] To him, employing the language of Hamlet, it comes "easy as lying."[46] Were older heads to give their attention
to the boy narratives that spell the ears of the happy groups that linger by the
school-house porch, or in the play-grounds, or on a Saturday out among the woods,
they would be surprised to discover, amidst so much of the frivolous and puerile,
so much that betrayed thought and talent in invention,—the invention or the capacity for structure invariably preceding the moral in the mind of the boy, and even
the thought by which what is simply moral in the story is educed or indicated; the
boldness of the fancy and the readiness of resource in the *raconteur*, still showing
themselves superior to the general crudeness of the conception, and the feeble and
common-place character of the materials. We are made to see the scheme in spite
of the agency; made to observe a fitness of parts and a symmetrical design, leading
through a thousand awkwardnesses and, obscurities to a really judicious moral. Of
course the moral as such forms no part of the object of the juvenile narrator, or his
more juvenile audience. The common aim is the story—the simple accumulation of
interesting incidents in relation to some hero for whom all sympathies are enlisted.
But as truthfulness is never wanting in its moral, and as the great end of every artist
is the approximation of all his fiction to a seeming truth, so unavoidably he incul-
cates a moral, of more or less value, whenever he tells a story. As the peculiar endowment which makes the *raconteur* is equally native and decided, so the passion for
his narratives, even among those who do not share his faculties, is equally true to
the moral instincts of his auditory. All listen with eagerness, and yield ready cre-
dence to all statements which keep within the verge of possibility; and with the eager and believing mind of youth, the limits of the possible are wonderfully flexile,
and oppose no unnecessary barriers to the ardent spirit and the free imagination.

It is this ready faith in the auditory which determines the legitimacy of the art—
which has been practised from the beginning of time, in all the nations and all the
ages of the earth. No people have ever lived without their authors of fictitious narrative. No people can live without them, since the faculties which find their utterance through this medium are the very faculties—the creative, the combining, and
the endowing—by which men are distinguished from all other animals. The art has
shown itself quite as decidedly among the savages of North America, as among the
most highly refined of the Asiatic nations. The inventions of our Six Nations, of the
Cherokees, Choctaws, and Catawbas, if inferior in polish and variety, do not seem
to have been less daring and original than those of the Arabians, to whom we are
indebted for some of the most admirable of those legends which seem particularly
designed to do their offices of tuition with a young and primitive people.[47] These
fictions, constituting some of the very loveliest conceptions which art has ever
drawn from the fountains of the imagination, were at first simple, and like those of
childhood. The additions of succeeding generations, the more elaborate efforts of
superior artists, have improved them for the delight of races more matured. At first
these performances were scenes and sketches rather than histories, and were employed upon such events of the common experience as were at once most natural

and impressive. But when religion began to act upon the imagination, the artist soon became tasked for higher exercises, and glimpses of the wild and spiritual were made to elevate the common-place and ordinary. This led to the machinery of superstition. Hence magic, as an agency by which romance was first begotten; hence *diablerie*,[48] by which the soul was made to startle at contact with a spiritual world, even when the doctrine of a future itself was left totally untaught, except as a purely speculative philosophy. In the phantoms of the imagination, the spectres of ignorant dread, and those vague and shadowy aspects that lurked in lonely places, among the woods, in the hollows of desolate hills, in the depths of lovely but forbidden waters, the various orders and denominations of Gnome, Kobold, Ondine, Sylph and Fairy, we behold the fantastic creations of a genius struggling constantly to pass from the oppressive chambers of the real, into the rare atmosphere of an ideal which suffered from no incumbrances.[49]

Gradually, as art continued to advance in the refinement of her own powers, and in the more facile employment of her own machinery, fiction became a thing of more complexity of form and of diminished imagination in respect to its conceptions. As the faith of the ignorant in the objects of former superstition became lessened and inflexible, the *raconteur* found it necessary to accommodate his fiction to the more rigid and exacting standards of the popular belief. To seem like truth was still, as it had always been in all ages, the object of the judicious artist; and the invention which had hitherto been exercised with the vague and supernatural, suffered no real or great diminution of its resources, when it felt itself compelled to turn its eye without rather than within for its materials; when the deeds of man, rather than his secret soul and speculative performances, afforded the substance of the chronicle; and the collective heart of the multitude, in its open exhibitions, served for the field of analysis, in place of the single individual, being, doing, or suffering, which hitherto had been the almost exclusive study. Histories of men— periods which betrayed large groups in active issues, such as the middle ages— naturally took the place of more primitive material. The romance of progress was the legitimate successor of that which illustrated the purely spiritual nature—which, by the way, was a romance of progress also, though in a sense very different from any other; and this, in turn, was followed just as naturally by the romance of society, or the ordinary novel of the present day.

In each of the latter classes of fiction, the chief object seems to have been so to delineate the aspects of real life, under certain conditions of society, as at once to preserve all their distinctive characteristics, and to invest with a biographical interest certain favorite studies of character and situation. These objects render necessary an admirable co-operation of the artist with the philosopher; the painter of detail with the poet of fine conceptions. It must be evident, even to persons of the most ordinary reflection and understanding, that to execute such a design with only moderate success, demands a very rare combination of moral attributes. Scarcely any intellectual performance, indeed, could task a greater variety of human powers. Keen perception, quick instincts, delicate tastes, strong good sense, a perfect knowledge of character, a nice appreciation of all that constitutes the sensibilities, and all that makes the virtues of the social man;—these are all absolute requisites for that artist, who, in the delineation of real life, in an atmosphere of fiction, must, to a certain extent, borrow faculties from every other department of human art. The poet must yield him fancy and imagination; the painter, an eye to the landscape; the sculptor, a just conception of form and attitude; the dramatist, combination and the art of trouping;—and even the lawyer and the historian must, or may be drawn upon,—the one for the capacity to argue out a case from certain premises and facts to a just conclusion,—to weigh the motives to action, and determine the awards of judgment; and the other, to sift the causes of social progress,—to estimate duly the morals of leading events, the effects which they should produce, and the principles to which, whether for good or evil, they are likely to give birth hereafter, affecting equally the condition of the community and the aspirations of the individual man. In a rare judgment all these faculties are necessarily found to unite. The artist in prose fiction, more than any other, must possess in large degree the constructive faculty. Poetry depends chiefly upon its courage and sentiment; the drama upon its passion; music upon its spirituality; and painting upon its happy distribution of light and shade, the harmony of its colors, and the symmetry of its forms. But, borrowing in some degree all these agencies, the artist in prose fiction makes them all ancillary to one particularly his own, and that we consider the constructive faculty. With this faculty it is that he frames and adapts his materials to whatever sort of edifice it is the particular aim of his genius to erect. That edifice may be a palace or a hovel, but it is required to be symmetrical, in compliance with laws growing out of the very conception which suggests the structure. The builder, to achieve the reputation of a master, must conceive boldly the plan and purpose of his fabric; and this requires a vigorous imagination. He must possess a lively fancy, else how should he adorn fitly and properly embellish the fabric which he has raised? He must be a person of great vigilance and freshness of resource, else how should he vary his entertainments for his guests according to their differing characteristics and desires? The flexibility of his intellectual vision must be great, else how should he be capable of that instinctive appreciation of character which is called for by the constant necessity of discriminating his *dramatis personae*, the great essential requisite for success in portraiture and for dramatic vitality in action? The first dawning of the humors of a period,—using the word in the sense of Ben Jonson,—its passing moods and fashions, its singular traits of moral and society, (which are mostly epidemical, and flit with the progress of a season), are among the minor but scarcely less necessary requisitions of his art; to execute which requires a rare versatility of talent. To this versatility no mere summary, like the present, could possibly do justice. Let it suffice that the great or successful worker in prose fiction must be, taking Walter Scott for our most obvious example, a person of equal imagination and cool common sense; of lively but healthy sensibilities; of great tact, (which is another word for admirable taste), and of equal vigilance and courage. He must be able to observe without effort,—so endowed by nature and so trained by practice as to achieve, so to speak, by the simple outpouring of his customary thoughts. His habitual mental exercise must be the acquisition of material, and its partial subjection to his purposes, though in detached and fragmentary conditions, susceptible of adaptation to more elaborate uses when his schemes ripen into design. Carrying the materials which he thus habitually realizes, without effort and almost without consciousness, to the alembic of his thought, he will extract from them by a process which, in the trained author, goes on without respite, all the sublimated essences which, thus resolved, become aggregated within himself and constitute the means and expedients of his own genius. He is original and inventive in due degree as he has incorporated these external elements in with his own thoughts, and the habitual workings of his own intellect.

To acquire such materials, and to attain these results, no mere fagging with a purpose can possibly avail. No mere drudgery under the stimulating force of will can possibly yield the habitual condition by which such accumulations go on, with all the regularity of advancing and returning hours. Cramming is no more likely to produce digestion in the case of the intellectual, than in that of the animal condition. On the contrary, as in the latter, the effect is unfavorable to the proper incorporation of the food with the healthy flesh and blood, and true nature of the recipient. And without the harmonious cooperation of the several powers and attributes,—unless the aliment taken in by the senses of the student and the inventor be kindred in quantity and quality with that upon which his genius may be supposed to feed, the latter is enfeebled rather than sustained by the innutritious supply, and the fruits of his labor lack equally congruity and health. If, as Milton hath it, the life of him who would write a poem must itself be a poem, so must the habitual tendency of observation and thought of him who deals in prose fiction, tend to the supply of means favorable in particular to his freshness, his invention, and his just appreciation of all the varieties of human character. Perhaps we may say all this, when we adopt the peculiar idiom of another nation, and say that for his art there must be a nature.

It is very clear that, of the thousand fine issues which belong to every action in the progress of a story, the trials of the heart, the displays of passion, the subtle combinations of wit, the logical results of judgment, the fancy which happily relieves the action in the proper place, the vivacity which keeps the interest astir, the invention which provides the impressive incident, and all the various and numerous faculties, of feeling and understanding, which need to have fulness and free play in the development and action of a scheme which embodies equally and all the characteristics by which society is moved and human sensibility excited; it must be very clear, we say, that there can be very few of these agencies, about which, as the necessity for their employment arises, the author could deliberately sit down to reason. It would be morally and physically impossible, were any such necessity to exist, that his labors should ever arrive at the honors of a single volume. On the contrary, his resources should be so equally ready and ample, that he shall be conscious, his progress once begun, of no let or hindrance, calling for long pause or hesitation in the prosecution of his scheme. There must be no need to stop, and study, and adjust, before he can conscientiously set down. His implements must all be at hand, and at his instant control. His mental constitution must be that of the poet. He must be born to his task. You cannot fashion him to it by any course of training. He works quite as much by intuition as by calculation and common reasoning. His plan once fairly conceived, his thoughts and fancies, to use the felicitous language of Milton, must, "like so many nimble and airy servitors, trip about him at command, and, in well-ordered files as he would wish, fall aptly in their own places."[50] He leaps to his conclusions as if upon a wing of equal certainty and fleetness; and the chief and difficult study before him is at the beginning, when reason demands that he should choose his ground and field of operations, with such a careful regard to his peculiar tastes, studies and experiences, as shall give free play to whatever is individual in his character and genius. Great freedom of speech, affording a ready flow in the narrative, a prompt fancy to meet emergencies and supply details, so that the action shall at no time falter or become flat; a quick and keen perception of the differing shades and degrees, in quality, of human character; a nice appreciation of the delicate and noble, the lofty and the low, the sublime and the ridiculous; an eye eager to seek and prompt to discern the picturesque; a facility in finding varieties and in the suggestion of lively contrasts; and that flexibility of mood, by which one, having a ready utterance, may individualize the several dialects of the *dramatis personae*—dialects which as completely distinguish the individual from his companions, as do the particular traits of his countenance, the sound of his voice and movement of his body; these are all, in greater or less degree, essential to the successful pursuit of his art by the novelist and writer of prose fiction. If held generally, and in large endowment, and exercised with corresponding industry, these faculties must render him an artist of the highest order,—remarkable, as the Germans have it, for the great faculty of Shakespeare, his many-sidedness, or catholicity,—a poet, a philosopher and dramatist, a painter, a seer, and a prophet! His words will flow from him like those of inspiration. His creations, from their equal majesty, grace and beauty, will seem worthy to have owned a divine original. His voice will swell, in due season, to a natural authority in every ear, and his works will gradually pass into the common heart, lifting it to an habitual appreciation of the high humanities which it is the becoming object of a genius so worthily endowed to teach.

The fabric of such an artist will be raised with an equal eye to its uses, its durability, and grandeur. It will be no mere pleasure-house. Its objects are never temporary. The true genius works not less for eternity than man. It is, indeed, in working for eternity that he works for man. He has but a slender appreciation of the importance of his race, who only sees them as they exist around him; who, satisfied with the present sounds that fill his ears, entertains no hungering thirst for that faint voice, sounding ever in the solitude, which comes slowly but surely up from the far-off abodes of his posterity. He, on the contrary, who properly esteems his vocation, feels indeed that successful working must always imply the future only. To be of and with the present only, to speak the voice with which it is already familiar, to go nothing beyond it, to have no mysteries which it shall not and cannot fathom; this is, surely, to forfeit all claim upon the future generations, with whom progress only is existence. But the true artist knows better than to toil for such barren recompense. His ambition, or we should rather say, his nature is governed by a more selfish instinct. He builds in compliance with laws and motives which do not seem to consider earth. His conceptions are caught from the *Highest*, and would seem to emulate his achievements. In what consists his material? The soul of man, his hopes and fears, his humanities; the inner nature, the spirit and the heart, where lie his most permanent and most valuable possession. And from what other of God's creations does he take the tributary forms and aspects which he groups around his subject as subservient to the action? The sky for beauty and repose; the sea for immensity; the forest for depth and intricacy; the rock and mountain for solidity and strength: such are the model forms and attributes that impress his soul from the beginning, and fashion, unconsciously to himself, all the shapes and creations of his genius. His fancies, in like manner, are controlled and counselled by the lovely and the sweet, the graceful and the bright, which the garden groups beneath his eye, or the groves cherish and encourage about his footsteps. And thus informed, insensibly to himself as it were, he models his own mind into images which posterity is fain to deify. Thus, while the *tout ensemble*[51] of his fabric will awe by its magnificence, the exquisiteness of its detail must persuade to a near delight which loves to linger upon the study of its cunning joinery; and this is the perfection of art, where the exquisite delicacy of the finish is not required to compensate for deficient majesty and greatness in the first conception.

The first conclusive proof that we have of the superior artist will be in the manifestation of *design*. The really great genius is conspicuous chiefly in this quality. It is talent that simply *finishes*. It is taste only that never offends. It is art that adapts with propriety. It is genius that creates! To be sure of this faculty in the artist, we must see that he works out a purpose of his own; and we estimate his strength by the resolution which he shows, under all circumstances, in the prosecution of his scheme. It will not do that he follows, however admirably, in the track of other masters. It will not do even should he rival them successfully, in a region which they had explored already. The world can never be persuaded of *his* superiority, who shall do nothing better than multiply specimens under well-known laws and models. He may triumph for a season; he may give a certain degree of pleasure always, as adroitness, aptness and ingenuity, the sources of the imitative faculty, are very apt to do; but there will always be apparent in his performances that want of courage and enterprise, which give to the original a masculine vigor and proportion which men esteem the most essential of all qualities in their guides and leaders. The admiration which hails the imitator is seldom of long duration. It lasts only while he seems like an original. It is by the strongest instincts that the world distinguishes between the substance and the shadow. Not to sink into a pun, they soon feel the difference between them. The discovery once made, they resent the deception. In due degree with the extent of the imposture, will be the scorn and indignation which follow its exposure; and the innocent follower in another's footsteps, who has unconsciously left his own tracks for a season more conspicuous than those of his predecessor, is made to pay, as an offense, for the passing favor of good fortune. Nor, even where the imitation is not apparent, but where the aim is inferior, will the results be finally otherwise. There may be an originality which is yet without a becoming purpose. To seek simply after the satisfaction of a listless mood; to strive, in stimulating a feverish and morbid appetite, to minister to vicious tastes, to drowsy faculties, by temporary expedients in art, by clever surprises, by glittering but unsubstantial shows, the slight fetches of a talent that is capable of small exertions only, will not suffice long for the gratification of an intellectual people. It is, as we have urged already, in the *design* only, in the fresh classical conception of a vigorous imagination, bold, rich, free, generous, comprehensive and ingenious, that admiration becomes permanent, and reputation grows into that fixed condition which the world finally calls fame. The design of the builder must be first apparent; the grand outlines, the great bulk upheaved upon the plain, massive but with what wondrous symmetry of proportion; a maze, but with what admirable simplicity of plan; showing, at a glance, the classical conception, the daring scheme, the appropriate thought, and that dependency of detail in all the parts upon the main idea, by which the mighty fabric of imagination and art is sustained and embellished. We must see in the work before us, not only that the builder himself knew what he was about, that he did not work blindly and at random; but we must be prepared to acknowledge, as we gaze, that his work is entirely his own; that his copy has not been set for him; that he has striven with a native birth, and struck his shaft into a hitherto unbroken soil with the vigor of an arm that obeyed an impulse equally noble and independent. We must behold that indubitable freshness in the conception, which we can liken to nothing already familiar to our fancies. We must see in the artist that eagerness of bent, that enthusiasm of mood, which proves his own conviction of a new discovery. And it must not be because we behold him, that he works. It must be because of a love for the labor, that he addresses himself to its execution. He builds neither for the shelter nor the recompense, scarcely for the praise and the fame, though these naturally suggest themselves to his mind, as proper influences that cheer him when he faints, and stimulate him to new exertions when he would shrink back from very weariness. He cannot help but build! It is because of the God working in his soul that he seeks to raise a temple. His struggle to erect the structure betrays his secret sense of properties in the true and beautiful, which his own nature entertains, and which he seeks to symbolize and to evolve, as well as he may, and in the best materials, for the delight and satisfaction of others. The decorations of his temple have an equal significance. They declare for the tastes, as the fabric itself speaks for the religion of the artist. The sentiments, which are only so many passions informed by the affections and subdued to a spiritual delicacy by the active intervention of the soul, now busy themselves in embellishing the apartments. The chambers are to be furnished, the high saloon, the lofty portico, the altar-place and the niche. Music and the dance are to be pre-

sent, to spell, with a seasonable soothing, the pauses between majestic lessons and
affectionate discourse. Intellect must make itself felt, superior and winning, through
some, if not all, of the human agencies. There must be eloquence, though it be that
of the passions only. There should be song, though it speaks as freely the language
of mere mirth and frivolity, as that of poetry and love; and we shall not quarrel with
the scheme of enjoyment, which is made to minister in a temple meant for so various an audience, if art demeans herself in some lowlier forms, to pleasure and to
persuade a class who are not yet worthy to penetrate the inner sanctuary. The muse
that stoops to elevate, does not degrade her dignity by the temporary concession to
the lowly and the mean. There will be a better life in consequence, more of an inner
life, in the humanity which is thus plucked from its wallow by the offices of art,
which will amply compensate for any reproach that might otherwise fall upon her
temples, from the admission of those who have been hitherto thought unworthy.
What we too frequently esteem as brutal, is nothing more than roughness; and we
must not forget that the noblest fabric of art is still meant as a place of refuge for
humanity. The cathedral loses none of its sacred character, because the vicious
sometime crawl along its aisles; and it lessens not the virtue in the offices of religion, because music is employed to appeal to the sensual nature. The heart is
reached through the senses, when we should vainly appeal to the intellect; and we
must be careful not to withhold from the stubborn the attractions of any influence,
the proper employment of which may make them accessible to yet higher teachings.
The sensual may still occupy a place within our temples—*must* be there, perhaps, so
long as humanity is the simple occupant; but the sensual may be trained to be the
minister of the ideal, and the spiritual man may have his regeneration on that
hearthstone where the worst passions of the heart may have laid themselves down
to sleep at nightfall. It is a miserable error and a bigotry of the worst blindness,
which presumes to repudiate the offices of art when they should minister to a better nature in the vicious heart of man. For, however rude and erring may be the
rites in her temples, they are still calculated to elevate the aims of such as seek their
ministrations. The very office of art is to purify, and her agency is still that of the
intellectual man. She still toils, whatever be her faults, in behalf of him who struggles—blinded it may be, and frequently overthrown in the attempt—to attain that
better condition to which the races, without their own consciousness, are for ever
addressing their endeavors. Genius, of whatever description, and however false,
under perverse influences, to its highest commission and eternal trusts, is still of an
immortal and endowing nature. It is because of this redeeming security for humanity which it possesses, that it commands the world's eye, and in some degree the
world's admiration, even when it most seems to practise against the world's happiness. It is the conviction that we feel, that the great fabric, though sometimes prostituted to the business of the brothel, is nevertheless a temple where thousands
drink in the influences of a purer and more grateful atmosphere than that to which
they are ordinarily accustomed. However unclean the structure, we yet behold in its
design and durableness the working of a rare and blessed divinity, the holiness of

whose altars we must recognize, though the god himself may be in exile. It is for us, not to abandon the shrine because the profligate have expelled him from it; but to endeavor to purify the temple that we may persuade him back to the altar, which we hallow with a purer service. It is in this spirit that we are to employ the offices and the temples of every from of art, to make them clean and holy; not surrender them, because of their partial degradation, wholly to this foul route to which, with a nicer regard to our tastes than our faith and duty, we have too early and too easily yielded them. Let us, more wisely, with the strong sense and the enthusiastic spirit of Martin Luther, determine that the devil shall not possess himself of all the fine music! To yield him up all the agencies by which the heart of man may be touched, in his hours of care or weariness or relaxation, is surely to contribute wonderfully to the spread of Satan's dominion, and to increase, with woful odds against them, the toils of the saints, in their warfare for the Church of Christ.

Such as we have endeavored to describe him is the Master of Fiction, and under such laws and motives will he bring forth his best performances. We have preferred setting forth his higher offices, and the more encouraging and elevating standards which enforce and regulate his labors. All of these belong to poetry—the noblest fashion of human art, whether we regard it in its epic, its lyrical, or dramatic forms. The same standards applied to prose narrative—the romance or the novel—are as legitimately desirable in these forms as in any other, by him who craves amusement and needs instruction. The aims of prose fiction are precisely those of poetry, simply contemplating another and a larger audience. Nay, the audience may be the very same. There are persons who care nothing for music,—who do not comprehend its happy harmonies, and those delicious flights of sound which, through a sensual medium, lift the soul to objects of divinest contemplation. Yet, to such persons, the same object is gained by other artists—the poet or the painter; and the spirit which the musician would deem utterly callous to all tender influences, is made to overflow with sympathy when appealed to through an agency which its affinities are naturally strong. And he who is insensible to the natural charms of poetry—"the measured file and metrical array" of art[52]—will yield himself very joyfully to the lessons which he rejects in verse, if his teacher will employ a more simple and less ambitions medium. Fortunately for the susceptibilities of the race, the Genius of Art, who addresses herself to its exigencies, is of vast compass and wonderful flexibility. She adapts herself to all conditions, and contrives a spell to make every affection, in some degree, her own. Nothing can stale her infinite variety; and, as her purpose and destiny are universal conquest, so she is empowered to adapt her ministry to the condition of the individual, so that his inner nature shall feel the touch of an influence by which his purification may begin. It is no less within her province to render classical—in other words, to make appropriate and becoming—every form of utterance and exhibition which will contribute in any measure to the attainment of her vital objects. This is the conclusive answer to all that one-sided class of critics, who narrow the province of the classical either to the simply prescriptive, or to that one single form of expression to which their tastes or their studies most incline them. They overlook entirely the catholic nature of art, which accommodates its lessons, like any other schoolmaster, to its several classes, and is careful to insinuate its wishes through a new medium, when it finds itself stubbornly resisted in the old. As there is no more good reason why a poem should be compassed in twelve books and the Spenserian stanza,[53] than in five acts and in the fashion of the drama,—so the plan of a romance in prose, in one, two, or three volumes, is not a whit less acceptable to the Genius of Classic Art, than if the same materials were wrought into heroics and tagged with the unnecessary but beautiful appendage of rhyme. We must insist upon this the more, because of the lamentable bigotry of certain literary purists—to say nothing of their ignorance in relation to this subject. Of course, we are not to be understood as arguing in respect to the abuses of the popular novel,—the low purposes to which it is put, and the inferior objects which are too frequently aimed at in its composition. All forms of art, all doctrines, all faith and custom—the offices of religion, the purest privileges of love and society—are, in like manner, subject to abuse, and not unfrequently employed thus for their own desecration and defeat. Our purpose is only to show that this particular form of fiction is quite as legitimate in its origin and quite as susceptible of general use and employment as any other. It is probable that the very same class of persons who now denounce prose fiction would be equally hostile to poetry— nay, are confessedly hostile to it in its dramatic forms, and as anxious now to exclude Shakespeare from use, as the more discriminating moralist would be to suppress the prurient writings of Sue and Paul de Kock. Dull men, who are at the same time vain men, are always to be found, to whom the beautiful in art appears only like a false syren, glozing in the ears of the unwary, and beguiling the ignorant from the secure paths. They would have the young voyager seal up his ears to any charming but their own; and the better to accomplish this object, they cloak their desires with shows of exterior morality, and, in the accents of the holiest mission, promote the objects of the worst. Perhaps there is no worse foe to purity and religion than mere dulness. The dulness which compels the attention of the young, when the heart is eager to go forth and be free in the sunshine, and in the pleasant atmosphere of birds and flowers, in process of time becomes a tyranny which compels men to seek in secret, and consequently with some degree of shame, that very Being who was dispatched to earth with the most beneficent commission of sympathy and love.

If you denounce prose fiction, such as we have indicated,—a fiction which contemplates the highest objects of art, and which is susceptible of the noblest forms to which art has ever yet given expression, you must equally denounce poetry and music. Its flexibility, greater than either of these, is yet equally subject to arbitrary standards—standards which exact equal obedience to certain principles of art, to say nothing of the laws of nature, inevitable in the case of all. That its privileges are larger, does not render its exercise less proper or becoming. Its aims may be quite as daring as those of poetry, its machinery as wild and wondrous, and—to employ a word the literalness of which might almost forbid its use in this connection—as *impossible* and visionary. It is not less true because of its impossibles. It is a truth in the seed, to germinate hereafter; a truth of the spiritual nature; that superior mood by which we are so imperfectly yet impressively informed, and of which, at present, we have such vague and unsatisfying glimpses. Our cravings furnish sufficient arguments to establish the truthfulness of fiction, and to prove its legitimacy as an universal element of delight and desire, natural to the hopes and to the imagination of mankind. Fiction, indeed, is neither more nor less than probable truth under intenser conditions than ordinary. It is quite as properly the organ of religion, one of the aids of faith, as any prayer that ever ascended from bearded patriarch, or any praise of the devotee that ever borrowed the wings of song to cleave the vaulted roof of the temple in making its way to heaven. It has been the frequent language of all religions. It is employed in the form of fable, and parable, and allegory, by Deity himself; and no more remarkable specimen of romance was ever framed for the wondering delight and instruction of man, than the noble drama embodied in the Scriptures which describes the cruel trials of the man of Uz![54] We say not these things with irreverence, but rather with an acute sense of the perfect propriety with which man may use those divinest forms of intellect which God has given him, and which have never been thought indecorously employed when celebrating the works, the glory, and the benevolence of God. That he should not degrade them to base uses, has been the leading motive of this essay. That modern fiction should incorporate a history of mortal loves and mortal disappointments; that it should be yielded up to a homely narrative of the thousand cares and vices that vex the wayward heart, and embitter its perverse struggles; that it should involve humiliating details of licentiousness and crime that it should portray passion in the form of its most wilful exercise, and depict the hopeless and various miseries which flow from its indulgence; no more lessens the propriety of its claims to minister for the good and safety, the direction and the reproof of man, than do like events in the career of David,—the man of such generous, but of so many wild and violent impulses,—the murderer of Uriah, the ravisher of Bathsheba,— the man who erred, and suffered, and atoned, as man is seldom found to do in the ordinary progress of an age.[55] There, indeed, in that sacred and startling history, do we find a model romance, than which none more terribly pleasing and instructive could be found in the whole compass of romantic fiction. But even through the corruption springs the flower. The history of man on earth, whatever be his crimes and errors, if it be honestly written, nothing extenuate, and nothing overwrought, is always a religious history. It is the history of his training for another state; and, whether he makes proper progress or falters by the wayside, does not impair the value of the history in its influence on other men. In the one case, it were a lamp to guide; in the other, a beacon to forewarn. The hues of romance which it is made to wear,—the purple lights and the soft attractive colors which constitute its atmosphere, and commend it to the heart which might shrink from the touch of a truth unskilfully applied,—do not diminish the value of the moral which it brings; do not lessen its healing attributes, or take from what is wholesome in the sting and bitter which it employs, to goad the slumbering conscience into sensibility. Nor is this atmosphere of poetry unreal or unnatural. It is the very atmosphere which marks the progress of passionate youth, and serves in some degree to retard the violence of the passions, when a more rigid morality has failed of its effect. Nor should it be urged against the arts of fiction that, for so long a season after youth has passed for ever, they bring back glimpses of its better hopes—its summer fancies—its skies without a cloud, and its songs without a murmur. Romance, in fact, would seem to be the handmaid whose affections are won by youth, that they should find a solace for it when youth is gone. She is employed to bring warmth to his bosom in age, even as the physical nature of the monarch-minstrel was kept in life by fresh contact with innocent girlhood. She is the restorer to the fancy of all that delicious atmosphere which hung about the heart in youth. She brings back to us all our first glowing and most generous conceptions; when the soul was least selfish, when the affections were most fond; ere strife had made the one callous, or frequent defeat and disappointment had rendered the other sour and suspicions. Beheld through her medium, there is nothing in life which is vulgar and degrading. All its fancies are pure, and show as luxuriantly as they are bright and fresh. It is not, indeed, through the fancies and the tastes that sin assails the heart. It is through the passions only, and in the utter absence of the fancy, and those tastes which the fancy usually originates, that wild and vicious appetites inflame the lowlier nature, and give it an ascendency over the superior, which it is the peculiar quality of all intellectual exercises to subdue and to correct. These find an aliment in the obvious nature which renders them indifferent to, and keeps them ignorant of, the prurient appetites of a morbid mood. The aspects of nature and man are equally grateful to the faith which looks confidingly to all things under the genial influence of a hope that takes its birth in the affections, and believes chiefly because it loves. And it is precisely such a confiding nature which is the soul and very secret of success in art. To its eye, nothing is absolutely unseemly, though all demands improvement, in the natural aspects of earth and man. The desert is no desert, spread out and sleeping beneath the broad, blue canopy of heaven. The sea is no terror, reposing in its delicious moonlight. The forest is no region of gloom and exile, but one rather of refuge and of shade, when the world threatens and the burning sun prevails. It is by an innate property that art is enable to crown nature with an aspect of her own;—nor inanimate nature only. The wild beast is stilled by, and crouches beneath, a look; the reptile is spelled by a sound, and uncoils himself; unharming, from his victim. And man himself— the savage man! He is savage, it may be, but not necessarily foul or beastly. Wild, but why vicious, unless you make, or suffer him to remain so? It is in your own hands to subject him to holier and happier laws, if you will only so far sympathize with his inferior nature, as to show him the pathway to a better promise. The serf— destined to an inferior condition, through which only can he rise into a better—is elevated, by his reverence and fidelity, into a being whom we reward not less with love than with food and raiment. To the catholic eye of art, high and humble are but relative dependencies, mutual in position, though differing in height and aspect. The beautiful and the obscure, the bright and the dark, are but natural foils of each other—in other words, parts of a system, in which variety is not simply a proof of the boundless resources of the Creator, but of his sense, also, of what is essential to the proper exercise the relief and the gratification of the soul. The philosophy which art teaches, is the faith with which youth begins; a faith which youth is but too apt to forget, in the more earthy cares of manhood; but which it is the becoming vocation of art, as tributary to religion, still to re-inspire. It is in this way that art is always young and original. Every generation discovers in her a new aspect. Novel forms, new guises, declare for her supremacy over the monotonous and tamely recurring aspects of ordinary time. It is because heedless of this peculiar virtue in the constitution of this catholic Muse, that we find the critic of hackneyed judgment, grown too subservient to the customary to appreciate the fresh, resenting as a vice the assumption of new phases in the very Genius which he has worshipped under another form. He seems unwilling to believe that there should be any longer a novelty in art, when there is no longer a freshness in his own nature.

4

NATHANIEL HAWTHORNE

Anonymous

International Magazine (1851).

The author of *The House of the Seven Gables* is now about forty-five years of age.[56] He was born in Salem, Massachusetts, and is of a family which for several generations has "followed the sea." Among his ancestors, I believe, was the "bold Hawthorne," who is celebrated in a revolutionary ballad as commander of the "fair American."[57] He was educated at Bowdoin College in Maine, where he graduated in 1825.

Probably he appeared in print before that time, but his earliest volume was an anonymous and never avowed romance which was published in Boston in 1832.[58] It attracted little attention, but among those who read it with a just appreciation of the author's genius was Mr. S. G. Goodrich, who immediately secured the shrouded star for *The Token,* of which he was editor, and through which many of Hawthorne's finest tales and essays were originally given to the public.[59] He published in 1837 and in 1842 the second volume of his *Twice-Told Tales*, embracing whatever he wished to preserve from his contributions to the magazines; in 1845 he edited *The Journal of an African Cruiser*; in 1846 published *Mosses from an Old Manse*, a second collection of his magazine papers; in 1850 *The Scarlet Letter*, and in the last month the longest and in some respects the most remarkable of his works, *The House of the Seven Gables.*[60]

In the introductions to the *Mosses from an Old Manse* and *The Scarlet Letter* we have some glimpses of his personal history. He had been several years in the Custom-House at Boston, while Mr. Bancroft[61] was collector, and afterwards had joined that remarkable association, the "Brook Farm Community," at West Roxbury, where, with others, he appears to have been reconciled to the old ways, as quite equal to the inventions of Fourier, St. Simon, Owen, and the rest of that ingenious company of schemers who have been so intent upon a reconstruction of the foundations of society.[62] In 1843, he went to reside in the pleasant village of Concord, in the "Old Manse," which had never been profaned by a lay occupant until he entered it as his home. In the introduction to *The Mosses* he says:

A priest had built it; a priest had succeeded to it; other priestly men, from time to time, had dwelt in it; and children, born in its chambers, had grown up to assume the priestly character. It was awful to reflect how many sermons must have been written there. The latest inhabitant alone—he, by whose translation to Paradise the dwelling was left vacant—had penned nearly three thousand discourses, besides the better, if not the greater number, that gushed living from his lips. How often no doubt, had he paced to and fro along the avenue, attuning his meditations, to the sighs and gentle murmurs, and deep and solemn peals of the wind, among the lofty tops of the trees! In that variety of natural utterance, he could find something accordant with every passage of his sermon, were it of tenderness or reverential fear. The boughs over my head seemed shadowy with solemn thoughts, as well as with rustling leaves. I took shame to myself for having been so long a writer of idle stories, and ventured to hope that wisdom would descend upon me with the falling leaves of the avenue; and that I should light upon an intellectual treasure, in the Old Manse, well worth those hoards of long-hidden gold, which people seek for in moss-grown houses. Profound treatises of morality—a layman's unprofessional, and therefore unprejudiced views of religion;—histories (such as Bancroft might have written, had he taken up his abode here, as he once purposed), bright with picture, gleaming over a depth of philosophic thought;—these were the works that might fitly have flowed from such a retirement. In the humblest event, I resolved at least to achieve a novel that should evolve some deep lesson, and should possess physical substance enough to stand alone. In furtherance of my design, and as if to leave me no pretext for not fulfilling it, there was, in the rear of the house, the most delightful little nook of a study that ever offered its snug seclusion to a scholar. It was here that Emerson wrote *Nature*; for he was then an inhabitant of the Manse, and used to watch the Assyrian dawn and the Paphian sunset and moon- rise, from the summit of our eastern hill.[63] When I first saw the room, its walls were blackened with the smoke of unnumbered years, and made still blacker by the grim prints of puritan ministers that hung around. These worthies looked strangely like bad angels, or, at least, like men who had wrestled so continually and so sternly with the devil, that somewhat of his sooty fierceness had been imparted to their own visages. They had all vanished now; a cheerful coat of paint, and gold tinted paper hangings, lighted up the small apartment; while the shadow of a willow-tree, that swept against the overhanging eaves, attempered the cheery western sunshine. In place of the grim prints there was the sweet and lovely head of one of Raphael's Madonnas, and two pleasant little pictures of the Lake of Como. The only other decorations were a purple vase of flowers, always fresh, and a bronze one containing graceful ferns. My books (few, and by no means choice; for they were chiefly such waifs as chance had thrown in my way) stood in order about the room, seldom to be disturbed.

In his home at Concord, thus happily described, in the midst of a few congenial friends, Hawthorne passed three years; and, "in a spot so sheltered from the turmoil of life's ocean," he says, "three years hasten away with a noiseless flight, as the breezy sunshine chases the cloud-shadows across the depths of a still valley." But at length his repose was invaded by that "spirit of improvement," which is so constantly marring the happiness of quiet-loving people, and he was compelled to look out for another residence.

Now came hints, growing more and more distinct, that the owner of the old house was pining for his native air. Carpenters next appeared, making a tremendous racket among the outbuildings, strewing green grass with pine shavings and chips of chesnut joists, and vexing the whole antiquity of the place with their discordant renovations. Soon, moreover, they divested our abode of the veil of woodbine which had crept over a large portion of its southern face. All the aged mosses were cleared unsparingly away; and there were horrible whispers about brushing up the external walls with a coat of paint—a purpose as little to my taste as might be that of rouging the venerable cheeks of one's grandmother. But the hand that renovates is always more sacrilegious than that which destroys. In fine, we gathered up our household goods, drank a fare-well cup of tea in our pleasant little breakfast-room—delicately fragrant tea, an unpurchasable luxury, one of the many angel-gifts that had fallen like dew upon us—and passed forth between the tall stone gate-posts, as uncertain as the wandering Arabs where our tent might next be pitched. Providence took me by the hand, and—an oddity of dispensation which, I trust, there is no irreverence in smiling at—has led me, as the newspapers announce while I am writing, from the old Manse into a Custom House! As a story-teller, I have often contrived strange vicissitudes for my imaginary personages, but none like this. The treasure of intellectual gold which I had hoped to find in our secluded dwelling, had never come to light. No profound treatise of ethics—no philosophic history—no novel, even, that could stand unsupported on its edges—all that I had to show, as a man of letters, were these few tales and essays, which had blossomed out like flowers in the calm summer of my heart and mind.

The Mosses from an Old Manse he declared the last offering of their kind he should ever put forth; "unless I can do better," he wrote in this Introduction, "I have done enough in this kind." He went to his place in the Custom House, in his native city, and if President Taylor's advisers had not been apprehensive that in his devotion to ledgers he would neglect the more important duties of literature, perhaps we should have heard no more of him; but those patriotic men, remembering how much they had enjoyed the reading of the *Twice-Told Tales* and the *Mosses*, induced the appointment in his place of a whig, who had no capacity for making books, and in the spring of last year we had *The Scarlet Letter*.[64]

Like most of his shorter stories, *The Scarlet Letter* finds its scene and time with the earlier Puritans. Its argument involves the analysis and action of remorse in the heart of a person who, himself unsuspected, is compelled to assist in the punishment of the partner of his guilt. This peculiar and powerful fiction at once arrested attention, and claimed for its author the eminence as a novelist which his previous performances had secured for him as a writer of tales. Its whole atmosphere and the qualities of its characters demanded for a creditable success very unusual capacities. The frivolous costume and brisk action of the story of fashionable life are easily depicted by the practised sketcher, but a work like *The Scarlet Letter* comes slowly upon the canvas, where passions are commingled and overlaid with the deliberate and masterly elaboration with which the grandest effects are produced in pictorial composition and coloring. It is a distinction of such works that while they are acceptable to the many, they also surprise and delight the few who appreciate the nicest arrangement and the most high and careful finish. *The Scarlet Letter* will challenge consideration in the name of Art, in the best audience which in age receives Cervantes, Le Sage, or Scott.

Following this romance came new editions of *True Stories from History and Biography,* a volume for youthful readers, and of the *Twice-Told Tales.*[65] In the preface to the latter, underrating much the reputation he has acquired by them, he says:

> The author of *Twice-Told Tales* has a claim to one distinction, which, as none of his literary brethren will care about disputing it with him, he need not be afraid to mention. He was for a good many years the obscurest man of letters in America. These stories were published in magazines and annuals, extending over a period of ten or twelve years, and comprising the whole of the writer's young manhood, without making (so far as he has ever been aware) the slightest impression on the public. One or two among them, the "Rill from the Town Pump," in perhaps a greater degree than any other, had a pretty wide newspaper circulation; as for the rest, he has no grounds for supposing that on their first appearance they met with the good or evil fortune to be read by any body. Throughout the time above specified he had no incitement to literary effort in a reasonable prospect of reputation or profit; nothing but the pleasure itself of composition—an enjoyment not at all amiss in its way, and perhaps essential to the merit of the work in hand, but which, in the long run, will hardly keep the chill out of a writer's heart, or the numbness out of his fingers. To this total lack of sympathy, at the age when his mind would naturally have been most effervescent, the public owe it (and it is certainly an effect not to be regretted, on either part), that the author can show nothing for the thought and industry of that portion of his life, save the forty sketches, or thereabouts, included in these volumes. Much more, indeed, he wrote; and some very small part of it might yet be rummaged out (but it would not be worth the trouble) among the dingy pages of fifteen or twenty year old periodicals, or within the shabby morocco covers of faded Souvenirs. The remainder of the works alluded to had a very brief existence, but, on the score of brilliancy, enjoyed a fate vastly superior to that of their brotherhood, which succeeded in getting through the press. In a word, the author burned them without mercy or remorse, and, moreover, without any subsequent regret, and had more than one occasion to marvel that such very dull stuff as he knew his own condemned manuscripts to be, should yet have possessed inflammability enough to set the chimney on fire! [....][66]

As he glances over these long-forgotten pages, and considers his way of life while composing them, the author can very clearly discern why all this was so. After so many sober years, he would have reason to be ashamed if he could not criticise his own work as fairly as another man's; and, though it is little his business and perhaps still less his interest, he can hardly resist a temptation to achieve something of the sort. If writers were allowed to do so, and would perform the task with perfect sincerity and unreserve, their opinions of their own productions would often be more valuable and instructive than the works themselves. At all events, there can be no harm in the author's remarking that he rather wonders how the *Twice-Told Tales* should have gained what vogue they did, than that it was so little and so gradual. They have the pale tint of flowers that blossomed in too retired a shade—the coolness of a meditative habit, which diffuses itself through the feelings and observations of every sketch. Instead of passion, there is sentiment; and, even in what purport to be pictures of actual life, we have allegory, not always so warmly dressed in its habiliments of flesh and blood as to be taken into the reader's mind without a shiver. Whether from lack of power or an unconquerable reserve, the author's touches have often an effect of tameness; the merriest man can hardly contrive to laugh at his broadest humor, the tenderest woman, one would suppose, will hardly shed warm tears at his deepest pathos. The book, if you would see anything in it, requires to be read in the clear, brown, twilight atmosphere in which it was written; if opened in the sunshine, it is apt to look exceedingly like a volume of blank pages. [....][67]

The author would regret to be understood as speaking sourly or querulously of the slight mark made by his earlier literary efforts on the public at large. It is so far to the contrary, that he has been moved to write this preface, chiefly as affording him an opportunity to express how much enjoyment he has owed to these volumes, both before and since their publication. They are the memorials of very tranquil and not unhappy years. They failed, it is true—nor could it have been otherwise—in winning an extensive popularity. Occasionally, however, when he deemed them entirely forgotten, a paragraph or an article, from a native or foreign critic, would gratify his instincts of authorship with unexpected praise—too generous praise, indeed, and too little alloyed with censure, which, therefore, he learned the better to inflict upon himself. And, by-the-by, it is a very suspicious symptom of a deficiency of the popular element in a book, when it calls forth no harsh criticism. This has been particularly the fortune of the *Twice-Told Tales*. They made no enemies, and were so little known and talked about, that those who read, and chanced to like them, were apt to conceive the sort of kindness for the book, which a person naturally feels for a discovery of his own. This kindly feeling (in some cases, at least) extended to the author, who, on the internal evidence of his sketches, came to be regarded as a mild, shy, gentle, melancholic, exceedingly sensitive, and not very forcible man. Hiding his blushes under an assumed name, the quaintness of which was supposed, somehow or other, to symbolize his personal and literary traits. He is by no means certain that some of his subsequent productions have not been influenced and modified by a natural desire to fill up so amiable an outline, and to act in consonance with the character assigned to him; nor, even now, could he forfeit it without a few tears of tender sensibility.   To conclude, however,—these volumes have opened the way to most agreeable associations, and to the formation of imperishable friendships; and there are many golden threads, interwoven with his present happiness, which he can follow up more or less directly, until he finds their commencement here; so that in his pleasant pathway among realities seems to proceed out of the Dream-Land of his youth, and to be bordered with just enough of its shadowy foliage to shelter him from the heat of the day. He is therefore satisfied with what the *Twice-Told Tales* have done for him, and feels it to be far better than fame.

That there should be any truth in this statement that the public was so slow to recognize so fine a genius, is a mortifying evidence of the worthlessness of a literary popularity. But it may be said of Hawthorne's fame that it has grown steadily, and that while many who have received the turbulent applause of the multitude since he began his career are forgotten, it has widened and brightened, until his name is among the very highest in his domain of art, to shine there with a lustre equally serene and enduring.

Mr. Hawthorne's last work is *The House of Seven Gables*, a romance of the present day. It is not less original, not less striking, not less powerful, than *The Scarlet Letter*. We doubt indeed whether he has elsewhere surpassed either of the three strongly contrasted characters of the book. An innocent and joyous child-woman, Phoebe Pyncheon, comes from a farm-house into the grand and gloomy old mansion where her distant relation, Hepzibah Pyncheon, an aristocratical and fearfully ugly but kind-hearted unmarried woman of sixty, is just coming down from her faded state to keep in one of her drawing-rooms a small shop, that she may be able to maintain an elder brother who is every moment expected home from a prison to which in his youth he had been condemned unjustly, and in the silent solitude of which he has kept some lineaments of gentleness while his hair has grown white, and a sense of beauty while his brain has become disordered and his heart has been crushed and all present influences of beauty have been quite shut out. *The House of Seven Gables* is the purest piece of imagination in our prose literature.

The characteristics of Hawthorne which first arrest the attention are imagination and reflection, and these are exhibited in remarkable power and activity in tales and essays, of which the style is distinguished for great simplicity, purity and tranquillity. His beautiful story of "Rappaccini's Daughter" was originally published in the *Democratic Review*, as a translation from the French of one M. de l'Aubépine, a writer whose very name, he remarks in a brief introduction, (in which he gives in French the titles of some of his tales, as "Contes deux foix raconties," "Le Culte du feu," etc.) "is unknown to many of his countrymen, as well as to the student of foreign literature."[68] He describes himself, under this *nom de plume*, as one who—

> Seems to occupy an unfortunate position between the transcendentalists (who under one name or another have their share in all the current literature of the world), and the great body of pen-and-ink men who address the intellect and sympathies of the multitude. If not too refined, at all events too remote, too shadowy and unsubstantial, in his mode of development, to suit the taste of the latter class, and yet too popular to satisfy the spiritual or metaphysical requisitions of the former, he must necessarily find himself without an audience, except here and there an individual, or possibly an isolated clique.

His writings, to do them justice, he says—

> Are not altogether destitute of fancy and originality; they might have won him greater reputation but for an inveterate love of allegory, which is apt to invest his plots and characters with the aspect of scenery and people in the clouds, and to steal away the human warmth out of his conceptions. His fictions are sometimes historical, sometimes of the present day, and sometimes, so far as can be discovered, have little or no reference either to time or space. In any case, he generally contents himself with a very slight embroidery of outward manners—the faintest possible counterfeit of real life,— and endeavors to create an interest by some less obvious peculiarity of the subject. Occasionally a breath of nature, a rain drop of pathos and tenderness, or a gleam of humor, will find its way into the midst of his fantastic imagery, and make us feel as if, after all, we were yet within the limits of our native earth. We will only add to this cursory notice, that M. de l'Aubépine's productions, if the reader chance to take them in precisely the proper point of view, may amuse a leisure hour as well as those of a brighter man; if otherwise, they can hardly fail to look excessively like nonsense.

Hawthorne is as accurately as he is happily described in this curious piece of criticism, though no one who takes his works in the "proper point of view," will by any means agree to the modest estimate which, in the perfect sincerity of his nature, he has placed upon them. He is original, in invention, construction, and expression, always picturesque, and sometimes in a high degree dramatic. His favorite scenes and traditions are those of his own country, many of which he has made classical by the beautiful associations that he has thrown around them. Every thing to him is suggestive, as his own pregnant pages are to the congenial reader. All his productions are life-mysteries, significant of profound truths. His speculations, often bold and striking, are presented with singular force, but with such quiet grace and simplicity as not to startle until they enter in and occupy the mind. The gayety with which his pensiveness is occasionally broken, seems more than anything else in his works to have cost some effort. The gentle sadness, the "half-acknowledged melancholy," of his manner and reflections, are more natural and characteristic.

His style is studded with the most poetical imagery, and marked in every part with the happiest graces of expression, while it is calm, chaste, and flowing, and transparent as water. There is a habit among nearly all the writers of imaginative literature, of adulterating the conversations of the poor with barbarisms and grammatical blunders which have no more fidelity than elegance. Hawthorne's integrity as well as his exquisite taste prevented him from falling into this error. There is not in the world a large rural population that speaks its native language with a purity approaching that with which the English is spoken by the common people of New England. The vulgar words and phrases which in other states are supposed to be peculiar to this part of the country are unknown east of the Hudson, except to the readers of foreign newspapers, or the listeners to low comedians who find it profitable to convey such novelties into Connecticut, Massachusetts, and Vermont. We are glad to see a book that is going down to the next ages as a representative of national manners and character in all respects correct.

Nathaniel Hawthorne is among the first of the first order of our writers, and in their peculiar province his works are not excelled in the literature of the present day or of the English language.

5

NATHANIEL HAWTHORNE

Henry T. Tuckerman

Southern Literary Messenger (1851).

Henry Theodore Tuckerman (1813-1871) was born in Boston but after 1845, wrote much of his literary criticism, sketches, poems, and books of romantic travel in New York. Tuckerman's writing includes *America and Her Commentators* (1864), a scholarly work on travel in America.

I passed an hour lately in examining various substances through a powerful microscope, with a man of science at my elbow, to expound their use and relations. It was astonishing what revelations of wonder and beauty in common things were thus attained in a brief period. The eye aptly directed, the attention wisely given and the minute in nature enlarged and unfolded to the vision, a new sense of life and its marvels seemed created. What appeared but a slightly rough surface proved variegated iris-hued crystals; a dot on a leaf became a moth's nest with its symmetrical eggs and their hairy pent-house; the cold passive oyster displayed heart and lungs in vital activity; the unfolding wings grew visible upon the seed-vessels of the ferns; beetles looked like gorgeously emblazoned shields; and the internal economy of the nauseous cockroach, in its high and delicate organism, showed a remarkable affinity between insect and animal life. What the scientific use of lenses—the telescope and the microscope—does for us in relation to the external universe, the psychological writer achieves in regard to our own nature. He reveals its wonder and beauty, unfolds its complex laws and makes us suddenly aware of the mysteries within and around individual life. In the guise of attractive fiction and sometimes of the most airy sketches, Hawthorne thus deals with his reader. His appeal is to consciousness and he must, therefore, be met in a sympathetic relation; he shadows forth,—hints,—makes signs,—whispers,—muses aloud,—gives the keynote of melody—puts us on a track;—in a word, addresses us as nature does—that is unostentatiously, and with a significance not to be realized without reverent silence and gentle feeling—a sequestration from bustle and material care, and somewhat of the meditative insight and latent sensibility in which his themes are conceived and wrought out. Sometimes they are purely descriptive, bits of Flemish painting—so exact and arrayed in such mellow colors, that we unconsciously take them in as objects of sensitive rather than imaginative observation; the "Old Manse" and the "Custom House"—those quaint portals to his fairy-land, as peculiar and rich in contrast in their way, as Boccaccio's sombre introduction to his gay stories—are memorable instances of this fidelity in the details of local and personal portraiture; and that chaste yet deep tone of colouring which secure an harmonious whole.[69] Even in allegory, Hawthorne imparts this sympathetic unity to his conception; "Fire Worship," "The Celestial Railroad," "Monsieur du Miroir," "Earth's Holocaust," and others in the same vein, while they emphatically indicate great moral truth, have none of the abstract and cold grace of allegorical writing; besides the ingenuity they exhibit, and the charm they have for the fancy, a human interest warms and gives them meaning to the heart.[70] On the other hand, the imaginative grace which they chiefly display, lends itself quite as aptly to redeem and glorify homely fact in the plastic hands of the author. "Drowne's Wooden Image," "The Intelligence Office," and other tales derived from common-place material, are thus moulded into artistic beauty and suggestiveness. Hawthorne, therefore, is a prose-poet. He brings together scattered beauties, evokes truth from apparent confusion, and embodies the tragic or humorous element of a tradition or an event in lyric music—not, indeed, to be sung by the lips, but to live, like melodious echoes, in the memory. We are constantly struck with the felicity of his invention. What happy ideas are embodied in "A Virtuoso's Collection" and "The Artist of the Beautiful"—independent of the grace of their execution! There is a certain uniformity in Hawthorne's style and manner, but a remarkable versatility in his subjects; and each as distinctly carries with it the monotone of a special feeling or fancy, as one of Miss Baillie's plays:— and this is the perfection of psychological art.

There are two distinct kinds of fiction, or narrative literature, which for want of more apt terms, we may call the melodramatic and the meditative; the former is in a great degree mechanical, and deals chiefly with incidents and adventure; a few types of character, and approved scenic material and what are called effective situations, make up the story; the other species, on the contrary, is modelled upon no external pattern, but seems evolved from the author's mind, and tinged with his idiosyncrasy; the circumstances related are often of secondary interest while the sentiment they unfold, the picturesque or poetic light in which they are placed, throw an enchantment over them. We feel the glow of individual consciousness even in the most technical description; we recognize a significance beyond the apparent, in each character; and the effect of the whole is that of life rather than history: we inhale an atmosphere as well as gaze upon a landscape; the picture offered to the mental vision has not outline and grouping, but color and expression, evincing an intimate and sympathetic relation between the moral experience of the author and his work, so that, as we read, not only scenes but sensations, not only fancies but experience seem borne in from the entrancing page.

There is a charm also essential to all works of genius which for want of a more definite term we are content to call the ineffable. It is a quality that seems to be infused through the design of the artist after its mechanical finish—as life entered the statue at the prayer of the Grecian sculptor.[71] It is a secret, indescribable grace, a vital principle, a superhuman element imparting the distinctive and magnetic character to literature, art and society, which gives them individual life; it is what the soul is to the body, luminous vapour to the landscape, wind to sound, and light to color. No analysis explains the phenomenon; it is recognized by consciousness rather than through direct intellectual perception; and seems to appeal to a union of sensibility and insight which belongs, in the highest degree, only to appreciative minds. Its mysterious, endearing and conservative influence hallows all works universally acknowledged as those of genius in the absolute significance of the word; and it gives to inanimate forms, the written page, the composer's harmony and the lyric or dramatic personation, a certain pervading interest which we instantly feel disarming criticism and attesting the presence of what is allied to our deepest instincts. It touches the heart with tender awe before a Madonna of Raphael; it thrilled the nerves and evoked the passions in the elocution of Kean;[72] it lives in the expression of the Apollo, in the characters of Shakespeare, and the atmospheres of Claude; and those once thus initiated by experience, know spontaneously the invisible line of demarcation which separates talent, skill and knowledge from genius by the affinity of impression invariably produced:—a distinction as clearly felt and as difficult to portray as that between the emotions of friendship and love. It would appear as if there was a provision in the minds of the highly gifted similar to that of nature in her latent resources; whereby they keep in reserve a world of passion, sentiment and ideas, unhackneyed by casual use and unprofaned by reckless display—which is secretly lavished upon their mental emanations:—hence their moral life, intense personality, and sympathetic charm. Such a process and result is obviously independent of will and intelligence; what they achieve is thus crowned with light and endowed with vitality by a grace above their sphere; the Ineffable, then, is a primary distinction and absolute token of genius; like the halo that marks a saintly head. Results like these are only derived from the union of keen observation with moral sensibility; they blend like form and color, perspective and outline, tone and composition in art. They differ from merely clever stories in what may be called flavor. There is a peculiar zest about them which proves a vital origin; and this is the distinction of Hawthorne's tales. They almost invariably possess the reality of tone which perpetuates imaginative literature;—the same that endears to all time Defoe, Bunyan, Goldsmith, and the old dramatists. We find in pictorial art that the conservative principle is either absolute fidelity to detail as in the Flemish, or earnest moral beauty as in the Italian school; the painters who yet live in human estimation were thoroughly loyal either to the real or the ideal—to perception or to feeling, to the eye or the heart. And, in literature, the same thing is evident. *Robinson*

Crusoe is objectively, and *Pilgrim's Progress* spiritually, true to nature; the *Vicar of Wakefield* emanated from a mind overflowing with humanity; and it is the genuine reproduction of passion in the old English plays that makes them still awaken echoes in the soul. It may be regarded as a proof of absolute genius to create a mood; to inform, amuse, or even interest is only the test of superficial powers sagaciously directed; but to infuse a new state of feeling, to change the frame of mind and, as it were, alter the consciousness—this is the triumph of all art. It is that mysterious influence which beauty, wit, character, nature and peculiar scenes and objects exert, which we call fascination, a charm, an inspiration or a glamour, according as it is good or evil. It may safely be asserted that by virtue of his individuality every author and artist of genius creates a peculiar mood, differing somewhat according to the character of the recipient, yet essentially the same. If we were obliged to designate that of Hawthorne in a single word, we should call it metaphysical, or perhaps soulful. He always takes us below the surface and beyond the material; his most inartificial stories are eminently suggestive; he makes us breathe the air of contemplation, and turns our eyes inward. It is as if we went forth, in a dream, into the stillness of an autumnal wood, or stood alone in a vast gallery of old pictures, or moved slowly, with muffled tread, over a wide plain, amid a gentle fall of snow, or mused on a ship's deck, at sea, by moonlight; the appeal is to the retrospective, the introspective, to what is thoughtful and profoundly conscious in our nature and whereby it communes with the mysteries of life and the occult intimations of nature. And yet there is no painful extravagance, no transcendental vagaries in Hawthorne; his imagination is as human as his heart; if he touches the horizon of the infinite, it is with reverence; if he deals with the anomalies of sentiment, it is with intelligence and tenderness. His utterance too is singularly clear and simple; his style only rises above the colloquial in the sustained order of its flow; the terms are apt, natural and fitly chosen. Indeed, a careless reader is liable continually to lose sight of his meaning and beauty, from the entire absence of pretension in his style. It is requisite to bear in mind the universal truth, that all great and true things are remarkable for simplicity; the direct method is the pledge of sincerity, avoidance of the conventional, an instinct of richly-endowed minds; and the perfection of art never dazzles or overpowers, but gradually wins and warms us to an enduring and noble love. The style of Hawthorne is wholly inevasive; he resorts to no tricks of rhetoric or verbal ingenuity; language is to him a crystal medium through which to let us see the play of his humor, the glow of his sympathy, and the truth of his observation.

Although he seldom transcends the limited sphere in which he so efficiently concentrates his genius, the variety of tone, like different airs on the same instrument, gives him an imaginative scope rarely obtained in elaborate narrative. Thus he deals with the tragic element, wisely and with vivid originality, in such pieces as "Roger Malvin's Burial" and "Young Goodman Brown"; with the comic in "Mr. Higginbotham's Catastrophe," "A Select Party," and "Dr. Heidegger's Experiment," and with the purely fanciful in "David Swan," "The Vision of the Fountain," and "Fancy's Show Box." Nor is he less remarkable for sympathetic observation of nature than for profound interest in humanity; witness such limning as the sketches entitled "Buds and Bird Voices," and "Snow-Flakes"—genuine descriptive poems, though not cast in the mould of verse, as graphic, true and feeling as the happiest scenes of Bryant or Crabbe. With equal tact and tenderness he approaches the dry record of the past, imparting life to its cold details, and reality to its abstract forms. The early history of New England has found no such genial and vivid illustration as his pages afford. Thus, at all points, his genius touches the interests of human life, now overflowing with a love of external nature, as gentle as that of Thomson, now intent upon the quaint or characteristic in life with a humor as zestful as that of Lamb, now developing the horrible or pathetic with something of Webster's dramatic terror, and again buoyant with a fantasy as aerial as Shelley's conceptions.[73] And, in each instance, the staple of charming invention is adorned with the purest graces of style. This is Hawthorne's distinction. We have writers who possess in an eminent degree, each of these two great requisites of literary success, but no one who more impressively unites them; cheerfulness as if caught from the sea-breeze or the green-fields, solemnity as if imbibed from the twilight, like colors on a palette, seem transferable at his will, to any legend or locality he chooses for a frame-work whereon to rear his artistic creation; and this he does with so dainty a touch and so fine a disposition of light and shade, that the result is like an immortal cabinet picture—the epitome of a phase of art and the miniature reflection of a glorious mind. Boccaccio in Italy, Marmontel in France, Hoffman and others in Germany, and Andersen in Denmark, have made the tale or brief story classical in their several countries; and Hawthorne has achieved the same triumph here.[74] He has performed for New England life and manners the same high and sweet service which Wilson has for Scotland—caught and permanently embodied their "lights and shadows."

Brevity is as truly the soul of romance as of wit; the light that warms is always concentrated, and expression and finish, in literature as in painting, are not dependent upon space. Accordingly the choicest gems of writing are often the most terse; and as a perfect lyric or sonnet outweighs in value a mediocre epic or tragedy, so a carefully worked and richly conceived sketch, tale or essay is worth scores of diffuse novels and ponderous treatises. It is a characteristic of standard literature, both ancient and modern, thus to condense the elements of thought and style. Like the compact and well-knit frame, vivacity, efficiency and grace result from this bringing the rays of fancy and reflection to a focus. It gives us the essence, the flower, the vital spirit of mental enterprise; it is a wise economy of resources and often secures permanent renown by distinctness of impression unattained in efforts of great range. We, therefore, deem one of Hawthorne's great merits a sententious habit, a concentrated style. He makes each picture complete and does not waste an inch of canvas. Indeed the unambitious length of his tales is apt to blind careless readers to their artistic unity and suggestiveness; he abjures quantity, while he refines upon quality.

A rare and most attractive quality of Hawthorne, as we have already suggested, is the artistic use of familiar materials. The imagination is a wayward faculty, and writers largely endowed with it, have acknowledged that they could expatiate with confidence only upon themes hallowed by distance. It seems to us less marvellous that Shakespeare peopled a newly discovered and half-traditional island with such new types of character as Ariel and Caliban;[75] we can easily reconcile ourselves to the enchanting impossibilities of Arabian fiction; and the superstitious fantasies of northern romance have a dreamlike reality to the natives of the temperate zone. To clothe a familiar scene with ideal interest, and exalt things to which our senses are daily accustomed, into the region of imaginative beauty and genuine sentiment, requires an extraordinary power of abstraction and concentrative thought. Authors in the old world have the benefit of antiquated memorials which give to the modern cities a mysterious though often disregarded charm; and the very names of Notre Dame, the Rialto, London Bridge, and other time-hallowed localities, take the reader's fancy captive and prepares him to accede to any grotesque or thrilling narrative that may be associated with them. It is otherwise in a new and entirely practical country; the immediate encroaches too steadily on our attention; we can scarcely obtain a perspective:

> Life treads on life and heart on heart:—
> We press too close in church and mart,
> To keep a dream or grave apart.[76]

Yet with a calm gaze, a serenity and fixedness of musing that no outward bustle can disturb and no power of custom render hackneyed, Hawthorne takes his stand, like a foreign artist in one of the old Italian cities,—before a relic of the past or a picturesque glimpse of nature, and loses all consciousness of himself and the present, in transferring its features and atmosphere to canvas. In our view the most remarkable trait in his writings is this harmonious blending of the common and familiar in the outward world, with the mellow and vivid tints of his own imagination. It is with difficulty that his maturity of conception and his finish and geniality of style links itself, in our minds, with the streets of Boston and Salem, the Province House and even the White Mountains; and we congratulate every New Englander with a particle of romance, that in his native literature, "a local habitation and a name," has thus been given to historical incidents and localities;[77]—that art has enshrined what of tradition hangs over her brief career—as characteristic and as desirable thus to consecrate, as any legend or spot, German or Scottish genius has redeemed from oblivion. The "Wedding Knell," the "Gentle Boy," the "White Old Maid," the "Ambitious Guest," the "Shaker Bridal," and other New England subjects, as embodied and glorified by the truthful, yet imaginative and graceful art of Hawthorne, adequately represent in literature, native traits, and this will ensure their ultimate appreciation. But the most elaborate effort of this kind, and the only one, in fact, which seems to have introduced Hawthorne to the whole range of American readers, is the *Scarlet Letter*. With all the care in point of style and authenticity which mark his lighter sketches, this genuine and unique romance, may be considered as an artistic exposition of Puritanism as modified by New England colonial life. In truth to costume, local manners and scenic features, the *Scarlet Letter* is as reliable as the best of Scott's novels; in the anatomy of human passion and consciousness it resembles the most effective of Balzac's illustrations of Parisian or provincial life, while in developing bravely and justly the sentiment of the life it depicts, it is as true to humanity as Dickens. Beneath its picturesque details and intense characterization, there lurks a profound satire. The want of soul, the absence of sweet humanity, the predominance of judgment over mercy, the tyranny of public opinion, the look of genuine charity, the asceticism of the Puritan theology,—the absence of all recognition of natural laws, and the fanatic substitution of the letter for the spirit—which darken and harden the spirit of the pilgrims to the soul of a poet—are shadowed forth with a keen, stern and eloquent, yet indirect emphasis that haunts us like "the cry of the human."[78] Herein is evident and palpable the latent power which we have described as the most remarkable trait of Hawthorne's genius;—the impression grows more significant as we dwell upon the story; the states of mind of the poor clergymen. Hester, Chillingworth and Pearl, being as it were transferred to our bosoms through the intense sympathy their vivid delineation excites;—they seem to conflict, and glow and deepen and blend in our hearts, and finally work out a great moral problem. It is as if we were baptized into the consciousness of Puritan life, of New England character in its elemental state; and knew, by experience, all its frigidity, its gloom, its intellectual enthusiasm and its religious aspiration. *The House of the Seven Gables* is a more elaborate and harmonious realization of these characteristics. The scenery, tone and personages of the story are imbued with a local authenticity which is not, for an instant, impaired by the imaginative charm of romance. We seem to breathe, as we read, the air and be surrounded by the familiar objects of a New England town. The interior of the House, each article described within it, from the quaint table to the miniature by Malbone;—every product of the old garden, the street-scenes that beguile the eyes of poor Clifford, as he looks out of the arched window, the noble elm and the gingerbread figures at the little shop window—all have the significance that belong to reality when seized upon by art. In these details we have the truth, simplicity and exact imitation of the Flemish painters. So life-like in the minutiae and so picturesque in general effect are these sketches of still-life, that they are daguerreotyped in the reader's mind, and form a distinct and changeless background, the light and shade of which give admirable effect to the action of the story: occasional touches of humor, introduced with exquisite tact, relieve the grave undertone of the narrative and form vivacious and quaint images which might readily be transferred to canvas—so effectively are they drawn in words; take, for instance, the street musician and the Pyncheon fowls, the judge balked of his kiss over the counter, Phoebe reading to Clifford in the garden, or the old maid, in her lonely chamber, gazing on the sweet lineaments of her unfortunate brother. Nor is Hawthorne less successful in those pictures that are drawn exclusively for the mind's eye and are obvious to sensation rather than the actual vision. Were a New England Sunday, breakfast, old mansion, easterly storm, or the morning after it clears, ever so well described? The skill in atmosphere we have noted in his lighter sketches, is also as apparent: around and within the principal scene of this romance, there hovers an alternating melancholy and brightness which is born of genuine moral life; no contrasts can be imagined of this kind, more eloquent to a sympathetic mind, than that between the inward consciousness and external appearance of Hepzibah or Phoebe and Clifford, or the Judge. They respectively symbolize the poles of human existence; and are fine studies for the psychologist. Yet this attraction is subservient to fidelity to local characteristics. Clifford represents, though in its most tragic imaginable phase, the man of fine organization and true sentiments environed by the material realities of New England life; his plausible uncle is the type of New England selfishness, glorified by respectable conformity and wealth; Phoebe is the ideal of genuine, efficient, yet loving female character in the same latitude; Uncle Venner, we regard as one of the most fresh, yet familiar portraits in the book; all denizens of our eastern provincial towns must have known such a philosopher; and Holgrave embodies Yankee acuteness and hardihood redeemed by integrity and enthusiasm. The contact of these most judiciously selected and highly characteristic elements, brings out not only many beautiful revelations of nature, but elucidates interesting truth; magnetism and socialism are admirably introduced; family tyranny in its most revolting form, is powerfully exemplified; the distinction between a mental and a heartfelt interest in another, clearly unfolded; and the tenacious and hereditary nature of moral evil impressively shadowed forth. The natural refinements of the human heart, the holiness of a ministry of disinterested affection, the gracefulness of the homeliest services when irradiated by cheerfulness and benevolence, are illustrated with singular beauty. "He," says our author, speaking of Clifford, "had no right to be a martyr; and beholding him so fit to be happy, and so feeble for all other purposes, a generous, strong and noble spirit would, methinks, have been ready to sacrifice what little enjoyment it might have planned for itself,—*it would have flung down the hopes so paltry in its regard—if thereby the wintry blasts of our rude sphere might come tempered to such a man*": and elsewhere: "Phoebe's presence made a home about her,— that very sphere which the outcast, the prisoner, the potentate, the wretch beneath mankind, the wretch above it, instinctively pines after—a home. She was real! Holding her hand, you felt something; a tender something; a substance and a warm one: *and so long as you could feel its grasp, soft as it was, you might be certain that your place was good in the whole sympathetic chain of human nature*. The world was no longer a delusion."

Thus narrowly, yet with reverence, does Hawthorne analyze the delicate traits of human sentiment and character; and open vistas into that beautiful and unexplored world of love and thought, that exists in every human being, though overshadowed by material circumstance and technical duty. This, as we have before said, is his great service; digressing every now and then, from the main drift of his story, he takes evident delight in expatiating on phases of character and general traits of life, or in bringing into strong relief the more latent facts of consciousness. Perhaps the union of the philosophic tendency with the poetic instinct is the great charm of his genius. It is common for American critics to estimate the interest of all writings by their comparative glow, vivacity and rapidity of action: somewhat of the restless temperament and enterprising life of the nation infects its taste; such terms as "quiet," "gentle" and "tasteful," are equivocal when applied in this country, to a book; and yet they may envelope the rarest energy of thought and depth of insight as well as earnestness of feeling; these qualities, in reflective minds, are too real to find melo-dramatic development; they move as calmly as summer waves, or glow as noiselessly as the firmament; but not the less grand and mighty is their essence; to realize it, the spirit of contemplation and the recipient mood of sympathy, must be evoked, for it is not external but moral excitement that is proposed; and we deem one of Hawthorne's most felicitous merits—that of so patiently educing artistic beauty and moral interest from life and nature, without the least sacrifice of intellectual dignity.

The healthy spring of life is typified in Phoebe so freshly as to magnetize the feelings as well as engage the perceptions of the reader; its intellectual phase finds expression in Holgrave, while the state of Clifford, when relieved of the nightmare that oppressed his sensitive temperament, the author justly compares to an Indian summer of the soul. Across the path of these beings of genuine flesh and blood, who constantly appeal to our most humane sympathies, or rather around their consciousness and history, flits the pale, mystic figure of Alice—whose invisible music and legendary fate overflow with a graceful and attractive superstition—yielding an Ariel-like melody to the more solemn and cheery strains of the whole composition. Among the apt though incidental touches of the picture, the idea of making the music-grinder's monkey an epitome of avarice, the daguerreotype a test of latent character, and the love of the reformer Holgrave for the genially practical Phoebe, win him to conservatism, strike us as remarkably natural yet quite as ingenuous and charming as philosophical. We may add that the same pure, even, unexaggerated and perspicuous style of diction that we have recognized in his previous writing, is maintained in this.

As earth and sky appear to blend at the horizon though we cannot define the point of contact, things seen and unseen, the actual and the spiritual, mind and matter, what is within and what is without consciousness, have a line of union, and, like the colours of the iris, are lost in each other. About this equator of life the genius of Hawthorne delights to hover as its appropriate sphere; whether indulging a vein of Spenserian allegory, Hogarth sketching, Goldsmith domesticity, or Godwin metaphysics, it is around the boundary of the possible that he most freely expatiates; the realities and the mysteries of life to his vision are scarcely ever apart; they act and re-act as to yield dramatic hints or vistas of sentiment. Time broods with touching solemnity over his imagination; the function of conscience awes while it occupies his mind; the delicate and the profound in love and the awful beauty of death transfuse his meditation; and these supernal he likes to link with the terrestrial influences—to hallow a graphic description by a sacred association or to brighten a commonplace occasion with the scintillations of humour—thus vivifying or chastening "the light of common day."[79]

6

ANGLO-AMERICAN LITERATURE AND MANNERS

Anonymous

International Magazine (1852). A review of *Anglo-American Literature and Manners,* by Philarete Chasles.

A volume of brilliant French criticism will be published in a few days by Charles Scribner, under the title of *Anglo-American Literature and Manners,* by Philarete Chasles, Professor in the College of France.[80] M. Chasles, in a book of five hundred pages, considers the literature and manners of the people of the United States— their institutions, capacity for self-government, actual condition and probable future—with all the sprightly grace of a Frenchman, and with a great deal of cleverness prosecutes his industrious researches from the landing of the *Mayflower* to the present day. He finds in the United States neither an Utopia, nor a land worthy merely of ridicule. He does not simply condemn, like some travellers, nor give us universal and unreasonable praise, as our egotism and contentment lead us to desire, but takes a fair view of the country, its claims, position, and prospects. In the beginning of his performance he considers that the most essential thing for the founding of a new common wealth, is moral force; this he finds in the Puritans, who possessed "sincerity, belief, perseverance, courage"; they could "wait, fight, suffer." Their energy, he thinks, comes from their Teutonic or Saxon blood; their indomitable perseverance is a fruit of Calvinism, added to which they are clannish, or mutual helpers one of another. This is the key to the philosophical, political and prophetic portion of his work. The literary part is honest criticism, freely spoken, by the aid of such light as happened to be around him. He begins with the landing of the Pilgrims, speaks of their literature, which, like all other American literature down to the present day, he regards as destitute of originality. Franklin, Jonathan Edwards, and others, all lack this quality. The author of the *American Cultivator* has the most of it;[81] but Franklin is made up of Fénelon, Bunyan, and Addison; Edwards partakes of Hobbes, Priestley, and in his better moments of the close reasoning Descartes.[82] He gives us then a politician, a journalist, and a gentleman, "the American Aristocrat" as he calls him, Gouverneur Morris, our minister at Paris during the old revolution. Brockden Brown is characterized as a copyist of Monk Lewis; and he comes then to Washington Irving, but while all the charms of this delightful writer are thoroughly appreciated and minutely described, it is denied that he has originality.[83] "In some square house in Boston, he sees in thought St. James's Park: in reveries he is led through the umbrageous alleys of Kensington—he talks with Sterne—he shakes hands with Goldsmith." "It is a copy, some what timid, of Addison, of Steele, of Swift." You would think of him as of "a young lady of good family, a slave to propriety, never elevating her voice, never exaggerating the *ton*,[84] never committing the sin of eloquence"; "a refined continuation of the style of Addison," &c. Nevertheless a dawn of freshness appears in his writings when they treat of forest scenes. This dawn advances into day in Cooper, upon whom we have an admirable critique. The author of *The Spy*, M. Chasles thinks, has a native vigor unknown to Irving. Paulding is dismissed with but very little consideration. Channing occupies the critic longer, but is found to be an unsatisfactory and too general reasoner. Audubon furnishes the most attractive chapter in the book, which closes with what is called the First Literary Epoch of the United States.[85]

The next division is of the *Literature of the People, and the falsely popular Literature of England and the States*. One thoughtful chapter is given to the infancy and future of America; the age and despair of Europe, of emigration, and colonization. Then, the popular movements in France and England are treated of, and the education of the masses. Crabbe, Burns, Elliott, Thomas Cooper and others serve as a text.[86] Popular literature is found to be less anarchical in America than in Europe. We have a chapter on Herman Melville; and then the Americans are viewed through the spectacles of Marryat, Trollope, Dickens, and their exaggerations are noted.[87] The force of public opinion and of the press conclude the section. Our poets have two chapters: I. Barlow, Dwight, Colton, Payne, Sprague, Dana, Drake, Pierepont; Female Poets; and Street and Halleck.[88] II. Bryant, Emerson, and Longfellow. *Tom Stapleton*, by an Irish Sunday newspaper reporter, and *Puffer Hopkins*, by Mr. Cornelius Matthews, one chapter;[89] Stephens, Silliman, and others represent the travellers;[90] a chapter is dedicated to Arnold and André;[91] Haliburton's *Sam Slick* concludes the criticism; and the book ends with *The Future of Septentrional America and the United States*—what a "Bee" is, how an American village is got up, the aggregative principles of Americans, the Lowell Lectures, Democrats and Whigs—and then, far-seeing prophetic talking, conclude what the author has to say about us.[92]

7

PIERRE; OR, THE AMBIGUITIES

Anonymous

A review of Herman Melville's *Pierre; or, The Ambiguities* (1852). *American Whig Review* (1852).

A bad book! Affected in dialect, unnatural in conception, repulsive in plot, and inartistic in construction. Such is Mr. Melville's worst and latest work.

Some reputations seem to be born of accident. There are common-place men who on some fine day light, unknown to themselves, upon a popular idea, and suddenly rise on the strength of it into public favor. They stride the bubble for a little while, but at last its prismatic hues begin to fade; men see that the object of their applause has after all but an unsubstantial basis, and when at length the frail foundation bursts, they fall back into their original obscurity, unheeded and unlamented. Mr. Melville has experienced some such success. A few years back, he gave to the world a story of romantic adventure; this was untrue in its painting, coarse in its coloring, and often tedious and prolix in its descriptive passages. But there was a certain air of rude romance about it, that captivated the general public. It depicted scenes in a strange land, and dealt with all the interests that circle around men whose lives are passed in peril. Nor were appeals to the grosser instincts of humanity wanting. Naked women were scattered profusely through the pages, and the author seemed to feel that in a city where the ballet was admired, *Typee*[93] would be successful.* Mr. Melville thought he had hit the key-note to fame. His book was reprinted in all directions, and people talked about it, as much from the singularity of its title as from any intrinsic merit it possessed.

This was encouraging, and Mr. Melville evidently thought so, for he immediately issued a series of books in the same strain. *Omoo, Mardi, White-Jacket, Redburn,* followed one another in quick succession; and the foolish critics, too blind to perceive

---

* Mr. Cornelius Mathews was, we believe, the first to designate this prurient taste under the happy and specific head of "the ballet-feeling."

that the books derived their chief interest from the fact of the scenes being laid in countries little known, and that the author had no other stock in trade beyond tropical scenery and eccentric sailors, applauded to the very echo.[94] This indiscriminating praise produced its usual effect. Mr. Melville fancied himself a genius, and the result of this sad mistake has been—*Pierre*.

As a general rule, sea-stories are very effective, and to those versed in nautical lore, very easy writing. The majority of the reading public are landsmen, and the events of an ocean-life come to them recommended by the charm of novelty. They cannot detect the blunders, and incongruity passes with them for originality. The author can make his vessel and his characters perform the most impossible feats, and who, except the favored few that themselves traverse the sea professionally, will be one bit the wiser? The scope for events is also limited, and this very limitation renders the task of writing a sea-tale more simple. A storm, a wreck, a chase and a battle, a mutiny, desertions, and going into and leaving port, with perhaps a fire at sea, form the principal "properties" of a salt-water artist. Considerable descriptive powers are, we admit, necessary to the management of these materials. The storm must be wild, the battle fierce, and the fire terrible; but these, after all, are broad outlines, and require little delicacy of handling to fill them in. Sometimes, as in the *Pilot*, one finds a veil of pathetic tenderness and grace flung over the characters, but as a general rule in nautical fictions, the wit is coarse, the pathos clumsy, and the most striking characters are invariably unnatural.[95]

It is when a writer comes to deal with the varied interests of a more extended life; when his hand must touch in harmonious succession the numberless chords of domestic sorrows, duties and affections, and draw from each the proper vibration; when he has to range among the ever-changing relations of every-day humanity, and set each phase of being down in its correct lineaments; it is then he discovers that something more is necessary for the task than a mere arrangement of strong words in certain forms,—or the trick of painting nature, until, like a ranting actress, she pleases certain tastes according as she deviates from truth.

Mr. Melville's previous stories, all sea-born as they were, went down the public throat because they were prettily gilt with novelty. There are crowds of people who will run after a new pill, and swallow it with avidity, because it is new, and has a long Greek name. It may be made of bread, or it may be made of poison; the novelty of the affair renders all considerations of its composition quite immaterial. They learn the name, eat the bolus, and pay the doctor. We have a shrewd suspicion that the uncouth and mysterious syllables with which Mr. Melville baptized his books had much to do with their success. Like Doctor Dulcamara, he gave his wares an exciting title, and trusted to Providence for the rest.[96] The enchantment worked. The mystic cabala of "*Omoo*, by the author of *Typee*," was enough in itself to turn any common novel-reader's brain, and the books went off as well as a collection of magic rings would in Germany, or the latest batch of *Agnus Deis* in an Italian village.[97] People had little opportunity of judging of their truth. Remote scenes and savage actors gave a fine opportunity for high coloring and exaggerated outline, of which Mr. Melville was not slow to avail himself, and hence Fayaway is as unreal as the scenery with which she is surrounded.

We do not blame Mr. Melville for these deviations from truth. It is not much matter if South Sea savages are painted like the heroes of a penny theatre, and disport themselves amid pasteboard groves, and lakes of canvas. We can afford Mr. Melville full license to do what he likes with *Omoo* and its inhabitants; it is only when he presumes to thrust his tragic *Fantoccini* upon us, as representatives of our own race, that we feel compelled to turn our critical Aegis upon him, and freeze him into silence.[98]

Pierre aims at something beyond the mere records of adventure contained in *Mardi* and *Omoo*. The author, doubtless pulled up by the very false applause which some critics chose to bestow upon him, took for granted that he was a genius, and made up his mind to write a fine book; and he has succeeded in writing a fine book with a vengeance. Our experience of literature is necessarily large, but we unhesitatingly state, that from the period when the Minerva press was in fashion, up to the present time, we never met with so turgid, pretentious, and useless a book as *Pierre*.[99] It is always an unpleasant and apparently invidious statement for a critic to make, that he can find nothing worthy of praise in a work under consideration; but in the case of *Pierre* we feel bound to add to the assertion the sweeping conclusion, that there we find every thing to condemn. If a repulsive, unnatural and indecent plot, a style disfigured by every paltry affectation of the worst German school, and ideas perfectly unparalleled for earnest absurdity, are deserving of condemnation, we think that our already expressed sentence upon *Pierre* will meet with the approval of every body who has sufficient strength of mind to read it through.

Mr. Pierre Glendinning, the hero of the book, and intended by the author to be an object of our mournful admiration, supports in the course of the story the arduous characters of a disobedient son, a dishonest lover, an incestuous brother, a cold-blooded murderer, and an unrepentant suicide. This *repertoire* is agreeably relieved by his playing the part of a madman whenever he is not engaged in doing anything worse.

This agreeable young gentleman is the only son of a widow lady of large fortune, who coquets in her old age with suitors about the same age as Pierre. And to render the matter still more interesting, Pierre by mutual consent sinks the son, and deports himself by word and look towards his mother as a lover; while she, charming coquette of fifty that she is, readily imitates this delightful *abandon*. The early character of Mr. P. Glendinning, as traced by our author, is exceedingly fine; we will, however, spare it to our readers, merely stating on Mr. Melville's authority, that in him might be observed "the polished steel of the gentleman, girded with Religion's silken sash"; which sash, his great-grandfather had somehow or other taught him, "should, in the last bitter trial, furnish its wearer with glory's shroud." Setting aside the little incompatibility of religion having anything to do, even in sashes, with martial glory, we cannot help thinking that the mere mention of making a shroud out of so scanty an article as a sash, is quite sufficient to scandalize any respectable under-taker.

Well, this be-sashed young gentleman, who lives alone with his mother at the family place of Saddle Meadows, is engaged formally to a very flighty young lady named Lucy Tartan. If there is anything to which we object particularly in this young couple, it is the painful habit they have contracted of *tutoyer*-ing[100] each other through whole pages of insane rhapsody. We cannot believe that the indiscriminate use of "thee" and "thou" makes the nonsense with which it is generally connected one atom more readable. On the contrary, it has a most unpleasant effect, for it deprives the mad passages in which it occurs of the only recommendation that can palliate insanity, that is, simplicity.

Notwithstanding Mr. P. Glendinning's being already supplied with a mother and a mistress, he is pursued by indefinite longings for a sister. His reason for this im-perious craving is rather a pugnacious one, and almost inclines us to believe that the young gentleman must have had some Celtic blood in his veins. If he had but a sister, he alleges he would be happy, because "it must be a glorious thing to engage in a mortal quarrel on a sweet sister's behalf!" This, it must be confessed, is a strange fancy, but we suppose it is to be accounted for by the fact of Saddle Mead-ows being rather a dull place, and Mr. Pierre believing that a little fighting was the best thing in the world for the blues.

By a chain of the most natural circumstances in the world—we mean in Mr. Melville's books—this sister is most unexpectedly supplied. In fact, though the author says nothing about it, we are inclined to think that he imported her direct from a lunatic asylum for the occasion. She proves to be an illegitimate daughter of Pierre's father, and judging from her own story, as well as we could understand it, appears to have been dry-nursed by an old family guitar; an allegory almost as fine as that of Romulus and Remus.[101] If we suppose this paternal instrument to have been out of tune at the time that it assumed the responsibility of the little Isabel, that young lady's singular turn of mind is at once accounted for; but if we go a little farther, and suppose the worthy instrument to have been cracked, we explain still more satisfactorily the origin of her very erratic conduct.

"Sister Isabel," being an illegitimate Glendinning, is of course inadmissible to the refined atmosphere breathed by the aristocratic Mrs. Glendinning, who has rather strong ideas upon such subjects. Accordingly, Pierre, who is afraid to mention to his mother the discovery he has made, and moved to compassion by the forlorn state of the young lady, who, lives with her faithful guitar in a charming cottage on the edge of a beautiful lake, takes compassion on her desolate condition, and de-termines to devote his life to her. He therefore conceives the sublime idea of obvi-ating all difficulties—for difficulties there must have been, or Mr. Melville would not say so, though we confess that we have not been so fortunate as to discover them—by presenting her to the world as his wife! The reasons alleged by this virtu-ous hero are detailed at some length by Mr. Melville, as if he knew that he could not apologize too much for presenting such a picture to the world. Firstly, Pierre wishes to conceal the fact of Isabel's being the offspring of his father's sin, and thereby protect his parent's reputation. Secondly, he is actuated by a desire not to disturb his mother's mind by any disclosure which would destroy the sacredness of her deceased husband's memory; and lastly, he entertains towards this weird sister feelings which Mr. Melville endeavors to gloss over with a veil of purity, but which even in their best phase can never be anything but repulsive to a well constituted mind.

Now, in this matter Mr. Melville has done a very serious thing, a thing which not even unsoundness of intellect could excuse. He might have been mad to the very pinnacle of insanity; he might have torn our poor language into tatters, and made from the shreds a harlequin suit in which to play his tricks;[102] he might have piled up word upon word, and adjective upon adjective, until he had built a pyramid of nonsense, which should last to the admiration of all men; he might have done all this and a great deal more, and we should not have complained. But when he dares to outrage every principle of virtue; when he strikes with an impious, though, happily, weak hand, at the very foundations of society, we feel it our duty to tear off the veil with which he has thought to soften the hideous features of the idea, and warn the public against the reception of such atrocious doctrines. If Mr. Melville had reflected at all—and certainly we find in him but few traces of reflection—when he was writing this book, his better sense would perhaps have informed him that there are certain ideas so repulsive to the general mind that they themselves are not alone kept out of sight, but, by a fit ordination of society, every thing that might be supposed to even collaterally suggest them is carefully shrouded in a decorous darkness. Nor has any man the right, in his morbid craving after originality, to strip these horrors of their decent mystery. But the subject which Mr. Melville has taken upon himself to handle is one of no ordinary depravity; and however he may endeavor to gloss the idea over with a platonic polish, no matter how energetically he strives to wrap the mystery in a cloud of high-sounding but meaningless words, the main conception remains still unaltered in all its moral deformity. We trust that we have said enough on this topic. It is a subject that we would gladly not have been obliged to approach, and which we are exceedingly grieved that any gentleman pretending to the rank of a man of letters should have chosen to embody in a book. Nor can we avoid a feeling of surprise, that professedly moral and apparently respectable publishers like the Messrs. Harper, should have ever consented to issue from their establishment any book containing such glaring abominations as *Pierre*.

But to return to the development of this chaotic volume. Mr. P. Glendinning, actuated by this virtuous love for his sister, informs his proud mother that he is married. She, knowing not the true relationship that binds them together, spurns her unworthy son from her house for having degraded the family name so far by making a *mésalliance*;[103] and the worthy young gentleman, after having nearly killed Miss Lucy Tartan, his betrothed, with the same intelligence, and left his mother in a fit of indignation which has every chance of becoming a fit of apoplexy, sets out with—we really do not know what to call her, for Mr. Melville has so intertwined and confused the wife with the sister, and the sister with the wife, that we positively cannot tell one from the other; so we may as well compromise the matter by calling her simply Isabel. He sets out then with Isabel, in a perfect enthusiasm of virtue, for the city, having first apprised a fashionable cousin of his, one Mr. Glendinning Stanly, that he was on his way, and requesting him to prepare his house for his reception. This fashionable cousin, however, takes very little trouble about the matter; and accordingly, when Pierre and Isabel arrive accompanied by a young lady of loose morals named Delly, they find no house or welcome. A series of incidents here follow, which are hardly worth reciting. They consist of Pierre's quarrel with Stanly, a scene in a police station, a row with a cabman, and ending by Pierre's taking rooms in some out-of-the way place, inhabited by a colony of poor authors, who bear the general denomination of Apostles. Just in this part of the book it comes out suddenly that Pierre is an author, a fact not even once hinted at in the preceding pages. Now the reader is informed, with very little circumlocution, and as if he ought to have known all about it long ago, that Mr. P. Glendinning is the author of a sonnet called the "Tropical Summer," which it seems has called forth the encomiums of the literati, and induced certain proprietors of certain papers to persecute him for his portrait. All this is told in a manner that proves it very clearly to be nothing more than an afterthought of Mr. Melville's, and not contemplated in the original plan of the book, that is, if it ever had a plan. It is dragged in merely for the purpose of making Pierre a literary man, when the author had just brought him to such a stage that he did not know what else to do with him.

Of course, under such circumstances, Mr. P. Glendinning, having the responsibility upon his back of Mrs.—Miss Isabel, his wife-sister, (as Mr. Melville himself would express it,) and the young lady of loose morals, and having no money wherewith to support them, can do nothing better than make his living by writing. Accordingly he writes away in his garret; and we cannot help thinking here, that if he wrote at all in the same style that he speaks, his MSS. must have been excessively original and amusing. Here in this poor place he starves his time away in company with Isabel and the young lady of loose morals. Meanwhile he hears of his mother's death, her bequest of all the property to his cousin Stanly, and the betrothal of that gentleman to his late mistress, Lucy Tartan. This intelligence, however, is soon followed by a remarkable event. Miss Lucy Tartan, true to her old habits of flightiness; conceives the resolution of coming to live with Pierre and Isabel, whom she believes to be his wife. Accordingly, she arrives at the haunt of the Apostles, and takes up her abode with her old lover, very much to the disgust of Madam Isabel, who acts much more like a jealous wife than a sister. In this comfortable state they all live together until Mr. Glendinning Stanly and Miss Lucy Tartan's brother arrive at Pierre's domicile to reclaim the fugitive. She refuses to go, however, and Mr. Pierre thrusts them out of the house. Immediately after he receives two notes: one from a bookseller, for whom he was writing a work, informing him that he is a swindler; the other from Messrs. Stanly and Tartan, putting him in possession of the fact that he is a liar and a scoundrel—all of which conclusions the reader arrives at long before this epoch.

Mr. P. Glendinning on reading these notes immediately proceeds to stand on them. This operation is minutely described by our author, and is evidently considered by him as a very effective piece of business. Putting a note under each heel of his boots, appears to be with Mr. P. Glendinning the very climax of vengeance. Having stood for a sufficiently long time upon the epistles, he proceeds to enter an Apostle's room, and burglariously abstract from thence a pair of pistols, which he loads with the unpleasant letters. Then marching into the street, he meets with, and is cowhided by, Mr. Stanly, and in consequence thereof shoots that individual with two distinct pistols. One would have been meagre, but two bullet-holes make the thing dramatic.

Mr. P. Glendinning now makes his appearance in prison; a place that, if fitness were any recommendation, he ought to have been in long ago. Here he raves about as usual in compound words and uncompounded ideas, until Lucy and Isabel enter, when there is a terrific amount of dying, and the usual vial of poison makes its appearance. How many persons give up the ghost in the last chapter of this exciting work, we are really unable to decide. But we have a dim consciousness that every body dies, save and except the young lady of loose morals.

Previous to entering more closely upon the singular merits of this book, we have endeavored, we fear but feebly, to give the reader some idea of the ground-work on which Mr. Melville has strung his farrago of words. If we have succeeded, so much the better, for our readers will perhaps appreciate more fully our approaching remarks. If we have not, it matters but little, for the reader will have lost nothing that is worth a regret.

We have already dismissed the immorality of Mr. Melville's book, which is as horrible in its tendency as Shelley's *Cenci*, without a ray of the eloquent genius that lights up the deformity of that terrible play; but we have yet another and less repulsive treat in store for the reader.[104] Mr. Melville's style of writing in this book is probably the most extraordinary thing that an American press ever beheld. It is precisely what a raving lunatic who had read Jean Paul Richter *in a translation* might be supposed to spout under the influence of a particularly moonlight night. Word piled upon word, and syllable heaped upon syllable, until the tongue grows as bewildered as the mind, and both refuse to perform their offices from sheer inability to grasp the magnitude of the absurdities. Who would have believed that in the present day a man would write the following, and another be found to publish it?

> Now Pierre began to see mysteries inter-pierced with mysteries, and mysteries eluding mysteries; and began to seem to see the mere imaginariness of the so supposed solidest principle of human association. Fate had done this for them. Fate had separated brother and sister, till to each other they somehow seemed so not at all.—Page 193.

There, public! there's a style for you! There, Mr. Hawthorne, you who rely so much upon the quiet force of your language, read that and profit by it! And you, Mr. Longfellow, who love the Germans, and who in *Hyperion* have given us a sam-ple of an ornate and poetical style, pray read it too, and tell us if it is a wise thing to bind 495 pages of such stuff together, and palm it off upon the public as a book![105] But here is a string of assertions that we think are not to be surpassed; it is positively refreshing to read them:

> Of old Greek times, before man's brain went into doting bondage, and bleached and beaten in Baconian fulling mills, his four limbs lost their barbaric tan and beauty; when the round world was fresh, and rosy, and spicy as a new-plucked apple; all's wilted now! In those bold times, the great dead were not, turkey-like, dished in trenchers, and set down all garnished in the ground to glut the damned Cyclop like a cannibal; but nobly envious Life cheated the glutton worm, and gloriously burned the corpse; so that the spirit up-pointed, and visibly forked to heaven.—Page 269.[106]

We pause here. And when our readers have sufficiently recovered their senses to listen, we will remark that until now we were quite unaware that it was the modern practice to bury people in cover dishes or soup tureens, after having garnished them with parsley. Mr. Melville however asserts it, so it must be correct. Neither do we see what the Cyclop has to do with the funereal ceremonies alluded to. A church-yard is the last place in which we should think of looking for Polyphemus.

It is rather a curious study, that of analyzing a man's style. By a little careful examination and comparison, we are always able to hunt out the lurking secret of a writer's diction. We can discover Bulwer's trick of culminating periods, and Dickens's dodge of impossible similes and startling adjectives. A perfectly plain and pure style is the only one which we cannot properly analyze. Its elements are so equally combined that no one preponderates over the other, and we are not able to discover the exact boundary line that separates the art of the author from the nature of the man. But who writes such a style now-a-days? We feel convinced that echo will not answer, "Mr. Melville."

The author of *Omoo* has his own peculiarities. The English language he seems to think is capable of improvement, but his scheme for accomplishing this end is rather a singular one. Carlyle's compound words and Milton's Latinic ones sink into insignificance before Mr. Melville's extraordinary concoctions. The gentleman, however, appears to be governed by a very distinct principle in his eccentricities of composition, and errs systematically. The essence of this great eureka, this philological reform, consists in "est" and "ness," added to every word to which they have no earthly right to belong. Feeling it to be our duty to give currency to every new discovery at all likely to benefit the world or literature, we present a few of Mr. Melville's word-combinations, in the hope that our rising authors will profit by the lesson, and thereby increase the richness and intelligibility of their style: flushfulness; patriarchalness; humanness; perfectest; heroicness; imaginariness; insolubleness; recallable; entangledly; unrunagate; magnifiedly; intermarryingly; solidest; uncapitulatable; ladylikeness; electricalness; ardentest; unsystemizable; youngness; unemigrating; undoffable.

After such a list, what shall we say? Shall we leave Mr. Melville to the tender mercies of the Purists, or shall we execute vengeance upon him ourselves? We would gladly pursue the latter course if we only knew how to accomplish it. As to destroying or abusing the book, we cannot make it appear worse than it is; and if we continue our remarks upon it, it is simply because we have a duty to perform by every improper work, which we have no right to leave unfinished. We shall, then, instead of turning executioners, simply assume the post of monitors, and warn all our little authors who are just now learning to imitate the last celebrity, to avoid Mr. Melville and his book, as they would some loathsome and infectious distemper.

Perhaps one of the most remarkable features in *Pierre*, is the boldness of the metaphors with which it is so thickly studded. Mr. Melville's imagination stops at nothing, and clears a six-barred simile or a twenty-word antithesis with equal dexterity and daring. It is no light obstacle that will bring him up in his headlong course, and he scoffs alike at the boundaries of common sense and the limits of poetical propriety. We have just caught an image which will serve our purpose, and transfix it, butterfly-like, on our critical pin, for the admiration of scientific etymologists. It is a fine specimen, and quite perfect of its kind. Fortunately for the world, however, the species is very rare:

> An infixing stillness now thrust a long rivet through the night, and fast nailed it to that side of the world!—Page 219.

This is a grand and simple metaphor. To realize it thoroughly, all we have to do is to imagine some Titantic upholsterer armed with a gigantic nail, and hammer to match, hanging one hemisphere with black crape.

His description of a lady's forehead is equally grand and incomprehensible. He says, "The vivid buckler of her brow seemed as a magnetic plate." Trephining is rather an uncommon operation, but we fancy that this lady's head must have undergone some such treatment, in order to warrant her forehead being likened to a "vivid buckler."

Mr. Melville, among other improvements, has favored us with a new substantive of his own invention. We are very grateful to him for this little attention, but our thankfulness would be rendered still more willingly if he had appended a little note explaining the meaning of this—no doubt very forcible—word. At page 252 we find the following sentence: "Thy *instantaneousness* bath killed her." On a first reading of this we hurriedly came to the conclusion that "instantaneousness" must be either some very old or some very new weapon of destruction. We judged simply from the fatal results attributed to it in the sentence. Can it be possible, thought we to ourselves, that the reign of the sanguinary Colt is over? that revolvers are gone out of fashion and "instantaneousnesses" come in? What can these new weapons be like? Have they six barrels, or are they worked by steam? In the midst of these perplexities we were still further bewildered by coming suddenly upon this passage, at page 248: "The strange, imperious instantaneousness in him."

Here in an instant was our whole theory upset. The hieroglyph on the Rosetta stone was not more puzzling than this noun of Mr. Melville's.[107] It was evident from the context in the last sentence that it could not be a weapon of destruction, so we immediately formed a conception that it must be some newly discovered magnetic power, which resided in the man, but could be used with fatal effect if necessary. Upon this hypothesis we were proceeding to build another theory, far more magnificent than our first, when we lit upon a third sentence that sent to the winds all previous speculations. It ran as follows: "That *instantaneousness* now impelled him."— Page 252.

Eureka! we shouted, we have it. Success has crowned our toil, and the enigma is for ever solved. "Instantaneousness" is a new motive power! We leave our readers to brood over this discovery.

Mr. Melville's lingual improvements do not stop here. He discards all commonplace words, and substitutes much better ones of his own in their stead. He would not for the world call the travelling from one place to another "a journey"—that would be far too common. In Mr. Melville's refined diction it becomes "a displacement." Every thing that is dim is with him "nebulous." Hence we have nebulous stories, nebulous landscapes, nebulous meanings, and though last, not least, Mr. Melville himself has given us a very nebulous book!

His descriptive passages are very vivid. The following "night piece" is somewhat after the manner of Callot:[108]

> The obscurely open window, which ever and anon was still softly illumined by the mild heat-lightning and ground lightning, that wove their wonderfulness without, in the unsearchable air of that ebonly warm and most noiseless summer night.—Page 203.

In the same page, a little further on, we find that: "The casement was suddenly and wovenly illumined."

This is no doubt fine to those that understand, but, strange as the confession may appear, we are foolhardy enough to acknowledge that we have not the remotest conception of what it all means. We cannot, by any mental process hitherto discovered, induce our reasoning faculties to accept "ebonly warm" and "wovenly illumined" as conveying any tangible idea. The first two words we do not recognize as belonging to any known language, and we have a shrewd suspicion that the idea—if the author intended any—is quite as undiscoverable.

Again, he hits off a lady's eyes after the following fashion. It may be poetical, but we cannot call it complimentary: "Her dry burning eyes of long-fringed fire."— Page 202.

This young lady must have been the original performer of the "lightning glance" and the "look of flashing scorn," once used so freely by a certain class of novelwriters.

At page 60 we find the following singular expression: "It was no wonder that Pierre should flush a bit, and *stammer in his attitudes* a little."

It was an old-fashioned idea that the disease of stammering was usually confined to the organs of speech. In modern times, however, it seems to embrace a wider sphere; and we shall, no doubt, soon hear of "stuttering legs" and "a man with a hesitation in his arm." Nor do we see why the converse should not be adopted, or why a man should not have a "club-tongue," or "bunions upon his conversation!"

We have been so far particular in pointing out Mr. Melville's faults. We have attached a certain degree of importance to each of them, from the fact that we are obliged to look upon him in the light of an experienced author, and cannot allow him that boyish license which we are always ready to grant to tyros who lose themselves for the first time amid the bewildering paths of literature. Mr. Melville has written good books, and tasted largely of success, and he ought to have known better. We regret that we are not able to temper our criticism with some unalloyed praise. Critics too often gain the reputation of deriving pleasure from the depreciation of others, but it is those who are ignorant of the art that say so. The true critic rejoices with a boyish enthusiasm when he meets with a work worthy of his admiration. The very nature of his avocation enhances the pleasure he feels at the recognition of original beauty. He that has been travelling for many a weary day over dry and dusty tracks of letter-press, strewn thickly with withered commonplaces, and enlivened only with newly-feathered platitudes, must experience a thrill of strange delight when he suddenly emerges from the desolate path he has been pursuing, and comes upon a rich and pleasant pasture of thought. Believe not, fair Public, that this weary critic will not do the fresh mend justice. Believe rather that in his wild pleasure at lighting upon this pure untrodden ground, where things do not smell of second-hand nature, he will rush madly into the extreme of praise, and search as sedulously for the hidden flowers of beauty as he did before for faults. Critics are not envious or malicious—they are simply just; and being just, they are obliged to condemn three fourths of the books that are submitted to their notice. It is not by any means with a view of proving our magnanimity that we quote the following passage from *Pierre* as a specimen of Mr. Melville's better genius. Even this very passage is disfigured by affectations and faults, which, in any other book, would condemn it to exclusion; but in a work like *Pierre*, where all else is so intensely bad, and this is probably the only passage in it that could be extracted with advantage, we feel that we would be doing our author an injustice if, after setting forth all his sins so systematically, we did not present to our readers some favorable specimen of his powers. The passage we subjoin is a description of old Pierre Glendinning, the grandfather of the young Pierre, our ambiguous hero:

Now this grand old Pierre Glendinning was a great lover of horses, but not in the modern sense, for he was no jockey. One of his most intimate friends of the masculine gender was a huge, proud, gray horse, of a surprising reserve of manner, his saddle-beast. He had his horses' mangers carved like old trenchers, out of solid maple logs: the key of the corn-bin hung in his library; and no one grained his steeds but himself; unless his absence from home promoted Moyar, an incorruptible and most punctual old black, to that honorable office. He said that no man loved his horses, unless his own hands grained them. Every Christmas he gave them brimming measures. "I keep Christmas with my horses," said grand old Pierre. This grand old Pierre always rose at sunrise; washed his face and chest in the open air; and then, returning to his closet, and being completely arrayed at last, stepped forth to make a ceremonious call at his stables, to bid his very honorable friends there a very good and joyful morning. Woe to Cranz, Kit, or Douw, or any other of his stable slaves, if grand old Pierre found one horse un-blanketed, or one weed among the hay that filled their rack. Not that he ever had Cranz, Kit, Douw, or any of them flogged—a thing unknown in that patriarchal time and country—but he would refuse to say his wonted pleasant word to them; and that was very bitter to them, for Cranz, Kit, Douw, and all of them loved grand old Pierre, as his shepherds loved old Abraham.

What decorous, lordly, gray-haired steed is this? What old Chaldean rides abroad? 'Tis grand old Pierre; who, every morning before he eats, goes out promenading with his saddle-beast; nor mounts him without first asking leave. But time glides on, and grand old Pierre grows old; his life's glorious grape now swells with fatness; he has not the conscience to saddle his majestic beast with such a mighty load of manliness. Besides, the noble beast himself is growing old, and has a touching look of meditativeness in his large, attentive eyes. Leg of man, swears grand old Pierre, shall never more bestride my steed; no more shall harness touch him! Then every spring he sowed a field of clover for his steed; and at midsummer sorted all his meadow-grasses, for the choicest hay to winter him; and had his destined grain thrashed out with a flail, whose handle had once borne a flag in a brisk battle, into which this same old steed had pranced with grand old Pierre; one waving mane, one waving sword!

Now needs must grand old Pierre take a morning drive. He rides no more with the old gray steed. He has a phaëton built, fit for a vast general, in whose sash three common men might hide. Doubled, trebled, are the huge S-shaped leather springs; the wheels seem stolen from some mill; the canopied seat is like a testered bed. From beneath the old archway, not one horse, but two, every morning now draw forth old Pierre, as the Chinese draw their fat god Jooh once every year from out his fane.

But time glides on, and a morning comes when the phaëton emerges not; but all the yards and courts are full; helmets line the ways; sword-points strike the stone steps of the porch; muskets ring upon the stairs; and mournful martial melodies are heard in all the halls. Grand old Pierre is dead; and, like a hero of old battles, he dies on the eve of another war; ere wheeling to fire on the foe, his platoons fire over their old commander's grave. In A.D. 1812 died grand old Pierre. The drum that beat in brass his funeral march, was a British kettle-drum, that had once helped to beat the vainglorious march for the thirty thousand prisoners led into sure captivity by that bragging boy, Burgoyne.[109]

Next day the old gray steed turned from his grain—turned round, and vainly whinnied in his stall. By gracious Moyar's hand he refuses to be patted now; plain as horse can speak, the old gray steed says, "I smell not the wonted hand; where is grand old Pierre? Grain me not, and groom me not; where is grand old Pierre?"

He sleeps not far from his master now; beneath the field he cropt, he has lain him softly down; and long ere this grand old Pierre and steed have passed through that grass to glory.

But his phaëton, like his plumed hearse, outlives the noble load it bore. And the dark bay steeds that drew grand old Pierre alive, and, by his testament, drew him dead, and followed the lordly lead of the led gray horse—those dark bay steeds are still extant, not in themselves, or in their issue, but in the two descendants of stallions of their own breed. For on the lands of Saddle-Meadows, man and horse are both hereditary; and this bright morning, Pierre Glendinning, grandson of grand old Pierre, now drives forth with Lucy Tartan, seated where his own ancestor sat, and reining steeds whose great-great-great-grandfathers grand old Pierre had reined before.—Pages 38-41.

We have dwelt long enough upon these "Ambiguities." We fear that it we were to continue much longer, we should become ambiguous ourselves. We have, we think, said sufficient to show our readers that Mr. Melville is a man wholly unfitted for the task of writing wholesome fictions; that he possesses none of the faculties necessary for such work; that his fancy is diseased, his morality vitiated, his style nonsensical and ungrammatical, and his characters as far removed from our sympathies as they are from nature.

Let him continue, then, if he must write, his pleasant sea and island tales. We will be always happy to hear Mr. Melville discourse about savages, but we must protest against any more Absurdities, misnamed "Ambiguities."

8

WILLIAM GILMORE SIMMS, LL.D.

P.

International Magazine (1852).

A steadily growing reputation for almost twenty years, justified by the gradually increasing evidence of those latent, exhaustless, ever-unfolding energies which belong to genius, has inwoven the name of Simms with the literature of America, and made it part of the heirloom which our age will give to posterity. Asking and desiring nothing to which he could not prove himself justly entitled, he has wrested a reputation from difficulty and obstacle, and conquered an honorable acknowledgement from opposition and indifference. Even if we had not proofs of genius in the treasury of thought and imagination constituted by his writings, still the nobility of the example of energy, perseverance, and high-toned hopefulness, which he has given, would deserve a grateful homage.

William Gilmore Simms is the second, and only surviving, of three brothers, sons of William Gilmore Simms, and Harriet Ann Augusta Singleton. His father was of a Scotch-Irish family, and his mother of a Virginia stock, her grandparents having removed to South Carolina long before the Revolution, in which they took an active part on the Whig side. He was born on the 17th of April, 1806. His mother died when he was an infant. His father, failing in business as a merchant, removed first to Tennessee, and then to Mississippi. While in Tennessee he volunteered and held a commission in the army of Jackson (in Coffee's brigade of mounted men), which scourged the Creeks and Seminoles after the massacre of Fort Mimms.[110] Our author, left to the care of a grandmother, remained in Charleston, where he received an education which circumstances rendered exceedingly limited. He was denied a classical training, but such characters stand little in need of the ordinary aids of the schoolmaster, and, with indomitable application, he has not only stored his mind with the richest literature, but has received an unsolicited tribute to his diligence and acquisitions, in the degree of Doctor of Laws, conferred upon him by the respectable University of Alabama.

At first it was designed that he should study medicine, but his inclination led him to the law. He was admitted to the bar of South Carolina when twenty-one, practised for a brief period, and became part proprietor of a daily newspaper, which, taking ground against nullification, ruined him—swallowing up a small maternal property, and involving him in a heavy debt which hung upon and embarrassed him for a long time after.[111] In 1832, he first visited the North, where he published *Atalantis*.[112] *Martin Faber* followed in 1834, and periodically the long catalogue of his subsequent performances.

There are few writers who have exhibited such versatility of powers, combined with vigor, originality of copious and independent ideas, and that faculty of condensation which frequently by a single pregnant line suggests an expansive train of reflection. As a poet, he unites high imaginative powers with metaphysical thought—by which we mean that large discourse of reason which generalizes, and which seizes the universal, and perceives its relations to individual phenomena of nature and psychology. His poems abound in appropriate, felicitous, and original similes. His keen and fresh perception of nature, furnishes him with beautiful pictures, the truthfulness and clearness of which are admirably presented in the lucid language with which they are painted, and, in his expression of deep personal feelings, we find a noble union of sad emotion and manliness of tone. He draws from a full treasury of varied experience, active thought, close observation, just and original reflection, and a spirit which has drunk deeply and lovingly from the gushing founts of nature. His inspiration is often kindled by the sunny and luxuriant scenery of the beautiful region to which he was born, and besides the freshness and glow which this imparts to his descriptive poetry, it makes him emphatically the poet of the South. Not only has he sung her peculiar natural aspects with the appreciation of a poet and the feeling of a son, but he has a claim to her gratitude for having enshrined in melodious verse her ancient and fading traditions.

Mr. Simms commenced writing verses at a very early period. At eight years of age he rhymed the achievements of the American navy in the last war with Great Britain.[113] At fifteen, he was a scribbler of fugitive verse for the newspapers, and before he was twenty-one he had published two collections of miscellaneous poetry, which his better taste and prudence subsequently induced him to suppress. Two other volumes of poems followed, in a more ambitious vein, which are also now beyond the reach of the collector, and were issued while he was engaged in the occupations of a newspaper editor and a student and practitioner of law.[114] These volumes were followed by *Atalantis*, a poem which has been highly praised by the best critics of our time.

As a prose writer, his vigorous, copious, and original ideas are clothed in a manly flexible, pure, and lucid style. His first production, *Martin Faber*, succeeded *Atalantis*. It was the initial of a series of tales, which we may describe as of the metaphysical and passionate or moral imaginative class. These, with two or more volumes of shorter tales, are numerous, and perhaps among the most original of his writings. They comprise *Martin Faber and Other Tales, Castle Dismal, Confessions; or, The Blind Heart, Carle Werner and other Tales,* and the *Wigwam and the Cabin.*[115] There are other compositions belonging to this category, and, it may be, not inferior in merit to any of these, which have appeared in periodicals and annuals, but have not yet been collected by their author.

The first novel of Mr. Simms belonged to our border and domestic history. This was *Guy Rivers;* and to the same class he has contributed largely, in *Richard Hurdis, Border Beagles, Beauchampe, Helen Halsey,* and other productions.[116] In historical romance, he has written *The Yemassee,* the *Damsel of Darien, Pelayo,* and *Count Julian,* each in two volumes.[117] The scenes of the two last are laid in Europe. His romances founded on our revolutionary history, are *The Partisan, Mellichampe,* and *The Kinsmen.*[118] In biography and history, he is the author of *The Life of Marion; The Life of Captain John Smith,* founder of Virginia; a *History of South Carolina;* a geography of the same State; a *Life of Bayard;* and a *Life of General Greene.*[119]

It is impossible to enumerate accurately his poetical productions, as many, published in periodicals, have never been printed together; but the collection of his poems now in course of publication at Charleston, will supply a desideratum to the lovers of genuine American letters and art. *Atalantis, Southern Passages and Pictures, Donna Florida, Grouped Thoughts and Scattered Fancies, Areytos, Lays of the Palmetto, The Cassique of Accabee and other Poems, Norman Maurice,* and "The City of the Silent," constituting distinct volumes, are, however, well known.[120]

The orations of Mr. Simms, which have been published, comprise one delivered before the Erosophic Society of the Alabama University, entitled, "The Social Principle—the True Source of National Permanence"; another before the town council and citizens of Aiken, South Carolina, on the Fourth of July, 1844, entitled, "The Sources of American Independence"; and one delivered before literary societies in Georgia, entitled "Self-Development."[121]

As a writer of criticism, Mr. Simms is known by numerous articles contributed to periodicals; by a review of Mrs. Trollope, in the *American Quarterly,* and of Miss Martineau in the *Southern Literary Messenger* (both subsequently republished in pamphlets, and received with general approval),[122] as well as by many others of equal merit—a selection from which, wholly devoted to American topics has been published under the title of *Views and Reviews in American History and Fiction.*[123]

Scarcely a production of Mr. Simms has been unmarked by a cordial reception from the best literary journals; and the praise of the London *Metropolitan* and *Examiner*—the former when under the conduct of Thomas Campbell, the latter of Albany Fonblanque[124]—was generously bestowed, especially on *Atalantis;* of which the *Metropolitan* said, "What has most disappointed us is, that it is so thoroughly English; the construction, the imagery, and, with a very few exceptions, the idioms of the language, are altogether founded on our own scholastic and classical models"; and Fonblanque, in reviewing a tale by Simms, entitled "Murder Will Out," said, "But all we intended to say about the originality displayed in the volume has been forgotten in the interest of the last story of the book, "Murder will Out." This is an American ghost story, and, without exception, the best we have ever read. Within our limits, we could not, with any justice, describe the whole course of its incident, and it is in that, perhaps, its most marvellous effect lies. It is the *rationale* of the whole matter of such appearances, given with fine philosophy and masterly interest. We never read anything more perfect or more consummately told."

But the testimony of the critical press, or even of the successful sale of an author's works, is not so suggestive of merit as the fact that his productions have entered into the popular mind; and this tribute Mr. Simms has received in the fact that in regions which he has identified with legends, created from them by his own genius, localities of his different incidents are pointed out with a sincere belief in their historical veracity. The dramatic powers manifested in his novels, have been still more largely displayed in his *Norman Maurice*, a play of singular originality, in design, character, and execution, the nervous language and felicitous turns of expression in which remind us of the best of the old dramatists. We have heretofore expressed in the *International* a conviction that *Norman Maurice* is the best American drama that has yet been published—the most American, the most dramatic, the most original.

As a member of the Legislature of his native State, and on various public occasions, Mr. Simms has vindicated a title to fame as an orator; and a recent nomination for the presidency of South Carolina College, although he declined being a candidate, is an evidence of the impression which his ability, information, and high character have produced on his fellow citizens.

His intense intellectual activity, united with a habitually reflective and philosophical mode of thought, and unwearied laboriousness, enable him to accomplish an almost incredible amount of literary labor. The catalogue of his works which is subjoined, gives but an inadequate idea of what he has really performed; for multifarious productions, many of them of the highest order in their respective classes, are scattered in the pages of periodicals, or still in manuscript; while the unceasing demands on his pen, with his arduous editorship, prevent him from accomplishing many fruitful designs, whose inception he has hinted in various ways.[125] To his intellectual gifts, he unites a brave, generous nature, a kindly, and strong heart, a genial, impulsive, yet faithful and determined disposition, warm affection and friendship, a spirit to do and to endure, and a soul as much elevated above the petty envies and jealousies which too often deform the *genus irritabile*, as it is in large sympathy with the beautiful, the true, the just—with humanity and with nature.

9

A KEY TO *UNCLE TOM'S CABIN*

George Frederick Holmes

A response to *Facts for the People: A Key to* Uncle Tom's Cabin, *Presenting the Original Facts and Documents upon which the Story is Founded, Together with Corroborative Statements, Verifying the Truth of the Work.* By Harriet Beecher Stowe. 1853. *Southern Literary Messenger* (1853).

George Frederick Holmes (1828-1897) was born in Georgetown, British Guyana, grew up in England, and travelled to Canada and the United States in his late teens to teach and practise law. He was president of the University of Mississippi for five months (1848-1849) and had written numerous articles, many of which appeared in the *Southern Quarterly Review*, before the age of twenty-five.

Ecce iterum Crispinus.[126] Mrs. Stowe obtrudes herself again upon our notice, and, though we have no predilections for the disgusting office of castigating such offences here, and rebuking the incendiary publication of a woman, yet the character of the present attack, and the bad eminence which she and her books have both won, render a prompt notice of the present encyclopaedia of slander even more necessary than any reply to her previous fiction.[127] Her second appearance on the stage of civil dissension and social polemics is much changed from what it was at the time when her first revelations were given to the world. She was then an obscure Yankee school-mistress, eaten up with fanaticism, festering with the malignant virus of abolitionism, self-sanctified by the virtues of a Pharisaic religion, devoted to the assertion of women's rights, and an enthusiastic believer in many neoteric heresies, but she was comparatively harmless, as a being almost entirely unknown.[128] She has now, by a rapid ascent and at a single dash, risen to unequalled celebrity and notoriety; and, though we believe with Dryden, that

Short is the date of all immoderate fame;[129]

yet at the present moment, she can give currency to her treacherous doctrines and her big budget of scandal by the prestige of unprecedented success. That success has been attained less by the imaginary merits of the fiction, though these have obtained unmeasured commendation, than by the inherent vice of the work. Its unblushing falsehood was its chief passport to popular acceptance. But, however acquired, she has certainly won a brilliant vantage-ground for the repetition of her assault upon the South. Is she not now hailed as the great prophetess of the wretched by the multitudes of the earth? Do not all the tongues of Babel, and all the hosannahs of ignorance unite in common acclaim to do her honor? Is she not venerated as the ancient Sibyl who points the way to realms of Saturnian bliss, if she can only unite the fanaticism and blind delusion of the world for the achieve-ment of a vicarious sacrifice at the expense of the South?[130] The Southern States of the Union and the institution of slavery are proposed as the scapegoat for the sins, and the expiation for the miseries of all humanity; and Mrs. Stowe is worshipped as the chosen messenger of heaven, to whom the revelation of this new and easy atonement has been committed, and who has been entrusted with the secret of the sole gate of salvation.[131] The Pharisees of Northern Abolitionism are taught a pleasant escape from the consciousness of their own iniquities and domestic disor-ders by magnifying the supposed guilt of their neighbours, and concentrating their whole attention upon the only sin in which they do not more zealously participate. The poverty-stricken, the wretched, the oppressed millions of Europe have their own real woes presented to their fancy in the picture of the imaginary wrongs of the slave: and the titled lords of the soil and greedy capitalists of England, after driving penury from its wretched home, sweeping miserable crowds from any foot-hold on the soil and wringing profits or selfish gratifications from the agonies of famished labour, wrap themselves in the warm mantle of self-delusion or hypocrisy; and thank Heaven that they are not as Southern men are. The harmonious concord of such influences lends strength and volume to that outpouring of applause which is lavished upon Mrs. Stowe and her book, and gives at this time to anything she may write a popularity and importance wholly unconnected with any intrinsic mer-its. This very consideration, however, should induce us not to accumulate our in-dignation on the head of the poor pander to the prurient appetite of the public, but to distribute our censure with liberal impartiality between the deceiver and the will-ingly deceived. Still, as Mrs. Stowe furnishes the text, she must be set up as the tar-get at which our arrows have necessarily to be aimed.

But if the position of the "author of *Uncle Tom's Cabin*"[132] is materially changed on her second manifestation in print, the mutation is not less between her two pro-ductions. The first work was a fiction designed as an embodiment of the truth—but possessing all the characteristics of fiction, and many that do not legitimately be-long even to romance. The second is professedly a compilation of facts for the purpose of sustaining the allegations of imagination, and of proving the reality to be worse than conjecture. The first was an intricate involution and convolution of fictions for the insinuation of slander; the second is a distortion of the facts and mutilation of the records, for the sake of giving substance to the scandalous fancy, and reduplicating the falsehood of the representation. *Uncle Tom's Cabin* is represented in the present work as "a mosaic of facts"—and *The Key* is now supplied to give access to the quarry from which the facts were taken. We think the designation of a fictitious mosaic of facts equally applicable to both romances, for the fancy, which was displayed before in false colouring and perverse arrangement, is now exercised in the congenial task of false representation and misinterpretation. It was a wise proverb of the Arabs, that there is no lie so black or dangerous as that which is founded upon the truth. Mrs. Stowe has illustrated two aspects of the aphorism, but she has not recognized the delusion and iniquity of either procedure. We endeavoured to expose briefly on a former occasion the pernicious fallacy of weaving a fiction out of the threads of life, and we shall now more briefly exhibit the sophistry of that easy and shallow process—the transmutation of facts into fiction. This, indeed, will constitute the principal aim and the larger portion of our present criticism.

Before touching the *Key*, however, we have a preliminary remark to introduce, which may seem foreign to our immediate subject, but is most intimately combined with it as explaining and perpetuating the agitation which Mrs. Stowe has been able to excite. It is a horrible thought that a woman should write or a lady read such productions as those by which her celebrity has been acquired. Are scenes of license and impurity, and ideas of loathsome depravity and habitual prostitution to be made the cherished topics of the female pen, and the familiar staple of domestic consideration or promiscuous conversation? Is the mind of woman to be tainted, seduced, contaminated, and her heart disenchanted of its native purity of sentiment, by the unblushing perusal, the free discussion, and the frequent meditation of such thinly veiled pictures of corruption? Can a lady of stainless mind read such works without a blush of confusion, or a man think of their being habitually read by ladies without shame and repugnance? It is sufficiently disgraceful that a woman should be the instrument in disseminating the vile stream of contagion; but it is intolerable that Southern women should defile themselves by bringing the putrid waters to their lips? If they will drink of them in secret, let them repent in secret, and not make vices unknown to the ears of the pure and upright of their sex, the subject of daily thought and conversation. Grant that every accusation brought by Mrs. Stowe is perfectly true, that every vice alleged occurs as she has represented, the pollution of such literature to the mind and heart of woman is not less—but perhaps even more to be apprehended. It may accord with the gross fancies and coarse nature of a Cincinnati school-mistress to revel over the imagination or the reality of corruptions, with which she is much more conversant than the majority of Southern gentlemen, but the license of a ribald tongue must be excluded from the sanctity of the domestic hearth. If Mrs. Stowe will chronicle or imagine the incidents of debauchery let us hope that women—and especially Southern women, will not be found poring over her pages. The gospels according to Fanny Wright and George Sand, the fashionable favour extended to the novels of the French School, and the woman's rights' Conventions, which have rendered the late years infamous, have unsexed in great measure the female mind, and shattered the temple of feminine delicacy and moral graces; and the result is before us in these dirty insinuations of Mrs. Stowe, and in the Christian address of the women of England.[133] If the annals of prostitution are to be raked over and republished, they should find no students or lecturers among women of refined feelings or respectable character. The Stowe-ic philosophy is a fatal contamination to woman.

The point was one of too immediate interest to the South, as well as to all portions of the world where female purity is sincerely prized, for us to suffer it to pass without notice, and it has a direct importance at the present time when the dowagers, duchesses, and countesses of England are engaged in the Christian duty of propagating slanders and inviting the co-operation of their American sisters to assist in redressing grievances which exist chiefly in imagination, by means of social revolution and servile war. We could not overlook this matter, as it is only one form of that masculine habit of thought, and that corrupting effrontery of speech and action, which is gradually spreading from the licentious atmosphere of European capitals, and stealing over the manners of women when the presence of the plague is least suspected. But, having rendered this service to the generals cause of morals, we will open the door to the horrors of *Uncle Tom's Cabin,* with the aid of Mrs. Stowe's *Key,* although its wards are not very nicely adjusted to the lock, and betray the rude contrivance of a felonious artist.

This second work is written to substantiate the representations of its predecessor, and to brand still deeper the mark of infamy with which she had previously endeavored to stigmatize the South. Mrs. Stowe intimates that *Uncle Tom's Cabin* was a very inadequate representation of slavery, because the reality was too dreadful for a work of art, and could afford no pleasure unless partially concealed by a veil. She now proposes to withdraw that veil, to exhibit all the sores and ulcers that prey upon the body of the institution, to present the alleged reality in blacker colours than it was exhibited in the fiction, to reply to the doubts and criticisms that have been occasioned by her book, and thus establish the veracity of her former delineations. This contemplated effort is ushered in with the very unnecessary and incredible declaration that "The writer has aimed, as far as possible, to say what is true, and only that, without regard to the effect which it may have upon any person or party." If this declaration is sincere, we can only say that the novelty of the attempt has not been rewarded by any discernible evidences of success; but truth is not easily lured back to the perch from which it had been ignominiously and systematically expelled. Yet, we must give her due credit for this rare visitation of a laudable desire, and regret her lamentable failure, when she "can only say that she has used the most honest and earnest endeavours to learn the truth"; and commends her new book of enormities "to the candid attention and earnest prayers of all true Christians throughout the world."

On a former occasion we refused to deny or call in question the particular facts which were woven into the texture of *Uncle Tom's Cabin;* we denied only the truth of the representation produced by the arrangement and colouring of those facts, and the justice of the inferences proposed to be drawn from them. We are thus relieved from any necessity to reply to or express our entire dissent from the present work, as it is entirely foreign to the only issue which we then made, and, we may add, to the only issue which can be effectually made. Mrs. Stowe limits her present labour of verification to the production of evidence that the facts previously employed were either substantially true, or were so nearly equivalent to the literal truth that they were not unwarrantably assumed in a work professedly of fiction. She shows that there are negro-traders like Haley; that there are quadroons and persons of white complexions, but black blood, who are held as slaves; that there are Shelbys and Legrees; Topsys and Quaker Abolitionists; St. Clares and excellent servants, not quite as good as Uncle Tom; and,—no, she fails to prove the verisimilitude of that Yankee anomaly, Miss Ophelia. She furnishes abundant evidence to prove that the slave laws of the South are exceedingly harsh and severe in the letter, especially to the ears of those who understand neither them nor any other laws, and that there are instances when they are exceedingly harsh in execution, as is the case with all laws. She exhibits enough to generate a more anxious desire for the amelioration of the servile condition, and to deepen our regret that every effort has been arrested and palsied by seditious intervention, and Northern Abolitionism. She proves that negroes are sold, that they are often taken to the South, and that there are frequent separations of families in consequence of the ordinary business transactions of life—but this is all that she does prove. It is certainly a triumphant vindication of *Uncle Tom's Cabin,* if the verification of that insidious libel depended upon the general truth of the separate incidents: it is utterly valueless as a confirmation, if the falsehood and pernicious character of the novel were wholly unconnected with the truth of the details, as we alleged them to be. The fact is that our former exposure of *Uncle Tom's Cabin* remains unassailed and unaffected by this long array of documentary evidence and conjectural interpretation; and that the real issue, which we alleged to have been overlooked by the respondents to Mrs. Stowe, is wholly unapproached by her cloud of witnesses. There was a great error in unnecessarily, and for the most part ignorantly, traversing the mere facts, instead of recurring to the more valid, more just, and more efficacious procedure of demurring to their pretended significance and their mischievous interpretation.

Under these circumstances we might with grace and propriety leave any further notice of Mrs. Stowe and her faggot of delusions to those who have sacrificed the cause of the South, notwithstanding their good intentions, and have afforded to her the prospect of an easy triumph by joining issue with her on the false grounds which her first work very dexterously suggested. The defence proposed by us is unmenaced; the works thrown up by them have been carried without difficulty on the first demonstration, and she will carry this pretence of victory to foreign lands, to communities ready to hail with exultation and to welcome with blind credulity every thing that strengthens their prejudices, or is in accordance with them. We might very appropriately leave to those who have injured the South—to the writers of replicant romances and inconclusive editorials—the duty of retrieving their errors, and reinstating the argument on a legitimate basis by defending themselves against the cogency of this rejoinder; but this is no merely literary controversy, and the interests at stake are too serious to be left in suspense for the decision of a wager of battle conducted on one side by those who have so foolishly yielded the vantage-ground before. We are fully aware how insufficient our defence must be, from the want of space, want of time, and perhaps want of ability; but at any rate we can promise that it will not fail from concurrence or collusion of sophistry, or from the occupancy of untenable grounds. We shall, however, so far take advantage of our own exemption from the attack or reply, that we will be exceedingly brief in our remarks, and will only furnish indications of the argument which others may meditate on, expand, and improve; and will not enter into any detailed examination of the present *Key*.

The issue formerly presented by us, which we now again propose, is that the evils ascribed to the institution of slavery are incident in a still greater extent to all social organizations whatever, and that they are changed in form only, while diminished in kind and degree by the prevalence of slavery. We illustrated this position before, and we now leave it to be developed by those who may honour our views with their approval. The merits of the question are contained in a nut-shell. The whole defence of the South lies in the single position, that the arguments and the line of reasoning adopted in *Uncle Tom's Cabin* and implied in the *Key*, are absolutely destructive of all forms of polity, civilized or savage. This position we think satisfactory and impregnable, but it requires a larger range of view, and greater profundity of investigation than are accorded to the subject by the ordinary assailants or defenders of slavery. However, the whole question must now be thoroughly re-examined; and we cannot regret that a sufficiently active and general excitement has been produced through the rash intermeddling of Mrs. Stowe, to call for such a complete discussion and exposition of the whole subject as may scatter to the winds the frivolous accusations of the abolitionists, and may tranquillize the weak minds and vacillating fancies of many sensitive slaveholders in the South. It is their lukewarm, shilly-shally convictions, "blown about with every wind of doctrine,"[134] and their temporizing uncertainty in a case where doubt is treason either to the negro or the South, which has armed our Abolition adversaries with the fire-brands which they are hurling into the combustible materials in ours midst. One way or the other this case of conscience must be decided promptly: this is no time for either hesitation or delay. If slavery be sinful, impolitic, or inexpedient, either with reference to the interests of the slave or those of his master, away with it. Let it be abolished to-morrow, or so soon as may be practicable with safety: but let there be no tampering with so great a subject, to unite the service of God and Mammon, and to frame excuses for ourselves, while living in conscious iniquity. But if, on the contrary, it be, as we are firmly convinced it is, an institution natural, just, and righteous, render this conviction universal, let all know with confident assurance that it is beneficial to both master and slave, but more especially to the latter, confirm the weak brethren in the faith by sober and thorough instruction, and then neither the powers of the earth nor the powers of hell can shake the institution, or seriously disturb our tranquillity.

We are, however, leaving ourselves too little space for even the brief and desultory remarks which we design making on this Book of the Testimonies.[135] Again, we concede the long string of alleged facts—all the stories—all the hearsay evidence—all the tattle of ignorant busy-bodies, and garrulous old ladies—all the advertisements treasured up through thirty years—all the slave laws, and judicial decisions—everything, except the use made of them and their interpretation. And this reservation we are assured is amply sufficient for the South. We do not mean to say that these statements are even possessed of isolated truth in all instances. Mrs. Stowe admits that she may have committed many errors—some very gross ones have already been pointed out; but we think it unimportant to the defence whether these things be literally true or not, and we may entrust to the local newspapers in each vicinage the task of exposing the misstatements, hoping that they will not disregard this duty, as they may render good service by exposing the eager credulity, the negligent rashness, and the shameless indifference to truth with which the indictment has been drawn up against a whole people, and the evidences of crime collected. But to our argument, it is a matter of trivial consequence whether these statements be separately true or not, the onus of the offence lies in their false interpretation, and the true defence in the explanation of their limited and real significance. We would venture to assert the partial or complete injustice of Mrs. Stowe's exposition of the evidence adduced by her in at least ninety-nine cases out of every hundred that possess any intrinsic importance.

For example. She has delineated Haley as the worst type of negro-trader:—we have ourselves heard of those who were even worse than he. She has adduced evidence to prove that there are such men. We would never have denied it. And then she charges it not on the callousness and depravity of the individual, but on the institution of slavery. The justice of so attributing it is what we deny, and what is the essential point in her intended proof. Slavery only furnishes the occasion and determines the form of the brutality; it neither generates it, nor would its abolition extirpate it. All that would be effected would be to transfer it to some other channel, perhaps to slime it over with the oily varnish of cunning greed, and compel it to pursue its career of darkness by the more terrible, because more effectual and secret means of cheating and legal oppression. There are worse Haleys in the large cities than on the Ohio river; there are more victims to the greed, the power, the depravity of the coarse-minded and merciless in the unnoted transactions of ordinary life, and in the general routine of commercial and manufacturing oppression, than are to be found in the pens of the negro traders. Because rascality is practised for gain, because murders, direct or consequential, are instigated by the desire of gold, shall we charge these things to the score of money, and agitate its entire abolition? Because murders can be wrought only on a living subject, shall we get rid of the crime by proposing the entire annihilation of life? Mrs. Stowe's doctrine runs naturally into absurdities. Because the African slave trade is carried on and perpetu-ated solely by commerce and navigation, shall we suppress both? It may be said with more than her ordinary degree of truth, that without the existence of slavery there would be no slave-trade, but does the existence of slavery at the South ac-count for the curious and disgraceful fact that nearly five-sixths of the slave vessels sail from Baltimore, and the Northern ports of the righteous free States, and none from the more Southern harbours? We do not think that this is attributable to Southern slavery, but to the greater greed, the more unscrupulous pursuits, the am-pler facilities for commercial enterprize in the Northern Cities, and in no slight de-gree to the ancient and persistent opposition of the Southern States to the African slave-trade, which was manifested at a time when the North was clamorous for its continuance and encouragement. If the vices of Haley and the sufferings of his victims are rightly attributable to the institution of slavery, we have certainly a right and a more reasonable right to refer to the absence of it in England, the evictions of the Duchess of Sutherland and company, and the distresses of the poor needle-women on which the London *Times* has so forcibly commented.[136] The absence of slavery is not the absence, but the certain multiplication of misery among the la-bouring classes. Yet it is by such grievous abuse and perversion of facts and reason-ing that Mrs. Stowe has filled this lugubrious volume with falser facts than ever ornamented her fiction.

We have not alluded to the North and to England with a view to refute crimina-tion by recrimination. And yet, it would be justifiable, not as a defence, but to ar-rest defamation on the part of those who had greater errors to correct than our-selves. But our motive has been to show that the evil assigned to slavery is equally or still more incident to societies where slavery does not exist, and that it is only the peculiar form of the evil which is the fruit of slavery. No doubt that form appears horrible to those unacquainted with it, and who see nothing distressing in the mul-tiplied sufferings and crimes which occur everywhere around them; but this unrea-sonable horror, thus springing from entire ignorance, which is more alarmed by its own frenzied imaginations than affected by more dismal but familiar realities, is the motive power which secures popular acceptance and gives plausibility to Mrs. Stowe's fictitious delineations and false constructions.

A word is all that we have time to give to each of the leading topics in this com-pilation of false testimony, and we shall follow Mrs. Stowe into the tangled laby-rinths of that lady-like study, the criminal law in regard to slaves. We are only sur-prised that her peculiar tastes should not have led her attention to the *causes célèbres*[137] in which the trials of negroes for rape are recorded. She might have found them in her ample pile of newspapers. But as these cases furnish stringent evidence on the other side of the question, like a promising apprentice to the law, she has omitted all allusion to them, as well as to the instances of murder, arson, and grave felonies committed by slaves. It is true these are of rarer occurrence among the negroes in Southern States, than amongst the white population in other countries, but they do occur, and might furnish a very pretty counterpart to Mrs. Stowe's juridical researches, and some explanation occasionally of the meaning and propriety of the laws which she cites. Thus she notes with becoming horror the lynching of Cornutt in Grayson, but makes no reference to the seditious and abolitionist doctrines of Bacon, to the insurrection of the negroes, or the murders previously committed by them. We have so little room to say what we wish to say, that we would request the papers throughout the South to take each case reported in Stowe's Reports, vol. III, which occurred and was tried in their respective neighbourhoods, and expose the misconstruction and misinterpretation of their present exposition. It should be honestly and impartially done, and executed with care, skill, and logical consideration. The *Richmond Times* or *Examiner* should do this in the case of the Commonwealth vs. Souther, the *Spirit of Jefferson* in the case of Col. Castleman, the *Wytheville Republican* in the case of Cornutt. It is only by this division of labour, and by the embodiment of the results of such separate inquiry in some New York or Washington Paper that any effectual refutation of these misrepresentations can be presented to those minds which most require it.

There is not a single available law-book within fifteen miles of us while we write, and under such circumstances we cannot pretend to speak very confidently about any details of legislation. But at one time, we were tolerably familiar with the slave law of both Virginia and South Carolina, and can trust our recollection of the latter at least so far as to state that the greater part of it is obsolete and is almost a dead letter on the books. It is sometimes referred to in aid of the judgment of juries, in order to regulate rather than govern their decisions, but we can safely say that any real or imaginary severity of the law is always mitigated by the verdict, except in obscure corners of the different districts, where ignorant magistrates and stupid jurymen lean with the natural tendency of all coarse natures to cruelty. Every effort is, however, made to bring all negro trials from the country to the Courthouses, where they are protected by the intelligence and good-feeling of an enlightened community. Mrs. Stowe complains of the bitter injustice of denying slaves the benefit of counsel and the advantage of trial by jury; the latter is granted by law, with the right of appeal, in all serious cases; the former is usually employed by the owner with a liberality entirely disproportioned to any pecuniary value of the slave, and is never refused, even without the hope of a fee, by the bar. This complaint of Mrs. Stowe is therefore entirely unfounded in fact. Yet such misstatements on so important a point connected with a question vitally affecting the peace of the Union, and the good name and tranquillity of the South are gravely introduced into these Facts for the People—which are no facts as interpreted by herself, and are fitted only for those people who invite deception and are prepared to welcome delusion and slander.

But it is not the falsehood of any particular facts that we would now object to, it is the general, and uniform fallacy or sophistry of their interpretation which is fatal to the credibility of the whole work. We wish we had the time to examine her exposition of the case of Mr. Rowand in Charleston, S. C., and to show the perverse ingenuity with which she conceals every thing that conflicts with her predetermined misconstruction, and distorts to wrong everything that admits of such misuse in the pliant hand of fanaticism. We will only remark that Henry Bailey, the Attorney General, was memorable for the undeviating fairness and unwavering justice with which he conducted all prosecutions, neither exaggerating nor extenuating anything, nor setting down aught in malice; that B. F. Hunt, who appeared for the defence, was born and raised in Massachusetts; and that Judge O'Neall,[138] who presided on the bench, was always suspected of undue leaning to the cause of the negro: and then add, that if Mrs. Stowe can find nothing in a cause tried by such lawyers before such a judge but material for vituperation, the objections alleged must be sought, not in the merits of the cause, but in the moral and mental obliquity, and in the deceiving prejudices of the commentator.

Before we leave this legal division, justice to the *Messenger* requires us to notice the compendious process by which Mrs. Stowe endeavours to escape from the cogency of an argument offered in the first criticism of *Uncle Tom's Cabin* in this Magazine. The Editor in that able review had illustrated the inaccuracy of Mrs. Stowe's representations, by adducing the Louisiana Law prohibiting the sale of children under ten years of age separately from their mothers, as a reason why the sale of Eliza in New Orleans at the age of eight or nine would have been entirely invalid. Mrs. Stowe attempts to evade this conclusive objection, by alleging that the owner might misrepresent the age of the child, which would be incapable of proof. The general tenor of Mrs. Stowe's argument in this *Key* to *Uncle Tom's Cabin* is that the slave-laws are so brutally severe, that even the best dispositions on the part of the slaveholders, who are represented as better than their laws, are ineffectual to redress or alleviate the miseries incident to slavery. But here she sails on the opposite tack, and endeavours to exculpate herself by intimating that even good laws are entirely nugatory in consequence of the fraud, the villainy, and the evasions of individuals. She has made a difficult dilemma for herself; either the laws are not enforced, and consequently furnish a defective and erroneous view of slavery, in which case she must abandon her whole train of deductions from the language of the laws: or they are enforced, in which event she must confess the invalidity of her reply to the *Messenger*, and the misrepresentation alleged. She must take one horn or the other; she cannot recur to either as suits her convenience; or, at any rate, if she extricates herself from her difficulties in this way, she must accord the same privilege to the advocates of the Southern cause, and thereby concede the fallacy of every separate thread in the elaborate indictment. It will not suffice to say that the laws may be sometimes enforced, and sometimes evaded; that position suits the South, and is a truth which the South would urge conclusively against all her attacks; it is the case with all laws, and is the reason that everywhere crime sometimes escapes punishment: but Mrs. Stowe is not content to test slavery on the incidents common to all human institutions, but will represent the mere letter of the law for the repression of crime, as the development of the spirit in which slaves must be treated. It is amusing to see Mrs. Stowe driven by the merciless consequences of this original fallacy into the horrible necessity of defending the murder of Uncle

Tom by Legree—an outrage which every Southern man would reprobate with indignant scorn—and probably punish by the summary application of Lynch law,
which may be sometimes profitably applied.

Mrs. Stowe, it is true, condemns Lynch law—without understanding either its
nature or operation any better than she understands any other sort of law—and her
ignorance of the latter subject is revealed at every step by the bald blunders with
which she translates the technical language of jurisprudence on every emergency
into the *niaiseries* of female tattle.[139] She speaks of the mobs and mobocracy at the
South. Such things are of very rare occurrence—and are entirely unknown except in
those cities where Yankee influences have crept in. But how are the facts in regard
to mobs in the Northern cities? They are of weekly occurrence in Philadelphia, and
are most sanguinary and ferocious: we have heard of the Macready and numerous
other riots in New York: and, even in the land of steady habits, they have not been
unfrequent at Boston.[140] The mob does not flourish at the South, it is pre-eminently
of Northern growth and culture.

The Fourth Part of Mrs. Stowe's calumnies we leave to the reverend Clergy at
the South: they are grossly slandered and abused, but they are able to reply for
themselves; and we will not interfere with their legitimate domain, though we confess our abstinence is due to no want of inclination to write in their defence, but
simply to the want of room. We will, however, trespass so far upon their sacred
office, as to ask permission to participate with them in administrating one rebuke.
Mrs. Stowe professes to be a Christian, she talks largely of Christianity, she throws
an ultra Christian hue over all her writings, she appeals to all Christians throughout
the world, and she arrogates to herself and her party the peculiar distinction of true
Christian views and Christian motives. Those who think with her are Christians,
those who dissent, or whose practice does not accord with her doctrines, are worse
than infidels.

For ourselves, we make no profession of excessive Christianity, and no pretension to extravagant religion; but we are disgusted and dismayed at the recklessness
with which the name of Christ is bandied about, and at the audacious blasphemy
which assumes a Christian motive as the cloak or excuse for every unlicensed and
malignant project, and for every fanatical purpose. While every principle of Christianity is openly set at defiance by the unrighteous aims and calumnious representations of Mrs. Stowe, she glozes over the treacherous deception by the asseveration
of a sanctity which exists only in her own imagination, and is cherished into a superficial conviction solely by habitual indulgence in consummate hypocrisy and self-
sufficient assurance. It is revolting to us, who have no sensitive Christianity like
Mrs. Stowe, to witness the sacred name of a divine religion assumed as a blind by
every rabid enthusiast, and every disorganizing dreamer; and used as a common
lure of deception to tempt the unreflecting favour of the populace to every scheme
of anarchy or delusion. The Abolitionists, the Communists, the Lippardists, the
Spiritual Rappers, and the whole confraternity of social humbugs, all claim to speak
as the oracles of heaven, and as special messengers entrusted with the authority of

Christ.[141] In that adorable name these fanatics busily prosecute the works of the devil. Like Ananias and Sapphira, they lie in the name of the Holy Ghost.[142] "It is not every one that saith Lord, Lord, shall enter into the kingdom of heaven."[143] But in our day, religion has been so mutilated, so defaced, so depraved, so travestied by the unhallowed chicanery of silly and turbulent charlatans, so blasphemed by the unholy mouths of self-constituted apostles, male and female, that any peculiar profession of pre-eminent Christianity may be legitimately regarded as presumptive evidence of unchristian motives and diabolical purposes. It is not enough that people should believe themselves to be in the right before agitating such questions: they are in duty bound to be actually right. It is not enough that they should suppose themselves undeluded in assigning Christianity to themselves or their projects: they can readily hatch that belief by systematic hallucinations, and nurture it by artificial fancies and a prolonged course of hypocrisy. The human mind is easily warped by its own deceitful manifestations. But they must be absolutely and indubitably right, or the Christianity professed is a vain and hollow pretence—the more sinful, and the more pernicious that it cannot be lightly suspected by charitable minds, and is never detected by weak intellects. We are very certain that all the "unco-righteous" schemes of Mrs. Stowe and her coadjutors, including the myriads who signed the Christian address of the Women of England, are presided over by the arch-spirit of the Infernal Gulf, and are guiltless of all Christianity, but the shameless prostitution of its sacred name; for there is not a single precept of revelation, which is not disregarded, discredited, and trampled under foot, when it conflicts with the development of their theories, or the execution of their unholy desires.

Mrs. Stowe's demonstration of deceit is suggestive, not so much in consequence of what it alleges, as in consequence of what it omits; not from the cogency and profundity of the argument, but from the depth of the error and the intricacy of the endless web of sophistry which it reveals. We have barely touched on a few salient points, we have not pretended to examine any topic thoroughly: we do not propose this notice as either an approximation to the full defence of the South, or as a refutation of the new volume: we had neither time nor space accorded to us for the performance of this task, and we have not touched it; we have only presented a few brief observations suggested by a cursory examination. We consign the whole subject to other and better hands; but in taking leave of that Christian-minded woman, Mrs. Stowe, we would commend to the serious meditation of herself and her Christian friends "throughout the world" a few verses from the Epistle of St. James, which they have probably never read, or have forgotten:

> If any man among you seem to be religious, and bridleth not his tongue, but deceiveth his own heart, this man's religion is vain.

> Pure and undefiled religion before God and the Father is this, To visit the fatherless and widows in their affliction, and to keep himself unspotted from the world.[144]

> Who is a wise man and endued with knowledge among you? Let him shew out of a good conversation his works with meekness of wisdom.

But if ye have bitter envying and strife in your hearts, glory not, and lie not against the truth.

This wisdom descendeth not from above, but is earthly, sensual, devilish.

For where envying and strife is, there is confusion and every evil work.

But the wisdom that is from above is first pure, then peaceable, gentle, and easy to be entreated, full of mercy and good fruits, without partiality, and without hypocrisy.[145]

10

PREFACE TO *THE YEMASSEE*

William Gilmore Simms

The *Yemassee* was first published in 1835; this preface, addressed to "Professor Samuel Henry Dickson, M. D., of South Carolina," was written for the 1853 edition.[146]

My Dear Dickson,—

It is now nearly twenty years since I first inscribed the Romance of *The Yemassee* with your name. The great good fortune which attended the publication in the favor of the public, the repeated editions which have been called for, and the favourable opinions of most of the critics, who, from time to time, have sat in judgement upon it, seem to justify me in endeavouring to retouch and perpetuate the old inscription in the new and improved edition of my various writings which it is meant to herald. You will see, if you do me the honour again to glance over the pages of this story, that I have done something towards making it more acceptable to the reader. I could not change the plan of the story in any wise. That is beyond my control. I could make no material alterations of any kind; such a labor is always undertaken with pain, and implies a minuteness of examination which would be excessively tedious to a writer who has long since dismissed the book from his thoughts, in the more grateful occupation of fresh imaginings and new inventions. It is my great regret that I can now do so little towards rendering the story more worthy of the favor it has found. I am now fully conscious of its defects and crudities. No one can be more so than myself. In reading it over, for the small revision which I have made, I am absolutely angry with myself, as Scott is reported to have been with Hogg while reading one of the stories of the Shepherd, at having spoiled and botched so much excellent material.[147] I see now a thousand passages, through which had I the leisure, and could I muster courage for the effort, I should draw the pen, with the hope to substitute better thoughts, and improved situations, in a more appropriate and grateful style. But I need not say to you how coldly and reluctantly would such a task be undertaken, by one who has survived his youth, and who must economize all his enthusiasm for the new creations of his fancy. I can only bestow a touch of the pruning knife here and there, cutting off the more obtrusive excrescences, and leaving the minor ones to the indifference or the indulgence of the reader.

Something, perhaps, should be said of the story as a whole. When I wrote, there was little understood, by readers generally, in respect of the character of the red men; and, of the opinions entertained on the subject, many, according to my own experience, I knew to be incorrect. I had seen the red men of the south in their own homes, on frequent occasions, and had arrived at conclusions in respect to them, and their habits and moral nature, which seemed to me to remove much of the air of mystery which was supposed to disguise most of their ordinary actions. These corrections of the vulgar opinions will be found unobtrusively given in the body of the work, and need not be repeated here. It needs only that I should say that the rude portraits of the red man, as given by those who see him in degrading attitudes only, and in humiliating relation with the whites, must not be taken as a just delineation of the same being in his native woods, unsubdued, a fearless hunter, and without any degrading consciousness of inferiority, and still more degrading habits, to make him wretched and ashamed. My portraits, I contend, are true to the Indian as our ancestors knew him at early periods, and as our people, in certain situations, may know him still. What liberties I have taken with the subject, are wholly with his mythology. That portion of the story, which the reverend critics, with one exception, recognised as sober history, must be admitted to be a pure invention—one, however, based upon such acts and analogies as, I venture to think, will not discredit the proprieties of the invention.

What I shall add to these statements, must be taken from the old preface, which I shall somewhat modify.

You will note that I call *The Yemassee* a romance, and not a novel. You will permit me to insist upon the distinction. I am unwilling that the story shall be examined by any other than those standards which have governed me in its composition; and unless the critic is prepared to adopt with me those leading principles, in accordance with which the book has been written, the sooner we part company the better.

Supported by the authority of common sense and practice, to say nothing of Pope—

> In every work regard the writer's end,
> Since none can compass more than they intend—[148]

I have surely a right to insist upon this particular. It is only when an author departs from his own standard (speaking of his labours as a work of art), that he offends against propriety and merits censure. Reviewing *Atalantis,* a fairy tale, full of fanciful machinery, and without a purpose, save to the embodiment to the mind's eye of some of those

> Gay creatures of the element,

> That, in the colour of the rainbow live,
> And play i'the flighted clouds—[149]

one of my critics—then a very distinguished writer—gravely remarked, in a very popular periodical, "Magic is now beyond the credulity of eight years; and yet the author *set out* to make a tale of magic, *knowing* it to be thus beyond the range of the probable—knowing that all readers were equally sagacious—and never, for a moment, contemplated the deception of any sober citizen."

The question briefly is—What are the standards of the modern Romance? What is the modern Romance itself? The reply is immediate. The modern Romance is the substitute which the people of the present day offer for the ancient epic. The form is changed; the matter is very much the same; at all events, it differs much more seriously from the English novel than it does from the epic and the drama, because the difference is one of material, even of fabrication. The reader who, reading *Ivanhoe*, keeps Richardson and Fielding beside him, will be at fault in every step of his progress. The domestic novel of those writers, confined to the felicitous narration of common and daily occurring events, and the grouping and delineation of characters in ordinary conditions of society, is altogether a different sort of composition; and if, in a strange doggedness, or simplicity of spirit, such a reader happens to pin his faith to such writers alone, circumscribing the boundless horizon of art to the domestic circle, the Romances of Maturin, Scott, Bulwer, and others of the present day, will be better than rhapsodical and intolerable nonsense.

When I say that our Romance is the substitute of modern times for the epic or the drama, I do not mean to say that they are exactly the same things, and yet, examined thoroughly, the differences between them are very slight.[150] These differences depend on the material employed, rather than upon the particular mode in which it is used. The Romance is of loftier origin than the Novel. It approximates the poem. It may be described as an amalgam of the two. It is only with those who are apt to insist upon poetry as verse, and to confound rhythm with poetry, that the resemblance is unapparent. The standards of the Romance—take such a story, for example, as the *Ivanhoe* of Scott, or the *Salathiel* of Croly,—are very much those of the epic.[151] It invests individuals with an absorbing interest—it hurries them rapidly through crowding and exacting events, in a narrow space of time—it requires the same unities of plan, of purpose, and harmony of parts, and it seeks for its adventures among the wild and wonderful. It does not confine itself to what is known, or even what is probable. It grasps at the possible; and, placing a human agent in hitherto untried situations, it exercises its ingenuity in extricating him from them, while describing his feelings and his fortunes in his progress. The task has been well or ill done, in proportion to the degree of the ingenuity and knowledge which the romancer exhibits in carrying out the details, according such proprieties as are called for by the circumstances of the story. These proprieties are the standards set up at his starting, and to which he required religiously to confine himself.

The Yemassee is proposed as an *American* romance. It is so styled as much of the material could have been furnished by no other country. Something too much of extravagance—so some may think,—even beyond the usual licence of fiction—may enter certain parts of the narrative. On this subject, it is enough for me to say, that the popular faith yields abundant authority for the wildest of its incidents. The natural romance of our country has been my object, and I have not dared beyond it. For the rest—for the general peculiarities of the Indians, in their ungraded condition—my authorities are numerous in all the writers who have written from their own experience. My chief difficulty, I may add, has risen rather from the discrimination necessary in picking and choosing, than from any deficiency of the material itself. It is needless to add that the historical events are strictly true, and that the outline is to be found in several chronicles devoted to the region of the country in which the scene is laid. A slight anachronism occurs in one of the early chapters, but it has little bearing upon the story, and is altogether unimportant.

But I must not trespass upon your patience, if I do not upon your attention. If you read *The Yemassee* now, with such changes of mood and judgment as I must acknowledge in my own case, I can hardly hope that it will please you as it did twenty years ago. And yet, my friend, could we both read it as we did then! Ah! how much more grateful our faith than our knowledge! How much do we lose by our gains—how much do our acquisitions cost us!

11

NOVELS: THEIR MEANING AND MISSION

Anonymous

Putnam's Monthly Magazine (1854).

The announcement of philosopher Fourier, that "Attractions are proportioned to destinies," albeit false in many, is, nevertheless, true in some respects.[152] Thus, in literature, every longing and every susceptibility of the soul, and, in fact, every mental want, creates for itself a satisfaction and a supply. So, too, we may regard every phasis of literature as a typal manifestation of some profounder necessity that underlies and procreates it. For example: The Epos gives utterance to all the untold heroisms of our nature;[153] and the *Iliad* is at once the embodiment of a nation's warlike daring, and the realization, to a certain extent, of a heroic ideal that finds its home and birth-place in every soul of man. Each man is, in a measure, an Achilles, and burns with the flame of his awful ire [Μῆνις Ουλόμένη];[154] but genius alone, in elevating everything she touches to the dignity of apotheosis, has touched with her mystic wand *this* side of the many-sided soul; and lo! it lives and breathes perennially.

History, again, develops the infinite in man; and, as Frederick Schlegel remarks, "replies to the first problem of philosophy—the restoration in man of the lost image of God; as far as this relates to Science."

So, both the physical and the metaphysical sciences respond to opposite and distinctive poles in our mental organism; while the fine arts, which hold a maesothetic position between the two, are, in all their provinces, an effort after the realization of that which finds full expression only in that absolute, which is the birth-place of the soul. Thus, the mind, unsatisfied with itself and subjective existences, ever struggles after objective forms and embodiment; for "nature," as Emerson tells us, "*will* be reported."[155]

But, besides those faculties and tendencies already named, and which find expression in some form or other, we have to take cognizance of that class which have relation to the imagination and the *fancy*; and which also find for themselves "a local habitation and a name," as well as a place in the world of letters.[156] I refer to romance literature.

That this species of composition is a normal and legitimate development of the mind, mankind have endorsed by the fact of every nation's having given birth to productions of this kind, and by the extreme avidity with which fabulous and romantic narratives have in all times been received. Finding its primeval home in the gorgeous East—amid scenes of vastness and of splendor, where the magnificence of nature's visible forms, and the voluptuous quiescence of life, invite to lolling repose, giving birth to dreamy fancies; while every balsamic breeze and Sabean odor wafts on its wings reveries of grandeur—it reached its full Eastern perfection in those wonderful phantasies: *The Thousand and One Tales*.[157]

Of Eastern romance, we may remark, *en passant*,[158] that it will be found the almost unmixed product of fancy (or phantasy). The tendency of the oriental mind was not sufficiently introspective to elevate them to the dignity of works of *imagination*; and, besides, everything in nature was symbolical and suggestive, and speech itself was nearly pure metaphor. The East is the home of the language of flowers, and the poetry of mathematics.

Transported to the West, romance assumed a more intellective and also a more emotional cast; losing many of its outer splendors, it clothed itself in a stronger garb, and partook of the active form of Western life. This is the hey-day of the European chivalry and romance epoch, displayed in the genial satire and the glorious humor of its brightest exponent, Miguel de Cervantes Saavedra; and the gallant or amatory harp of the Troubadours and the Minnesingers.[159]

The subsequent course of romance literature, down to the present time, is known to every one, and need not here be pursued; as it modified its original form, and extended the boundaries of its province of action—now taking in one field, and again another—jutting out in strange extravagances and *outre*[160] developments, and then rising to the natural and the true; till now, when its domain embraces infinity and absorbs every subject of human feeling and action, thought and emprise. Carlyle says that romance has not ceased to exist; that, on the other hand, it is now in its full meridian splendor. And verily, we are inclined to believe it—if not in life, yet in literature.

Nothing is more easy or gratuitous than the vituperative condemnation and contempt that have so often been lavished on novels and novel writing. They are "trash," "yellow-covered literature," "wishy-washyism, namby-pambyism," &c., &c.[161] The guardian makes it a point to keep his ward as carefully from a novel as from the measles, and would as lief that she would dose herself with rats-bane as devour a romance. Our venerated ancestor (peace to his manes), who, in early manhood, was so annoyed by the flirtations of his gay younger sister, which seemed always to succeed profound and long-continued brooding over the pages of the novels sent her from London, had, one should say, some reason for cautioning us, among his last words of advice, to "Beware of novels."

Uncle Greybeard, too, imagines that he has completely annihilated the whole tribe when he utters a "Pshaw!" and something about "vapid sentimentality," and "man-millinerism." True, O grave Greybeard; those which chiefly filled the shelves of your village library were most deserving of the epithets, and even at the present day many a heated press labors day and night to satiate the public appetite for just such "*trash.*"

The truth, however, is, that the domain of romance-composition has been so materially extended within the last quarter of a century, the fields of thought and feeling commented upon so altered, and the type of popular novels so completely changed, that what could, to a great extent, be very well predicated of novels fifty years ago, is totally false in its sweeping application to our present species. We have now no desire for the extravagances of sentiment and action that, with a few brilliant exceptions, characterized English novels of former times. On the other hand, we are disgusted with such productions, and covet, above all, the natural in thought and feeling. What is wanted to constitute a good modern novel, is not a monstrous assemblage of grotesquely illusive pictures of life and nature, interlarded with inconceivable sentiments, unheard-of adventures, and impossible exploits. Not at all. We demand that they be veritable and veracious segments of the great life-drama, displaying Nature and Man as they are, sentiments as they are felt, and deeds as they are done. Novels are judged as Art products, and as little sympathy is felt with the *bizarreries* that are heaped together, for the gratification of very weak brains, as for the fantastic adornings of a Dutch house, or the architectural proportions of a Chinese pagoda.

We are now-a-days really very little interested in the history of that amiable creature, Miss Angelica Celestina Sugarheart, with whom that equally generous gent, Peter Giraldine Gingerbread, fell in love. The life-views and vicissitudes of this sentimental pair—how Ma was opposed to it, how Peter (poor Peter!) took to melancholy and the sea, and, after innumerable prodigious adventures with pirates on the Gulf of Mexico, returned just in time to shoot a rival, and espouse Angelica Celestina, who afterwards lived, in great connubial felicity, in a charming cottage by the side of a lovely lake. Even Miss Blandish would not declare that this is quite "divine" now-a-days. On the whole, we have come to receive these overwhelming communications with very considerable *sang froid.*[162] Novels are now, many of them, the productions of men of the highest intellectual and moral worth, and are at present more generally read, and probably exercise a greater influence than any or all other forms of literature together. Then, in the name of truth and common sense, let us throw down the *baton,* and cry "Halt!" to sneers and sneerers at novels. Rather would we endeavor to investigate the nature and legitimate field of novel writing, and point out the meaning and the mission of such works.

A few words prefatory, however, on the subject of a name.

There is no more unfortunate circumstance than the lack of an appropriate and experienced name for that kind of composition to which we are necessitated, in lieu of a better, to affix the appellation Novels, Romances, &c. They are total misnomers, every one of them. The fact is, that the thing itself has repeatedly changed, while the name has not, and thus thing and name are mutual contradictions. And, indeed, it is very much to be desiderated that Samuel Taylor Coleridge, instead of racking his and our brains with *Exemplastics,* and other such, had given us a good title for this very important class of works which are, even to the present day, denied Christian baptism.[163] *Novel* is just *quelque chose de nouvelle*—something new, novel; and thus is as applicable to one thing as to another. *Romance,* as the word itself imports,* is confined to the middle ages; and *Fiction,* though originally a harmless enough word, and, in fact rather expressive, denoting the result of mental *picturing*—(*fingo*) imagining—has now come to be symbolical simply of a *fib.*

Only this, and nothing more.[164]

On the other hand, you can scarcely, with strict propriety, call them works of imagination or fancy: for, in so doing, we include, under that term, poetry, oratory, and everything else to some extent. We shall, then, have to be satisfied with the old names—earnestly desiring that a new and more interpretative term may be speedily devised.

The domain of the novel ranges over the entire field of the real and the ideal, and thus touches at every point of man's consciousness—in the evolution of individual character, and the development of human life and nature, in their actual phases. And in these points, it is coordinate and co-extensive, at once, with poetry and the drama. With poetry, in being a veritable ποίησο[165]—an art-creation; and with the drama, in its plan or plot—the involution of circumstance, character, and passion, and the evolution from the complexity of these life-and-death commingling scenes of grand vital results and important practical lessons. Thus, novels, especially those that are the transcendent productions of the imagination, take hold of everything that is in *rapport* with the infinite in man. The artist who created them

Builded better than he knew;**

for, in displaying the phenomenal, an enticing hint has, at times, been thrown out that led us on with winning smiles to the home of the real: one touch of the human harp-chord, the Infinite, has set a-thrilling the old "Eternal Melodies." For so it is, that everything in life has a relation at once to the me and the not-me; and while the obverse carries the relative, the reverse bears the stamp of the absolute.

Regarding these idealistic creations, a remark or two may, at the present moment, not be inappropriate.

There be persons to whom nothing is comprehensible but what comes through the gross palpabilities of the senses. They can appreciate nothing that comes not in positive cuffs and downright hard blows. Now with these it is no intention of ours

---

* The word is French. The language was then called *Lingua Romana,* and any book written in that tongue received the name of *livre Romans* (liber Romanus), or simply Romans; that is, Romans book— romans, whence *romance.*

** Emerson's *Poems*—"The Problem." [1839]

to discuss the question as to the comparative value of the real and the ideal—the practical and the theoretic. We have but to say that there are two worlds: there be two sides to everything in this world and out of it. There is the world of which your senses are cognizant—that which your eyes see, and your ears hear, and your hands handle— the physical. We will even become sensationalists enough to admit, that you have a solid frame of integument, muscle, and adipose tissue surrounding you, and an epigastric region somewhere about the middle of said framework; we will accede to your proposition, that the earth you tread on has a solidity and a reality (contingent); and admit that if you apply a loaded pistol to your head, and pull the trigger, it will stand a chance of blowing out what nature meant for your brains. There is no denying your creed so far. But, if you insist that *that* is all, then we cry "halt," in heaven's name! To your doctrine, friend, we can't subscribe *Credo!*[166] Nay, on that score we are utter σκεπτικοί—unbelievers. And if ye were not

> ———Quanti cerci
> Si della mente———*

so *squint-eyed* in mind, you could not help knowing that there is another world—the world of your longings and your dreadings and your imaginings— the spiritual. Where roam

> Those thoughts that wander through eternity,[167]

with fields and blessed isles of its own, and an infinite blue concave stretching all around. As for the predilection for the real and the practical, it might be well to remember that theory ever stands at the base of practice; and the ideal, being the greater, includes the real. And, indeed, Leigh Hunt, in one of his papers, argues that it would be extremely difficult to prove that imaginings have not as real an existence as those to which we are in the habit of applying that rather ambitious title. Besides, if the *dictum* of our great master-philosopher be true, that

> —we are such stuff
> As dreams are made of, and our little life
> Is rounded with a sleep,—[168]

why may not those remembered characters that jut out with a glorious psychal existence, be as veracious to me as any of the shadows in buckram by which I am surrounded. Apply sensuous tests to them. Were you never influenced most materially by a book-character? Were you never stopped—physically arrested—by a thought? Were you never "*struck*" by some purely brain-delineation? Did Sir John Falstaff never sit and swear with you at your drinking bouts;[169] or what do you think of a poor Burns carrying in his pocket a copy of *Paradise Lost* to fortify his mind and stay himself up with the defiant courage of Milton's Satan? Aha! my friend, you will have to come to the confession that:—

---

* Dante's *Inferno*, Canto VII. ver. 40- I. ["How many circles. Yes, of the mind." *The Comedy*, later *The Divine Comedy*, consists of three books: *Inferno, Purgatorio*, and *Paradiso; Inferno* was completed c.1314.]

> There are more things in Heaven and Earth
> Than are dreamt of in your philosophy.[170]

What a glorious cloud of spiritual and intellectual witnesses have we all around us and taking up their home with us! To whom we refer as precedents in every action—with whom, consciously or otherwise, we advise every course of conduct, and from whom we draw untold consolations and benefits.

We think of a heroic Patience-man—Prometheus Vinctus—chained to the craggy rock—enduring the gnawings of the vulture, and still exclaiming:

> Κρεισον γαρ οιμαι τηδε λατρυειον πετφω
> Η πατρι φυναι Ζηνι πιστον αγγεον.*

or of his parallel *Samson Agonistes;*[171] we think of

> The great Achillies whom we knew,**

of Dante and paradises and the inferno; of blundering yet sage old Don Quixote; of the hurrying words of Shakespeare's metropolitan brain; we go on adventures with Tom Jones, or dwell in desert isles with Robinson Crusoe; we philosophise with Moses (*Vicar of Wakefield*) and exclaim "Prodigious!" with Dominie Sampson; we muse with Manfred or we curse with Mephistopheles.[172] And so it is throughout every province of human action—we are never without our *compagnons de voyage.*[173] They hover around us or dwell with us, and perhaps there could be no more noble tribute paid to the glory and veritability of such genius-creations.

Such and so vast is the scope of novel-composition taking in the Unseen and the Eternal as well as the Temporal; embracing at once the life that now is, and that which is to come. Their name is Legion—numbered by the million—while thousands of Ann street presses teem with untold quantities more—diurnally. Of every possible species—and of every grade of merit—from a *Pirate's Revenge* or an *Alamance* (which may be taken as minimum) up to a *Vanity Fair*, or a *Wilhelm Meister* (which approach to the maximum)—a distance that you and I, friend, would rather not travel over.[174] So, to assist us, we shall endeavor to make a few great general divisions, under which all Romance productions may be included.

It is worthy of note that the terms "Novel" and "Romance," though often confounded—are, in a general signification, analogous to the philosophico-metaphysical divisions, "Imagination" and "Fancy." "The fancy," says Coleridge in his *Biographia Literaria*, "combines, the imagination creates." Now this, though perhaps not a rigidly philosophical distinction, is yet capital as a general definition. Putting them side by side, then, we have Fancy—Romance; Imagination—Novel; that is, the term Romance is indicative of a *combination* of wonderful deeds and darings; outreisms and bizarreries; while novel (not the *name*—for that is senseless in such an application—but the thing) carries the idea of an Art-creation; not an ac-

---

* Aeschylus [c.525-c.456 B.C.], *Prometheus Vinctus.*(996).

** [Alfred, Lord] Tennyson's [1809-1892] *Poems—Ulysses.* [1842]

cretion of circumstances and particulars from without, but an inly production of the mind in its highest imagining or poetic moods. Of course, it is not intended to be insinuated that they are not found in constant affiliation—as are all the mental tendencies—yet the preponderance of the faculty will run in the direction above indicated. And more particularly is this true in regard to Novels since the rise of our present new and better school of imaginative writers, who have elevated this species of composition to its true dignity—and regarding which school, we have a few words to remark by and by. But, in the mean time to our divisions.

I. The purely *Romantic:* 1. The *Apologue*—the didactic; 2. *Extravaganzas;* 3. Romance *Sentimental:*

II. The *Novel* proper: 4. *Historico-Descriptive;* 5. Novels *Analytic*—of *Men* and *Manners;* 6. Novels *Idealistic.* Besides which classes, it will be necessary to include Novels—*Philosophical—Political, Religious—Eclectic.*

The first three divisions, namely, the Apologue, Extravaganza, and Sentimental productions, have relation to the class we call Romances; the last three, and the minor subdivisions, are what we may with propriety name *Novels,* taking that term as indicating imaginative in opposition to fanciful works. And, whether intentionally or otherwise, we find that we have with considerable correctness, given them place in the order of their development in actual literature. For it is a fact that tales, having their foundation in the fancy, ever precede the noble flights of imagination. Even as in the individual, the fancy precedes, in relation of time, the imagination; so in the adolescence of a national literature, we have the grotesque and the arabesque before the lofty idealistic.

The first division, the *Apologue,* is one of the earliest developments in all literature. For the order of progression seems to be thus:—The madrigal—the primal form—merges into fable or allegory, and this continues until a higher type takes its place. And here again the circumstance in literature finds its analogue in life, for at no time are persons so didactic as in youth, except when a garrulous senility has brought back a second childhood. This fact is abundantly illustrated in European literature. There was first the troubadour and chivalric period, when all was song. When "believers," says Tieck, "sang of faith; lovers of love; knights described knightly actions and battles; and loving, believing knights were their chief audience."[175] But the age of chivalry passed away, the world awoke to the sternness and the reality, the mystery and the majesty of life, and they asked to be taught. And so arose the Fable, the Allegory, the Analogue.

Of this class of writing, no finer type could be desired than that marvellous *Gesta Romanorum,* or that exquisite German, *Reinecke der Fuchs,* Reynard the Fox.[176] This form of writing is, however, by no means a desirable one, and is always indicative of a transition state in literature.

The second division is that to which we have given the name of *Extravaganzas.* Under which we may include not only those *jeux d'esprit*—the innumerable *voyages imaginaires* of former times[177]—exemplified lately in another field, that of astronomy, by Locke's "Moon Hoax," and the "Hans Phaall" of Edgar A. Poe,[178] but also the *bizarreries* of Mrs. Radcliffe, Kotzebue,[179] and numerous other German and French writers—those terrifico-ghostly, blood-and-thunder books, as well as the stories of exploit and adventure, e.g., Captain Marryat's tales; and also productions which owe their effect to the illustration of *practical jokes*, such as *Charles O'Malley* and *Harry Lorrequer*, *Valentine Vox* and *Stanley Thorn*.[180] As a political extravaganza, the *Utopia* of Sir Thomas More is undoubtedly the most capital thing extant.[181]

Of the *third* division, we need fortunately say but little, as they are so perfectly familiar to every one, as to require no illustration. They are usually well seasoned with "molasses," and generally conclude with the moral—*"And they lived happily all the rest of their days."* They are still the bane of our literature, and are the chaff among which are found a few golden-grained products of true genius.

There is, however, another class of sentimental works, or rather (for that term is abused in its present application) works of sentiment, or (if the term be endurable) aesthetical productions, which have their foundation in heart-feelings, and make their thesis the emotional. These are some of the quiet home books of Grace Aguilar, Mrs. Kirkland, Elizabeth Oakes Smith, and (to be brief) Ike Marvel, as seen in his *Dream-Life* and *Reveries of a Bachelor*; while of the sentimental, in its boldest and most analytical point of view, Rousseau and Bernardin de St. Pierre are undoubtedly to be taken as the most excellent representatives.[182]

Division *four* brings us to the most prolific and popular type of novels—the Historico-Descriptive. Under this head there is such a multiplicity of writers, that the enumeration of any other than typal representatives is out of the question.

At the head of this class, in both its departments, stands, without doubt, Sir Walter Scott. He has *harried* not only every nook and cranny of Scottish life and manners, but has rummaged almost every salient point of history for material. If Scott, and Professor Wilson, and Mrs. Ferrier be the illustrators of Scotland and the Scotch, in their great national, peculiarities, assuredly so may Mrs. Hall be considered of Ireland and the Irish, in the home-life of that people, while Charles Lever displays its more farcical phases.[183] The English "Upper Ten" find at once a satirist and an exponent in Hook and Thackeray, while "John Bull" never had a more jolly appreciator, or more faithful chronicler, than Dickens; the salient and spirited soul of Parisian life is not so salient as to elude the grasp of a Balzac, nor so spirited as not to be seized by a Paul de Kock; German life has its thousand expositors; Italy its faithful Manzoni, and its eloquent Madame de Staël; while Northern Europe is familiar to us as household scenes through the felicitous sketches of Miss Bremer; and the East, in all its grandeur and gorgeousness, is ours through the pages of *Anastasius* and *Eöthen*.[184]

America has no national novel, for the very good reason that there is no such thing as American society. Particular portions, indeed, and particular sides thereof have found interpreters. Western and Indian life has a Cooper; Southern, a Kennedy; and New England, a Hawthorne and a Sedgwick; but her "idea" has never yet been embodied—her pulse, the state of it, has never yet been recorded; for the reason that arterial circulation has hardly yet commenced; her "mission" has not quite got itself evolved; and *the* American Novel, like her "Coming Man," is only a "coming."

In a far higher than a historico-descriptive sense are Dickens and Thackeray, Rousseau and Bernardin de St. Pierre, Hawthorne and Mrs. Stowe, Richter and Goethe; novelists, as recorders, not of phases of society and national characteristics, merely, but of (5) *men and manners*; as students of elemental human nature; and observers and reporters of this great life-drama. This it is that brings them into *rapport* with Shakespeare and the heart of universal life; this is their crown of glory—every one of them; and that which will not allow them to perish, like the ephemeral productions of romance, but give them a lasting interest: an interest co-extensive with that human nature which they depict, and elevate them to the dignity of classics.

Closely allied with the former division are those works that have for their object a purely idealistic aim—which are not so much analyses of human nature as art-products—with a tendency purely ποιητικός—creative; having the subjective as their basis, and, as thesis, the development of a subjective state in its connection with objective realities. These have their value in the involution of the mystic—ποιητικός—in the sense of the Schlegels.[185] In regard to which productions, says Poe: "With each note of the lyre is heard a ghostly, and not always a distinct, but an august and soul-exalting *echo*. In every glimpse of beauty presented, we catch, through long and wild vistas, dim and bewildering visions of a far more etherial beauty *beyond*. A Naiad voice addresses us *from below*. The notes of the air of the song tremble with the according tones of the accompaniment."[186]

This form is to be found in full perfection in the exquisite imaging of Jean Paul Richter, in the etherial *Undine* of De La Motte Fouqué—analogous, in a different form, to that magnificent tragic embodiment of Aeschylus, *Prometheus Vinctus*, or the "Comus" of Milton, or Coleridge's "Christabel," or Shelley's "Alastor."[187] Poe, too, has given us some curious specimens of ideal fantasying; and, like that of Paganini, it is fantasying on *one* string.[188] No one could better push to its utmost a hoping or a dreading, or a vague longing, or a tendency of the mind or of the emotions, or an idiosyncrasy of character. Witness his "Gold Bug," or "Ligeia," or the "Fall of the House of Usher."[189]

The characteristic and the glory of the new school of novelists is, without doubt, its vigor and earnest veracity. As we before observed, a quarter of a century has had the effect of completely revolutionizing this department of literature. By some this happy movement is referred to the influence of one writer, and by others to another. Some say Godwin's *Caleb Williams* led the way; others make Fielding its great prototype; and so on. But the true secret of the new impulse is with greater probability to be sought for in the more profoundly earnest spirit of the age. We note, amid the crudities and absurdities of this era, the primal movement towards a radically stronger and nobler theorem of life and literature in all their departments—of a deeper theosophy and a more transcendent philosophy. The world's "Idea" now is the *true*. This idea it is that is leading us back to the search after a more satisfactory solution of all the problems that affect human existence and its concerns; that makes physical science the offspring of the nineteenth century; that has turned criticism upside down; that has given us an Emerson and a Carlyle—a Schiller and a Goethe; and that has swept away the "old drowsy shop" of Aristotelian logic and ontology, and erected—or, at least, laid the foundation—of that splendid fabric, of which some of the master-builders are Sir William Hamilton, and Kant, and Fichte, and Schelling, and the Schlegels, and Novalis, and Jean Paul Richter.[190] And this idea has at last taken possession of the field of imaginative writing—of novels; and is leading us back to the ultimate principles of the art, which are truth itself, to the investigation of the true, with reference to society and the legitimate field of the ideals. It is giving us, instead of the puling sentimentality of those eternal love-developments, true home-sentiments and honest heart-feelings; instead of solemn pedantry, true knowledge—all understood and clearly elaborated; instead of a conglomeration of fantastic bizarreries, fit only to bamboozle one, and cause him to wonder where he is straying, presenting us with high ideals of life, and pointing out to us the heroism of doing and daring. We will not take hyperism—we demand honesty. And hence our love for Bernardin de St. Pierre, and Mme. de Staël, and Manzoni, and Defoe, and Goldsmith, and Dickens, and Thackeray, and Kingsley, and Hawthorne, and Cooper, and Mrs. Stowe. Dickens, and Thackeray, and Kingsley, and Goldsmith, are universally satisfactory, just because they are faithful to life throughout its various phases; Defoe and Cooper and Manzoni we glory in on account of their minutiae and likeness of detail—in the forest or on the sea they never fail us; Tieck and Hawthorne and Simms are artistic to a fault; while with Miss Bremer and Hans Andersen, we are delighted on account of the quietude and unwarped simplicity of their depiction of still life.[191]

So much for the meaning of novels. Their mission, we think, is palpable enough. We spoke, in the introduction, of every desire and proclivity of the mind being the prediction of its satisfaction in literature. Novels (we think it will, by this time, be understood what class we mean) are the filling up and the satisfying of that in the soul which otherwise would be blank and vacant.

And peculiarly are they the product of this nineteenth era when there is such a fecundity and such an overflowing of mental and psychal life. They are one of the "features" of our age. We know not what we should do without them. And, indeed, there is a class of writers who, if they did not develop in this way, would find no other mode of utterance whatever. How *could* Kingsley have written except through *Alton Locke* and *Yeast?*[192] What vehicle could Dickens have found for the communication of just his class of ideas but that of *Nicholas Nickleby*, of *David Copperfield*, or of *Hard Times?*[193] How *could* Thackeray have given us his pictures of society, but through the *camera obscura* of *Vanity Fair* and *Pendennis*, and *The Newcomes?*[194]

But still they (novels) are not the whole of literature. Assuredly not! no more than *sauce piquante* makes a dinner, or the hours we spend in jocularity and abandon a life.[195] They are didactic; but it is philosophy wearing a smiling face, and holding out a winning invitation. They are the *Utile* clothed in the garb of the *Dulce*.[196] And in this dulcet manner, they touch human consciousness at every possible point.

They have already absorbed every field of interest. As pictures of life, and as developments of the passions, they have almost entirely superseded the drama; while every subject of interest, every principle of science, of art, of politics, of religion, finds a graceful appreciator and interpreter through the popular novel.

So that, do you wish to instruct, to convince, to please? Write a novel! Have you a system of religion or politics or manners or social life to inculcate? Write a novel! Would you have the "world" split its sides with laughter, or set all the damsels in the land a-breaking their hearts? Write a novel! Would you lay bare the secret workings of your own heart, or have you a friend to whom you would render that office? Write a novel! Have you "fallen out"—got into a consquabulation with your wife (as an English baronet, a famous novelist, did), and are you fain to give her a public castigation (as the English baronet desired)? Write a novel! (The English baronet did so.) Or, on the other hand, should any wife feel like Caudleising and retaliating on her husband? Again we say, write a novel! (By the way, the baronet-novelist's lady did so, also.) Have you any tit-bits of wit or humor—any morceaux of fun or frolic—any "insight" into art or aesthetics? Why, write a novel! Do you wish to create a sensation? Write a novel! And, lastly, not least, but loftiest, would you make (*magnum et venerabile nomen!*)—would you make money?[197] Then, in Pluto's and Mammon's name! write a novel!

12

ADVERTISEMENT TO *RICHARD HURDIS*

William Gilmore Simms

Appeared in *Richard Hurdis: A Tale of Alabama* (1855).

It might be of some use to such of our young authors as are just about to begin their career in letters, were I to state the reasons which governed me, some eighteen years ago, in giving this story, with several others of the same family, to the public, anonymously. But I am not prepared, just yet, to enter the confessional. The matter is a sort to keep. I treasure up much curious literary history, the fruit of a protracted experience, in reserve for a day and volume of greater leisure and deliberation. Enough now, to say that I had my interest—ay, and fun too—in the mystery with which the publication of the work was originally clothed; and, if I had one counsel, over all, to impart to the young beginner, it should be to cling to the anonymous in literature as long as it will afford him a decent cover. Were I now, for the first time, beginning my own career, with the possession of the smallest part of my present experience, my left hand should never know what my right is doing. I should not only keep the public in ignorance of my peculiar labors, but I should, quiet as religiously, keep the secret from my friends and associates. This is especially necessary, if you would be safe; if you would have anything like fair play; if you would escape from a thousand impertinences; if you would hope for any honest judgments. There are very few friends, indeed, to whom you can trust any of your secrets; and this of authorship, is one, which, of all others, is least easy to keep. Your friend is vain on your account—or on his own—which is much the most likely—and must blab, with even the slightest precautions than were taken by the barber of King Midas.[198] Even if he honestly keeps your secret, what is the profit to you in letting it out of your own hand? You must employ an agent in finding your way to the press, but this need not be one of those whom you rank among your friends. A business transaction may be kept secret; but a confidence, gratuitously given, is rarely safe. If you reveal a secret, unless from the necessity of the case, you may reasonably be supposed to desire its farther circulation. So friends mostly understand it.—And, do not deceive yourself with the notion, that, by confiding to the persons nearest to you, and who most share your sympathies, you can possibly derive and advantage from it. They can seldom serve you in any way. They can give no help to a reputation which is to be founded on your own real merits; no counsel, of any value in an art which they themselves do not profess, but which they are still very prone to teach; exercise no influence which is not apt, in some way, to prove pernicious; and, whether they praise or blame, are generally the worst judges to whom you could submit your productions. Go to your cook in preference. Your friends always find your own personality conflicting, in their minds, with your productions. They never separate *you* from your writings. Their personal and local associations perpetually start up to baffle the free influence of your works upon their thoughts and hearts; and they weigh your opinions, or your imaginations, or your designs and inventions, with a continual reference to *yourself*, as you appear in ordinary society. In society, you are perhaps nothing; silent as Gibbon—without any of the small change of conversation—that clinking currency which best passes among ordinary people, and which need not be true coin, at all—though you may be able to draw for a thousand pounds: and you thus socially appear at great disadvantage with the very persons to whom you confide your secret, and trustingly declare your labors. What can be the result? Your friend, who have known you only in social relations, is required to feel surprise at your performances, or to speak very qualifiedly of their merits. He is reduced to this alternative.—If he admits himself to be surprised, it is equivalent to confessing that he has not had the capacity to discover your peculiar endowment. His self-esteem will oppose any such admission, and he disparages it accordingly. "He has always known that you had a certain talent";—"but—it was surely a little too bold of you to undertake a book!" And this will be thought and said without any wilful desire to harm; simply from what seems necessary to self-respect and the maintenance of old positions and the old social relations. And, you do not see, that, if you continue presumptuously to write books, it is possible—barely possible—that you will outgrow your circle? Every chatty, conceited, "talking potato" of it, is personally interested in preventing such a growth. The instincts of mediocrity are always on the watch and easily alarmed; and it perpetually toils to keep down any growth which is calculated to fling a shadow over itself. And this is all very natural—not to be complained of, or quarreled with. The safest way to avoid any of these perils, and much annoyance, is to keep your secret, and let your book find its way alone. Let the book win the reputation before you claim authorship.

Of all this, something hereafter. My own humble experience in authorship, of some twenty-five years growth, will some day furnish ample materials for a volume of literary anecdote, which, I promise the reader, will not be found less valuable for its lessons, because so well calculated to provoke frequent merriment. I shall make the attempt, in more elaborate pages, to indicate the true reason which serve to keep the masses of mankind from any direct intercourse with their authors:—show why society, itself, works to this very end, as if moved by a common necessity, and governed by a positively selfish interest.

Richard Hurdis was singularly successful with the public in spite of much hostile criticism. It was objected, to the story, that it was of too gloomy and savage a character. But the entire aspect of a sparsely-settled forest, or mountain country, is grave and saddening, even where society is stationary and consistent; and, where society is only in process of formation the saddening and the grave in its aspect are but too apt to take on even sterner features, and to grow into the gloomy and ferocious. It is quite enough, in answer to the objection, to say that the general portraiture is not only a truthful one, in the present case, but that the materials are really of historical character. The story is a genuine chronicle of the border region where the scene is laid, and of the period when the date is fixed. Its action, throughout, is founded on well-known facts. Its personages were real, living men; being, doing, and suffering, as here reported. Nothing has been "extenuate," nothing has been "set down in malice." A softer coloring might have been employed, and, more frequently, scenes of repose might have been introduced for relieving the intense and fierce aspects of the story; but these would have been out of place in a narrative so dramatic of cast, and where the action is so rapid.

Some doubts have been expressed touching the actual existence of the wild and savage confederacy which I have here described; but nobody, at all familiar with the region and period of the story, can possible entertain a question of the history. There are hundreds of persons, now living, who knew, and well remember, all the parties; and the general history of the outlawry prevailing in the Mississippi valley, twenty years ago, can hardly have escaped the knowledge, in some degree, of every inhabitant of the southwest, during that period. I knew Stuart, the captor of Murrell, personally; and had several conferences with him, prior to the publication of his narrative. I have also met certain of the *dramatis personae*, during my early wanderings in that wild country. The crimes here recorded, were then actually in progress of commission; and some of my scenes, and several of my person, were sketched from personal observation, and after the current reports from the best local authorities. I repeat, briefly, that the facts here employed are beyond question, and still within the memory of living men. I need scarcely add, that, as a matter of course, I have exercised the artist's privilege of placing my groups, in action, at my own pleasure; using what accessories I thought proper, and dismissing others; suppressing the merely loathsome; bringing out the heroic, the bold and attractive, into becoming prominence, for dramatic effect; and, filling out the character, more or less elaborately, according to the particular requisitions of the story, without regarding the individual claims of the subordinate. Let me say, further,—though this, perhaps, is scarcely necessary—that, in most cases, I have used other than the true names, and altered certain localities, simply that living and innocent affections should not be unnecessarily outraged.

One other matter. It will be seen that there is a peculiarity in the arrangement of the story. The hero tells, not only what he himself performed, but supplies the events, even as they occur, which he yet derives from the report of others. Though quite unusual, the plan is yet strictly within the proprieties of art. The reader can readily be made to comprehend that the hero writes after a lapse of time, in which he had supplied himself with the necessary details, filling up the gaps in his own experience. I have persuaded myself that something is gained by such a progress, in the more energetic, direct and dramatic character of the story; and the rapidity of the action is a necessary result, from the exclusion of all circuitous narration. The hero and author, under plan, become identical;—a union which the reader will be pleased to believe only fictitious: while the real writer was unknown, it was of little consequence whether the parties were confounded or not. Even now, the dis-claimer is hardly necessary; since nobody need be mystified in the matter, unless it be some inveterate Dogberry, who prides himself on the length of his ears, and insists upon the whole road in his daily crossing of the *Pons Asinorum.*[199]

There are two other stories—*Border Beagles,* and *Beauchampe,*—which belonged originally to this unnamed family. These will succeed to *Richard Hurdis,* in the pre-sent classification of my writings.

13

AN INQUIRY INTO THE PRESENT STATE OF SOUTHERN LITERATURE

Anonymous

Southern Literary Messenger (1856).

There has been no question so often asked, and so variously answered of late years as this, "shall the South have a literature of her own?" It is one of vital importance to her social and political interests, a question on which hangs the integrity of her peculiar institutions, and on which is based the preservation of her social and political independence.

We look in vain elsewhere for any national literature whose object it is to aim a blow at the existence of the very social fabric which supports it. What for example, would be thought of a history of Great Britain whole chapters of which were devoted to an eloquent denunciation of monarchy? What would be thought of a feuilleton published within sight of the Tuilleries, designed to ridicule the pretensions of Napoleon III and to rear upon the tumbling ruins of his dynasty the regime of the Bourbons?[200] What would be thought of a political essay emanating from the press of a Harper or a Redfield, designed to show the utter failure of republican institutions and eloquently recommending a return to the colonial vassalage of England?[201]

And yet "'tis true 'tis pity, but pity 'tis 'tis true"[202] that the literature which the South has adopted as her own, which helps to form her libraries, to allure her youth, or to teach her children is devoted in a great measure to a crusade against an institution, the destruction of which, as she verily believes would impoverish her purse, cripple her power and corrupt her morals.

We are prepared to sustain what we say. George Bancroft has been elevated, whether justly or not, to the high rank of the historian of the United States. His book, or rather his books, for their name is Legion, are in the hands of every well read man in the South. They are placed in the hands of children as the fountain from which they may draw the most reliable information concerning their country and her institutions. Yet has he devoted one entire chapter to an assault on the institution of slavery, besides many insidious side blows at the same object of his wrath, distributed throughout the work. Nor do we mean to complain very much of Mr. Bancroft's course. He had an undoubted right, and indeed it was his bounden duty to treat the subject according to his own peculiar views; and it was perhaps but natural that, with the bias of his section, and the narrow feelings and prejudices of a New England author, he should entertain the views which he has expressed. There might, indeed, without a sacrifice of the dignity of the historian, have been a little less of the prejudice of the partizan, and a little more of the impartiality of the profound statesman in his style. It might have been a little more just to the people of half the republic of which he wrote, had he given to the world at least some of their reasons in support of an institution which they sustained. Mr. Macaulay, partizan as he is, gives us at least an insight into the merits of both sides of every question. Mr. Bancroft however sees but one side of the shield, and he must not therefore be surprised if there should rise up a champion in defence of the other. But it was not to charge Mr. Bancroft with unfairness, nay, not even to refute his flimsy logic, and milk sop philanthropy, that we cited his authority. It was to lament that his history should be placed in the hands of the people of the South, without any counteracting influence—it was to deplore the madness of those who gulp the poison, yet neglect the antidote. Is it wise in a people to recognize as authority a book which wilfully misrepresents their interests? Is it politic to disseminate principles calculated to shake the very foundation of our social fabric? Is it just to instil into the minds of our children a distaste for an institution which we believe divine in its origin, and conservative in its influence, and which they may at no very distant day be called upon to defend with their blood?

But it is not in the dignified and impressive language of history alone, that our literature seeks to prejudice the institution of Slavery. Evil as is the tendency of history when perverted from its true channel of impartial justice, it is harmless when compared with falsehood arrayed in the attractive garb of romance and poetry. History finds its place for the most part in the libraries of the thoughtful and the learned prepared to refute its sophisms, or to reject its falsehoods. But fiction diffuses itself through all the avenues of social life, and fastens itself upon the heart and the fancy of the young, the guileless, and the romantic. History must needs to be at all consistent, confine itself to deductions drawn from an observation of a general system. Fiction may take exceptional cases as examples of a class, and present a falsehood in the garb of truth. To illustrate this proposition let us look for a moment at Massachusetts, the nursery of the poisonous literature to which we refer. History would have to say of the character of the people of that State, that they were for the most part orderly, law-loving and law-abiding. Fiction might select from the chronicles of the Courts the tragedy of Webster and Parkman, and, throwing over the dark picture a flood of genius, might well fill the mind of the reader with horror for any society where such a miser or such a villain could have been nurtured.[203] Or take the case of the Southern master and his slave for an illustration. History, if true to its high mission of truth, would be compelled to say that that relation was marked by kindness almost parental on the one hand, and by grateful obedience almost filial on the other. Mrs. Harriet Stowe, true to her low mission of falsehood, might search the newspapers of the South for an exceptional case of cruelty and oppression, stamped with the detestation and indignant reprobation of all society, and with the colours which she has borrowed from the pallet of Charles Dickens, and the pencil which she has stolen from Mrs. Sherwood, might paint a scene which might well excite the fancy, and wring the heart of the reader.[204] False as such a picture is, it is no less effective than if true. As well might you judge of the beauties of a garden, by some nettle overlooked by the gardener. As well might you judge of the purity and innocence of Eden, by the trail of that serpent whose insidious wiles "brought death into the world."[205] And yet it is a melancholy truth that by such arts impressions have been made, which it is almost impossible to eradicate.

It cannot be denied, and we would be the last to deny it, that Henry W. Longfellow is the first of our living American poets. We are proud to recognize him as such, for so long as his muse devotes herself to her true mission of interpreting the kinder feelings of the heart, of inspiring the young to patient and enduring toil, as in the "Psalm" or "Excelsior"; of teaching a beautiful lesson of religious dependence, and innocent virtue as in his charming picture of *Evangeline*; of illustrating, like a true American poet, the annals of that proud aboriginal race, which has passed away, as in "Hiawatha," so long do we recognize him as the truthful teacher, and the tender minstrel.[206] But he too must pervert his genius to our injury, he too must administer in the attractive draught of his poetry the poison of abolition, he too must strike his harp, strung as it is to tenderness, into harsh notes of discord with the South, and inspire to new hostility those whom he might have controlled. We lay down his volume with a sigh, at finding that one whom we had loved to recognize as a brother, nourishes in his heart a fraternity like that of Cain.[207]

But there is another department of literature even more injurious in its tendencies than those which we have mentioned. We refer to those books which are placed in the hands of children at a time when the mind is not strengthened to resist, but quick to receive influences. These come mostly from the north, nor does fanaticism overlook so admirable an opportunity for instilling pernicious sentiments into the minds of the unwary youth. Take up almost any book that you will designed to amuse and instruct children, and you will find a plausible homily against slavery, an exaggerated narrative of the sufferings of the slave, and a touching account of some young philanthropist, redolent of the odour of sanctity at six years old, who persuades papa to liberate his unhappy negroes. Take up any volume of elegant extracts designed to instruct our youth in the graces of Yankee eloquence, or the cadences of Yankee reading, and you will find it filled with attacks upon slavery, and with such trash as Bryant's "African Chief."[208] What must be the inevitable effect of such a system of education? Will it not make such an impression upon the minds of many as will be impossible to eradicate in after years? But even if such were not the result, it is disgraceful to support and encourage by our patronage a literature designed to break down one of the established institutions of our State. Slavery is as essential a social institution in Virginia, as is marriage. It is controlled and regulated by laws, it involves private rights even above the just action of law, it is divine in its origin, it is permanent in its nature. Like marriage it cannot even be dissolved except by compliance with the regulations of law. If this be all so, and that it is so, no candid man can deny, is it not as unwise to tamper with an institution thus lying at the very basis of our social fabric, as with the holy institution of marriage? And can there be an interference more dangerous and fatal than by a literature designed to instil prejudice in the minds of the young, and to ripen it in the minds of the adult? The justification of these impertinent intermeddlers in the concerns of their neighbors, is to be found in the hackneyed and perverted maxim of the Roman dramatist,

Homo sum, humani nihil a me alienum puto.[209]

A maxim which, when thus perverted, justifies theft, which encourages discord, which nourishes treason. A maxim which dictates a systematic persecution of an Anglo-Saxon brother, for the imaginary relief of an African slave. A maxim which prompts the benevolent "Homo" to turn with scorn and contempt from the want and misery around him, and, like another Mrs. Jellaby, to reserve his sympathies and philanthropy for the happy and contented negro of the South.[210] A maxim which having served the turn of the Jacobins of France, bathed a nation in blood, and blackened it with atheism, emigrates to New England, and develops itself in new crimes committed in the name of Religion and Virtue.[211] Well that such a philanthropist declares himself a man, lest haply the horrified spectator of his crimes might mistake him for a fiend. As it is, who is not ready, after beholding so much enormity in the name of humanity, and so much vice in the name of virtue, to exclaim with Ensign Northington, "Damn Homo."

But we have been betrayed into a digression from the original purpose with which we took up the pen. So far we have attempted to show the importance, the vital necessity of a Southern literature. We are aware that there are many obstacles in the way of its establishment. We confess with candour, that many of these obstacles have been imposed by ourselves. But we deny emphatically that our inferiority in literary attainment proceeds from any inferiority in capacity to the North. There are several causes at work to retard our progress in this respect, to two of which we propose to advert.

The facility with which political distinction may be attained in a republic, naturally allures young men of genius and education to that arena. The applause of a mob, for wiser men than Garrick have mistaken the puff of a dunce for fame, the prestige of a place in Congress or in our legislative halls, the panting, struggling aspirations for eminence in the nation, all present far greater attractions to youth than that quiet path along the cool sequestered vale of literature.[212] And yet this very proclivity which drives men into political life, furnishes us with a successful answer to those who taunt us with backwardness in literary attainment. In the councils of the nation the South has furnished us with our wisest and most accomplished statesmen. The palm of intellectual superiority has been tacitly but freely accorded to the South in this department of science and learning. Who can say what brilliant contributions might not have been added to our polite literature by the dramatic genius, and splendid eloquence of Henry Clay? And what a great reservoir of thought and instruction is presented to the mind in the works of that distinguished Carolinian, who was as familiar with every spring and function in the fabric of social government as the skilful anatomist with the nerves and organs of the human body.

This devotion of the talent of the South to the field of politics has, in a great measure, been the result of necessity. The systematic warfare of the North against the institution of slavery, has induced those who might otherwise have pursued a calmer but not less brilliant career to rush to the defence of their interests. The agitation thus produced has been general and continuous. Not confined to the more cultivated classes of society, it has been diffused through the masses, and thus has materially diminished the number of readers, as well as the number of authors, of polite literature. A period of political agitation, or of civil strife, is not a period for the cultivation of Belles Lettres. When the rights of property are assailed, when the fireside is in danger, there is but little time for the study of philosophy or the pursuit of literature. The only authors who are then produced, are those who make it their province to analyze the social compact, to proclaim political freedom and rights, and to exhort their countrymen to a steadfast assertion and unyielding defence of those rights. During the revolution in England, which established the Protectorate on the ruins of royalty, the young Latin secretary of Cromwell arose to some eminence as a political writer. But it was not until the storm had passed away, and order was once more restored to the distracted realm, that the unfading fame of *Paradise Lost* eclipsed the political distinction of John Milton, the defender of the Liberty of the Press.[213] In the department of literature which such civil strife produces, we boldly and confidently challenge a comparison between the two sections. Until New England can rival the fame of Jefferson and Madison; or the more modern disciples of the Dana school achieve something worthy to be compared with the searching disquisitions of Calhoun, the South may rest quietly under the taunts of inferiority which *one of her own sons*, a few years ago, hurled against her in order to curry favour with the modern Athenians of Boston.

The other cause to which we referred, which has retarded the rise of literature in the South, is to be found in the active enterprise of her sons, urging them to seek their fortune in some new home in the far West. This has prevented that growth of population which is essential to the maintenance of a home literature. Those who have thus left their homes, immersed in the struggle for independence in a new country, have but little time or inclination for the pursuit of letters, while by their voluntary absenteeism they sap the population which might otherwise sustain such pursuits at home. Nor is this tendency to emigration due, as has been charged, to the institution of slavery. It produces the impoverishment at home of which it seems to be the result, and is thus, to our minds, a subject of regret. It proceeds from the restless spirit of adventure so remarkable in Southern youth, and from that ardent love of political distinction which we consider the bane of our society. They meet, it is true, with their reward, for it is a fact worthy of notice, that a large majority of the aspiring emigrants to new countries, who have attained the preferment which they sought, have been originally from the Southern States.

He is an unwise physician who can only form a diagnosis of disease, without skill to suggest a remedy. If we have succeeded in pointing out the importance of a literature to the South, and in alluding to some of the causes which have prevented its development, we have but half fulfilled our duty until we suggest a remedy for the evil which exists. Indeed, in these remedies are embodied other causes which have prevented the attainment of this desirable object, for the neglect of duty involves consequences as deplorable as the positive commission of wrong.

In order, then, to build up a Southern literature, we would urge upon the South the importance of sustaining exclusively her literary institutions. We doubt whether all other causes combined have done more essential injury to the prosperity of the South, than the neglect of her colleges for Northern institutions. In the item of capital, the most important in a political aspect, who can calculate the loss which the South has sustained by such a suicidal policy? The capital thus expended beyond her borders is never again heard of, unless, perchance, in the circulation of abolition documents, or the furnishing of Sharpe's rifles and revolvers for Kansas emigrants.[214] But it is not in its political aspect that we desire to consider this question. By the encouragement of our own institutions, we elevate the general standard of intelligence, we improve the character of our common schools; and for the Yankee pedagogue and old-field school, we substitute a Southern teacher, born and reared amongst us, and devoting his energies and talents to the formation and advancement of literature. Nor is this all. A literary class is established in our midst—a corps of Alumni, bound together by a common devotion to Alma Mater, are dispersed through our State. A thirst for literature is engendered, libraries are built up and encouraged, and young men, who would never have heard of a collegiate education elsewhere, are every year introduced into society to elevate its tastes and adorn its circles. We venture to say that there can never be a home literature where there is not a reading public, and every step that is taken toward promoting the general intelligence of the community, is a new incentive to the exertions of genius. We rejoice to see that a disposition thus to encourage our own colleges and universities is growing up at the South. It is founded, indeed, on a different principle than that for which we are contending, but yet a just and noble principle of self-preservation. Let it be continued, and while the capital expended in education will be retained at home; while our youth will be educated better for the stations which they may be severally called upon to fill, while a blow, prompted by just resentment, will be thus struck at the Northern nurseries of abolition, it will not be the less grateful to Southern pride to know that we will be pursuing the surest policy to build up a sound and wholesome literature.

Scarcely less important than this is the encouragement of Southern literary periodicals. Let the market for Southern talent be in a Southern magazine. These periodicals are the nests from which young genius first tries its wing before it braves the atmosphere of a chilling public opinion. We speak that which we know when we assert that there are the elements of a Southern literature now in our midst. Properly supported, a Southern magazine would teem monthly with the emanations from aspiring citizens of the republic of letters. Is it asking too much of the true Southerner, who recognizes the importance of what we have said, that out of his abundance he would contribute something to the accomplishment of such an end? We conjure the thinking men, the reading men of the South, to come forward to the support of that periodical, through the medium of whose columns we now address them. But a short time since a magnificent donation was bestowed upon the prosperous Agricultural Society of the State. All honour to the generous donor, all success to the useful recipient. But is it not of equal importance that Southern enterprise should be directed to the cultivation of letters? If a generous interest were taken in the *Southern Literary Messenger*, which has already done much for the honour of the State, and of which Virginia and the South may well be proud, and also in a similar enterprise about to be established in Charleston, it would tend more than aught else to stimulate the literature of the entire South.[215] Thus would we have to boast of our glorious old State as of a column founded upon the affections of a brave and honest people as on a rock, rising in the Doric simplicity of her political structure, strong massive and elegant, and adorned by the graceful Corinthian capital of a pure and classic literature.

14

A PERCEPTIBLE FALLING OFF OF "SENSATION BOOKS": WHAT IS LIKELY TO TAKE THEIR PLACE?

Anonymous

Putnam's Monthly Magazine (1856).

It is with no small pleasure that we hear, from many booksellers, the announcement of a perceptible falling off in that class of books which go among the trade by the name of "sensation-books." They are generally of the sort advertised as "thrilling," "exquisite," "intensely interesting," and which are said to run through editions of twenty and thirty thousand copies in less than a month. We have so often, within the last year, taken occasion to let our readers know the character of these publications, that we have no need now to explain it at length. Suffice it to say, that they may be, for the most part, succinctly described as trash. Without original merit of any kind, and appealing merely to sensibilities and not to the reason and conscience, they were a species of debauched literature, and every one must be glad that the day for their disappearance has come. They engendered bad habits of writing among authors, and bad habits of thought and feeling, among readers, and, unless something worse takes their place—a result which we do not anticipate—it will be a happy riddance.

But what is likely to take their place—ah! who can tell? What kind of reading will be furnished to that vast mass of readers who have been accustomed to waste their time on the wretched novels whose downfall we chronicle? It is impossible to say; the taste of the reading public is apt to be capricious, and, when it tires of one stimulant, readily looks about for another. But we can say what class of works ought to be advanced to the vacant niches; for the world already so abounds in good books, and men of genius, capable of writing good books, are so numerous, that no intellectual curiosity need be starved. There are capital novels extant, which, though not new, will prove, we warrant, a refreshment to those who undertake them—there are grand and exquisite poems in our English literature—there are histories, of all times, and almost all men, that have more interest than the most brilliant works of fiction—and there are innumerable essayists and travelers, whom to encounter, is to achieve a pleasure for life. Let the disconsolate lovers of the paper-covered nonsense, now demised, turn to these for solace. They will find them less easy reading, at first, but infinitely better, in the end. They will find that their taste improves and grows by what it feeds on, until, having acquired a true appreciation of what is really good in books, they will wonder that they could ever have fed upon the sentimental husks which had once been their nutriment.

Nor need our young writers despair of a field for the proper exercise of their talent. Our whole American life is a comparatively untrodden ground; and if they must write fiction, let them try their hands upon the rich and suggestive materials lying everywhere about them. Have we, as yet, besides *Uncle Tom*, a genuine novel of American life? Has anything like justice yet been done to the peculiarities of the several parts of the nation? Are not the experiences of the emigrant and the settler full of tragic incident, full of pathos, full of stirring adventure, and not without their humorous side? Besides, how much of human history is to be rewritten—from the new modern standpoints—with a new sense of its picturesque effects, and a new philosophy of its bearing and significance? In fact, there is no end to the topics, which a skillful writer may make both entertaining and instructive, if he will but give his mind and his time to the task. The same expenditure of labor and thought, which is now given to some ephemeral romance—to a work which will scarcely outlive the proverbial nine days of wonder—if devoted to a nobler undertaking, would not produce, perhaps, so profitable a work for the nonce, but it would lead to a greater work in the end, and acquire for the author, instead of a transient and hollow notoriety, a lasting fame. Be this as it may, however, we are sure that the public would gain a great advantage, in the possession of a sounder, purer, and more vigorous literature.

We throw out these few words simply as hints. Our experience in the magazines here convinces us that there is an almost incredible amount of intellectual activity in this country, which, rightly directed, would soon create a brilliant literature for us. The great defect in it, however, is want of maturity and taste. Our writers do not take time to learn the secret of their own powers, to husband them with discretion, and to apply them with the most effectiveness and concentration. As the general life of the nation, so the literary life, is hurried. A certain rawness and want of depth, a certain superficial elegance, in lieu of true beauty, marks too many of our efforts. But there is great strength at the bottom of us—a luxuriance of force even—which shows that there is no deficiency of genius, and only the absence of culture and care. We are an intense people, and intensity passes with us, often, for real vigor, for that calm and masterly control of the powers which is the sign of true greatness of mind. The mistake lies in supposing spasmodic violence an indication of strength, whereas it is rather an indication of disease.

15

PORTRAIT OF SIR WALTER SCOTT, BY GEO. W. CURTIS OF *PUTNAM'S MAGAZINE*

Anonymous

Southern Literary Messenger (1856). Appended to the title is the following note: "The Editor of the Messenger deems it proper to say that this article, though written after the forms of the editorial plural, is from the pen of a contributor."

We have lately fallen in with a report of a lecture upon Charles Dickens, Esq., by Mr. Curtis, in which, by way of a foil to his hero, the lecturer has undertaken to present his idea of Scott.[216] According to his view, the Wizard of the North was "a border baron of literature," "a man who accepted his social superiority as a fixed fact," one "who had no sympathy with men as men," but "as a landlord with his tenants," who was "the last laureate of feudalism," and finally a "Sir Roger de Coverley of genius"—and that is all.[217]

On the other hand, Mr. Dickens is the representative man of the age, the Columbus of Humanity, the discoverer of the great truth that the poor, the degraded, the vicious, and the criminal, are still men and women, bone of our bone and flesh of our flesh, heirs of a common mortality and immortality with ourselves. Mr. Dickens is the Shakespeare of novelists, and his characters alone are realities, like Hamlet, Mercutio and Imogen.[218]

We must stop by the way to remark that, of all points of comparison, Mr. Curtis has certainly been most unlucky in selecting this. Let him make the most of his examples. Pickwick, Sam Weller, the Fat Boy, Pecksniff, and the Infant Phenomenon,—with what class of readers do these names call up such vivid and distinct personages as the characters of Scott?[219] Where are Henry Morton, Cuddie Headrigg, and Ephraim Macbriar? Jonathan Oldbuck and Edie Ochiltree? Dominie Sampson and Bailie Nicol Jarvie? Pleydell and Dandie Dinmont, and Dirk Hatteraick? Richard Moniplies and Jenkin Vincent? Brian de Bois Guilbert, Isaac the Jew, the clerk of Copmanhurst, and the inimitable Wamba?[220] But we forbear—our little closet has no room for the crowds of people, from the king to the beggar, who start up at the name of the mighty magician, and greet us with the familiarity of old acquaintance.

Walter Scott wanting in hearty sympathy with his fellow men! He, whose "common sense" was declared to be his leading characteristic by one who knew him most intimately from his boyhood till near the close of his life! He, with whom the peasant at the plough or the turf-digging was wont to exchange a pinch of snuff, pausing from his labor "to hae a crack wi'the Shirra." He, who was idolized by his countrymen in the vale of Tweed, and by the populace in Edinburgh! whose judicious charities gave to so many of the poor around him employment, independence, self-respect! whose most frequent thought, in his hour of adversity, was for the faithful and affectionate servants, whom the change of fortune affected equally with himself!

It is true that people are to be found in all countries, insensible to merit which they cannot appreciate, and envious of all that is superior to them in the social scale. It is true that, even in the lifetime of Scott, his political opinions drew upon him the hostility and hatred of such as these—the mobs, who burned stacks of grain and destroyed machinery—who, inflamed by the artful suggestions of men more cunning and wicked than themselves, in the attempt to cure or avenge the evils which they felt, would have pulled down the fabric of society and deluged it with blood. To such men as these he was obnoxious in Scotland. To such as these he might have been hateful elsewhere, to Red Republicans in France, to Anti-Renters and Fillibusters in America, to destructives, who declare that property is robbery, and who spurn at all the restraints of religion, morality, law and social order. But we utterly disbelieve and deny, that in his feelings or his conduct, there was wanting aught that a true lover of human nature should have possessed or exercised.

Let us grant that he was a Tory and a Loyalist—that his opinions in favor of hereditary monarchy and aristocracy were overstrained—that his personal reverence for royalty exceeded the limits of sober reason. Were these other than natural results of his birth, his education, and the experience of the tumultuous times in which he lived? With the terrible anarchy of the French revolution before his eyes, and the iron despotism of Napoleon which followed it—the alarming riots which disturbed the peace and menaced the integrity of his own country—and the convulsions which have not yet subsided in the rest of Europe—is it unpardonable that he should cling with undue tenacity to the forms which invested the conservative principles of his own government? And after all, was he ever untrue to the duties of a real patriot? Was he ever a flatterer of the court, a time-server, a seeker of place and emolument? Let the answer be found in his *Letters of Malachi Malgrowther*, in which he opposed the government, and cooled the attachment of his own political friends, at the very moment when his reverse of fortune would have induced a meaner man to conciliate the patronage of the one and the interest of the other.[221] Let it be found in the universal respect and confidence which he enjoyed, at the hands of his opponents, from "Frank Jeffrey's buff and blue" down to all except the anarchists to whom we have alluded.[222] That political opinions have often much to do with our social relations is not denied. But even, in our own country, we have examples enough to prove, that the widest theoretical democracy may consist with the most exclusive pride of caste—and the highest toned Federalism, as in the case of the illustrious Marshall, with the utmost simplicity of manners and the purest benevolence.[223] How far does the lecturer himself propose to carry his doctrines of equality? Does he level all distinctions of education, refinement and intelligence? Does Mr. Curtis ask his butcher to dinner of a Sunday? Does he invite his printer boys to his bachelor entertainments? Does he walk into his club arm in arm with "Boots?" or put on his white kid gloves and escort his laundress to the opera? We put these questions in profound ignorance of his domestic habits—but we feel quite sure of an answer in the negative. And we beg further to inquire, if not in this way, how does Mr. Curtis or Mr. Dickens, or any apostle of their school, manifest *in action* the peculiar devotion which they feel for the rights of the million? One writes a long serial novel, which pays him fabulous profits. The other edits a very popular magazine, with a most productive subscription list, or delivers brilliant lectures to an applauding audience "for a consideration." We claim no right to know how far their time, talents and income are employed for the relief of their fellow creatures. But when one of them thus arraigns before the bar of public opinion, as a feudal aristocrat, destitute of human sympathy, the man who stood among the foremost, if not the very first, of all the literary men of his time, in unpretending, but active and practical, well-doing, there ought to be no small show of good deeds to justify the broad phylactery and the sonorous thanksgiving.

To be explicit, it strikes us that there is a good deal of *cant* in this production. We yield to no man in reverence for the memory of Thomas Hood, the humorist, whose heart was as kind and tender, as his fancy was sportive and facetious. But Mr. Curtis' periods have not the ring of his metal. The sentiment of the "eloquent lecturer" recalls to us the accessories of the theatre, the actor ranting on the stage, the gas lights at his feet, the *claqueurs*[224] under the chandelier. We may do him injustice, and for his sake we hope it is so: but the whole performance suggests the idea of something got up for effect. It seems forced and overstrained. Was there really no philanthropy in England before Charles Dickens? Had we not heard of Howard?[225] Were there not private individuals, public associations, parliamentary committees, striving in all ways to alleviate suffering, to reclaim offenders, to solve the difficult problems of social misery and evil, and to apply the fit remedies to each? No well informed man can be ignorant of these facts. But either Mr. Curtis was ignorant, or it better served his purpose of canonizing Mr. Dickens, that they should be ignored. To bring out all the brilliancy of his phantasmagoria, the rest of the house must be darkened.

The literary criticisms of the lecturer are not more felicitous than the moral. Scott has done nothing more than summon all the world to witness the last tournament. His great failure (but he has the honor to share this with Mr. Dickens) is in the delineation of women. So says Mr. George W. Curtis.

One might suppose that our critic had confined his reading of Scott to the poems and one or two novels—say *Ivanhoe* and *The Talisman*.[226] How else to account for the first assertion we know not. It is impossible to name the *Waverley* novels, without remembering the series which has illustrated the history and the life of England and Scotland, from the days of Queen Bess and Mary, Queen of Scots, throughout the reigns of the Stuarts and the Hanoverian princes, down to the middle of the 18th century. There are *Kenilworth*, and the *Abbot*, and the *Monastery*—*Peveril of the Peak*, and *Woodstock*—*The Legend of Montrose* and *Old Mortality*—and the *Fortunes of Nigel*, which slipped out of its place in our counting up.[227] What says Macaulay? Our readers, we are sure, will pardon the quotation:

> At Lincoln Cathedral there is a beautiful painted window, which was made by an apprentice out of the pieces of glass which had been rejected by his master. It is so far superior to every other in the church that, according to the tradition, the vanquished artist killed himself from mortification. Sir Walter Scott, in the same manner, has used those fragments of truth which historians have scornfully thrown behind them, in a manner which may well excite their envy. He has constructed out of their gleanings works, which, even considered as histories, are scarcely less valuable than theirs. But a truly great historian would reclaim those materials which the novelist has appropriated. The government and the history of the people would be exhibited in that mode in which alone they can be exhibited justly, in inseparable conjunction and intermixture. We should not then have to look for the history of the wars and votes of the Puritans in Clarendon, and for their phraseology in *Old Mortality*; for one half of King James in Hume, and for the other half in the *Fortunes of Nigel*.[228]

Apart from the historical novels, how many thousands and tens of thousands, in all civilized lands and in some that can scarce be called so, have dwelt with delight, not only upon the originals, but on the translations in many tongues, of his other fictions? on the exquisite creations of a fancy, whose fertility was exhaustless, while its productions, however luxuriant, were always true to nature and to life. Nor is anything more remarkable in them, than the fidelity with which each character is supported, whether belonging to the upper, the middle, or the lower classes of society. All move and speak so like real men and women, that we forget they are but puppets of the imagination, and look upon their sayings and doings, their loves and hatreds, their griefs and joys, as upon those of the actual world in which we live. Can such work as this come from the hand of a man, without a heart for his kind? Let us call a single witness: stand up Jeanie Deans! and tell us whether Walter Scott was capable of reverencing truth and virtue in the humblest position, of depicting the love, the constancy, the purity, the fortitude, the delicacy, the self-devotion, of a true woman's nature! Shall we introduce any more of the "womankind?" There are plenty in waiting: Die Vernon and Edith Bellenden, Lady Peveril the gentle, and the high-souled Rebecca, Green Mantle and Margaret Ramsay, Jenny Dennison, Mrs. Saddletrees, and Mrs. Meg Dodds! Let no one be alarmed at the landlady, her tongue will utter no harsh words on this occasion, especially in presence of Bessie

Maclure, whom neither poverty nor misfortune, the slaughter of her own sons, nor the cruelty and coldness of all the world, can provoke into unholy hatred or revenge, or remove from her firm (though humble) trust in the Lord whom she worships.[229]

In all seriousness we wonder, whether Mr. Curtis has *read* the novels of Sir Walter Scott, to say nothing of his miscellanies, histories, and biographies—or has he, as Sydney Smith humorously suggested to be the proper course for an impartial reviewer, abstained from so doing in fear of being prejudiced? Or is he afflicted with a morbid defect of vision, as some unfortunates are, who cannot distinguish colors? If the latter, his case is hopeless. If the former, he has before him, if he please to accept it a wealth of enjoyment of which he has no conception. Let him read Scott for two or three years (in connection with Lockhart's biography)[230] and then try his hand at another lecture.[231]

16

THE DUTY OF SOUTHERN AUTHORS

W. R. A.

Southern Literary Messenger (1856).

Through no more appropriate channel can we convey our thoughts upon the subject we have selected, than through the columns of a periodical devoted to the South, and to the maintenance of her literature and institutions. And if there should be found anything of force in what we shall urge, we could ardently hope that the seeds thus sown in diffidence and weakness, might, under the skilful culture of abler minds, germinate and grow to a tree bearing useful fruit. If there is any wish for the accomplishment of which we could breathe forth our most earnest prayers, it is for the establishment of a Southern literature, standing secure and independent upon its own pedestal, lighting up the threshold of its temple with the refulgent beams of its self-illumination. If there is any enterprise, towards the successful achievement of which the energy of every southern mind ought to be bent in unrelaxing effort, it is such an enterprise as will give to the South a literature that will command the respect and admiration of the world. If there is any duty, more than all others incumbent upon the Southern people, the performance of which they cannot neglect without discredit to themselves and injury to posterity, it is the duty of rewarding by their approbation, and stimulating by their praise, the literary creations of the genius of their section. It is the literature of a country that gives her people a position among the nations of the earth, and to this source must she look for the place she is destined to fill in the eyes of future generations. He who would refute error and advance truth, who would create light and dispel darkness, who would gain renown and benefit his kind, who would wield a power greater than the sword—he, we say, who would do all this, should devote himself to the task of elevating the literature of his country.

While it is the imperative duty of the authors of all nations to let the light shine that God has given them—to contribute, like so many springs, to swell the great stream of human knowledge and happiness, till it overflows its banks with the waters of truth—to worship wisdom and learning for their own sakes—while such motives, and such promptings as these, should inspire the heart, and kindle the genius of every author; yet to the Southern writer, besides all these, there should be other inducements and incentives to literary labors. Graver and more solemn considerations than a mere thirst for fame and distinction, should impel him to drive his pen. He lives in a community in which African slavery subsists. We, of the South, recognize it as a great social, moral and political blessing—beneficial alike to us and to the slave. We see in it a great pillar of conservatism, and we regard it as the best and most enduring basis for Republican institutions. But the rest of Christendom stands united against us, and are almost unanimous in pronouncing a verdict of condemnation. Wild crusades have been set on foot against our institutions, and amid the clamors and uproar of false philanthropy the still, small voice of truth is unheeded and unheard. The great question of African slavery is not understood in the outside world, whose prejudices are against it. Its great truths have not been fully presented and sustained; nor have its advocates been sufficiently untiring in their efforts to write its history in such letters that even those "who run may read." It is because of the world's ignorance of African slavery, as it exists at the South, that the world is arrayed against it. Let there be light upon this subject—let it be understood—and we need not fear to stand alone; for then, against the fanatical tide that threatens to overwhelm us, there will be raised a great moral break-water in our defence. As literature has been the most powerful weapon which the enemies of African slavery have used in their attacks, so, also, to literature we must look for the maintenance of our position, and our justification before the world. Let Southern authors, men who see and know slavery as it is, make it their duty to deluge all the realms of literature with a flood of light upon this subject. Let them dispel with the sun of genius the mists and clouds which ignorance and fanaticism have thrown around slavery, purposely involving it in an obscurity and darkness, through which men will not grope to find the truths upon which it reposes. This, then, is the "Duty of Southern Authors." The field for their labors is wide. Upon their efforts may depend the destiny of the South, and the preservation of her institutions. Their exertions should not be spasmodic and periodical, but constant and continuous. The press should teem with productions upon slavery, with as steady and unceasing an action, as it does with writings upon religion. The true features of slavery should be described in works of endless succession. Thus, by a constant agitation of the streams of literature, with the elements of truth, we shall be able to make the world view both sides of this great question, and see how we have been wronged and misrepresented. On the 29th of June, 1853, an address was delivered by Professor James P. Holcombe, before the Society of Alumni of the University of Virginia, containing thoughts that should recommend themselves to the grave and earnest consideration of every Southern man.[232] It was our good fortune to hear that address. Every one should read it. It contains wise and comprehensive views, which, when fully carried out, will mark the commencement of a new era in the history of our noble State University. It also contains appeals in behalf of a native Southern literature, which, if listened to, would arouse the sleeping intellects of our section, and make them create new stars to shine "forever in the firmament of letters." As it was the impression made by this speech which first led us to think upon the subject we are now presenting, we shall quote the eloquent language of the able and learned speaker, so far as it is applicable and auxiliary to our theme. We shall invoke the bright blaze of his genius to warm with inspiration the hearts of Southern men, and illuminate the path along which lies "the Duty of Southern Authors." Professor Holcombe says:

> Domestic slavery has impressed such distinct and peculiar features upon Southern society, that it can never be comprehended or appreciated by the rest of the world, without a class of native authors, Southern born and Southern bred, to interpret between us and them. Northern men, of the most enlarged patriotism, seldom visiting us at home, and then in a ceremonious way, looking at us through imperfect lights, and judging us by false standards, catch only the sharp points which rise up above the face of our institutions, and are unable to form a fair and intelligent estimate of our character. Hence our history, our moral and social habits, our opinions, all the circumstances of our condition, are discolored by the partial and broken medium of that Northern literature, through which they are now exhibited to the world....We want a native literature to vindicate the integrity of history, and preserve from oblivion the fame of our fathers.

Southern literati, read here your duty to the South, your duty to yourselves and to posterity! With the great moral force of literature overturn the unholy citadel erected by the slander, fanaticism, and malignity of your enemies, from whose unconsecrated towers, arrows steeped in the poison of falsehood and infamous libel, are shot at your institutions. There never was a field that promised a more deathless immortality to the author than this, nor greater benefits to his country and race. The success of *Uncle Tom's Cabin*, is an evidence of the manner in which our enemies are employing literature for our overthrow. Is that effusion, in which a woman, instigated by the devil, sows the seed of future strife between the two sections of her country, likely to be the last? No. The literary workshops of the North are even now resounding with the noisy and fanatical labors of those who, with Mrs. Stowe as their model, are forging calumnies, and hammering falsehood into the semblance of truth. Southern men, learn that the arms with which they assail you are the best for your defence. In the great armories and arsenals of literature, if you will look for them, there are more weapons for you than for your adversaries; because you will use them in the cause of reason and of truth, while your opponents wield them in behalf of prejudice and fanaticism. The sacred Book of God sustains you; reason and conscience sustain you; the annals of the world upon the subject of slavery sustain you; the immutable and eternal fiats of Nature and Nature's laws sustain you. Why should you hesitate, or doubt that victory will be yours, when on the side of slavery all these stand arrayed, with nothing to oppose them but ignorance, passion, and a spirit of fanaticism, as mad as it is mischievous?

But listen again to the stirring and eloquent words of Professor Holcombe, and recognize the groves through which Southern literature must wander, if it would fain gather enduring laurels for its brow while living, and chaplets to deck its tomb when dead.

We can no longer cover the salient points of our institutions through the halls of Congress. The voice of the statesman and orator cannot reach the masses, with whom lie the issues of life and death. Literature alone can dispossess the demon of fanaticism by its sweet compulsion. Let us appeal to her varied forms, of poem, drama, novel, history and essay, to enter every cottage in the land, and disperse the delusions which invest this whole subject of domestic slavery. Let them vindicate it before the reason and conscience of our people, and hallow it as a great instrumentality of Providence in their affections. Let them declare how earnestly we resisted its original imposition, how consistently we have labored for its subsequent amelioration, how uniformly we have sustained every measure of policy which promised for it a peaceful euthanasia, and how fiercely those who still roll in the unblessed wealth of that bloody commerce from whence it sprung, have sought to close every avenue for its gradual extinction, and hem it in, to perish amid social and national convulsion. Let them point out in characters of light, which all who run may read, that human wisdom has yet devised no scheme for its abolition, which does not call upon a great and enlightened people to sacrifice all the civilization which makes life valuable, for the mockery of conferring an empty freedom upon a race unfit for its enjoyment. Let them show, that although the same imperious necessity, which suspends ordinary laws in times of peril, forbids us to banish from the statute book the provisions which uphold the power of the master over his slave; yet all human laws receive their form and pressure from the spirit of a people, and, like the atmosphere we breathe, although possessing a weight more crushing than iron, may be made to bear lightly as the gossamer film of summer. Let them exhibit the mighty though noiseless features of public opinion in softening the harsher features of slavery, and converting its elements of danger and suffering into springs of refinement and virtue. Let them deliver to an immortality of honest scorn, the libeller who has raked through the prison records of a nation, that she might hold up the isolated and exceptional cases of cruelty to be found scattered over the tract of half a century, among its millions of population, as types of a whole people and generalizations of their character. Let them rid us of the superstition that slavery is a cleaving mischief, and by contrasting the general comfort, content and virtue of our people with the misery, suffering and vice of Europe and the Northern States, show that our domestic institutions are a blessing, and constitute a great conservative bulwark against the inroads of those destroying agencies that have consigned ancient empires, republics and kingdoms to the tomb, and are now slowly working the destruction and overthrow of free society both in the Old World and the New.

Let Southern scholars but be true to the responsibilities of our time and place, and the darkness will no longer dare affront the light. We shall divide the public opinion of the world, break the force of its sympathy, and by pouring through the bosoms of our people the living tide of hope, strengthen their hearts for the day of trial, and cover our land and its institutions with a shield of fire. We should raise up a native literature, if it could perform no other function than be our witness before posterity. If our institutions are ever to be overthrown, let no interposing cloud of fanaticism cover the truth from the view of future ages. Let us catch the inspiration of that sublime prayer, which the father of poetry puts into the mouth of Ajax, in the very extremity of Grecian distress, when hostile deities had shifted the fortunes of war; a prayer instinct with the spirit which gives immortality to the dying hero:

> If Greece must perish, we thy will obey,
> But let us perish in the face of day.[233]

We have quoted the above extracts from Professor Holcombe's brilliant address, because they bear directly upon our subject, and in its elucidation, are superior to anything that we can write. We hope that such alterations and interpolations of our own, as we thought necessary to introduce between the detached extracts we have selected, may not have marred the beauty, symmetry and strength of the Professor's argument.

We have, up to this point, endeavored to direct the gaze of the reader to that vast and unexplored ocean of truth, upon whose bosom we would urge Southern intellects to embark. Over its boundless surface let them sail on voyages of discovery, and visiting new isles and continents of light and knowledge, let them gather wisdom from every region of the earth, that its blended rays may illumine and vindicate the institutions of the South, and teach fanatics that in assailing slavery they seek to overthrow an ordinance of God, and to subvert one of the pillars of society and government.

But while we are lamenting the absence of such a literature at the South as would defend us for the present, and speak for us before posterity, let us not forget to award all honor and praise to those pioneers, whose writings upon slavery have prepared the field for the firm and steady tread of the Southern literary corps. Over the early grave of the lamented Dew, let the Southern slaveholder drop a sorrowing tear, to testify his grief at the untimely end of the able defender of our institutions.[234] Let him cherish with pride the names of Bledsoe and Fitzhugh, whose batteries of logic the advocates of abolition dare not face.[235] To Professor Wm. A. Smith, of Randolph Macon, the thanks of the South are due for his able and eloquent maintenance of the great truth, that "slavery is the normal condition of society."[236] Each of these, and many others, have done much for the institutions of the South. They have done their duty. In respect to slavery, they have performed the office of "hewers of wood and drawers of water" to those who are to follow in their footsteps.[237] They have furnished the materials for others to carry on the great work, until the impregnable citadel of Southern institutions shall be completed. They have collected the timbers of the edifice, which it is the duty of others to raise up. By their labors they have enabled those who shall follow them to stand upon a vantage ground.

Although all of the works upon slavery, to whose authors we have alluded, are powerful in logic, deep in research, and valuable to the South, yet their value and utility, in a great degree, will depend upon their being made the united basis of a *slavery literature*, so to speak. Isolated they do but little for the South; because, from the very nature of domestic slavery, no one author has been able, as yet, for want of the material and industry, to give us a book that would exhibit to the world a complete view of our institutions, in every aspect and position; so as to make them thoroughly understood by a kind of self-illumination, as it were. Each author has contemplated slavery from some particular stand-point, or has discussed it in one particular branch. The theme is one of such magnitude, that no one has been industrious enough to pursue a different course. Hence, when their books have been read by those who desired to inform themselves of slavery, and expected to find an exposition, complete and entire, the readers have been disappointed in finding that the subject is treated only partially, *ex parte*, is considered only in respect to a particular feature, relation or branch.[238] Thus, nothing, or comparatively little, is learned of the institution, because those who are ignorant of it, and seek light, cannot supply for themselves what the author does not give them. It is like expecting a child to read who is only furnished with half of the alphabet.

Let us illustrate. We shall then be better enabled, from our knowledge of what is wanting, to suggest how the deficiency is to be remedied.

Take Dew on *Slavery*. What is the character of the book? It is an examination of slavery as we find it existing in the nations of antiquity. It justifies slavery by showing *precedents*—by an appeal to the authority of the past. What does Fitzhugh do? He most ably demonstrates the "failure of Free society"; and by contrasting it with slave society, shows by a kind of *reductio ad absurdum*, the superiority of the latter. Professor Bledsoe, after handling Blackstone pretty roughly (and deservedly so too) for his blundering definitions, proceeds to crush to atoms, in the most masterly manner, every argument of the abolitionists against slavery. He then justifies the institution by appeals to Scripture, and defends it by "arguments from the public good," concluding with an examination of the Fugitive Slave Law.[239] Now, all of these works (we take these as samples, and as being the most conspicuous,) are exceedingly able and powerful in their arguments for slavery. But they benefit us but little in the outside anti-slavery world; for this reason: that to be fully understood and appreciated, they require an acquaintance with the institution of domestic slavery, as it exists at the South, which the outside world does not possess. They strengthen and confirm the convictions of the slaveholder, because his acquaintance with slavery enables him to see the truth and power of what is advanced, and to supply what is necessary for comprehending the subject. Not so with the man who knows nothing of slavery, but is seeking light upon it. A New Englander, or an Englishman, may learn from Dew what slavery was among the ancients, but he will not learn enough from that book to justify and defend the modern institution. He may read *Sociology for the South*, and see there that Free Society has failed, and is failing, but he will not the less deem African slavery a curse.[240] He may peruse *Liberty and Slavery*, and see the overwhelming collection of Scriptural authority adduced in defence of slavery. But his ignorance of the institution, of its moral, social, political and religious features, will prevent his recognizing the force and application of what is urged. The "arguments from the public good" will not penetrate his mind with conviction, because it is not proved to him that they are founded upon, and sustained by the facts of slavery; and he has no access to those facts. Consequently the great power and ability of the work are thrown away upon his mind; nor are his prejudices against slavery shaken or removed.

When we would *convince* men, we must store their minds with *facts*, upon which to base and support she arguments we intend employing for their conviction. Until we do *that*, the strength of our logic will neither be felt nor acknowledged; because the world is ignorant, or misinformed as to slavery at the South, and cannot perceive the truth, nor understand the premises of our theoretical reasonings, however correct and irrefragable they may be.

What is it then that we want, and have long wanted? A GREAT AND COMPREHENSIVE HISTORY OF AFRICAN SLAVERY AT THE SOUTH—a work that would take up the subject from the first introduction of slaves in 1620,[241] by a Dutch frigate, and bring it down to the present day. A History of Slavery would be its strongest defence, and its clearest vindication before the world. Such a work by the light of its truths would dispel the darkness which invests this great question, and refute the slanders which the ignorance and malignity of our enemies have perpetrated upon us. Such a book would be a great fulcrum upon which to place the levers of literature that must be used to overturn the opposing wall that error, prejudice and fanaticism have flung around us, to obscure and conceal the truth. Such a book would make all the works that have been written on our side intelligible to the world, and by blending and converging the rays of light from every source to a focal centre, would illuminate our position, and in the collection of weapons for our defence from every arsenal of reason, would arm a phalanx to stand in unbroken ranks around our institutions, and hurling defiance at the enemy, to laugh to scorn their impotent rage as they fell stunned and wounded from the impregnable battlements of reason. From such a book, as from a great literary fountain, the streams of poetry and the drama would flow; fiction, too, would then come and deck the honest forms of history with the gorgeous and attractive robes of the ideal. This, then, is the "Duty of Southern Authors"; to elevate the literature of the South, to repel the libel, "that no Southern work is worth reading"; to commence their labors by giving to the world a History of African Slavery—one that will recommend itself to the patriots and statesmen of the North, and to the sages of other lands; and by the embodiment of the facts of slavery, show it in its true colors, and vindicate it before mankind. And in the wake of history, let all the auxiliary forces of literature, to which we have alluded, follow, and diffuse their influence wherever a book is opened or a paper read, till a knowledge of our institutions shall pervade all ranks of society, and extend to every land. Nor let the efforts of Southern authors be altogether defensive. Scipio saved Rome by attacking Carthage; so let southern authors protect slavery by attacking free society.[242] Let them hold up its abominations and iniquities to the world, and tearing away the flimsy veil of its hypocrisy, let them point to the fearful magazine of explosive vices and corruptions underlying their whole social fabric, and threatening the destruction of religion and government. Let them speak of the impending conflict between the labor and capital of Free Society at the North, and paint "the fierce confederate storm of sorrow, barricaded evermore in her great cities."[243] Let them place in the background of the horrid picture of Free Society, the dark and shadowy hosts of advancing isms, with No Property, No Religion, No Slavery, No Marriage, and No Government, inscribed upon their unconsecrated banners; uttering blasphemies against God, denouncing the laws of Nature, and threatening to destroy everything that men hold dear. Let them, on the other hand, paint a picture for the South, that by its striking contrast and comparison with the other, may vindicate her institutions in the happiness, repose and virtue that characterize her condition. Let them show that it is to the institution of slavery, in its great conservative influence, that we owe our superiority in morals, politics, religion, and obedience to the law; that it is to this source we must look, to account for our freedom from all the social disorders and convulsions of the North. Let them show its blessings to us and its benefits to the world, that it is a great and necessary feature of conservatism in our government, and that its abolition would be attended with ruin and disaster to both sections of the Union, and with consequences that would be felt throughout Christendom. Let them prove by evidence, that the veriest skeptic cannot doubt, that this same institution of slavery will secure to the South permanent peace, prosperity and happiness, when, from inevitable causes in operation, destruction shall brood over the wrecks of Free Society,

> While Desolation, on their grass-grown streets,
> Expands her raven-wing; and up the wall
> Hisses the gliding snake, through hoary weeds
> That clothe the mouldering ruin.[244]

In an age when the power of the pen exceeds that of the sword, purse and tongue, let us not be idle. It has been truly said, that the bloodless conquests of the pen surpass in grandeur and extent, the triumphs of war; that the empire of Aristotle survived that of Alexander; that Napoleon did not alter the face of Europe more than Bacon; that the order of the Jesuits recovered more easily from the blows aimed at them by kings and councils, than from the strokes of Pascal.[245] With such a mighty power at its command, and such boundless fields before them for its exercise, why is Southern genius idle? While their institution of slavery affords them so much leisure for thought and literary activity, and assures every advantage of order and security, why are our authors oblivious of their duty to the slandered South and to the fame of their fathers?

17

IDEALS IN MODERN FICTION

Anonymous

Putnam's Monthly Magazine (1857). Preceding the article is the following editorial observation: "The views of this writer differ from those entertained, and sometimes expressed, by the *Monthly*; but the article is quite able to stand by itself."

Thought rules the world. Old dynasties have gone out, one after another. That of commerce is uncrowned by literature, which is the growing power; and in the kingdom of literature, the third estate is represented by a multitude of novels. These have not the patrician elegance, or the old renown and lofty pretensions, of the poem, but find compensation in a firmer hold upon a greater number of minds. We must go quite out of our way to meet the poet. The novelist comes to seek us. With the poet we must fly on unaccustomed wings of music and enthusiasm. The novelist will walk with us in daily paths, and we are astonished to find that, after so easy an ascent by his side, we are standing on the same eminence to which the poet was wont to drag us, dizzy and gasping, through the air. We are never quite comfortable in our relation to these winged thinkers. They carry us as a kite carries a hare, but do not often enable us to fly. Sometimes they even drop and abandon us in mid-career, and, in general, we find their ascension by rhythms and rhymes, by circumlocution and gyration, to be a little tedious—to be a labor rather than a festival or refreshment.

Our fine arts are too fine. Our poems do not lead us gently from the hearth, but jerk us suddenly to the remotest corners of the earth, or beyond the limits of the visible mundane sphere. Milton transports his reader as far as the kingdom of Chaos and old Night. Dante hurries him away from the green earth, from the blue heaven, to walk among the damned, among the purified. The shock is almost too great for healthy nerves. The poet tears me from my seat by the fire, from the bright circle of home, from the interests of my estate, my neighborhood, my culture. Out of every liberal enterprise, he snatches me and whirls me away as far as

Purgatory, as far as Paradise, before he will drop me a word of wisdom, and when he speaks, all his music and eloquence cannot quite overcome a lingering home-sickness which half occupies my mind. I shall not do the work or reap the pleasure of to-morrow in Hades or in Heaven, but here in the midst of my friends and neighbors, in the studies, endeavors, and relations which surround me. I am build-ing a house, planting a garden, striving to organize a reading club, a musical society, a lyceum, to elevate the tone of my own circle, to carry forward the civilization of our parish. Such an undertaking demands every faculty, engrosses my time and attention, involves the solution of every moral problem, the application of all spiri-tual laws to the affairs of life, and I cannot afford to be spirited away from it into the upper or the nether deep, to grope my way, among conditions which do not belong to me—to ends remote from the purpose of my working day.

But the novelist comes to my hearthstone; with him I am at home. Instead of the "cherubic host in thousand choirs," and the "loud uplifted angel trumpets," he gives me a comfortable concert, such as I may hope and live to hear.[246] He gives me the music of Mozart and Beethoven, or the joyful, earnest vocal harmony of the German four-part song, which lifts me as high as I am capable of mounting hon-estly, upon wings of my own emotion.[247] The novelist represents a healthy natural-ism, a return from the lawless excursions of barbaric fancy to the plain level of facts and forces, out of which our ideal world is to be fashioned by practical endeavor. The poets have rather separated than joined the ideal and actual. They should have bridged the chasm and offered us hope and encouragement. The novelists push them aside, and show that to all we dream and desire, to fair relations, cheerful in-fluences, and worthy opportunity, we may find or make a way, not through chaos, or the seven heavens, or the siege of Troy, or the court of King Arthur, but through the very conditions and circumstances in which we find ourselves engaged.

The poets must share this tendency. They must learn to walk upon firmer ground, and to commend the highest, by ability to speak the lowest truth. So much commonsense as a man has, so much currency he can give to his superior sense. The poets have lost power by every liberty they have taken with the facts of nature and history. Could they not see the significance of ordinary events of experience common to all. These alone are great. Birth, death, love, marriage, the home circle, the struggle for a livelihood, the search after truth in a world full of rumors and traditions, have these no interest that I must busy myself with dragons and en-chanters, with vagabond knights-errant, with dwarfs, and giants, and genii, and the thousand children of a fancy which builds castles in the clouds and dodges the work of the world? The wise heart finds more beauty and promise in the humblest history, than in all these nebulous splendors. The little black boy at my foot, if the meaning of his poor obstructed life could be shown, is more worthy of attention than all the angels and archangels of song. No destiny can be higher than that of the little black boy. He will not have wings in a hurry, he will not be like the black ginn who takes the fancy of children by his stature and his flight through the dark-ness, bearing beautiful princes in his arms, but he will be a man. Who can tell us what it is to be a man, even the most unfortunate; a man in ordinary circumstances, with ordinary advantages? Who has tried? Hardly the poet. He is even now addressing himself to the task. In England, the noblest of the nobility are endeavoring to take up new and democratic honors before the old hereditary dignity falls quite away.

A lord is lecturing, a thousand men of rank are busy with problems of labor and education. So the poets are obliged to abandon their old privilege of playing in the air to show like eagles their spread of wings and majesty of motion.

They must help us to lift what we are obliged to carry. We will not set noblemen or poets any longer on high, to be idle and admired, as early ages were content to do. They must help directly, or we turn to men who will help, and leave them, where they can neither shine nor sing, in a vacuum of neglect.

The novelists have made an honest effort. They have told such truth as they found to tell. We take occasion, first to thank them heartily for good service rendered, and then to inquire whether, on the whole, they have been large-minded enough to give us a fair and just picture of life in this planet. I have been born into certain stubborn conditions. My parents are moderately stupid, or narrow, or violent, and they stand in the way of my growth. My companions are busy, or greedy, or hard-natured, and do not understand my aims. I must get bread and shelter. I must establish a moral relation to my fellows, must stand for something and be a centre of influence, better or worse. The books, the newspaper, the preachers hinder and help. Sometimes I think my labor would be lighter, if no man had ever thought, or offered explanation which needs again to be explained.

The attempt to dispose orderly of stories, rumors, traditions, and theories afloat in the air, is like the first organization of chaos. Yet the creative impulse is strong in every child. He must struggle in his lot to conform the disorder of the actual to the order of the mind. This effort of the soul to find expansion, to find a field for free activity for expression, and reinforcement, we name the ideal tendency, and the object of our poetry and novel writing is to show the certain, though arduous, victory of the spirit over all obstructions. If, in any work, the soul appears superior to matter, able to overrule conditions, and make where it cannot find an opportunity to do its work, and take its joy in living—that work is ideal.

Ideality is manifested not in avoiding inevitable laws, but in revealing a force able to control them and make them servants of thought and affection.

There are two elements to be considered in our review of a work of art: the positive force exhibited, and the more or less obstinate resistance to it by fate and society—the strength of supernatural, and the impediment of natural laws. The balance between these old antagonists makes either a hard and well won, or an easy and cheerful, victory. The work, which shows a desperate struggle, is helpful to every reader whose life is yet a battle. That which represents a large success, is dear to all who have secured the ordinary advantages of fortune—who have comfort and culture, and are masters of leisure and of society. For this last class few books are written. We put in a petition for them. They are very much in need of help. Their enemies are ennui and luxury. They have no longer the stimulus of poverty and con-tempt. They are housed, and fed, and flattered, and too well content. These democ-rats, the novelists, are thoughtful first of their own order, and they are not yet ready to remember the poor rich man, the poor pedant, the poor doctors of law and medicine and divinity, the poor professors of logic and anatomy. The learned, who feed laboriously upon saw-dust, are as grateful as the ignorant hungry for a draught from the bottle of the idealist, who proposes to break up all routine—to burst every barrier which confines the fermenting liquor of life.

Look at all the novels, and consider how many are directly helpful to the readers of this article.

We find only *Wilhelm Meister* and *The Elective Affinities* distinctly addressed to the cultivated mind.[248] When the warm-hearted Novalis read *Meister* for the first time, he declared it a thoroughly prosaic work. But we learn that, being drawn to take up the book again, he continued, during his life, to read it regularly twice a year. He was at first repelled by the coldness and simplicity of diction, the absence of senti-mentality, and the commonplace character of many scenes, actors, and motives in the plot. Students, making a just demand, continue to complain that the most ear-nest desires of the race are not represented in the book; that the religion of a "fair saint" is exhibited from an intellectual and exterior, not a vital point of sight, and that, excepting Mignon, who is dear even to the cold heart of criticism, there is no character to be loved in all the brilliant company. Still the idealism of the work is not to be denied. We have here displayed the effort of a young man to find culture and exercise for his artistic faculties; and though he falls into the society of moun-tebanks and harlequins, he also draws to himself many noble hearts. He establishes relations with men of widely-different pursuits, engages the interest of a society whose object is a liberal culture and coöperation, and the whole atmosphere of the book is that of intellectual and aesthetic activity. Since *Wilhelm Meister* was pub-lished, the world has been flooded with novels. But they offer no picture or sugges-tion of a society which we can freely enjoy. And yet, the novel, like poetry, should submit the "shows of things to the desires of the mind,"[249] and give us some hint of the manners and enterprises which ought to fill our tedious days.

From the satirist, or critic in fiction, we do not expect poetry.

Dickens attacks abuses, unroofs the debtor's prison, crucifies the Barnacle fam-ily, astonishes the Circumlocution Office, petrifies bigotry, and fills the margin of his picture with specimens of petty knavery and very exasperated snobbery in high and low life.[250] Among some thirty characters, he gives us, perhaps, five, with whom we should not, decidedly, object to associate, although, it must be confessed, their company is a little dull. The knaves and fools give animation to the work. They are only tedious because they fill so many pages, and have everything so en-tirely their own way. The highest ideal in the book is that of common honesty and common kindness—an affectionate daughter, an affectionate father, a friendly, considerate young man, are given us to admire, and they are approachable only through the crowd of ignorant, selfish, vulgar semi-savages. The hero of Dickens is like that temperance lecturer, whose drunken brother accompanied him, to serve as a shocking example, and persisted in occupying more than his share of the attention of the audience.

But from Dickens, from Thackeray, we do not demand ideality. If they give us a little sentiment, we receive it thankfully as a gratuity—as a dish not promised in the bill of fare. From these men we look for exploration of dark corners, and we are glad to see their wretched inhabitants lighted by the sunshine of sympathy, not scorched with a flame of reprobation.

The French novels are also critical, not ideal. They expose an abyss of sensuality and ferocity, so that reading the *Mysteries of Paris* is like looking into a den of fierce and filthy beasts, rendered more horrible by the transparent human faces which express their lusts and passions.[251] We do not laugh over these scenes. We hardly expend even pity on the characters we meet in them. They corrupt their readers into a frantic excitement and degraded sympathy, or repel him into healthy disgust. They show the somewhat extravagant virtue of one or two favorite characters struggling for self-preservation in an ocean of corruption. The young heart—the best heart—is almost drowned in this whirlpool. Madame Sand can with difficulty keep her *Consuelo* pure.[252] She is obliged to confess that youth, health, and opportunity, conspiring with the ardor of a lover, are enemies to virtue almost irresistible. This child, though blessed with the coldest temperament and a strong ideal tendency, conquers with difficulty, and after a doubtful struggle with the fire of temptation in her blood and in her thought.

It is well that every ulcer should be probed. But our interest in the operation shows how little we expect from life. The basest activity is more entertaining than our own enterprises. So we read Balzac and Eugène Sue, and are surprised to learn how much there is, after all, to admire and enjoy in a life of sentimental beastliness. French novels are like brandy and water and cigars. They reach and irritate a brain which is impervious to finer influences.

But George Sand, in *Consuelo*, has offered us a distinct ideal. The elevating, purifying influence of the art impulse she has felt. She knows that it is no mere self-indulgence, or seeking after beauty and pleasure, which makes the artistic temperament, but a sense of the Infinite—a haunting presence of perfection which, in proportion to its power, subordinates the senses and delivers man to a life that is not only beautiful, but good. Still her artist is alone in the world, thwarted, misunderstood, suspected, imprisoned, and hated; is taken for a lunatic or a fool. Neither Albert nor Consuelo have their natural influence. They do not control circumstances or reorganize the society around them, as every ideal element tends to do. Their art serves only to keep vital heat in themselves, to separate them from vice and folly. It should animate a circle of lovers, and quicken other ideal forces flowing out into new expression in sculpture, painting, poetry, and the conduct of life. We know very well how little art has done for Europe or the world, but Madame Sand recognizes the ascension and true power of music. Why has she never given us a picture of that power in exercise? Why are her artists thrown, one into the bottom of a dry well, which serves him for a lunatic asylum, the other into that court, which the egotism of Frederic converted into a prison, even for his sister.

We complain that in all our novels there is too much fate, too much accident and brute force, too much repression and too little power. The spiritual energy revealed in them is not strong enough to procure for itself success and acceptance. The aspiration of every hero is baffled. He is not able to organize a serene and helpful activity, but is beaten down by suspicion and conservatism, and is poorly consoled for the failure of his life by some sugar-plum, by a suitable marriage or a timely inheritance.

What does Jane Eyre propose to do with Mr. Rochester after she has married and adopted him?[253] He is a poor, broken, shipwrecked mariner, on the waters of passion and self-indulgence, whom she, with the strength and courage of an angel, has drawn to shore. This burnt-out bully, after worrying and insulting the dependent girl, whose love was no secret to him, is now thoroughly subdued by misfortunes. He begins life anew, a tiger deprived of teeth and claws, dependent for every pleasure on the heroic heart beside him—a heart always so much stronger, so much deeper than his own.

In *Jane Eyre*, as in Charlotte Brontë, the grandest natural endowment, the utmost heroism, is barely able to sustain itself and make life tolerable in the midst of crushing neglect and discouragement.

The book *Jane Eyre* is a cry of agony. It is a protest against shocking injustice and injury. In Christian England, three young girls, daughters of a clergyman, are starved at school, and left, lonely and unregarded, to eat out their young hearts in activity at home. These children cry out of cold and darkness. *Jane Eyre* is a passionate appeal to common humanity against the civilization of England, which commits the education of children to such machinery as the system of boarding-schools, and degrades all culture, in the person of the despised governess, "That dreadful dummy," as Curtis calls her, "in the English game of life."

There is, in the novels of Goethe himself, no woman able to accomplish what Jane Eyre has done. The tranquil, thoughtful, and tender Ottilie, whose nature is like the upper sky, filled only with sunbeams, which kindle the very clouds into forms and fountains of light, would have lacked that concentrated energy which commands the respect and admiration of Rochester.[254] Ottilie could not live and leave the object of a love forbidden by her moral sense. In *Jane Eyre*, we see the struggle, and predict the victory of a force, more mighty than any revealed in the world of the German master, yet the heroes and heroines of Goethe expand like flowers in sunshine, and, however crossed by circumstance, their natural tendencies are developed both by good and evil fortune. He shows the triumph of an ideal which is not the highest, and gives us so much more of hope and courage.

Mrs. Gaskell has written a novel which deserves to be read. In *North and South*, the attraction of incident is subordinated to that of character, and the principal figures are titanic in strength and simplicity.[255]

We are made acquainted with two large-natured lovers, but the book affords no outlook beyond their marriage. This happy event, which ought to be the beginning of a life worth studying and showing, is made a blank wall, and terminates our view. Children may be satisfied when Margaret is folded in the arms of Mr. Thornton; but men and women know that the power of love in these young hearts is yet to be tried. Will it lead to a gradual adjustment of moral forces, in two natures which have encountered happily at a single point? Formal marriage is common enough, and we all know that the road to it winds through Paradise, and passes the margin of the pit—but is true marriage possible? Can there be conjunction of thought and will without loss of personal independence—without destruction of the charm of remoteness and virginity of spirit? Can there be union yet freedom and spontaneity of impulse? Can blind tenderness become clear-sighted and not die? Can the energies of chosen companions be harmonized and directed together to the highest ends? To these questions our novelists and poets have given no answer.

In *John Halifax* we have a picture of married life.[256] No modern writer has painted more forcibly the dawn of love's morning—no one has more magnified the expectation with which a noble heart awaits and entertains its sacred ray.

Yet the marriage is here a point of departure, and introduces the career of one "gentleman." The idealism of this hook is intense but narrow. There is in it no society, no festival, no influence of art or literature. The life of the hero is strictly domestic and moral, full of the sternness of duty and the bitterness of a long struggle with misfortune and injustice. For this is another protest against the inequality of social conditions in England. It is a strong book, but affords no large view of life. In it only the moral element is developed—only devotion to duty is honored—not love of beauty or of truth. While reading, we are in church and not in nature. It is a world like the heaven of Swedenborg, wherein the secular sun is displaced by a moral luminary, whose ray is neither intelligence nor joy, but a sentiment of unmingled obligation.[257]

We have a single American novel, *Margaret*.[258] Its criticism is directed against the old dogmatic theology of New England. Its ideal element is the expansion of a young mind, so dear to nature that it will not be contained in such a system. Yet the heroine is only delivered from dogma to dogma, and in the end of the book we are outraged by the advent of a sentimental millennium. The author is a theologian, who has broken the shell of a narrow creed, but could not throw off the creed-making tendency and become a poet.

Miss Bremer's page is healthy though her circle is small. In her conception of home she is happy, and has made, perhaps, the best contribution toward a solution of the vexed question of woman's destiny. She has shown true poetic power, giving interest and significance to common events by disclosing their relation to life, and to the development of character. There is ideality in her young heroines. They have a vague consciousness of powers unexercised of rudimentary wings. In every house there is a plain sister, who solaces herself as no young woman ever twice attempted to do, by reading Plato in solitude.

In *Bertha*, however, we have the old complaint, the old despair. She is another lonely victim, only reaching to prophesy and prepare a better condition for her sex. The influence of woman is crushed in the house of her hard father. The early history of his children is dismal "skip." Tragedy, to be tolerable, must be grand and imposing. Great calamities may be endured in fiction or reality, but the death in life, which falls upon gentle natures subjected to the tyranny of dogmatism, selfishness, and conceit, is too dismal to contemplate. If the tragic element be employed in art, it should not largely enter in the shape of "moaning women, hard-eyed husbands, and deluges of Lethe." [259]

We will not accuse novelists, especially women, of aiming at a vulgar effect, and seeking to excite and agitate feeble minds. They plainly celebrate sorrows they have felt, injuries they have borne. We ask them only to consume in private their private griefs, and publicly to do some justice to the general joy.

From every partial report of the tendency of human nature toward perfection, we return with pleasure to the broad and sunny page of Goethe. He is open-eyed to the infinite variety of interests in life. His characters are not emphasized as saints, as heroes, as lovers, because they have a widely-diversified activity which prevents the morbid concentration of force upon a single point. Some example we have here of every kind of spiritual development. The interest of the tale is distributed among many actors; their peculiarities are marked and significant. In each is exhibited a moral activity, whose direction is carefully shown. When once the bias, impulse, and motive of character is distinctly indicated, the artist stops. He will not carry out any tendency to extreme results, but leave the mind of the render to complete that history. The curious, experimenting, impressible Wilhelm is assisted by older observers and actors.[260] We cannot afford to lose the company of one of these men— of one of these women. In each is revealed an element that must be cultivated in us— that must be limited and guarded. They have virtues, they have vices; but, at the worst, they live, and act, and grow. Here is reinforcement of character, which in nature is always amelioration; here is growth in wisdom and skill, for truly in every breast there is some measure of aspiration—some freedom and obedience to the attraction of beauty, truth, and excellence in one or other of their innumerable manifestations. We may demand of the novelist, since Goethe has furnished so high a standard, that the ideal tendency which he exhibits shall have fair play, and not be overwhelmed or exhausted in a struggle with conditions. We will be grateful to those who, like Charlotte Brontë, show us the central fire of the inextinguishable spirit expanding under the burden of mountains and continents, which it cannot yet upheave for its own deliverance; but we need to see the same element sustaining the happy world of organization and intelligence.

The power of heat is shown, not in volcanic convulsions, but in its vital relation to plants, and animals, and man. The strength of Jane Eyre, and Rochester, and Consuelo is condensed like that of pent-up lightning in a cloud. We need to see the same force diffused, like the electricity which stirs in the air and water, in the sap and in the blood. For the ideal should visit us not to make misery tolerable, but to render common life a cheerful satisfaction. We want imaginary companions who will draw near to us on the level of every-day experience—who will take up all that is best in culture and endeavor, and walk in advance of us, hearing our burdens. The wise have accepted such companions, instruments, and enterprises as they find in the world, and are striving and learning to use them. Upon many abuses, judgment is speedily passed. Our novels are hot arguments upon questions no longer open in any sane mind. We concede to the author of *Uncle Tom's Cabin*, that slavery, if not a bad, is at least an unfortunate relation. Then that book falls to the ground. We are all democrats in principle; we despise castes and classes in society; we agree with Thackeray and Dickens, that common honesty and common decency are necessities of life. We dispose of several tons of fiction by simply declaring that a self-respect superior to snobbery, and a social system which affords equal opportunity to all, are decidedly desirable, and very few people doubt it. But who will tell me what to do with my day? I am haunted by a suspicion that it is as good as any day; that it would be no better if it were filled with "moving accidents." They would only, as we say, "divert" me—that is, draw me off from the way of enduring happiness. I want a permanent and large activity, and there is surely work enough to be done in every village before society will be possible among men. I want sympathy and coöperation, and I see in the breasts of my neighbors a latent humanity whose extent is incalculable, and which points toward everything dear to me. If I could be taught to take hold on what is so near me, something great and beautiful might yet be done even here.

I have passed the period of romance. Only children wait for adventures. I do not look for sudden wealth or poverty. I do not expect to fall in love with a princess, a beggar, or an opera-dancer. I can earn my bread, and am not exposed to great misery in any turn of the wheel of fortune. Is life, then, for me no longer worth living?

After the dragons are all killed, what shall we do? The great poet, only, can answer this question. He can show power in his figures, without throwing them into convulsions—can exhibit in sunshine the energy which is capable of fronting every storm. It is surely better worth while to see men helpful, than to see them contending. Civility is fairer to behold than barbarism. What mind will outrun the confusion that roars around and fills the noisy century, to anticipate the next ages, and show to what good result our best mental and moral effort is conducting man? The right novel, the true poem, is a hand that points forward. It will show the manhood, not the childhood, of the race. It will not need to elaborate a black background of misfortune to serve as a foil for doubtful happiness, but will exhibit an activity so splendid that it must shine in relief upon the dingy gray of ordinary circumstances, duties, and relations.

18

SOUTHERN LITERATURE

Anonymous

Putnam's Monthly Magazine (1857).

Since the *Pickwick Papers*, there has been no such delightful reading as the *Journal* of the late Southern Convention at Savannah. The world is greatly indebted to the gentlemen who engaged with such alacrity in this seasonable *divertissement*,[261] and whose eloquent naïveté equalled that of Snodgrass, Tupman, and Winkle in their palmiest moments.[262] After the grave excitement of a presidential election,[263] the convention came in as naturally as a farce after a drama—*Raising the Wind*, for instance, after *Old Heads and Young Hearts*.[264] The whole affair sprang out of the charity of generous souls who wished to give the country a laugh, to treat us all to a good Christmas burlesque, and atone, by their impromptu performance, for the lamentable absence, in American amusements, of clown, harlequin, and pantaloon. A chivalric paper, with even more perception than the *Eatanswill Gazette*, entered fully into the sly humor of the performance, and announced that the convention passed resolutions which would be recorded and filed as the basis of future resolutions at future conventions.[265]

The success of the exhibition was signal. We congratulate all the performers upon having given the country a heartier laugh than it has enjoyed for many months. We are quite sure that the spectacle was more ludicrous than the actors themselves conceived, and the Pickwick Club might have learned many a valuable lesson from its Savannah rival. It was a matter of regret that a distinguished amateur clown from Virginia, whose ground and lofty tumblings, during the summer season, had won him such merited consideration, should have been unavoidably prevented from appearing, by a little job of cabinet-work which he had undertaken. But the country was reconciled to the absence of the South Carolina pet, knowing how exhausted he had been by his recent striking performance in that absurd old farce, *My Uncle*, in which he was so appropriately supported by a collection of sticks from his native state.[266] The Georgia bragger, although a good deal hackneyed in his part, came in, toward the end of the performance, with a tolerable joke, which served, at least, to show his capacity. But, in general, the whole spectacle was of the freshest character, scarcely any of the actors having ever before been heard of.

Of all the good jokes perpetrated by the Savannah Pickwickians, none seems to us more purely humorous than the debate upon a "southern literature." Resolved, say these lovely wags, that there is no southern literature. Resolved, that there ought to be a southern literature. Resolved, that there shall be a southern literature. Resolved—this time the delighted reader is sure they are going to authorize W. Gilmore Simms LL. D., to construct a southern literature. Not at all. The very best of the joke is, that his name is omitted altogether, and sundry other gentlemen are requested to take the matter in hand. Dr. Simms is destined, this year, to be a victim. He went away from New York some time since, and was announced as a martyr in some sympathetic newspaper. But here there was a grave question—whether the martyrdom on that occasion was in the pulpit or in the pews. At home, however, there can be no doubt that he was deliberately sacrificed. It is now many years since Dr. Simms and his writings have done duty—and well, too—as the southern author and a southern literature. If an unwary critic ever chanced to suggest that, haply, "the spirit of the free states seemed to be more conducive to literary affluence and excellence than that of the slave states," the outraged press of the latter scoffed at him bitterly, and soon silenced him with Simms. And yet, at the very moment when there is question of creating a southern literature upon the great scale, by a vote of the Savannah Pickwickians, the name of W. Gilmore Simms, LL. D., is ruthlessly omitted!

It appears, according to the Savannah club, that neither English nor American authors are capable of producing this "southern literature," and for once the gentlemen who want it must turn to and help themselves. One of the practical humorists of the club, a very Tracy Tupman, remarked plaintively—"They had at one time a literary publication in South Carolina, but where was it now?" and, having thus exposed the probable success of the effort to establish a "southern literature," the delightful Tupman proceeds with the most brilliant *non sequitur*[267] upon record:

> It was important that the South should have a literature of her own, to defend her principles and her rights. He thought they could get text-books at home, without going either to Old England or to New England for them. These resolutions would do no harm, but he thought that, instead of passing resolves, it would be better for each man to determine hereafter to encourage no northern books or papers. [Applause.] *Let the country understand, that the South had talent enough to do anything that needs to be done, and independence enough to do it.* Let southern children be kept from northern educational institutions, and northern instructors be excluded from the south. Let southern colleges and manufacturing establishments be built up. A thousand commercial conventions would not do as much towards making the south independent of New England as one good college or manufacturing establishment.

"Her principles and her rights," which the southern literature is to be established to illustrate and defend, are, the *principle* that a man is a thing, and the *right* of selling him and his children into perpetual slavery. And with an elaboration of humor which Grimaldi,[268] not to say Sam Weller, would have envied, this good Tupman continues—

> He did not know in what part of Europe they could expect to get text-books that would suit the southern country. Certainly not in England where their own language was spoken and written.

So far Tupman was certainly correct. But if he be determined to look abroad for the foundation of the "southern literature," notwithstanding that the country is to take notice that "the south has talent enough to do anything that needs to be done," why should he not look into Russian or Turkish letters? Certainly a judicious selection of works might be made from those literatures, which, under the careful supervision and excision of the American Tract Society, and protected by the laws of South Carolina, Louisiana, Virginia, Georgia, etc., against education, might be cautiously introduced as the nucleus of the enterprise.[269] We commend this suggestion to the attention of the numerous gentlemen, whom, as scholars and literary men, we congratulate upon their appointment, by men who find the literature of Shakespeare and Milton not fit for their purposes, to

> prepare such a series of books in every department of study, from the earliest primer to the highest grades of literature and science, as may seem to them best qualified to elevate and purify the education of the South.

These are the gentlemen—but why did not the facetious Tupman, who remembered that there "had been" a literary publication in South Carolina, recall that there is a literary man there, and do justice to the martyr Simms ?—

> Profs. Bledsoe, McGuffey, of Va.; President Smith, of Randolph and Weaver College, Va.; Hon. Geo. E. Badger, and D. L. Swain, of N. C.; Rt. Rev. Bishop Elliott, and J. Hamilton Cooper, of Ga.; Prof. John Lecompte, Rev. J. H. Thornwell, Rev. J. W. Miles, and Rev. Dr. Curtis, of S. C.; President Tallman, of Ga.; Dr. Lacey, of N. C.; Ashbel Smith, of Texas; President Longstreet, of Miss.; Dr. Garland, of Ala.; Charles Gayarre, of La.; Dr. Richard Fuller, of Ind.; and Dr. Alonzo Church, of Ga.[270]

There was no especial time mentioned in which the southern literature must be completed by these gentlemen; and that is a little defect in the humor of the joke. Why not have resolved, for instance, that the article must be delivered at the next meeting of the Pickwickians at Knoxville? But, meanwhile, Winkle, of Georgia, submitted the following additional resolution:

> *Resolved*, That it is recommended to the legislatures of the southern states to withhold, from all schools and academies that use northern textbooks or employ northern teachers, any portion of the school fund.
> This, he thought, would be striking at the root of the evil; but so long as they permitted northern "school-marms" and school-teachers to come here, they could, of course, select injurious books for their scholars. He was for excluding such people and their books altogether. [Applause.]

Winkle, of Georgia, is evidently stern but sagacious. Sagacious, because, while northern books and "school-marms" come in, the chances of the southern literature may languish; but stern, because his method would restrict the reading public of "the south" to that literature which, by the terms of the joke, does not yet exist. Does Winkle mockingly mean to recommend to southern readers the "literary publications" which "they had at one time" in South Carolina? He insisted that the state legislatures should exclude the "northern literary publications," which would consequently force into the field "the talent enough to do anything," to which Tupman gracefully alluded.

But Augustus Snodgrass, of South Carolina, took a bolder, sweep, and by implication called Winkle and Tupman spoons. Augustus Snodgrass said:

> He was opposed to this child's play—these resolves not to subscribe to northern periodicals, or buy northern goods. It was nothing but a miserable subterfuge, and would amount to nothing practical. Whatever resolves this convention might adopt, southern ladies would continue to read *Godey's Lady's Book* and *Arthur's Home Magazine*, no matter what sentiments they might advance; the ladies wanted the fashions and their hoops, and they would have them. [Laughter.] They could get these things at the north, but not at the south. Northern publishers employed the talent of the south and of the whole country to write for them, and poured out thousands annually for it; but southern men expected to get talent without paying for it. The *Southern Quarterly Review* and the *Literary Messenger* were literally struggling for existence, for want of material aid. But these journals were as well supported at the south as northern periodical were. It was not the south that built up northern literature; *they did it themselves*. There was talent, and mind, and poetic genius enough in the south to build up a literature of a high order; but southern publishers could not get money to assist them in their enterprises, and, therefore, the south had no literature. He regarded these resolutions as mere child's play.

Snodgrass agrees with Tupman's theory of "talent enough to do anything," by declaring that there "is talent, and mind, and poetic genius enough in the south to build up a literature of a high order," if it were only encouraged. The wag never asks why it is not encouraged. The droll Snodgrass never hints that there is a choice of mental as well as other food, and that a man or woman, even in "the south," will read what seems most interesting and able. The Pickwickian jokers at Savannah must, of course, have their little biennial joke, but the great laws of nature will perversely continue to operate. Calhoun's works, and Jefferson's works, and Benton's works are published in the free states.[271] The works of W.Gilmore Simms, LL. D., are also published there; and we invite Tupman's attention, and that of the whole club, to this curious fact, that Mr. De Bow,[272] who moved the names of the gentlemen who were to prepare a southern literature, is himself the editor of a review which is printed in New York* and that the first gentleman upon his list, Professor Bledsoe, is also the author of a work designed to show the great and glorious character of human slavery, and that this book is published in Philadelphia. The fact

---

* We wish to do no injustice. No names, either of the printer or publisher, appear upon the Magazine, but we have the statement upon good authority.

is—whatever the joke may be—that where there is a large reading public, there will be authors and publishers. The Pickwickians might as well have appointed a committee to secure summer in January, as to create a literature. They can, indeed, make police regulations. They can institute a vast censorship, as in Rome, and publicly condemn and burn books. And we recommend to the jokers, as a suitable candidate for grand inquisitor of this holy office for the condemnation of any book which tended to disseminate the heresy of human brotherhood, the superintendent of common schools of North Carolina, who, in his letter to school committees, dated April 14, 1856, remarking upon certain schoolbooks, says:

> The houses which publish these works have high national characters they are not connected with the sectional agitations that are now having such pernicious influence, and they have manifested the most enlightened and liberal kind of enterprise, by trying to promote their interests in a way to benefit us [....][273] I can, therefore, cheerfully recommend them to the patronage of our citizens, as well as to their confidence; and, as an instance of the importance of carrying out, in the selection of books, the suggestions of those who have given anxious attention to the whole subject, I may mention that I knew a merchant of our state recently to purchase readers which contain an article strongly reflecting on the south, and are published by bitter and bigoted abolitionists. I am not blaming the merchant; he only knew the books were used in his section, and, doubtless, had little acquaintance with their contents or with the character of publishers—matters to which I have given special attention.

What thoughtful tenderness is here! The Hon. C. H. Wiley does not blame the merchant![274] Amiable Hon. C. H. Wiley! He (the merchant) only knew the books were used in his section. They might have been bibles, not yet purgated and prepared by the Hon. C. H. Wileys. They might have been books which said God made man in his image; Love thy brother as thyself; Do as you would be done by—instead of, "God made every man in his image—except the black man; Love thy brother as thyself—unless he be a negro;[275] Do as you would be done by—and you know, little dears, if you were Africans, you would wish to be sold as slaves, to enjoy Christian privileges." Such "readers" would not be connected with sectional agitations, and might supply a broad foundation of the proper sentiment on which to rear a southern literature. But unless the Hon. C. H. Wileys are suffered to burn and banish books that are written out of "the south," they will pertinaciously come in. Among others, *Putnam's Monthly* will come in, because there are plenty of readers at "the south" who are interested in the country and its development, and plenty of writers at the south whose articles Maga is always glad to publish—if they are good—and liberally to pay for.[276]

The chances of a literature technically southern, that is, uninspired by any spirit of liberty, and directly advocating slavery, may be inferred from the fact, that the Hon. C. H. Wiley, whom we have just quoted, is the superintendent of schools in North Carolina—that Professor Hedrick was banished from a university in that state last summer, for saying what might be construed into a condemnation of the system of slavery; and that, in general, a man speaks and writes there in favor of the natural freedom of man at his peril;[277] and yet North Carolina is generally considered as milder in its feeling upon the great question, than any other of the slave states. Mr. Wiley says, that "of the growing *white* population, it will not be one in fifteen, perhaps, not one in twenty, who cannot read or write." He allows that in 1840, "one in every seven and a half of our adult population could not read and write, of whom every two-thirds were women, the mothers, guardians, and first teachers of the citizens of the state." If it is remembered that the white population is only two-thirds of the inhabitants of the state, the ratio of people who cannot read and write is proportionably changed.

In Massachusetts, in the year 1850, there was only one in every 446 of the whole population who could not read and write; and the same number of the School Journal, which contains Mr. Wiley's statement, also contains parts of a "Fourth of July" speech at Raleigh, in which the orator feelingly says: "We may deplore the overthrow of other systems; we may shed tears of sorrow and of patriotic anguish over the disastrous darkness which, even now, seems to be settling on the star of Massachusetts; yet, happen what may, let us be true to ourselves." And he alludes to the glorious "right of free-speech," enjoyed by the citizens of the state—Professor Hedrick, for example—forgetful of the Revised Statutes of North Carolina, which set forth, ch. 34, § 74, p. 209, that a white man may be fined or imprisoned for attempting to teach any slave to read or write.

Further than this, which is unpromising for the number of indigenous readers— at least, for the new southern literature—let the Savannah Tupmans and Snodgrasses look for a moment at the actual performance, in "the south," of the "talent enough to do anything" in the way of a literature. Here is our contemporary for December, 1856—the *Southern Literary Messenger*. Its editorial appeal, at the close of the year, says: "The magazine has never been worthier of the hearty support of the southern public than at present," and again: "The editor asks, with a reasonable confidence, that an augmented share of southern patronage may be granted to a work which has, for twenty-two years vindicated the intellectual reputation of the southern people, and upheld their social institutions under every species of assault."

Now, let us see in what manner this number vindicates the intellectual reputation of the southern people. It has six prose articles, one of which is merely an account of the circumstances attending the painting of a copy of "The School of Athens,"[278] for the Virginia University, three of the others are stories of the most ordinary lady-magazine character; and the two papers in the number which have any value at all, are both selected from English publications. There are seven poems, and, excepting one little song, with a French refrain, they are such verse as is easily written and read with difficulty. This is distinctively the southern magazine. Does the most credulous Pickwickian believe that, if northern books and periodicals and "school-marms" are banished, the delights of life in slave regions will become more patent?

We say such things in no possible spirit of unkindness to our contemporary, but that contemporary, in appealing so entirely to a "southern," rather than a national or American support, directly challenges scrutiny into its claims and character.

But we have still another specimen of the "talent enough to do whatever is wanted," in the way of "southern literature," and this is purely "southern," in the most technical sense. It is a signal example of that kind of literature for which Tupman need not "go to Old or New England." It is the sort which may be freely had when "northern books and papers" are definitively excluded, and is of the kind, in the words of the resolution, "best qualified to elevate and purify the education of the south."

This is the literature to cling to, while the weeping state of North Carolina, with the Hon. C. H. Wiley at its head, holding a cambric handkerchief to his eyes, "may deplore the overthrow of other systems, and may shed tears of sorrow and patriotic anguish over the disastrous darkness which, even now, seems to settling upon the star of Massachusetts." This is the literature which that eminent superintendent will not "blame" merchants for vending and reading. This effort of the "southern" genius, to which we invite the attention of the reader, is entitled, *The Hireling and the Slave: Chicora, and Other Poems.* By William J. Grayson, Charleston, 1856."[279] The argument of the poem is thus stated. The human mind attends with delight:

> Slavery is that system of labor which exchanges subsistence for work, which secures a life-maintenance from the master to the slave, and gives a life-labor from the slave to the master. The slave is an apprentice for life, and owes his labor to his master; the master owes support, during life, to the slave. Slavery is the negro system of labor. He is lazy and improvident. Slavery makes all work, and it insures homes, food, and clothing for all. It permits no idleness, and it provides for sickness, infancy, and old age. It allows no tramping or skulking, and it knows no pauperism.

Who makes the slave "an apprentice for life," and by what claim, and in what manner, "he owes his labor," the gentle Grayson does not say or sing. But he continues:

> All Christians believe that the affairs of the world are directed by Providence for wise and good purposes. The coming of the negro to North America makes no exception to the rule. His transportation was a rude mode of emigration—the only practicable one in his case—not attended with more wretchedness than the emigrant ship often exhibits even now, notwithstanding the passenger law. What the purpose of his coming is we may not presume to judge. But we can see much good already resulting from it—good to the negro in his improved condition; to the country whose rich fields he has cleared of the forest, and made productive in climates unfit for the labor of the white man; to the continent of Africa in furnishing, as it may ultimately, the only means for civilizing its people.

Very "ultimately," we would say.

The implication of this statement is, that slavery is good for the soul of the African, by opening to it a chance for the glorious liberty wherewith Christ hath made us free. It is a great Christian scheme. Every native African, who absents himself from the slave barracoon, and refuses to undergo the "rude mode of emigration" to America and heaven, deliberately declines salvation, and must, therefore, be saved against his wicked will. If it is true of one African, it is true of all. The slave-trade is a great missionary institution; and the genius of Christianity, having saved the rest of the world, finally invited Africa to sit down with the redeemed. Now we wish to call Tupman's attention, and that of the gentle Grayson, to the fact, that there is a most reprehensible partiality in this selection of candidates for salvation.

The present writer, "a northern school-marm" of an uncertain age, and the gentle Grayson, the bard of slavery and salvation, have an equal right to Christian privileges—although the school-marm may be deeply dun in her color, and the son of song of that lovely pallor peculiar to the unmixed races. In the same way ought not the African, whether young or old, sick or well, to be admitted to the chances of Christianization? Now, we protest it is not so. That eminent missionary, Captain Canot, originally sent out by some West Indian saints to catch bodies and save souls in Africa, in his work, describing his experience in furthering the designs of Providence upon the slave-coast, remarks:

> Upon one occasion, to my great astonishment, I saw a stout and apparently powerful man, discarded by Ormond as utterly worthless. His full muscles and sleek skin, to my unpracticed eye, denoted the height of robust health. Still, I was told that he had been medicated for the market with bleating drugs, and sweated with powder and lemon-juice to impart a gloss to his skin. Ormond remarked that these jockey-tricks are as common in Africa as among horse-dealers in Christian lands; and, desiring me to feel the negro's pulse, I immediately detected disease, or excessive excitement. In a few days I found the poor wretch, abandoned by his owner, a paralyzed wreck in the hut of a villager at Bangalang. When a slave becomes useless to his master in the interior, or exhibits signs of failing constitution, he is soon disposed of to a peddler or broker. These men call to their aid a quack, familiar with drugs, who, for a small compensation, undertakes to refit an impaired body for the temptation of greenhorns. Sometimes the cheat is successfully effected; but experienced slavers detect it readily by the yellow eye, swollen tongue, and feverish skin.[280]

We put it to all Christians, including the gentle Grayson, whether a man should lose his candidacy for Christian salvation merely because of bleating drugs and sweating unto sleekness with lemon-juice and gunpowder, which can but affect the perishable body?

We can merely give an idea of the rare beauty and character of this work, which is entirely worthy of its inspiration. Consider the truthfulness of this picture of African candidates who have survived "the rude mode of emigration."

> And yet the life, so unassailed by care,
> So blessed with moderate work, with ample fare,
> With all the good the starving pauper needs,
> The happier slave on each plantation leads;
> Safe from harassing doubts and annual fears,
> He dreads no famine in unfruitful years;
> If harvests fail, from inauspicious skies,
> The master's providence his food supplies;
> No paupers perish here for want of bread,
> Or lingering live, by foreign bounty fed;
> No exiled trains of homeless peasants go,
> In distant climes to tell their tales of woe:
> Far other fortune, free from care and strife,

For work, or bread, attends the negro's life,
And Christian slaves may challenge as their own,
The blessings claimed in fabled states alone—
The cabin home, not comfortless though rude,
Light daily labor, and abundant food,
The sturdy health that temperate habits yield,
The cheerful song that rings in every field,
The long, loud laugh, that freemen seldom share,
Heavens boon to bosoms unapproached by care,
And boisterous jest and humor unrefined,
That leave, though rough, no painful sting behind;
While, nestling near, to bless their humble lot,
Warm social joys surround the negro's cot,
The evening dance its merriment imparts,
Love, with its rapture, fills their youthful hearts,
And placid age, the task of labor done,
Enjoys the summer shade, the winter sun,
And, as through life no pauper want he knows,
Laments no poor-house penance at its close.

We invite the attention of robust carpenters, and masons, and farmers, and laborers of every kind, whose market-value cannot be less than $1,500, if they are only black enough (the state of Virginia, we believe, allows a sixteenth part black blood to qualify for slavery), to the superior advantages of this aspect of the Christian scheme.

We cite, now, some toothsome bits of the gentle Grayson's milder and even more Christian strain. He is speaking of the wicked revilers of slavery—but mark how tenderly he entreats them:

There, chief and teacher, Gerrit Smith appears,
here Tappan mourns, like Niobe, all tears,
Carnage and fire mad Garrison invokes,
And Hale, with better temper, smirks and jokes;
There Giddings, with the negro mania bit,[281]
Mouths and mistakes his ribaldry for wit,
His fustian speeches into market brings,
And prints and peddles all the paltry things;
The pest and scorn of legislative halls,
No rule restrains him, no disgrace appalls;
Kicked from the House, the creature knows no pain,
But crawls, contented, to his seat again,
Wallows with joy in slander's slough once more,
And plays Thersites[282] happier than before;
Prompt from his seat—when distant riots need
The Senate's aid—he flies with railway speed,
Harangues, brags, bullies, then resumes his chair,
And wears his trophies with a hero's air;
His colleagues scourge him; but he shrewdly shows
A profitable use for whips and blows—
His friends and voters mark the increasing score,
Count every lash, and honor him the more.

There supple Sumner, with the negro cause,
Plays the sly game for office and applause;
What boots it if the negro sink or swim?
He wins the Senate—tis enough for him.
What though he blast the fortunes of the state
With fierce dissension and enduring hate?
He makes his speech, his rhetoric displays,
Trims the neat trope, and points the sparkling phrase
With well-turned period, fosters civil strife,
And barters for a phrase a nation's life;
Sworn into office, his nice feelings loathe.
The dog-like faithfulness that keeps an oath;*
For rules of right the silly crowd may bawl,
His loftier spirit scorns and spurns them all;
He heeds nor court's decree nor Gospel light,
What Sumner thinks is right alone is right.
On this sound maxim sires and sons proceed,
Changed in all else, but still in this agreed:
The sires all slavers, the humaner son
Curses the trade, and mourns the mischief done.
For gold they made the negroes slaves, and he,
For fame and office, seeks to set them free;
Self still the end in which their creeds unite,
And that which serves the end is always right.

There Greeley,[283] grieving at a brother's woe,
Spits with impartial spite on friend and foe;
His negro griefs and sympathies produce
No nobler fruits than malice and abuse;
To each fanatical delusion prone,
He damns all creeds and parties but his own,
Brawls, with hot zeal, for every fool and knave,
The foreign felon and the skulking slave;
Even Chaplin,[284] sneaking from his jail, receives
The Tribune's sympathy for punished thieves,
And faction's fiercest rabble always find
A kindred nature in the Tribune's mind;
Ready each furious impulse to obey,
He raves and ravens like a beast of prey,
To bloody outrage stimulates his friends,
And fires the Capitol for party ends.

There, Seward[285] smiles the sweet perennial smile,
Skilled in the tricks of subtlety and guile;
The slyest schemer that the world e'er saw;
Peddler of sentiment and patent law;

---

* "Is thy servant a dog that he should do this thing ?"—Mr. Sumner's answer, when asked whether he would obey the Constitution as interpreted by the authorities of the country.—Grayson. [Charles Sumner (1811-1874), lawyer, senator, and vehement opponent of the "Fugitive Slave Law" and the "Kansas-Nebraska Bill." Two days after delivering his "The Crime Against Kansas" speech (May 1856) in the Senate, he was physically assaulted there.]

Ready for fee or faction to display
His skill in either, if the practice pay,
But void of all that makes the frank and brave,
And smooth, and soft, and crafty like the slave;
Soft as Couthon[286] when, versed in civil strife,
He sent his daily victims to the knife,
Women proscribed with calm and gentle grace,
And murdered mildly, with a smiling face
Parental rule in youth he bravely spurned,
And higher law with boyish wit discerned
A village teacher then, his style betrays
The pedant practice of those learned days,
When boys, not demagogues, obeyed his nod,
His higher law the tear-compelling rod;
While Georgia's guest, a pleasant life he led,
And slavery fed him with her savory bread,
As now it helps him, in an ampler way,
With spells and charms that factious hordes obey.

There Stowe, with prostituted pen, assails
One half her country in malignant tales;
Careless, like Trollope,[287] whether truth she tells,
And anxious only how the libel sells,
To slander's mart she furnishes supplies,
And feeds its morbid appetite for lies
On fictions fashioned with malicious art,
The venal pencil, and malignant heart,
With fact distorted, inference unsound,
Creatures in fancy, not in nature found—
Chaste quadroon virgins, saints of sable hue,
Martyrs, than zealous Paul more tried and true,
Demoniac masters, sentimental slaves,
Mulatto cavaliers, and Creole knaves—
Monsters each portrait drawn, each story told!
What then? The book may bring its weight in gold;
Enough! upon the crafty rule she leans,
That makes the purpose justify the means,
Concocts the venom, and, with eager gaze,
To Glasgow flies for patron, pence, and praise,
And for a slandered county finds rewards
In smiles or sneers of duchesses and lords.

For profits and applauses poor as these,
To the false tale she adds its falser Keys[288]
Of gathered slanders—her ignoble aim,
With foes to traffic in her country's shame. [....][289]

A moral scavenger, with greedy eye,
In social ills her coarser labors lie;
On fields where vice eludes the light of day,
She hunts up crimes as beagles hunt their prey;
Gleans every dirty nook—the felon's jail,
And hangman's mem'ry, for detraction's tale,
Snuffs up pollution with a pious air,

Collects a rumor here, a slander there;
With hatred's ardor gathers Newgate's spoils,
And trades for gold the garbage of her toils.

In sink and sewer thus, with searching eye,
Through mud and slime unhappy wretches pry;
In fetid puddles dabble with delight,
Search every filthy gathering of the night;
Fish from its depths, and to the spacious bag
Convey with care the black, polluted rag;
With reeking waifs secure the nightly bed,
And turn their noisome stores to daily bread.

With this chivalric burst of the gentle Grayson, we leave that pleasing bard.

This is a fair specimen of the "southern literature" that is intended in the elaborate joke of the Pickwickians at Savannah. The simple truth was stated by Snodgrass. Publishers at the north pay liberally, and therefore, the books that are written at "the south" are not published there. The reason is, that the free spirit of the north encourages and fosters every kind of mental development; and, as one of the instinctive convictions of the human mind is, that men are born free, wherever it is a crime to say so there will never be any literature, and publishers and authors will be few, poor, and unknown. Those Savannah wags knew it as well as anybody. It is literature itself they oppose. The poor dear "south," of which the club take such care, is full of readers. Those readers may deplore what they call the eternal agitation of the great question; but they must also see that, as it will be agitated until it is settled, they must make up their minds to it, and, in their magazine reading, omit such articles as this, and enjoy such as precede and follow it. They must dine, although there be a skull on the table. They must read what the authors of our time and of all time write, and they know very well that all the greatest men have been lovers and laureates of liberty. If the condition of the perpetuity of slavery were that "the south" should feed upon such literature as may be called, in Tupman's sense, "southern"—the harpings of the gentle Grayson, for example—slavery would be abolished to-morrow. We observe that some southern newspaper shakes the whip over the head of Willis, because that gentleman said he should vote for Frémont, and announces that his pen has lost its charm for southern minds.[290] But, if that were so, it is high time for Professor Bledsoe & Co. to go to work; for there can be no doubt in the mind of every intelligent southern reader that the literature of this country cares no longer to duck, and compliment, and omit, but will speak louder and louder every day, directly and indirectly, against human slavery. The first proper novel in American literature, *Uncle Tom's Cabin*, is the greatest literary protest against it. That novel is scarcely six years old, and it strikes the key-note of a strain that will not cease. The whole spirit of modern literature is directly humane. There are, therefore, but three ways open to Tupman & Co.—first, to give up reading altogether; second, to read a humane literature, which is, in its very essence, anti-slavery; or, third, to insist that the "talent enough to do what is wanted" shall begin to do it.

We speak for the literature of the country when we say it no longer intends to shiver and turn pale when it speaks of "the south" or southern institutions. It will treat them as it treats "the north" and northern institutions. That is to say, it will honor the honorable, and scorn and satirize what is mean. It will treat slavery as a great moral, social, and political blight. It will point to "southern literature," and laws, and education, as illustrations of the truth of what it says. Tupman says, "Southern men ought to stop their subscriptions" to our pea-green Maga. Tupman is a droll Pickwickian. Does he suppose that our readers, who live in slave states, necessarily consider slavery sacred, and will content themselves with reading the gentle Grayson? They must have the best in the market for their money. Men in slave states send us valuable articles. They write well, and like to read what is well written. Go to, Tupman! you are speaking in a purely Pickwickian sense when you say we traduce "the south." Is "the south," slavery? We do speak ill of slavery, and we shall often do so. We shoot folly as it flies, and wherever it flies, and wherever it perches. And if folly bloats into crime or fuddles into fury, we shall still shoot away.

19

CAROLINE M. KIRKLAND

John S. Hart

From *The Female Prose Writers of America.* 3rd ed. 1857

John Seely Hart (1810-1877), a professor at Princeton who wrote on grammar, the classics, and poetry, among other subjects, is credited with having taught the first course on American literature. *A Manual of American Literature for Schools and Colleges* was published in 1872.

Mrs. Kirkland, formerly Miss Caroline M. Stansbury, was born and bred in the city of New York. After the death of her father, Mr. Samuel Stansbury, the family removed to the western part of the State, where she was married to Mr. William Kirkland, an accomplished scholar, and at one time professor in Hamilton College. After her marriage she resided several years in Geneva, and in 1835 removed to Michigan; lived two years in Detroit, and six months in the woods—sixty miles west of Detroit. In 1843 she returned to New York, where she has lived ever since, with the exception of a visit abroad in 1849, and another in 1850. Mr. Kirkland died in 1846.

She was first prompted to authorship by the strange things which she saw and heard while living in the backwoods. These things always presented themselves to her under a humorous aspect, and suggested an attempt at description. The descriptions, given at first in private letters to her friends, proved to be so very amusing that she was tempted to enlarge the circle of her readers by publication. *A New Home—Who'll Follow?* appeared in 1839; *Forest Life,* in 1842; and *Western Clearings* in 1846. These all appeared under the assumed name of "Mrs. Mary Clavers," and attracted very general attention. For racy wit, keen observation of life and manners, and a certain air of refinement which never forsakes her, even in the roughest scenes, these sketches of western life were entirely without parallel in American literature. Their success determined in great measure Mrs. Kirkland's course of life, and she has become an author by profession.

An "Essay on the Life and Writings of Spenser," prefixed to an edition of the first book of the *Fairy Queen,* in 1846, formed her next contribution to the world of letters. The accomplished author appears in this volume quite as shrewd in her observations, and as much at home, among the dreamy fantasies of the great idealist, as she had been among the log cabins of the far west.

In July, 1847, the *Union Magazine* was commenced in New York under her auspices as sole editor. After a period of eighteen months, the proprietorship of the Magazine changed hands, its place of publication was transferred to Philadelphia, and its name changed to *Sartrain's Union Magazine.* Under the new arrangement, Mrs. Kirkland remained associate editor, her duties being limited, however, almost entirely to a monthly contribution. This arrangement continued until July, 1851. Her whole connexion with the Magazine runs through a course of four years, and much of the marked success of that periodical is due to the character of her articles. Having been myself resident editor of the Magazine during the last two years of that time, and conducted its entire literary correspondence, I suppose I have the means of speaking with some confidence on this point, and I have no hesitation in saying, that of all its brilliant array of contributors, there was not one whose articles gave such entire and uniform satisfaction as those of Mrs. Kirkland. During her first visit to Europe, she wrote incidents and observations of travel, which were published, first in the Magazine, and afterwards in book form, under the title of *Holidays Abroad; or, Europe from the West,* in two volumes, 1849. Excepting these, and one or two stories, her contributions have been in the shape of essays, and they form, in my opinion, her strongest claims to distinction as a writer.

20

CATHARINE M. SEDGWICK

John S. Hart

From *The Female Prose Writers of America.* 3rd ed. 1857

Miss Sedgwick holds about the same position among our female prose writers that Cooper holds among American novelists. She was the first of her class whose writings became generally known, and the eminence universally conceded to her on account of her priority, has been almost as generally granted on other grounds. Amid the throng of new competitors for public favour, who have entered the arena within the last few years, there is not one, probably, whose admirers would care to disturb the well-earned laurels of the author of *Redwood* and *Hope Leslie.*

Miss Sedgwick is a native, and has been much of her life, a resident of Stockbridge, Massachusetts. Her father was the Hon. Theodore Sedgwick, of Stockbridge, who served his country with distinguished reputation in various stations, and particularly in the Congress of the United States, as Speaker of the House of Representatives, and afterwards as Senator, and who, at the time of his death, was one of the Judges of the Supreme Court of his own State.[291] Her brothers, Henry and Theodore, have both been distinguished as lawyers and as political writers.[292] On the mother's side, she is connected with the Dwight family, of whom her grandfather, Joseph Dwight, was a Brigadier-General in the Massachusetts Provincial forces, and actively engaged in the old French war of 1756.[293]

Judge Sedgwick died in 1813, before his daughter had given any public demonstration of her abilities as a writer. Her talents seem to have been from the first justly appreciated by her brothers, whose judicious encouragement is very gracefully acknowledged in the preface to the new edition of her works, commenced by Mr. Putnam, in 1849.

Miss Sedgwick's first publication was *The New England Tale.* The author informs us in the preface, that the story was commenced as a religious tract, and that it gradually grew in her hands, beyond the proper limits of such a work. Finding this to be the case, she abandoned all design of publication, but finished the tale for her own amusement. Once finished, however, the opinions and solicitations of her friends prevailed over her own earnest wishes, and the volumes were given to the world, in 1822. The original intention of this book led the author to give special prominence to topics of a questionable character for a professed novel, and the unfavourable portraiture which she gives, both here and elsewhere, of New England Puritanism, has naturally brought upon her some censure. The limited plan of the story did not give opportunity for the display of that extent and variety of power which appear in some of her later productions. Still it contains passages of stirring eloquence, as well as of deep tenderness, that will compare favourably with anything she has written. Perhaps the chief value of *The New England Tale* was its effect upon the author herself. Its publication broke the ice of diffidence and indifference, and launched her, under a strong wind, upon the broad sea of letters.

Redwood accordingly followed in 1824. It was received at once with a degree of favour that caused the author's name to be associated, and on equal terms, with that of Cooper, who was then at the height of his popularity; and, indeed, in a French translation of the book, which then appeared, Cooper is given on the title-page as the author. *Redwood* was also translated into Italian, besides being reprinted in England.

The reputation of the author was confirmed and extended by the appearance, in 1827, of *Hope Leslie*, the most decided favourite of all her novels. She has written other things since, that in the opinion of some of the critics are superior to either *Redwood* or *Hope Leslie*. But, these later writings have had to jostle their way among a crowd of competitors, both domestic and foreign. Her earlier works stood alone, and *Hope Leslie,* especially, became firmly associated in the public mind with the rising glories of a native literature. It was not only read with lively satisfaction, but familiarly quoted and applauded as a source of national pride.

The subsequent novels followed at about uniform intervals; *Clarence, a Tale of our Own Times,* in 1830; "Le Bossu," one of the *Tales of the Glauber Spa,* in 1832; and *The Linwoods, or Sixty Years Since in America,* in 1835.[294]

In 1836, she commenced writing in quite a new vein, giving a series of illustrations of common life, called *The Poor Rich Man, and the Rich Poor Man.* These were followed, in 1837, by *Live and Let Live,* and afterwards by *Means and Ends,* a *Love Token for Children,* and *Stories for Young Persons.*[295]

In 1838, Miss Sedgwick went to Europe, and while there, wrote *Letters from Abroad to Kindred at Home.* These were collected after her return, and published in two volumes.

She has written also a *Life of Lucretia M. Davidson,* and has contributed numerous articles to the Annuals and the Magazines. Some of her recent publications have been prepared expressly for children and young persons. *The Boy of Mount Rhigi,* published in 1848, is one of a series of tales projected for the purpose of diffusing sentiments of goodness among the young.[296] The titles of some of her other small volumes are *Facts and Fancies, Beatitudes and Pleasant Sundays, Morals of Manners, Wilton Harvey, Home, Louisan and her Cousins, Lessons Without Books,* &c.[297]

The quality of mind that is most apparent in Miss Sedgwick's writings is that of strength. The reader feels at every step that he has to do with a vigorous and active intellect. Another quality, resulting from this possession of power, is the entire absence of affectation of every kind. There is no straining for effect, no mere verbal prettiness. The discourse proceeds with the utmost simplicity and directness, as though the author were more intent upon what she is saying than how she says it. And yet, the mountain springs of her own Housatonic do not send up a more limpid stream, than the apparently spontaneous flow of her pure English. As a novelist, Miss Sedgwick has for the most part wisely chosen American subjects. The local traditions, scenery, manners, and costume, being thus entirely familiar, she has had greater freedom in the exercise of the creative faculty, on which, after all, real eminence in the art mainly depends. Her characters are conceived with distinctness, and are minutely individual and consistent, while her plot always shows a mind fertile in resources and a happy adaptation of means to ends.

21

HARRIET BEECHER STOWE

John S. Hart

From *The Female Prose Writers of America.* 3rd ed. 1857

Harriet Elizabeth Beecher is the daughter of the Rev. Lyman Beecher D. D., and seems to have inherited much of the splendid talents of her father. She was born at Litchfield, Connecticut, June 15, 1812. She went to Cincinnati with her father's family in the autumn of 1832. In the winter of 1836 she was married to Professor Calvin E. Stowe, of the Theological Seminary of that place.[298] In 1850 Professor Stowe accepted a professorship in Bowdoin College, Brunswick, Maine, where the family resided for one or two years, when he transferred to a chair in the Theological Seminary, at Andover, Massachusetts.

Mrs. Stowe's writings are found principally in the various literary and religious periodicals of the country, and in a volume of tales, called *The Mayflower,* published in 1843. She has not written so much as some of our female authors, but what she has written has left a profound impression. She is remarkable for the qualities of force and clearness. Few readers can resist the current of her argument, and none can mistake her meaning. She possesses also a great fund of wit, and a delicate play of fancy not inferior to our most imaginative writers.

The foregoing paragraphs were published in 1851, the year before the appearance of Mrs. Stowe's great work. In revising our article for the present edition (1854), we have concluded to let the verdict stand unaltered, merely adding, in the briefest possible manner, such remarks as subsequent events seem to call for.

Uncle Tom's Cabin was published in March, 1852, Its success was unprecedented in the annals of literature. In less than nine months, the sale had exceeded a million copies; the author and her publishers had made fortunes out of it; more than thirty rival editions of it had been published in London alone, besides numerous other editions in different parts of Scotland and Ireland; it was translated into every living language that possessed a popular literature; and Harriet Beecher Stowe, before comparatively unknown even in her own country, became as familiar a name in every part of the civilized world, as Homer or Shakespeare.

It is absurd to attribute such extraordinary success to the abolition character of the book. This feature of the work has probably repelled quite as many readers as it has attracted. The anti-slavery sentiment, obtruded by the author in her own person, is the greatest blemish of the book as a work of art. It is an undoubted proof of the extraordinary skill of the author in other respects, that she has been able so completely to fascinate millions of readers, to whom her anti-slavery opinions have been utterly offensive. The whole secret of the matter simply is, Mrs. Stowe is a woman of genius, and her book is one of consummate skill. No living writer equals her in abilities as a mere story-teller, seizing the reader's attention, as she does, on the very first page, and holding it captive, without any let-up to the very last. Her delineations of character are perfectly life-like. Even those personages that are introduced incidentally in a single scene, stand out clear and distinct upon the canvas, like the charcoal sketches in the contours of a great master. Of her dramatic power—generally considered the highest walk of genius—it is superfluous to speak, when hundreds of theatres have been kept thronged for months in succession, by the exhibition of her story even in the crude form given to it by some bungling playwright. Her mastery of pathos is apparently unbounded. The springs of emotion are touched at will; the heart throbs, the eyes swim, without a moment's notice, and without any apparent effort or preparation on the part of the writer.

Blackwood, in an article of more than thirty pages, devoted to the examination of the literary merits of *Uncle Tom's Cabin,* viewing it solely as a work of art, and apart entirely from the social and political questions which it suggests, thus sums up its opinion of the author.

"Mrs. Stowe is unquestionably a woman of genius; and that is a word which we always use charily: regarding genius as a thing *per se*—different from talent, in its highest development, altogether, and in kind. Quickness, shrewdness, energy, intensity, may, and frequently do accompany, but do not constitute genius. Its divine spark is the direct and special gift of God: we cannot completely analyze it, though we may detect its presence, and the nature of many of its attributes, by its actions; and the skill of high criticism is requisite, in order to distinguish between the feats of genius and the operation of talent. Now, we imagine that no person can read *Uncle Tom's Cabin,* and not feel in glowing contact with genius—generally gentle and tender, but capable of rising, with its theme, into very high regions of dramatic power. This Mrs. Stowe has done several times in the work before us—exhibiting a passion, an intensity, a subtle delicacy of perception, a melting tenderness, which are as far out of the reach of mere talent, however well trained and experienced, as the prismatic colours are out of the reach of the born blind. But the genius of Mrs. Stowe is of that kind which instinctively addresses itself to the affections; and though most at home with the gentler, it can be yet fearlessly familiar with the fiercest passions which can agitate and rend the human breast.

With the one she can exhibit an exquisite, tenderness and sympathy; watching the other, however, with stern but calm scrutiny, and delineating both with a truth and simplicity, in the one case touching, in the other really *terrible*.

In 1853, *Uncle Tom* being then in the very acme of his renown, the author visited England, and several countries of Europe. The enthusiasm of her reception abroad is still too fresh upon the minds of all to need repetition. In the British Isles, particularly, it was a regular ovation. Since her return, she has prepared and published a book of travels, called *Sunny Memories of Foreign Lands,* now just from the press.[299] It is in two volumes, 12mo., and is having a rapid sale. These volumes are very unequal in style and execution. Parts of them are devoted to the exposition of the various religious and philanthropic institutions of Great Britain. These are of course plain and practical, as they should be. But in those parts, as in the visits to Melrose Abbey, to Abbortsford, to Stratford-upon-Avon, to Warwick Castle, and to various other places and persons of historical renown, the imaginative temperament of the author has had free play, and she has written in a manner not surpassed by anything in *Uncle Tom*. One would have supposed it impossible to write with such freeness on such hackneyed topics. The incidental remarks, interspersed here and there in the midst of her narrative, contain some of the finest specimens of aesthetic criticism to be found anywhere. What she says, for instance of Shakespeare, and of Gothic architecture, as exhibited in the various cathedrals which she visited, is in the very highest style of criticism. These criticisms, oftentimes profound as they are brilliant, seem to gush forth in the simplest and most natural manner, as if from an over-flowing fountain, giving an indescribable charm to the parts of her book in which they occur.

22

LYDIA M. CHILD

John S. Hart

From *The Female Prose Writers of America.* 3rd ed. 1857

The maiden name of this accomplished writer was Lydia Maria Francis. She is native of Massachusetts, and a sister of the Rev. Convers Francis, D.D., of Harvard University.[300]

Mrs. Child commenced authorship as early as 1824. Her first production was *Hobomok.*[301] It was a novel based upon New England colonial traditions, and was suggested to her mind by an article in the *North American Review,* in which that class of subjects was urgently recommended as furnishing excellent materials for American works of fiction. Probably, the example of Cooper, who was then in the height of his popularity, and still more, that of Miss Sedgwick, whose *Redwood* was then fresh from the press, had also some influence upon the new author. Her work was well received, and was followed in 1825 by *The Rebels,* a tale of the Revolution, very similar in character to the former.[302] Both of these works are now out of print. A new edition of them would be very acceptable.

Her next publication, I believe, was *The Frugal Housewife,* containing directions for household economy, and numerous receipts.[303] For this she had some difficulty in finding a publisher, in consequence of the great variety of cookery books already in the market. But it proved a very profitable speculation, more than six thousand copies having been sold in a single year.

Mrs. Child's versatility of talent, and the entire success with which she could pass from the regions of fancy and sentiment to those of fact and duty, still further, appeared in her next work, which was on the subject of education. It was addressed to mothers, and was called *The Mother's Book*[304] It contains plain, practical directions for that most important part of education which falls more immediately under the mother's jurisdiction. It has gone through very numerous editions, both in this country and in England, and continues to hold its ground, notwithstanding the number of excellent books that have since appeared on the same subject. It was published in 1831.

The *Girl's Book*, in two volumes, followed in 1832, and met with a similar success.[305] Its object was not so much the amusement of children, as their instruction, setting forth the duties of parent and child, but in a manner to attract useful readers.

She wrote about the same time *Lives of Madame de Staël and Madame Roland*, in one volume; *Biographies of Good Wives*, in one volume; and the *History of the Condition of Women in all Ages*, in two volumes.[306] All these were prepared for the "Ladies' Family Library," of which she was the editor. They are of the nature of compilations, and therefore do not show much opportunity for the display of originality. But they do show, what is a remarkable trait in all of Mrs. Child's writings, an earnest love of truth. The most original work of the series us the *History of the Condition of Women*. They are very useful and valuable volumes.

In 1833, Mrs. Child published an *Appeal for that Class of Americans called Africans*. It is said to be the first work that appeared in this country in favour of immediate emancipation. It made a profound impression at the time.

In the same year, Mrs. Child published *The Coronal*.[307] It was collection of small pieces of prose and verse, most of which had appeared before in periodicals of various kinds.

One of the most finished and original of Mrs. Child's works, though it has not been the most popular, appeared in 1835. It was a romance of Greece in the days of Pericles, entitled *Philothea*.[308] Like the *Prophet of Ionia*, and some of her other classical tales, the *Philothea* shows a surprising familiarity with the manners, places, and ideas of the ancients. It seemed, indeed, more like a translation of a veritable Grecian legend, than an original work of the nineteenth century. While all the externals of scenery, manners, and so forth, are almost faultlessly perfect, perhaps not inferior in this respect to the *Travels of Anacharsis*, the story itself has all the freedom of the wildest romance.[309] It is, however, romance of a purely ideal or philosophical cast, such as one would suppose it hardly possible to have come from the same pen that had produced a marketable book on cookery, or that was yet to produce such heart-histories as "The Umbrella Girl," or "The Neighbour-in-law."[310] Indeed, the most remarkable thing in the mental constitution of Mrs. Child, is this harmonious combination of apparently opposite qualities—a rapt and lofty idealism, transcending equally the conventional and the real, united with a plain common sense that can tell in homely phrase the best way to make a soup or lay a cradle—an extremely sensitive organization, that is carried into the third heavens at the sound of Ole Bull's violin, and yet does not shrink from going down to Lispenard street to see old Charity Bowery.[311]

Mrs. Child conducted for several years a "Juvenile Miscellany," for which she composed many tales for the amusement and instruction of children. These have since been corrected and re-written, and others added to them, making three small volumes, called *Flowers for Children*. One of these volumes is for children from four to six years of age; one, for those from eight to nine; and one, for those from eleven to twelve.

In 1841, Mr. and Mrs. Child went to New York, where they conducted for some time the *Anti-Slavery Standard*. Mrs. Child wrote much for this paper, not only upon the topic suggested by the title, but on the miscellaneous subjects.

In the same year, 1841, she commenced a series of "Letters to the Boston Courier," which contain some of the finest things she has ever written. They were extensively copied, and were afterwards collected into a volume, under the title of *Letters from New York*. This was followed by a second series in 1845.[312]

These *Letters* are exceedingly various. They contain tales, speculations, descriptions of passing events, biographies, and essays, and bring alternately tears and laughter, according to the varying moods of the writer.

In 1846, she published a volume called *Fact and Fiction,* consisting of tales that had previously appeared in Magazines and Annuals. These are of a miscellaneous character, somewhat like the *Letters,* only longer.

23

MATTER OF FACT AND MATTER OF FICTION

Ignatius

Harper's New Monthly Magazine (1857).

If I announce myself as a matter-of-fact person, I by no means wish to imply that I am one of the dry, feelingless individuals that your practical people always are—in novels. No: I simply mean to say that I am a being of this real work-a-day world of facts, and not of fiction; and I wish humbly and seriously to inquire why it is that these worlds are so different and distinct each from each, that it is almost a matter of course that whoso belongs to the one cannot belong to the other. Why is it that in this year of grace, 1857, the large majority of our imaginative writers are in the habit of holding such a very cracked mirror, made of such very bad glass, up to poor Nature, that we can only get a distorted, or at best a partial view of her dear old face?

Why is it, I say again? Why is it that plays, poems, and especially novels, those final *bétes noirs* of careful mothers and sober governesses, for the most part, even when admirable in other respects, deal with people and events so confessedly alien from the ordinary course of things, that, "like a man in a play" is our instinctive epithet for a man who looks or behaves unnaturally, stiltedly, affectedly; and, "like an incident in a novel" is the phrase by which we distinguish something very unlike an incident of everyday life?

I am prepared to admit that we seem to be growing more sensible of these incongruities, and that the life of fiction is becoming more natural than it has been; but this is saying little. Human sense could not be supposed to stand out long against such fierce outrages as have been made upon it by diverse novelists now almost forgotten. The young lady, clad in a simple robe of white muslin, who thought nothing of leaving her home, so costumed, amidst the most terrific convulsions of the elements, and who, finding a haven in some remote cottage, or haply in the miserable garret of a London by-street, invariably found her harp transported thither before her, to the accompaniment of which instrument she immediately proceeded to pour forth her woes in song—this class of damsel has, we believe, entirely departed from three-volume life.

With her has disappeared the interesting young nobleman, tall, dark, and with a forehead of purest ivory, whose ordinary costume consisted of a large cloak, and a hat pulled over his brows, and whose conversation abounded in such colloquialisms as, "Hear me, Amanda!" "By yonder azure vault I swear." "Wouldst thou then, base traitor?" etc., etc.

The filial relations of novel-writers may also be supposed to have grown happier of late, if we are to believe that their former illustrations were drawn from personal experience. When was the first father introduced into a story who was not a harsh and inexorable tyrant, deaf to sighs and entreaties, blind to tears and the evidently failing health of his offspring (even when the blue veins streaked the lily skin, and the form was so fragile that a south breeze might be expected to waft it away), and only bent on uniting his daughter to the gentleman whose estate joined his own, or to the son of his friend to whom he had betrothed her while yet in her cradle; or to the man (the villain of the history, with black hair and mustache, deep-set eyes, a powerful frame, and a propensity for eaves-dropping and pocket pistols), to whom he has lost all his property, at *piquet* or *rouge et noir?*

And talking of villains, what has become of that personage who really had arrived at a sort of respectability from the mere fact of age and long use—the stage villain, the melodramatic ruffian, with a rolling voice and eyes to match, who was always flinging the end of his mantle over his shoulder, and who wore a large-brimmed, low-crowned hat, with a feather in it—who never took an evening walk without the accompanying attention of thunder and heavy rain from the orchestra—who would stamp away, with a lady hanging fainting on his arm, a pistol in each hand, and a dagger between his teeth; and who sometimes disappeared at the end of the piece, down a trap, with red fire issuing from beneath, in the most literal and orthodox manner?[313]

Well, these are of the past, and the credulity of readers and audiences is not taxed after this fashion nowadays. Still there remain plenty of incongruities to assimilate, many improbabilities to correct, before our fictitious literature (as a school, always allowing for one or two noble exceptions) can be held as really valuable, not only as an elevating moral influence, but as a picture of character and manners, proper to the time they profess to describe.

For instance, in novels the chief end and aim of existence is, of course, love. Nothing else is thought of, nothing else is lived for, by all men and women under thirty, in three-volume life. That respectable age, indeed, if we allow ourselves the latitude prescribed by a certain recent class of fiction, will not serve as the limit beyond which passionate and engrossing devotion—a life-long ardor, and so forth—may not be expected as a matter of course. In novels, your lovers of middle age, with slightly-grayed hair, and a spirit worn by encounter with the world, are the most desperate, unreasoning, and unreasonable of all. Experience, the cares of life, and the loss of youth, appear to have been unavailing to quench their fire, assuage their anguish, or teach them a soberer philosophy than the "Without *thee*" (meaning Amanda) "life is a blank"—that absolute creed of all noveldom, not to subscribe to which is to be put out of the pale of sentimental orthodoxy. And these lovers, both youthful and elderly, proceed to comport themselves after a most striking and peculiar fashion, in evidence of their fine feelings and unusual circumstances. Most of his time the three-volume lover, especially the middle-aged one, is under the influence of strong passion, suppressed emotion, stony calm, or resigned dejection. Does he put on his hat, he tightens his lip, bends his heavy brows, gives a flashing glance around him, and strides forth wearing a mocking mask of cheerfulness for the world, but with a heart full of anguish, doubt, anxiety, jealousy, as the case may be—all for and on account of the aforesaid Amanda. Alack! that Spartan boy of old time has much to answer for! He was the undoubted origin of what may be termed the compressed-lip style of hero—from which we have hardly known peace of late years. Why didn't he cry out and have done with it, and so permitted Messrs. Montgomery & Co., when suffering from headache or outraged confidence, to cry out too—instead of going wandering about with bent brows, galvanic smiles, and luridly-sparkling eyes—such being the sort of aspect which the world of fiction appears to consider most natural and unremarkable in its citizens?

Again, don't we all know the heroic lady of the same genus—distinguished for drawing herself up to her full height, throwing back her head with a haughty gesture, flashing an instantaneous glance of anger, tenderness, or astonishment, and then relapsing into her ordinary manner and bearing, which we should think must reflect credit on the professor of calisthenics who was privileged to train her deportment in early youth? Yes, we are familiar with that dignified maiden who rarely condescends to show any feeling except to the omniscient eye of the narrator, who constantly perceives beneath that quiet aspect, that marble calm, or majestic indifference (take your choice of phrase, ladies and gentlemen—they are all excellent, have seen service, and are warranted to wear well) the most turbulent emotion seething furiously, a frenzy of anguish, all the more poignant that it is voiceless, or the disturbance of a spirit well-nigh lashed to madness!

But to return to our heroes. We are aware how invariably and entirely love enters into all the details of these gentlemen's lives. They take it with them not only to such poetical localities as the study, the camp, the secluded home, but to the stock-exchange, the bank, and the various courts of law. Not only does it nerve the warrior's arm in the deadly fight, causing him to slay unheard-of numbers with that right hand which his Amanda's touch has rendered sacred; not only does it inspire the poet with sonnets, and the painter with wonderful artistic conceptions, which, when exhibited on the walls of the Royal Academy, cause professors and connoisseurs to go into raptures, and some eminent patron of art to purchase for vast sums; not only this, but the same absorbing sentiment makes the barrister's speech bristle with eloquence, and his arguments in the cause of Kiggins *versus* Kellogg (the great trespass case) to come home to the hearts of the jurymen, and crown his client with success; while the commercial man pursues his speculations, trudges away in the city, and is shrewd, prudent, and money-making—all for love.

Now, without wishing to depreciate that excellent article, Man, I humbly contend that this version of him and his characteristics is, in one sense, as much above his deserts as in every other it is below them. Ordinary man is neither so little nor so great as novelists would have us believe. Ordinary man is not in the habit of striding about the world, clenching his hands and grinding his teeth, with disheveled hair, and a soul torn by contending emotions, because Amanda has refused him or been cross to him, or kind to somebody else, or has a cold, or any other mischance has occurred that fictitious flesh is heir to. That microcosm, the masculine ego, holds too much for one idea, even the dearest, to be able to engross it so solely, and entirely, and continuously. Moreover, ordinary man is not so invariably apt at conceiving that unselfish devotion—earnest, persevering, and self-sacrificing, which is the usual style with which he loves—in Three Volumes.

Probably this misconception, and the undue elevation of the masculine ideal in this respect, arises from the predominance of female writers of fiction, who, in describing man under these circumstances, involuntarily delineate themselves. But it will not do—the substitution will be detected. The nature of the best man that ever lived would, I believe, be found inferior to that of woman in this one particular. Devotion, tenderness, so absorbing and self-forgetting, is not the breath of life to a man (though he may love truly and well, after his manner), as it is to a genuine woman. The sons of Adam may think best, work best, write best, and reason best; but the daughters of Eve will always be insomuch nearer the divine ideal as to love best.

Then most men at least have to do with the actual and tangible difficulties of life; their thoughts are busy about such mundane interests as their advancement in their several vocations, their success among their brethren and the like matters, which however unromantic and unworthy a hero of a novel, are neither unnecessary nor degrading, when not all-absorbing, to a flesh-and-blood man of this busy, working world. They have not even the *time* to be continually feeling desperately, deeply, and intensely those sentimental grievances that form the staple of manly trials in three-volume life. Their heads are too well filled and too well cultivated, for their hearts to endanger them so liberally. So much for ordinary man. But even when you take the exceptional man from this real life, and compare him with his prototype in three volumes, you find almost as marked a difference. The gentleman who sits beside you at dinner is probably one of this class, with more depth of feeling, more earnestness of soul, a more sensitive and impassioned nature, than falls to the lot of ninety-nine hundredths of his brethren. His circumstances may also be propitious to the manufacture of a hero; and he may have opportunities of showing himself a faithful lover, a self-sacrificing friend, a brave struggler with difficulties. But this man, of all others, is the very last to behave in the way that is appropriate to a novel and imposing on paper; and in the first place, his looks, be assured, will not answer to popular predilections. He will probably be an undersized man; or, if he be tall, is almost certain not to be possessed of that "graceful and dignified bearing" which it is only easy to bestow on a post-octavo wearer of broadcloth. Possibly his features will neither be noble and refined, nor massive and grim, but just ordinary intelligent features, lit up not by wonderful dark eyes, or soul-piercing gray ones, but by that light of frankness and kindliness which is reserved for subordinate characters in three-volume life. In fact, though I would by no means wish to insinuate that a handsome or athletic man can not be a heroical one, it is certain that nature, unlike novelists, has a loving yearning after the theory of compensations, and dearly likes to set a noble soul in a physical frame of little external significance. Apollo and Antinous (she doubtless concludes) are sufficiently well dowered by the mere casket, and there is no need of a superlatively shining jewel within.[314]

Howbeit—and whether beautiful or not, broad-chested or slender and straight, given your real-world hero, and see how he conducts himself. Watch him, and try to detect the occasions on which he strides forth into the night—bares his heated brows to the cool, caressing breeze—shakes in every limb as he makes some indifferent remark to Amanda—or bites his lip in suppressed anguish till the blood flows freely. See if he wastes his life by "immolating it upon the altar of one black and bitter memory"—or renders himself unfit for general society by his absorbing desire for the special companionship of the fair girl or majestic woman on whom he has set his affections. No—he has does none of these things. A true man, in love or out of it, is manly, straightforward, sincere. He is neither theatrical nor "effective" in his bearing—be has no idea of dramatic fitness, or picturesqueness, or well-sounding phrases. The romance and poetry in his nature lie deep down—far beyond the ken even of that "quick observer" who is able to detect so much in fiction. The throes and struggles of the passionate part of him are evidenced by no convulsions of the body or contortions of the features: no length of stride, no amount of maltreatment of the lips, is likely to help *him* better to endure a grief or overcome an emotion. He is altogether another order of being from your novel hero.

As different, we would hope, are the higher types of our real-world women from the portraits purporting to be of them that we find in the generality of novels. Defend us, kind fates, from actual contact with such startling ladies as it has been often our lot to read about. May we never know more intimately than through the three-volume medium that tall and haughty damsel with the flashing eye and curling lip, who moves majestically whenever she moves at all; who never leaves a room, but sweeps from it; who, with the proud reserve, the icy reticence, manifest in her manner and tone of voice, crushes into utter misery the hapless lover, or the meek sister, or adoring parent with whom she comes in contact. True, she is generous as the sunlight: true, she is ready to give up her fortune to the poor little sister: true, she will cheerfully die for the lover to whom she hasn't a kind word to say: true, she is the most devoted, energetic, and self-sacrificing of friends, daughters, or wives, when the dire occasion arises; but who would not rather have less of a heroine and more of a woman for his actual comfort and home-treasure? Who would not rather possess a household angel such as, thank Heaven, there are many in real life—who know nothing of those dramatic accomplishments in which the heroine of the haughty genus is so well versed; who do not suffer injuries, real or fancied, to rankle silently in their hearts; and who, when they are sorrowful, dare to look sad as nature bids them; and when they are joyful, suffer their joy to manifest itself simply, sweetly, and unconsciously, without any undercurrent of thought or suspicion to "arrest the smile ere it curled the red lip," or "cloud the transient brightness of the dark eyes," etc., etc., etc.? Let us have less of the great sacrifices these ladies are so apt at performing, if they can only be purchased by their failing in all the endearing *little* duties of daily life. Let us have less of those picturesque but uncomfortable qualities, both good and bad, if you please, excellent Company of Novelists—and a little more of homely, household sweetness, of simple, natural *womanhood* in short, the faults of which are patent, salient, and heartily repented—unlike those hypocritical sins which wrap themselves in the garments of grandeur, and strive to look fine and heroic, instead of showing themselves as they truly are—ignoble and paltry.

We protest against these self-conscious dames of fiction, who conduct themselves like so many Melpomenes in private life, whose phraseology is tragic, inflated, and involved, their manners impassible, and their aspect enigmatic.[315]

On the other hand, we have not much sympathy with a second and no less favorite ideal of novel-writers—the "girlish, laughing thing," who bounds into the room, tosses her golden hair back upon her shoulders, and claps her lily hands in childish glee at the smallest provocation. We are tired of being told how, when she is happy, the smiles dimple about her exquisite mouth, and living lustre arises from the depths of her blue eyes; and how, when she is grieved, the full red lip pouts like that of a chidden child, and the large tears slowly fall down the rounded cheeks. We are tired also of the details of her utter unconsciousness when somebody comes and falls madly, irretrievably, fiercely in love with her; how she treats the unhappy being who is thus terribly circumstanced with the innocent familiarity of a petted child, never dreaming of such a thing as a lover till the gentleman declares himself in due form; that is to say, with the accompanying ceremonies of strained gaze, passionately clasped hands, haggard countenance, disheveled hair, and a voice "low but distinct, and full of an indescribable and mysterious power which compelled her to listen." We are tired of all this. Give us something new, we beseech.

There are many other remarks which I would much like to make to the creators of fictitious humanity, but they are too numerous to be offered now. I beg to submit these for their present consideration, and in the mean while rest (for I don't scruple to confess that I owe some of the pleasantest hours of my life to their lucubrations) their obliged and obedient servant,

IGNATIUS.

24

NATHANIEL HAWTHORNE

E. P. *Whipple*

Atlantic Monthly (1860).

Edwin Percy Whipple (1819-1886), author, literary critic, and lecturer, was born in Gloucester, Massachusetts. His editorial work and criticism (much of it unsigned and still unidentified) was greatly influential: twelve editions of *Essays and Reviews*, 2 vols. (1848-1849) appeared by 1888. From the 1840s, he acted as a consultant for the publishing house Ticknor, Reed, and Fields, and in that capacity he was involved in the publication of Nathaniel Hawthorne's *The Scarlet Letter* (1850).

The romance of *The Marble Faun* will be widely welcomed, not only for its intrinsic merits, but because it is a sign that its writer, after a silence of seven or eight years, has determined to resume his place in the ranks of authorship.[316] In his preface he tells us, that in each of his previous publications he had unconsciously one person in his eye, whom he styles his "gentle reader." He meant it "for that one congenial friend, more comprehensive of his purposes, more appreciative of his, success, more indulgent of his short-comings, and, in all respects, closer and kinder than a brother,—that all-sympathizing critic, in short, whom an author never actually meets, but to whom he implicitly makes his appeal, whenever he is conscious of having done his best." He believes that this reader did once exist for him, and duly received the scrolls he flung "upon whatever wind was blowing, in the faith that they would find him out." "But," he questions, "is he extant now? In these many years since he last heard from me, may he not have deemed his earthly task accomplished, and have withdrawn to the paradise of gentle readers, wherever it may be, to the enjoyments of which his kindly charity on my behalf must surely have entitled him?" As we feel assured that Hawthorne's reputation has been steadily growing with the lapse of time, he has no cause to fear that the longevity of his gentle reader will not equal his own. As long as he writes, there will be readers enough to admire and appreciate.

The publication of this new romance seems to offer us a fitting occasion to attempt some description of the peculiarities of the genius of which it is the latest
offspring, and to hazard some judgments on its predecessors. It is more than
twenty-five years since Hawthorne began that remarkable series of stories and essays which are now collected in the volumes of *Twice-Told Tales, The Snow Image and
other Tales,* and *Mosses from an Old Manse.*[317] From the first he was recognized by such
readers as he chanced to find as a man of genius, yet for a long time he enjoyed, in
his own words, the distinction of being "the obscurest man of letters in America."[318] His readers were "gentle" rather than enthusiastic; their fine delight in his
creations was a private perception of subtle excellences of thought and style, too
refined and self-satisfying to be contagious; and the public was untouched, whilst
the "gentle" reader was full of placid enjoyment. Indeed, we fear that this kind of
reader is something of an Epicurean,[319]—receives a new genius as a private blessing, sent by a benign Providence to quicken a new life in his somewhat jaded sense
of intellectual pleasure; and after having received a fresh sensation, he is apt to be
serenely indifferent whether the creator of it starve bodily or pine mentally from
the lack of a cordial human shout of recognition.

There would appear, on a slight view of the matter, no reason for the little notice
which Hawthorne's early productions received. The subjects were mostly drawn
from the traditions and written records of New England, and gave the "beautiful
strangeness" of imagination to objects, incidents, and characters which were familiar facts in the popular mind. The style, while it had a purity, sweetness, and grace
which satisfied the most fastidious and exacting taste, had, at the same time, more
than the simplicity and clearness of an ordinary school-book. But though the subjects and the style were thus popular, there was something in the shaping and informing spirit which failed to awaken interest, or awakened interest without exciting delight. Misanthropy, when it has its source in passion,—when it is fierce, bitter,
fiery, and scornful,—when it vigorously echoes the aggressive discontent of the
world, and furiously tramples on the institutions and the men luckily rather than
rightfully in the ascendant,—this is always popular; but a misanthropy which
springs from insight,—a misanthropy which is lounging, languid, sad, and depressing,—a misanthropy which remorselessly looks through cursing misanthropes and
chirping men of the world with the same sure, detecting glance of reason,—a misanthropy which has no fanaticism, and which casts the same ominous doubt on
subjectively morbid as on subjectively moral action,—a misanthropy which has no
respect for impulses, but has a terrible perception of spiritual laws,—this is a misanthropy which can expect no wide recognition and it would be vain to deny that
traces of this kind of misanthropy are to be found in Hawthorne's earlier, and are
not altogether absent from his later works. He had spiritual insight, but it did not
penetrate to the sources of spiritual joy; and his deepest glimpses of truth were calculated rather to sadden than to inspire. A blandly cynical distrust of human nature
was the result of his most piercing glances into the human soul. He had humor, and
sometimes humor of a delicious kind; but this sunshine of the soul was but sun-

shine breaking through or lighting up a sombre and ominous cloud. There was also observable in his earlier stories a lack of vigor, as if the power of his nature had been impaired by the very process which gave depth and excursiveness to his mental vision. Throughout, the impression is conveyed of a shy recluse, alternately bashful in disposition and bold in thought, gifted with original and various capacities, but capacities which seemed to have developed themselves in the shade, without sufficient energy of will or desire to force them, except fitfully, into the sunlight. Shakespeare calls moonlight the sunlight sick;[320] and it is in some such moonlight of the mind that the genius of Hawthorne found its first expression. A mild melancholy, sometimes deepening into gloom, sometimes brightened into a "humorous sadness," characterized his early creations. Like his own Hepzibah Pyncheon, he appeared "to be walking in a dream"; or rather, the life and reality assumed by his emotions "made all outward occurrences unsubstantial, like the teasing phantasms of an unconscious slumber."[321] Though dealing largely in description, and with the most accurate perceptions of outward objects, he still, to use again his own words, gives the impression of a man "chiefly accustomed to look inward, and to whom external matters are of little value or import, unless they bear relation to something within his own mind." But that "something within his own mind" was often an unpleasant something, perhaps a ghastly occult perception of deformity and sin in what appeared outwardly fair and good; so that the reader felt a secret dissatisfaction with the disposition which directed the genius, even in the homage he awarded to the genius itself. As psychological portraits of morbid natures, his delineations of character might have given a purely intellectual satisfaction; but there was audible, to the delicate ear, a faint and muffled growl of personal discontent, which showed they were not mere exercises of penetrating imaginative analysis, but had in them the morbid vitality of a despondent mood.

Yet, after admitting these peculiarities, nobody who is now drawn to the *Twice-Told Tales*, from his interest in the later romances of Hawthorne, can fail to wonder a little at the limited number of readers they attracted on their original publication. For many of these stories are at once a representation of early New-England life and a criticism on it. They have much of the deepest truth of history in them. "The Legends of the Province House," "The Gray Champion," "The Gentle Boy," " The Minister's Black Veil," "Endicott and the Red Cross," not to mention others, contain important matter which cannot be found in Bancroft or Grahame.[322] They exhibit the inward struggles of New-England men and women with some of the darkest problems of existence, and have more vital import to thoughtful minds than the records of Indian or Revolutionary warfare. In the "Prophetic Pictures," "Fancy's Show-Box," "The Great Carbuncle," "The Haunted Mind," and "Edward Fane's Rose-Bud," there are flashes of moral insight, which light up, for the moment, the darkest recesses of the individual mind; and few sermons reach to the depth of thought and sentiment from which these seemingly airy sketches draw their sombre life. It is common, for instance, for religious moralists to insist on the great spiritual truth, that wicked thoughts and impulses, which circumstances prevent from passing into wicked acts, are still deeds in the sight of God; but the living truth subsides into a dead truism, as enforced by commonplace preachers. In "Fancy's Show-Box," Hawthorne seizes the prolific idea; and the respectable merchant and respected church-member, in the still hour of his own meditation, convicts himself of being a liar, cheat, thief; seducer, and murderer, as he casts his glance over the mental events which form his spiritual biography. Interspersed with serious histories and moralities like these, are others which embody the sweet and playful, though still thoughtful and slightly saturnine action of Hawthorne's mind, like "The Seven Vagabonds," "Snow-Flakes," "The Lily's Quest," "Mr. Higginbotham's Catastrophe," "Little Annie's Ramble," "Sights from a Steeple," "Sunday at Home," and "A Rill from the Town-Pump."

The *Mosses from an Old Manse* are intellectually and artistically an advance from the *Twice-Told Tales*. The twenty-three stories and essays which make up the volumes are almost perfect of their kind. Each is complete in itself, and many might be expanded into long romances by the simple method of developing the possibilities of their shadowy types of character into appropriate incidents. In description, narration, allegory, humor, reason, fancy, subtlety, inventiveness, they exceed the best productions of Addison; but they want Addison's sensuous contentment and sweet and kindly spirit. Though the author denies that he has exhibited his own individual attributes in these *Mosses*, though he professes not to be "one of those supremely hospitable people who serve up their own hearts delicately fried, with brain-sauce, as a titbit for their beloved public,"—yet it is none the less apparent that he has diffused through each tale and sketch the life of the mental mood to which it owed its existence, and that one individuality pervades and colors the whole collection. The defect of the serious stories is, that character is introduced, not as thinking, but as the illustration of thought. The persons are ghostly, with a sad lack of flesh and blood. They are phantasmal symbols of a reflective and imaginative analysis of human passions and aspirations. The dialogue, especially, is bookish, as though the personages knew their speech was to be printed, and were careful of the collocation and rhythm of their words. The author throughout is evidently more interested in his large, wide, deep, indolently serene, and lazily sure and critical view of the conflict of ideas and passions, than he is with the individuals who embody them. He shows moral insight without moral earnestness. He cannot contract his mind to the patient delineation of a moral individual, but attempts to use individuals in order to express the last results of patient moral perception. Young Goodman Brown and Roger Malvin are not persons; they are the mere, loose, personal expression of subtle thinking. "The Celestial Rail Road," "The Procession of Life," "Earth's Holocaust," "The Bosom Serpent," indicate thought of a character equally deep, delicate, and comprehensive, but the characters are ghosts of men rather than substantial individualities. In the *Mosses from an Old Manse*, we are really studying the phenomena of human nature, while, for the time, we beguile ourselves into the belief that we are following the fortunes of individual natures.

Up to this time the writings of Hawthorne conveyed the impression of a genius in which insight so dominated over impulse, that it was rather mentally and morally curious than mentally and morally impassioned. The quality evidently wanting to its full expression was intensity. In the romance of *The Scarlet Letter* he first made his genius efficient by penetrating it with passion. This book forced itself into attention by its inherent power; and the author's name, previously known only to a limited circle of readers, suddenly became a familiar word in the mouths of the great reading public of America and England. It may be said, that it "captivated" nobody, but took everybody captive. Its power could neither be denied nor resisted. There were growls of disapprobation from novel-readers, that Hester Prynne and the Rev. Mr. Dimmesdale were subjected to cruel punishments unknown to the jurisprudence of fiction,—that the author was an inquisitor who put his victims on the rack,—and that neither amusement nor delight resulted from seeing the contortions and hearing the groans of these martyrs of sin; but the fact was no less plain that Hawthorne had for once compelled the most superficial lovers of romance to submit themselves to the magic of his genius. The readers of Dickens voted him, with three times three, to the presidency of their republic of letters; the readers of Hawthorne were caught by a *coup d'état*, and fretfully submitted to a despot whom they could not depose.

The success of *The Scarlet Letter* is an example of the advantage which an author gains by the simple concentration of his powers on one absorbing subject. In the *Twice-Told Tales* and the *Mosses from an Old Manse* Hawthorne had exhibited a wider range of sight and insight than in *The Scarlet Letter*. Indeed, in the little sketch of "Endicott and the Red Cross," written twenty years before, he had included in a few sentences the whole matter which he afterwards treated in his famous story. In describing the various inhabitants of an early New-England town, as far as they were representative, he touches incidentally on a "young woman, with no mean share of beauty, whose doom it was to wear the letter 'A' on the breast of her gown, in the eyes of all the world and her own children. And even her own children knew what that initial signified. Sporting with her infamy, the lost and desperate creature had embroidered the fatal token in scarlet cloth, with golden thread and the nicest art of needle-work; so that the capital 'A' might have been thought to mean Admirable, or anything, rather than Adulteress." Here is the germ of the whole pathos and terror of *The Scarlet Letter*; but it is hardly noted in the throng of symbols, equally pertinent, in the few pages of the little sketch from which we have quoted.

Two characteristics of Hawthorne's genius stand plainly out, in the conduct and characterization of the romance of *The Scarlet Letter*, which were less obviously prominent in his previous works. The first relates to his subordination of external incidents to inward events. Mr. James's "solitary horseman" does more in one chapter than Hawthorne's hero in twenty chapters; but then James deals with the arms of men, while Hawthorne deals with their souls.[323] Hawthorne relies almost entirely for the interest of his story on what is felt and done within the minds of his characters. Even his most picturesque descriptions and narratives are only one-tenth matter to nine-tenths spirit. The results that follow from one external act of folly or crime are to him enough for an *Iliad* of woes. It might be supposed that his whole theory of Romantic Art was based on these tremendous lines of Words-worth:

> Action is momentary,—
> The motion of a muscle, this way or that:
> Suffering is long, obscure, and infinite.[324]

The second characteristic of his genius is connected with the first. With his insight of individual souls he combines a far deeper insight of the spiritual laws which govern the strangest aberrations of individual souls. But it seems to us that his mental eye, keen-sighted and far-sighted as it is, overlooks the merciful modifications of the austere code whose pitiless action it so clearly discerns. In his long and patient brooding over the spiritual phenomena of Puritan life, it is apparent, to the least critical observer, that he has imbibed a deep personal antipathy to the Puritanic ideal of character; but it is no less apparent that his intellect and imagination have been strangely fascinated by the Puritanic idea of justice. His brain has been subtly infected by the Puritanic perception of Law, without being warmed by the Puritanic faith in Grace. Individually, he would much prefer to have been one of his own "Seven Vagabonds" rather than one of the austerest preachers of the primitive church of New England;[325] but the austerest preacher of the primitive church of New England would have been more tender and considerate to a real Mr. Dimmesdale and a real Hester Prynne than this modern romancer has been to their typical representatives in the world of imagination. Throughout *The Scarlet Letter* we seem to be following the guidance of an author who is personally good-natured, but intellectually and morally relentless.

The House of the Seven Gables, Hawthorne's next work, while it has less concentration of passion and tension of mind than *The Scarlet Letter*, includes a wider range of observation, reflection, and character; and the morality, dreadful as fate, which hung like a black cloud over the personages of the previous story, is exhibited in more relief. Although the book has no imaginative creation equal to little Pearl, it still contains numerous examples of characterisation at once delicate and deep. Clifford, especially, is a study in psychology, as well as a marvellously subtle delineation of enfeebled manhood. The general idea of the story is this,—"that the wrong-doing of one generation lives into the successive ones, and, divesting itself of every temporary advantage, becomes a pure and uncontrollable mischief";[326] and the mode in which the idea is carried out shows great force, fertility, and refinement of mind. A weird fancy, sporting with the facts detected by a keen observation, gives to every gable of the Seven Gables, every room in the House, every burdock growing rankly before the door, a symbolic significance. The queer mansion is haunted,—haunted with thoughts which every moment are liable to take ghostly shape. All the Pyncheons who have resided in it appear to have infected the very timbers and walls with the spiritual essence of their lives, and each seems ready to pass from a memory into a presence. The stern theory of the author regarding the hereditary transmission of family qualities, and the visiting of the sins of the fathers on the heads of their children, almost wins our reluctant assent through the pertinacity with which the generations of the Pyncheon race are made not merely to live in the blood and brain of their descendants, but to cling to their old abiding-place on earth, so that to inhabit the house is to breathe the Pyncheon soul and assimilate the Pyncheon individuality. The whole representation, masterly as it is, considered as an effort of intellectual and imaginative power, would still be morally bleak, were it not for the sunshine and warmth radiated from the character of Phoebe. In this delightful creation Hawthorne for once gives himself up to homely human nature, and has succeeded in delineating a New-England girl, cheerful, blooming, practical, affectionate, efficient, full of innocence and happiness, with all the "handiness" and native sagacity of her class, and so true and close to Nature that the process by which she is slightly idealized is completely hidden.

In this romance there is also more humour than in any of his other works. It peeps out, even in the most serious passages, in a kind of demure rebellion against the fanaticism of his remorseless intelligence. In the description of the Pyncheon poultry, which we think unexcelled by anything in Dickens for quaintly fanciful humor, the author seems to indulge in a sort of parody on his own doctrine of the hereditary transmission of family qualities. At any rate, that strutting chanticleer, with his two meagre wives and one wizened chicken, is a sly side fleer at the tragic aspect of the law of descent. Miss Hepzibah Pyncheon, her shop, and her customers, are so delightful, that the reader would willingly spare a good deal of Clifford and Judge Pyncheon and Holgrave, for more details of them and Phoebe. Uncle Venner, also, the old wood-sawyer, who boasts "that he has seen a good deal of the world, not only in people's kitchens and back-yards, but at the street-corners, and on the wharves, and in other places where his business" called him, and who, on the strength of this comprehensive experience, feels qualified to give the final decision in every ease which tasks the resources of human wisdom, is a very much more humane and interesting gentleman than the Judge. Indeed, one cannot but regret that Hawthorne should be so economical of his undoubted stores of humor,—and that, in the two romances he has since written, humor, in the form of character, does not appear at all.

Before proceeding to the consideration of *The Blithedale Romance*, it is necessary to say a few words on the seeming separation of Hawthorne's genius from his will.[327] He has none of that ability which enabled Scott and enables Dickens to force their powers into action, and to make what was begun in drudgery soon assume the character of inspiration. Hawthorne cannot thus use his genius; his genius always uses him. This is so true, that he often succeeds better in what calls forth his personal antipathies than in what calls forth his personal sympathies. His life of General Pierce, for instance, is altogether destitute of life; yet in writing it he must have exerted himself to the utmost, as his object was to urge the claims of an old and dear friend to the Presidency of the Republic.[328] The style, of course, is excellent, as it is impossible for Hawthorne to write bad English, but the genius of the man has deserted him. General Pierce, whom he loves, he draws so feebly, that one doubts, while reading the biography, if such a man exists; Hollingsworth, whom he hates, is so vividly characterized, that the doubt is, while we read the romance, whether such a man can possibly be fictitious.

Midway between such a work as the *Life of General Pierce* and *The Scarlet Letter* may be placed *The Wonder-Book* and *Tanglewood Tales*.[329] In these Hawthorne's genius distinctly appears, and appears in its most lovable, though not in its deepest form. These delicious stories, founded on the mythology of Greece, were written for children, but they delight men and women as well. Hawthorne never pleases grown people so much as when he writes with an eye to the enjoyment of little people.

Now *The Blithedale Romance* is far from being so pleasing a performance as *Tanglewood Tales*, yet it very much better illustrates the operation, indicates the quality, and expresses the power, of the author's genius. His great books appear not so much created by him as through him. They have the character of revelations,—he, the instrument, being often troubled with the burden they impose on his mind. His profoundest glances into individual souls are like the marvels of clairvoyance. It would seem, that, in the production of such a work as *The Blithedale Romance*, his mind had hit accidentally, as it were, on an idea or fact mysteriously related to some morbid sentiment in the inmost core of his nature, and connecting itself with numerous scattered observations of human life, lying unrelated in his imagination. In a sort of meditative dream, his intellect drifts in the direction to which the subject points, broods patiently over it, looks at it, looks into it, and at last looks through it to the law by which it is governed. Gradually, individual beings, definite in spiritual quality, but shadowy in substantial form, group themselves around this central conception, and by degrees assume an outward body and expression corresponding to their internal nature. On the depth and intensity of the mental mood, the force of the fascination it exerts over him, and the length of time it holds him captive, depend the solidity and substance of the individual characterizations. In this way Miles Coverdale, Hollingsworth, Westervelt, Zenobia, and Priscilla become real persons to the mind which has called them into being. He knows every secret and watches every motion of their souls, yet is, in a measure, independent of them, and pretends to no authority by which he can alter the destiny which consigns them to misery or happiness. They drift to their doom by the same law by which they drifted across the path of his vision. Individually, he abhors Hollingsworth, and would like to annihilate Westervelt, yet he allows the superb Zenobia to be their victim; and if his readers object that the effect of the whole representation is painful, he would doubtless agree with them, but profess his incapacity honestly to alter a sentence. He professes to tell the story as it was revealed to him; and the license in which a romancer might indulge is denied to a biographer of spirits. Show him a fallacy in his logic of passion and character, point out a false or defective step in his analysis, and he will gladly alter the whole to your satisfaction; but four human souls, such as he has described, being given, their mutual attractions and repulsions will end, he feels assured, in just such a catastrophe as he has stated.

Eight years have passed since *The Blithedale Romance* was written, and during nearly the whole of this period Hawthorne has resided abroad. *The Marble Faun*, which must, on the whole, be considered the greatest of his works, proves that his genius has widened and deepened in this interval, without any alteration or modification of its characteristic merits and characteristic defects. The most obvious excellence of the work is the vivid truthfulness of its descriptions of Italian life, manners, and scenery; and, considered merely as, a record of a tour in Italy, it is of great interest and attractiveness. The opinions on Art, and the special criticisms on the masterpieces of architecture, sculpture, and painting, also possess a value of their own. The story might have been told, and the characters fully represented, in one-third of the space devoted to them, yet description and narration are so artfully combined that each assists to give interest to the other. Hawthorne is one of those true observers who concentrate in observation every power of their minds. He has accurate sight and piercing insight. When he modifies either the form or the spirit of the objects he describes, he does it either by viewing them through the medium of an imagined mind or by obeying associations which they themselves suggest. We might quote from the descriptive portions of the work a hundred pages, at least, which would demonstrate how closely accurate observation is connected with the highest powers of the intellect and imagination.

The style of the book is perfect of its kind, and, if Hawthorne had written nothing else, would entitle him to rank among the great masters of English composition. Walter Savage Landor is reported to have said of an author whom he knew in his youth, "My friend wrote excellent English, a language now obsolete."[330] Had *The Marble Faun* appeared before he uttered this sarcasm, the wit of the remark would have been pointless. Hawthorne not only writes English, but the sweetest, simplest, and clearest English that ever has been made the vehicle of equal depth, variety, and subtlety of thought and emotion. His mind is reflected in his style as a face is reflected in a mirror; and the latter does not give back its image with less appearance of effort than the former. His excellence consists not so much in using common words as in making common words express uncommon things. Swift, Addison, Goldsmith, not to mention others, wrote with as much simplicity; but the style of neither embodies an individuality so complex, passions so strange and intense, sentiments so fantastic and preternatural, thoughts so profound and delicate, and imaginations so remote from the recognized limits of the ideal, as find an orderly outlet in the pure English of Hawthorne. He has hardly a word to which Mrs. Trimmer would primly object,[331] hardly a sentence which would call forth the frosty anathema of Blair, Hurd, Kames, or Whately, and yet he contrives to embody in his simple style qualities which would almost excuse the verbal extravagances of Carlyle.[332]

In regard to the characterization and plot of *The Marble Faun*, there is room for widely varying opinions. Hilda, Miriam, and Donatello will be generally received as superior in power and depth to any of Hawthorne's previous creations of character; Donatello, especially, must be considered one of the most original and exquisite conceptions in the whole range of romance; but the story in which they appear will seem to many an unsolved puzzle, and even the tolerant and interpretative "gentle reader" will be troubled with the unsatisfactory conclusion. It is justifiable for a romancer to sting the curiosity of his readers with a mystery, only on the implied obligation to explain it at last; but this story begins in mystery only to end in mist. The suggestive faculty is tormented rather than genially excited, and in the end is left a prey to doubts. The central idea of the story, the necessity of sin to convert such a creature as Donatello into a moral being, is also not happily illustrated in the leading event. When Donatello kills the wretch who malignantly dogs the steps of Miriam, all readers think that Donatello committed no sin at all; and the reason is, that Hawthorne has deprived the persecutor of Miriam of all human attributes, made him an allegorical representation of one of the most fiendish forms of un-mixed evil, so that we welcome his destruction with something of the same feeling with which, in following the allegory of Spenser or Bunyan, we rejoice in the hero's victory over the Blatant Beast or Giant Despair. Conceding, however, that Do-natello's act was murder, and not "justifiable homicide," we are still not sure that the author's conception of his nature and of the change caused in his nature by that act, are carried out with a felicity corresponding to the original conception.

In the first volume, and in the early part of the second, the author's hold on his design is comparatively firm, but it somewhat relaxes as he proceeds, and in the end it seems almost to escape from his grasp. Few can be satisfied with the concluding chapters, for the reason that nothing is really concluded. We are willing to follow the ingenious processes of Calhoun's deductive logic, because we are sure, that, however severely they task the faculty of attention, they will lead to some positive result; but Hawthorne's logic of events leaves us in the end bewildered in a laby-rinth of guesses. The book is, on the whole, such a great book, that its defects are felt with all the more force.

In this rapid glance at some of the peculiarities of Hawthorne's genius, we have not, of course, been able to do full justice to the special merits of the works we have passed in review; but we trust that we have said nothing which would convey the impression that we do not place them among the most remarkable romances produced in an age in which romance-writing has called forth some of the highest powers of the human mind. In intellect and imagination, in the faculty of discerning spirits and detecting laws, we doubt if any living novelist is his equal; but his genius, in its creative action, has been heretofore attracted to the dark rather than the bright side of the interior life of humanity, and the geniality which evidently is in him has rarely found adequate expression. In the many works which he may still be expected to write, it is to be hoped that his mind will lose some of its sadness of tone without losing any of its subtlety and depth; but, in any event, it would be un-just to deny that he has already done enough to insure him a commanding position in American literature as long as American literature has an existence.

25

JAMES FENIMORE COOPER

G. S. Hillard

Atlantic Monthly (1862).

George Stillman Hillard (1808-1879), clergyman, politician, miscellaneous author, and occasional orator, was born in Machias, Maine. He wrote a number of wide-ranging reviews, mostly for the *North American Review* and the *Christian Register* (which he also edited), a biography of Captain John Smith (1834), and edited a five-volume edition of Edmund Spenser (1839).

The publication, now brought to a close, of a new edition of the novels of Cooper[*] gives us a fair occasion for discharging a duty which Maga has too long neglected, and saying something upon the genius of this great writer, and, incidentally, upon the character of a man who would have been a noticeable, not to say remarkable, person, had he never written a line. These novels stand before us in thirty-two goodly duodecimo volumes, well printed, gracefully illustrated, and, in all external aspects, worthy of generous commendation. With strong propriety, the publishers dedicate this edition of the "first American novelist" to "the American People." No one of our great writers is more thoroughly American than Cooper; no one has caught and reproduced more broadly and accurately the spirit of our institutions, the character of our people, and even the aspects of Nature in this our Western world. He was a patriot to the very core of his heart; he loved his country with a fervid, but not an undiscerning love: it was an intelligent, vigilant, discriminating affection that bound his heart to his native land; and thus, while no man defended his country more vigorously when it was in the right, no one reproved its faults more courageously, or gave warning and advice more unreservedly, where he felt that they were needed.

---

[*] We refer to the new edition of the novels of Cooper by Messrs. W. A. Townsend & Co., with illustrations by Darley. [Stringer & Townsend published a thirty-four volume edition of the novels, carefully revised, in 1855.]

This may be one reason why Cooper has more admirers, or at least fewer disparagers, abroad than at home. On the Continent of Europe his novels are everywhere read, with an eager, unquestioning delight. His popularity is at least equal to that of Scott; and we think a considerable amount of testimony could be collected to prove that it is even greater. But the fact we have above stated is not the only explanation of this. He was the first writer who made foreign nations acquainted with the characters and incidents of American frontier and woodland life; and his delineations of Indian manners and traits were greatly superior in freshness and power, if not in truth, to any which had preceded them. His novels opened a new and unwrought vein of interest, and were a revelation of humanity under aspects and influences hitherto unobserved by the ripe civilization of Europe. The taste which had become cloyed with endless imitations of the feudal and mediaeval pictures of Scott turned with fresh delight to such original figures—so full of sylvan power and wildwood grace—as Natty Bumppo and Uncas.[333] European readers, too, received these sketches with an unqualified, because an ignorant admiration. We, who had better knowledge, were more critical, and could see that the drawing was sometimes faulty, and the colors more brilliant than those of life.

The acute observer can detect a parallel between the relation of Cooper to America and that of Scott to Scotland. Scott was as hearty a Scotchman as Cooper an American: but Scott was a Tory in politics and an Episcopalian in religion; and the majority of Scotchmen are Whigs in politics and Presbyterians in religion. In Scott, as in Cooper, the elements of passion and sympathy were so strong that he could not be neutral or silent on the great questions of his time and place. Thus, while the Scotch are proud of Scott, as they well may be, while he has among his own people most intense and enthusiastic admirers,—the proportion of those who yield to his genius a cold and reluctant homage is probably greater in Scotland than in any other country in Christendom. "The rest of mankind recognize the essential truth of his delineations, and his loyalty to all the primal instincts and sympathies of humanity;" but the Scotch cannot forget that he opposed the Reform Bill, painted the Covenanters with an Episcopalian pencil, and made a graceful and heroic image of the detested Claverhouse.[334]

The novels of Cooper, in the dates of their publication, cover a period of thirty years: beginning with *Precaution*, in 1820, and ending with *The Ways of the Hour*, in 1850. The production of thirty-two volumes in thirty years is honorable to his creative energy, as well as to the systematic industry of his habits. But even these do not constitute the whole of his literary labors during these twenty-nine years. We must add five volumes of naval history and biography, ten volumes of travels and sketches in Europe, and a large amount of occasional and controversial writings, most of which is now hidden away in that huge wallet wherein Time puts his alms for Oblivion. His literary productions other than his novels would alone be enough to save him from the reproach of idleness. In estimating a writer's claims to honor and remembrance, the quantity as well as the quality of his work should surely be taken into account; and in summing up the ease of our great novelist to the jury of posterity, this point should be strongly put.

Cooper's first novel, *Precaution,* was published when he was in his thirty-first year. It owed its existence to an accident, and was but an ordinary production, as inferior to the best of his subsequent works as Byron's *Hours of Idleness* to *Childe Harold.*[335] It was a languid and colorless copy of exotic forms: a mere scale picked from the surface of the writer's mind, with neither beauty nor vital warmth to commend it. We speak from the vague impressions which many long years have been busy in effacing; and we confess that it would require the combined forces of a long voyage and a scanty library to constrain us to the task of reading it anew.

And yet, such as it was, it made a certain impression at the time of its appearance. The standard by which it was tried was very unlike that which would now be applied to it: there was all the difference between the two that there is between strawberries in December and strawberries in June. American literature was then just beginning to "glint forth" like Burns's mountain daisy, and rear its tender form above the parent earth.[336] The time had, indeed, gone by—which a friend of ours, not yet venerable; affirms he can well remember—when school boys and collegians, zealous for the honor of indigenous literature, were obliged to cite, by way of illustration, such works as Morse's *Geography* and Hannah Adams's *History of the Jews;* but it was only a faint, crepuscular light, that streaked the east, and gave promise of the coming day.[337] Irving had just completed his *Sketch-Book,* which was basking in the full sunshine of unqualified popularity. Dana, in the thoughtful and meditative beauty of *The Idle Man,* was addressing a more limited public.[338] Percival had just before published a small volume of poems; Halleck's *Fanny* had recently appeared; and so had a small duodecimo volume by Bryant, containing "The Ages," and half a dozen smaller poems.[339] Miss Sedgwick's *New England Tale* was published about the same time. But a large proportion of those who are now regarded as our ablest writers were as yet unknown, or just beginning to give sign of what they were. Dr. Channing was already distinguished as an eloquent and powerful preacher, but the general public had not yet recognized in him that remarkable combination of loftiness of thought with magic charm of style, which was soon to be revealed in his essays on Milton and Napoleon Bonaparte. Ticknor and Everett were professors in Harvard College, giving a new impulse to the minds of the students by their admirable lectures; and the latter was also conducting the *North American Review.*[340] Neither had as yet attained to anything more than a local reputation. Prescott, a gay and light-hearted young man,—gay and light-hearted, in spite of partial blindness,—the darling of society and the idol of his home, was silently and resolutely preparing himself for his chosen function by a wide and thorough course of patient study. Bancroft was in Germany, and working like a German. Emerson was a Junior in College. Hawthorne, Longfellow, Holmes, Whittier, and Poe were school-boys; Mrs. Stowe was a school-girl; Whipple and Lowell were in the nursery, and Motley and the younger Dana had not long been out of it.[341]

Precaution, though an indifferent novel, was yet a novel; of the orthodox length, with plot, characters, and incidents; and here and there a touch of genuine power, as in the forty-first chapter, where the scene is on board a man-of-war bringing her prizes into port. It found many readers, and excited a good deal of curiosity as to who the author might be.

Precaution was published on the 25th of August, 1820, and *The Spy* on the 17th of September, 1821. The second novel was a great improvement upon the first, and fairly took the public by storm. We are old enough to remember its first appearance; the eager curiosity and keen discussion which it awakened; the criticism which it called forth; and, above all, the animated delight with which it was received by all who were young or not critical. Distinctly, too, can we recall the breathless rapture with which we hung over its pages, in those happy days when the mind's appetite for books was as ravenous as the body's for bread-and-butter, and a novel, with plenty of fighting in it, was all we asked at a writer's hands. In order to qualify ourselves for the task which we have undertaken in this article, we have read *The Spy* a second time; and melancholy indeed was the contrast between the recollections of the boy and the impressions of the man. It was the difference between the theatre by gas-light and the theatre by day-light: the gold was pinchbeck, the gems were glass, the flowers were cambric and colored paper, the goblets were gilded pasteboard. Painfully did the ideal light fade away, and the well-remembered scene stand revealed in disenchanting day. With incredulous surprise, with a constant struggle between past images and present revelations, were we forced to acknowledge the improbability of the story, the clumsiness of the style, the awkwardness of the dialogue, the want of Nature in many of the characters, the absurdity of many of the incidents, and the painfulness of some of the scenes. But with all this, a candid, though critical judgment could not but admit that these grave defects were attended by striking merits, which pleaded in mitigation of literary sentence. It was stamped with a truth, earnestness, and vital power, of which its predecessor gave no promise. Though the story was improbable, it seized upon the attention with a powerful grasp from the very start, and the hold was not relaxed till the end. Whatever criticism it might challenge, no one could call it dull: the only offence in a book which neither gods nor men nor counters can pardon. If the narrative flowed languidly at times, there were moments in which the incidents flashed along with such vivid rapidity that the susceptible reader held his breath over the page. The character of Washington was an elaborate failure, and the author, in his later years, regretted that he had introduced this august form into a work of fiction; but Harvey Birch was an original sketch, happily conceived, and, in the main, well sustained. His mysterious figure was recognized as a new accession to the repertory of the novelist, and not a mere modification of a preëxisting type. And, above all, *The Spy* had the charm of reality; it tasted of the soil; it was the first successful attempt to throw an imaginative light over American history, and to do for our country what the author of *Waverley* had done for Scotland. Many of the officers and solders of the Revolutionary War were still living, receiving the reward of their early perils and privations in the grateful reverence which was paid to them by the contemporaries of their children and grandchildren. Innumerable traditionary anecdotes of those dark days of suffering and struggle, unrecorded in print, yet lingered in the memories of the people, and were told in the nights of winter around the farm-house fire; and of no part of the country was this more true than of the region in which the scene of the novel is laid. The enthusiasm with which it was there read was the best tribute to the substantial fidelity of its delineations. All over the country, it enlisted in its behalf the powerful sentiment of patriotism; and whatever the critics might say, the author had the satisfaction of feeling that the heart of the people was with him.

Abroad, *The Spy* was received with equal favor. It was soon translated into most of the languages of Europe; and even the "gorgeous East" opened for it its rarely moving portals. In 1847, a Persian version was published in Ispahan; and by this time it may have crossed the Chinese wall, and be delighting the pig-tailed critics and narrow-eyed beauties of Pekin.

The success of *The Spy* unquestionably determined Cooper's vocation, and made him a man of letters. But he had not yet found where his true strength lay. His training and education had not been such as would seem to be a good preparation for a literary career. His reading had been desultory, and not extensive; and the habit of composition had not been formed in early life. Indeed, in mere style, in the handling of the tools of his craft, Cooper never attained a master's ease and power. In his first two novels the want of technical skill and literary accomplishment was obvious; and the scenery, subjects, and characters of these novels did not furnish him with the opportunity of turning to account the peculiar advantages which had come to him from the events of his childhood and youth. In his infancy he was taken to Cooperstown, a spot which his father had just begun to reclaim from the dominion of the wilderness. Here his first impressions of the external world, as well as of life and manners, were received. At the age of sixteen he became a midshipman in the United States navy, and remained in the service for six years. A father who, in training up his son for the profession of letters, should send him into the wilderness in his infancy and to sea at sixteen, would seem to be shooting very wide of the mark; but in this, as in so many things, there is a divinity that shapes our rough-hewn ends.[342] Had Cooper enjoyed the best scholastic advantages which the schools and colleges of Europe could have furnished, they could not have fitted him for the work he was destined to do so well as the apparently untoward elements we have above adverted to; for Natty Bumppo was the fruit of his woodland experience, and Long Tom Coffin of his sea-faring life.

The Pioneers and *The Pilot* were both published in 1823; *Lionel Lincoln* in 1825; and *The Last of the Mohicans* in 1826. We may put *Lionel Lincoln* aside, as one of his least successful productions; but the three others were never surpassed, and rarely equalled, by any of his numerous subsequent works. All the powerful, and nearly all the attractive, qualities of his genius were displayed in these three novels, in their highest degree and most ample measure. Had he never written any more,—though we should have missed many interesting narratives, admirable pictures, and vigorously drawn characters,—we are not sure that his fame would not have been as great as it is now. From these, and *The Spy*, full materials may be drawn for forming a correct estimate of his merits and his defects. In these, his strength and weakness, his gifts and deficiencies, are amply shown. Here, then, we may pause, and without pursuing his literary biography any farther, proceed to set down our estimate of his claims as a writer. Any critic who dips his pen in ink and not in gall would rather praise than blame; therefore we will dispose of the least gracious part of our task first, and begin with his blemishes and defects.

A skilful construction of the story is a merit which the public taste no longer demands, and it is consequently fast becoming one of the lost arts. The practice of publishing novels in successive numbers, so that one portion is printed before another is written, is undoubtedly one cause of this. But English and American readers have not been accustomed to this excellence in the works of their best writers of fiction; and therefore they are not sensitive to the want of it. This is certainly not one of Scott's strong points. Fielding's *Tom Jones* is, in this respect, superior to any of the "Waverley Novels," and without an equal, so far as we know, in English literature. But, in sitting in judgment upon a writer of novels, we cannot waive an inquiry into his merits on this point. Are his stories, simply as stories, well told? Are his plots symmetrically constructed and harmoniously evolved? Are his incidents probable? and do they all help on the catastrophe? Does he reject all episodical matter which would clog the current of the narrative? Do his novels have unity of action? or are they merely a series of sketches, strung together without any relation of cause and effect? Cooper, tried by these rules, can certainly command no praise. His plots are not carefully or skilfully constructed. His incidents are not probable in themselves, nor do they succeed each other in a natural and dependent progression. His characters get into scrapes from which the reasonable exercise of common faculties should have saved them; and they are rescued by incredible means and impossible instruments. The needed man appears as unaccountably and mysteriously as if he had dropped from the clouds, or emerged from the sea, or crept up through a fissure in the earth. The winding up of his stories is often effected by devices nearly as improbable as a violation of the laws of Nature. His personages act without adequate motives; they rush into needless dangers; they trust their fate, with unsuspecting simplicity, to treacherous hands.

In works of fiction the skill of the writer is most conspicuously shown when the progress of the story is secured by natural and probable occurrences. Many events take place in history and in common life which good taste rejects as inadmissible in a work of imagination. Sudden death by disease or casualty is no very uncommon occurrence in real life but it cannot be used in a novel to clear up a tangled web of circumstance, without betraying something of a poverty of invention in the writer. He is the best artist who makes least use of incidents which lie out of the beaten path of observation and experience. In constructive skill Cooper's rank is not high; for all his novels are more or less open to the criticism that too frequent use is made in them of events very unlikely to have happened. He leads his characters into such formidable perils that the chances are a million to one against their being rescued. Such a run is made upon our credulity that the fund is soon exhausted, and the bank stops payment.

For illustration of the above strictures we will refer to a single novel, *The Last of the Mohicans*, which everybody will admit to be one of the most interesting of his works,—full of rapid movement, brilliant descriptions, hair-breadth escapes, thrilling adventures,—which young persons probably read with more rapt attention than any other of his narratives. In the opening chapter we find at Fort Edward, on the head-waters of the Hudson, the two daughters of Colonel Munro, the commander of Fort William Henry, on the shores of Lake George; though why they were at the former post, under the protection of a stranger, and not with their father, does not appear. Information is brought of the approach of Montcalm, with a hostile army of Indians and Frenchmen, from the North; and the young ladies are straightway hurried off to the more advanced, and consequently more dangerous post, when prudence and affection would have dictated just the opposite course. Nor is this all. General Webb, the commander of Fort Edward, at the urgent request of Colonel Munro, sends him a reinforcement of fifteen hundred men, who march off through the woods, by the military road, with drums beating and colors flying; and yet, strange to say, the young ladies do not accompany the troops, but set off, on the very same day, by a by-path, attended by no other escort than Major Heyward, and guided by an Indian whose fidelity is supposed to be assured by his having been flogged for drunkenness by the orders of Colonel Munro. The reason assigned for conduct so absurd that in real life it would have gone far to prove the parties having a hand in it not to be possessed of that sound and disposing mind and memory which the law requires as a condition precedent to making a will is, that hostile Indians, in search of chance scalps, would be hovering about the column of troops, and so leave the by-path unmolested. But the servants of the party follow the route of the column: a measure, we are told, dictated by the sagacity of the Indian guide, in order to diminish the marks of their trail, if, haply, the Canadian savages should be prowling about so far in advance of their army! Certainly, all the sagacity of the fort would seem to have been concentrated in the person of the Indian. How much of this improbability might have been avoided, if the action had been reversed, and the young ladies, in view of the gathering cloud of war, had been sent from the more exposed and less strongly guarded point of Fort William Henry to the safe fortress of Fort Edward! Then the smallness of the escort and the risks of the journey would have been explained and excused by the necessity of the case; and the subsequent events of the novel might have been easily accommodated to the change we have indicated.

One of the best of Cooper's novels—as a work of art perhaps the very best—is *The Bravo*. But the character of Jacopo Frontoni is a sort of moral impossibility, and the clearing up of the mystery which hangs over his life and conduct, which is skilfully reserved to the last moment, is consequently unsatisfactory. He is represented as a young man of the finest qualities and powers, who, in the hope of rescuing a father who had been falsely imprisoned by the Senate, consents to assume the character, and bear the odium, of a public bravo, or assassin, though entirely innocent. This false position gives rise to many most effective scenes and incidents, and the character is in many respects admirably drawn. But when the end comes, we lay down the book and say,—"This could never have been: a virtuous and noble young man could not for years have been believed to be the most hateful of mankind; the laws of Nature and the laws of the human mind forbid it: so vast a web of falsehood could not have been woven without a flaw: we can credit much of the organized and pitiless despotism of Venice, but could it work miracles?"

Further illustrations of this same defect might easily be cited, if the task were not ungracious. Neither books, nor pictures, nor men and women should be judged by their defects. It is enough to say that Cooper never wrote a novel in regard to which the reader must not lay aside his critical judgment upon the structure of the story and the interdependence of the incidents, and let himself be borne along by the rapid flow of the narrative, without questioning too curiously as to the nature of the means and instruments employed to give movement to the stream.

In the delineation of character, Cooper may claim great, but not unqualified praise. This is a vague statement and to draw a sharper line of discrimination, we should say that he is generally successful—sometimes admirably so—in drawing personages in whom strong primitive traits have not been effaced by the attritions of artificial life, and generally unsuccessful when he deals with those in whom the original characteristics are less marked, or who have been smoothed by education and polished by society. It is but putting this criticism in another form to say that his best characters are persons of humble social position. He wields his brush with a vigorous hand, but the brush itself has not a fine point. Of all the children of his brain, Natty Bumppo is the most universal favorite,—and herein the popular judgment is assuredly right. He is an original conception,—and not more happily conceived than skilfully executed. It was a hazardous undertaking to present the character backwards, and let us see the closing scenes of his life first,—like a Hebrew Bible, of which the beginning is at the end; but the author's genius has triumphed over the perils of the task, and given us a delineation as consistent and symmetrical as it is striking and vigorous. Ignorant of books, simple, and credulous, guileless himself, and suspecting no evil in others, with moderate intellectual powers, he commands our admiration and respect by his courage, his love of Nature, his skill in woodland lore, his unerring moral sense, his strong affections, and the veins of poetry that run through his rugged nature like seams of gold in quartz. Long Tom Coffin may be described as Leatherstocking suffered a sea-change,—with a harpoon instead of a rifle, and a pea-jacket instead of a hunting-shirt. In both the same primitive elements may be discerned; the same limited intellectual range combined with professional or technical skill; the same generous affections and unerring moral instincts; the same religious feeling, taking the form at times of fatalism or superstition. Long Tom's love of the sea is like Leatherstocking's love of the woods; the former's dislike of the land is like the latter's dislike of the clearings.

Cooper himself, as we are told by his daughter, was less satisfied, in his last years, with Long Tom Coffin than most of his readers,—and, of the two characters, considered that of Boltrope the better piece of workmanship. We cannot assent to this comparative estimate; but we admit that Boltrope has not had full justice done to him in popular judgment. It is but a slight sketch, but it is extremely well done. His death is a bit of manly and genuine pathos; and in his conversations with the chaplain there is here and there a touch of true humor, which we value the more because humor was certainly not one of the author's best gifts.

Antonio, the old fisherman, in *The Bravo*, is another very well drawn character, in which we can trace something of a family likeness to the hunter and sailor above mentioned. The scene in which he is shrived by the Carmelite monk, in his boat, under the midnight moon, upon the Lagoons, is one of the finest we know of in the whole range of the literature of fiction, leaving upon the mind a lasting impression of solemn and pathetic beauty. In *The Chainbearer*, the Yankee squatter, Thousandacres, is a repulsive figure, but drawn with a powerful pencil. The energy of character, or rather of action, which is the result of a passionate love of money, is true to human nature. The closing scenes of his rough and lawless life, in which his latent affection for his faithful wife throws a sunset gleam over his hard and selfish nature, and prevents it from being altogether hateful, are impressively told, and are touched with genuine tragic power.

On the other hand, Cooper generally fails when he undertakes to draw a character which requires for its successful execution a nice observation and a delicate hand. His heroes and heroines are apt to abuse the privilege which such personages have enjoyed, time out of mind, of being insipid. Nor can he catch and reproduce the easy grace and unconscious dignity of high-bred men and women. His gentlemen, whether young or old, are apt to be stiff, priggish, and commonplace; and his ladies, especially his young ladies, are as deficient in individuality as the figures and faces of a fashion-print. Their personal and mental charms are set forth with all the minuteness of a passport; but, after all, we cannot but think that these fine creatures, with hair, brow, eyes, and lips of the most orthodox and approved pattern, would do very little towards helping one through a rainy day in a country-house. Judge Temple, in *The Pioneers*, and Colonel Howard, in *The Pilot*, are highly estimable and respectable gentlemen, but, in looking round for the materials of a pleasant dinner-party, we do not think they would stand very high on the list. They are fair specimens of their class,—the educated gentleman in declining life,—many of whom are found in the subsequent novels. They are wanting in those natural traits of individuality by which, in real life, one human being is distinguished from another. They are obnoxious to this one general criticism, that the author is constantly reminding us of the qualities of mind and character on which he rests their claims to favor, without causing them to appear naturally and unconsciously in the course of the narrative. The defect we are adverting to may be illustrated by comparing such personages of this class as Cooper has delineated with Colonel Talbot, in *Waverley*, Colonel Mannering and Counsellor Pleydell, in *Guy Mannering*, Monkbarns, in *The Antiquary*, and old Osbaldistone, in *Rob Roy*. These are all old men: they are all men of education, and in the social position of gentlemen; but each has certain characteristics which the others have not: each has the distinctive individual flavor—perceptible, but indescribable, like the savor of a fruit—which is wanting in Cooper's well-dressed and well-behaved lay-figures.

In the delineation of female loveliness and excellence Cooper is generally supposed to have failed,—at least, comparatively so. But in this respect full justice has hardly been done him; and this may be explained by the fact that it was from the heroines of his earlier novels that this unfavorable judgment was drawn. Certainly, such sticks of barley-candy as Frances Wharton, Cecilia Howard, and Alice Munro justify the common impression.[343] But it would be as unfair to judge of what he can do in this department by his acknowledged failures as it would be to form an estimate of the genius of Michelangelo from the easel-picture of the "Virgin and Child" in the Tribune at Florence.[344] No man ever had a juster appreciation of, and higher reverence for, the worth of woman than Cooper. Towards women his manners were always marked by chivalrous deference, blended as to those of his own household with the most affectionate tenderness. His own nature was robust, self-reliant, and essentially masculine: such men always honor women, but they understand them better as they grow older. There is so much foundation for the saying, that men are apt to love their first wives best, but to treat their second wives best. Thus the reader who takes up his works in chronological order will perceive that the heroines of his later novels have more spirit and character, are drawn with a more discriminating touch, take stronger hold upon the interest, than those of his earlier. Ursula Malbone is a finer girl than Cecilia Howard, or even Elizabeth Temple.[345] So when he has occasion to delineate a woman who, from her position in life, or the peculiar circumstances into which she is thrown, is moved by deeper springs of feeling, is obliged to put forth sterner energies, than are known to females reared in the sheltered air of prosperity and civilization,—when he paints the heart of woman roused by great perils, overborne by heavy sorrows, wasted by strong passions,—we recognize the same master-hand which has given us such powerful pictures of character in the other sex. In other words, Cooper is not happy in representing those shadowy and delicate graces which belong exclusively to woman, and distinguish her from man; but he is generally successful in sketching in woman those qualities which are found in both sexes. In *The Bravo*, Donna Violetta, the heroine, a rich and high-born young lady, is not remarkable one way or the other; but Gelsomina, the jailer's daughter, born in an inferior position, reared in a sterner school of discipline and struggle, is a beautiful and consistent creation, constantly showing masculine energy and endurance, yet losing nothing of womanly charm. Ruth, in *The Wept of the Wish-ton-Wish*, Hetty Hutter, the weak-minded and sound-hearted girl, in *The Deerslayer*, Mabel Dunham, and the young Indian woman, "Dew of June," in *The Pathfinder*, are further cases in point. No one can read the hooks in which these women are represented and say that Cooper was wanting in the power of delineating the finest and highest attributes of womanhood.

Cooper cannot be congratulated upon his success in the few attempts he has made to represent historical personages. Washington, as shown to us in *The Spy*, is a formal piece of mechanism, as destitute of vital character as Maelzel's automaton trumpeter. This, we admit, was a very difficult subject, alike from the peculiar traits of Washington, and from the reverence in which his name and memory are held by his countrymen. But the sketch, in *The Pilot*, of Paul Jones, a very different person, and a much easier subject, is hardly better.[346] In both cases, the failure arises from the fact that the author is constantly endeavoring to produce the legitimate effect of mental and moral qualities by a careful enumeration of external attributes. Harper, under which name Washington is introduced, appears in only two or three scenes; but, during these, we hear so much of the solemnity and impressiveness of his manner, the gravity of his brow, the steadiness of his gaze, that we get the notion of a rather oppressive personage, and sympathize with the satisfaction of the Whartons, when he retires to his own room, and relieves them of his tremendous presence. Mr. Gray, who stands for Paul Jones, is more carefully elaborated, but the result is far from satisfactory. We are so constantly told of his calmness and abstraction, of his sudden starts and bursts of feeling, of his low voice, of his fits of musing, that the aggregate impression is that of affectation and self-consciousness, rather than of a simple, passionate, and heroic nature. Mr. Gray does not seem to us at all like the rash, fiery, and dare-devil Scotchman of history. His conduct and conversation, as recounted in the fifth chapter of the novel, are unnatural and improbable and we cannot wonder that the first lieutenant did not know what to make of so melodramatic and sententious a gentleman, in the guise of a pilot.

Cooper, as we need hardly say, has drawn copiously upon Indian life and character for the materials of his novels and among foreign nations much of his reputation is due to this fact. Civilized men and women always take pleasure in reading about the manners and habits of savage life; and those in whom the shows of things are submitted to the desires of the mind delight to invest them with those ideal qualities which they do not find, or think they do not, in the artificial society around them. Cooper had enjoyed no peculiar opportunities of studying by personal observation the characteristics of the Indian race, but he had undoubtedly read everything he could get hold of in illustration of the subject. No one can question the vividness and animation of his sketches, or their brilliant tone of color. He paints with a pencil dipped in the glow of our sunset skies and the crimson of our autumn maples. Whenever he brings Indians upon the stage, we may be sure that scenes of thrilling interest are before us: that rifles are to crack, tomahawks to gleam, and arrows to dart like sunbeams through the air; that a net of peril is to be drawn around his hero or heroine, from the meshes of which he or she is to be extricated by some unexpected combination of fortunate circumstances. We expect a succession of startling incidents, and a rapid course of narrative without pauses or languid intervals. We do not object to his idealizing his Indians: this is the privilege of the novelist, time out of mind. He may make them swift of foot, graceful in movement, and give them a form like the Apollo's; he may put as much expression as he pleases into their black eyes; he may tessellate their speech as freely as he will with poetical and figurative expressions, drawn from the aspects of the external world: for all this there is authority, and chapter and verse may be cited in support of it. But we have a right to ask that he shall not transcend the bounds of reason and possibility, and represent his red men, as moved by motives and guided by sentiments which are wholly inconsistent with the inexorable facts of the case. We confess to being a little more than skeptical as to the Indian of poetry and romance: like the German's camel, he is evolved from the depth of the writer's own consciousness. The poet takes the most delicate sentiments and the finest emotions of civilization and cultivation, and grafts them upon the best qualities of savage life; which is as if a painter should represent an oak-tree bearing roses. The life of the North-American Indian, like that of all men who stand upon the base-line of civilization, is a constant struggle, and often a losing struggle, for mere subsistence. The sting of animal wants is his chief motive of action, and the full gratification of animal wants his highest ideal of happiness. The "noble savage," as sketched by poets, weary of the hollowness, the insincerity, and the meanness of artificial life, is really a very ignoble creature, when seen in the "open daylight" of truth. He is selfish, sensual, cruel, indolent, and impassive. The highest graces of character, the sweetest emotions, the finest sensibilities,—which make up the novelist's stock in trade,— are not and cannot be the growth of a so-called state of Nature, which is an essentially unnatural state. We no more believe that Logan ever made the speech reported by Jefferson, in so many words, than we believe that Chatham ever made the speech in reply to Walpole which begins with, "The atrocious crime of being a young man";[347] though we have no doubt that the reporters in both cases had something fine and good to start from. We accept with acquiescence, nay, with admiration, such characters as Magua, Chingachgook, Susquesus, Tamenund, and Canonchet;[348] but when we come to Uncas, in *The Last of the Mohicans*, we pause and shake our heads with incredulous doubt. That a young Indian chief should fall in love with a handsome quadroon like Cora Munro—for she was neither more nor less than that—is natural enough; but that he should manifest his passion with such delicacy and refinement is impossible. We include under one and the same name all the affinities and attractions of sex, but the appetite of the savage differs from the love of the educated and civilized man as much as charcoal differs from the diamond. The sentiment of love, as distinguished from the passion, is one of the last and best results of Christianity and civilization in no one thing does savage life differ from civilized more than in the relations between man and woman, and in the affections that unite them. Uncas is a graceful and beautiful image; but he is no Indian.

We turn now to a more gracious part of our task, and proceed to say something of the many striking excellences which distinguish Cooper's writings, and have given him such wide popularity. Popularity is but one test of merit, and not the highest,—gauging popularity by the number of readers, at any one time, irrespective of their taste and judgment. In this sense, *The Scottish Chiefs* and *Thaddeus of War-*

saw were once as popular as any of the Waverley Novels.[349] But Cooper's novels have enduring merit, and will surely keep their place in the literature of the language. The manners, habits, and costumes of England have greatly changed during the last hundred years; but Richardson and Fielding are still read. We must expect corresponding changes in this country during the next century; but we may confidently predict that in the year 1962 young and impressible hearts will be saddened at the fate of Uncas and Cora, and exult when Captain Munson's frigate escapes from the shoals.[350]

A few pages back we spoke of Cooper's want of skill in the structure of his plots, and his too frequent recurrence to improbable incidents to help on the course of his stories. But most readers care little about this defect, provided the writer betrays no poverty of invention, and succeeds in making his narratives interesting. Herein Cooper never lays himself open to that instinctive and unconscious criticism, which is the only kind an author need dread, because from it there is no appeal. It is bad to have a play hissed down, but it is worse to have it yawned down. But over Cooper's pages his readers never yawn. They never break down in the middle of one of his stories. The fortunes of his characters are followed with breathless and accumulating interest to the end. In vain does the dinner-bell sound, or the clock strike the hour of bed-time: the book cannot be laid down till we know whether Elizabeth Temple is to get out of the woods without being burned alive, or solve the mystery that hangs over the life of Jacopo Frontoni. He has in ample measure that paramount and essential merit in a novelist of fertility of invention. The resources of his genius, alike in the devising of incidents and the creation of character, are inexhaustible. His scenes are laid on the sea and in the forest,—in Italy, Germany, Switzerland, and Spain,—amid the refinements and graces of civilization and the rudeness and hardships of frontier and pioneer life; but everywhere he moves with an easy and familiar tread, and everywhere, though there may be the motive and the cue for minute criticism, we recognize the substantial truth of his pictures. In all his novels the action is rapid and the movement animated: his incidents may not be probable, but they crowd upon each other so thickly that we have not time to raise the question: before one impression has become familiar, the scene changes, and new objects enchain the attention. All rapid motion is exhilarating alike to mind and body; and in reading Cooper's novels we feel a pleasure analogous to that which stirs the blood when we drive a fast horse or sail with a ten-knot breeze. This fruitfulness in the invention of incidents is nearly as important an element in the composition of a novelist as a good voice in that of a singer. A powerful work of fiction may be produced by a writer who has not this gift; but such works address a comparatively limited public. To the common mind no faculty in the novelist is so fascinating as this. *Caleb Williams* is a story of remarkable power; but *Ivanhoe* has a thousand readers to its one.

In estimating novelists by the number and variety of characters with which they have enriched the repertory of fiction, Cooper's place, if not the highest, is very high. The fruitfulness of his genius in this regard is kindred to its fertility in the invention of incidents. We can pardon in a portrait-gallery of such extent here and there an ill-drawn figure or a face wanting in expression. With the exception of Scott, and perhaps of Dickens, what writer of prose fiction has created a greater number of characters such as stamp themselves upon the memory so that an allusion to them is well understood in cultivated society? Fielding has drawn country squires, and Smollett has drawn sailors; but neither has intruded upon the domain of the other, nor could he have made the attempt without failure. Some of our living novelists have a limited list of characters; they have half a dozen types which we recognize as inevitably as we do the face and voice of an actor in the king, the lover, the priest, or the bandit: but Cooper is not a mere mannerist, perpetually copying from himself. His range is very wide: it includes white men, red men, and black men,—sailors, hunters, and soldiers,—lawyers, doctors, and clergymen,—past generations and present,—Europeans and Americans,—civilized and savage life. All his delineations are not successful; some are even unsuccessful: but the aberrations of his genius must be viewed in connection with the extent of the orbit through which it moves. The courage which led him to expose himself to so many risks of failure is itself a proof of conscious power.

Cooper's style has not the ease, grace, and various power of Scott's,—or the racy, idiomatic character of Thackeray's,—or the exquisite purity and transparency of Hawthorne's: but it is a manly, energetic style, in which we are sure to find good words, if not the best. It has certain wants, but it has no marked defects; if it does not always command admiration, it never offends. It has not the highest finish; it sometimes betrays carelessness: but it is the natural garb in which a vigorous mind clothes its conceptions. It is the style of a man who writes from a full mind, without thinking of what he is going to say; and this is in itself a certain kind of merit. His descriptive powers are of a high order. His love of Nature was strong; and, as is generally the case with intellectual men, it rather increased than diminished as he grew older. It was not the meditative and self-conscious love of a sensitive spirit, that seeks in communion with the outward world a relief from the burdens and struggles of humanity, but the hearty enjoyment of a thoroughly healthy nature, the schoolboy's sense of a holiday dwelling in a manly breast. His finest passages are those in which he presents the energies and capacities of humanity in combination with striking or beautiful scenes in Nature. His genius, which sometimes moves with "compulsion and laborious flight"[351] when dealing with artificial life and the manners and speech of cultivated men and women, here recovers all its powers, and sweeps and soars with victorious and irresistible wing. The breeze from the sea, the fresh air and wide horizon of the prairies, the noonday darkness of the forest are sure to animate his drooping energies, and breathe into his mind the inspiration of a fresh life. Here he is at home, and in his congenial element: he is the swan on the lake, the eagle in the air, the deer in the woods. The escape of the frigate, in the fifth chapter of *The Pilot*, is a well-known passage of this kind; and nothing can be finer. The technical skill, the poetical feeling, the rapidity of the narrative, the distinctness of the details, the vividness of the coloring, the life, power, and animation which breathe and burn in every line, make up a combination of the highest order of literary merit. It is as good a sea-piece as the best of Turner's; and we cannot give it higher praise.[352] We hear the whistling of the wind through the rigging, and the roar of the pitiless sea, bellowing for its prey; we see the white caps of the waves flashing with spectral light through the darkness, and the gallant ship whirled along like a bubble by the irresistible current we hold our breath as we read of the expedients and manoeuvres which most of us but half understand, and heave a long sigh of relief when the danger is past, and the ship reaches the open sea. A similar passage, though of more quiet and gentler beauty, is the description of the deer-chase on the lake, in the twenty-seventh chapter of *The Pioneers*. Indeed, this whole novel is full of the finest expressions of the author's genius. Into none of his works has he put more of the warmth of personal feeling and the glow of early recollection. His own heart beats through every line. The fresh breezes of the morning of life play round its pages, and its unexhaled dew hangs upon them. It is colored throughout with the rich hues of sympathetic emotion. All that is attractive in pioneer life is reproduced with substantial truth; but the pictures are touched with those finer lights which time pours over the memories of childhood. With what spirit and power all the characteristic incidents and scenes of a new settlement are described,—pigeon shooting, bass fishing, deer-hunting, the making of maple-sugar, the turkey shooting at Christmas, the sleighing-parties in winter! How distinctly his landscapes are painted,—the deep, impenetrable forest, the gleaming lake, the crude aspect and absurd architecture of the new-born village! How full of poetry in the ore is the conversation of Leatherstocking! The incongruities and peculiarities of social life which are the result of a sudden rush of population into the wilderness are also well sketched; though with a pencil less free and vivid than that with which he paints the aspects of Nature and the movements of natural man. As respects the structure of the story, and the probability of the incidents, the novel is open to criticism; but such is the fascination that hangs over it, that it is impossible to criticize. To do this would be as ungracious as to correct the language and pronunciation of an old friend who revives by his conversation the fading memories of school-boy and college life.

Cooper would have been a better writer, if he had had more of the quality of humor, and a keener sense of the ridiculous; for these would have saved him from his too frequent practice of introducing both into his narrative and his conversations, but more often into the latter, scraps of commonplace morality, and bits of sentiment so long worn as to have lost all their gloss. In general, his genius does not appear to advantage in dialogue. His characters have not always a due regard to the brevity of human life. They make long speeches, preach dull sermons, and ventilate very self-evident propositions with great solemnity of utterance. Their discourse wants not only compression, but seasoning. They are sometimes made to talk in such a way that the force of caricature can hardly go farther. For instance, in *The Pioneers*, Judge Temple, coming into a room in his house, and seeing a fire of maple-logs, exclaims to Richard Jones, his kinsman and factotum,—"how often have I forbidden the use of the sugar-maple in my dwelling! The sight of that sap, as it *exudes* with the heat, is painful to me, Richard." And in another place, he is made to say to his daughter,—"Remember the heats of July, my daughter; nor venture farther than thou canst *retrace before the meridian*." We may be sure that no man of woman born, in finding fault about the burning of maple-logs, ever talked of the sap's "exuding"; or, when giving a daughter a caution against walking too far, ever translated getting home before noon into "retracing before the meridian." This is almost as bad as Sir Piercie Shafton's calling the cows "the milky mothers of the herds."[353]

So, too, a lively perception of the ludicrous would have saved Cooper from certain peculiarities of phrase and awkwardnesses of expression, frequently occurring in his novels, such as might easily slip from the pen in the rapidity of composition, but which we wonder should have been overlooked in the proof-sheet. A few instances will illustrate our meaning. In the elaborate description of the personal charms of Cecilia Howard, in the tenth chapter of *The Pilot*, we are told of "a small hand which *seemed to blush at its own naked beauties*." In *The Pioneers*, speaking of the head and brow of Oliver Edwards, he says,—"The very air and manner with which the member *haughtily maintained itself* over the coarse and even wild attire," etc. In *The Bravo*, we read,—"As the stranger passed, his *glittering organs rolled over* the persons of the gondolier and his companion," etc.; and again, in the same novel, — "The packet was received calmly, though *the organ* which glanced at its seal," etc. In *The Last of the Mohicans*, the complexion of Cora appears "charged with the color of the rich blood that *seemed ready to burst its bounds*." These are but trivial faults; and if they had not been so easily corrected, it would have been hypercriticism to notice them.

Every author in the department of imaginative literature, whether of prose or verse, puts more or less of his personal traits of mind and character into his writings. This is very true of Cooper; and much of the worth and popularity of his novels is to be ascribed to the unconscious expressions and revelations they give of the estimable and attractive qualities of the man. Bryant, in his admirably written and discriminating biographical sketch, originally pronounced as a eulogy, and now prefixed to *Precaution* in Townsend's edition, relates that a distinguished man of letters, between whom and Cooper an unhappy coolness had for some time existed, after reading *The Pathfinder,* remarked,—"They may say what they will of Cooper, the man who wrote this book is not only a great man, but a good man." This is a just tribute; and the impression thus made by a single work is confirmed by all. Cooper's moral nature was thoroughly sound, and all his moral instincts were right. His writings show in how high regard he held the two great guardian virtues of courage in man and purity in woman. In all his novels we do not recall a single expression of doubtful morality. He never undertakes to enlist our sympathies on the wrong side. If his good characters are not always engaging, he never does violence to virtue by presenting attractive qualities in combination with vices which in real life harden the heart and coarsen the taste. We do not find in his pages those moral monsters in which the finest sensibilities, the richest gifts, the noblest sentiments are linked to heartless profligacy, or not less heartless misanthropy. He never palters with right; he enters into no truce with wrong; he admits of no compromise on such points. How admirable in its moral aspect is the character of Leatherstocking! he is ignorant, and of very moderate intellectual range or grasp; but what dignity, nay, even grandeur, is thrown around him from his noble moral qualities,—his undeviating rectitude, his disinterestedness, his heroism, his warm affections! No writer could have delineated such a character so well who had not an instinctive and unconscious sympathy with his intellectual offspring. Praise of the same kind belongs to Long Tom Coffin, and Antonio, the old fisherman.[354] The elements of character—truth, courage, and affection—are the same in all. Harvey Birch and Jacopo Frontoni are kindred conceptions: both are in a false relation to those around them; both assume a voluntary load of obloquy; both live and move in an atmosphere of suspicion and distrust; but in both the end sanctifies and exalts the means; the element of deception in both only adds to the admiration finally awakened. The carrying out of conceptions like these—the delineation of a character that perpetually weaves a web of untruth, and yet through all maintains our respect, and at last secures our reverence—was no easy task; but Cooper's success is perfect.

Cooper was fortunate in having been born with a vigorous constitution, and in having kept through life the blessing of robust health. He never suffered from remorse of the stomach or protest of the brain and his writings are those of a man who always digested his dinner and never had a headache. His novels, like those of Scott, are full of the breeze and sunshine of health. They breathe of manly tastes, active habits, sound sleep, a relish for simple pleasures, temperate enjoyments, and the retention in manhood of the fresh susceptibilities of youth. His genius is thoroughly masculine. He is deficient in acute perception, in delicate discrimination, in fine analysis, in the skill to seize and arrest exceptional peculiarities; but he has in large measure the power to present the broad characteristics of universal humanity. It is to this power that he owes his wide popularity. At this moment, in every public and circulating library in England or America, the novels of Cooper will be found to be in constant demand. He wrote for the many, and not for the few; he hit the common mind between wind and water; a delicate and fastidious literary appetite may not be attracted to his productions, but the healthy taste of the natural man finds therein food alike convenient and savory.

In a manly, courageous, somewhat impulsive nature like Cooper's we should expect to find prejudices; and he was a man of strong prejudices. Among others, was an antipathy to the people of New England. His characters, male and female, are frequently Yankees, but they are almost invariably caricatures; that is, they have all the unamiable characteristics and unattractive traits which are bestowed upon the people of New England by their ill-wishers. Had he ever lived among them, with his quick powers of observation and essentially kindly judgment of men and life, he could not have failed to correct his misapprehensions, and to perceive that he had taken the reverse side of the tapestry for the face.

Cooper, with a very keen sense of injustice, conscious of inexhaustible power, full of vehement impulses, and not largely endowed with that safe quality called prudence, was a man likely to get involved in controversies. It was his destiny, and he never could have avoided it, to be in opposition to the dominant public sentiment around him. Had he been born in Russia, he could hardly have escaped a visit to Siberia; had he been born in Austria, he would have wasted some of his best years in Spielberg. Under a despotic government he would have been a vehement Republican; in a Catholic country he would have been the most uncompromising of Protestants. He had full faith in the institutions of his own country; and his large heart, hopeful temperament, and robust soul made him a Democrat; but his democracy had not the least tinge of radicalism. He believed that man had a right to govern himself, and that he was capable of self-government; but government, the subordination of impulse to law, he insisted upon as rigorously as the veriest monarchist or aristocrat in Christendom. He would have no authority that was not legitimate; but he would tolerate no resistance to legitimate authority. All his sentiments, impulses, and instincts were those of a gentleman; and vulgar manners, coarse habits, and want of respect for the rights of others were highly offensive to him. When in Europe, he resolutely, and at no little expense of time and trouble, defended America from unjust imputations and ignorant criticism; and when at home, with equal courage and equal energy, he breasted the current of public opinion where he deemed it to be wrong, and resisted those most formidable invasions of right, wherein the many combine to oppress the one. His long controversy with the press was too important an episode in his life to be passed over by us without mention; though our limits will not permit us to make anything more than a passing allusion to it. The opinion which will be formed upon Cooper's course in this matter will depend, in a considerable degree, upon the temperament of the critic. Timid men, cautious men, men who love their ease, will call him Quixotic, rash, imprudent, to engage in a controversy in which he had much to lose and little to gain; but the reply to such suggestions is, that, if men always took counsel of indolence, timidity, and selfishness, no good would ever be accomplished, and no abuses ever be reformed. Cooper may not have been judicious in everything he said and did; but that he was right in the main, both in motive and conduct, we firmly believe. He acted from a high sense of duty; there was no alloy of vindictiveness or love of money in the impulses which moved him. Criticism the most severe and unsparing he accepted as perfectly allowable, so long as it kept within the limits of literary judgment; but any attack upon his personal character, especially any imputation or insinuation involving a moral stain, he would not submit to. He appealed to the laws of the land to vindicate his reputation and punish his assailants. Long and gallant was the warfare he maintained,—a friendless, solitary warfare,—and all the hydra-heads of the press hissing and ejaculating their venom upon him,—with none to stand by his side and wish him God-speed. But he persevered, and, what is more, he succeeded: that is to say, he secured all the substantial fruits of success. He vindicated the principle for which he contended: he compelled the newspapers to keep within the pale of literary criticism; he confirmed the saying of President Jackson, that "desperate courage makes one a majority."

Two of his novels, *Homeward Bound* and *Home as Found,* bear a strong infusion of the feelings which led to his contest with the press. After the publication of these, he became much interested in the well-known Anti-Rent agitation by which the State of New York was so long shaken; and three of his novels, *Satanstoe, The Chainbearer,* and *The Redskins,* forming one continuous narrative, were written with reference to this subject. Many professed novel-readers are, we suspect, repelled from these books, partly because of this continuity of the story, and partly because they contain a moral; but we assure them, that, if on these grounds they pass them by, they lose both pleasure and profit. They are written with all the vigor and spirit of his prime; they have many powerful scenes and admirably drawn characters; the pictures of colonial life and manners in *Satanstoe* are animated and delightful; and in all the legal and ethical points for which the author contends he is perfectly right. In his Preface to *The Chainbearer* he says,—"In our view, New York is at this moment a disgraced State; and her disgrace arises from the fact that her laws are trampled under foot, without any efforts—at all commensurate with the object being made to enforce them." That any commonwealth is a disgraced State against which such charges can with truth be made no one will deny; and any one who is familiar with the history of that wretched business will agree, that, at the time it was made, the charge was not too strong. Who can fail to admire the courage of the man who ventured to write and print such a judgment as the above against a State of which he was a native, a citizen, and a resident, and in which the public sentiment was fiercely the other way? Here, too, Cooper's motives were entirely unselfish: he had almost no pecuniary interest in the question of Anti-Rentism; he wrote all in honor, unalloyed by thrift. His very last novel, *The Ways of the Hour,* is a vigorous exposition of the defects of the trial by jury in cases where a vehement public sentiment has already tried the question, and condemned the prisoner. The story is improbable, and the leading character is an impossible being; but the interest is kept up to the end,—it has many most impressive scenes,—it abounds with shrewd and sound observations upon life, manners, and politics,—and all the legal portion is stamped with an acuteness and fidelity to truth which no professional reader can note without admiration.

Cooper's character as a man is the more admirable to us because it was marked by strong points which are not common in our country, and which the institutions of our country do not foster. He had the courage to defy the majority: he had the courage to confront the press: and not from the sting of ill-success, not from mortified vanity, not from wounded self-love, but from an heroic sense of duty. How easy a life might he have purchased by the cheap virtues of silence, submission, and acquiescence! Booksellers would have enriched him; society would have caressed him; political distinction would have crowned him: he had only to watch the course of public sentiment, and so dispose himself that he should seem to lead where he only followed, and all comfortable things would have been poured into his lap. But he preferred to breast the stream, to speak ungrateful truths. He set a wholesome example in this respect; none the less valuable because so few have had the manliness and self-reliance to imitate him. More than twenty years ago De Tocqueville said,—"I know of no country in which there is so little true independence of mind and freedom of discussion as in America": words which we fear are not less true today than when they were written.[355] Cooper's dauntless courage would have been less admirable, had he been hard, cold, stern, and impassive: but he was none of these. He was full of warm affections, cordial, sympathetic, and genial; he had a woman's tenderness of heart; he was the most faithful of friends; and in his own home no man was ever more gentle, gracious, and sweet. The blows he received fell upon a heart that felt them keenly; but he bared his breast none the less resolutely to the contest because it was not protected by an armor of insensibility.

But we must bring this long paper to a close. We cannot give to it the interest which comes from personal recollections. We saw Cooper once, and but once. This was the very year before he died, in his own home, and amid the scenes which his genius has made immortal. It was a bright midsummer's day, and we walked together about the village, and around the shores of the lake over which the canoe of Indian John had glided. His own aspect was as sunny as that of the smiling heavens above us; age had not touched him with its paralyzing finger: his vigorous frame, elastic step, and animated glance gave promise of twenty years more of energetic life. His sturdy figure, healthy face, and a slight bluffness of manner reminded one more of his original profession than of the life and manners of a man of letters. He looked like a man who had lived much in the open air,—upon whom the rain had fallen, and against whom the wind had blown. His conversation was hearty, spontaneous, and delightful from its frankness and fulness, but it was not pointed or brilliant; you remembered the healthy ring of the words, but not the words themselves. We recollect, that, as we were standing together on the shores of the lake,— shores which are somewhat tame, and a lake which can claim no higher epithet than that of pretty,—he said: "I suppose it would be patriotic to say that this is finer than Como, but we know that it is not." We found a chord of sympathy in our common impressions of the beauty of Sorrento, about which, and his residence there, he spoke with contagious animation. Who could have thought that that rich and abundant life was so near its close? Nothing could be more thoroughly satisfying than the impression he left in this brief and solitary interview. His air and movement revealed the same manly, brave, true-hearted, warm-hearted man that is imaged in his books. Grateful are we for the privilege of having seen, spoken with, and taken by the hand the author of *The Pathfinder* and *The Pilot*: "it is a pleasure to have seen a great man." Distinctly through the gathering mists of years do his face and form rise up before the mind's eye: an image of manly self-reliance, of frank courage, of generous impulse; a frank friend, an open enemy; a man whom many misunderstood, but whom no one could understand without honoring and loving.

26

WAR AND LITERATURE

John Weiss

Atlantic Monthly (1862).

John Weiss (1818-1879), Unitarian minister and literary critic, was born in Massachusetts. His translations of Schiller (1845) played a crucial role in the introduction of the literature of German idealism into New England.

It would be a task worthy of a volume, and requiring that space in order to be creditably performed, to show how war affects literature, at what points they meet, where they are at variance, if any wars stimulate, and what kinds depress the intellectual life of nations. The subject is very wide. It would embrace a discussion of the effects of war when it occurs during a period of great literary and artistic splendor, as in Athens and in the Italian Republics; whether intellectual decline is postponed or accelerated by the interests and passions of the strife; whether the preliminary concentration of the popular heart may claim the merit of adding either power or beauty to the intellectual forms which bloom together with the war.

These things are not entirely clear, and the experience of different countries is conflicting. The Thirty Years' War, though it commenced with the inspiration of great political and religious ideas, did not lift the German mind to any new demonstrations of truth or impassioned utterances of the imagination.[356] The nation sank away from it into a barren and trivial life, although the war itself occasioned a multitude of poems, songs, hymns, and political disquisitions. The hymns of this period, which are filled with a sense of dependence, of the greatness and awfulness of an invisible eternity, and breathe a desire for the peaceful traits of a remote religious life, are at once a confession of the weariness of the best minds at the turmoil and uncertainty of the contest and a permanent contribution of the finest kind to that form of sacred literature. But princes and electors were fighting as much for the designation and establishment of their petty nationalities, which first checkered the map of Europe after the imperial Catholic power was rolled southwardly, as they were for the pure interest of Protestantism. The German intellect did eventually gain something from this political result, because it interrupted the literary absolutism which reigned at Vienna; no doubt literature grew more popular and German, but it did not very strikingly improve the great advantage, for there was at last exhaustion instead of a generously nourishing enthusiasm, and the great ideas of the period became the pieces with which diplomatists carried on their game. The *Volkslied* (popular song) came into vogue again, but it was not so fresh and natural as before; Opitz, one of the best poets of this period, is worth reading chiefly when he depicts his sources of consolation in the troubles of the time.[357] Long poetical bulletins were written, in the epical form, to describe the battles and transactions of the war. They had an immense circulation, and served the place of newspapers. They were bright and characteristic enough for that; and indeed newspapers in Germany date from this time, and from the doggerel broadsides of satire and description which then supplanted minstrels of whatsoever name or guild, as they were carried by post, and read in every hamlet.* But the best of these poems were pompous, dull, and tediously elaborated. They have met the fate of newspapers, and are now on file. The more considerable poets themselves appeared to be jealous of the war; they complained bitterly that Mars had displaced Apollo; but later readers regret the ferocious sack of Magdeburg, or the death of Gustavus Adolphus, more than the silencing of all those pens.[358]

On the other hand, Spain, while fighting for religion and a secure nationality, had her Cervantes, Lope de Vega, and Calderon, all of whom saw service in the field, and other distinguished names, originators of literary forms and successful cultivators of established ones.[359] They created brilliant epochs for a bigoted and cruel country. All that was noble or graceful in the Spanish spirit survives in works which that country once stimulated through all the various fortunes of popular wars. But they were not wars for the sake of the people; the country has therefore sunk away from the literature which foretold so well how great she might have become, if she had been fortunate enough to represent, or to sympathize with, a period of moral and spiritual ideas. Her literary forms do not describe growth, but arrested development.

A different period culminated in the genius of Milton, whose roots were in that golden age when England was flowering into popular freedom. He finally spoke for the true England, and expressed the vigorous thoughts which a bloody epoch cannot quench. Some of his noblest things were inspired by the exigencies of the Commonwealth, which he saw "as an eagle nursing her mighty youth, and kindling her undazzled eyes at the full mid-day beam."[360]

---

* Newspapers proper appeared as early as 1615 in Germany. But these rhymed gazettes were very numerous. They were more or less bulky pamphlets, with pithy sarcastic programmes for titles, and sometimes a wood or copper cut prefixed. A few of them of Catholic origin, and one, entitled *Pest-Bote,* (*The Express,*) is quite as good as anything issued by the opposite party.

The Dutch people, in their great struggle against Philip II, seemed to find a stimulus in the very exhaustions of war.[361] The protesting ideas for which they fought drew fresh tenacity from the soil, wet with blood and tears, into which generous passion and resolution sank with every death. Here it is plain that a milder conflict, carried on by intrigue and diplomatic forms alone, for peaceable separation from the Catholic interest, would not have so quickened the intelligence which afterwards nourished so many English exiles and helped to freight the *Mayflower*. And we see the German mind first beginning to blossom with a language and a manifold literature during and after the Seven Years' War, which developed a powerful Protestant State and a native German feeling. Frederic's Gallic predilections did not infect the country which his arms had rendered forever anti-Gallic and anti-Austrian.[362] The popular enthusiasm for himself, which his splendid victories mainly created, was the first instinctive form of the coming German sense of independence. The nation's fairest period coincided with the French Revolution and the aggressions of the Empire. *Hermann and Dorothea* felt the people's pulse, which soon beat so high at Jena and Leipsic with rage and hope.[363] The hope departed with the Peace of 1815, and pamphleteering, pragmatic writing, theological investigation, historical research, followed the period of creative genius, whose flowers did not wither while the fields ran red.[364]

A war must be the last resort of truly noble and popular ideas, if it would do more than stimulate the intelligence of a few men, who write best with draughts of glory and success. It must be the long-repressed understanding of a nation suffused with strong primitive emotions, that flies to arms to secure the precious privilege of owning and entertaining its knowledge and its national advantages. And in proportion as any war has ever been leavened with the fine excitement of religion or humanity, however imperfectly, and though tyrannized over by political selfishness, we can see that the honest feeling has done something to obliterate the traces of violence, to offer the comfort of worth in the cause to wounded lips. When the people themselves take to fighting, not for dynastic objects to secure the succession of an Infant to the throne, to fix a Pope in his chair, or to horse a runaway monarch around their necks, not to extort some commercial advantage, or to resist a tampering with the traditional balance of power, but to drive back the billows of Huns or Turks from fields where cities and a middle class must rise, to oppose citizen-right to feudal-right, and inoculate with the lance-head Society with the popular element, to assert the industrial against the baronial interest, or to expel the invader who forages among their rights to sweep them clean and to plant a system which the ground cannot receive, then we find that the intense conviction, which has been long gathering and brooding in the soul, thunders and lightens through the whole brain, and quickens the germs of Art, Beauty and Knowledge. Then war is only a process of development, which threatens terribly and shakes the locks upon its aegis in the face of the brutes which in fest its path. Minerva is aware that wisdom and common sense will have to fight for recognition and a world: she fends blows from her tranquil forehead with the lowering crest; the shield is not always by her side, nor the sword-point resting on the ground. What is so vital as this armed and conscious intelligence? The pen, thus tempered to a sword, becomes a pen again, but flows with more iron than before.

But the original intellectual life begins while the pen is becoming tempered in the fires of a great national controversy, before it is hard enough to draw blood. Magnetic streams attract each slender point to a centre of prophesying thought long before the blood-red aurora stains suddenly the midnight sky and betrays the influence which has been none the less mighty because it has been colorless. Sometimes a people says all that it has in its mind to say, during that comfortless period while the storm is in the air and has not yet precipitated its cutting crystals. The most sensitive minds are goaded to express emphatically their moral feeling and expectation in such a rude climate, which stimulates rather than depresses, but which is apt to fall away into languor and content. This only shows that the people have no commanding place in history, but are only bent upon relieving themselves from sundry annoyances, or are talking about great principles which they are not in a position, from ethnical or political disability, to develop. Such is all the Panslavic literature which is not Russian.* But sometimes a people whose intellect passes through a noble pre-revolutionary period, illustrating it by impetuous eloquence, indignant lyrics, and the stern lines which a protesting conscience makes upon the faces of the men who are lifted above the crowd, finds that its ideas reach beyond the crisis in its life into a century of power and beauty, during which its emancipated tendency springs forward, with graceful gestures, to seize every spiritual advantage. Its movements were grand and impressive while it struggled for the oppor-

---

* Some cultivated Bohemians who can recall the glories of Ziska [John Ziska, c.1370-1424] and his chiefs, and who comprehend the value of the tendency which they strove to represent, think that there would have grown a Bohemian people, a great centre of Protestant and Slavonic influence, if it had not been for the Battle of Weissenberg in 1620, when the Catholic Imperialists defeated their King Frederic [Frederick V (1596-1632), or Frederick I (elector Palatine of the Rhine)]. A verse of a popular song, *The Patriot's Lament*, runs thus, in Wratislaw's translation [Henry Albert Wratislaw, 1822-1892]:

> Cursed mountain, mountain white!
> Upon thee was crushed our might;
> What in thee lies covered o'er
> Ages cannot back restore.

If there had been a Bohemian people, preserving a real vital tendency, the Battle of the White Mountain would have resulted differently, even had it been a defeat. [In this battle, Catholic forces prevailed at the gates of Prague, and Bohemia was delivered into the hands of the Holy Roman Emperor, Ferdinand II (1578-1637.]

Other patriots, cultivated enough to be Panslavists, indulge a more cheerful vein. They see a good time coming, and raise the cry of *Hej Slovanè*!

> Hey, Slavonians! our Slavonic language still is living,
> Long as our true loyal heart is for our nation striving;
> Lives, lives, the Slavonic spirit, and 't will live forever:
> Hell and thunder! vain against us all your rage shall shiver.

This is nothing but a frontier feeling. The true Slavonic centre is at St. Petersburg; thence will roll a people and a language over all kindred ground.

tunity to make known the divine intent that inspired it; but when the fetters burst, and every limb enjoys the victory and the release, the movements become unbounded, yet rhythmical, like Nature's, and smite, or flow, or penetrate, like hers. To such a people war comes as the disturbance of the earth's crust which helps it to a habitable surface and lifts fair slopes to ripen wine and grain.

After all, then, we must carefully discover what a war was about, before we can trace it, either for good or for evil, into the subsequent life of a nation. There can be such thing as exhaustion or deterioration, if the eternal laws have won the laurel of a fight; for they are fountains of youth, from which new blood comes rushing through the depleted veins. And it soon mantles on the surface, to mend the financial and industrial distress. Its blush of pride and victory announces no heady passion. It is the signal which Truth waves from the hearts of her children.

If we wish directly to consider the effect of war upon our own intellectual development, we must begin by asking what ideas of consequence are suggested by our copious use of the word Country. What a phrase is that—Our Country—which we have been accustomed for eighty years to use upon all festivals that commemorate civic rights, with flattering and pompous hopes! We never understood what it meant, till this moment which threatens to deprive us of the ideas and privileges which it really represents. We never appreciated till now its depth and preciousness. Orators have built up, sentence by sentence, a magnificent estimate of the elements which make our material success, and they thought it was a patriotic chord which they touched with the climax of their fine periods. It was such patriotism as thrives in the midst of content and satisfactory circumstances, which loves to have an inventory made of all the fixtures and conveniences and the crude splendor of a country's housekeeping,—things which are not indeed to be despised, for they show what a people can do when cast upon their own resources, at a distance from Governmental interference, free to select their own way of living, to be fervent in business, in charities, in the cause of education, in the explorations which lay open new regions to the emigration of a world, in the inventiveness which gives labor new pursuits and increases the chances of poor men, in the enterprise which has made foundries, mines, workshops, manufactories, and granaries of independent States. We have loved to linger over the praises of our common schools and our voluntary system of congregational worship, to count the spires which mark every place that man clears to earn his living in. It has been pleasant to trace upon the map the great arteries of intercommunication, flowing east and west, churned by countless paddle-wheels, as they force a vast freight of wealth, material, social, intellectual, to and fro, a freshet of fertilizing life to swell every stream. We love to repeat the names which self-taught men have hewn out in rude places, with the only advantage of being members of Mankind, holding their own share in the great heart and soul of it, and making that itself more illustrious than lineage and fortune. Every element of an unexhausted soil, and all the achievements of a people let loose upon it to settle, build, sow, and reap, with no master but ambition and no dread but of poverty, and a long list of rights thrust suddenly into their hands, with

liberty to exercise them,—the right to vote, to speak, to print, to be tried by jury,—
all this margin for unfettered action, even the corresponding vastness of the country itself; whose ruggedest features and greatest distances were playthings of the
popular energy,—to love and extol these things were held by us equivalent to having a native land and feeding a patriotic flame. But now all at once this catalogue of
advantages, which we were accustomed to call "our country," is stripped of all its
value, because we begin to feel that it depends upon something else, more interior
and less easy to appraise, which we had not noticed much before. Just as when
suddenly, in a favorite child, endowed with strength, beauty, and effective gifts of
every member, of whom we were proud and expected great things, and whom we
took unlimited comfort in calling our own, there appears the solemn intention of a
soul to use this fine body to express its invisible truth and honor, a wonderful revelation of a high mind filled with aspirations which we had not suspected,—a sudden
lifting of the whole body like an eyelid before an inner eye, and we are astonished at
the look it gives us so this body of comfort and success, which we worshipped as
our country, is suddenly possessed by great passions and ideas, by a consciousness
that providential laws demand the use of it, and will not be restrained from inspiring the whole frame, and directing every member of it with a new plan of Unity,
and a finer feeling for Liberty, and a more generous sense of Fraternity than ever
before. Lately we did as we pleased, but now we are going to be real children of
Liberty. Formerly we had a Union which transacted business for us, secured the
payment of our debts, and made us appear formidable abroad while it corrupted
and betrayed us at home,—a Union of colporteurs, and caucuses, and drummers of
Southern houses; not a Union, but a long coffle of patriotic laymen, southerly clergymen, and slaves. Now the soul of a Democracy, gazing terribly through eyes that
are weeping for the dead and for indignation at the cause of their dying, holds the
thing which we call Union, and determines to keep its mighty hold till it can be
informed with Unity, of which justice is the prime condition. See a Country at last,
that is, a Republican Soul, making the limbs of free states shiver with the excitement of its great ideas, turning all our comfortable and excellent institutions into
ministers to execute its will, resolved to wring the great sinews of the body with the
stress of its awakening, and to tax, for a spiritual purpose, all the material resources
and those forms of liberty which we had pompously called our native land. A people in earnest, smarting with the wounds of war and the deeper inflictions of
treachery, is abroad seeking after a country. It has been repeating with annual con-
gratulations for eighty years the self-evident truths of the document which declared
its independence; now it discovers that more evidence of it is needed than successful trading and building can bring, and it sends it forth afresh, with half a million of
glittering specialities to enforce its doctrines, while trade, and speculation, and all
the ambitions of prosperous men, and delicately nurtured lives, and other lives as
dearly cherished and nursed to maturity, are sent out with an imperative commission to buy, at all hazards, a real country, to exchange what is precious for the sake
of having finally what we dreamed we had before,—the most precious of all earthly

things,—a Commonwealth of God. Yes, our best things go, like wads for guns, to bid our purpose speak more emphatically, as it expresses the overruling inspiration of the hour.

Is this really the character of our war, or is it only an ideal picture of what the war might be? That depends solely upon ourselves.

Our soldiers kindle nightly their bivouac fires from East to West, and set their watch. They are the advance posts of the great idea, which is destined to make a country as it advances southwardly, and to settle it with republicans. If we put it in a single sentence, "Freedom of industry for hand and brain to all men," we must think awhile upon it before we can see what truths and temporal advantages it involves. We see them best, in this night of our distress and trial, by the soldiers' watch-fires. They encroach upon the gloom, and open it for us with hopes. They shine like the stars of a deeper sky than day affords, and we can see a land stretching to the Gulf, and lying expectant between either sea, whose surface is given to a Republic to people and civilize for the sake of Man. Whoever is born here, or whoever comes here, brought by poverty or violence, an exile from misery or from power, and whatever be his ethnological distinction, is a republican of this country because he is a man. Here he is to find safety, cooperation, and welcome. His very ignorance and debasement are to be welcomed by a country eager to exhibit the plastic power of its divine idea,—how animal restrictions can be gradually obliterated, how superstition and prejudice must die out of stolid countenances before the steady gaze of republican good-will, how ethnic peculiarities shall subserve the great plan and be absorbed by it. The country no longer will have a conventional creed, that men are more important than circumstances and governments: we always said so, but our opinion was at the mercy of a Know-Nothing club,[365] a slaveholding cabal, a selfish democracy: it will have a living faith, born with the pangs of battle, that nothing on earth is so precious as the different kinds of men. It will want them, to illustrate its pre-eminent idea, and it will go looking for them through all the neglected places of the world, to invite them in from the by-lanes and foul quarters of every race, expressly to show that man *is* superior to his accidents, by bringing their bodies into a place where their souls can get the better of them. Where can that be except where a democracy has been waging a religious war against its own great evil, and has repented in blood for having used all kinds of men as the white and black pawns in its games of selfish politics, with its own country for the board, and her peace and happiness lying in the pool for stakes? Where can man be respected best except here, where he has been undervalued most, and bitterness and blood have sprung from that contempt?

This is the first truly religious war ever waged. Can there be such a thing as a religious war? There can be wars in the interest of different theologies, and mixed wars of diplomacy and confessions of belief, wars to transfer the tradition of infallibility from a pope to a book, wars of Puritans against the divine right of kings in the Old World and the natural rights of Indians in the New, in all of which the name of God has been invoked for sanction, and Scripture has been quoted, and

Psalms uplifted on the battle-field for encouragement. And it is true that every conflict, in which there are ideas that claim their necessary development against usage
and authority, has a religious character so far as the ideas vindicate God by being
good for man. But a purely religious war must be one to restore the attributes and
prerogatives of manhood, to confirm primitive rights that are given to finite souls
as fast as they are created, to proclaim the creed of humanity, which is so far from
containing a single article of theology, that it is solely and distinctively religious
without it, because it proclaims one Father in heaven and one blood upon the
earth. Manhood is always worth fighting for, to resist and put down whatever evil
tendency impairs the full ability to be a man, with a healthy soul conscious of rights
and duties, owning its gifts, and valuing above everything else the liberty to place its
happiness in being noble and good. Every man wages a religious war, when he attacks his own passions in the interest of his own humanity. The most truly religious
thing that a man can do is to fight his way through habits and deficiencies back to
the pure manlike elements of his nature, which are the ineffaceable traces of the
Divine workmanship, and alone really worth fighting for. And when a nation imitates this private warfare, and attacks its own gigantic evils, lighted through past
deficiencies and immediate temptations by its best ideas, as its human part rallies
against its inhuman, and all the kingly attributes of a freeborn individual rise up in
final indignation against its slavish attributes, then commences the true and only
war of a people, and the only war of which we dare say, though it have the repulsive features that belong to all wars, that it is religious. But that we do say; for it is
to win and keep the unity of a country for the great purposes of mankind, a place
where souls can have their chances to work, with the largest freedom and under the
fewest disabilities, at the divine image stamped upon them,—to get here the tools,
both temporal and spiritual, with which to strike poverty and misery out of those
glorious traces, and to chisel deep and fresh the handwriting where God says, This
is a Man!

Here is a sufficient ground for expecting that intellectual as well as political
enlargement will succeed this trial of our country. It is well to think of all the approaching advantages, even those remote ones which will wear the forms of knowledge and art. For it is undeniable, that a war cannot be so just as to bring no evils in
its train,—not only the disturbance of all kinds of industry, the suppression of
some, the difficulty of diverting, at a moment's notice, labor towards new objects,—not only financial embarrassment and exhaustion, and the shadow of a
coming debt,—not the maiming of strong men and their violent removal from the
future labors of peace, nor the emotional suffering of thousands of families whose
hearts are in the field with their dear ones, tossed to and fro in every skirmish,
where the balls slay more than the bodies which are pierced: not these evils
alone,—nor the feverish excitement of eighteen millions of people, whose gifts and
intelligence are all distraught, and at the mercy of every bulletin,—nor yet the possible violations of private rights, and the over-riding of legal defences, which, when
once attempted in a state of war, is not always relinquished on the return of peace.

These do not strike us so much as the moral injury which many weak and passionate minds sustain from the necessity of destroying life, of ravaging and burning, of inflicting upon the enemy politic distresses. There will be a taint in the army and the community which will endure in the relations of pacific life. And more than half a million of men, who have tasted the fierce joy of battle, have suffered the moral privations and dangers of the camp, are to be returned suddenly to us, and cast adrift, with no hope of finding immediate employment, and hankering for some excitements to replace those of the distant field. If little truth and little conscience have been at stake, these are the reasons which make wars so demoralizing: they leave society restored to peace, but still at war within itself, infested by those strange cravings, and tempted by a new ambition, that of waging successful wars. This will be the most dangerous country on the face of the earth, after the termination of this war; for it will see its own ideas more clearly than ever before, and long to propagate them with its battle-ardors and its scorn of hypocritical foreign neutralities. We have the elements to make the most martial nation in the world, with a peculiar combination of patience and impulse, coldness and daring, the capacity to lie in watchful calm and to move with the vibrations of the earthquake. And if ever the voice of our brother, crying out to us from the ground of any country, shall sigh among the drums which are then gathering dust in our arsenals, the long roll would wake again, and the arms would rattle in that sound, which is part of the speech of Liberty. But it is useless to affirm or to deny such possibilities. It is plain, however, that we are organizing most formidable elements, and learning how to forge them into bolts. The spirit of the people, therefore, must be high and pure. The more emphatically we declare, in accordance with the truth, that this war is for a religious purpose, to prepare a country for the growing of souls, a place where every element of material success and all the ambitions of an enthusiastic people shall only provide fortunate circumstances, so that men can be educated in the freedom which faith, knowledge, and awe before the Invisible secure, the better will it be for us when peace returns. A great believing people will more readily absorb the hurts of war. Spiritual vitality will throw off vigorously the malaria which must arise from deserted fields of battle. It must be our daily supplication to feel the religious purport of the truths for which we fight. We must disavow vindictiveness, and purge our hearts of it. There must be no vulgar passion illustrated by our glorious arms. And when we say that we are fighting for mankind, to release souls and bodies from bondage, we must understand, without affectation, that we are fighting for the slaveholder himself, who knows it not, as he hurls his iron disbelief and hatred against us. For we are to have one country, all of whose children shall repeat in unison its noble creed, which the features of the land itself proclaim, and whose railroads and telegraphs are its running-hand.

How often we have enumerated and deprecated the evils of war! The Mexican War, in which Slavery herself involved us, (using the power of the Republic against which she conspired to further her conspiracy), gave us occasion to extol the benefits of peace, and to draw up a formidable indictment against the spirit which lusted for the appeal to arms.[366] We have not lusted for it, and the benefits of peace seem greater than ever; but the benefits of equity and truth seem greater than all. Show me justice, or try to make me unjust,—force upon me at the point of the sword the unspeakable degradation of abetting villainy, and I will seize the hilt, if I can, and write my protest clear with the blade, and while I have it in my hand I will reap what advantages are possible in the desolation which it makes.

Among these advantages of a war waged to secure the rights of citizenship to all souls will be the excitement of a national intellectual life, which will take on the various forms of a national literature. This is to be expected for two reasons. First, because our arms will achieve unity. By this is meant not only that there will be a real union of all the States, consequent upon an eventual agreement in great political and moral ideas, but also that this very consent will bring the different characteristic groups of the country so near together, in feeling and mutual appreciation, and with a free interchange of traits, that we shall begin to have a nationality. And there can be no literature until there is a nation; when the varieties of the popular life begin to coalesce, as all sections are drawn together towards the centre of great political ideas which the people themselves establish, there will be such a rich development of intellectual action as the Old World has not seen. Without this unity, literature may be cultivated by cliques of men of talent, who are chiefly stimulated to express themselves by observing the thought and beauty which foreign intellects and past times produced; but their productions will not spring from the country's manifold life, nor express its mighty individuality. The sections of the country which are nearest to the intelligence of the Old World will furnish the readiest writers and the most polished thinkers, until the New World dwarfs the Old World by its unity, and inspires the best brains with the collected richness of the popular heart. Up to the period of this war the country's most original men have been those who, by protesting against its evils and displaying a genius emancipated from the prescriptions of Church and State, have prophesied the revolution, and given to America the first rich foretaste of her growing mind. The thunder rolled up the sky in the orator's great periods, the lightning began to gleam in the preacher's moral indignation, the glittering steel slumbered uneasily and showed its half-drawn menace from the subtle lines of poets and essayists who have been carrying weapons these twenty years; their souls thirsted for an opportunity to rescue fair Liberty from the obscene rout who had her in durance for their purposes, and to hail her accession to a lawful throne with the rich gifts of knowledge, use, and beauty, a homage that only free minds can pay, and only when freedom claims it. We do not forget the literary activity with which a thousand ready intellects have furnished convenient food for the people: there has been no lack of books, nor of the ambition to attempt all the intellectual forms. Some of this pabulum was not good for a growing frame; the excuse for offering it may be found in the exigencies of squatter-life. We are a notable people for our attachment to the frying-pan, and there is no doubt that it is a shifty utensil: it can be slung at the saddle-bow or carried in a valise, it will bear the jolting of a corduroy road, and furnish a camp mess in the minimum of time out of material that was perhaps but a moment before sniffing or pecking at its rim. A very little blaze sets the piece of cold fat swimming, and the black cavity soon glows and splutters with extemporaneous content. But what dreams howl about the camp-fires, what hideous scalping-humor creeps from the leathery supper into the limbs and blood of the adventurous pioneer!

No better, and quite as scrofulous, has been the nourishment furnished by the rhetorical time-servers and polished conventionalists, whose gifts have been all directed against the highest good of the country's mind, to offer sweets to its crying conscience, and draughts of fierce or languid cordials to lull the uneasy moods of this fast-growing child of Liberty. Such men are fabricators of smooth speech; they have brought their gilding to put up on the rising pillars of the country, instead of strength to plant them firmly in their places and to spread the protecting roof. This period of storm will wash off their dainty work. When the clean granite stands where it should to shelter the four-and-thirty States as they walk the vast colonnades together, intent upon the great interchanges of the country's thought and work, this tinsel will not be missed; as men look upon the grave lines that assure them of security, they will rejoice that the time for the truly beautiful has arrived, and hasten to relieve the solid space with shapes as durable as the imagination which conceives.

There must be a great people before there can be a great character in its books, its instructions, or its works of art. This character is prophesied only in part by what is said and thought while the people is becoming great, and the molten constituents are sparkling as they run in to their future form. We have been so dependent upon traditional ideas that we suppose an epic, for instance, to be the essential proof that a people is alive and has something to express. Let us cease to wonder whether there will ever be an American poem, an American symphony, or an American *Novum Organon*.[367] It is a sign of weakness and subservience: and this is a period crowded with acts of emancipation. We cannot escape from the past, if we would; we have a right to inherit all the previous life of men that does not surfeit us and impede our proper work, but let us stop our unavailing sighs for Iliads. The newspaper gathers and circulates all true achievements faster than blind poets can plod round with the story. The special form of the epic answered to a state of society when the harper connected cities with his golden wire, slowly unrolling its burden as he went. Vibrations travel faster now; men would be foolish to expect that the new life will go journeying in classic vehicles. When the imagination becomes free, it can invent forms equally surprising and better adapted to the face of the country.

There is no part of this country which has not its broad characters and tendencies, different from anything ever seen before, imperfect while they are doomed to isolation, during which they show only a maimed and grotesque vitality. The religious tendency is different; the humor is different, the imagination differs from anything beyond the Atlantic. And the East differs from the West, the North from the South; and the Pacific States will have also to contribute gifts peculiar to themselves, as the silt of the Sacramento glitters unlike that of the Merrimac or the Potomac. We are not yet a People; but we have great, vivid masses of popular life, which a century of literary expression will not exhaust. All these passionate characters are running together in this general danger, having seized a weapon: they have found an idea in common, they are pervaded by their first really solemn feeling, they issue the same word for the night from East to West. The nationality thus commenced will introduce the tendency to blend in place of the tendency to keep apart, and each other's gifts will pass sympathetically from hand to hand.

The heightened life of this epoch is another cause which shall prepare a great development of intellectual forms. Excitement and enthusiasm pervade all classes of the people. All the primitive emotions of the human heart—friendship, scorn, sympathy, human and religious love—break into the liveliest expression, penetrate every quarter of society; a great river is let loose from the rugged mountain-recesses of the people; its waters, saturated with Nature's simple fertility, cover the whole country, and will not retire without depositing their renewing elements. A sincere and humble people is feeling the exigency. A million families have fitted out their volunteers with the most sumptuous of all equipments, which no Government could furnish, love, tears of anxiety and pride, last kisses and farewells, and prayers more heaven denying than a time of peace can breathe. What an invisible cloud of domestic pathos overhung for a year the course of the Potomac, and settled upon those huts and tents where the best part of home resided! what an ebb and flow of letters, bearing solemnity and love upon their surface! what anxiety among us, with all its brave housekeeping shifts, to keep want from the door while labor is paralyzed, and the strong arms have beaten their ploughshares into swords! What self-sacrifice of millions of humble wives and daughters whose works and sorrows are now refining the history of their country, and lifting the popular nobleness: they are giving *all that they are* to keep their volunteers in the field. The flag waves over no such faithfulness; its stars sparkle not like this sincerity. The feeling and heroism of the women are enough to refresh and to re-mould the generation. Like subtle lightning, the womanly nature is penetrating the life of the age. From every railroad station the ponderous train bore off its freight of living valor, amid the cheers of sympathizing thousands who clustered upon every shed and pillar, and yearned forward as if to make their tumultuous feelings the motive power to carry those dear friends away. What an ardent and unquenchable emotion! Drums do not throb like these hearts, bullets do not patter like these tears. There is not a power of the soul which is not vitalized and expanded by these scenes. But long after the crowd vanishes, there stands a woman at the corner, with a tired child asleep upon her shoulder the bosom does not heave so strongly as to break its sleep. There are no regrets in the calm, proud face no, indeed!—for it is the face of our country, waiting to suffer and be strong for liberty, and to put resolutely the dearest thing where it can serve mankind. In her face read the history of the future as it shall be sung and written by pens which shall not know whence their sharpened impulse springs; the page shall reflect the working of that woman's face, daughter of the people; and when exulting posterity shall draw new patriotism from it, and declare that it is proud, pathetic, resolved, sublime, they shall not yet call it by its Christian name, for that will be concealed with moss upon her forgotten head-stone.

27

OBSERVATIONS ON OUR LITERARY PROSPECTS

Samuel D. Davies

Southern Literary Messenger (1863).

Samuel D. Davies, lawyer, poet, and literary critic, was born in Virginia (1839); he wrote some poems and numerous articles, mostly for the *Southern Literary Messenger*.

The wild Scottish heath suddenly yielding forth its brood of hidden warriors at the summons of the Alpine chieftain, may not inaptly illustrate the literary, as well as the military aspect of our own country, under the wide-spread and deeply penetrating influences which the war has all at once generated in our midst. These impulses, if we may so term them, are manifested not only in the increased industrial energy of our people, so far as it is now practiced, but the national mind also participates in the powerful and energizing vibrations which are thus propagated from a common centre.

We observe the press now plied with a degree of activity hitherto unexampled, and writers yet "to fame unknown,"[368] are constantly entering upon the various fields of literary labor, with the promise of ultimately creating for us a national literature marked by all the distinctive characteristics of the Southern temperament. It will be remarked that material and psychological phenomena, especially when appearing in conjunction with each other, seem frequently to obey the same general laws, and may often be traced to the same principle of causation. This becomes more apparent on reflecting that while we had access to the markets of the world, our domestic production, so far as it depended upon human skill, continued in a state of comparative inactivity, while original literature was so rare among us, that the appearance of a new Southern book always gave rise to no small amount of sensation. Thus the labor of other countries administered to our several wants, and we seldom had occasion to inquire into our own ability to meet them.

The war, however, by interrupting our foreign intercourse, has compelled us to draw upon our own resources and the wants of the army, furnishing the strongest of all incentives to varied and energetic exertion, have caused us to turn our attention more patiently to the different departments of mechanical labor. Accordingly, our success in eliminating from the crude materials with which nature has supplied us, the means of satisfying our most urgent necessities, is equalled only by the promise of similar success from the active manner in which our literary tendencies have revealed themselves. The same circumstances which forced us to seek within our own territorial limits, the means of gratifying our intellectual wants. But it remains to be proven what will be the future character of these wants, and what sort of means we shall have for supplying them; in other words, whether we are to have a refined and elevated national taste, and whether our literature is likely to correspond with it. That it is possible to secure these very desirable objects admits of no reasonable doubt. The natural genius of our people is susceptible of the very highest development that has ever yet been realized by the human faculties; and although the English, French and Germans, forming with us one grand ethnological family, excel us for the present in the extent of their acquirements, yet our intellectual basis is as broad and deep, our capacities for improvement are as full and diversified as theirs. It is therefore merely a question of the will with us whether we shall exhibit the same amount of intellectual power or not.

The manifold appliances for accomplishing this result, may be reduced, we think, to one general head—that is, a high standard of education. And by this we mean not only intellectual instruction, but aesthetical culture, which presupposes the introduction of art into the catalogue of our studies. We shall thus acquire what is termed good taste, and this will insure such capability for appreciative criticism as will establish the proper relation between our literature and the requirements of the public mind. This may, perhaps, be more clearly expressed by saying that the supply of literary matter will be regulated both as to quantity and quality by the nature of the demand, and in all communities, whether partially or thoroughly educated, the production must, in every respect, conform to the consumption.

Good literature will be produced and encouraged wherever the public taste is capable of rejecting the opposite, and where this delicate sense of appreciation does not exist, there we shall find the most popular style of literature to be that which it is least desirable should be so. Thus, with all their boasted superiority of refinement, our Northern enemies must confess that their literature has formed itself.

We have yet to form a literature, and it would be well for us to take warning from their example. Let us not tolerate the slightest manifestation of the "unclean spirit" of the North, but by a rigid enforcement of enlightened critical rules, regulate our literature according to the principles of good taste and sound morality.

Some special consideration, however, seems due to the subject of criticism as applicable to our literature in its present state.

Horace, in his metrical treatise *de Arte Poetica*, seemingly complains, that he should be denied the indulgence once accorded to the earlier Roman writers in the coinage and application of terms. From this incidental remark we observe that, although the art of criticism, or perhaps more properly, the *science of taste*, so far from being an innate *a priori* product of the reason, is necessarily derivative, and does not operate *ab initio*[369] with the force of regulative law, still, it finally enlarges itself into a system of general principles or rules which are subsequently applied to the very examples from which they were originally deduced. This refers more properly to the antiquated rules of epic and dramatic composition, derived from the works of Homer and the Greek tragedians. Thus we find the critic condemning at one period what received the sanction of another, and in general, exhibiting all the phenomena of improvement which belong to every other branch of science. Ennius and Varius,[370] like Chaucer, Shakespeare and others, were honored and admired as poets, even while the license and irregularity which characterized their compositions were regarded as totally incompatible with the spirit of a more enlightened esthetical culture afterwards attained, thus demonstrating, that although the science of taste rises primarily on an empirical basis, yet it seeks ultimately to bring into its service the abstract principles of beauty, harmony and truth.

The works of Homer and Shakespeare have withstood the violence of critical censure, because they everywhere bear the impress of eternal truth, and accredit themselves as authorized revelations of the Deity, so far as his purposes are discernible in the visible creations by which we are surrounded. And here we refer more particularly to that rare and accurate appreciation of human life and character, which only genius is permitted to arrive at, and which is true for every age and condition of our race. Take, for example, the character of Miranda, as portrayed in *The Tempest*, and "Elaine, the lily maid of Astolat," so tenderly and beautifully drawn in the *Idylls of the King.*[371] Mr. Tennyson doubtless is endued with a genius of extraordinary quality, but nowhere is the sublime pre-eminence of Shakespeare more strikingly illustrated than in this particular instance. Here we have two maidens, reared alike in seclusion from the world, and retaining, in unsullied purity and natural perfection, all the delicate attributes of the female character. Each is at last brought face to face with one of the opposite sex, and love, with sudden grasp, takes possession of them like a strong mysterious instinct, to which they yield at once, unable and unwilling to resist it. So far, they may be said to coincide. But Elaine no longer serves as the type of her sex; like Copperfield's Dora, she departs "from honest nature's rule" and discovers scarcely a single trait appropriate to her situation.[372] Not so, however, with Miranda; love only supplies the full measure of her development; feelings, hitherto unknown, are awakened into life, and from her childlike simplicity she rises by a sudden though graceful transition to the "divine perfection of a woman."[373] Now, the superiority of Shakespeare consists in his furnishing a more faithful portraiture of the true womanly nature than Mr. Tennyson, and we are almost convinced that we behold in it a perfect realization of the purpose which the Creator contemplated with the sex, while Elaine, not quite deformed by her too exquisite sentimentalism, delights us only as the pure embodiment of a poet's dream. The one, grand and unapproachable as the "priest of nature" strikes us with overpowering awe as he unveils the features of the Deity, while the other, less aspiring in his purpose, charms us to ecstasy with the most beautiful creations of the human imagination. Inexpressibly sweet and touching beyond question, is that mournful story of the maiden's passionate love and Lancelot's cold indifference and cruelty, but we doubt if there is now, or ever was, a woman who could truthfully admit that Elaine was a fair representative of herself.

But, to return, criticism like logic, is strictly formal; it can no more originate the elements of beauty or sublimity, than the syllogism can invent a truth which had no previous existence. This must be the work of Genius, and Genius is "law unto itself." Accordingly, the old established rules of criticism have gone into disuse, and we now judge an author, not by any particular system of principles and maxims, but according to the teachings of our own experience in the affairs of actual life. We have wisely thrown off our former allegiance to the requirements of arbitrary law, and have invested the imagination with its natural right, of freedom, without which it must ever wear an ignoble form. This is, indeed, most proper, since we often find the true and the beautiful even where the rules of logic and the maxims of nice criticism were totally unknown, and this is especially true of the productions of unenlightened ages. The precious substance, like the native diamond, really exists there, but it remains for a higher civilization to give it shape and polish. It is a commonplace truism, that in new communities, where the process of intellectual development was just commenced, and works of taste and fancy begin to make their appearance, the disposition, as well as the ability to criticize, is wholly wanting; because in such situations men are more willing to receive entertainment and instruction than to take the trouble of finding out and establishing the laws according to which they should be imparted. And fortunate it is that such is the case. The fruits of the imagination, like those of the earth, flourish and mature only under the fostering influence of favourable seasons; there must be warmth and sunlight, kindness and encouragement, or the soil remains lifeless and unproductive. Had the earliest efforts of Grecian or Roman genius been met by a chilling storm of critical censure and depreciation, it is impossible to estimate the injurious consequences which might have ensued to the interests of polite literature. No one, however gifted, would have ventured to expose himself to the animadversions of an arbitrary and unrelenting tribunal, whose judgment might have inflicted on him the penalty of irretrievable disgrace—a penalty all the more aggravated and distressing, in being thus rendered the subject of universal notoriety and comment. Probably Lord Byron's history may illustrate, in some measure, the evils arising from injudicious, or rather from unseasonable criticism, and although no harm, perhaps, was done in a purely literary point of view, yet the effects on his temper were such as might better have been averted. His song, at first, was sad or joyous, ever changing with the facile versatility of a nature fresh, impressible and unperverted. But ridicule and depreciation began the long, protracted work of his ruin; or may we not better say, they impelled his genius to those lofty and imposing manifestations which otherwise might never have immortalized his name. Most others would have been crushed into silence by the rude and ungenerous reception which met his first appearance before the public, and would have been content to pass their remaining years in the gloom of unconsoled disappointment and mortification. But he was not formed for tame submission to the arrogant retentions of an authority which he despised. His proud, defiant spirit catching strength and inspiration from the bitter feeling, of his wrongs, and the intensity of his irrepressible scorn, enabled him to blast his deriders with a sudden and overwhelming revelation of his wondrous powers, which fully vindicated his insulted genius, and settled the basis of his future fame. Yet we may not be very wrong in saying that he never recovered from the effect, of first failure, and noisy malignity with which his faults were ever sounded in his ears, but sedulously cherishing the evil passions thus aroused, he was doomed, like the unfortunate princess in the Arabian story, to perish at last in the flames of his own enkindling. Still, all are not Byrons, and if they were, it would be folly and crime to presume too much on his example. Criticism is but too apt to intimidate and discourage; it is only the intrepid who can defy its tongue, while the more modest and unpretending are forced to keep themselves in the background for fear of being made the objects of popular derision. "Courage," says Lord Jeffrey, "is at least as necessary as genius to the success of a work of fiction; since without this, it is impossible to attain that freedom and self-possession, without which no talents can ever have fair play, and far less that inward confidence and exaltation of spirit which must accompany all the higher acts of the understanding. The earlier writers had, probably, less occasion for courage to secure them these advantages, as the public was far less critical on their day, and much more prone to admiration than to derision."

Let us now endeavor to apply the foregoing observations to the present state of literature in our own country.

In this, as in the useful and ornamental arts, we have heretofore been too much disposed to rely upon external sources of supply, and at the same time to neglect our own internal development. But the manifold inconveniencies of this mistaken policy, as the sequel has in a great measure proven it to be, will teach us a salutary lesson, and we must henceforth be more attentive to domestic improvement, if we would escape a repetition of our present evils. It has been said that the general policy of governments should not be regulated exclusively, or even chiefly, so as to meet the possible exigencies of the war, but it must be confessed that the recent history of the South exhibits this doctrine in a light which renders its advantages at least questionable. We do not purpose, however, to discuss any political problem that may arise in this connection. The habit of drawing our literary supplies from foreign sources caused us to be left, at the outbreak of hostilities, without a literature, and we had no other alternative than to set about creating means for supplying the deficiency. It is enough, therefore, to state that the isolation and the necessities resulting from the war, by limiting us to our own resources and compelling us to bring them into use, have caused us to recognize the vast extent of our hitherto undeveloped strength, and have thus given an impetus and a basis to our future growth and power, that probably would not have been imparted under any other circumstances. Thus, while the great work of our commercial and political independence is progressing to its consummation, and we observe as already stated, the intellectual advancement of people assuming *pari passu*,[374] and from the same causes, a distinct and prominent shape, it becomes us to watch its tendencies and turn them in the proper direction. The active enterprize of our publishers, and the liberality with which their efforts have been seconded by the reading and writing portions of our people, claim our attention as objects worthy of no slight consideration. Indeed, there is no want of a disposition to write and publish, and this disposition was perhaps never so strongly and so generally felt as it is at the present time. We have, as it were, newly discovered the immense treasures of intellectual wealth, which have so long lain hidden in the Southern mind, and we are eagerly hastening to draw it forth in one form or other, and place it, before the public vision. Much earth will necessarily accompany the genuine metal, and much will be mistaken and circulated for it. Now, we already have among us several writers of established reputation, whose abilities compelled an acknowledgement even from the arrogance and prejudice of our Northern rivals. Yet it is equally true that a large proportion of our writers are mere beginners in the pursuit of literary honours, and cannot, therefore, be expected to give such evidences of disciplined and well-digested learning as might be required by the highest standards of taste and education. But though admitting the fact, let not those among us, who are qualified for the office of critic, undertake to check the impulse which is now at work, by testing too severely these first fruits of our national literature. We do not advocate either unlimited license on the one hand, or too great leniency on the other, but we take the liberty of advising our literary censors to exercise that wise forbearance which they have hitherto shown, until they may interfere with manifest advantage to the public interests. We believe the policy of *laissez-faire*[375] to be the proper one, just now, notwithstanding the difficulty which many less liberal and tolerant observers may experience in resisting the temptation to adopt the opposite course. Some weeds must necessarily flourish, else in plucking them up, we may destroy the delicate plants we wish to cultivate. And however desirable it may seem to purify and elevate our literature at its birth, and all at once to imbue the reading public with the spirit of a correct and highly cultivated taste, yet such an idea is simply impracticable, and these results must follow from the improving influences of the time.

But while we deprecate the application of severe criticism to remedy any seeming abuse of the privileges which are now within the reach and aim of almost every one, it must, at the same time, be obvious that a most important responsibility attaches itself to the office of the editor. It is he, and not the publisher, who is the recognized authority to whom we look for guidance and instruction in matters of a literary nature; it is he who is to provide us with intellectual food, and he is responsible for its purity and wholesomeness. And although in our present sense, his function is, merely passive; although be may simply reject a contribution without discouraging the author by unfavourable comment, he will be able, nevertheless, to exercise a very appreciable influence in elevating our literature, and keeping it up to the proper standard, by a firm adherence to the requirements of good taste in mak-

ing his selections for publication; provided, however, his contributions are so numerous and varied as to admit of such discrimination. Of course he must do the
best he can with what his contributors furnish, and if they are wanting in ability, he
at least, is not to blame. In a word, our magazines ought to contain the standard
literature of the country, and with this end in view, they should be liberally supported by all the means necessary to their success. Two lengthy poems, founded on
the war, have made their appearance here, within the last eighteen months, which, if
critically reviewed, could not be regarded as very valuable contributions to our poetical literature, and probably no editor in the South would have published them in
his pages had they been submitted to his judgment. But although they have been
placed before the public, through another medium, it is useless to pass judgment on
them now, for the reason that nothing would be gained, and it might deter others
from similar undertakings, which would possibly reflect credit on our literary character.

For the present, we must not let our requirement or our expectations run too
high, and thus find fault with what is allotted to us. When we shall have original
productions of such striking excellence, as will entitle them to be regarded as examples worthy of imitation, then we may with propriety condemn whatever falls
below the standard thus erected. This, however, will not follow immediately. In the
meantime, if we *must* exercise our critical faculties, let us do so in examining the
literary productions of Europe, as they fall into our hands, content that the domain
of letters should remain with us, as heretofore, a republic, whose honors, not too
high for the aspiration of any, may be subject to the competition of all.

Now, in regard to the immediate introduction of foreign literature into the country, it must be confessed, that, however desirable it may appear at first view, it will,
nevertheless, be attended by certain disadvantages which, we believe, will outweigh
the benefits resulting from it; this we shall endeavor to explain. Probably the finest
literature of England, France and Italy, was produced at a period when the international diffusion of literary works was far more limited than it is at the present time.
Each literature therefore, grew as a purely indigenous production deriving but little,
if any material assistance, from outward sources. But from being thus confined to
national limits and preserved for the most part from foreign intermixture, it became
essentially characterized by the peculiarities of the people, among whom it had its
origin and was thus rendered national and distinctive in its most prominent features. Until the present time, we have never had such an opportunity to form a
national literature of our own, because we have never been sufficiently restricted to
ourselves. We have, however, at least, made a start in this direction, and if we now
permit foreign books to interfere and divert us from our self-cultivation, before we
have fairly begun it, the consequence will, in all probability, be that we shall relapse
into our former state of inactivity and dependence. Yet, we shall not insist upon
this objection. Many compensating advantages may be urged in favor of such a
policy, many will, unquestionably, follow from it. The ancient Roman and modern
German literature, arose under circumstances similar to those by which our own is

now surrounded; they had to *contend against* the influences of superior intellectual culture, in the neighbouring counties. But a marked difference is observable in the final development of the two. The literature of the Romans, is so largely compounded of the Grecian element, that absolute originality can scarcely be claimed for any of it. The Germans, on the contrary, have triumphed over these disadvantages in preserving their distinctive national identity, and the poetry and philosophy which form so large a portion of it, are noble monuments to the honor of Germany, for which she is indebted to her native genius alone. Our literary history may perhaps be similar.

In comparing our literature with that of the Europeans, why is it that the former is so far inferior to the latter? The simple reason is, that we are not so well educated as they are, and this is due to one of two other reasons; either because our means of education are more limited, or because, our temper is such, that we are unwilling to expend the time and labor necessary for acquiring the proficiency of our learned contemporaries.

Sir William Hamilton, in one of his elegant essays, shows that the conditions of classical learning in a community, are more or less reducible to the degree of proficiency in the classics required for graduation and practice in the learned professions.[376] On the same rationale, will the education of a community be found to influence its literature. They are correlative and reciprocally active. Where the public taste is cultivated, there will an appropriate style of literature be required, and there will it be produced. Thus, the distinguished writers of France and England, would never consent to write after the manner of some of our mot popular authors, nor would the most highly cultivated reading classes of these two countries, be satisfied with a great deal that satisfies the corresponding classes in America. Their tastes and habits of thought, exact more liberal and elaborate exhibitions of intellectual power. It may be answered, that we have reason to congratulate ourselves on escaping the necessities which, in so crowded a population as that of England, have imposed upon many of her more noted authors the painful burdens of mental labor, to which they owed their living, no less than their celebrity. This, however, is not the case with all. Besides, if we mistake not, the English university system, far more liberal and humane than ours, affords advantages and inducements for prosecuting scientific or literary studies, which nowhere exist in our own country.

Four years' rapid passage over the academical curriculum here, brings the students to the termination of his studies, he receives his diploma and leaves the seat of learning forever. But follow him still further. If he has wealth, this immediately takes possession of his time and thoughts, and he becomes unable to interest himself in any object not connected with his business or his pleasure. If, on the other hand, he has not wealth, then whatever may be his aspirations, he must devote himself to some occupation in which the further advancement of his studies is either impossible or useless. The two general facts, the want of a disposition and the want of opportunity to explore beyond the beaten tracks of knowledge, must, while they continue, keep us far behind the rest of the world, in the pursuits of science, and we must be content to follow on and receive from others that which might be our own by the right of original discovery. It may well be asked, how long we shall remain in this state of dependence. But whether it is not exactly what might be expected from a community, not yet advanced to the second stage of its national existence; whose physical and intellectual energies, finding sufficient employment in their surroundings, have not yet given place to abstract studies, or where there is a natural insolence about us that renders us averse to undertaking the labor of original investigation, and, at the same time, make us willing to adopt the results of labors not our own, these questions we shall not attempt to answer. But we may add, that if all we owe to the natural philosophers, the metaphysicians and the philologists of England, France and Germany, were taken away from our stock of learning, we might then appreciate the extent of our deficiencies. Originality, energy and self-reliance, are what we have never shown, until the pressure of circumstances calls them forth, and nothing has ever done this so effectually as war.

Yet the glory of a successful contest against our powerful enemies, will not suffice the destiny that awaits us. Having exhibited the firmness, the energy and the heroism of the Romans, we must not be slothful in attaining that philosophic habit of thought, and that exquisitely refined taste, which must ever associate the name of Greece with all that is noble in the mind, or beautiful in the creations of art. Says Victor Hugo in a late work: "At this day, when Waterloo is only a clicking of sabres, above Blucher, Germany has Goethe, and above Wellington, England has Byron.[377] A vast uprising of ideas is peculiar to our century, and in this aurora, England and Germany have a magnificent share. They are majestic because they think. The higher plane which they bring to civilization, is intrinsic in them; it comes from themselves, and from an accident."

We forebear to follow this profound and suggestive observation to its various conclusions. *They are majestic, because they think.* This is the true solution of the problem at the hands of a philosopher. But by a law of our being, we always *feel,* before we think. Great public commotions similar to that by which we are now surrounded, and comparatively so common in Europe, cause men to undergo a succession of feelings far more deep and powerful and diversified than could ever arise in the ordinary experience of a uniform and peaceful mode of life. Men are thus brought to a more intense consciousness of their mental existence, the intellect is excited to activity and they begin to reflect and reason. Consequently such periods are generally rich in intellectual phenomena. We are now unconsciously obeying this law; our fully aroused feelings have given us a deep insight into our spiritual nature, and we there behold elements of that higher civilization which shall finally vindicate our descent from a race that destiny has appointed to hold the sceptre among men. We therefore look forward with confident anticipation to such triumphs of mind and material power as will amply compensate for our past inactivity and comparative unproductiveness.

28

JANE AUSTEN

R. C. Waterson

Atlantic Monthly (1863).

R. C. Waterson was a minister in Boston. His works include *An Address on Pauperism, its Extent, Causes, and the Best Means of Prevention* (1844) and *A Service Book for the Church of the Savior* (1846).

In the old Cathedral of Winchester stand the tombs of kings, with dates stretching back to William Rufus and Canute; here, too, are the marble effigies of queens and noble ladies, of crusaders and warriors, of priests and bishops.[378] But our pilgrimage led us to a slab of black marble set into the pavement of the north aisle, and there, under the grand old arches, we read the name of Jane Austen.[379] Many colored as the light which streams through painted windows, came the memories which floated in our soul as we read the simple inscription: happy hours, gladdened by her genius, weary hours, soothed by her touch; the honored and the wise who first placed her volumes in our hand; the beloved ones who had lingered over her pages, the voices of our distant home, associated with every familiar story.

The personal history of Jane Austen belongs to the close of the last and the beginning of the present century. Her father through forty years was rector of a parish in the South of England.[380] Mr. Austen was a man of great taste in all literary matters; from him his daughter inherited many of her gifts. He probably guided her early education and influenced the direction of her genius. Her life was passed chiefly in the country. Bath, then a fashionable watering-place, with occasional glimpses of London, must have afforded all the intercourse which she held with what is called "the world." Her travels were limited to excursions in the vicinity of her father's residence. Those were days of post-chaises and sedan-chairs, when the rush of the locomotive was unknown. Steam, that genie of the vapor, was yet a little household elf singing pleasant tunes by the evening fire, at quiet hearthstones; it has since expanded into a mighty giant, whose influences are no longer domestic. The circles of fashion are changed also. Those were the days of country dances and India muslins; the beaux and belles of "the upper rooms" at Bath knew not the whirl of the waltz, nor the ceaseless involvements "of the German." Yet the measures of love and jealousy, of hope and fear, to which their hearts beat time, would be recognized to-night in every ballroom. Infinite sameness, infinite variety, are not more apparent in the outward than in the inward world, and the work of that writer will alone be lasting who recognizes and embodies this eternal law of the great Author.

Jane Austen possessed in a remarkable degree this rare intuition. The following passage is found in Sir Walter Scott's journal, under date of the fourteenth of March, 1826:

> Read again, and for the third time at least, Miss Austen's finely written novel of "Pride and Prejudice."[381] That young lady had a talent for describing the involvements and feelings and characters of ordinary life, which is to me the most wonderful I ever met with. The Big Bow-wow strain I can do myself like any now going; but the exquisite touch which renders ordinary commonplace things and characters interesting from truth of the description and the sentiment is denied to me.[382]

This is high praise, but it is something more when we recur to the time at which Sir Walter writes this paragraph. It is amid the dreary entries in his journal of 1826, many of which make our hearts ache and our eyes overflow. He read the pages of Jane Austen on the fourteenth of March, and on time fifteenth he writes, "This morning I leave 39 Castle Street for the last time." It was something to have written a book sought for by him at such a moment. Even at Malta, in December, 1831, when the pressure of disease, as well as of misfortune, was upon him, Sir Walter was often found with a volume of Miss Austen in his hand, and said to a friend, "There is a finishing-off in some of her scenes that is really quite above everybody else."

Jane Austen's life world presented such a limited experience that it is marvellous where she could have found the models from which she studied such a variety of forms. It is only another proof that the secret lies in the genius which seizes, not in the material which is seized. We have been told by one who knew her well, that Miss Austen never intentionally drew portraits from individuals, and avoided, if possible, all sketches that could be recognized. But she was so faithful to Nature, that many of her acquaintance, whose characters had never entered her mind, were much offended, and could not be persuaded that they or their friends had not been depicted in some of her less attractive personages: a feeling which we have frequently shared; for, as the touches of her pencil brought out the light and shades very quietly, we have been startled to recognize our own portrait come gradually out on the canvas, especially since we are not equal to the courage of Cromwell, who said, "Paint me as I am."

In the *Autobiography* of Sir Egerton Brydges we find the following passage: it is characteristic of the man:—

> I remember Jane Austen, the novelist, a little child. Her mother was a Miss Leigh, whose paternal grandmother was a sister of the first Duke of Chandos. Mr. Austen was of a Kentish family, of which several branches have been settled in the Weald, and

some are still remaining there. When I knew Jane Austen, I never suspected she was an authoress; but my eyes told me that she was fair and handsome, slight and elegant, with cheeks a little too full. The last time, I think, I saw her was at Ramsgate, in 1803; perhaps she was then about twenty-seven years old. Even then I did not know that she was addicted to literary composition.[383]

We can readily suppose that the spheres of Jane Austen and Sir Egerton could not be very congenial; and it does not appear that he was ever tempted from the contemplation of his own performances, to read her "literary compositions." A letter from Robert Southey to Sir Egerton shows that the latter had not quite forgotten her. Southey writes, under the date of Keswick, April, 1830:—

> You mention Miss Austen; her novels are more true to Nature, and have (for my sympathies) passages of finer feeling than any others of this age. She was a person of whom I have heard so much, and think so highly, that I regret not having seen her, or ever having had an opportunity of testifying to her the respect which I felt for her.

A pleasant anecdote, told to us on good authority in England, is illustrative of Miss Austen's power over various minds. A party of distinguished literary men met at a country-seat; among them was Macaulay, and, we believe, Hallam;[384] at all events, they were men of high reputation. While discussing the merits of various authors, it was proposed that each should write down the name of that work of fiction which had given him the greatest pleasure. Much surprise and amusement followed; for, on opening the slips of paper, seven bore the name of *Mansfield Park*,—a coincidence of opinion most rare, and a tribute to an author unsurpassed.[385]

Had we been of that party at the English country-house, we should have written, "The *last* novel by Miss Austen which we have read"; yet, forced to a selection, we should have named *Persuasion*.[386] But we withdraw our private preference, and, yielding to the decision of seven wise men, place *Mansfield Park* at the head of the list, and leave it there without further comment.

Persuasion was her latest work, and bears the impress of a matured mind and perfected style. The language of Miss Austen is, in all her pages, drawn from the "wells of English undefiled."[387] Concise and clear, simple and vigorous, no word can be omitted that she puts down, and none can be added to heighten the effect of her sentences. In *Persuasion* there are passages whose depth and tenderness, welling up from deep fountains of feeling, impress us with the conviction that the angel of sorrow or suffering had troubled the waters, yet had left in them a healing influence, which is felt rather than revealed. Of all the heroines we have known through a long and somewhat varied experience, there is not one whose life-companionship we should so desire to secure as that of Anne Elliot. Ah! could she also forgive our faults and bear with our weaknesses, while we were animated by her sweet and noble example, existence would be, under any aspect, a blessing. This felicity was reserved for Captain Wentworth. Happy man! In *Persuasion* we also find the subtle Mr. Elliot. Here, as with Mr. Crawford in *Mansfield Park*, Miss Austen deals dexterously with the character of a man of the world, and uses a nicer discernment than is often found in the writings of women, even those who assume masculine names.

Emma we know to have been a favorite with the author.[388] "I have drawn a character full of faults," said she, "nevertheless I like her." In Emma's company we meet Mr. Knightley, Harriet Smith, and Frank Churchill. We sit beside good old Mr. Woodhouse, and please him by tasting his gruel. We walk through Highbury, we are patronized by Mrs. Elton, listen forbearingly to the indefatigable Miss Bates, and take an early walk to the post-office with Jane Fairfax. Once we found ourselves actually on "Box Hill," but it did not seem half so real as when we "explored" there with the party from Highbury.

Pride and Prejudice is piquant in style and masterly in portraiture. We make perhaps too many disagreeable acquaintances to enjoy ourselves entirely; yet who would forego Mr. Collins, or forget Lady Catherine de Bourgh, though each in their way is more stupid and odious than any one but Miss Austen could induce us to endure. Mr. Darcy's character is ably given; a very difficult one to sustain under all the circumstances in which he is placed. It is no small tribute to the power of the author to concede that she has so managed the workings of his real nature as to make it possible, and even probable, that a high-born, high-bred Englishman of Mr. Darcy's stamp could become the son-in-law of Mrs. Bennett. The scene of Darcy's declaration of love to Elizabeth, at the Hunsford Parsonage, is one of the most remarkable passages in Miss Austen's writings, and, indeed, we remember nothing equal to it among the many writers of fiction who have endeavored to describe that culminating point of human destiny.

Northanger Abbey is written in a fine vein of irony, called forth, in some degree, by the romantic school of Mrs. Radcliffe and her imitators. We doubt whether Miss Austen was not over-wise with regard to these romances. Though born after the Radcliffe era, we well remember shivering through the *Mysteries of Udolpho* with as quaking a heart as beat in the bosom of Catherine Morland. If Miss Austen was not equally impressed by the power of these romances, we rejoice that they were written, as with them we should have lost *Northanger Abbey*. For ourselves, we spent one very rainy day in the streets of Bath, looking up every nook and corner familiar in the adventures of Catherine, and time, not faith, failed, for a visit to Northanger itself. Bath was also sanctified by the presence of Anne Elliot. Our inn, the "White Hart," (made classic by the adventures of various well-remembered characters), was hallowed by exquisite memories which connected one of the rooms (we faithfully believed it was our apartment) with the conversation of Anne Elliot and Captain Harville, as they stood by the window, while Captain Wentworth listened and wrote. In vain did we gaze at the windows of Camden Place. No Anne Elliot appeared.

Sense and Sensibility was the first novel published by Miss Austen.[389] It is marked by her peculiar genius, though it may be wanting in the nicer finish which experience gave to her later writings.

The Earl of Carlisle, when Lord Morpheth, wrote a poem for some now forgotten annual, entitled "The Lady and the Novel."[390] The following lines occur among
the verses —

> Or is it thou, all-perfect Austen? here
> Let one poor wreath adorn thy early bier,
> That scarce allowed thy modest worth to claim[391]
> The living portion of thy honest fame:
> Oh, Mrs. Bennett, Mrs. Norris, too,
> While Memory survives, she'll dream of you;
> And Mr. Woodhouse, with abstemious lip,
> Must thin, but not too thin, the gruel sip;[392]
> Miss Bates, our idol, though the village bore,
> And Mrs. Elton, ardent to explore;
> While the clear style flows on without pretence,
> With unstained purity, and unmatched sense.[393]

If the Earl of Carlisle, in whose veins flows "the blood of all the Howards," is
willing to acknowledge so many of our friends, who are anything but aristocratic,
our republican soul shrinks not from the confession that we should like to accompany good-natured Mrs. Jennings in her hospitable carriage, (so useful to our young
ladies of sense and sensibility), witness the happiness of Elinor at the parsonage,
and the reward of Colonel Brandon at the manor-house of Delaford, and share
with Mrs. Jennings all the charms of the mulberry-tree and the yew arbor.

An article on "Recent Novels," in *Fraser's Magazine* for December, 1847, written
by Mr. G. H. Lewes, contains the following paragraphs:[394]

What we most heartily enjoy and applaud is truth in the delineations of life and character. .... To make our meaning precise, we would say that Fielding and Miss Austen are
the greatest novelists in our language .... We would rather have written *Pride and Prejudice*, or *Tom Jones*, than any of the "Waverley Novels." .... Miss Austen has been called
a prose Shakespeare,—and among others, by Macaulay. In spite of the sense of incongruity which besets us in the words prose Shakespeare, we confess the greatness of
Miss Austen, her marvellous dramatic power, seems, more than anything in Scott, akin
to Shakespeare.

The conclusion of this article is devoted to a review of *Jane Eyre*, and led to the
correspondence between Miss Brontë and Mr. Lewes which will be found in the
memoir of her life. In these letters it is apparent that Mr. Lewes wishes Miss Brontë
to read and to enjoy Miss Austen's works, as he does himself. Mr. Lewes is disappointed, and felt, doubtless, what all true lovers of Jane Austen have experienced, a
surprise to find how obtuse otherwise clever people sometimes are. In this instance,
however, we think Mr. Lewes expected what was impossible. Charlotte Brontë
could not harmonize with Jane Austen. The luminous and familiar star which
comes forth into the quiet evening sky when the sun sets amid the amber light of
an autumn evening, and the comet which started into sight, unheralded and unnamed, and flamed across the midnight sky, have no affinity, except in the Divine
Mind, whence both originate.

The notice of Miss Austen, by Macaulay, to which Mr. Lewes alludes, must be, we presume, the passage which occurs in Macaulay's article on Madame D'Arblay, in the *Edinburgh Review*, for January, 1843. We do not find the phrase, "prose Shakespeare," but the meaning is the same; we give the passage as it stands before us:—

> Shakespeare has neither equal nor second; but among writers who, in the point we have noticed, have approached nearest the manner of the great master, we have no hesitation in placing Jane Austen, as a woman of whom England is justly proud. She has given us a multitude of characters, all, in a certain sense, commonplace, all such as we meet every day. Yet they are all as perfectly discriminated from each other as if they were the most eccentric of human beings. There are, for example, four clergymen, none of whom we should be surprised to find in any parsonage in the kingdom,—Mr. Edward Ferrars, Mr. Henry Tilney, Mr. Edward Bertram, and Mr. Elton.[395] They are all specimens of the upper part of the middle class. They have been all liberally educated. They all lie under the restraints of the same sacred profession. They are all young. They are all in love. Not any one of them has any hobby-horse, to use the phrase of Sterne.[396] Not one has any ruling passion, such as we read in Pope. Who would not have expected them to be insipid likenesses of each other? No such thing. Harpagon is not more unlike Jourdain, Joseph Surface is not more unlike Sir Lucius O'Trigger, than every one of Miss Austen's young divines to all his reverend brethren.[397] And almost all this is done by touches so delicate that they elude analysis, that they defy the powers of description, and that we know them to exist only by the general effect to which they have contributed.

Dr. Whately, the Archbishop of Dublin, in the *Quarterly Review*, 1821, sums up his estimate of Miss Austen with these words:

> The Eastern monarch who proclaimed a reward to him who should discover a new pleasure would have deserved well of mankind, had he stipulated it should be blameless. Those again who delight in the study of human nature may improve in the knowledge of it, and in the profitable application of that knowledge, by the perusal of such fictions. Miss Austen introduces very little of what is technically called religion into her books, yet that must be a blinded soul which does not recognize the vital essence, everywhere present in her pages, of a deep and enlightened piety.

There are but few descriptions of scenery in her novels. The figures of the piece are her care; and if she draws in a tree, a hill, or a manor-house, it is always in the background. This fact did not arise from any want of appreciation for the glories or the beauties of the outward creation, for we know that the pencil was as often in her hand as the pen. It was that unity of purpose, ever present to her mind, which never allowed her to swerve from the actual into the ideal, nor even to yield to tempting descriptions of Nature which might be near, and yet aside from the main object of her narrative. Her creations are living people, not masks behind which the author soliloquizes or lectures. These novels are impersonal; Miss Austen never herself appears; and if she ever had a lover, we cannot decide whom he resembled among the many masculine portraits she has drawn.

Very much has been said in her praise, and we, in this brief article, have summoned together witnesses to the extent of her powers, which are fit and not few. Yet we are aware that to a class of readers Miss Austen's novels must ever remain sealed books. So be it. While the English language is read, the world will always be provided with souls who can enjoy the rare excellence of that rich legacy left to them by her genius.

Once in our lifetime we spent three delicious days in the Isle of Wight, and then crossed the water to Portsmouth. After taking a turn on the ramparts in memory of Fanny Price, and looking upon the harbor whence the *Thrush*[398] went out, we drove over Portsdown Hill to visit the surviving member of that household which called Jane Austen their own.[399]

We had been preceded by a letter, introducing us to Admiral Austen as fervent admirers of his sister's genius, and were received by him with a gentle courtesy most winning to our heart.

In the finely-cut features of the brother, who retained at eighty years of age much of the early beauty of his youth, we fancied we must see a resemblance to his sister, of whom there exists no portrait.

It was delightful to us to hear him speak of "Jane," and to be brought so near the actual in her daily life. Of his sister's fame as a writer the Admiral spoke understandingly, but reservedly.

We found the old Admiral safely moored in that most delightful of havens, a quiet English country-home, with the beauty of Nature around the mansion, and the beauty of domestic love and happiness beneath its hospitable roof.

There we spent a summer day, and the passing hours seemed like the pages over which we had often lingered, written by her hand whose influence had guided us to those she loved. That day, with all its associations, has become a sacred memory, and links us to the sphere where dwells that soul whose gift of genius has rendered immortal the name of Jane Austen.

29

LITERATURE, LOVE, AND MARRIAGE

Orestes A. Brownson

Boston Quarterly Review (1864).

The question we raised in our *Review* last April, as to what works are to be called literary works, may receive a more restricted answer than we give it. Literature is frequently taken by modern writers in the sense of polite literature, or what the French call *Belles-lettres.* In this more restricted sense, it does not include professional works, or works devoted specially to science or the sciences. It must express something universal, and be addressed to the common understanding and common sentiments of all cultivated readers. There is, if we may so speak, a certain universal mind in all men who think, and certain sentiments common to all men who feel. It is to these common sentiments and this universal mind that polite literature is addressed, and these it must aim to embody or express in its creations. Not that the literary man is not free to express individualities, or to describe local manners, usages, habits, and customs, but he must do it always under some relation to the common and the universal. The common and the universal are the sources of his inspiration and the principles of his judgments. These common sentiments and this universal mind embrace what goes ordinarily under the name of common sense, good sense, taste, or good taste. To determine their existence, or their authority beyond human nature as we find it, is the province of science, not of general or polite literature.

The philosopher, as we show in the foregoing essay, knows that in this universal mind, and in these common sentiments, there is the intuition of an ideal that transcends human nature, that transcends all created nature, identical with Him who is "First True, First Good, and First Fair"; without which the human mind could neither exist nor operate, the human soul neither feel nor aspire, neither know nor love. But the literary man, as such, takes no account of this, and is contented to express human nature and its ideal without looking beyond it, and to embody the best he can the intuition, the sentiments, the beliefs, the convictions which he finds to be common to all men. He practices art without giving its philosophy. He who is truest to this common and universal nature, and expresses it with the most vividness, clearness, distinctness, vigor, and energy, is the prince of literature, as the homage rendered by all men who read them, to Homer, Dante, and Shakespeare amply testifies.

As this common and universal nature is in every living and full-grown man, the true artist, whether he writes or paints, sings or sculptures, pronounces an oration or designs a temple, is he who best expressed what is truest, deepest, richest, and broadest in his own human nature. He who only copies the convictions, sentiments, or ideal of others, without having found them in himself, or made them his own by his life and experience, is unworthy of the noble name of artist, however successful he may be as a copyist or an imitator. He must draw from the well within himself, from his own inspiration, his own life and experience, his own ideal, or an ideal that he has really assimilated and made his own. So of the literary man. A literature which is simply copied or imitated from a foreign model is no literature at all, in its artistic sense. Hence, we can assign no high rank to the Italian Sannazaro, notwithstanding the exquisite beauty, rhythm, and polish of his Latin verse, for he is only a servile imitator of Virgil, and Virgil himself ranks below Lucretius, and even Ovid, to say nothing of Horace and Catullus, for he servilely copies Homer and other Greek poets.[400]

It is not meant by this, that the literary man, to be original, must say nothing that has been said before him, for that would imply that no modern can be original. It is doubtful if there remains anything to be said that has not been said a thousand times over already, and better said than any one can now say it. The author often finds, on extending his reading, that even in the very passages in which he honestly believed that he was saying something new, he had been anticipated ages ago. You can find little even in Shakespeare that is not, in some form, to be found in his predecessors. Originality does not consist in saying things absolutely new, or which no one has said before, but in expressing in our own way, from our own mind, what we ourselves have really thought, felt, or lived.

Our American literature wants, generally speaking, originality, freedom, and freshness. It lacks spontaneity, is imitative, and, for the most part, imitative of the English. Those of our writers who are free, racy, original, as some of them are, lack culture, polish, are rude and extravagant. We, as a people, are educated up to a certain point, better educated up to that point, perhaps, than any European people, but we are not highly educated nor a highly cultivated people. A certain number of our scholars, historians, poets, and novel writers have a mental and social culture that places them on a level with the cultivated men of Europe; but, in general, our easy classes have more instruction than cultivation, while our poorer classes, excluding those of European birth, if better informed, are less well trained than those even of England. In literature and art we are provincials, striving to ape metropolitan fashions. Hence our literature is constrained and stiff, and has a certain vulgar air and tone. Like the American people themselves, it lacks free, manly, independent thought. It is licentious enough, at times, in doctrine and speculation, but there is all the difference in the world between license and freedom. In many sections we can find impudence enough, not unfrequently taken for independence; but, as a people, we have very little real independence of character, far less, in fact, that we had before 1776. *What will they say?* has more influence with us than with any other people on earth. My wife has constantly the fear of Mrs. Grundy[401] before her eyes, and is afraid to consult her own taste, convenience, or means in furnishing her house, or in selecting and shaping her dresses. In politics we go with our party, and never dare think beyond it or differently from it; and hence it would be difficult to find a civilized nation on earth so destitute of scientific and thorough-bred statesmen as our own. Not a man amongst us was found, at the breaking out of the present formidable Rebellion, able to solve a single one of the great problems it presented for practical solution. We have seen no statesmanship in either the Administration or Congress, or even in any of the leading journals and periodicals of the country. In religion we believe, or do not believe, with our sect, denomination, or church, accept or reject its symbols alike without thought, without reason, and without any perception of their meaning. In literature we copy, or try to copy, the English, the French, or the German, seldom venturing to give free play to our own original powers, or even suspecting that we have any. There is even in our best literature a constant effort to conform to a foreign standard, to write or sing not as we want to write or sing, but as somebody else has written or sung. Ralph Waldo Emerson is almost the only original writer of distinction that we can boast. His friend, Theodore Parker, thought and wrote as a sectarian, and was a rhetorician and sometimes a declaimer, but never a free, original thinker, and has produced nothing that will live.[402]

We have any quantity of fictitious literature, fictitious in all the senses of the term, produced chiefly by women, and therefore weak, sentimental, preventing instead of aiding high national culture. We prize woman as highly as do any of our contemporaries, but we have no great liking for feminine literature, whichever sex has produced it. Woman has a noble and important intellectual mission, but she performs it by her conversational rather than by literary gifts. Her genius may emit flashes which penetrate even farther into the surrounding darkness than the slower intellect of man, but the light is not steady enough, and is too transient, to enable us to seize even the outlines of the objects it momentarily illumines. Man can penetrate farther and rise higher by her aid than without it. Yet even the light she flashes, and which is so serviceable to him, has been struck out by her collision with the masculine intellect, and the problems she helps to solve she could never have conceived if man had not first suggested them and prepared her to grasp them. She can aid man, but can do nothing without him. She was made for him, and in herself is only inchoate man. The effort of "our strong-minded women" to raise their sex from the position of drudge, plaything, or an article of luxury, is praiseworthy and well deserving our sympathy and co-operation; but when they go farther, and attempt to make her as independent of man as he is of her, they forget the respective provinces of the sexes, and simply attempt to reverse the laws of nature, and assign to the female of the species the office of male. It is not conventionalism, but God, that has made the man the head of the woman, and not the woman the head of the man, and every day's experience proves that the men who lend themselves to the silly woman's rights movement are precisely the men the least acceptable to women. A woman wants a man, not a woman, for her husband, and a man wants a woman, not a man, for his wife.

The curse of the age is its femininity, its lack, not of barbarism, but of virility. It is the age of woman-worship. Women are angels; men are demons. Our modern literature, not our brave old English tongue, makes all the virtues feminine and all the vices masculine. A well-formed, fair-faced, sweet-tempered and gentle-spoken woman, if young and accomplished, is an angel; her sentimental tears are angel's tears, though her heart is cold, selfish, incapable of a single generous emotion or heroic virtue,—an angel, though utterly regardless of the misery she needlessly inflicts on any accepted lover, if her caprice only calls her to suffer also. Sweet angels are the dear creatures, if we may believe modern literature, though they made all connected with them thoroughly wretched, if they have gentle manners, pretty faces, and sweet voices. Yet it must be conceded that we have no class of writers who draw so much from themselves, in their writings, as our literary women. They draw from themselves, and draw themselves, and present woman, under the veil of pretended female modesty, which prevents her from being open, frank, truthful, honest, as self-willed, capricious, passionate, rash, artful, artificial, false, servile, tyrannical, exaggerating mole-hills into mountains, and seeing every thing through the distorting medium of a morbid sensitivity. Their fault, a feminine fault, is, that they exaggerate, and write themselves down infinitely worse than they are. Though moderately well read in feminine literature, we cannot call to mind a single heroine, drawn by a female hand, that is really frank and truthful, unless it be Jane Eyre, and Dinah in *Adam Bede,* and no one that a sensible man could love or wish for his wife.[403]

But literature is the exponent of the life and character of the people who produce it. The stream cannot rise higher than its fountain. Our authors, whether male or female, have labored, and still labor, under many disadvantages. The American people have the germs of romance in them as have every people, but they have not as yet been developed. Our country is new, and our people, as a distinct, free, and independent people, have hardly, as yet, attained to a consciousness of their own existence. The materials of romance have not yet been furnished to us. We are removed from the old homestead, have lost its legends, traditions, and associations, and have too recently settled in the wilderness to have created them anew for ourselves. There is little mystery in our ordinary life, and we have, save in the South Atlantic States, acquired no deep attachment to the soil, and are, if not a nomadic race, at least a moving, and a migratory, rather than a sedentary people. We have a rich, varied, and magnificent natural scenery, though rarely equalling that of

Europe, Mexico, or South America; but no human memories hallow it, and render it either poetical or romantic, and, as a people, we are not nature-worshippers. We have not that intense love of external nature which the English have, or affect to have. We are too familiar from our childhood up with woods and fields, pastures and meadows, winding brooks, water-falls, precipices, sheep feeding, lambs frolicking, cattle browsing, partridges whirring, quails whistling, birds singing, to go into ecstasies over them. If we are capable of being impressed by them, we have seen and felt more than the poet can express in his song, or the romancer seize and embody in his description. We have our rivers, our lakes, our forests, our mountains; but these, to serve the purpose of literature, must be associated with man, and consecrated by human joy or sorrow, human affections, or the fierce struggle of human passions. The wild Indian was a resource, but it has been exhausted by Cooper; and, besides, the Indian is himself the least romantic of mortals, and the memory of his treachery, his cruelty, and the fierce struggle for life which our pioneer settlers have had to sustain with him, is too recent to be poetical or romantic. We have a glorious nature, no doubt, but it is barren of legends, traditions, human associations, unpeopled with fairies, even with dwarfs; descriptions of it soon become wearisome to the mind, fatiguing to the soul, as do our immense and treeless prairies to the eye. In traversing these prairies, we long for a hill, a tree, or anything that can break the monotony. Nature, without man, or human association, as Byron well maintained, is not poetical, and cannot sustain a literature that does not soon becoming fatiguing and repulsive. We have never been able to admire Cole's picture of *The Voyage of Life*; for, though the human is there, it is dwarfed and crushed beneath the wild and massive nature overhanging it.[404] The human is too feeble to transform it, or to clothe it with the bright and unfading hues its own immortal spirit.

Most even, who live in the cities, have been born and brought up in the country, and our cockney class, to whom nature is a novelty, is very small. Our cities themselves are mostly huge market-towns, where people congregate to trade, not to live. They are, with two or three exceptions, of which New York is not one, provincial in their tastes, manners and habits; looking to some foreign city, chiefly London or Paris, as their metropolis. The commercial spirit dominates, and the commercial spirit is always and everywhere the most positive spirit in the world, so positive and hard, that it is only by a figure of speech that we can call it a *spirit* at all. The commercial classes, engrossed in business, intent on making, increasing, or retrieving their fortunes, have little leisure, and less taste for general literature, and absorb whatever of poetry or romance they may have in their nature in business operations or hazardous speculations. Our country residents are mostly country people. They have some education, but the mass of them, even when great readers, though characterized by much natural shrewdness and quickness of apprehension, have not much mental culture, or intellectual development or refinement. Their tastes are crude and coarse, and after the journals become a necessity of American life, crave yellow-covered literature, what are called "sensation novels," or works addressed specially to the sentiments, emotions, or passions. The more cultivated, but much smaller portion, who have wealth, leisure, and taste for polite literature of a higher order, rely principally on the supply from England, France, Italy, and Germany, or content themselves with re-perusing the classics.

The Americans as a people are Colonists and *parvenus*.[405] We have never yet felt that we are a nation, with our own national metropolis. Washington is only a village where are the government offices, and where Congress meets; it gives no tone to our literature, and only partially even to our politics. Boston is more of a literary capital than Washington, but it is the capital of New England rather than of the nation. New York and Philadelphia are great book manufacturing cities, but no great literary centres, like London or Paris. New York especially is the Leipsig of America, but the population of which it is the business centre, is hardly counted by the trade in their calculations of the sale of a book. New York subscribed for just one-eighth as many copies of Agassiz's great work on the Natural History of the United States as Boston.[406] In our cities, so numerous and so wealthy before the breaking out of the rebellion, and so marked by their hurry and bustle, luxurious tastes, and frightful extravagance, the great majority of the wealthy citizens have become rich by their own exertions and successful speculations. They had sometimes, and sometimes had not, a good business education to begin with, but in general as little mental culture or refinement as wealth. Engrossed in money-getting, they have had little time and less disposition to supply their early literary deficiencies. Their brains exhausted in their business pursuits, they cannot find relaxation in a literature that makes any demands on their intellects. They must seek their relaxation either in light, flashy, emotional novels, or in gross sensual pleasures. As parvenus, we seek rather to forget than to recall our own past. We are in a position which were not born to, which we were not brought up to, and which we feel that we may at any moment lose. We do not feel ourselves at home, or settled for life; we are ill at ease; care sits on our brow, anxiety contracts and sharpens our features. We have no freedom, no leisure to cultivate the mind, to develop and purify our tastes, to find enjoyment in intellectual and spiritual pleasures. With fine original mental constitutions, with an unequalled cerebral activity, which unhappily tells on our bills of mortality, save in special or professional studies, there is perhaps no civilized people that is not above us in the higher intellectual culture, and in the development of thought. We are in this respect below Great Britain, and Great Britain is below most of the Continental nations. Even the Irish and the German peasants who migrate hither soon come to leave our old American population in the lurch, and to govern the country.

Such a public is not favorable to high literary culture, and it is no wonder that American literature is no great thing. In these days, when the public are the only literary patrons, literature of a high, generous, and ennobling character cannot be produced without a high, generous, and cultivated literary public, that finds its amusement and relaxation from business or dissipation in literature, in works of taste, in the creations of thought and imagination. As yet we have as a people no real artistic culture. The literary man is not independent of his medium. He can never be formed, by himself alone, without living, breathing, and moving in a literary atmosphere. Man cultivates man, and cultivated society is essential to the production and growth of a genuine, high-toned literature. The society and conversation of virtuous, refined, and cultivated women are also indispensable. Woman cannot be a literary man herself; but no literary man of correct taste, and of broad, elevated, and generous views and sentiments can be formed without her.

Some of these disadvantages are, no doubt, common to all modern society, so universally pervaded by what the late Emperor Nicholas so justly stigmatized as the "mercantile spirit," which makes all things venal, and estimates a man by what he has, not by that he is.[407] Worth, now-a-days, means hard cash, or what can be exchanged for hard cash. But this "mercantile spirit," which turns even religion into a speculation, and coins genius into money—of which Barnum, if a vulgar, is yet a real impersonation—is more rife in our country, and finds less to counteract or temper it than elsewhere.[408] Here it coins the blood of our brave and heroic defenders, the widow's desolation, the mother's grief, and the orphan's wail into money, which our shoddy nabobs display in the form of silks, laces, and jewellery, with which they deck out their vulgar wives and daughters, as we are learning by an experience that will, in the end, be as bitter as it has hitherto seemed sweet. It is hard for genuine literary men to be formed in such a medium, and still harder for them to find a large appreciative public. Nevertheless, our literary artists must not despair; they must struggle manfully against the false taste and false tendencies of the age and nation, not by preaching against them, as we do in our capacity of critic, or as Cooper did in his later novels; but by laboring to produce fitting and attractive examples of what literature should be, by careful self-culture, by acquiring habits of independence, and by avoiding all servile imitation—not study—of foreign models whether ancient or modern. No man writes well unless he writes freely from his own life. Above all, let them bear in mind that a literature destined to live, and to exert an ennobling influence on the national character, must entertain the ideal, be replete with thought, inspired by earnest purpose, and addressed to the understanding as well as to the affections, passions, and emotions. Truth has a bottom of its own, and can stand by itself; but beauty cannot, for it exists only in the relation of the true to our sensibility or imagination, as a combination of intellect and sense. The form of ancient classic literature is unsurpassable, but that literature finds it vital principle, that which preserves it as a living literature today, chiefly in its thought, in the truth which it expresses to the understanding, though under the form of the beautiful to our sensitive nature. Hence all efforts to exclude the study of the classics from our schools and colleges have failed and will fail. The neglect of the ancient classics marks simply the advance of barbarism.

Some of the remarks we have made have been suggested by reading *Hannah Thurston,* a story of American life, by Bayard Taylor, late Secretary of the American Legation at the Court of St. Petersburg.[409] Mr. Taylor enjoys a high reputation as a literary man. He is said to be a poet; but whether so or not, we are unable to judge, for, to our loss, no doubt, we have read only two or three of his occasional songs, of which we did not think much. He has been a great traveller, has seen much, and relates well what he has seen. But we really know him only by his *Hannah Thurston,* and can judge him only as the author of that work. As the author of *Hannah Thurston,* he has most of the faults of American writers in general, and very few of the merits of such writers as Irving, Cooper, Hawthorne, Kennedy, Bird, and Gilmore Simms; and he even ranks below several of our female writers, such as Miss Sedgwick and the author of *Miriam* and *Husks.*[410] He strikes us as a feminine man. The virile element in him, apparently, is weak, and he writes more as a man of sentiment than as a man of thought. His story is well conceived, and is conducted with artistic skill to its conclusion. His intention has been good, and he deserves high praise for it. His book may be read once, if not with intense interest, without fatigue; but we broke down in our attempt to read it a second time. It is unlike Thackeray's novels, which interest more on a second than on a first perusal. His book shows some experiences of life, fine powers of observation, some humour, and, now and then, unobtrusive wit; but it lacks strength—free, vigorous, masculine thought. It is called *A Story of American Life,* and American it is, and none but an American could have written it; for none but an American could have shown us the same evident effort to write like an Englishman, without ever attaining to the real English manner. The American who does not try to write like an Englishman, and is contented to write as a man whose mother tongue is English, will catch more of the English manner than the one who does.

Mr. Taylor is unmistakably American. His style has the peculiarly American nasal twang. We, Americans, lack the English *aplomb,* the English *selbstandichkeit,* and the English round and full pronunciation.[411] We do not feel ourselves full-blooded Englishmen, are afraid to be ourselves, and seldom speak out, like men, our own mother tongue in a full round voice. We speak through the nose, in a thin, sharp voice, as if afraid to speak with an open mouth. This is especially true of us in the Northern States; in the South and the West we find more individual independence. As a rule, we both write and speak our common language with more grammatical correctness than do the English, but rarely with the same ease, fluency, and idiomatic grace. Our writers have as much genius, ability, and knowledge as the English, but less mental culture and less self-confidence, as any can feel who compares the *North American* with the *Quarterly,* or the *Atlantic* with *Blackwood.* There is almost always something of the plebeian and the provincial about us, and we act as if afraid of committing some solecism, or of neglecting some conventional usage which we have heard of but are unfamiliar with. This is easily explained by the fact that English writers themselves had, at the epoch of the founding of the Anglo-American colonies, very little of that high-bred and metropolitan air which the better class of them have now; and by the further fact that the first settlers of the colonies were chiefly provincials, plebeians, and dissenters from the national church, to which adhered the aristocratic and ruling classes of the mother country. The American people have sprung, in so far as of English blood, chiefly from the middle and

lower classes of England, for, as Mr. Bancroft has justly remarked, royalty and nobility did not emigrate, and the larger portion of the colonial gentry, such as we had,
abandoned the colonies when they declared their independence of Great Britain.
The objections to the air and tone of our literature, apply more especially to New
England and the Middle States; the writers of the Southern States have the temper
and tone of a slaveholding community, are independent enough, but are too florid,
too wordy, and incline to the pompous; Western writers are free enough, but inflated, turgid, bombastic, and neglectful of the graces and proprieties of our mother
tongue. Indeed, we are daily losing throughout the Union the purity, the simplicity,
and directness demanded by the English genius, as is also the fact in England, owing to the extraordinary development of journalistic and periodical literature, and to
the influence of Hibernian and feminine writers. The writers for our leading journals are in no small proportion Irishmen, and for our popular magazines women, or
what is far worse, feminine men, who have great fluency and little thought.

Mr. Taylor has a touch of the nasal twang of the Middle States, which is very distinguishable from that of New England, but not a whit more agreeable or manly.
The real "Down East" vernacular has been rendered classic by our excellent friend
Seba Smith, Esq., in his famous *Jack Downing Letters*, the only man who has yet written it. Haliburton, in his *Sam Slick*, Smith of this city, in his counterfeit Jack Downing, and Professor Lowell, of Cambridge, in his *Biglow Papers*, write it as a language
they have learned, as many Americans, ourselves especially, do English, never as
their mother tongue.[412] With Mr. Smith the language of "Down East" is really vernacular, and he writes it as naturally, as gracefully, as idiomatically as Burns on Scott
writes broad Scotch, or Gerald Griffin the Munster brogue.[413] We ought to be a
good judge in this matter, for the Down East dialect was our mother tongue, and
we never heard any other spoken till we were a right smart lad. Mr. Taylor writes
English, very correct English, but with an American twang, all the more remarkable, for he evidently tries to write English as an Englishman. We find no fault with
any writer for writing according to his own national character. Americans are not
inferior to Englishmen, as we may one day prove, by a fierce war on the sea and on
the land, if we have not done it already, and the inferiority of our literature is due to
our fear to be ourselves. Human nature is as broad, as rich, as living in us as in
Englishmen; their mother tongue is ours, and we can write it as well as they, if we
only write as they do, from our own minds and hearts, and learn to express our
own thoughts and sentiments in our own way, with frankness, directness, naturalness, and simplicity. Mr. Taylor's fault is, being an American, in trying to play the
Englishman.

Mr. Taylor is a practised writer, and writes with much facility, but he is neither a
profound nor a vigorous writer. Still he is a shrewd observer, and, if he does not go
to the bottom of things, he skims gracefully over their surface. His satire is free
from malice; he is pleasant, bright, good-humored, and never ruffles your temper,
or offends your taste. There are passages even, in this book, which indicate that he
has a deeper nature than he displays, and has thought more than he pretends. It is,

after all, only the smallest, and that not the best part of the man, that the author is able to express, and there are few men or women whose experience is not deeper and richer than can be found in the pages of the truest, deepest, and richest romance. Never yet has fiction been able to match the romance of real life. Mr. Taylor is unquestionably far superior to his book, but he does not, after all, strike us as a man of deep feeling or of original and far-reaching thought. He designs well, constructs not unhappily the outlines of his story, gives us its dry bones, properly arranged, and proves himself a good literary anatomist; but he succeeds not in clothing them with living flesh, nor in breathing a soul into the body, and bidding it live, which Heinrich Heine says is the grand defect of English literature in general.[414] The English nature has more heart than soul, and is more remarkable for a deep sensibility, which it masks under a rough and bluff exterior, than for spirituality, and Americans in this respect, especially in the Free States, share largely in the English nature. But no man is to be censured for not giving to the offspring of his brain what he himself has not to give.

Mr. Taylor lays the scene of his story in the interior of the State of New York, in the pleasant village of Skaneateles,—Ptolemy, as he calls it,—on the borders of the beautiful Skaneateles Lake, one of the most charming lakes in a State that should be called Lake State, and his design has been to satirize gently, very gently, yet keenly and effectively, certain faults and follies into which our Anglo-Saxon nature betrays us. He points his wit and humor at several classes of philanthropists and world-regenerators, far more numerous and rampant before the outbreak of the Rebellion than they are now. He laughs, and bids us laugh, moderately, at sewing-societies and tea-parties among our spinsters and some not spinsters, to make dresses for a pupil or two of the missionary schools in India, or to clothe half a dozen negro children in the interior of Africa, as yet unvisited by any traveller, European or American, though in this he has been preceded and surpassed by Dickens in his *Bleak House*. He takes off admirably the one-sidedness of the original abolitionists, the folly of Fourierism, the vain pretensions and immoral tendencies of Mesmerism,[415] modern Spiritism, and Free-Lovism, and discourses at length, philosophically, politically, economically, and aesthetically on Woman's Rights, all of which had some years since numerous advocates in the village named, and in or near it was founded an experimental establishment or community for the general and particular improvement of the human species, and giving the finishing stroke to the Creator's work. This part of his novel is happily conceived and well executed, and deserves for the author the warm gratitude of the public.

But we cannot say as much of the love-story. Hannah Thurson, who gives her name to the book, is the daughter of Quaker parents, has herself been brought up a Quaker, but has strayed beyond the limits prescribed by George Fox and Robert Barclay, and can hardly be said to be a Quaker at all.[416] She has made humanity her God, and philanthropy her worship. She has devoted herself body and soul to the assertion of woman's rights, and insists that woman has the right to be treated as a man, to enter public life, or upon any public career, as a man, and to vote and be voted for as a man. She is, or wishes to be, a man-woman, and to force all men to recognize and respect her manly claims, which would be very well, if she were a man, and not a woman. She is tall, well-formed, very handsome, intellectual, passably educated, and on some subjects well instructed, refined in her tastes and feelings, liberal, generous, benevolent, but intolerant and unyielding where her principles and sense of justice are not acknowledged. She is about thirty years of age, has had several offers of marriage, which she has rejected, because she wishes to remain free to devote herself to the cause of humanity, so grossly and shamefully outraged in the degraded position in which society places her sex. The hero and lover is a certain Maxwell Woodbury, an American gentleman just returned from India, at the age of thirty-seven, where he has acquired wealth, or at least independence. He becomes acquainted at a tea-party with Hannah, whose views on woman's rights he combats. We have no space to follow the sharp and protracted discussions which took place between them. The author manages them passably well on both sides, but, so far as the logic goes, he gives the advantage decidedly to Hannah, who proves herself the better man. Indeed, she argues her cause bravely, and maintains her ground firmly, successfully,—Lucretia Mott herself could not have done better; and makes more progress in converting him than he does in converting her,— which is the best possible argument against her side of the question. They quarrelled almost from their first meeting, and for a long time quarrel as often as they meet, each obstinately refusing to see the other's side. The quarrels, at first, excite mutual dislike, then they excite mutual interest, and end in each falling desperately in love with the other. Hannah triumphs in the argument, as women always do, but is vanquished by love. Her head is strong, but her heart is weak. Max promises to inquire, to look closer into the question, and she is sure if he does he will agree with her. They in fact both inquire—into the state of their own hearts, find they have great "harmony of sentiment," and a true "union of hearts," conclude the best thing they can do is to marry, and the great question is settled, in the way women and feminine men settle all great questions, not by reason, but by love, the grand conciliator. He, poor man, lets her have her own way, and she, proud woman, loves him, and when in due time she adds to her love as his wife her love as mother, she does his pleasure, for she finds that in pleasing him she best pleases herself.

There is much truth to nature, especially to woman's nature in all this, but not to the nature of Hannah Thurston, who has lived to the age of thirty totally ignorant of the first motions of what is called love. The Hannah Thurston whom we knew, and we knew her well, though under another name, and when she was some years younger, never betrayed such weakness. She was more beautiful, as well as more majestic than Mr. Taylor has described her. She was tall, well formed, graceful in all her motions, and dignified in her whole deportment; her features were large, but of the purest classic type; her complexion was the fairest and richest that we have ever seen, and her large, deep blue eyes expressed rare sweetness, strength and energy. Her manner was gentle, quiet, self-possessed, proud, commanding, not haughty or disdainful. She had tenderness, but no sentimental effusion, and never dissolved in tears. She appeared to be above all human weakness, self-poised, and self-sufficing, and conscious of ability to govern a household or empire. You never thought of her as lovely, but regarded her as queenly. She married when about twenty-five, not because she loved, but because she wanted a servant, and was willing to pay him wages. Love, in Mr. Taylor's sense of the word, she could not, and obey any will but her own she would not, even were it the will of Heaven. Such was the real Hannah Thurston of our acquaintance, from whom Mr. Taylor has modelled his heroine, and therefore we insist that her falling in love with Max Woodbury, and marrying him as her husband, her lord, not as her servant, is a fiction. The real Hannah Thurstons are ideal, not sentimental, and sentiment in their vocabulary does not mean love; and though they may sometimes fall through the senses, through the sentiments never. They are born with lofty natures, the choice souls of their sex; even if they love at all it is only in the ideal, with that sublime affection of the soul which Plato discourses with so much eloquence, or unfolds with that poetic charm which takes captive even the most unwilling of his readers.

People laugh at Plato's love, which, according to him, is one of the two wings on which the soul soars to the Empyreum; but it is very real, and all the love into which it does not enter is an intoxication of the senses, or weak, variable, and transitory sentiment.[417] Hence, that admonition to husbands to love their wives, and wives their husbands "in the Lord," and, hence the benediction which the Church bestows in the Christian spouses. But as this mystic love does not necessarily nor always prove a guarantee against the movement of the senses, it is always dangerous to cultivate it between the sexes, where the marriage relation does not exist, and is out of the question; and hence the justice of the warnings of all the moralists against so-called Platonic attachments. Mr. Taylor's mistake is in giving us a Hannah Thurston of this high ideal character, who can love only with this ideal love, and then making her succumb to sentiment, and fall in love with Max Woodbury, and marry him as an ordinary woman, or a sentimental girl, just out of the nursery. We protest against this as not true to Hannah's nature. She could more easily have become Max Woodbury's mistress than his sentimentally loving wife. Women of her caste may sometimes be moved through the senses, and become the slaves as well as the tyrants of men they loathe; but there is no moving and binding them through the sentiments. They have sense and reason, body and soul, flesh and spirit. Their souls aspire to the highest ideal, which they find and can find in no man. They have no sentimental illusions, and in their love either rise to heaven or sink to hell.

The real Hannah Thurstons, when developed under the safeguard of religion, under the influences of the Christian faith, and the sense of duty, become the glory of their sex. If unmarried, or widows, they found or reform convents, govern religious houses or communities, found institutions for the relief of the poor, the redemption of captives, or the restoration of the fallen; aid in changing the face of society, in advancing religion and civilization; and when they die are canonized, and presented to the veneration of a grateful and admiring prosperity: such are, in

Catholic countries, the St. Catherines, the St. Theresas, the St. Clares, the St. Frances de Chantals.[418] If developed without that safeguard, without positive religion, without the Christian ideal, and the Christian sense of duty; if taught, or suffered, to look upon duty as a vulgar restraint, as a trammel upon natural liberty, or the natural freedom of the soul, and worthless, because not spontaneous or instinctive, they become the shame of their sex and are remembered only for their loose manners and disorderly lives. They give us an Aspasia, a Laïs, a Thaïs, a Sappho, a Cleopatra, a Julia, a Fulvia, a Messalina, a Ninon de l'Enclos, a Catherine II, a George Sand.[419] They become notorious for their outrage upon law and private morals, and sometimes upon public decency. Now and then one of them may be converted, and edify the world by her sublime repentance and her grand expiations, like St. Mary Magdalene or St. Mary of Egypt.[420] Hannah Thurston had Christian manners, but no positive Christian faith, and only an instinctive morality. She was engrossed with the cause she had espoused, and found in that a measurable protection, but she had no well-grounded principles, that could have given her the power of resistance in the moment of strong temptation.

The author makes the same mistake with regard to his hero, in whom are the types of two very different classes of men. To be what the author wished to represent him, Max Woodbury should be a man of high moral principle, who acts always from faith and duty, and never from mere sentiment. He should be as little sentimental as sensual; yet, though he has honorable instincts, elevated and generous feeling, good sense, and good breeding, he is sentimental rather than ideal: and if, to a certain extent, independent in his views, with the courage, in spite of village associations, to smoke his hookah, and take his glass of old sherry with his dinner or a friend, he has no religious principles, no positive convictions, and acts from no high moral or ideal motives. When Mrs. Merryfield leaves her husband, and runs off with a scamp to join the Free Love community, he insists on her return, indeed, but not from a sense of duty, or for reasons addressed to her conscience. She must do it to avoid scandal, to prevent the village gossip, and because her husband loves her, is a more agreeable man than she thinks, and there is less incompatibility of temper between them than she has suffered herself to believe. She would miss her husband and her children, and, at her age, and with her memories and associations, she would not find the society of the Free Lovers as agreeable as she fancies. Her husband is a worthy man, and she can never be happy in reflecting that she has left him desolate, and her children worse than motherless. He so well manages her self-love, that she fancies that it is she who shows herself generous and self-sacrificing in returning to the home she has abandoned; not her husband in receiving and reinstating her in her position as wife and mother, without a world or a look of reproach.

Governed by a sense of propriety, by his good taste and generous feeling, by sentiment rather than by reason, wealthy, independent in his position, a returned East Indian, comparatively young, in the full vigor of his manhood, endowed with robust health and true manly beauty, Max Woodbury could never have contracted a sentimental marriage, or what is called a marriage of love, with Hannah Thurston, who is older, as a woman, than he is as a man, and all of whose associations, habits, tastes, and sentiments are at variance with his own. He might have dispensed with wealth, but not, at his age, with youth. That he could have done only as a youth himself. He could no more have married for love a woman thirty years old, who from early youth had mingled with all sorts of men, sat with them on the same platform, and, throwing aside the veil of her modesty, addressed public meetings in defence of political, social, and domestic changes, all of which offended his taste or conviction, and some of which he regarded even as immoral, than he could a cast-off mistress or a notorious courtezan. He could as best have married her only to get a housekeeper, or someone to make his tea and coffee, to bring him his slippers and light his pipe. If they had the high ideal character the author wished to give them, they would have been above all sentimental illusions; and if they had married, it would have been for other reasons and with other views than those assigned. Taken as they are represented, as sentimentalists, and above all mercenary motives, their marriage was simply impossible.

Mr. Taylor, and nearly all our popular writers on love and marriage, commit the mistake of placing the highest ideal of love in the sentimental order, and expecting the happiness of the married life from the sentimental union of two hearts. The most unhappy marriages are usually sentimental marriages, and we have never heard of a love-match that was not an unhappy match. A real union of hearts there may be, and there often is, but not a sentimental union. The harmony of sentiment the author speaks of is an illusion, and never yet existed between two individuals of the same sex or of opposite sexes. It sometimes appears to exist between two young lovers, and they are persuaded that it does exist, but they are deceived in themselves and in each other, for they heed only the sentiments which tend to unite them, and take no account of those which are mutually repellent, and which not seldom gain the mastery before the end of the honey-moon, if not suppressed by a sense of duty and a strong effort of the will. Then nothing is more uncertain, variable, and fickle, than sentiment. It depends more on physical than rational causes, and the finest imaginable sentimental union may be sundered forever by a rainy day, a fit of indigestion, a nervous headache, an idle word heedlessly dropped by an idle friend or acquaintance, a misapprehended jest, look, or gesture, or any assignable or unassignable cause whatever. All sentiments, taken alone, are purely selfish, and in sentimental love we love only our own sentiments. Sentiments are the affections of the sensitive soul, merely modes of our own interior life, and never go out of it. We attain to a reality out of us by sense and reason, never by sentiment, and therefore in sentiment we love never another, but simply ourselves, or our momentary state of feeling. The feeling changed, the union is dissolved, and the love gone.

The necessity of woman's nature, and equally so of man's nature, is to love. But all love is worship; and the fine or high-sounding talk of the woman, that she would be loved as for herself alone, and of the man, that he wants to be loved for what he is in himself, when it is not simply a protest against a purely mercenary marriage, proceeds from the sentiment of pride, and is a demand that each shall regard the other as God. Two young lovers under the illusion of the sentiment of love, when it first becomes conscious of itself, may, in the intoxication of the moment, regard each the other as divine, but they both become, in each other's estimation, very mortal after the intimacy of married life. Men and women, say what we will, are imperfect creatures, and love can tolerate no imperfection in its object. No woman is worthy to be loved in and for herself alone, not even the purest, noblest, loveliest, holiest, the most beautiful and charming of her sex, not even the Blessed Virgin herself, for such love were idolatry; and no man is in himself and for himself alone worthy of love; even humanity is worthy of love, the supreme homage of the soul, only as elevated through the Incarnation to be the nature of God, and forever separable from the divine Personality. Men and women, the great no less than the small, are creatures, and do not suffice for themselves; and how then can a love which stops with the creature, which on the part of the man stops with the woman, and on the part of the woman stops with the man, suffice for itself? Husband and wife may and should be all in all to each other, in relation to other men and women, but they never in themselves alone suffice for their own mutual love.

The error of supposing love as a sentiment suffices for the basis of a happy marriage is productive of much misery in our own modern society. Women, save in the lower classes, are very generally educated, and intellectually as well as sentimentally. They are educated beyond the harem of the Turk and the gyneceum of the Greek, and in several branches of literature compete not unsuccessfully with men.[421] Their education has raised them above a mere instinctive life, and developed in them wants which cannot be satisfied in the sentimental order. They can satisfy their craving to love and to be loved only in an order that transcends the finest and most generous sentiments as well as the senses. Yet their education does not supply the ideal wants it develops. It makes them aware of the necessity of the ideal to their happiness, and then sends them to seek it in the sentiments, where it is not to be found. The young girl is hardly out of the convent or the boarding-school before her sentimental illusions are dispelled, and, supplied with a clear understanding of nothing higher, she becomes cold, dry, hard, unloving and unlovely; she looks upon marriage as a purely mercenary thing, and coolly calculates for how much she can afford to sell herself or consent to be sold. Once married, she insists on receiving her price, which she proceeds to spend in such dissipations as she has a taste for, or as are within her reach, always in search of a "new sensation." Or, if the illusion continues till after marriage, the result is no better. Married in the expectation of finding happiness in the union of hearts and the harmony of sentiments, she soon finds that she has wants that these pretty things do not satisfy—the ideal wants which they cannot meet—and she either suffers from the interior craving to love with no object to love, the most lively image of hell that human imagination can form, or she tries, like her sister who married without love or expecting love, to find relief or forgetfulness in some sort of sensual dissipation. The evil is not confined to women; men suffer from it hardly less than women, for the need as well as the power of loving and being loved in man is even greater than in woman, and hence the chief reason why she almost always controls him, never yielding her will to his, and seldom failing to make him yield his to her. Woman's nature is lighter, more superficial than man's, and she is incapable of the strong, deep, and abiding affection which he experiences. Hence she can always, if she chooses, gamble on his love, and be his tyrant. A great deal of needless commiseration is bestowed on women, as if they were always the victims of man's tyranny or brutality. What women most love is their own will, and they generally contrive to have it. Men suffer more than women, but they do not make so much fuss about it.

The age does not err in its demand for the ideal; its error is in confounding the ideal with the sentimental. Love-matches are, we have said, usually unhappy, and however parents may have abused their power in individual cases, we have no doubt that in former times, and in countries where the old custom continues, the average of happy marriages, arranged by parents and guardians, was and is much higher than with us, where the young people take the matter into their own hands, barely condescending, when they have settled it, to inform the "Governor" or the "Landlady" of the fact, or going through the formality of asking consent when it is too late to withhold it. But a good custom become obsolete can never be revived, for it becomes obsolete because the course of events has left it behind. The age, again, does not err in setting a high value on sentiment, for the sentimental has its place in human nature, especially Anglo-Saxon nature, and its function in human life. The error is in supposing that it does or can suffice for itself; in supposing that love is fatal, is destiny, uncontrollable by intelligence and will; in not understanding that all love is worship, and that the creature can be safely loved only in the Ideal, in the Creator. To love the creature in the Creator, or one another in God, in whom we live, and move, and have our being, is not to love one another less, but is to give love a rational and solid basis, a real substance, to complete it, and to render it constant, abiding, and immortal as the human soul itself.

The age craves the Ideal, suffers for the want of it, but does not know that in the nature of things it can be supplied only by Christian faith, hope, and charity. The soul is spiritual, and the sensible and the sentimental can satisfy it only as it integrates them or sees them integrated in the Ideal, in God, the beginning and end of all things. The Christian religion is the revelation of the Ideal, and it places it within the reach of all who are not turned away from it by false doctrines or a false education. The age misconceives both religion and its necessity. It patronises religion, asserts its utility, its necessity even for savage and barbarous tribes, for nations in the infancy of civilization, for the lower classes, for the simple, the illiterate, the ignorant, and for women and children even in our old civilized communities, but by no means for the enlightened, the cultivated, the highly civilized, the learned, the scientific, and the strong. It comprehends not that the nearer we approach to the animal world, the less do we feel the need of religion; and that the higher we rise in the scale of civilization, the more educated and enlightened we become, the deeper and more pressing are the wants developed in us, which cannot be satisfied either

with the sensible or the sentimental, and which imperatively demand the ideal order, which transcends them, and brings us into immediate relation with the origin
and end of all things. Religion does not recede as science advances, and the more
we know of the universe, the intenser becomes our consciousness of the need of
knowing and loving it in its principle and cause. Ignorance and barbarism are the
greatest of all obstacles to religion, and it is almost impossible to get savages and
barbarians to accept any religion but a gross and debasing superstition, founded on
fear or dread, not on intelligence and love. The ignorant fear the wrath of the angry
gods, and seek to appease them with costly presents, and painful, often cruel, sacrifices. This sort of religion, rather of superstition, no doubt, recedes as science advances; but not true religion, the religion founded on love, and which meets the
soul's craving for the ideal. The greater the advance of civilization, the less can men
and women enjoy themselves, find interior peace and serenity, without religion.

No doubt, the age, in words, insists on religion, and formally teaches it in its
schools, but as something foreign to the human soul, imposed from abroad, enjoin-
ing a round of duties only arbitrarily connected with human life, and not needed or
fitted to satisfy the wants that education has developed in the soul, and of which we
are so painfully conscious. Our popular authors have learned that all worship is
love, and all love is worship; but they teach us to love the Creator in the creature,
and do not understand that when we love God only in loving creatures, we are
simply idolaters; and that all idolatry is not only sin, but slavery, that degrades and
debases, instead of purifying and elevating the soul. They should reverse their doctrine, and while holding all love to be worship, understand that we love not God in
creatures, nor creatures in themselves, but creatures in the Creator, in whom they
live, move, and have their being, and without whom they are nothing, and can neither love nor be loved. The unsatisfactory nature of the love which seeks to love
the creature in itself, is due to the fact that in itself, or out of God, the creature is
nothing, and presents no object to love. The love is necessarily, therefore, an empty
sentiment, a simple interior craving which finds only itself to feed upon.

This loving of creatures in God is a love which has a real object, unfailing and
unbounded for the creature in God is perfect, complete, infinite, and may receive
the full love or supreme homage of the soul. Marriage based on this love is sacred,
holy, and can never, whatever the imperfections of the spouses, be utterly miserable, because it can never leave the mind utterly empty, and the soul to devour herself. In this sense all love—the sensible, the sentimental, the ideal, is holy, and marriage, in all its mysterious rites and relations, is as pure, as high, as laudable as virginity; for in all the soul offers her supreme homage to her Maker. The whole
meaning of all this is, that in love and marriage reason or the ideal is primary, and
the happiness is sought from the cheerful and faithful performance of the duties
which belong to the married state, and to the state of the married in life. The faithful and loving performance of these duties secures repose and serenity of soul, even
where the sentiments of the spouses do not happen to be perfectly harmonious.
That delicate young girl, just from school, who, from a sense of duty and filial piety,

marries, in obedience to her parents' wishes, a man whom she has never before seen, and whose sentiments, tastes, habits are by no means accordant with her own, may, at first recoil, but she is not necessarily miserable, and the marriage may turn out to be a happy one, because nothing not within the power of good-will is necessary to make it so. The affections do not precede it, they follow it, because it was not entered into from sentimental illusion, and because nothing is demanded that, with God's grace, it is not possible on either side to give. The fine sentiments, the deep gushing feeling, the French woman's *la grande passion,* is not necessary to the happiness of the married life, and indeed would never answer for the ordinary duties of our state, and we suspect the truest and noblest Christian wives and mothers, they who have been dearest to their husbands, and are held in the most grateful and touching recollection by their children, have never felt it. We think the less one knows of it, the better. Poor friend Thurston, Hannah's mother, was all the better for the mistake with regard to her husband, which she so feelingly confesses to her daughter, and which she discovered not till he was dying. *La grande passion* may do for a woman who forgets what she owes to her husband, and takes up a forbidden lover; but it will never do for a wife. Sentiments, at best, are only the condiments; they can never be substantial *pieces* of the feast, which must be good sense, intelligence, and duty. A man would soon starve on curry or London Club sauce.

We have said here nothing new; the parson, in his sermon, has said it all, my dear, a hundred times. I have only given you the philosophy of his sermon, and shown you it accords with the nature of things, save in accordance with which neither you nor I, however wise I am, or beautiful and angelic you are, can be happy, married or unmarried. So take what I have said kindly; for if I am old now, I have been young, and remember too well the follies of youth.

30

NOVELS AND NOVEL-WRITING

Samuel D. Davies

Southern Literary Messenger (1864).

The art of fictitious narrative appears to have its origin in the same principles of selection by which the Fine Arts in general are created and perfected. Dunlop. *Hist. Fiction.*[422]

It may be doubted whether, in its ordinary meaning, Truth is stranger than Fiction, but however that may be, we are very sure it is hardly ever so acceptable to the imagination. It is this after all which popularly determines the merits of a work of art, whose strangeness is too frequently the only basis of its value. Sober-minded, intelligent people, however, will not have this wayward faculty gratified at the expense of reason and consistency. And if they sometimes countenance extravagant fancies and caprices in the forms of art, it is done with the rarity and caution with which they seek enjoyment on the race-course, or in the drinking-saloon, and not with the regularity of habitual indulgence.

It is, therefore, a matter of no small importance for the artist to know exactly how far he may venture beyond the boundaries of reality in order to produce a work that, shall be both rational and pleasing. Should he copy literally from real life, it is obvious that in a majority of instances his work would be intolerably dull and unattractive. Should he, on the other hand, resort to startling and fantastical inventions, he runs the equal risk of being condemned by grave and earnest critics. And thus, whichever way he turns, in seeking to avoid one fault, he is liable to find himself falling directly on the opposite extreme. Yet this problem, difficult as it may seem, has not remained unsolved, and especially in that department of artistic performance which aims at reproducing social life in any of its multifarious aspects. Shakespeare, Fielding, Thackeray, and a few other dramatists and novelists, have succeeded in representing "the many-sided creature, man," in portraitures so wonderfully charming and withal so simple and so truthful, that we express our highest estimate of their genius when we say that their characters are true to life. But we are very soon convinced that this is not the only secret of their excellence. Life-like characters and incidents compose our daily experience, and we call them common-place, nor is it at all conceivable that they should become essentially more pleasing, when presented second-hand, except under certain conditions, which will presently be stated. Indeed, there are hundreds of incidents and objects which, in real life, possess a positive interest for us, and yet to find them, paraded on the stage or in a novel, without that magical effect which Genius throws into its works, would give us a very poor opinion of the author's ingenuity and fancy, which could find noth-ing better for our amusement than what had already become wearisome and stale by reason of its familiarity.

Now, if we will insist on having real life, why not ask the favor of our friends to tell us all they have seen and felt and acted since they first enjoyed the conscious-ness of being men and women? Suppose a physician, a lawyer, or a merchant. We may return to his youthful days of single blessedness and describe his personal ap-pearance, his disposition and his habits, vouchsafing a similar distinction to the maiden destined for his wife. We may give a circumstantial narrative of his court-ship, marriage and early-wedded life, and draw an accurate picture of the house he afterwards selected for his dwelling. We may then follow up his history and show him in the years of his maturity and soberness—tell how, every morning after breakfast, he repairs to his counting-room, or office; how he visits a patient, or is visited by a client or a creditor; describe the persons who meet him on the streets or elsewhere, and repeat their conversation with him—all these, and a thousand other little particularities, would doubtless make up a very respectable duodecimo of unquestionable life realities, and yet how often would it be a volume which any one would have the patience to go through with? Such, nevertheless, is real life; still we sigh for novelty and pine away with *ennui* in the very circumstances which we affect most highly to admire in works of fiction.

We may, therefore, be pardoned for saying, that when this almost formulary ex-pression is applied by way of compliment to a plausible story which has afforded us an unusual amount of pleasure, we cannot help suspecting that it is not so much to the real life it contains as to the "tricksy spirit" of art that we address our praises.[423] For with that disregard of critical analysis so common among habitual novel-readers, we are too apt to confound the subject matter with the mode of treatment, and to overlook the claims of the artist whose genial inspiration renovates and beautifies what would otherwise be commonplace and homely.

True it is, that from the time of Aristotle to the present day, we have been mo-notonously taught "to hold as 'twere the mirror up to nature."[424]

"*C'est la nature en tout qu'on admire et qu'on amie,*" says Boileau, and yet if nature al-ways means reality, we have seen already how little there is in its naked representa-tion to make it interesting either to our feelings or our reason.[425] What then is the meaning of this literary maxim? The Grecian philosopher designated the fine arts by a general term, μίμησις or imitation, as if the artist had only to imitate what he saw around him in the ordinary phases of moral and material existence, in order to fulfil the purposes of his art. And in this he may have been historically correct, for in its earlier stages art is satisfied to imitate. Homer's representation of men and manners, in the heroic age of Greece, are doubtless faithful ones, and there is no reason to suppose that in describing the hospitalities of Alcinous,[426] or the combats of his favorite heroes, he was very greatly indebted to his imagination.[*] There is, indeed, a miraculous power of fancy in his glowing portraitures and striking epithets, which he himself seems scarcely conscious of; but even the divine personages and sacred localities which occupy so large a space in his descriptions, were never recognized by him as fanciful creations, but rather as undoubted realities, confirmed by long tradition and contemporary faith. He recounted history as he received it, and knew not that he was composing a grand, imperishable poem. The definition of Aristotle is still further justified when we reflect that before the age of Phidias, no statuary had succeeded in reproducing the forms of the commonest animals even for religious purposes, still less in giving forth those noble expressions of ideal beauty which only cultivated geniuses and rare mechanical skill would be capable of realizing. Thus far it may be said that art was imitation, or at least, that it aspired no higher than to reach the limit of reality—to copy objects in their actual forms. But as taste and intellectual refinement gradually increased, the imagination claimed an interest in the realm of art, and reality was no longer followed with the same unvarying precision. The tendency of the imitative arts from original realism to ultimate idealism, and back again to their primal starting point, has been luminously and concisely demonstrated by an English writer.[**] But we think this observation especially true of the descriptive arts—poetry and novel writing. First we have the minute and circumstantial method of description, in which articles of apparel, the affairs of the *cuisine*, and other immaterial details, are noted with the most tedious exactitude as in our earlier legends and romances. Next we find the actual superseded almost entirely by the imaginative, and hideous monsters, enchanted castles, and impossible heroes, engage the chief attention of the author. But realism finally recovers its former sway, because reality itself—the sum of human action and experience—becoming elevated and enriched by the influences of civilization,

---

[*] It may be asked whence came those grand and beautiful conceptions which constitute the highest excellences of the *Odyssey* and *Iliad*, and for which there is no corresponding type in the natural world, if they were not originated in the imagination of the poet. Our readers will remember that Boccaccio, in his *Vita di Dante*, [*Vita di Dante Alighieri* is the popular title of *Trattatello in Laude di Dante*: "*Little Tractate in Praise of Dante*" (1351)] shows by quite an elaborate argument, that poetry originated in the religious sentiments and aspirations of mankind. The imagination, seeking to embody the vague speculations of unenlightened reason, did indeed, at first invent a Hades, but the idea once invented and popularized, came subsequently to be regarded as a positive reality, suggesting clear and refined images to the mind. And therefore, when Homer unveils the invisible world, he only reproduces an idea so familiar to the public mind, that his descriptions are little more than imitation.

[**] *Blackwood,* Feb. 1856.

is rendered susceptible of an idealization of its own, and thus made subservient to the purposes of art. And it is this idealization of the real and the artificial which distinguishes our modern fictions, and which we have learned to look for in our novels.

We conclude, then, that the term nature is not limited to actuality, but that it embraces the probable, the possible, the rational; and with this interpretation, we properly understand what is meant by holding the mirror up to nature. Plain reality and arbitrary exaggeration may be regarded as the Scylla and Charybdis which novelists have equal reason to avoid in steering through the unmeasured sea of fiction.[427] We do not ask them for prodigies and wonders as in the *Castle of Otranto*, *Kenneth*, *The Three Spaniards*, and we may add, the *Strange Story* of the great English novelist, but we do require of them something more than a more repetition of what we daily see and have around us.[428] We may admire an accurate picture of some familiar landscape, and provided there be no particular association connected with it to arouse our interest or emotions, the feeling of admiration will be found to rest not on the subject itself, but rather on the consummate skill with which it has been imitated. So we may delight in a dramatic representation of the commonest incidents and characters of life, but it is not in *them* alone that we find the groundwork of our pleasure, but on the contrary, in the close and accurate observation of human nature, together with the faculty of mimicking its different manifestations that enables the artist who has genius to move us by his books and words and gestures. The same is true of those novels which claim to be representations of real life. This is not what we seek when we resort to works of fiction—nay, by this very act we turn our backs on real life, and like Dante, guided by the shade of Virgil, we follow the genial author into his own ideal world, to be aroused and recreated by its brighter hues and warmer temperature. Passive, yet with every sense awake, we move through changing scenes of cloudless beauty or tender gloom, exalted with a loftier happiness, or mourning with a deeper melancholy; viewing man as through a microscope, his wisdom and his follies, his honor and his shame, brought out in clear and prominent relief. It is this uniform expansion of the real, this contemplating human passions as through a magnifying medium, that awakens our sympathies in all their fulness, and fills us with an intensified consciousness of life.

Here, then, we make a grand distinction; we discriminate between the actual and the possible, between what is and what might be, without overrating the capabilities of nature. The portraiture of one who had been reared in the midst of luxury and dissipation, might exhibit only a depraved and heartless sensualist, or at least an insignificant sum in the sun of society. But place him amid the fearful, soul-stirring scenery of the battle-field, or some other situation which would evolve the nobler elements of his humanity, and it is not impossible that he should appear before us in the character of a hero or a philanthropist. Here the consistency of nature is not violated. But represent him as transforming himself into a lion, an elephant, or an improbable shadow, as controlling the elements of nature, or subjecting to his service the inhabitants of the invisible world, and we at once reject the fiction as equally unnatural and unreasonable. This remark, however, does not apply to poetry, for the supernatural agencies employed in some of the finest efforts of poetical genius are well known to constitute not the least notable of their excellences, and those who are familiar with *The Tempest, Midsummer Night's Dream*, or any of the great national epics from the siege of Troy to the age of Milton, need not be reminded of the fact. We conclude, then, that the grand purpose of the statuary and pictorial arts consists in developing the possible in man and nature as material forms, combining only so much of the spiritual element as may be expressed by fixed and permanent figures. The ultimate purpose of the novelesque and dramatic arts consists in evolving the possible in man as a moral and dynamical intelligence, (if we may so express it), viewed under certain modifying conditions, arising from his relations to society. It does not seek, or rather is not bound to copy his actual manifestation as a reality, for this is properly the work of history and biography. But art, we must remember, is the "child of freedom," *die Tochter der Freiheit*, and will not be trammelled in the enjoyment of her prerogative.[429]

Let us now enquire what limitation the artist is expected to observe. Between reality and possibility extends the domain of natural truth; what hovers beyond, and much that lies within it, is interdicted to the artist who would move our deepest sympathies, and fill us with a sober, rational enjoyment. The poet alone may pass beyond these limits; he may bid defiance to the law of gravitation, as well as to the conventionalities of civilized life; he may select his theme wherever the universe extends its "void immense,"[430] wherever human passion, in its freest ecstasies, reveals in man the glory of a divinity, or the deformity of a fiend. But the novelist is the artist of society. He seeks to interest us, not by arbitrary hypotheses of improbable or impossible existence, as in poetry, but by rational representations of social life as we observe or know it to exist. He brings his subject nearer to our sympathies and comprehension, and deals with human destiny not as a general abstract conception, but as a living concrete reality, more or less affected by certain other realities—the usages and maxims of society. His characters are people with the same instincts and capacities, the same sentiments and prejudices as our own; moving in the same atmosphere, and subject to the same accidents and influences and conditions of existence as ourselves except that these belong here exclusively to the artist, who is at liberty, and, indeed, in duty bound, to invent such situations and relations as, without being inconsistent with the possibilities of real life, yet serve to throw out in stronger relief the virtues and the vices, the sorrows and the pleasures in which we have all, to a greater or less extent, participated. Sir Walter Scott was singularly fortunate in selecting the time and place for the exhibition of his hero, Waverley. We see him first in the elegant ease of his quiet English home, so circumstanced that we might look upon him almost in the light of familiar acquaintanceship. And when we are invited to accompany him to scenes as romantic as the most sentimental could desire, we find them so tempered to a rational consistency, that without losing the essential charm of their character, they come upon us with all the gracefulness of some pleasing adventure of our own.

The duties and proprieties of enlightened social intercourse are, in general, the rule and measure of the novelistic art. Not that the author is required, like the older French tragedians, (as we once before observed), to sacrifice all genuine passion and emotion to a false and fatal notion of decorum, for this would be denying the primary attributes of art. *Famam sequere*, in its fullest meaning, expresses the true idea of his calling.[431] All social conventionalisms, whether of character or manners, are subject to his requisition, but he must be governed by a certain respect for the sentiments of his readers, so as not to offend them by coarse and sickening descriptions. A hero or a heroine, in a serious story of modern society, who exhibited the native propensities and manners of an Esquimaux or Hottentot, might indeed be regarded as a novelty, but we should be very strongly tempted to believe that the author had utterly mistaken his vocation. Thus, even the possible in nature is not always entitled to a place in the field of artistic representation, because it is not always compatible with the refinement of prevailing sentiments. And here the author must be guided by his own good taste.

But real life itself is not uniformly synonymous with the idea of nature. We find much therein which the Germans call *unnatur*, resulting from a false and defective education, which sadly perverts and deforms humanity, and is no part of its legitimate development. People who are described as artificial, eccentric, affected, etc., are common both in real life and novels, but the very words which we apply to them will be found to contain an idea exactly opposite to that of naturalness.

Notwithstanding, however, all the rules and principles which may be laid down for the guidance of the artist, we cannot ignore the fact that the human mind delights in what is strange; and by this we mean, what exceeds the limit of its own experience. "Fiction," says Lord Bacon, "strongly shows that a greater variety of things, a more perfect order, a more beautiful variety, *than can anywhere be found in nature*, is pleasing to the mind. Heroes and heroines who see and feel and act exactly what we ourselves do, cannot possibly excite our interest, because we seek their society, so to speak, in order to have our thoughts, our feelings and perceptions stimulated, deepened and extended."

Regarding the foregoing observations as correct in theory, we propose to examine from this standpoint some of the foreign works of fiction which have been republished in this country since the outbreak of the war, and which we presume are now familiar to our readers.

The startling impossibilities of *The Strange Story*, the singular caprices and infelicities of Mr. Collins' last novel, the unwomanly destiny which Miss Braddon dispenses to her heroines, the purity, elegance, and beautiful simplicity of Octave Feuillet, and the bold, refreshing originality of Victor Hugo, are worthy the special consideration of those who own an interest in the affairs of light literature.[432]

The Strange Story, so essentially different as it is from every other work of its distinguished author, seems like the splendid freak of an imperial intellect sporting in the consciousness of its superior nobleness and power. It exhibits neither the reckless profligacy and romantic sentimentalism of his earlier performances, nor the

calm, contemplative spirit of his later works. It is less a novel than a scientific treatise; it is less a representation of social life than the demonstration of a philosophical theorem, and we finish reading it with a sentiment very near akin to that of
Hamlet, when he made that oft repeated observation to Horatio.[433]

Rousseau somewhere tells us that we are not authorized to pronounce any phenomenon a miracle, simply because we do not understand the cause and principle
of its being, or because it varies from the line of our common experience.[434] This,
we know, was uttered in contradiction of the miraculous events recorded in the
sacred Scriptures, as examples of the direct exercise of Divine power. But Bulwer,
with a loftier purpose, and aiming a vigorous blow at the skeptical rationalism of
the age, teaches that there are mysterious and inexplicable phenomena in nature,
and by easy inference in the records of Divine revelation, which are none the less
true by reason of their being incomprehensible. He further exposes, in the history
of Allan Fenwick, the shallow foundation, as well as the incidental perplexities of
that self-sufficient unbelief, which, claiming to settle all questions by the tests of
science, would summarily expunge from the catalogue of facts whatever was found
to be irreconcilable with established scientific laws.

Allan Fenwick may be regarded as the representative of this particular kind of
skepticism, inasmuch as he seeks to reduce all phenomena to certain principles, and
contemptuously rejects whatever cannot be brought within the scope of logical
demonstration. He therefore denies the sacred authority of the Bible, and particularly the doctrine of spiritual immortality—of life beyond the grave. His conversion
from this state of unbelief to a more liberal and less arrogant habit of judgment
seems to be the paramount object of the story, and is obviously foreshadowed in
the dying words of Dr. Lloyds.

This result is effectuated indirectly by the agency of that daring hypothesis, that
wonderful impossibility, that open and defiant contradiction of all the known elements of scientific truth—embodied in the character of Margrave. In order, therefore, that the mysterious attributes of this singular being should be brought more
particularly under the observation of Fenwick, he is made to fall in love with Lilian
Ashleigh, who soon afterwards, being thrown in the presence of the "mystical Fas-
cinator," develops that unaccountable sympathy, which gives him so formidable an
influence over her destiny, and excites so deeply the interest and anxiety of Fenwick.

Here we have Skepticism, Mystery, Love; and from these the fourth term of the
proposition—Faith—is eliminated in the sequel of the story. Margrave is a mystery;
equally so is the Sein-Laeca; but deep and inexplicable as they are, they are brought
to bear on Fenwick's mind in such a manner that he cannot possibly ignore them.
They are facts of which he has the evidence of his senses, and he can no more deny
than he can comprehend them. And because his love, his happiness, are deeply and
dangerously involved in them, he is compelled, by the all-controlling passion, to
recognize them in all the terror of their truthfulness, and thus to study, with increasing application and solicitude, what he would otherwise have overlooked with

feelings of indifference or scorn. So that at last he acknowledges the power of the Infinite, after the impressive teachings of a long and painful experience, and humbles himself to the admission that there are mysterious truths, and among them the immortality of the soul, which, being beneficently veiled from our comprehension, by Omniscient Wisdom, can never be penetrated by the subtlest analyses and the most refined abstraction that the mind of man is capable of making. Margrave, we think, is merely the symbol of mystery, or rather of occult truth. Dr. Faber's special office seems to consist in reconciling these mysterious phenomena with scientific truth so far as they are susceptible of such elucidation. Mrs. Col. Poynts, and the other *dramatis personae* are introduced apparently with the view of sobering down with the semblance of reality, the otherwise exaggerated aspect of the story; and though only of secondary importance to the main design, they are all distinguished by the compact and symmetrical mould of Bulwer's genius.

With this imperfect and doubtless unsatisfactory notice, and without attempts to penetrate the mysteries of mesmerism, electro-biology, clairvoyance, or whatever it may be which constitutes the strangeness of the story, we pass on to the consideration of Mr. Wilkie Collins' last novel. We deem it proper to remark that the grouping of authors here presented, is due entirely to the circumstance that their work happened to appear among us at the same time, and not to any fancied similarity or equality of character or merit. And first, then, Mr. Collins strikes us as being guilty of a grievous fault: the fault of being elaborately loathsome and disgusting; in a word, be has very bad taste. Moreover, his fondness for strange and startling fancies, for results which could not be deduced by any process of reasoning from any previous examples of human character and conduct, has led him not indeed beyond the range of possibility, but certainly beyond the limits of reasonable probability.

No Name is unquestionably a work of considerable interest, but it fails, we think, most signally, in awakening the sympathy of the reader. For sympathy and interest express two very different ideas, and it is the combination of them that realizes the highest purpose of the art. We are, indeed, amused and entertained in witnessing the ingenious schemes and counter-schemes of Capt. Wragge and Mrs. Lecount, but we cannot sympathize with them, because we do not feel that we could ever be actuated by the same principles and motives. Magdalen Vanstone has doubtless disappointed many readers, though she seems to be a tolerably fair specimen of what Mr. Collins can accomplish in the way of character-painting. There was at first a singular fascination in her portraiture; a beauty and a freshness rarely met with in her wonderful exuberance of vitality, in her sudden vicissitudes of dove-like gentleness and wild impetuosity, of rapturous exhilaration and almost mournful earnestness, of womanly dignity and childlike simplicity—a brilliant, startling antithesis, an exquisite enigma, whose solution we eagerly awaited, that we might comprehend it in the unity and fullness of its meaning. But its meaning turned out nothing, after all. In the first place, we were disappointed in finding her already in love with that detestable milksop, who so obediently verified the evil predictions of his philosophical parent. We would greatly have preferred witnessing the first effects of the grande passion on a nature so "marvellously wrought" as hers, but this we were denied. And even this might have been tolerated, had it been the only blunder. But when she sternly and inexorably dedicates herself to the unworthy purpose of recovering, at any sacrifice, the wealth of which she had been cheated, while manifesting a comparative indifference to the unfortunate circumstances of his birth; when we see her deliberately laying aside the soft and winning qualities of womanhood, and assuming the severe, ungenial spirit of a confirmed enthusiast; when we see her, at the critical moment, yielding to her fatal passion, and consenting to the friendship and familiarity of an acknowledged villain, and the loathsome creature which he called his wife; and lastly, when she crowns her unnatural folly by marrying that pitiable, sickly, half-witted manikin, Noel Vanstone, we must needs confess that neither her motives, nor the occasional glimpses which she gives us of a generous womanly heart, can in the least degree explain, or justify, this monstrous inconsistency, this flagrant outrage against the spirit of social decorum, and we had almost said against the rule of natural possibility itself. Nora is simply a negative, presenting only a passive contrast to the stronger minded heroine. As to Frank Clare, we can only regret, in the language of Faulconbridge—

> That there should be
> In such a love so vile a lout as he.[435]

We forbear, for want of space, from noticing the other characters. Mr. Collins doubtless has genius, but it is not by such abrupt and anomalous exhibitions as these that he can expect to do it justice. However, we look forward with much interest to his future works, with the expectation of finding them more in keeping with the vast abilities of the author.

That Miss Braddon writes a very entertaining story, all are, doubtless, willing to admit: and in addition to this merit, she employs a style which for purity and gracefulness, is scarcely surpassed by that of, Fielding or of Smollett. Her conception of female destiny, however, is not an original one, and seems embraced in the single idea of suffering. There is much, though, in her development of this idea, to call forth a very high order of artistic talent, and to inspire us with a deep and sympathetic interest. Her heroines have all the delicacy of feeling and purity of motive, as well as the pardonable infirmities which we usually ascribe to woman. Aurora Floyd, notwithstanding her ignoble maternity, for which, by the way, we can discover no reasonable necessity whatever, is a very interesting personage, and we feel a positive gratification rather than a sentiment of compassion in witnessing the terrible retribution which her youthful error ultimately brought upon her.[436] Talbot Bulstrode, who illustrates an idea of manhood peculiar to a certain class of ladies, only acted towards Aurora as every other sensible man would have done under similar circumstances, and we rather approve his choice of the young lady with pink eye-lids, who usurped the sovereignty which the redoubtable Flora had established over his affections. John Mellish, that good, fat, even-tempered simpleton, is another purely feminine conception, realizing the true idea of a lover and a husband—who should sacrifice everything in deference to the woman he professes to adore. Indeed, we suspect from the evident gusto and complacency with which this agreeable authoress dwells upon his silly words and actions, that she is only inculcating some favorite notions of her own. *Darrell Markham*, is a story of the same general cast, though we observe a sort of antipodal contrast between the uxorious Mellish and the cold hearted, tyrannical Captain Duke.[437] Millicent is quite distinct in character from Aurora Floyd, and is, we think, a far more loveable and womanly impersonation. Markham is a revised edition of Bulstrode, and is obviously improved by the revision. We have not space for a full critical analysis of these works, and must therefore, leave a great deal that is worthy of remark, unnoticed. Altogether, these books are very readable ones, and evince much more than the average amount of talent observable in the ordinary fictions of the day.

It is difficult, on reading the *Romance of a Poor Young Man*, to determine whether Octave Feuillet is more of novelist than poet.[438] With a heart made up of the most refined sensibilities, a fancy of wonderful fertility and delicacy, a fine morality and a chivalrous sentiment of honor, he diffuses over his narrative an atmosphere of romantic elegance, simplicity and freshness, which are equalled only by the noble cast of his impersonations, and the skilful management by which he moves and keeps alive our interest. It may be a mere fancy, but there seems to be so decided a resemblance between the hero of this story and Victor Hugo's Marius, that we might almost suppose them to have originated in the same imagination.[439] The manly, dignified fortitude with which Maximilian met and endured the sad misfortunes which came so suddenly upon him; his miserable destitution, his tender devotion to his little sister, and their painfully interesting interviews, the scrupulous propriety and modesty of his deportment while employed in the household of Mde. Laroque, the gradual and irresistible growth of his love for Marguerite, their excursions to the waterfall, the adventure in the ruined castle, his pride, his despair; in a word, every scene and incident recorded in the narrative, is so exquisitely painted, that we recognize in them all, the magic touches of a master hand. The rare and fascinating character of Marguerite, is not inferior to the finest of Sir Walter Scott's impersonations, and the perfect naturalness of Mdlle. de Porhoet is as pleasing in itself as it is gracefully subservient to the happy issue of the plot. M. Laubepin, M. Bevalian, Mde. Laroque, Helouin, and the other characters, have all the spirited individuality and completeness of real personages, while their mutual relations, constantly varying but never wanting in interest, attest the elevated dramatic spirit, and expression of the author. Indeed, if we may judge of M. Feuillet from this little story, we cannot conclude otherwise than that he is one of the most genial and delightful authors of the age, notwithstanding he is presented to us in a language not his own, and we sincerely hope that we shall have frequent occasion hereafter to call attention to the productions of his genius.

And now we come to Victor Hugo,[440] who combines in his single personality, the diverse characteristics of novelist, historian and political philosopher. But it is only in the first of these three different aspects that we propose to estimate his merits and that, too, with a degree of brevity which we would reluctantly consent to, had not this pleasing duty been already satisfied. We must be permitted, never-theless, to offer another tribute to the singular beauties of this remarkable perform-ance. If Dumas,[441] by his somewhat fanciful interpretation of Victor Hugo's name*, incurred the sneers of certain English critics ten years ago, he now stands fully vin-dicated by the last performance of this gifted author. His powerful illustration of the tyranny of social usages and maxims, of the antagonism of society and nature, of opinion and truth, his masterly representations of the human heart, in its most touching or revolting aspects, of conscience in the sublimest manifestations of its power, or in the mournful degradation of its weakness, the dramatic vividness of his scenery, his depth and delicacy of feeling, and the irresistible effect of his anti-thetical collocations of good and evil, of innocence and guilt, of purity and deprav-ity, all are monuments at once of his elevated humanity and the massive greatness of his genius. We linger at the very entrance of the narrative, to contemplate the noble virtues of Monsieur Charles de Bienvenu, for there is an atmosphere of holi-ness about this generous, kind-hearted Bishop, that makes him savor more of heaven than earth. His faithful rendering unto God the things that are God's, while scrupulously fulfilling his duties to mankind; his earnest, active sympathy with the wants and sufferings of humanity, and the zeal, humility and self-forgetfulness with which he gave his own worldly and spiritual means to their relief are qualities that must command our deepest love and veneration. But more than this, he was a hero of the loftiest stamp. The perilous journey which he voluntarily undertook from Chastelar to the little shepherd-parish beyond the mountains, beautifully illustrates that trustful court, or rather, that outrageous resignation to the will of Providence, with which the sense of duty so thoroughly inspires some men that fear and danger seem but words of blasphemy. The conception and artistic treatment of this, and indeed of all the other characters, are unquestionably of the highest order. The Bishop's kindness to the unhappy, self-despised criminal, when scorned and re-jected wherever he sought for pity, and struggling with a fierce and torturing de-spair, he repaired with doubt and hesitation to the dwelling of his subsequent bene-factor, vividly contrasts the simple, heartfelt philanthropy of this godly man, with the harshness and injustice of those social maxims which, so often wanting in the spirit of charity, deny what heaven itself delights to grant, forgiveness and redemp-tion to the penitent.

The reformation wrought by the purifying influences of the Bishop's virtues, in the character of Jean Valjean; his ultimate elevation to a position of usefulness and power, in which he seems to have inherited the noble spirit of his benefactor; his lamentable downfall, consecrated by the sublime self-devotion with which he vol-untarily yielded himself to the sacrifice, his subsequent adventures, the sad history of Fantine, the stern, conscientious and inexorable Javert, the cunning and perfidi-ous Thenardiers, the gentle, though manly character of Marius, the kind, eccentric M. Gillenormand, the feminine sweetness and purity of Cosette, so far as we are yet

---

* Hugo, in old German, signifies *spirituous, breath, soul, spirit*; coupling the name of Victor, we have "victorious mind," "triumphant soul," "conquering spirit."

acquainted with her, the jealous affection with which her aged guardian dotes upon her—and a thousand scenes and incidents and sentiments come crowding so closely on us, that we are prevented by want of space from indulging, for the present, in more than a passing glance at them. Indeed, a volume of commentaries might be written on them. We will only add, for the benefit of those who have been deterred from reading the work, by the abstract reasonings and historical allusions, so thickly interspersed throughout the narrative, that the story is in fact distinct from them, constituting a perfect unity in itself.

31

MISS RAVENEL'S CONVERSION FROM SECESSION TO LOYALTY

William Dean Howells

A review of John W. De Forest's *Miss Ravenel's Conversion from Secession to* Loyalty (1867). *Atlantic Monthly* (1867).[442]

William Dean Howells (1837-1920) was born in Martin's Ferry, Ohio, and began his working life setting type for his father, a printer. He wrote around 200 books, including thirty-six novels and five autobiographical volumes, and many hundreds of essays and reviews. Howells worked on the *Nation* (New York) for a short time before becoming assistant editor of the *Atlantic Monthly* in 1866, a post he resigned in 1881 so that he could concentrate on fiction. In 1885, Howells signed a lucrative contract with the publishing house Harper & Brothers: in return for an annual salary of $10,000, he was to write a novel a year (to be serialized in *Harper's Monthly*) and a monthly column, "The Editor's Study"; the column ran from January, 1886 until March, 1892.

The light, strong way in which our author goes forward in this story from the first, and does not leave difficulty to his readers, is pleasing to those accustomed to find an American novel a good deal like the now extinct American stage-coach, whose passengers not only walked over bad pieces of road, but carried fence-rails on their shoulders to pry the vehicle out of the sloughs and miry places. It was partly the fault of the imperfect roads, no doubt, and it may be that our social ways have only just now settled into such a state as makes smooth going for the novelist; nevertheless, the old stage coach was hard to travel in, and what with drafts upon one's good nature for assistance, it must be confessed that our novelists have been rather trying to their readers. It is well enough with us all while the road is good,—a study of individual character, a bit of landscape, a stretch of well-worn plot, gentle slopes of incident; but somewhere on the way the passengers are pretty sure to be asked to step out,—the ladies to walk on ahead, and the gentlemen to fetch fence rails.

Our author imagines a Southern loyalist and his daughter sojourning in New Boston, Barataria, during the first months of the war. Dr. Ravenel has escaped from New Orleans just before the Rebellion began, and has brought away with him the most sarcastic and humorous contempt and abhorrence of his late fellow-citizens, while his daughter, an ardent and charming little blonde Rebel, remembers Louisiana with longing and blind admiration. The Doctor, born in South Carolina, and living all his days among slaveholders and slavery, has not learned to love either; but Lillie differs from him so widely as to scream with joy when she hears of Bull Run.[443] Naturally she cannot fall in love with Mr. Colburne, the young New Boston lawyer, who goes into the war conscientiously for his country's sake, and resolved for his own to make himself worthy and lovable in Lillie's blue eyes by destroying and desolating all that she holds dear. It requires her marriage with Colonel Carter—a Virginia gentleman, a good-natured drunkard and *roué*[444] and soldier of fortune on our side—to make her see Colburne's worth, as it requires some comparative study of New Orleans and New Boston, on her return to her own city, to make her love the North. Bereft of her husband by his own wicked weakness, and then widowed, she can at last wisely love and marry Colburne; and, cured of Secession by experiencing on her father's account the treatment received by Unionists in New Orleans, her conversion to loyalty is a question of time duly settled before the story ends.

We sketch the plot without compunction, for these people of Mr. De Forest's are so unlike characters in novels as to be like people in life, and none will wish the less to see them because he knows the outline of their history. Not only is the plot good and very well managed, but there is scarcely a feebly painted character or scene in the book. As to the style, it is so praiseworthy that we will not specifically censure occasional defects,—for the most part, slight turgidities notable chiefly from their contrast to the prevailing simplicity of the narrative.

Our war has not only left us the burden of a tremendous national debt, but has laid upon our literature a charge under which it has hitherto staggered very lamely. Every author who deals in fiction feels it to be his duty to contribute towards the payment of the accumulated interest in the events of the war, by relating his work to them; and the heroes of young-lady writers in the magazines have been every-where fighting the late campaigns over, again, as young ladies would have fought them. We do not say that this is not well, but we suspect that Mr. De Forest is the first to treat the war really and artistically. His campaigns do not try the reader's constitution, his battles are not bores. His soldiers are the soldiers we actually know,—the green wood of the volunteers, the warped stuff of men torn from civilization and cast suddenly into the barbarism of camps, the hard, dry, tough, true fibre of the veterans that came out of the struggle. There could hardly be a better type of the conscientious and patriotic soldier than Captain Colburne; and if Colonel Carter must not stand as type of the officers of the old army, he must be acknowledged as true to the semi-civilization of the South. On the whole he is more entertaining than Colburne, as immoral people are apt to be to those who suffer nothing from them. "His contrasts of slanginess and gentility, his mingled audacity and *insouciance* of character, and all the picturesque ins and outs of his moral architecture, so different from the severe plainness of the spiritual temples common in New Boston," do take the eye of peace-bred Northerners, though never their sympathy. Throughout, we admire, as the author intends, Carter's thorough and enthusiastic soldiership, and we perceive the ruins of a generous nature in his aristocratic Virginian pride, his Virginian profusion, his imperfect Virginian sense of honor. When he comes to be shot, fighting bravely at the head of his column, after having swindled his government, and half unwillingly done his worst to break his wife's heart, we feel that our side has lost a good soldier, but that the world is on the whole something better for our loss. The reader must go to the novel itself for a perfect conception of this character, and preferably to those dialogues in which Colonel Carter so freely takes part; for in his development of Carter, at least, Mr. De Forest is mainly dramatic. Indeed, all the talk in the book is free and natural, and, even without the hard swearing which distinguishes the speech of some, it would be difficult to mistake one speaker for another, as often happens in novels.

The character of Dr. Ravenel, though so simple, is treated in a manner invariably delightful and engaging. His native purity, amiability, and generosity, which a lifelong contact with slavery could not taint; his cordial scorn of Southern ideas; his fine and flawless instinct of honor; his warm hearted courtesy and gentleness, and his gayety and wit; his love of his daughter and of mineralogy; his courage, modesty, and-humanity,—these are the traits which recur in the differing situations with constant pleasure to the reader.

Miss Lillie Ravenel is as charming as her adored papa, and is never less nor more than a bright, lovable, good, constant, inconsequent woman. It is to her that the book owes its few scenes of tenderness and sentiment; but she is by no means the most prominent character in the novel, as the infelicitous title would imply, and she serves chiefly to bring into stronger relief the traits of Colonel Carter and Doctor Ravenel. The author seems not even to make so much study of her as of Mrs. Larue, a lady whose peculiar character is skilfully drawn, and who will be quite probable and explicable to any who have studied the traits of the noble Latin race, and a little puzzling to those acquainted only with people of Northern civilization. Yet in Mrs. Larue the author comes near making his failure. There is a little too much of her,—it is as if the wily enchantress had cast her glamour upon the author himself,—and there is too much anxiety that the nature of her intrigue with Carter shall not be misunderstood. Nevertheless, she bears that stamp of verity which marks all Mr. De Forest's creations, and which commends to our forbearance rather more of the highly colored and strongly flavored parlance of the camps than could otherwise have demanded reproduction in literature. The bold strokes with which such an amusing and heroic reprobate as Van Zandt and such a pitiful poltroon as Gazaway are painted, are no less admirable than the nice touches which portray the Governor of Barataria, and some phases of the aristocratic, conscientious, truthful, angular, professorial society of New Boston, with its young college beaux and old college belles, and its life pure, colorless, and cold to the eye as celery, yet full of rich and wholesome juices. It is the goodness of New Boston, and of New England, which, however unbeautiful, has elevated and saved our whole national character; and in his book there is sufficient evidence of our author's appreciation of this fact, as well as of sympathy only and always with what is brave and true in life.

32

MISS RAVENEL'S CONVERSION

Henry James

A review of John W. De Forest's *Miss Ravenel's Conversion from Secession to Loyalty* (1867). *Nation* (1867).

Henry James (1843-1916) was born in New York City; he was educated in an unsystematic, even chaotic, manner in Europe and America (this including an unlikely year at Harvard studying law), spending almost a third of his life in Europe by the time he reached eighteen. James left America for Paris in 1875 and settled in England the following year, where he was to remain, apart from frequent trips to continental Europe and sporadic returns to America, until his death; he became a naturalized British citizen shortly before his death in 1916. James, who wrote twenty-two novels (two were unfinished), 112 short stories, some extraordinarily bad plays, volumes of criticism and reviews, and a bewildering number of letters, had, and continues to have, an inestimable impact on European and American literature. James's first short stories and reviews, the means by which he honed his early style, appeared in 1866.

Mr. De Forest, who has written other books, but whose acquaintance we make for the first time in this novel, is a very lively writer. He is hardly to be called a young man, but as he appears in this story one would take him to be a man just at the end of his youth, tolerably well satisfied with himself, tolerably well satisfied, therefore, with the world, courageous, clear-headed, bright-minded, witty, yet whose wit, if analyzed, would not seldom appear to be one of the order of Lord Dalgarno's—which, says Scott, was sometimes levity and sometimes the play of abundant animal spirits[445]—a quick-eyed observer, and, to describe him briefly, a man, so far as concerns his habits of thought, his opinions, his culture, who is the product of an excellent New England town. As a novelist, we may add that, so far as concerns the more striking characteristics of his style, a not injudicious but decided admiration for Charles Reade has had something to do with his production.[446]

All this is talk about the author and is not in strictness reviewing his book. But the book is full of Mr. De Forest. We say so not meaning the words to be understood in their bad sense. But Mr. De Forest's plan of writing, like Mr. Reade's, admits of the constant presence of the author upon the stage as manipulator of the figures; like Mr. Reade, he is constantly favoring the reader with his own reflections and comments upon the action as it goes on, button-holing him, so to speak, and taking him into his confidence—a practice of which the tendency is sometimes in the other direction, but most frequently, we believe, tends to make the figures seem puppets; finally—and here is his weakest point as a novelist—he certainly fails to give his personages so much life and separate individuality as to make us accept them for real and forget the writer. So, after reading the story, we find ourselves pleased with Mr. De Forest, willingly ascribing praise to him, and thinking of him rather than of his characters, Dr. Ravenel and Miss Ravenel and the captain in love with her—we really have to reopen the book to get his name—Captain Edward Colburne.

One exception we make to this assertion regarding the personages of the story. Carter is well depicted; daguerreotyped from nature. We all have seen just such men, and all can recognize Mr. De Forest's accurate and spirited portraiture. He is a Virginian, a graduate of the school at West Point, a good soldier, not well furnished with brains originally, and somewhat demoralized in intellect and more demoralized in character by the stupid dissipations into which our army officers were so often driven by the dull life in frontier ports and Southern arsenals. We all remember how, in the beginning of the war, such men were gladly taken by our Northern governors for colonels of volunteer regiments; how they were apt to McClellan-ize;[447] how, in spite of an aversion to negroes and a weakness for whiskey, they became, by dint of knowing their business and by hard fighting, first brigadiers and then major-generals, and how occasionally some of them as well as some volunteers were suspected of worse faults than cursing the Radicals, too courteously entreating "true Southern gentlemen," and indulging a weakness for wine and women. A good specimen of this class, with its mingled virtues and faults—chief of the latter being the misfortune of having been born a fool—Mr. De Forest has given us in his John T. Carter, colonel, and by-and-by brigadier-general of volunteers. The character is not one of abounding subtleties, enough of its traits can be painted from the surface indications, but, such as it is, Mr. De Forest has set it before us vividly.

This handsome officer with his thirty-five years, his ruddy-bronze complexion, his audacious eye, his mighty mustachios, his easy assurance, his manners not unlike those of her native Louisiana, captivates Miss Lillie Ravenel. She is a small, female secessionist, eighteen or nineteen years old, whose father, a staunch Unionist, has been forced to fly from New Orleans at the very beginning of the troubles, and has "refugeed," as they used to say, in the new city of Boston, which is in New England State of Barataria—a city and a State which some people believe to be New Haven and Connecticut. Miss Ravenel, for her part, makes prize of the heart, not so case-hardened as the colonel's, of a good young man, Edward Colburne, a graduate of the college at New Boston, an attorney not yet in good practice, a good fellow as well as a good man, but a little colorless, commonplace, young, and, on the whole, of no consequence, though like many other such youth he turns out to be a valiant and enduring soldier. After Bull Run the governor of Barataria commissions Carter as a colonel and Colburne as a captain, their regiment being the 10th Barataria, and the two men say good-bye to the Ravenels and put to sea under sealed orders which consign them to Butler's expedition against New Orleans.[448] The city is taken, and the doctor and his daughter go back to their old home, where at once Miss Ravenel's conversion from secession to Loyalty takes place. It consists in this simply: that an empty-headed young lady, who had liked the secessionists partly because she was born empty-headed and partly because she was born in Louisiana, undergoes a change of feeling when she discovers that her father's Unionism makes him and herself odious to their former acquaintants. The book is ill named, from a circumstance which is in itself trifling, and which is in no way of the least importance to the story. The Ravenels, of course, continue their acquaintance with the colonel and the captain; the young lady, a good deal against the wishes of her father, who likes Colburne, marries Carter; her husband is by-and-by led into temptation by a creole lady—a Frenchwoman of Louisiana—and falls; she discovers his faithlessness, and, while he is away campaigning, goes back to New Boston; he is by-and-by killed in battle, and the widow of course marries Colburne.

The plot, then, is of the simplest; as we have said, the characters we find not interesting, and with one exception not well drawn—in fact, it would be saying too little not to say that they are, for the most part, the old familiar figures; yet the book is a readable book, and the author is, on the whole, to be congratulated on his success. So much nowadays is packed into a novel that it is possible for us to say all this, and not be inconsistent with ourselves. These are some of the things that will make the book liked, and on account of which we have read it with some pleasure, and recommend its perusal to our readers: First of all, the author is a lively and quite agreeable companion. Then there is, in the first chapters, a rather good satirical description of the society which supports existence in our better sort of college towns. We hear it whispered by the way that New Haven is not well pleased with this part of the new novel, but, we suppose, several other towns in more than one other State of the Union have an equal right with New Haven to be offended. Perhaps this passage may serve as well as any for a specimen of this portion of the book:

> The Whitewood house was of an architecture so common in New Boston that in describing it I run no risk of identifying it to the curious. Exteriorly it was a square box brick, stuccoed to represent granite; interiorly it consisted of four rooms on each floor, divided by a hall up and down the centre. This was the original construction, to which had been added a greenhouse, into which you passed through the library. Trim, regular, geometrical, one half of the structure weighing to an ounce just as much as the other half, and the whole perhaps forming some exact fraction of the entire avoirdupois of the globe, the very furniture distributed at measured distances, it was precisely such a building as the New Boston soul would naturally create for itself. Miss Ravenel

noticed this with a quickness of perception as to the relations of the mind and matter which astonished and amused Mr. Colburne.

"If I should be transported on Aladdin's carpet," she said, "fast asleep, to some unknown country, and should wake up and find myself in such a house as this, I should know that I was in New Boston. How the professor must enjoy himself here! This room is exactly twenty feet one way by twenty feet the other. Then the hall is just ten feet across by just forty in length. The professor can look at it and say, Four times ten is forty. Then the greenhouse and the study balance each other like the paddle boxes of a steamer. Why will you all be so square?"

Then there is some interesting reading descriptive of the days when Butler and Banks[449] ruled and reigned in New Orleans, and not a little peculating and debauchery went on there. The account of Chief-Quartermaster Carter's cotton "speculation," and his purchase of steamboats, will help people to understand what the Department of the Gulf was in the days of military rule. We quote with pleasure—part of which only is due to the cracker story—this little picture of a major-general in New Orleans. The time of the occurrence is after the removal of General Butler, and the picture is very good so far as it goes:

"Is the major-general pleasant?" asked Lillie with an inconsequence which was somewhat characteristic of her. She was more interested in learning how a great dignity looked and behaved than in hearing what were his opinions on the subject of freemen's labor.

"I don't know that a major-general is obliged to be pleasant, at least not in war time," answered the doctor, a little annoyed at the interruption to the train of his ideas. "Yes, he is pleasant enough; in fact something too much of deportment. He put me in mind of one of my adventures among the Georgia Crackers.[450] I had to put up for the night in one of those miserable up-country log shanties where you can study astronomy all night through the chinks in the roof, and where the man and wife sleep one side of you and the children and dogs on the other. The family, it seems, had had a quarrel with a neighboring family of superior pretensions, which had not yet culminated in gouging or shooting. The eldest daughter, a ragged girl of seventeen, described to me with great gusto an encounter of the hostile tribe. Said she, 'Miss Jones, she tried to come the dignerfied over mar. But that she found her beater, My mar is hell on dignerty.'—Well, the major-general runs rather too luxuriantly to dignity. But his ideas on the subject of reorganizing labor are excellent, and have my earnest respect and approbation. I believe that under his administration the negroes will be allowed and encouraged to take their first certain step towards civilization. They are to receive some remuneration—not for the bygone centuries of forced labor and oppression—but for what they will do hereafter."

We get also some satire on the custom which prevailed among our Northern governors of dispensing military patronage not with an eye single to the advantages of military service, but with a side glance, necessary we suppose, to the exigencies of politics. And finally, to put the best last, there is some excellent description of campaigning in the terrible swamps and forests of Louisiana and in the trenches of Port Hudson and the repulse, and the stirring battle-piece where we witness the brave death of Carter. It is as a picture of the military service in the Department of the Gulf, "a novel of the war," that we think best of the book. So considered, it deserves more praise, we think, than any of its numerous rivals for popular favor, and is so well worth reading that, though we are constrained to pronounce the work a poor novel, we are quite willing to say that it is a poor novel with a deal of good in it.

This first edition contains a great many typographical errors, some of them so gross as only to be accounted for by supposing gross carelessness in the proof-reader.

33

THE DECLINE OF THE NOVEL

Anonymous

Nation (1868).

The young man of literary aspirations who came up to London in the days of Elizabeth and James found the companies of players his best publishers and the theatre his best field of fame. It was the time of the drama's reign, and there was hardly a pretender to the throne. When James's son was beheaded the drama was also deposed, and when his grandson was restored to Whitehall the drama—which also was none the better for its sojourn in foreign parts—came back with him and likewise enjoyed its own again.[451] But, like the political restorations, the literary restoration was followed by a forced abdication, and the literature of England, like England herself, passed under the dominion of the adopted foreigner. The reign of William of Orange was the beginning of a period in English literature which may be described as the reign of translation.[452] From his time on through that of Anne and two of the Georges,[453] was the period when the authors of Greece and Rome were done in English. Tradition still put into the pocket of the literary adventurer coming up from the provinces or the universities the tragedy or comedy that was to make his fortune, but generally the young man's allegiance was soon transferred from the manager to the publisher. If he had little genius of his own, he set about earning the reverse of Durham's compliment to Cowley:[454]

> Horace's wit and Virgil's state
> He stole, but did not emulate,

or he leased himself to a bookseller and became an "eminent hand." If he were a man of native ability, still he had to follow the classical fashion—make love with the help of Venus, lash the town with the adaptations of Juvenal, laugh at it in imitations of Horace, lampoon his enemies as Atossa and Sporus, teach criticism out of Quintilian, and agriculture, as Evelyn would have taught it in his projected technical school, out of Varro and Calamella.[455]

Between the second of the two periods, which we have roughly described as the dramatic age and the age of translation, between this and the present time, which we call the period of ascendancy of the novel, there was an interregnum when the crown was, so to speak, in commission; when the authority of the kingdom was wielded by a regency of which, as regards power and influence, the members were very nearly equal. The novels of Fielding, Richardson, and Smollett; the social, moral, and humorous essay—descended from the noble house of *The Spectator,* once near the throne; the political pamphlet and gazette; the controversial or doctrinal religious treatise—each of these had pretensions to the chief place quite as great as the translation could offer, perhaps greater, at the moment when, as the eighteenth century ended, two more powerful claimants, one shortly after the other, appeared in the field. Genuine poetry, brought forward by Thomson, Cowper, and Burns, made a bold push for the throne, and was, indeed, momentarily set upon it by help of Byron, Scott, Moore, Southey, Coleridge, Campbell, and their fellows. But almost immediately she yielded to Scott and his host of followers, who gave us for our ruler the prose fiction, our *de facto* monarch at the present time.

But it may be fairly questioned, we think, if the empire of the novel is not now beginning to decline. Its life, of course, is not threatened; the question is only of the continuance of its predominance and supremacy. From the dawn of literature there have been stories, and, till the end of time, the story-telling instinct will exist and be powerful. Each age will delight to see its characteristic features set before it in portraits of individual men and women; man will always be fascinated by the vivid portrayal of human passions, and interested in analysis of the characters, and narrations of the fortunes and misfortunes, of beings who can be made to seem to each man more like himself than the actual beings whom the sight of his bodily eye conceals from him. We may be sure that the novel in its essentials will never cease from among men. But, if we understand the matter, the novel, never again perhaps to be less than powerful, has been paramount and sovereign so long, not in virtue of what it is essentially, but by reason of other causes, the operation of which is of late beginning to be less influential.

Once the theatre in London, as once in Athens, was the field for literary activity, because the stage furnished then the best and almost the only opportunity for the publishing of thought. Afterwards literature in England was chiefly translation, because the largest audience within reach of the literary man was composed of the court, the bar, and the universities, and the demand of the audience was for classical literature. The limits of the audience had gradually been enlarging and gradually had included greater and greater numbers of that class whose most pronounced literary inclination is a liking for stories, when there appeared opportunely a writer whose genius for story-telling was nothing less than marvellous; and since Scott then elevated the novel to the first place in literature it has been maintained there be an almost unnumbered host of able writers, whose efforts have been spurred by the requirements of a constantly increasing multitude of novel readers, until now there is hardly a character within the range of humanity, or an incident possible of occurrence in our civilization, or that of any historic period, which has not been presented to our attention over and over again with every degree of ability; but, of course, oftenest by unskilful artists. What "cause" is there which has not been treated of by the democrats, or aristocratic, or Caesarist novelist; or the Pedobaptist, or Catholic, or Rationalist, or Ritualistic, or "muscular Christian," or "nervous pagan," or mystical novelist; or the woman's spherical novelist; or the totally abstinent or bacchanalian novelist; or the musical novelist; or the Pre-Raphaelite, or shaping imagination, or Gothic, or classicist novelist; or the military or naval novelist; or the mediaeval, or prophetic, or realistic, or observant novelist; or the Hebrew, or Anglo-Saxon, or Norman, or Oriental, or Aboriginal Indian novelist; or the phrenological, or fox-hunting, or gambling, or bigamist, or forging, or murdering, or saintly, or diplomatic, or federal, or secessionist, or Jacobite, or Puritanical, or villatic, or romantic, or medical, or horsey, or some other sort of novelist? There is literally no end to the varieties and sub-varieties of sociological, artistic, scientific, theological, political, historical, and other sermons, which now for a quarter of a generation have been preached to the world under cover of the life and adventures of the two lovers, their parents, friends, and enemies.

There may be a Frenchman to come who will discover and ventilate some fresh, yet unknown improper relation of the sexes. And incest was hardly exhausted by Chateaubriand. And the great American novel remains unaccomplished. For years we have had Mr. Street, an author favorably situated at the head of sloop navigation on the right bank of a stream which shames the Rhine; and Mr. Whitman has for years contemned the comma and every badge of subserviency to foreign literature,[456] but still we are without anything that can be called the jubilant, expansive novel of Libertad and These States, and which does justice to the new human and topographical nature discovered by Columbus and invented by Thomas Jefferson. But if we except these two, why should we not say that all possible fields for the novel writer have been so often cropped, as the farmers say, that nobody will be able to get much from any one of them unless he is a cultivator of very rare ability; one of a hundred thousand; a man able to put into the ground as much as he expects to get out of it, more than a dozen ordinary farmers would be worth if all their possessions were taken together.

One is justified, then, in taking it for true that just now all possible methods of working up the novelist's materials are familiar to the point of weariness, and that there is in the mind of the reader a sort of disgust—perhaps only sub-conscious in many cases, only momentary in many cases, and in some cases not just—at the very appearance of the novelistic poem. And probably it is true, too, that the literary insufficiency of the vast majority of mechanical people who set themselves to producing what has long been the most popular of literary products, has had the effect of indisposing really able, ambitious workmen to range themselves as fellow-workmen in the decaying fraternity. But on these two reasons, as not going very far towards the root of the matter, we are not inclined to insist with any strenuousness. Looking further for a cause of that decline in the novel's authority which we seem to see, we settled on what we think the real one. It is possible to make a rough but not false division of the public interested in general reading into two classes, of which the superior is that whose tastes and wishes give direction to the literary activity of the better sort of writers, while the inferior is composed of persons seeking merely for amusement, and satisfied with the service of writers correspondingly inferior. Of course, let us here remark, we speak in a very general way—of what is called general literature, of the mass of workers in general literature, and of its readers in the mass. Now, just at present that class of general readers who have some claim to be called thinkers, have begun to discuss earnestly—that is to say, with a view of forming opinions, with a determination more or less definite of acting on the opinions they may form, with a wish, then, for exactness as regards facts and arguments—thus we say, they have begun the discussion of a vast number of difficult questions, questions which, for a generation or two, while yet they were new and in the merely picturesque stage, made the subject-matter of the novel, and also were the cause why the novel supported itself so long in the position where the great founder of its dominion was able to place it. Because these questions were in the picturesque stage, the novelist seized upon them; because they were new to the public, their devotees turned novelists in order to put them in a pleasing form before the audience which it was hoped to persuade, or whose attention, at all events, it was desired to gain.

This attention has been gained, and the discussion of so many of these questions has been entered on, and entered on so seriously, that, apparently, we are on the eve of radical changes, or, rather, we are, apparently, on the eve of the beginnings of radical changes, in the structure and even the very foundation of our social and political system. The woman question, which once Miss Mulock greatly agitated,[457] is nowadays debated in the legislatures of two countries; trades unions and co-operation occupy the minds of responsible senators instead of confusing the readers of "The Wandering Jew";[458] the negro in the State in many parts of the country where once he was a happy, dancing figure in "The White Slaves" and "Uncle Tom's Cabins as they are,"[459] and sits in political conventions and divides parties in States where, not so long ago, his most eye-filling position was that of a Gospel-saint or an Old-Testament prophet in the genuine *Uncle Tom's Cabin* or the *Dreds*;[460] the troubled seeker of Newman's *Loss and Gain*[461] is today represented by the Ritualist who confounds Convocation and editorially hopes for an invitation for Bishop Coxe to go with Archbishop Manning to the next general council;[462] the right of the former party-of-the-second-part in a courtship to be the party-of-the-first-part, once asserted by implication only in the "*Cousin Stellas*" of ten years ago, is today supported by weekly papers with regular, or irregular, financial articles and all the political news.[463] We are all getting to be sociologists, and sociology now leaves the novel where it used to amuse us, and which it used to make so interesting and important, and becomes the staple of the more serious, earnest, regularly appointed "organ of opinion."

The successor of the novel, in the chief of the literary places of power, will doubtless be the family of weekly and monthly journals. It is a family of respectable antiquity. When the novel was but a humble dependant upon the romance, the periodical devoted to literary and social subjects suddenly gained a very honorable and influential position, which, to be sure, was not, in Addison's time, capable of permanent occupation. It existed, however, and existed in good repute beside the other forces over which the translation dominated; and in the half-century since the novel attained the highest rank, has gradually been drawing to its standard greater and greater numbers of the ablest writers, till now, in this age of business done by steam and telegraph; in this age, therefore, of news brought by steam and lightning from every quarter of the earth; in this age, therefore, of business newspapers read daily by millions who more and more insist that the daily newspaper shall more and more exclusively devote itself to news; in this age which naturally, then, makes of the newspaper a type to which literature naturally may and, indeed, necessarily must conform itself if it is to reach the reader—in this age the quarterly, monthly, and weekly press, aided by its kinship with its immensely powerful unliterary brother, seems destined to an easy conquest of the throne.

That this is well, we are optimistic enough to believe. In Adam's fall we sinned all, to be sure; but it was once for all, we imagine, that the race then made universal lapse; since Adam's day, when we have moved altogether it has been upwards, we suppose, towards laudable ends, and with tolerably good results. At any rate, it is permitted to hope so; and as to the matter in hand, we presume the decay of the novel and the rise of good essays in magazines—or in weekly papers, say—does not make very forcibly in favor of the pessimist's view. However, the question of the loss and gain to literature consequent on the change of dynasty which we expect, we do not intend considering at present. To such ambitious writers as do not possess special qualifications for creating what we have called the essential novel, who is not a heaven-born genius in the story-telling way, or in the invention of characters, or in the analysis of the soul of man—to such writers we feel like saying that, should they very much longer continue coming up to the market with novels in hand, they will very probably—almost certainly in fact, and sometime soon—find themselves arrived a day too late for the fair.

34

LITERATURE TRULY AMERICAN

Anonymous

Nation (1868).

It is very common to hear it said that a magazine or a newspaper, or other periodical published in this country, ought to be "truly American"; that this or that poem is truly American; that somebody ought to write a truly American novel; and Mr. Eugene Benson[464] and Mr. Walt Whitman are so far from being the only persons who declare that they crave a literature that shall be truly American, that perhaps half of us who have turned our thoughts in that direction would admit that we are of Mr. Whitman's and Mr. Benson's mind. We, for our own part, confess that we do not know with exactness just what is meant by these words so often heard. It is not to be doubted that there is some idea, more or less clear, of what it is that he wants in every man's mind who says that our literature ought to be truly national. But we may as well acknowledge that in our belief this idea is oftener very vague than at all well defined. We seriously doubt if the man who is in the habit of saying that he would like his family paper or his magazine to be American from the very first line to the last, would not be obliged to sit mute if called on suddenly to state accurately what he means by a magazine to be American from the first line to the last. Yet there must be something at the bottom of so common an expression: and we have given the subject some consideration, with intent to fix, if possible, upon the meaning of it—some of the meanings of it, rather; for when we constantly see that phrases of precise definition have all sorts of various meanings given them, it is not to be hoped that a phrase which extremely often is used without any thought will not be found to have very various senses.

If Mr. A. B. Street should say that he wanted our literature to be purely American, we should know what he desired.[465] He would want, we suppose, descriptive prose and poetry devoted to the panther or American lion, to the soaring of the bald-headed eagle, to the Palisades, to Washington and Lafayette, to Mount Hood,

Weehawken, and Qommunipaw, to the rush of the indigenous buffalo besides the north fork of the Platte River, to the Red man and his canoe, to the Falls of Niagara—though the Mammoth Cave of our own Kentucky, as not being partly in a British province, might appear a better theme for patriotic bards. We all know very well what constitutes a truly American literature in the opinion of those persons of whom we have chosen to make Mr. Street the exemplar. They seem to think America is square miles of natural scenery, and a fauna and flora entirely different from the fauna and flora of certain despotic countries that we might name.

Then akin to these are the people who, in the plenitude of a genuine love of country, and, it is true, in the plenitude of a lack of knowledge on almost all subjects, seem to have a notion that Columbus's discovery of America necessitated the invention of a new world of literature. Not very long ago the people of Utica, in this State, laughed with derision at an Irishman who, when a certain Mr. Price set up an opposition band, remarked that, "Now there was a new band, there'd be new music entirely," as if the blessed Saint Cecilia[466] were about to descend in the interest of Mr. Price and his new sax-horns. But our Irish fellow-citizen, even under the misconstruction of the Sassenach, was certainly not more foolish than many of his unnaturalized compatriots. It is not improbable that if Utica had on one of those old days been polled on the question, Shall we have a purely American science of pure mathematics? a large minority of the legal voters would have thought upon the national emblem and voted in the affirmative. But there is little need of speaking about these classes of friends of an American literature, for they now have little influence and are disappearing with rapidity, and their works follow them with even space.

Then there are men among us who, when they demand that out literature shall be national, seem to have in mind, as distinctively American literature, literature printed on a Hoe press in four or five editions daily. They give a great and honest admiration to the Washington correspondents of our enterprising journals. Anything more moderate in tone or more polished in style than the ordinary reckless newspaper writing seems to them somehow foreign and aristocratic, and to be distrusted, if not denounced, as "un-American." Trying literary performance by this standard, the only standard which they use, they have serious doubts if it is desirable that a prospective editor should go to college. Generally they think that the best training for men who are to supply their fellow-citizens with opinions morally and intellectually sound, who are to wield the influence of several thousand ordinary men as regards most political and social questions—the best training for the editor, in short, is to go into a printing-office when he is twelve years old, get thoroughly grounded in Mr. Greeley's tabulated election returns, and, generally, feed his mind on newspaper cuttings, party platforms, orations, lives and speeches of "little giants," "prominent statesmen," "first men," and "grand public men," and things of that kind. Many men have been trained in this way, some to honors, none, so far as we know, to dishonor, as men count dishonor, but none either, so far as we know, to be of any service to literature, unless one thinks literature is made fresh every night and delivered by carriers every morning. People who do conceive of it so, when they talk of un-American literature mean most literature—all which their peculiar training has unfitted them to estimate aright.

Then there are many men, more than one not unfamiliar with the rural districts one would imagine, who remember very well the time when no foreigner had anything but insolence and contempt to bestow upon the American government and people, and who, being not so much wider-minded than the calumniators of America, got themselves into a condition of bitter hostility to the country's enemies and have hardly yet begun to get out of it, but are still painfully patriotic in all the relations of life. It is of one of these that the story is told that, presiding in a justice's court in the West, he indignantly rebuked a young attorney for citing English decisions on a common law point in the court of a man whose father had fought in the Revolutionary war, and who himself had been present as the battle of New Orleans. The sort of literature which would seem truly American to Americans of this kind is well known. Not to mention too many branches of literature, it is for them the poetry is fearfully and wonderfully made which describes the making of the national colors with the "milky baldric of the skies,"[467] the flush of aurora, and the azure of the mid-day heavens. The books of travel are written for them which describe Pompeii and call to mind the highly creditable record of our native land in the matter of volcanoes; which compute in dollars and cents the enormous annual expenses of the British royal family, and compare them with the cost to this country of the establishments of President Polk or President Taylor;[468] and, in general, books are written for them which not only set forth a justifiable pride in the United States, but a more or less unjustifiable contempt for all things not American. Of course much of this contempt is due to the spirit of uncorrected brag which infests the hearts of most men, American or otherwise; we would not say that it all has so creditable an origin as a natural wish to resist and offset foreign calumny and misconception. But whether born of uninstructed patriotism or of ignorance, it exists—most of it existed—and what would truly be an American literature, tried by this standard, it is easy to see.

Disregarding the notions of those who entertain so inadequate a conception of what America is as to suppose that all is said when one gives its boundaries on the map; or, when one thinks of it as a democracy, and of a democracy as ignorance and vulgarity; when one has celebrated our peculiar autumn foliage, and vindicated the superiority of the Hudson to the Rhine, and substituted as poetical properties the mocking-bird for the nightingale and Tecumseh for Sir Lancelot;[469] or when one has sufficiently hated the Queen's birthday and exalted the twenty-second of February[470]—disregarding these and similar ideas of the true American and the truly American in literature, we come to an idea of which Mr. Whitman may as well be made the representative, and which, if not over wise, is not altogether foolish, and is to be spoken of with some respect.

Although, as men and women have for some centuries agreed to talk to each other, orally and in print, Mr. Whitman is to be called indecent in speech; and although, as able men have for all these centuries been talking to us for the common benefit, one would say that he lacks a pinch or so of brains; and although it may be said that in his poems he has an artist leads a very intermittent life, and is generally non-existent, still there is this to be said of him, that he has so heartily and honestly, with such belief in it and such love for it, "sounded his barbaric yawp,"[471] as he happily phrases it, in behalf of the greatness of mere manhood and the consequent perfect equality of every man with every other, that he may very well be honored as a preacher of democracy—democracy in its wider, humanitarian sense—as it is perhaps to exist in "these States." For the poet of democracy we, for our own part, feel as if we should have to wait, and, thinking of what poetry is, we feel as if we should wait willingly. What Mr. Whitman wants when he speaks of an American literature we can easily understand, and to a certain extent we can join with him in the desire for its coming. That every power of the mind of man may be allowed free activity, that no laws or institutions of human invention may be suffered to trammel man's faculties in any field of human endeavor, that men may believe in themselves, respecting each other democratically, and neither feudally oppressing nor pitying any one, that the feeling of brotherhood may become the basis of society—all this is good. We like to believe that in America, sooner than elsewhere, and better than elsewhere, it may all come to pass, and there is a reason why a literature that should reflect Mr. Whitman's hope in this regard, might, with no great impropriety, be styled distinctively an American literature.

Not to take up more time in considering special traits that it may be desirable our literature should or should not possess, it is safe to say that American literature, to use figurative language, ought to express America. But it is safe, too, to say that it will; that it cannot help doing just that, whatever that may be. Literature, as somebody says, all literature whatsoever, is the thought of thinking souls. And whatever it is that souls in American are thinking, whether concerning democracy, or the color of the leaves in the fall, or wild-fowl on Seneca lake, or what not, is perfectly sure to get itself expressed. We may be absolutely confident that just so far as America is American, the literature of America will be American, and whosoever wants more than this is not wise, and, for another thing, will certainly be disappointed; and people who are anxious that our literature should be American may rest assured that it cannot be anything else.

35

POE AND HAWTHORNE

Eugene Benson

Galaxy (1868).

Eugene Benson (1839-1908), painter, art critic, and essayist, was born in Hyde Park, New York; he moved to New York City in 1856 to study at the National Academy of Design. Benson supported his studies and painting by writing; through his contributions to the New York *Evening Post*, he quickly became known as a leading art critic. Notwithstanding his admiration for French culture (he was an early advocate of Baudelaire's poetry), Benson was fiercely committed to the importance of American literary nationalism. In 1873, Benson settled permanently in Italy with his wife; he continued to paint, but with little financial reward.

Poe and Hawthorne are two brilliant exceptions in American literature. Among Americans, they are the only two literary men who have had the sense of beauty and the artist's conscience in a supreme degree. They belonged to the haughty and reserved aristocracy of letters. Hawthorne was like a magician, hidden from the world, creating his beautiful phantasms; Poe was like a banished spirit, abased among men, exercising an intellect, and drawing upon a memory that implied a clearer and higher state of being than that of material and common life. His mental perspicacity and unerringness suggest a super-mortal quality, and make the simple narrative of "The Gold Bug" appalling; for you will remark that the sentiment of strangeness and terror which it begets is excited without any of Poe's usual resources—that is, of death or murder in any form. One is appalled by the *precision* of the intellect revealed, which is unmatched by any English story-writer.

But it is because of the beauty that Poe created, because of his knowledge of its harmonious conditions, because of his admirable style, the pure and strange elements of his nature, his general and minute method, rather than because of his puzzles, or curious intellectual *inventions* that he is a type of exquisite and brilliant genius. The interest of his inventions would be exhausted at the first reading, if they were not contained in a beautiful literary form—if they were not set before us with a fine literary art, that charms even while it is the medium of the exceptional, and often of the repugnant!

Poe was dominated by intellectual conscience; Hawthorne was dominated by moral conscience. For the proper objects of intellect, Poe had an intellectual passion. Hawthorne's *passion*, on the contrary, spent itself upon moral subjects; you will notice that the texture of his stories is woven about a question of moral responsibility and the transmission of traits. The problem of sin engaged Hawthorne; the processes of crime—that is, pure intellect in action— engaged Poe.

Very few persons have a definite idea of the difference between the unique and unrivalled genius of these two men, who still had positive, if hidden, bonds of sympathy with each other. They were radically, though not obviously different in their work and in the spring of their being. Both had an exquisite sense of the music of thought; both loved the mysterious and *bizarre*; both labored to paint the exceptional and dominate our intellects with an intimate sense of the spiritual and unseen.

Poe began his work in a natural but emphatic tone. He was direct. He took his reader from particular to particular, exercising a power like that of the Ancient Mariner upon the wedding guest.[472] He arrested his reader upon a particular *word*. The emphasis with which he pronounces it, gives a foretaste of the lurking *dénouement*. With particular words he struck the key-tone of his tale; with particular words he rapidly and ominously indicated the unaccustomed road upon which he urged your mind.

Hawthorne works in a different fashion. He deepens the tone of *his* stories by flowing and unnoticeable phrases. He avoids emphasis; by gentle speech he lures you on and on into the depressing labyrinth of human motives and human character, touching with exquisite grace, elaborating a trait, at all times letting you but faintly see the connection of events, but always establishing the fact of the subtle relationships of his characters, and making you feel that his subject has its roots deep in the fluid depths of the ancient, unseen, and baffling world of the past, which the intellect cannot sound, but only dive into, and come forth to tell strange tales of its shadowy experience. To Poe, nothing was shadowy. On the contrary, everything was fearfully distinct and real and positive to his tenacious and penetrating intellect. In Hawthorne, moral conscience was abnormal in its development. In Poe, it did not even exist. Hawthorne, in his method, was an idealist; Poe, in his method, was a realist. But Poe realized the unreal, and Hawthorne idealized the real. But for Poe's poetic sense, he would have been as prosaic and literal, *at all times*, as Defoe. But for Hawthorne's poetic sense, he would have been a droning moralist. Poe confronted the mind with the appalling; Hawthorne begot in it a sense of the unstableness and ungraspableness of human experience. He aimed to give us glimpses of the moral ramifications and far-reaching influence of human actions.

Both Poe and Hawthorne were alike and splendidly endowed with imagination; but Poe had more *invention*—in fact, a most marvellous faculty of invention—and he was the more purely intellectual of the two. Hawthorne was a man of delicate sentiment, of mystical imagination; Poe was a man of little sentiment, but great delicacy of intellectual perception, and had a realistic imagination. Hawthorne incessantly lures the mind from the visible and concrete to the invisible and spiritual. To him, matter was transparent; in his stories he paints material bodies, and gradually resolves them into abstractions; they become allegorical, typical—uncertain incarnations of certain affinities, traits, qualities. Poe never is vague, never indefinite. His most weird and arbitrary imagination is made palpable and positive to the reader. The predominating sentiment of Hawthorne is sad and depressing; that of Poe is melancholy and ominous.

Poe's intellect was direct, inevitable, and unerring; Hawthorne's was indirect, easily turned from its object, and *seemed* purposeless; Poe's always seemed instinct with intense purpose. Hawthorne would have preferred to *hide* all his processes of creation; he shunned observation; he was isolated; happy in evoking beautiful figures, but having no desire to let you see *how* he did it. But Poe, like all *inventors*, took pains to let you see the whole process of his mind; he laid bare his mechanism; he took his listener step by step with him, well aware that he *must* admire a skill and ingenuity so superior to all he had known.

The action of Hawthorne's mind was like a limpid stream that, fed from hidden springs, glints and glides through sunshine, darkens in shadow, loses itself only to surprise you again with the same placid and dark-flowing waters. In point of style Hawthorne is serene and elusive. Poe is nervous, and terse, and positive. Hawthorne's style is characterized by exquisite sequence of thought and imperceptible gradations of tone and sentiment. Poe's is more salient, has a more rapid and impassioned, and always tense expression.

We are to understand Poe by his stories of "The Gold Bug," "Ligeia," "Eleanora," "The Oblong Box," "The Murders in the Rue Morgue," "The Fall of the House of Usher," and "The Black Cat;" we are to understand Hawthorne by *The House of the Seven Gables*, *The Scarlet Letter*, "The Minister's Black Veil," and *Mosses from an Old Manse*.[473]

Poe's "House of Usher," "Ligeia" and "Eleanora" are the most beautiful examples of his prose, and show the positive influence of De Quincey's *Opium Eater*. They have great beauty of diction, as well as great *precision* of expression, which is the chief characteristic of the style of "The Gold Bug." His word-palette seems to be full and rich, and he uses it to produce sombre and beautiful pictures. He produces all the effects of poetry, save that of flowing and musical sounds.

Poe was unquestionably under the first impression of De Quincey's magazine writings when he wrote his most imaginative stories. They have the same full and impressive diction—long and mournful breathings of an over-burdened *memory*, associated with a wish to define, to explain, to analyze. In "The Gold Bug," in "The Murders in the Rue Morgue," and in "The Black Cat," Poe attained an original expression, and his own mind, pure from all foreign influence, seems to be in full action. It is in them that he narrates and analyzes, but gives no room for the reverie and the dream which add so much to the haunting beauty of his "House of Usher" and "Ligeia."

De Quincey and Poe had a remarkable tendency to reverie, which was, in both cases, always checked by a passion for analysis. De Quincey, who is the subtlest of all English critics, often broke out of his finest dreams, and interrupted his most perfect analyses, to indulge a trivial and colloquial habit of his mind. Poe never made the same mistake. He never was trivial or garrulous in a story designed to produce a particular impression. In a few words, Poe's intellectual moods were always *in keeping*. But I believe that De Quincey first put in full play Poe's expressional faculties, and first subjected him to the fascination, and showed him the novelty of subtle and sustained analysis as a literary process at the command of the story writer.

But if Poe, by intellectual sympathy, derived his first style from De Quincey, he did not make himself guilty of De Quincey's defects; and, later, his final and original style, which attained its perfection in "The Gold Bug," has no relation to any writer, but is the result of his peculiar mental endowments.

In his earlier stories, Poe was brilliant and exuberant. Miss Prescott is not more extravagant than he is in "The Assignation."[474] But if he was extravagant, he was also charmingly and beautifully romantic; and in "Ligeia," and in "The House of Usher," intense and pervading thought satisfies the understanding, while the imagination is impressed by splendid descriptive phrases.

Hawthorne's earlier style shows no positive foreign influence. He was always subdued and restrained; he was pervaded by a fine thoughtfulness. The action of his thought was not intense and incessant, like Poe's, but gentle and diffused. Hawthorne indicated himself at the beginning as a man of intellectual *sentiment*; Poe as a man of intellectual *passion*. The distinction to be made between the *effect* of the literary expression of the two minds is, that Hawthorne charms, and Poe enchains the reader. That Hawthorne has left us a larger quantity of perfect artistic work than Poe, we must attribute to the happier conditions of his life. Hawthorne may have been a little chilled by the want of the pleasant sun of popularity; but Poe was embittered by the success of others, and pre-eminently unfortunate in his destiny. Nothing that he ever wrote begot a sentiment of love; but the gentle and friendly genius of Hawthorne awakens a responsive spirit in the reader.

Hawthorne never seems to feel or think very deeply; he thought comprehensively. Compared with hearty writers like Dickens or Irving, or with impassioned writers like De Quincey or George Sand, he is the chilliest, the most elusive of spirits, and his only merit seems to be that of a graceful habit of thinking, and of a temperate illustration and expression of his subject. His delicate humor oftenest is like the fantasy of an invalid; the merriment is pathetically contrasted with a sad and time-stricken face.

Hawthorne was not closely related to his contemporaries. The vivid and near, and all that characterizes the social life of New England today, seem as remote from him as the ghost of a memory. He is our American type of the "Dreamer"—a being who could have no place in our thoughts of American life but for Hawthorne.

While Theodore Parker was accumulating facts, and fulminating against a people swayed hither and thither by conscience and selfishness; while Emerson was affronting the formalists and the literalists, Hawthorne was dreaming. He brooded over his thoughts; he spent season after season in reverie—reverie which is foreign to our idea of the American man. Out of his loneliness, out of his reveries, out of his dreams, he wove the matchless web of a style which shows what Lowell calls the rarest creative intellect, in some respects, since Shakespeare.

The *Passages from Hawthorne's Note Books* let us see how he perfected his art, and taught himself to use, with such inimitable clearness and delicacy, his means of expression.[475] They are the answer to the question why we never discover shallow or dry or meagre places in his perfectly sustained, evenly flowing, harmoniously and exquisitely *toned* style. Hawthorne seems to have had but one activity, and that activity was the activity of the artist. He used his mind to mirror nature. To see, to feel, to reflect, was his whole life—all of which is contained in the single word *reverie*. The observations of nature which enrich his literary work are not the observations of an active, restless, or acquisitive mind; in his work they seem accidental; they lend themselves, without any effort on his part, to accent his work, to break the monotony of his mood. Many of his pages show great sweetness of temper, an almost feminine feeling toward nature and life.

The alembic of his genius gave forth the material consigned to it colored and mellowed, and often saddened in hue, by his unique and pervading personality.

Hawthorne, a descendant of the Puritans, living in a Puritan state, in a Puritan town, without making himself the historian of Puritanism, rendered it with force, gave the spirit and sentiment of its life, in an intense and powerful story which contains the very soul of its faith. Hawthorne, in *The Scarlet Letter*, has made the work of the historian and judge superfluous as an examination and decision upon Puritanism as a *social fact*. The most intense work of our greatest romancer, without a word of indignation, without an aggressive phrase, embodies Puritanism in a story, and leaves it with a stigma more terrible than the scarlet letter it seared upon the heart of the wretched Dimmesdale, and fixed upon the black robe of the heroic martyr, Hester Prynne. With what fine and beautiful art he lets you see the monstrous pretensions of the legal spirit, which was the soul of Puritanism, and its brutal blunder in intruding itself between a woman's heart and its most sacred need—"sacred even in its pollution." In the treatment of his theme, how fine, how elevated, how comprehensive is Hawthorne! With what indulgence and sympathy, with what reverence does he consider the mournful and mute woman, blank-eyed and helpless before her judges, who seek to unmask the secret of her heart. Poor Hester Prynne! how different her treatment from the treatment of the Syrian Magdalen! Noble and outraged, much suffering, silent woman! victim of legal, obtuse and mechanical minds, she shall forever exist as the type of her sex wronged by bigotry, victim of a harsh, unelastic social faith!

Among Hawthorne's *creations*, it seems to me that Clifford in *The House of Seven Gables*, and Donatello in *The Marble Faun*, are the most remarkable. Clifford is an example of portrait art; Donatello is a beautiful and palpable creation. They illustrate the two phases of his genius. The portrait of Clifford in the chapter entitled "The Guest," is in every particular an uncommon and impressive piece of work. Poe never did anything so subtle, so floating and vague, and at the same time vivid and sure, as the description and analysis of Clifford. You shall judge.

> The expression of his countenance—while, notwithstanding it had the light of reason in it—seemed to waver and glimmer, and nearly to die away, and feebly to recover itself again. It was like a flame which we see twinkling among half-extinguished embers; we gaze at it more intently than if it were a positive blaze, gushing vividly upward— more intently, but with a certain impatience, as if it ought either to kindle itself into satisfactory splendor, or be at once extinguished .... Continually, as we may express it, he faded away out of his place; or, in other words, his mind and consciousness took their departure, leaving his wasted, grey, and melancholy figure—a substantial emptiness, a material ghost—to occupy his seat at table. Again, after a blank moment, there would be a flickering taper-gleam in his eye-balls. It betokened that his spiritual part had returned, and was doing its best to kindle the heart's household fire, and light up intellectual lamps in the dark and ruinous mansion, where it was doomed to be a forlorn inhabitant .... His old faded garment, with all its pristine brilliancy extinct, seemed, in some indescribable way, to translate the wearer's untold misfortune, and make it perceptible to the beholder's eye. It was the better to be discerned, by this exterior type, how worn and old were the soul's more immediate garments; that form and countenance, the beauty and grace of which had almost transcended the skill of the most exquisite of artists. It could the more adequately be known that the soul of the man must have suffered some miserable wrong from its earthly experience. There he seemed to sit, with a dim veil of decay and ruin between him and the world, but through which, at flitting intervals, might be caught the same expression, so refined, so softly imaginative, which Malbone, venturing a happy touch with suspended breath— had imparted to the miniature. There had been something so innately characteristic in this look, that all the dusky years, and the burden of unfit calamity which had fallen upon him, did not suffice utterly to destroy it.

After this matchless rendering of traits, Hawthorne gives a matchless analysis of Clifford's nature—than which I know of nothing more finely distilled in expression, more discriminating in thought. It is Hawthorne's masterpiece, with which his *Faun* only is comparable.

You will observe that in all of Hawthorne's works the remarkable and characteristic thing is the incessant action of the moral faculty, exquisitely toned by the artistic sentiment. The moral sense and the artistic sense make of him a channel of issue, and it is their incessant play of expression which begets the distrust and doubt of the reader upon all the old, creed-closed questions of life. He is the finest distillation of the New England mind, and he has idealized all that is local in New England life. No marble can be too white or too exquisitely sculptured to symbolize his pure and beautiful genius, and suggest the gratitude which his countrymen owe to him.

Edgar A. Poe, the gift of the South to American literature, was more selfish, and more unfortunate in his life than Hawthorne. In him the moral faculty had no play—everything was concentrated to feed his sense of beauty and strangeness. He was no shifting questioner and elusive thinker, but ardent, intense and his mind was the intellectual centre of the anomalous! But what an imperial imagination, and how august and music-voiced was his memory! *The Raven* and the prose poem, "Ligeia," are magical in their influence.[476] All that there is of beauty and regret and strangeness to be employed by the literary artist was employed by Poe in "Ligeia." He awakens the imagination, touches the profoundest emotions of an impassioned lover, and by associating his creation with the idea of death, produces that wild melancholy, that rebellious and protesting sentiment of regret, which possesses us at the memory of a beautiful, beloved, but vanished object!

Charles Baudelaire, the French poet, who has given the best literary portrait and the briefest and best analysis of Poe's genius with which I am acquainted, remarks that, in none of his works did he express the sanguine and sensual side of love. "To Poe the divine passion of love appeared magnificent, star-like, and always veiled with melancholy. His portraits of women are *aureoled*; they shine in the midst of a supernatural vapor, and are painted in the emphatic manner of an adorer .... His women, luminous and sick, dying of strange ailments, and speaking with a voice that resembles music, correspond with the nature of their Creator—by their strange aspirations, by their knowledge, by their incurable melancholy, they participate in his being, and resemble him."[477]

As a critic, Poe was illiberal and perverse, burning incense before second- rate writers, and stinging the author he professed to admire. His article on Hawthorne, like Antony's oration, with its blasting phrase, "Yet Brutus was an honorable man,"[478] leaves an impression contrary and fatal to the frequent professions of high appreciation which make the refrain of his article. As a critic, Poe spent himself upon questions of detail, and, in all cases, belittled his subject. He did not exercise the most engaging faculties of his mind. He is brilliant, caustic, stinging, personal without geniality, expressing an irritated mind. Reading his criticisms, we think his literary being might be said to resemble a bush that blossoms into a few perfect flowers, but always has its thorns in thickest profusion. Poe was what may be called a *technical critic*. He delighted to involve his reader in the mechanism of poetry, and convict his victim of ignorance, while he used his knowledge as a means to be exquisitely insolent. He was like an art critic stuffed with the jargon of studios, talking an unknown language; careless about the elements of the subject which, properly, are the chief and only concern of the public. That Poe was acute, that he was exact, that he was original, no one can question; but he was not stimulating, and comprehensive, and generous, like the more sympathetic critics, as, for example, Diderot or Carlyle.[479] It was his misfortune to have been called to pronounce upon the ephemera of literature, conscious that he was expected to think them fixed stars.

His critical notices of American men of letters show the incessant struggle of a supreme scorn muffled and quieted from time to time in the acknowledgment of mitigating circumstances to excuse the literary criminals that he had assembled. When he wishes to be indulgent and generous, it is the indulgence and generosity of a cat stroking a mouse—the claw is felt by the breathless victim. He probably tore his subject more than any critic that ever lived. In his criticisms, the sentences are sharp, stinging, pointed, and sparkling; they are like so many surgical knives—they lay open the living subject, quivering and fainting, to the bone. Poe had no indulgence for literary offenders. He had the instincts of a mole slaking its thirst over its prey. Poe scratched almost every one of his literary contemporaries, and, in nine cases out of ten, he was right in his destructive work. But he was virulent, mocking, incensing, seeming to be animated with a personal animosity for his subject; he was like a literary pirate, sparing neither friend nor foe, always accusing other people of stealing, while his own hands were not pure. There is no question but that Poe had a monomania upon the subject of plagiarism. He was so skilful in hiding his own literary thefts that he seems to have been impelled to accuse others, and talk incessantly of a vice known best to himself—it was an example of his perverseness of nature. Although the arrogant and incensing elements of Poe's nature had full play in his remarks on American writers; they were only the accidental expression of his literary genius, and should not determine our critical conclusions. Poe had what I may call, pre-eminently, a beautiful mind—all its highest and characteristic manifestations were harmonious and enchaining. His combination of the strange or the unusual with the lovely or symmetrical, is his claim to be considered original. No writer ever reached a more personal expression of the beautiful than Poe. He was modern in all his traits, romantic as no other American writer, delighting in the horrible as the natural antithesis of his radiant and mournful ideal beauty. The women that live in his stories, the ideal women of a modern epoch, pale, sick, luminous, wide-eyed, preyed upon by "incurable melancholy," versed in the most recondite knowledge, vibrative, and "speaking with a voice that resembles music," and as from profound depths, have no existence outside of Poe's beautiful and strange imagination. He created them as Eugène Delacroix created his women, who are remarkable, impassioned, profound, and make you think. Poe's "Lenore," "Ligeia" and "Morella," are the creations of a poet—ideal and natural as the Venus of Milo[480] is ideal and natural, but in no sense realistic, and having no relation to the photographic and literal portraits of women such as we find in modern novels.[481] It is for them that Poe has drawn upon his poetical nature; they are the issue of his sense of beauty, which in him was more imperative in its needs, and more creative in its energy than the same sense in Hawthorne. Among Americans, I repeat, Poe and Hawthorne are the only two literary men who have had the sense of beauty and the artist's conscience in a supreme degree; and in Poe it was more isolated, or unalloyed, than in Hawthorne.

36

THE GREAT AMERICAN NOVEL

John W. De Forest

Nation (1868).

John William De Forest (1826-1906) was born in Seymour, Connecticut and wrote two comparatively undistinguished novels, as well as a work of history and two travel books, between 1851 and 1859. After raising a company of volunteers for the Union at the start of the Civil War, he was commissioned a captain in 1862. His war-time experiences formed the basis of one of the most compelling Civil War novels, and De Forest's only successful work, *Miss Ravenel's Conversion from Secession to Loyalty* (1867). (See 2: No. 31 and 2: No. 32.) De Forest left the army in 1868 to turn to writing professionally, but earned little from novels that pandered to a readership with which he was out of touch. The following essay became a major focus for debates about American literary nationalism and popularized the phrase "great American novel" in subsequent responses and reactions.

A friend of ours, a fairly clever person, and by no means lacking in common sense on common subjects, has the craze in his head that he will some day write a great American novel.

"If I can do it," he says, "I shall perform a national service, and be hailed as a national benefactor. It will be acknowledged that I have broken another of the bonds which make us spiritually colonists and provincials. Who does not like to have his portrait taken? If I ever can give expression to the idea which is in my brain, the American people will say, 'That is my picture,' and will lavish heart and pocket in remuneration. It is a feat worthy of vast labor and suffering."

During eight or ten years he has struggled for his prize. He has published two or three experiments which have been more or less well spoken of by the critics, and rather more than less neglected by the purchasing public. Now and then, collared by the material necessities of life, or by some national enthusiasm even stronger than his own, he has turned aside into other pursuits, has fought at the front, has aided in the work of reconstruction, has written articles and other things which he calls trivialities. But at every leisure moment he returns to his idea of producing "the Great American Novel."

Will he produce it? Will anyone of his generation produce it? It is very doubtful, for the obstacles are immense. To write a great American poem is at present impossible, for the reason that the nation has not yet lived a great poem. It cost unknown centuries of Greek faiths and fightings to produce the *Iliad*. It cost all the Roman kings and all the Roman republic to produce the *Aeneid*. The *Divine Commedia* is the result of a thousand years of the Papal Church. Europe had to live critically through the crusades and the feudal system before it could earn the *Gerusalemme Liberata* and the *Orlando Furioso*.[482] *Paradise Lost* is the summary of all gnosticism and Protestantism. We may be confident that the Great American Poem will not be written, no matter what genius attempts it, until democracy, the idea of our day and nation and race, has agonized and conquered through the centuries, and made its work secure.

But the Great American Novel—the picture of the ordinary emotions and manners of American existence—the American *Newcomes* or *Misérables* will, we suppose, be possible earlier "Is it time?" the benighted people in the earthen jars of commonplace life are asking. And with no intention of being disagreeable, but rather with sympathetic sorrow, we answer, "Wait." At least we fear that such ought to be our answer. This task of painting the American soul within the framework of an American novel has seldom been attempted, and has never been accomplished further than very partially—in the production of a few outlines. Washington Irving was too cautious to make the trial; he went back to fictions of Knickerbockers and Rip Van Winkles and Ichabod Cranes; these he did well, and we may thank him for not attempting more and failing in the attempt.[483] With the same consciousness of incapacity Cooper shirked the experiment; he devoted himself to Indians, of whom he knew next to nothing, and to backwoodsman and sailors, whom he idealized; or where he attempted civilized groups, he produced something less natural than the wax figures of Barnum's old museum. If all Americans were like the heroes and heroines of Cooper, Carlyle might well enough call us "eighteen millions of bores."[484] As for a tableau of American society, as for anything resembling the tableaux of English society by Thackeray and Trollope, or the tableaux of French society by Balzac and George Sand, we had better not trouble ourselves with looking for it in Cooper.

There come to us from the deserts of the past certain voices which "syllable men's names"[485]—names that seem to sound like "Paulding," "Brown," "Kennedy"—and we catch nothing further. These are ghosts, and they wrote about ghosts, and the ghosts have vanished utterly. Another of these shadowy mediums, still living, if we are not misinformed, is W. Gilmore Simms, of whom the best and worst thing to be said is this—that he is nearly as good as Cooper, and deserves fame nearly as much.

Thus do we arrive, without frequent stoppage, at our own time. Hawthorne, the greatest of American imaginations, staggered under the load of the American novel. In *The Scarlet Letter, The House of the Seven Gables,* and *The Blithedale Romance* we have three delightful romances, full of acute spiritual analysis, of the light of other worlds, but also characterized by only a vague consciousness of this life, and by graspings that catch little but the subjective of humanity. Such personages as Hawthorne creates belong to the wide realm of art rather than to our nationality. They are as probably natives of the furthest mountains of Cathay or of the moon as of the United States of America.[486] They are what Yankees might come to be who should shut themselves up for life to meditate in old manses. They have no sympathy with this eager and laborious people, which takes so many newspapers, builds so many railroads, does the most business on a given capital, wages the biggest war in proportion to its population, believes in the physically impossible and does some of it. Hawthorne's characters cannot talk. Certainly not in the style of this western world; rather in the language of men who never expressed themselves but on paper, and paper in dreams. There is a curious lack of natural dialogue in Hawthorne's books and with this, of course, a lack of almost all other signs of the dramatic faculty. Besides, his company is so limited. New Englanders they profess to be: to be sure, they are of the queerest; men and women of the oldest, shyest, most recluse nature, and often creatures purely ideal; but they never profess to be other than New Englanders. The profoundest reverence for this great man need prevent no one from saying that he has not written "the Great American novel."

The nearest approach to the desired phenomenon is *Uncle Tom's Cabin.* There were very noticeable faults in that story; there was a very faulty plot; there was (if idealism be a fault) a black man painted whiter than the angels, and a girl such as girls are to be, perhaps, but are not yet; there was a little village twaddle. But there was also a national breadth to the picture, truthful outlining of character, natural speaking, and plenty of strong feeling. Though comeliness of form was lacking, the material of the work was in many respects admirable. Such Northerners as Mrs. Stowe painted we have seen; and we have seen such Southerners, no matter what the people South of Mason and Dixon's line may protest; we have seen such negroes, barring, of course, the impeccable Uncle Tom—uncle of no extant nephews, so far as we know. It was a picture of American life, drawn with a few strong and passionate strokes, not filled in thoroughly, but still a portrait. It seemed, then, when that book was published, easy to have more American novels. But in *Dred* it became clear that the soul which a throb of emotion had enabled to grasp the whole people was losing its hold on the vast subject which had so stirred us. Then, stricken with timidity, the author shrank into her native shell of New England. Only certain recluse spirits, who dwell between the Dan and Beersheba[487] of Yankeedom, can care much for Doctor Hopkins as he goes through his exercises in *The Minister's Wooing,* while the attempt to sketch Aaron Burr as a contrast to the clerical hero shows most conclusively happy ignorance of the style of heartless men of the world.[488] *The Pearl of Orr's Island* is far better.[489] It is an exquisite little story, a thoroughly finished bit of work, but how small! There, microscope in hand over the niceties of Orr's Island, we wait for another cameo of New England life. But what special interest have Southerners and Westerners and even New Yorkers in Yankee cameos?

There was another dainty and by no means feeble story about a still further north-eastern realm of rocks and sand and fog. A brother of James Russell Lowell, a poet in soul, though he writes in prose, went to Newfoundland in search of the ideal and wrote *The New Priest in Conception Bay*.[490] A few choice, critical souls praised it, we believe, and we believe the purchasing public hardly noticed it. It should not have been let die, and its author should have been called on for more novels. True, large, and kindly portraits of rustic souls were in it, and, as we judge of such things, the best landscape pictures ever done by an American, unless we except Thoreau.[491] Story there was almost none, and no more passion than in a Fra Angelico.[492] What can be hoped for such books in presence of a popular taste which accepts Headley as a Tacitus, and J. S. C. Abbot as a Livy, and Dr. Holland as a Virgil?[493] One is tempted, even as Congressmen often are, to fall back on "lore," and cry "O tempora! O mores!"[494] We mention this book partly to call attention to the fact that its author, like so many of his competitors, evaded the trial of sketching American life and fled abroad for his subjects.

We shall always be grateful to Oliver Wendell Holmes for *The Autocrat of the Breakfast Table,* and hardly less grateful for *The Professor*.[495] Lighter, brighter, keener, defter prose has rarely been written in America. It would not be unworthy of a Parisian; it would not be scorned by Taine or Veuillot or Henri de Rochefort.[496] He has also created a personage or two whom we shall not forget. A truer American than "the young man called John" never breathed. We would not let him vote anywhere on the mere credit of his ideas. If men and angels should swear to us that he was born abroad, we would not believe them. He is one of us, and was from conception. If he lives, he reads the *Ledger* and John S. C. Abbott, and does not read *The New Priest in Conception Bay*.[497] Heaven prosper him and give him more wisdom! There is true picturing of intelligent and unintelligent Eastern Americans in *The Autocrat* and *The Professor*. But when the author undertakes a novel, he enters upon a field where passion is needed, to say nothing of his lack of what the poor despised phrenologer calls "constructiveness," and in that he is lacking. We have carefully watched his efforts, not in hardness of spirit, but with sympathy; we know how much easier it is to look on than to run. We acknowledge that *Elsie Venner* and *The Guardian Angel* are interesting books.[498] They show us faithfully the exterior of commonplace New England life, and they travesty the solemnities of New England's spiritual life with an amusing manual dexterity. But the artist is hampered by his scientific theories and by his lack of fervent emotional sympathy. His characters do not go; they do not drag him along; they do not drag us. We seem to see that they disappoint their creator; that they do not move as he thought they would when he devised them; that they do not fulfil the double purpose of living for themselves and for him. From time to time he stops and rubs one up, seeking to galvanize it into life and action. We have little doubt that he was far better satisfied with *The Guardian Angel,* for instance, when he commenced it than when he wrote the closing lines.

Moreover, these two tales are not American novels; they are only New England novels; they are localisms. We shall not be suspected of desiring to belittle New England, of denying its moral strength, keen intellect, and wide influence. But Dr. Holmes has not sketched that Yankeehood which goes abroad and leavens the character of the Republic. The Yankeehood which he exhibits is that which stays in corners, speechless and impotent—a community of old maids, toothless doctors, small-souled lawyers, village poets, and shelved professors; the coterie of an antique borough, amusing, queer, and of no account. We do not say that he should have put a Wendell Phillips or an Emerson on the canvas; we only say that he has given no prominence to those moral characteristics of New England which produce such moves of the national heart and teachers of the national intellect.[499] He has scarcely alluded to the kind of society which made these men what they are, unless we allow an exception in favor of the suggestiveness of Byles Gridley.[500] Thus his stories are not only provincial in scene and in the form of the dialogue, but provincial to the very depths of the spirit which animates them.

Of *Waiting for the Verdict* we have little to add beyond what we have already said.[501] While acknowledging anew the breadth of the plan, we must reiterate our abhorrence of the execution. In reading it we remember with wicked sympathy the expression of a bachelor friend, "I hate poor people's children," and we are attempted to add, "and poor people." We do not believe that "the poor and lowly of God's creatures" are his chosen; we hold that, if he has any preference, it must be for the wisest, sweetest, and noblest. It is dreadful to have low, tattered, piebald, and stupid people so rubbed into one. Remembering Mr. Dolls, we feel a desire to burn a rag under the noses of Mrs. Davis's characters. The mild sermonizing twaddle of the *Hills of the Shatemuc* was better than this pertinacious exhibition of moral dwarfs, bearded women, Siamese twins, and headless calves.[502] Bad taste in the selection of minor features and a rushing of adjectives to the head spoil a book which, in its table of contents, gives grand promise of an American novel.

There are other experiments. There are novels by Mr. Mitchell, and Mr. Bayard Taylor, and Mr. Beecher, and many more, but none is better than those already mentioned and few are nearly as good.[503] Is there in the whole catalogue a *Newcomes,* a *Vanity Fair,* a *Misérables,* or even a *Little Dorrit* or a *Small House at Allington*?[504] Is there, in other words, a single tale which paints American life so broadly, truly, and sympathetically that every American of feeling and culture is forced to acknowledge the picture as a likeness of something which he knows? Throwing out *Uncle Tom's Cabin,* we must answer, Not one!

And why not? There are several reasons, some material, some spiritual, some pertaining to the artists, some to the subject. It is not necessary to dwell upon the fact that, as we produce few books of any kind, we must consequently produce a duly small proportion of good ones. Another cause of barrenness is not less obvious, but it has been upheld by selfishness, short-sightedness, and national prejudice; it has been so strenuously defended that argument is pardonable. For lack of an international copyright the American author is undersold in his own market by the stolen brain labor of other countries. The ordinary reader, wanting a book and not caring what, providing it will amuse him, steps into a bookstore and finds *Little Dorrit* alongside *Elsie Venner*. He is pretty sure that both are good, but he sees that the former costs a dollar and three-quarters, and the latter two dollars. He buys the cheaper because it is the cheaper. *Little Dorrit* is stolen and sold without any profit to Dickens; and *Elsie Venner* remains unsold, to the loss of Holmes. Nine readers out of ten do this; each one is glad of the twenty-five cents saved; then he wonders "why we don't have an American literature." Depend upon it that, if *Little Dorrit* were the dearest, more Elsie Venners would be sold, and Dr. Holmes would give more time to planning and perfecting novels. The American reader must have his book cheap. He will pay high for his coat, his sofa, his piano, his portrait; but the furniture and clothing and adornment of his minds must be cheap, even if nasty. To charge the English price for a good novel might provoke an indignation meeting, if not a riot. When the "young man called John" buys a book for two dollars, he wants very nearly the worth of his "stamps" in paper and binding. The intellectual or moral value of his purchase is a trifle in his estimation, and he does not mean to pay much for it. In short, the American author has first a small sale, and second a small profit on his sale. His business does not keep him, and so he works carelessly at it, or he quits it. His first book is marked by inexperience; his second is produced in haste to meet a board-bill; and he stops disgusted before he has learned his trade. If he could make a living, and if in addition he saw a chance, the merest chance, of doing as well as a grocery merchant, he would go on and perhaps be our glory; who knows?

We do not say that he would do miraculously well, even under favoring pecuniary circumstances. The child of a community which is given to estimating the claims of books by their cheapness, his culture is not of the highest. Clever, but not trained, he knows better what to write than what not to write. Just consider the educational advantages of an English writer of by no means the highest rank, Miss Thackeray, the author of *The Village on the Cliff*.[505] Surrounded from infancy by such men as the creator of *Vanity Fair*, the creator of *David Copperfield*, and their compeers, she may be said to have inherited the precious knowledge of what not to write. You can see it in her books; there is no great power, but there is nothing threadbare, nothing sophomorical; there is a careful, intelligent workmanship, like that of an old hand. The power of an author is frequently, if not generally, no more than the expression of the community which produced him. Have we as yet the literary culture to educate Thackerays and Balzacs? Ah! we only buy them—cheap.

So much for the artist; now for the sitter. Ask a portrait-painter if he can make a good likeness of a baby, and he will tell you that the features are not sufficiently marked nor the expression sufficiently personal. Is there not the same difficulty in limning this continental infant of American society, who is changing every year not only in physical attributes, but in the characteristics of his soul? Fifteen years ago it was morality to return fugitive slaves to their owners—and now? Five years ago everybody swore to pay the national debt in specie—and now? Our aristocracy flies through the phases of Knickerbocker, codfish, shoddy, and petroleum. Where are the "high-toned gentlemen" whom North and South gloried in a quarter of a century since? Where are the Congresssmen who could write *The Federalist?* Where is everything that was? Can a society which is changing so rapidly be painted except in the daily newspaper? Has any one photographed fireworks or the shooting-stars? And then there is such variety and even such antagonism in the component parts of this cataract. When you have made your picture of petrified New England village life, left aground like a boulder near the banks of the Merriman, does the Mississippian or the Minnesotian or the Pennsylvanian recognize it as American society? We are a nation of provinces, and each province claims to be the court.

When Mr. Anthony Trollope commences a good novel, he is perplexed by no such kaleidoscopic transformations and no such conflicting claims of sections. Hundreds of years ago English aristocracy assumed the spiritual nature which it holds with little change to the present day. It had made its code of honor; it had established its relations with the mass of the nation; it had become the model for all proper Englishmen. At this time it is a unit of social expression throughout the kingdom. A large class of people go up to London at the same season, go into the country at the same season, lead very nearly the same lives, have the same ideas and tastes. There you have something fixed to paint; there you have the novelist's sitter; there you have his purchaser. All successful English romances are written with reference to this class; they may attack it, they may defend it, they always paint it. Wealthy, it pays high prices for books; anxious to be amused, it buys them freely. For such a sitter who would not, if possible, learn to paint well? Thus, also, in France, only that the subject is always in your studio, for the studio is Paris. If George Sand writes a provincial novel, she does it not for the people of the province described but for the Parisians, who occasionally like a novelty. But the French author need not know more than that one city to have his subject and his public. In divided Germany there have been few good novels. In distracted Italy there has been, perhaps but one—*I Promessi Sposi*—and that historical, the result of half a lifetime, the task of a great poet.[506] Even Manzoni found it a mighty labor to depict the life of a nation of provinces.

Well, what are our immediate chances for a "great American novel?" We fear that the wonder will not soon be wrought unless more talent can be enlisted in the work, and we are sure that this sufficient talent can hardly be obtained without the encouragement of an international copy right. And, even then, is it time?

37

AMERICANISM IN LITERATURE

Thomas Wentworth Higginson

Atlantic Monthly (1870).

Thomas Wentworth Higginson (1823-1911), minister, reformer, soldier, and man of letters, was born in Cambridge, Massachusetts. He became a Unitarian minister in 1847 and actively campaigned against the Fugitive Slave Act (see 2: n.238); he was one of the "Secret Six" who funded John Brown's (1800-1859) attempt to foment a slave insurrection at Harper's Ferry, Virginia. Higginson, who went on to write a vast quantity of essays, history, and some fiction, was a major contributor to the *Atlantic Monthly* from the early 1860s. In response to his "Letter to a Young Contributor" (April, 1862), in which he exhorted women to submit work, Emily Dickinson sent Higginson four poems, and thus began a long correspondence between the two. Although Higginson discouraged Dickinson from publishing poetry during her lifetime, he edited some of her poems (much "correcting" and dislocating them in the process) in two posthumous volumes (1890 and 1891). In November, 1862, Higginson had accepted a Civil War commission as colonel of the First South Carolina Volunteers, which consisted of slaves freed by Union forces; later in life, he continued to maintain his social commitment, welcoming the establishing of the National Association for the Advancement of Colored People and the racial activism of W. E. B. Du Bois.

The voyager from Europe who lands upon our shores perceives a difference in the sky above his head; the height seems loftier, the zenith more remote, the horizon-wall more steep; the moon appears to hang in middle air, beneath a dome that arches far beyond it. The sense of natural symbolism is so strong in us, that the mind unconsciously seeks a spiritual significance in this glory of the atmosphere. The traveller is not satisfied to find the sky alone enlarged, and not the mind,— *coelum, non animum*.[507] One wishes to be convinced that here the intellectual man inhales a deeper breath, and walks with bolder tread; that philosopher and artist are here more buoyant, more fresh, more fertile; that the human race has here escaped at one bound from the despondency of ages, as from their wrongs.

And the true and healthy Americanism is to be found, let us believe, in this attitude of hope; an attitude not necessarily connected with culture nor with the absence of culture, but with the consciousness of a new impulse given to all human progress. The most ignorant man may feel the full strength and heartiness of the American idea, and so may the most accomplished scholar. It is a matter of regret if thus far we have mainly had to look for our Americanism and our scholarship in very different quarters, and if it has been a rare delight to find the two in one.

It seems unspeakably important that all persons among us, and especially the student and the writer, should be pervaded with Americanism. Americanism includes the faith that national self-government is not a chimera, but that, with whatever inconsistencies and drawbacks, we are steadily establishing it here. It includes the faith that to this good thing all other good things must in time be added. When a man is heartily imbued with such a national sentiment as this, it is as marrow in his bones, and blood in his veins. He may still need culture, but he has the basis of all culture. He is entitled to an imperturbable patience and hopefulness, born of a living faith. All that is scanty in our intellectual attainments, or poor in our artistic life, may then be cheerfully endured: if a man sees his house steadily rising on sure foundations, he can wait or let his children wait for the cornice and the frieze. But if one happens to be born or bred in America without this wholesome confidence, there is no happiness for him; he has his alternative between being unhappy at home and unhappy abroad; it is a choice of martyrdoms for himself, and a certainty of martyrdom for his friends.

Happily, there are few among our cultivated men in whom this oxygen of American life is wholly wanting. Where such exist, for them the path across the ocean is easy, and the return how hard! Yet our national character develops slowly; we are aiming at something better than our English fathers, and we pay for it by greater vacillations and vibrations of movement. The Englishman's strong point is a vigorous insularity which he carries with him, portable and sometimes insupportable. The American's more perilous gift is a certain power of assimilation, through which he acquires something from every man he meets, but runs the risk of parting with something in return. For the result, greater possibilities of culture, balanced by greater extremes of sycophancy and meanness. Emerson says that the Englishman of all men stands most firmly on his feet. But it is not the whole of man's mission to be found standing, even at the most important post. Let him take one step forward,—and in that advancing figure you have the American.

We are accustomed to say that the war and its results have made us a nation, subordinated local distinctions, cleared us of our chief shame, and given us the pride of a common career. This being the case, we may afford to treat ourselves to a little modest self-confidence. Those whose faith in the American people carried them hopefully through the long contest with slavery will not be daunted before any minor perplexities of Chinese immigrants or railway brigands or enfranchised

women. We are equal to these things; and we shall also be equal to the creation of a
literature. We need intellectual culture inexpressibly, but we need a hearty faith still
more. "Never yet was there a great migration that did not result in a new form of
national genius." But we must guard against both croakers and boasters; and above
all, we must look beyond our little Boston or New York or Chicago or San Francisco, and be willing citizens of the great Republic.

The highest aim of most of our literary journals has thus far been to appear English, except where some diverging experimentalist has said, "Let us be German," or
"Let us be French." This was inevitable; as inevitable as a boy's first imitations of
Byron or Tennyson. But it necessarily implied that our literature must, during this
epoch be chiefly second-rate. We need to become national, not by any conscious
effort, implying attitudinizing and constraint, but by simply accepting our own life.
It is not desirable to go out of one's way to be original, but it is to be hoped that it
may lie in one's way. Originality is simply a fresh pair of eyes. If you want to aston-
ish the whole world, said Rahel, tell the simple truth.[508] It is easier to excuse a thousand defects in the literary man who proceeds on this faith, than to forgive the one
great defect of imitation in the purist who seeks only to be English. As Wasson has
said,—"The Englishman is undoubtedly a wholesome figure to the mental eye; but
will not twenty million copies of him do, for the present?"[509] We must pardon
something to the spirit of liberty. We must run some risks, as all immature creatures
do, in the effort to use our own limbs. Professor Edward Channing used to say that
it was a bad sign for a college boy to write too well; there should be exuberances
and inequalities. A nation which has but just begun to create a literature must sow
some wild oats. The most tiresome vaingloriousness may be more hopeful than
hypercriticism and spleen. The follies of the absurdest spread-eagle orator may be
far more promising, because they smack more of the soil, than the neat Londonism
of the city editor who dissects him.

It is but a few years since we have dared to be American in even the details and
accessories of our literary work; to make our allusions to natural objects real, not
conventional; to ignore the nightingale and skylark, and look for the classic and
romantic on our own soil. This change began mainly with Emerson. Some of us
can recall the bewilderment with which his verses on the bumblebee, for instance,
were received, when the choice of subject seemed stranger than the words themselves.[510] It was called "a foolish affectation of the familiar." Happily the illusion of
distance forms itself rapidly in a new land, and the poem has now as serene a place
in literature as if Andrew Marvell had written it.[511] The truly cosmopolitan writer is
not he who carefully denudes his work of everything occasional and temporary, but
he who makes his local coloring forever classic through the fascination of the
dream it tells. Reason, imagination, passion, are universal; but sky, climate, costume,
and even type of human character, belong to some one spot alone till they find an
artist potent enough to stamp their associations on the memory of all the world.
Whether his work be picture or symphony, legend or lyric, is of little moment. The
spirit of the execution is all in all.

As yet we have hardly begun to think of the details of execution in any art. We do not aim at perfection of detail even in engineering, much less in literature. In the haste of American life, much of our literary work is done at a rush, is something inserted in the odd moments of the engrossing pursuit. The popular preacher becomes a novelist; the editor turns his paste-pot and scissors to the compilation of a history; the same man must be poet, philanthropist, and genealogist. We find a sort of pleasure in seeing this variety of effort, just as the bystanders like to see a street-musician adjust every joint in his body to a separate instrument, and play a concerted piece with the whole of himself. To be sure, he plays each part badly, but it is such a wonder he should play them all! Thus, in our rather hurried and helter-skelter literature, the man is brilliant, perhaps; his main work is well done; but his secondary work is slurred. The book sells, no doubt, by reason of the author's popularity in other fields; it is only the tone of our national literature that suffers. There is nothing in American life that can make concentration cease to be a virtue. Let a man choose his pursuit, and make all else count for recreation only. Goethe's advice to Eckermann is infinitely more important here than it ever was in Germany: "Beware of dissipating your powers; strive constantly to concentrate them. Genius thinks it can do whatever it sees others doing, but it is sure to repent of every ill-judged outlay."[512]

In one respect, however, this desultory activity is an advantage: it makes men look in a variety of directions for a standard. As each sect in religion helps to protect us from some other sect, so every mental tendency is the limitation of some other. We need the English culture, but we do not need it more evidently than we need the German, the French, the Greek, the Oriental. In prose literature, for instance, the English contemporary models are not enough. There is an admirable vigor and heartiness, a direct and manly tone; King Richard still lives: but Saladin also had his fine sword-play; let us see him.[513] There are the delightful French qualities,—the atmosphere where literary art means fineness of touch. "Où il n'y a point de délicatesse, il n'y a point de littérature. Un écrit où ne se rencontrent que de la force et un certain feu sans éclat n'annonce que le caractère."[514] But there is something in the English climate which seems to turn the fine edge of any very choice scimitar till it cuts Saladin's own fingers at last.

God forbid that I should disparage this broad Anglo-Saxon manhood which is the basis of our national life. I knew an American mother who sent her boy to Rugby School in England, in the certainty, as she said, that he would there learn two things,—to play cricket and to speak the truth. He acquired both thoroughly, and she brought him home for what she deemed, in comparison, the ornamental branches. We cannot spare the Englishman from our blood, but it is our business to make him more than an Englishman. That iron must become steel; her, harder, more elastic, more polished. For this end the English stock was transferred from an island to a continent, and mixed with new ingredients, that it might lose its quality of coarseness, and take a finer and more even grain.

As yet, it must be owned, this daring expectation is but feebly reflected in our books. In looking over any collection of American poetry, for instance, one is struck with the fact that it is not so much faulty as inadequate. Emerson set free the poetic intuition of America, Hawthorne its imagination. Both looked into the realm of passion, Emerson with distrust, Hawthorne with eager interest; but neither thrilled with its spell, and the American poet of passion is yet to come. How tame and manageable are wont to be the emotions of our bards, how placid and literary their allusions. There is no baptism of fire; no heat that breeds excess. Yet it is not life that is grown dull, surely; there are as many secrets in every heart, as many skeletons in every closet, as in any elder period of the world's career. It is the inter-preters of life who are found wanting, and that not on this soil alone, but through-out the Anglo-Saxon race. It is not just to say, as some one has said, that our lan-guage has not in this generation produced a love-song, for it has produced Brown-ing; but was it in England or in Italy that he learned to sound the depths of all hu-man emotion?[515]

And it is not to verse alone that this temporary check of ardor applies. It is often said that prose fiction now occupies the place held by the drama during the Eliza-bethan age. Certainly this modern product shows something of the brilliant profu-sion of that wondrous flowering of genius; but here the resemblance ends. Where in our imaginative literature does one find the concentrated utterance, the intense and breathing life, the triumphs and despairs, the depth of emotion, the tragedy, the thrill, that meet one everywhere in those Elizabethan pages? What impetuous and commanding men are these, what passionate women; how they love and hate, struggle and endure; how they play with the world; what a trail of fire they leave behind them as they pass by! Turn now to recent fiction. Dickens's people arc amusing and lovable, no doubt; Thackeray's are wicked and witty; but how under-sized they look, and how they loiter on the mere surfaces of life, compared, I will not say with Shakespeare's, but even with Chapman's and Webster's men.[516] Set aside Hawthorne in America, with perhaps Charlotte Brontë and George Eliot in England, and there would scarcely be a fact in prose literature to show that we modern Anglo-Saxons regard a profound human emotion as a thing worth the painting. Who now dares delineate a lover, except with good-natured pitying sar-casm, as in *David Copperfield* or *Pendennis?* In the Elizabethan period, with all its un-speakable coarseness, hot blood still ran in the veins of literature; lovers burned and suffered and were men. And what was true of love was true of all the passions of the human soul.

In this respect, as in many others, France has preserved more of the artistic tra-dition. The common answer is, that in modern French literature, as in the Elizabe-than, the play of feeling is too naked and obvious, and that the Puritan self-restraint is worth more than all that dissolute wealth. I believe it; and here comes in the intel-lectual worth of America. Puritanism was a phase, a discipline, a hygiene; but we cannot remain always Puritans. The world needed that moral bracing, even for its art; but, after all, life is not impoverished by being ennobled; and in a happier age, with a larger faith, we may again enrich ourselves with poetry and passion, while wearing that heroic girdle still around us. Then the next blossoming of the world's imagination need not bear within itself, like all the others, the seeds of an epoch of decay.

I utterly reject the position taken by Matthew Arnold, that the Puritan spirit in America was essentially hostile to literature and art.[517] Of course the forest pioneer cannot compose orchestral symphonies, nor the founder of a state carve statues. But the thoughtful and scholarly men who created the Massachusetts Colony brought with them the traditions of their universities, and left these embodied in a college. The Puritan life was only historically inconsistent with culture; there was no logical antagonism. Indeed, that life had in it much that was congenial to art, in its enthusiasm and its truthfulness. Take these Puritan traits, employ them in a more genial sphere, adding intellectual training and a sunny faith, and you have a soil suited to art above all others. To deny it is to see in art only something frivolous and insincere. The American writer in whom the artistic instinct was strongest came of unmixed Puritan stock. Major John Hathorne, in 1692, put his offenders on trial, and generally convicted and hanged them all. Nathaniel Hawthorne held his more spiritual tribunal two centuries later, and his keener scrutiny found some ground of vindication for each one. The fidelity, the thoroughness, the conscientious purpose, were the same in each. Both sought to rest their work, as all art and all law must rest, upon the absolute truth. The writer kept, no doubt, something of the sombreness of the magistrate; each, doubtless, suffered in the woes he studied and as the one "had a knot of suffering in his forehead all winter" while meditating the doom of Arthur Dimmesdale, so may the other have borne upon his own brow the trace of Martha Corey's grief.[518]

No, it does not seem to me that the obstacle to a new birth of literature and art in America lies in the Puritan tradition, but rather in the timid and faithless spirit that lurks in the circles of culture, and still holds something of literary and academic leadership in the homes of the Puritans. What are the ghosts of a myriad Blue Laws compared with the transplanted cynicism of one *Saturday Review*?[519] How can any noble literature germinate where young men are habitually taught that there is no such thing as originality, and that nothing remains for us in this effete epoch of history but the mere recombining of thoughts which sprang first from braver brains? It is melancholy to see young men come forth from the college walls with less enthusiasm than they carried in; trained in a spirit which is in this respect worse than English toryism,—that it does not even retain a hearty faith in the past. It is better that a man should have eyes in the back of his head than that he should be taught to sneer at even a retrospective vision. One may believe that the golden age is behind us or before us, but alas for the forlorn wisdom of him who rejects it altogether! It is not the climax of culture that a college graduate should emulate the obituary praise bestowed by Cotton Mather on the Rev. John Mitchell of Cambridge, "a truly aged young man." Better a thousand times train a boy on Scott's novels or the *Border Ballads* than educate him to believe, on the one side, that chiv-

alry was a cheat and the troubadours imbeciles, and on the other hand, that universal suffrage is an absurdity and the one real need is to get rid of our voters.[520] A
great crisis like a civil war brings men temporarily to their senses, and the young
resume the attitude natural to their years, in spite of their teachers; but it is a sad
thing when, in seeking for the generous impulses of youth, we have to turn from
the public sentiment of the colleges to that of the workshops and the farms.

It is a thing not to be forgotten, that for a long series of years the people of our
Northern States were habitually in advance of their institutions of learning, in courage and comprehensiveness of thought. There were long years during which the
most cultivated scholar, so soon as he embraced an unpopular opinion, was apt to
find the college doors closed against him, and only the country lyceum—the people's college—left open. Slavery had to be abolished before the most accomplished
orator of the nation could be invited to address the graduates of his own university.
The first among American scholars was nominated year after year, only to be re-
jected, before the academic societies of his own neighborhood. Yet during all that
time the rural lecture associations showered their invitations on Parker and Phillips;
culture shunned them, but the common people heard them gladly. The home of
real thought was outside, not inside, the college walls. It hardly embarrassed a professor's position if he defended slavery as a divine institution; but he risked his
place if he denounced the wrong. In those days, if by any chance a man of bold
opinions drifted into a reputable professorship, we listened sadly to hear his voice
grow faint. He usually began to lose his faith, his courage, his toleration,—in short,
his Americanism,—when he left the ranks of the uninstructed.

That time is past; and the literary class has now come more into sympathy with
the popular heart. It is perhaps fortunate that there is as yet but little *esprit de corps*
among our writers, so that they receive their best sympathy, not from each other,
but from the people. Even the memory of the most original author, as Thoreau, or
Margaret Fuller Ossoli, is apt to receive its sharpest stabs from those of the same
guild.[521] When we American writers find grace to do our best, it is not so much
because we are sustained by each other, as that we are conscious of a deep popular
heart, slowly but surely answering back to ours, and offering a worthier stimulus
than the applause of a coterie. If we once lose faith in our audience, the muse
grows silent. Even the apparent indifference of this audience to culture and high
finish may be in the end a wholesome influence, recalling us to those more important things, compared to which these are secondary qualities. The indifference is
only comparative; our public prefers good writing, as it prefers good elocution; but
it values energy, heartiness, and action more. The public is right; it is the business of
the writer, as of the speaker, to perfect the finer graces without sacrificing things
more vital. "She was not a good singer," says some novelist of his heroine, "but she
sang with an inspiration such as good singers rarely indulge in." Given those positive qualities, and I think that a fine execution does not hinder acceptance in America, but rather aids it. Where there is beauty of execution alone, a popular audience,

even in America, very easily goes to sleep. And in such matters, as the French actor, Samson, said to the young dramatist, "sleep is an opinion."[522]

It takes more than grammars and dictionaries to make a literature. "It is the spirit in which we act that is the great matter," Goethe says. "Der Geist aus dem wir handeln ist das Höchste." Technical training may give the negative merits of style, as an elocutionist may help a public speaker by ridding him of tricks. But the positive force of writing or of speech must come from positive sources,—ardor, energy, depth of feeling or of thought. No instruction ever gave these, only the inspiration of a great soul, a great need, or a great people. We all know that a vast deal of oxygen may go into the style of a man; we see in it not merely what books he has read, what company he has kept, but also the food he eats, the exercise he takes, the air he breathes. And so there is oxygen in the collective literature of a nation, and this vital element proceeds, above all else, from liberty. For want of this wholesome oxygen, the voice of Victor comes to us uncertain and spasmodic, as of one in an alien atmosphere where breath is pain; for want of it, the eloquent English tones that at first sounded so clear and bell-like now reach us only faint and muffled, and lose their music day by day.[523] It is by the presence of this oxygen that American literature is to be made great We are lost if we leave the inspiration of our nation's life to sustain only the journalist and the stump-speaker, while we permit the colleges and the books to be choked with the dust of dead centuries and to pant for daily breath.

Perhaps it may yet be found that the men who are contributing most to raise the tone of American literature are the men who have never yet written a book and have scarcely time to read one, but by their heroic energy in other spheres are providing exemplars for what our books shall one day be. The man who constructs a great mechanical work helps literature, for he gives a model which shall one day inspire us to construct literary works as great. I do not wish to be forever outdone by the carpet-machinery of Clinton or the grain-elevator of Chicago. We have not yet arrived at our literature,—other things must come first; we are busy with our railroads, perfecting the vast alimentary canal by which the nation assimilates raw immigrants at the rate of half a million a year. We are not yet producing, we are digesting: food now, literary composition by and by: Shakespeare did not write *Hamlet* at the dinner-table. It is of course impossible to explain this to foreigners, and they still talk of convincing, while we talk of dining.

For one, I cannot dispense with the society which we call uncultivated. Democratic sympathies seem to be mainly a matter of vigor and health. It seems to be the first symptom of biliousness to think that only one's self and one's cousins are entitled to consideration, and constitute the world. Every refined person is an aristocrat in his dyspeptic moments; when hearty and well, he demands a wider range of sympathy. It is so tedious to live only in one circle and have only a genteel acquaintance! Mrs. Trench, in her delightful letters, complains of the society in Dresden, about the year 1800, because of "the impossibility, without overstepping all bounds of social custom, of associating with any but *noblesse*."[524] We order that matter otherwise in America. I wish not only to know my neighbor, the man of fashion, who strolls to his club at noon, but also my neighbor, the wheelwright, who goes to his dinner at the same hour. One would not wish to be unacquainted with the fair maiden who drives by in her basket-wagon in the afternoon; nor with the other fair maiden, who may be seen at her wash-tub in the morning. Both are quite worth knowing; both are good, sensible, dutiful girls: the young laundress is the better mathematician, because she has been through the grammar school; but the other has the better French accent, because she has spent half her life in Paris. They offer a variety, at least, and save from that monotony which besets any set of people when seen alone. There was much reason in Horace Walpole's coachman, who, having driven the maids of honor all his life, bequeathed his earnings to his son, on condition that he should never marry a maid of honor.

I affirm that democratic society, the society of the future, enriches and does not impoverish human life, and gives more, not less, material for literary art. Distributing culture through all classes, it diminishes class-distinction and develops distinctions of personal character. Perhaps it is the best phenomenon of American life, thus far, that the word "gentleman," which in England still designates a social order, is here more apt to refer to personal character. When we describe a person as a gentleman, we usually refer to his manners, morals, and education, not to his property or birth; and this change alone is worth the transplantation across the Atlantic. The use of the word "lady" is yet more comprehensive, and therefore more honorable still; we sometimes see, in a shopkeeper's advertisement, "Saleslady wanted." Now the mere fashionable novelist loses terribly by the change: when all classes may wear the same dress-coat, what is left for him? But he who aims to depict passion and character gains in proportion; his material is increased tenfold. The living realities of American life ought to come in among the tiresome lay-figures of average English fiction like Steven Lawrence into the London drawing-room: tragedy must resume its grander shape, and no longer turn on the vexed question whether the daughter of this or that matchmaker shall marry the baronet. It is the characteristic of a real book that, though the scene be laid in courts, their whole machinery might be struck out and the essential interest of the plot remain the same. In Auerbach's *On the Heights*, for instance, the social heights might be abolished and the moral elevation would be enough.[525] The play of human emotion is a thing so absorbing that the petty distinctions of cottage and castle become as nothing in its presence. Why not waive these small matters in advance, then, and go straight to the real thing?

The greatest transatlantic successes which American novelists have yet attained—those won by Cooper and Mrs. Stowe—have come through a daring Americanism of subject, which introduced in each case a new figure to the European world,—first the Indian, then the negro. Whatever the merit of the work, it was plainly the theme which conquered. Such successes are not easily to be repeated, for they were based on temporary situations, never to recur. But they prepare the way for higher triumphs to be won by a profounder treatment,—the intro-

duction into literature, not of new tribes alone, but of the American spirit. To analyze combinations of character that only our national life produces, to portray dramatic situations that belong to a clearer social atmosphere,—this is the higher
Americanism. Of course, to cope with such themes in such a spirit is less easy than
to describe a foray or a tournament, or to multiply indefinitely such still-life pictures
as the stereotyped English or French society affords; but the thing when once done
is incomparably nobler. It may be centuries before it is done: no matter. It will be
done, and with it will come a similar advance along the whole line of literary labor,
like the elevation which we have seen in the whole quality of scientific work in
America, within the past twenty years.

We talk idly about the tyranny of the ancient classics, as if there were some special peril about it, quite distinct from all other tyrannies. But if a man is to be
stunted by the influence of a master, it makes no difference whether that master
lived before or since the Christian epoch. One folio volume is as ponderous as another, if it crush down the tender germs of thought. There is no great choice between the volumes of the Encyclopaedia. It is not important to know whether a
man reads Homer or Dante: the essential point is whether he believes the world to
be young or old; whether he sees as much scope for his own inspiration as if never
a book had appeared in the world. So long as he does, he has the American spirit;
no books, no travel, can overwhelm him, but these can only enlarge his thoughts
and raise his standard of execution. When he loses this faith, he takes rank among
the copyists and the secondary, and no accident can raise him to a place among the
benefactors of mankind. He is like a man who is frightened in battle: you cannot
exactly blame him, for it may be an affair of the temperament or of the digestion;
but you are glad to let him drop to the rear, and to close up the ranks. Fields are
won by those who believe in the winning.

38

AMERICAN NOVELS

Thomas Sergeant Perry

North American Review (1872).

Thomas Sergeant Perry (1845-1928) was born in Rhode Island and educated at Harvard. After studying in Germany (along with William James) he tutored at Harvard (1868-1872) in French and German. Perry joined the staff of the *North American Review* in 1872 and left it to take up a post in English at Harvard (1877-1882). Perry's books include *English Literature in the Eighteenth Century* (1883) and *A History of Greek Literature* (1890). His essays, often on realism and contemporary foreign fiction, appeared in the *Nation,* the *North American Review*, and elsewhere. Perry's influence on writers such as William Dean Howells and Henry James was immense: he partly fuelled their interest in Ivan Turgenev, and his commitment to "dramatic fiction" and the attenuation of the narrative voice helped shape Henry James's views on narration.

We have often wondered that the people who raise the outcry for the "Great American Novel" did not see that, so far from being of any assistance to our fellow-countryman who is trying to win fame by writing fiction, they have rather stood in his way by setting up before him a false aim for his art, and by giving the critical reader a defective standard by which to judge his work. Whenever this so-longed-for novel does appear, we may be sure that our first impression will not be that it is American. It may be American, without a doubt, but it will not be ostentatiously so; that will not be its chief merit. If it is written in this country and about this country, there will be of course a flavor of the soil, which is to be desired, but the epicure does not want his coffee muddy. There is an American nature, but then there is human nature underlying it, and to that the novel must be true before anything else. That is what is of importance; it is that alone which makes the novel great, which causes it to be read in all times and in all countries. If the author so far forgets this, his first duty, as to imagine that the simple rehearsal of the barrenest external phenomena of life and nature in this country can be of any real interest to the reader, he makes as great a mistake as would an actor who should fancy that nothing more was needed for representing Hamlet than to dress in black, wear a light wig, and to powder his cheeks to look pale. It is the bane of realism, as of all isms, to forget that it represents only one important side of truth, and to content itself, as complacently as an advocate, with seeing its own rules obeyed, and, generally, with the narrowest construction of the law. By insisting above all things on the novel being American, we mistake the means for the end; we have a perfect right to demand accuracy in the writer,—in spite of Mrs. Spofford, we cannot read about castles in New England,[526]—but we should not regard it as anything but the merest machinery, the least part of a novel; it is a *sine qua non*, to be sure, but so in man is the spinal marrow; we think no more of a friend on account of his having a spinal marrow.[527] So long as we over-estimate the value of this formal accuracy, it will be possible for any one to prove to his own satisfaction and to ours that such and such a novel is the best. "See here," he will say, "so-and-so makes the Connecticut River two hundred and fifty miles long, while 'Civis Americanus' gives it its proper length; and then 'Geographicus' says on page 343, just before the Boston horse-car conductor declares his love to the Nova Scotia servant of the selectman, that Vermont has thirty-five inhabitants to the square mile; he was thinking of New Hampshire; he's no novelist." No one fancies a novel that can be proved to be better than another, like a manual of geometry. Nor do we care for one that loses its value at every census. It may be well that novels should be of temporary interest, but they should at least outlast the year's almanac.

It might not be amiss to pause for a moment to consider the origin of this expression, "The great American novel." Critics would differ about the great English novel or the great French novel; why should America have one? Nevertheless, novelists have striven for this prize, genial critics have imperilled their reputations by rashly awarding it to various writers, who have as rapidly faded into oblivion, and we are as far from unanimity about it as we ever were. We imagine that it is a term that has come down to us from the time, a generation or two ago, when, America having an army and navy, consideration in the eyes of Europe for its material strength and future importance, the absence of a fully developed literature was keenly felt. Literature, too, was considered a branch of manufactures and not a thing of growth. We were to have an American Byron; possibly with good Presidents and a proper tariff, an American Shakespeare; and then the public, detecting the great differences between the society of Europe and that of this country, cried aloud for the novel that should do for us what Fielding had already, and Thackeray has since, done for England. That this should be done is indeed desirable; but our hopes will be vain unless our writers, with keener vision than the public, see the uselessness of a mere outside resemblance to their models.

That a novel is not good by simply being un-American, one can see by recalling a by no means unreadable story—*Miss Van Kortland*—that appeared about four or five years ago.[528] The effect of reading to excess the modern English novel was here clearly seen. There was the general air of English country life barely disguised by American names. Congress was made exactly like Parliament. It was an English bottom sailing under American colors. Of the elaborate Americanism of *Lady Judith*, we need not speak.[529] The reader could not help being reminded of the Yankees in Punch's caricatures, who would be arrested as suspicious characters in the backwoods of Maine, nor could their apt use of "old hoss" save them. Such hybrids we may trust will be soon forgotten; but in vastly the greater number of the American novels of the present day we find perhaps equally damaging faults, although of a different kind. Let us take, for example, Mr. De Forest's novels. In his writings we find a great deal that is American, but not so much that goes to the making of a really great novel. His stories have certain undeniable merits, and if the great American novel needed only to be American, he would easily bear off the palm. *Miss Ravenel's Conversion, Overland, Kate Beaumont,*[530] are three novels that could have been written in no other country; but such geographical criticism wholly leaves their real value out of the question, as if Charles Reade were to be exalted for having written the "great Australian novel," "Never too Late to Mend," or Defoe for his "great Juan Fernandez novel."[531] In the true novel the scene, the incidents, are subordinated to the sufferings, actions, and qualities of the characters. They are for the time living beings, and our greatest sympathy is necessarily given to those who deserve it from some internal reason, not from the number of miles they may have travelled, or the number of times they may have been shot at in the dark. Such incidents lend an interest, it is true, but it is not of the highest kind. The geology, the botany, the ethnography, may be accurate to date, the reader may be in perpetual shivers from the urgency of the dangers that threaten every one in the novel, but the real story lies beneath the hats and bonnets of those concerned, not in the distant cataracts that wet them, nor the bullets that scar them. It would seem as if the author had contented himself too readily with but one side, and that not the most valuable, of the novelist's work. He should retain the skill that he now possesses and use it, not as a thing of lasting value in itself, but as an aid to the representation of what is more genuine art. We should be sorry, however, if we did not do justice to the vividness with which he has drawn many of his side-characters, especially in his latest novels and in many of his less ambitious magazine sketches. As a simple narrator he is deserving of much praise; he can draw admirably the less important personages, so that one only notices more sharply his smaller degree of success when he undertakes to represent that more difficult character, a man under the influence of some all-controlling passion. What he can see he can write down for our reading, and this is certainly a rare gift, but his eye is stronger than his imagination. It is when he comes to this more delicate part of his work that the reader is disappointed, and all the more, as we have said, from his skill elsewhere.

Of the society novel this is the more common form. One takes the manly A and represents some possible complications of his "heart-agony," and that of the lovely C, from the persecution of flinty-hearted parents, loss of money, jealousy, etc. One would be averse to saying that his own country cannot supply as good material for

such novels as any other. There are here pretty women and good men. In spite of
our race for wealth, our early marriages, our bolting our meals and consequent dys-
pepsia, the devious course of what is strangely called the tender passion may still be
observed by those who watch their kind. Lovers languish and rejoice, hearts
threaten to break and then grow indifferent, as truly here as in any German village,
where the full moon shines every night of the year. But can any one name a good
American love-story? With the exception of *Esmond* it might be hard to find one in
the language; but let us consider America alone.[532] What are the American novels of
society, in which we might suppose love-making would have full sway? Those of
Mrs. Stowe suggest themselves at once. We cannot believe that her great popularity
is due entirely to her wonderful success with *Uncle Tom's Cabin.* To her youngest
readers that book must be already a thing of the past; but we fancy that it is because
she has succeeded in catching certain traits of American life that she is so widely
read. Besides, with all her faults, she is a humorist, and is often entertaining enough;
but what could be more ignoble than her last two novels of society, *Pink and White
Tyranny,* and *My Wife and I?*[533] It is profound criticism to call Thackeray a cynic;
perhaps Mrs. Stowe is one in disguise, but no man would dare show his head in a
drawing- room after describing such a character as the heroine of the last of these
novels. One would have to be disappointed in love a great many times before
young ladies made upon him such an impression of furbeloved, curled, food-
despising, thin-voiced flirts as one finds here. The men are the infant heroes of
Mrs. Sherwood's tales grown up. As for the manners of these people, their giggling,
their love-making, it is what one imagines to be the romance of a "calico and neck-
tie ball." For example, we find in Chapter XXX of *My Wife and I:*

> "O, you know!—this inextricable puzzle,—what does ail a certain person? Now he
> didn't come at all last night, and when I asked Jim Fellows where his friend was (one
> must pass the compliment of inquiring, you know), he said, 'Henderson had grown
> dumpy lately,' and he couldn't get him out anywhere."
>
> "Well, Eva, I'm sure I can't throw any light on the subject. I know no more than
> you."
>
> "Now, Ida, let me tell you, this afternoon when we stopped in the park, I went into
> that great rustic arbor on the top of the hill there, and just as we came in on one side, I
> saw him in all haste hurrying out on the other, as if he were afraid to meet me."
>
> "How very odd."
>
> "Odd! well, I should think it was; but what was worse, he went and stationed himself
> on a bench under a tree where he could hear and see us, and there my lord sat—
> perhaps he thought I didn't see him, but I did."
>
> "Lillie and Belle Forester and Wat Jerrold were with me, and we were having such a
> laugh! I don't know when I have had such a frolic, and how silly it was of him to sit
> there glowering like an owl in an ivy-bush, when he might have come out and joined
> us, and had a good time! I'm quite out of patience with the creature, it's so vexatious
> to have him act so!"

Further on we find:

> (*Enter* ALICE *with empressement.*)

"Girls, what do you think? Wat Sydney came back and going to give a great croquet party out at Clairmont, and of course we are all invited with notes in the most resplendent style, with crest and coat of arms, and everything—perfectly "*mag.*" There's to be a steamboat, with a band of music, to take the guests up, and no end of splendid doings; marquées and tents and illuminations and fireworks, and to return by moonlight after all's over; isn't it lovely? I do think Wat Sydney's perfectly splendid, and its all on your account, Eva, I know it is," etc., etc.

And so they artlessly prattle on. This is by no means an extract, which, taken away from its context, seems unduly ridiculous; far from it, it is a very good specimen of the whole tone of the book. Be these the manners of good society? Is there nothing nobler in life than a horse-car flirtation? Is it necessary that society novels should be like fashion-plates, with the same jaunty ease and simpering gentility that mark those illustrations of the happy life of the rich and great? If the people are tawdrily dressed, if their talk is empty enough to shame the silliest school-girl that ever chattered until she gasped for breath, if their manners are either rude or pompously haughty, how can one take a genuine interest in the story? Let their manners be as bad as possible, their clothes and grammar in tatters, provided they have one trait, one quality, be it one that makes or mars human beings, and then we can read the story. To be interested in characters in fiction, as with human beings in life, our sympathy must be aroused; for beings who simply giggle and pout, indifference is kindness.

Most American writers are afraid of their heroes and heroines. They give them homes by the side of imaginary rivers, in impossible cities. They are as shy of fairly introducing their characters as if we were all strangers at a watering-place hotel, and were very nervous about tainting our tender gentility. That this is the result of attempting to represent in this country, with its changing, uncertain classes, what in England is clear enough from its fixed social laws, is highly probable. But a novel to be good may well let good society alone. The best that Mrs. Stowe has done leaves the dancing master out entirely. For the English novel the task is greatly simplified by the fact that every man in that country is much more closely connected with the whole social system than is the case with us. In their novels we are introduced to distinct characters, say to a barrister, an officer, a young lord. Besides, whatever personal characteristics may belong to each of these persons, they all stand in a certain definite relation to society at large. Each carries a certain atmosphere with him. With us when we read about a lawyer in one of our stories, nothing more is told us than if we were informed that he always wore Roman scarves, perhaps not so much. We have all sorts of lawyers; no one man is a representative of the class. Occasionally we find that a good word is given to an omniscient professor who sits by a lamp and dabbles in Sanscrit, botany, metaphysics, chemistry, anatomy, zoology, etc., etc. He generally wears a long beard, has acquired patience by his severe studies, and is especially remarkable for the unexpected way in which he makes an offer of marriage after nourishing an untold and unsuspected love for a long time, while he pretended to be looking out words in the dictionary. Occasionally, we say, this representative of the quiet ideal appears in fiction, but he is an uncertain and artificial creation. In spite of the young girl's rapture over hops at West Point, an officer is not always an entrancing lover in fiction. There is, possibly, a vague Bohemian glamour around the artist, but even that is by no means certain. Since in general this deficiency exists, the task of the writer is rendered more difficult. Our democracy certainly equalizes us: it enlists us, as it were, into a vast army, but a peaceful, unheroic army, and to make any fictitious person interesting the author is put to the greater task of distinctly drawing his character as a man; he gets no aid from his surroundings. One would say that the natural tendency of the American novelist would be toward romance; that the very uniformity of our social life would offer nothing tempting to the writer, unless, indeed, to the satirist, who should turn to ridicule the shallowness, greedy pretence, and emptiness which he might see about him. In spite of the contumely that is thrown upon the frivolities of fashion in *Pink and White Tyranny* and in *My Wife and I*, it may be said that it is not given to every one to be a satirist. No satire is keener than that which tells the truth. One is only tender about his favorite vice. To call a selfish man a murderer, or a pirate, would be as idle as to write odes in praise of an honest bank clerk. And so in these stories Mrs. Stowe has overshot her mark by caricaturing what only needed to be shown in its real dulness to appear worthless. To her, and to many others, American society seems frivolous, but it is only exalted when a writer wastes his powder by attacking it as he would a dangerously false religion.

While the American writer finds these difficulties in the way of the "novel of society," it may be just that those tales should be considered that take up man from some other point of view than that which controls the respectable matron who is making out a list of invitations for her daughter's party. There are the dry-humored Yankees, the Yankee-despising, self-praising Westerners, and the lordly Southerners, who hate both. What has been done with such characters as these?

In hardly any book do we get more of the Yankee than in the novel *Margaret*, by Sylvester Judd. It is a story of life in New England nearly a hundred years ago, and, although it stands in about the same relation to most novels that Burton's *Anatomy of Melancholy* does to ordinary manuals of anatomy, it has a certain interest of its own.[534] This is, to be sure, hardly great enough to beguile the reader to the reading of the book, which is written in defiance of every rule of literary composition; but yet, in spite of a crabbed style, as rough as a corduroy road, of tedious and impossible conversations, of great delays in the telling of the story, the reader can readily see a sincerity in the writer that is often much less evident in the works of much cleverer writers. As an example of its artistic crudeness we quote the following conversation:

Another day Mr. Evelyn came to the Pond. Margaret watched his approach with composure, and returned his greeting without confusion.

> "You have been at the Head," said she, "and I must take you to other places today. First the Maples."
> "This is a fine mineralogical region," said he, as they entered the spot. "I wish I had a hammer."
> "I will get one," said she. "Let me go for it."

"You are not in health, you told me, and you do not look very strong. I must go by all means. I will be back in a trice. You will have quite as much walking as you can master before the day is through."

"I fear I shall be more tired wandering than in going."

"See this," said he, exposing a hollow stone filled with rare crystals, which he found and broke during her absence.

"I thank you, I thank you," she replied. "The master has given me an inkling of geology, but I never imagined such beauty was hidden here."

"With definite forms and brilliant texture these gems vegetate in the centre of this rough rusty stone."

"Incomparable mystery! New anagogics! I begin to be in love with what I understand not."

"Humanity is like that."

"What is humanity?"

"It is only another name for the world that you asked me about."

"I am perplexed by the duplicity of words. He is humane who helps the needy."

"That is one form of humanity. I use the term as expressing all men collectively viewed in their better light. Much depends upon this light phase, or aspect, what subjectively to us is by the Germans called stand-point. Indian's Head, in one position, resembles a human face; in another, quite as much a fish's tail. Man, like this stone, is geodic,—such stones, you know, are called geodes."

"Have you the skill to discover them?"

"It is more difficult to break than find them. Yet if I could crack any man as I do this stone, I should open to crystals."

"Any man?"

"All men."

"Passing wonderful! I would run a thousand miles for the hammer! I have been straining after the stars, how much there is in the stones! Most divine earth, henceforth I will worship thee! Geodic Androids! What will the master say?"

"I see traces of more gems in these large rocks. Let me rap here, and lo! a beryl; there is an agate, yonder is a growth of garnets."

"Let me cease to be astonished, and only learn to love."

"An important lesson, and one not too well learned."

"Under this tree I will erect a temple to the god of rocks. Was there any such? Certes, I remember none."

"The god of rocks is God."

"You sport enigmas. Let us to Diana's Walk."

We will not follow them. Their talk flows on as easily and naturally as in the extract given above, closely resembling the conversations in the chapters in the phrase-book for advanced pupils. But with all these obvious faults, and an almost impossible plot, the writer shows a genuine love of nature, and an appreciation of character that is really poetical. It is a book that is good in spite of itself, but yet it is barely readable. Its merits are those that are hardly evident enough to tempt the ordinary reader, who, naturally enough, wishes the way made easy before him. He takes a novel as he takes a walk, for amusement; he does not care for ruggedness,—that wearies him, everyday life gives him that,—any more than he does for an afternoon stroll through the thickets of the untrodden forest.

In Dr. Holmes's novels,—if we can call them novels,—in spite of his way of treating his characters like pathological or anatomical specimens, and in Mr. Henry

Ward Beecher's *Norwood*, we find the humorous Yankee admirably given.[535] But, while *Elsie Venner* is in its way a well-constructed romance, and Hiram in *Norwood* is an amusingly and accurately drawn character, neither novel deserves the highest praise. They are both very clever attempts by men who are not novelists. Sam Lawson, in Mrs. Stowe's *Old Town Stories*, is an extremely amusing person.[536] This lady has certainly, to a remarkable extent, the power of detecting the humorous side of what she sees and of representing it. The Yankee in her writings is an admirable copy of an original that can be found in almost every New England village,—a man, namely, of greater or less worthlessness, but with a wisdom, or rather shrewdness, that makes him far superior to the ordinary people around him. It is part of the novelist's work to introduce just such characters. They are, so to speak, picturesque, and yet true to nature. Of the immense superiority of a story that contains one personage that is really a human being, it would be needless to speak. Most novels leave as shadowy an impression of the genuineness of their heroes and heroines upon the minds of their readers, as does the pictured Quaker of the advertisements of the soundness of his religious views. But the introduction of a character that is only of dramatic importance, that is to say, who is more truly drawn as a representative of a class than as a human being, does not of itself make a good novel. The reader is more easily satisfied with a superficial sketch in the former case than he would be in the latter. A man may be well drawn as a village loafer, he may give us the very impression that the genuine idler makes upon us, and to do this is no light task; it is one for which a writer deserves high praise, and this no one would deny to Mrs. Stowe. But there is beyond this a feeling in the reader's mind that he has a right to expect a solution of more difficult characters, a representation not only of one or two persons, but also of some probable and well-connected incidents. In the better sort of novels we get some human beings, but we also demand a story, a plot that shall be probable and interesting. One character, no matter if very lifelike, in an awkwardly constructed story is as out of place as would be a poet on a desert island. But still it cannot be denied that it is the drawing of a character which is the most difficult part of the novelist's task, and if he succeeds he has thereby the surest hold upon his readers. If he fails in this, he fails indeed, for even the most imaginative are cold to the dangers that threaten even the most carefully dressed puppets. But a well-drawn character, one which we feel to be an accurate representation of what a human being might be, one who seems to us not merely what we fancy fellow-travellers, for instance, are, but who is a consistent creation, moved by passion, with feelings of his own, and his own special temptations, who may differ entirely from ourselves, but yet of the truth of whose delineation every one can instinctively be sure, is a rare person in fiction. For creating him there are no infallible rules, any more than there are for painting a good portrait in oils. It all depends upon the writer's brains. But if he is successful, if he creates a character with whom we can feel any sympathy, although the feeling may not be one of admiration, we are sure that the writer has done something of which he may well be proud.

The story that is to be told is another thing for which no definite *a priori* rules can be given. Great tragedies can be utterly spoiled and the humblest incidents can be exalted by the attitude which the writer's mind takes toward them. To argue from analogy is often unsafe, because the argument generally begins where the analogy ceases; but a Bierstadt can choose for himself in the whole wide world the most wonderful spot to paint, with mountains, rivers, lakes, and forests—such as poets are said to dream of—before him, but his canvas, when he has done his best, leaves us as cold as if we had been looking at a new drop-curtain in the theatre; while Millet can paint a little rustic scene, a woman driving sheep into their pen, a dim road in a dark wood, that we can never forget.[537] It is not what the writer selects that moves us, but his way of treating it. A vulgar mind can degrade *King Lear*, and a poet can throw a charm over the tritest line in the copy-book.

We need not go far for illustrations of what we have been saying; it is only necessary to recall some of the fantastic stories for which Southern novelists often betray a fondness. For example, there is one which is both described and criticised by its title, *Heart-Hungry*.[538] We need not go into a special examination of that novel, however, for the same thing may be said of the whole class, that they deal with the most tremendous manifestations of the power of love and jealousy, which combine to poison young lives and lead to the most heinous crimes. The books are, so to speak, thunder-storms in print, and seem to be written to make the way easy for some future Taine in a history of American literature to illustrate his remarks on the influence of hot climates upon the tastes of writers. But there is already good authority against tearing a passion to tatters. It has been widely acknowledged, and for a long time, that bombast is not the most effective means that a writer can use.

Of novels that fail from their dulness, whether caused by their photographic accuracy, or by the sluggish imagination of the author, we are sure that no examples need be given, especially in a land of circulating-libraries. All that we have tried to do is to set before our readers some of the more obvious faults of some of our popular writers. To do this it is by no means necessary to discuss at length all the American novels of recent years. They are, naturally, of different degrees of merit, from these weird visions of the Southern novelist to the innocently prattling stories for which *Harper's Magazine* is famous. The great novel is yet unwritten. We hope that he who shall attempt to write it will see the simplicity, the singleness of the problem that lies before him. The surer he is of this, the better will be his work. The less conscious he is of trying to be American, the more truly will he succeed in being so. Self-consciousness does not make a strong character, and so it is with this quality of the novelist. Lay the scene on the limitless prairie or in limited Fifth Avenue, but let the story rise above its geographical boundaries; let the characters be treated as human beings, not simply as inhabitants of such or such a place, with nothing to distinguish them from the beasts that perish, except certain peculiarities of dress and language. They must dwell somewhere, but they must be something besides citizens. Fantastic creatures dwelling in pure ether are not what the reader demands, but beings true, not to fashion, but to those higher laws and passions that alone are real, that exist above all the petty, accidental caprice of time and place. The real novelist, he who is to write the "great American novel," must be a poet; he must look at life, not as the statistician, not as the census-taker, nor yet as the newspaper reporter, but with an eye that sees, through temporary disguises, the animating principles, good or bad, that direct human existence; these he must set before us, to be sure, under probable conditions, but yet without mistaking the conditions for the principles. He must idealize. The idealizing novelist will be the real novelist. All truth does not lie in facts.

39

MIDDLEMARCH

Henry James

A review of *Middlemarch* (1872), by George Eliot. *Galaxy* (1873).

Middlemarch is at once one of the strongest and one of the weakest of English novels. Its predecessors as they appeared might have been described in the same terms; *Romola*,[539] is especially a rare masterpiece, but the least *entraînant* of masterpieces.[540] *Romola* sins by excess of analysis; there is too much description and too little drama; too much reflection (all certainly of a highly imaginative sort) and too little creation. Movement lingers in the story, and with it attention stands still in the reader. The error in *Middlemarch* is not precisely of a similar kind, but it is equally detrimental to the total aspect of the work. We can well remember how keenly we wondered, while its earlier chapters unfolded themselves, what turn in the way of form the story would take—that of an organized, moulded, balanced composition, gratifying the reader with a sense of design and construction, or a mere chain of episodes, broken into accidental lengths and unconscious of the influence of a plan. We expected the actual result, but for the sake of English imaginative literature which, in this line is rarely in need of examples, we hoped for the other. If it had come we should have had the pleasure of reading, what certainly would have seemed to us in the immediate glow of attention, the first of English novels. But that pleasure has still to hover between prospect and retrospect. *Middlemarch* is a treasure-house of details, but it is an indifferent whole.

Our objection may seem shallow and pedantic, and may even be represented as a complaint that we have had the less given us rather than the more. Certainly the greatest minds have the defects of their qualities, and as George Eliot's mind is pre-eminently contemplative and analytic, nothing is more natural than that her manner should be discursive and expansive. "Concentration" would doubtless have deprived us of many of the best things in the book—of Peter Featherstone's grotesquely expectant legatees, of Lydgate's medical rivals, and of Mary Garth's delightful family. The author's purpose was to be a generous rural historian, and this very redundancy of touch, born of abundant reminiscence, is one of the greatest charms of her work. It is as if her memory was crowded with antique figures, to whom for very tenderness she must grant an appearance. Her novel is a picture— vast, swarming, deep-colored, crowded with episodes, with vivid images, with lurking master-strokes, with brilliant passages of expression; and as such we may freely accept it and enjoy it. It is not compact, doubtless; but when was a panorama compact? And yet, nominally, *Middlemarch* has a definite subject—the subject indicated in the eloquent preface. An ardent young girl was to have been the central figure, a young girl framed for a larger moral life than circumstance often affords, yearning for a motive for sustained spiritual effort and only wasting her ardor and soiling her wings against the meanness of opportunity. The author, in other words, proposed to depict the career of an obscure St. Theresa. Her success has been great, in spite of serious drawbacks. Dorothea Brooks is a genuine creation, and a most remarkable one when we consider the delicate material in which she is wrought. George Eliot's men are generally so much better than the usual trowsered offspring of the female fancy, that their merits have perhaps overshadowed those of her women. Yet her heroines have always been of an exquisite quality, and Dorothea is only that perfect flower of conception of which her predecessors were the less unfolded blossoms. An indefinable moral elevation is the sign of these admirable creatures; and of the representation of this quality in its superior degrees the author seems to have in English fiction a monopoly. To render the expression of a soul requires a cunning hand; but we seem to look straight into the unfathomable eyes of the beautiful spirit of Dorothea Brooks. She exhales a sort of aroma of spiritual sweetness, and we believe in her as in a woman we might providentially meet some fine day when we should find ourselves doubting of the immortality of the soul. By what unerring mechanism this effect is produced—whether by fine strokes or broad ones, by description or by narration, we can hardly say; it is certainly the great achievement of the book. Dorothea's career is, however, but an episode, and though doubtless in intention, not distinctly enough in fact, the central one. The history of Lydgate's *ménage*, which shares honors with it, seems rather to the reader to carry off the lion's share.[541] This is certainly a very interesting story, but on the whole it yields in dignity to the record of Dorothea's unresonant woes. The "love-problem," as the author calls it, of Mary Garth, is placed on a rather higher level than the reader willingly grants it. To the end we care less about Fred Vincy than appears to be expected of us. In so far as the writer's design has been to reproduce the total sum of life in an English village forty years ago, this common-place young gentleman, with his somewhat meagre tribulations and his rather neutral egotism, has his proper place in the picture; but the author narrates his fortunes with a fulness of detail which the reader often finds irritating. The reader indeed is sometimes tempted to complain of a tendency which we are at loss exactly to express—a tendency to make light of the serious elements of the story and to sacrifice them to the more trivial ones. Is it an unconscious instinct or is it a deliberate plan? With its abundant and massive ingredients *Middlemarch* ought somehow to have depicted a weightier drama. Dorothea was altogether too superb a heroine to be wasted; yet she plays a narrower part than the imagination of the reader demands. She is of more consequence than the action of which she is the nominal centre. She marries enthusiastically a man whom she fancies a great thinker, and who turns out to be but an arid pedant. Here, indeed, is a disappointment with much of the dignity of tragedy; but the situation seems to us never to expand to its full capacity. It is ana-lyzed with extraordinary penetration, but one may say of it, as of most of the situa-tions in the book, that it is treated with too much refinement and too little breadth. It revolves too constantly on the same pivot; abounds in fine shades, but it lacks, we think, the great dramatic *chiaroscuro*. Mr. Casaubon, Dorothea's husband (of whom more anon) embittered, on his side, by matrimonial disappointment, takes refuge in vain jealousy of his wife's relations with an interesting young cousin of his own and registers this sentiment in a codicil to his will, making the forfeiture of his property the penalty of his widow's marriage with this gentleman. Mr. Casaubon's death befalls about the middle of the story, and from this point to the close our interest in Dorothea is restricted to the question, will she or will not marry Will Ladislaw? The question is relatively trivial and the implied struggle slightly facti-tious. The author has depicted the struggle with a sort of elaborate solemnity which in the interviews related in the two last books tends to become almost ludicrously excessive.

The dramatic current stagnates; it runs between hero and heroine almost a game of hair-splitting. Our dissatisfaction here is provoked in a great measure by the insubstantial character of the hero. The figure of Will Ladislaw is a beautiful attempt, with many finely-completed points; but on the whole it seems to us a failure. It is the only eminent failure in the book, and its defects are therefore the more striking. It lacks sharpness of line and depth of color; we have not found ourselves believing in Ladislaw as we believe in Dorothea, in Mary Garth, in Rosamond, in Lydgate, in Mr. Brooke and Mr. Casaubon. He is meant, indeed, to be a light creature (with a large capacity for gravity, for he finally gets into Parliament), and a light creature certainly should not be heavily drawn. The author, who is evidently very fond of him, has found for him here and there some charming and eloquent touches; but in spite of these he remains vague and impalpable to the end. He is, we may say, the one figure which a masculine intellect of the same power as George Eliot's would not have conceived with the same complacency; he is, in short, roughly speaking, a woman's man. It strikes us as an oddity in the author's scheme that she should have chosen just this figure of Ladislaw as the creature in whom Dorothea was to find her spiritual compensations. He is really, after all, not the ideal foil to Mr. Casaubon which her soul must have imperiously demanded, and if the author of the "Key to all Mythologies" sinned by lack of order, Ladislaw too has not the concentrated fervor essential in the man chosen by so nobly strenuous a heroine. The impression once given that he is a *dilettante* is never properly removed, and there is slender poetic justice in Dorothea's marrying a *dilettante.* We are doubtless less content with Ladislaw, on account of the noble, almost sculptural, relief of the neighboring figure of Lydgate, the real hero of the story. It is an illustration of the generous scale of the author's picture and of the conscious power of her imagination that she has given us a hero and heroine of broadly distinct interests—erected, as it were, two suns in her firmament, each with its independent solar system. Lydgate is so richly successful a figure that we have regretted strongly at moments, for immediate interests' sake, that the current of his fortunes should not mingle more freely with the occasionally thin flowing stream of Dorothea's. Toward the close, these two fine characters are brought into momentary contact so effectively as to suggest a wealth of dramatic possibility between them; but if this train had been followed we should have lost Rosamond Vincy—a rare psychological study. Lydgate is a really complete portrait of a *man,* which seems to us high praise. It is striking evidence of the altogether superior quality of George Eliot's imagination that, though elaborately represented, Lydgate should be treated so little from what we may roughly (and we trust without offence) call the sexual point of view. Perception charged with feeling has constantly guided the author's hand, and yet her strokes remain as firm, her curves as free, her whole manner as serenely impersonal, as it; on a small scale, she were emulating the creative wisdom itself. Several English romancers—notably Fielding, Thackeray, and Charles Reade—have won great praise for their figures of women: but they owe it, in reversed conditions, to a meaner sort of art, it seems to us, than George Eliot has used in the case of Lydgate; to an indefinable appeal to masculine prejudice—to a sort of titillation of the masculine sense of difference. George Eliot's manner is more philosophic— more broadly intelligent, and yet her result is as concrete or, if you please, as picturesque. We have no space to dwell on Lydgate's character; we can but repeat that he is a vividly consistent, manly figure—powerful, ambitious, sagacious, with the maximum rather that the minimum of egotism, strenuous, generous, fallible, and altogether human. A work of the liberal scope of *Middlemarch* contains a multitude of artistic intentions, some of the finest of which become clear only in the meditative after-taste of perusal. This is the case with the balanced contrast between the two histories of Lydgate and Dorothea. Each is a tale of matrimonial infelicity, but the conditions in each are so different and the circumstances so broadly opposed that the mind passes from one to the other with that supreme sense of the vastness and variety of human life, under aspects apparently similar, which it belongs only to the greatest novels to produce. The most perfectly successful passages in the book are perhaps those painful fireside scenes between Lydgate and his miserable little wife. The author's rare psychological penetration is lavished upon this veritably mulish domestic flower. There is nothing more powerfully real than these scenes in all English fiction, and nothing certainly more *intelligent.* Their impressiveness, and (as regards Lydgate) their pathos, is deepened by the constantly low key in which they are pitched. It is a tragedy based on unpaid butchers' bills, and the urgent need for small economies. The author has desired to be strictly real and to adhere to the facts of the common lot, and she has given us a powerful version of that typical human drama, the struggles of an ambitious soul with sordid disappointments and vulgar embarrassments. As to her catastrophe we hesitate to pronounce (for Lydgate's ultimate assent to his wife's worldly programme is nothing less than a catastrophe). We almost believe that some terrific explosion would have been more probable than his twenty years of smothered aspiration. Rosamond deserves almost to rank with Tito in *Romola* as a study of a gracefully vicious, or at least of a practically baleful nature. There is one point, however, of which we question the consistency. The author insists on her instincts of coquetry, which seems to us a discordant note. They would have made her better or worse—more generous or more reckless; in either case more manageable. As it is, Rosamond represents, in a measure, the fatality of British decorum.

In reading, we have marked innumerable passages for quotation and comment; but we lack space and the work is so ample that half a dozen extracts would be an ineffective illustration. There would be a great deal to say on the broad array of secondary figures, Mr. Casaubon, Mr. Brooke, Mr. Bulstrode, Mr. Farebrother, Caleb Garth, Mrs. Cadwallader, Celia Brooke. Mr. Casaubon is an excellent invention; as a dusky *repoussoir* to the luminous figure of his wife he could not have been better imagined. There is indeed something very noble in the way in which the author has apprehended his character. To depict hollow pretentiousness and mouldy egotism with so little of narrow sarcasm and so much of philosophic sympathy, is to be a rare moralist as well as a rare story-teller. The whole portrait of Mr. Casaubon has an admirably sustained greyness of tone in which the shadows are never carried to the vulgar black of coarser artists. Every stroke contributes to the unwholesome, helplessly sinister expression. Here and there perhaps (as in his habitual diction), there is a hint of exaggeration; but we confess we like fancy to be fanciful. Mr. Brooke and Mr. Garth are in their different lines supremely genial creations; they are drawn with the touch of a Dickens chastened and intellectualized. Mrs. Cadwallader is, in another walk of life, a match for Mrs. Poyser, and Celia Brooke is as pretty a fool as any of Miss Austen's. Mr. Farebrother and his delightful "womankind" belong to a large group of figures begotten of the super abundance of the author's creative instinct. At times they seem to encumber the stage and to produce a rather ponderous mass of dialogue; but they add to the reader's impression of having walked in the Middlemarch lanes and listened to the Middlemarch accent. To but one of these accessory episodes—that of Mr. Bulstrode, with its multiplex-ramifications—do we take exception. It has a slightly artificial cast, a melodramatic tinge, unfriendly to the richly natural coloring of the whole. Bulstrode himself—with the history of whose troubled conscience the author has taken great pains—is, to our sense, too diffusely treated; he never grasps the reader's attention. But the touch of genius is never idle or vain. The obscure figure of Bulstrode's comely wife emerges at the needful moment, under a few light strokes, into the happiest reality.

All these people, solid and vivid in their varying degrees, are members of a deeply human little world, the full reflection of whose antique image is the great merit of these volumes. How bravely rounded a little world the author has made it—with how dense an atmosphere of interests and passions and loves and enmities and strivings and failings, and how motley a group of great folk and small, all after their kind, she has filled it, the reader must learn for himself. No writer seems to us to have drawn from a richer stock of those long-cherished memories which one's later philosophy makes doubly tender. There are few figures in the book which do not seem to have grown mellow in the author's mind. English readers may fancy they enjoy the "atmosphere" of *Middlemarch*; but we maintain that to relish its inner essence we must—for reasons too numerous to detail—be an American. The author has commissioned herself to be real, her native tendency being that of an idealist, and the intellectual result is a very fertilizing mixture. The constant presence of thought, of generalizing instinct, of *brain,* in a word, behind her observation, gives the latter its great value and her whole manner its high superiority, it denotes a mind in which imagination is illumined by faculties rarely found in fellowship with it. In this respect—in that broad reach of vision which would make the worthy historian of solemn fact as well as wanton fiction—George Eliot seems to us among English romancers to stand alone. Fielding approaches her, but to our mind, she surpasses Fielding. Fielding was didactic—the author of *Middlemarch* is really philosophic. These great qualities imply corresponding perils. The first is the loss of simplicity. George Eliot lost hers some time since; it lies buried (in a splendid mausoleum) in *Romola.* Many of the discursive portions of *Middlemarch* are, as we may say, too clever by half. The author wishes to say too many things, and to say them too well; to recommend herself to a scientific audience. Her style, rich and flexible as it is, is apt to betray her on these transcendental flights; we find, in our copy, a dozen passages marked "obscure." *Silas Marner* has a delightful tinge of Goldsmith—we may almost call it; *Middlemarch* is too often an echo of Messrs. Darwin and Huxley.[542] In spite of these faults—which it seems graceless to indicate with this crude rapidity—it remains a very splendid performance. It sets a limit, we think, to the development of the old-fashioned English novel. Its diffuseness, on which we have touched, makes it too copious a dose of pure fiction. If we write novels so, how shall we write History? But it is nevertheless a contribution of the first importance to the rich imaginative department of our literature.

40

MARK TWAIN

George L. Ferris

Appleton's Journal (1874).

One of the pleasantest offices of cultivated thought is the study of contrasts in the literatures of different peoples. The trained power of the artist-eye derives no greater pleasure in its discriminating observance of landscapes than that resulting from the arrangement and grouping of the recorded forms of national thought and sentiment, considered purely from the picturesque stand-point.

If this be true of poetry, philosophy, and art in general, it is peculiarly so of national humor. For humor is a direct product from the life-blood. It sucks its ingredients from each hidden taint and essential virtue; from intellectual perversity and moral insight; from external environment and from internal fact.

Other forms of thought are the outcome of single phases, standing together as symmetrical fragments of the individual or the people. Humor comes the nearest to being the one complete revelation, which subtends all the complex secrets of Nature and habit.

The poet sings sweet songs to the world that thrill or soften. But, behind the cloudy forms which his incantations evoke and his genius illumines, the individual fades away. The orator storms, or pleads, or reasons, but the attention slips by the man to fasten on what he says or thinks. The essayist challenges interest for the most part by appeals from the special to the universal.

Not so the humorist, whether the mouthpiece of his age and country, or the mere witness of himself. Harlequin may wear a mask, but under the shallow fold the face plays hide-and-seek in vain. The heart beams out in the mirth that quivers on the edge of pathos, or the grotesque laugh, which needs only a little deeper tone to become melancholy. It is the intense humanity and lifelikeness of humor, that set the ultimate stamp, on its charm and significance.

Our literary inheritance from the princes of humor is full of finger-marks, index-signs, and marginal notes. We like to query whether Dean Swift, with his terrible scowl and blighting satire, which seems as if inspired from some Dantean depth, where devils mock and laugh, ever had the unctuous enjoyment of roast-beef and mighty ale, that shows in Dick Steele, Charles Lamb, and Charles Dickens? It is pleasant to speculate whether Heine, with his acute French wit sparkling on the current of deep German humor, ever recovered from his infatuation for frisky champagne and Parisian grisettes?[543] Or, if Jean Paul, "the only one," whose imagination pirouetted on earth with as much agility and swiftness as it cleft the upper abysses eagle-winged, never had the vertigo?

Would we not have known exactly how Hogarth looked, his grim features softened by a funny twist of the mouth, even had he never painted himself with an exceeding honest-faced but belligerent-looking bull-dog squatted by his side? How we should like to have heard Rabelais, after he had set a nation in a, roar of laughter, reading the *Adventures of Pantagruel* to the jolly old abbot![544]

Or, again, let us overleap the wide abyss of centuries, and stand amid the vast prairies, the gloomy cañons, and the grand forests of the far West. There in mining-camp or squatter settlement we see the figures of Mark Twain, Bret Harte, or John Hay, casting long shadows before them.[545] In the tedious entr'actes between fiery whiskey, coffee, and buckwheat "slapjacks," we can hear them make merry over adventures and fancies, which, vitalized by the breath of genius, were soon to ripple the world's face with laughter.

Such whimsical caprices never cease to haunt the students of the humorous in books with a sense of nearness and intimacy in their favorites. We are impertinently curious about them, make them mental bedfellows, as it were, because we love them. The laugh in literature is the "one touch of Nature" (above all others) "which makes the whole world akin."[546]

America has of late years bristled with humorous writers, as does the porcupine with quills. But few of these quills have been pungent in point or well feathered for flight. Yet what persistent jokers! They have sought to off set failures at the lawyer's brief, the doctor's pill-box, the counter-jumper's measuring-tape, the carpenter's plane, or what not. Still, amid a legion of quacks, there are some who have been crowned and anointed with the true "laying-on of hands."[547]

In surveying the distinctive and peculiar American humor, it becomes necessary to banish two highly-gifted men, Holmes and Lowell. *The Hosea Biglow Papers* have all the pungent wit of Pope, the meaty and athletic vigor of Swift. The genial front of the "autocrat" shines like a fixed star. But their passports are not properly *viséd* by the home stamp. In spite of the use of dialect and other forged earmarks, with which they would cunningly hoodwink us, we say to these magnificent impostors: "Get you gone, you belong to the world, not to America; you are giants truly, but your national angles, prejudices, and crudities, have been so ground down in the social mill, so polished away in the intellectual workshop, that your humor is that of the cosmopolite. It self-registers as much for any other Anglo-Saxon as for the American."

Mark Twain and Bret Harte may, on the whole, be pronounced our most marked types of humorists. Each one has a noble constituency, but in many respects they are at the antipodes from each other. The latter is impelled to create and idealize, even when most faithful to externals. His plummet feels for the deep heart of hidden mysteries, and finds love, sweetness, and self-sacrifice, beneath what is odd, grotesque, and barbaric. True, he deals largely with suffering, crime, and misery, in his most vigorous and characteristic sketches, yet is it with that sunny charity, which is the moral equivalent of searching insight. He has learned a lesson of the mining-camp, and knows where to look for gold in unsightly places. The essentially dramatic spirit, to which his instincts of form in art lead him, is no doubt partly responsible for the vividness of light and shade which intensifies his stories both in prose and rhyme. Yet, underlying form and method, seems to be a subtle feeling for the truth that good and evil are facts that melt and glide into each other imperceptibly, a recognition of which in painting human life is the tap-root of the soundest philosophy and the deepest humour.

Mark Twain, on the other hand, rarely touches the latent springs of human sentiment, nor is his style more than narrative and descriptive. He strolls in the open, breezy sunshine, happy-go-lucky fashion, yet with a keenness of vision that allows nothing in his horizon to escape him. But, before any further study of the author, let us briefly sketch the man, who was generally known to his little circle as Samuel L. Clemens, before the world coddled and petted him as Mark Twain.

He was born in Missouri in 1835, and got but scanty gleanings of early education. He became a printer's apprentice when his father died, and found that setting type at the case was by no means a bad school. After a few years, most of which were spent in itinerating from one country newspaper to another, young Clemens became a pilot on a Mississippi steamboat running between St. Louis and New Orleans. The picturesque life which he saw in this new business seems to have stimulated his literary faculties, for we soon find him writing for the newspapers. One day while he was pondering as to what *nom de plume* he should attach to his articles, he heard a sailor, who was taking soundings of the river, call out, "Mark twain!" The phrase tickled the fancy of our young literary pilot, and he adopted it for his own.

After seven years of this river-life, in which Mark Twain sedulously cultivated the art of writing, he went to Nevada Territory as private secretary of his brother, who had been appointed Secretary of the Territory. The chance was peculiarly grateful to one who had a keen thirst for adventure, and a vivid appreciation of the ludicrous. Nevada was just then beginning to swarm with reckless and quaint people, who had shot off at a tangent from the established order of society. Bankrupt tradesmen, young college-graduates who, tired of grubbing for Greek roots, would now grub for gold and silver, thieves and murderers escaped from justice—these and a thousand other off-scourings of life collided and made frontier society lively.

The fashionable toilet consisted of an eight-inch Colt, an Arkansas tooth-pick, jackboots, and an "insectivorous" shirt. The pet amusements were drinking bad whiskey, playing "draw-poker," and practising at human targets. Such paradisiacal conditions were surely enough to make any reasonable man happy. That our hero was so may be deduced from the fact that, what was originally projected as a pleasure-trip, lasted for seven years. During his life in the mining region he passed through diverse experiences, now exploring and prospecting, now editing a newspaper, now working on days' wages in a quartz-mill. Many of the sketches after incorporated in the "Jumping Frog" and *Roughing It* were published at this time in local or Eastern journals.[548] During a considerable time he was city editor of the *Virginia City Enterprise*, and some of the quaintest and brightest things which have appeared under his name originally enlivened its crimson catalogue of brutal murders and "Judge Lynch" executions.

From Virginia City Mark Twain drifted to San Francisco. Bad luck continued to follow him persistently. What money he had made while oscillating between the editor's quill and the gold-digger's pick had been invested in Nevada mining-stock. Wall Street, however, whispered gently to the wilderness, and there was a sudden collapse in-values. He then became interested with Bret Harte in the conduct of the *Californian*, and the two humorists hobnobbed for the first time. The nomadic taint, however, ran riot in the blood of both these "imps of Fortune," and they soon deserted the paste-pot and scissors for another delusive experiment in mining for gold. On returning to San Francisco, Mark Twain, his health now being poor, obtained a commission to go to the Sandwich Islands. Here the delicious climate and *dolce far niente* life built him up again in health, and an absence of a few months brought him back again to San Francisco with renewed health and spirits. A short lecturing tour through California and Nevada was successful, and so replenished his pockets as to furnish sufficient funds for a trip to New York. In 1867 he published *The Jumping Frog*, a collection of his best fugitive works, and immediately aroused public attention, not only in America but in England.[549]

The peculiar humor was a revelation to the conservative British mind, and the little work was even more talked of across the ocean than at home. The "Quaker City" excursion to the different seaports of Southern Europe and the Orient gave our rising author an opportunity of which he made abundant use. The amusing record of his experiences was presented to the world in a book which made a very remarkable sensation—*The Innocents Abroad*. In the second part of this work—*The New Pilgrim's Progress*—readers were made acquainted with the genesis of a Bunyan of a different type from the old Baptist dreamer.[550]

This publication justified the expectations of a public ever on the alert for something to laugh at, and Mark Twain rose on a flood-tide of popularity. When he returned to America, he betook himself again for a short time to journalism, and became connected with the Buffalo *Express*. The confinement of office-work, however, did not suit his free Bohemian spirit, and the swelling results of his literary venture soon put it in his power to break loose from the slavery of the editor's desk and follow his own intellectual caprices. His next book was *Roughing It*, published in 1873, recording, in elaborate form, his early experiences in the mining-country and the Sandwich Islands. This was speedily followed by the novel, *The Gilded Age*, written in collaboration with Charles Dudley Warner.[551] Our author is now residing at Hartford, and is in the very prime of his life and power. Before dismissing the mere material facts of Mark Twain's life, some allusion to the very remarkable pecuniary success of his books will be of interest. During the five years which have elapsed since the issue of *The Innocents Abroad*, the aggregate sale of our author's works has reached two hundred and forty-one thousand copies, representing a money-value of nine hundred and fifty thousand dollars. Though a large sale is by no means the only or even the best measure of literary excellence, the above-mentioned fact is so remarkable as to be almost unparalleled.

The differences between wit and humor have been elaborated by numerous essayists. These have said many bright things and many stupid ones on the subject. But, after all, the essence of it eludes definition and analysis. We see the effects, but fail to reach the ultimate force. This, at all events, we know, that wit is purely intellectual, and that humor is deeper and wider in its sources and powers. Wit sparkles in instantaneous gleams. It is the point of collision and also of union between opposites. Thackeray somewhere says that "humor is wit and love"; that "the best humor is that which contains the most humanity; that which is flavored throughout with the most tenderness and kindness."[552]

Of humor in its highest phase, perhaps Bret Harte may be accounted the most puissant master among our contemporary American writers. Of wit, we see next to none. Mark Twain, while lacking the subtlety and pathos of the other, has more breadth, variety, and ease. His sketches of life are arabesque in their strange combinations. Bits of bright, serious description, both of landscape and society, carry us along till suddenly we stumble on some master-stroke of grotesque and irresistible form. He understands the value of repose in art. One tires of a page where every sentence sparkles with points, and the author is constantly attitudinizing for our amusement. We like to be betrayed into laughter as much in books as in real life. It is the unconscious, easy, careless gait of Mark Twain that makes his most potent charm. He seems always to be catering as much to his own enjoyment as to that of the public. He strolls along like a great rollicking school-boy, bent on having a good time, and determined that his readers shall enjoy it with him. If Bret Harte has remarkable insight, Mark Twain has no less notable outsight. And yet perhaps the great popularity of the latter writer is as much the consequence of his defects as of his powerful gifts. He is representative because he embodies, to a striking extent, in his mode of constructing the forms of humor, the peculiar style of the average American journalist. Journalism on this side of the water has two unique types: the professional funny man, and the police-court reporter. Both these are strongly-marked national characters, and the style in which they serve up dishes for the public breakfast is well known. Hardly a newspaper appears but that it contains a variety of such paragraphs as the following:

John Smith had a beautiful stallion, who was so amiable in his temper that he would always caress the air with an affectionate gesture of his steel-clad hoofs when a stranger approached from behind. Squire Robinson bought the horse. The gorgeous funeral which Deadhead, the undertaker, supplied for the squire a few days after, enabled our respected fellow-citizen, who presides with such dignity in front of the mourners, to fit out his wife and daughter with the latest spring fashions.

It would be unjust to our author to say that he is either one or the other of these types in full flower. And yet how frequently do we see both these gentlemen surreptitiously stealing away out of sight under the cover of Mark Twain's coat-tails! Or perhaps it is only a literary illustration of Darwin's doctrine of rudimentary organs and limbs by which he explains changes in structural type. Mark Twain's early literary training was that of a writer for newspapers, where news was scarce and hard to get, and the public demanded their intellectual fare dressed with the hottest, strongest condiments. Is it not natural that we should see distinct and powerful traces of this method in all his later work?

In spite of this fault, our writer is so thoroughly genial, so charged with rich and unctuous humor, that we forget the lack of finesse and delicacy in its breadth and strength. Its tap-root takes no deep hold in the subsoil, and we may not always find a subtle and penetrating fragrance in its blooms. But these are so lavish, bright, and variegated, that we should be ungrateful indeed not to appreciate our author's striking gifts at their full worth. *The Innocents Abroad*, and *Roughing It*, are the most thoroughly enjoyable examples of Mark Twain's humor. While they are not to be altogether admired as intellectual workmanship, the current of humor is so genuine and fresh, so full of rollicking and grotesque fun, that it is more than easy to overlook fault both in style and method. Like most of the American humorists, Mark Twain depends chiefly on exaggeration as the effective element in his art. This has long been acknowledged the peculiar characteristic in our humorous processes. The clean-cut, sinewy force, so common to foreign writers, and no less evident in such men as Holmes and Lowell, is wanting in our distinctive Americans of this guild of literature. Their strength, on the other hand, is large, loose-jointed, and clumsy, the vigor of Nature and free exercise, not that of the gymnasium and fencing-school. It is humor which runs abroad with rambling, careless steps, not the humor which selects deliberately a fixed goal, and disembarrasses itself of every superfluity before commencing the race. What we lose, however, in energy, point, momentum, we gain in freshness and spontaneity.

In using exaggeration as a force in art, Mark Twain exaggerates not characters but circumstances. As a consequence, he is never a caricaturist. We recognize, even in his most extraordinary statements and descriptions, therefore, a flavor of reality, which takes strong hold of the imagination. Many of the unique people, whom he delineates, indeed, in his Western scenes, seem to have stepped right out of life into the printed page, veritable photographs in large and showy settings.

Mark Twain's latest book, *The Gilded Age*, was written in conjunction with Mr. Warner. Our author contributed to this joint production the career of the Hawkins family, and of Colonel Sellers, occupying the first eleven chapters, and twenty-two other chapters, scattered throughout the book. The rest of the composite story must be credited to the accomplished author of *Backlog Studies* and *Saunterings*.[553] We have the word of the authors that there was no intention of making it humorous, the sole purpose being that of bitter satire, true and honest to the core. Some of the best detached descriptions which have ever emanated from Mark Twain's pen may be found in this book. They show that the author's powers are at their best working capacity, and that the world has a right to look for liberal fruits from them.

41

GROWTH OF THE NOVEL

George Parsons Lathrop

Atlantic Monthly (1874).

George Parsons Lathrop (1851-1898) was born near Honolulu, Oahu, Hawaiian Islands (his father was a diplomat), and was educated there, in New York City, and Dresden, where he met Rose Hawthorne, the daughter of Nathaniel Hawthorne; they married in 1871. Lathrop became an associate editor of the *Atlantic Monthly* (1876) under Howells; but they soon quarreled, and Lathrop moved to the *Boston Courier* in 1877. In addition to poetry and some fiction, Lathrop wrote *A Study of Hawthorne* (1876) to which Henry James acknowledged his debt in his own *Hawthorne* (1879). The following essay, together with "The Novel and its Future" (2: No. 42) and Thomas Sergeant Perry's "Ivan Turgénieff" (2: No. 43), anticipates ideas about narration and the "dramatic novel" for which Henry James, among others, is often given a little too much credit.

Criticism has not kept pace with the novel in its more recent manifestations. A remarkable indolence prevails, not only with the greater number of novel-readers, but also on the part of too many among those industrious journalists under whose inspection works of this class fall, in regard to the inquiry by what principles the variously modified forms of the novel now extant are to be judged, and relegated each to its proper place. A large proportion of the criticisms upon new novels contain only vague and fragmentary allusions to novelty of incident, verisimilitude of the picture, theories of life involved in the story, or the freshness and "piquancy"—terms which these jaded reviewers apparently hold to be synonymous—of the whole, without an attempt to draw comprehensive conclusions; in short, these criticisms present whatever issues from the chance critic's chance taste, rather than a ray thrown out from the strong, central light of systematic meditation. The impression exists, too, that anybody, without having subjected himself to artistic discipline, can write a novel. We see men turning aside from the course of regular and

professed activities, to spin some slight web of fiction that shall attract a few admirers, and something of that spendthrift praise which it apparently becomes every day
easier to obtain. Even the most unlikely persons are subject, at any moment, to
infection with the prevalent disorder, and the facility with which mediocre and inferior work, in this branch of literature, attains to an exaggerated prominence, makes
it necessary that skilled judgment should be more generally applied in such matters
than at present; that a thoughtful endeavor should be made to penetrate the significance of the novel, and to determine some of the principles by which its further
progress should be guided.

The exigencies of an epoch cause poetical forms to undergo certain modifications; and by watching the influence of these exigencies, we shall discover the relative importance of particular forms at different periods, determining also the rate
and direction of their progress. The novel deals perforce most prominently with the
surface of life, the appearances of things; yet it has rendered no small service if it
succeed in rescuing from nothingness these ephemeral appearances, the beautiful or
amusing trivialities through which we daily take our way. Moreover, the great ideas
and great deeds of this world come upon us unawares, whether it be today or to-
morrow; and for their sake also the processes of each unfolding day are worth observing. But we do not commonly remember, in taking up our volumes of modern
every-day romance or comedy, that the hasty stitches at the back are in reality attached to a thread leading into a very remote past, and furnishing a clew to the real,
historically accretive nature of these volumes. We forget that the novel comes to us
with the marks of a long and laborious culture upon it.

Perhaps the earliest remaining productions which bear any distinguishable likeness to the more complex and more highly inflected novels of our own time are the
Greek romances of Heliodorus and his followers, in the opening centuries of the
Christian era. The Theagenes and Chariclea may, I suppose, be regarded as the immediate progenitor of that long line of fiction which has held enduring sway over
the human mind from the time of Heliodorus's writing up to the present.[554] But
this work is on a very low plane. It is utterly deficient in true dramatic method, and
not so much a breathing and speaking image of life, as a tiresome piece of carpen-
try. For us, it is like an obsolete plaything, and furnishes hardly more delight than
may be had in the taking apart of one of those Japanese toys, made to resemble an
egg, which is found to consist of a surprising number of thin wooden tissues, revealing, when stripped off, a tiny kernel at the centre. In like manner, the small seed
of circumstance from which the Thessalian romancer's story springs is hidden away
under numerous thin shells of implicate adventure, each very similar to all the rest;
and the entertainment consists in the leisurely removal of these husks. The whole
interest rests upon surprise, and surprise of the cheapest kind. "What have been
your adventures?" is the first question one character puts to another, on meeting,
all the way through. It is not necessary to pass in review consecutively the gradual
advances made in the art of fiction, from the time of this blunt-edged beginning—
if, indeed, we may assume that fiction can be traced to a beginning at all—up to

that of the brilliant achievements of Fielding and Sir Walter Scott. We have only to look so far into them, as to recognize that the tendency of those advances was distinctly toward the increase of a dramatic spirit and dramatic methods in novel-writing.

The Renaissance breathed a fresh life into the dry works of the Greek romancers, and they put forth new and sprightlier shoots. Boccaccio and Bandello engaged in the composition of short tales so new to the time that they were called simply novels; and these contained the germ of that intricate organism which we now recognize under the same generic name.[555] But in the hands of Boccaccio and his school, the novel did not get beyond the first pulpy and amorphous stage of its growth. Boccaccio cared little, or not at all, for that subtle differentiation of human character which constitutes the underlying science of our modern novel-art. He was content with a witty anecdote, recounted in a polished style, within the limits of a few folds of paper. Nevertheless, his legacy was an invaluable one. The heirs of his invention laid out their riches to rare advantage. The Elizabethan dramatists caught these stories, and expanded them to a fuller stature of imaginative existence, Shakespeare, above all, rounding the contour, and completing the figures with infinite variety of proportioned power, such as made his plays adequate to the representation of life both entire and particular. In the mean time, Rabelais and Cervantes had introduced a new element into fiction, namely, that of satire and artistically managed symbolism. Of the two, Cervantes exercised the most influence upon the subsequent development of the novel, for he understood the genuine and simple delineation of individual character. In this, though writing a century earlier than Le Sage, he far outstripped the author of *Gil Blas*. Heading the reaction against those exaggerated romances of chivalry, which had sprung from the metrical romances of the twelfth century, he made a greater advance in *Don Quixote* than he himself was aware of, perhaps. That he hardly estimated its bearing upon the subsequent history of fiction; regarded it simply as an amusing satire on the abuse of romance-reading,—a romance ridiculing romances,—we are disposed to conclude, from his composing immediately afterward a serious romance modeled on that of Heliodorus. He had previously written a pastoral romance, *Galatea*, and his *Exemplary Novels*.[556] As yet, the term novel was restricted to short stories which might be introduced episodically in the course of a ponderous romance, like the novel of "The Curious Impertinent," in *Don Quixote*. It was not surprising that the extent of Cervantes's advances in the direction of the modern novel should not be at once appreciated, either by his public or himself. But we may safely assign to him a considerable influence in the century which elapsed before the production of *Gil Blas*.

Wearied with preposterous fables and languid pastorals, a series of reactionary writers took the field, in the seventeenth century, and foremost among them was Le Sage, with his epic of luck and loose living, *Gil Blas*,—an attempted panorama of life, in which, however, the persons were rather typical than individual, and again *figurative*, if one may so describe it, rather than typical. A second reaction had come, but this time there was no Cervantes to take the lead. In England, however, the use to which the masters of the Elizabethan stage had put the Italian novels of the fourteenth century, had insured that accelerated dramatic tendency of the novel which here demands our attention. In the century immediately ensuing upon that in which Shakespeare died, Fielding, more than any other before him, threw light upon the course which fiction was thereafter to pursue. Beginning, before his majority, as a writer of plays, he spent a good deal of time in getting out hasty adaptations from the French, as well as numerous comedies of his own; but though these comedies are still extant, they are hardly less entirely forgotten than the poles and canvas of the flimsy booth itself in Smithfield, wherein they first strutted before the world, in the days of *Bartholomew Fair*.[557] But it is not unreasonable to suppose, that his practice in this kind of writing had its effect upon the romances which at a later period he made the basis of his only real celebrity. In the production of these he declared himself, and with some reason, to be founding "a new province of writing." For, although he in fact only filled out and enlivened a form which had been some hundreds of years constructing for him, the result was something substantially new. Richardson had begun to write novels, chiefly for the sake of his epistolary style. A story indicated in letters always contains something of dramatic management; but, if it be at all extended, it involves more of repetition and improbability. Richardson's people seem first of all to be concerned that their various troubles and experiences, with the accompanying sentiments, should be transferred in full to note-paper, so as to make up a good, readable book, afterward. And previously to Richardson's writing, the stage had usurped the attention of genius; the novels of Lodge and Greene were not progressive.[558] But when the theatre had lost its masters, and suffered a long decline, Fielding, as if conscious that a lively genius could appear to advantage only in some new guise, threw himself into the novel—or, as he called it, the romance—with all the fervor of his really gifted mind. The artistic impulse which sustained him, as it found expression in his last and perhaps most finished work, *Amelia*, was this: "To observe minutely the several incidents which tend to the catastrophe or completion of the whole, and the minute causes whence these incidents are produced."[559] Here we have the root of dramatic development; and it was the application of this method that brought the novel into a familiar and affectionate relation to life, which no form of imaginative writing had up to that time enjoyed. Looking at his persons in this way, it was necessary that Fielding should pay the closest attention to their utterances and actions, from first to last, and calculate with some nicety the interaction of individuals one upon another. Conversation, instead of being thrown in here and there, as heretofore, simply to delay bringing to a close some little train of incident, or with a view to making the story real enough to be rend with comfort, became in his hands a just expression of every participator in it, and a light reflected upon the speakers, as well as a subtle cause of subsequent conduct, in a manner approaching that of its operation in real life. But, although Fielding was dramatic, in so far as conversation and incident led the story on from point to point with a certain degree of system, combined with spontaneity, he did not carry the dramatic movement far enough. When all was over, his tale would remain but a rambling, aimless concatenation, terminating in nothing but an end of the adventures. His great power lay in the observation of manners and natures; but he was content to offer the results of this observation in a crude, digressive form, somewhat lacking—if it may be said—in principle. He was fond of whipping in and out among his characters, in person, and did so with a sufficiently cheery and pleasant defiance of all criticism; but the practice injured his art, nevertheless. In a word, he seems to have written as much for his own amuse-ment as for that of his reader; and although he sedulously endeavored to identify these two interests, he did not hesitate, when he felt like discharging a little disserta-tion on love, or classical learning, or what not, to do this at any cost, either of artis-tic propriety or the reader's patience. And, worst of all, he frequently dissected his *dramatis personae* in full view of the audience, giving an epitome of their characters off-hand, or chatting garrulously about them, when the mood took him. These shortcomings withheld from him the possibility of grouping his keen observations firmly about some centre of steady and assimilative thought. With Fielding, nothing crystallized, but all was put together in a somewhat hastily gathered bundle; and the parts have a semi-detached relation. He hardly dreamed of that suggestive and deeply significant order of novel which our own day has seen almost perfected in the hands of George Eliot. And yet, what a brilliant retinue has Fielding had! Scott, Dickens, Thackeray—George Eliot herself—and many more besides, have fol-lowed in the path which he opened. He had an alert and energetic mind, and heart-ily and impartially enjoyed life, wherever and whatever it might be found; and this capacity for a healthy participation in the business of the people who surround him remains now, as it then was, an indispensable qualification in the novelist. But the best allegiance to Fielding must move men to further explorations in that province which he, in his day, so despotically governed. His greatest successors in empire have done this; but in what degrees, it will be interesting to consider. If, too, we find their efforts crowned by a constant though gradual progress, we shall perhaps think the conclusion justified, that new avenues to new goals of art remain yet to be adventured on.

It was only a dozen years after Fielding had ceased to write, that *The Vicar of Wakefield* suddenly took its place among those calm perpetuities which from time to time stand forth out of the dissolving cloud of ephemeral fiction. Nothing more exquisite of its kind than this novel of Goldsmith's has ever been given to us. The objective rendering of good Doctor Primrose is perfect. Goldsmith seems here to have reached an eminence in novel-art hitherto attained by no one, and to which few have since aspired. Only Thackeray's *Henry Esmond* presents itself as worthy of comparison with it, and even this perhaps falls short, in point of simple humor and native sweetness. But the sober richness with which Goldsmith's chief personage is elaborated is not of the showy style calculated to make headway with the many. And it is true that the range of a novel conceived as this is must be somewhat lim-ited; variety of characterization being not so much the aim, as a complete study and full objective presentation of the hero. Nevertheless it is certain that, in this book,

Goldsmith secured some of the purest dramatic results attainable through the novel; and that it will accordingly always remain a source of the most wholesome inspiration.

It was reserved for Scott to enlarge the mechanical apparatus, and extend the sympathies of the novel, beyond all precedent. The brilliancy of his advent into the field of fiction was in great measure due to his wider appreciation of character, as compared with that of the writers who had gone before. He treated all sorts of persons with the same genuine enjoyment of personality, whatever it might be; and if his heroes were sometimes rather colorless, and his women molded too exclusively by generalized conceptions of femininity, he still succeeded in showing that human nature remains fundamentally the same, beneath all the shifting and superimposed conditions of history, and demonstrated the applicability of the novel to life in past periods. As for mechanism, he contrived many clever little devices for moving stories on to an end; he dispensed with those long, introduced narratives which Heliodorus employed, and which Fielding relied upon too willingly—sometimes carrying them on from one chapter to another by means of a pumping question from the listener, not inappropriately followed by a gush of tears from the narrator. In his conversations, Scott sometimes seems, by his nice discriminations, to give the slightest shades of meaning, and the very accent of the voice; though he is as often melodramatic and unreal. But, with all his merits, and overlooking his rather musty antiquarian devotions to costume, Scott remains much too conscious, it strikes me, in his characterization. Frequently, having effected some ingenious stroke of delineation, he is so well pleased that he instantly repeats it in more diffuse terms. This at once dulls the edge of his wit, and makes us aware of an obtrusive presence among the fictitious personages. The author cannot restrain himself from jovial participation in his reader's amusement; he must ever peep out from behind the side-scenes, to exchange a sly Caledonian wink with us. To avoid this subtle error, a writer should seek always to lose himself more and more, in giving life to his imaginary persons. Dramatic effect of the highest and most sterling quality cannot be obtained without a resolute act of self-renunciation on the part of the author. And in proportion as the novelist intervenes, visibly, between the reader and the characters of his story, he detracts from the realness of the latter. For example, it is a prominent defect in Dickens that he is antic in the extreme. He appears to have been conscious of the necessity which existed for curbing himself, as in one of his letters he alludes to the "preposterous sense of the ridiculous" which he was obliged to contend with, in order that he should not write extravagantly.

Not less injurious, in its way, to dramatic perfection is the system of minute and deliberate analysis pursued by George Eliot. It makes us look to her books rather for instances of her remarkable acumen, and the terse statement of her perceptions, than for a sympathetic rendition of human nature that shall charm and soothe us, at the same time that it instructs or educates. Her writing does not soothe, because she keeps so constantly before us the stern effort she is making, not to swerve from strict analysis. The authoress presides too watchfully over the progress of our acquaintance with the imaginary beings to whom she has introduced us; and we should be more at ease, if she would omit some of the more wordy of her examinations into their mental status at each new turn of the story. There are instances of fine dramatic handling in her books, from which we may cite those culminating scenes between Stephen Guest and Maggie Tulliver, in *The Mill on the Floss*.[560] But these superior passages only throw forward upon our notice the too frequent consciousness and restraint which disturb her work. The novelist, it is true, must observe a certain economy, holding back the more telling dramatic effects for particular passages. But the difference should be in the degree, rather than in the quality, of dramatic force; a kind of difference well exemplified in Hawthorne's *Scarlet Letter*. George Eliot's open analysis, too, has a tendency to lead her insensibly into partiality, a thing which she is by this very means strenuously trying to avoid. That tendency she has almost wholly overcome in *Middlemarch*; which is distinguished for a fine impartiality. But it is in this same crowning work that we find, perhaps more strongly exemplified than in any other of her books, the final defect of her system. In a book of this kind all that can be said about the characters is said; but, after all, the result is not so good as if something had been withheld, for our imaginations to reach after. Despite the vigorous bloom, the insistent life of *Middlemarch*, do we not feel that there is an overwrought completion about it? The persons of the story are elaborated almost to exhaustion; there appears to be a lack of proportion in the prominence so fully accorded to each individual in his or her turn, for minor characters are dwelt upon too much in detail; and there is little or no mystery of distance about any of the figures, at any time. We have struck bottom, with these people, beyond hope of recalling that thought of illimitably profound humanity which indicates the unknown quantity in character, and which gives Shakespeare's personages their lasting title to our love or consideration. The secret of dramatic effect is simply this, that in real life ultimate truth seldom finds a pure utterance. In drama, therefore, we have a situation presented as nearly as possible (subject to aesthetic laws) in the way in which it would present itself in the fact; the involved truths of the whole proceeding being illustrated by the partial expressions of each individual, on his own behalf or in estimating his fellows; so that the final, fleeting essence of the matter lies within the scope of inference only. And in proportion as dramatic skill is successful, it stimulates in us the disposition and ability to make such inference. But George Eliot would cut us off from this last spiritual, intangible result, by reducing everything to absolute statement, and endeavoring to fix the final issues in penetrating and permanent phrases. I would not underrate the magnificent obligations which George Eliot has laid upon the race; my admiration of her brave and noble genius is in no way lessened by the opinion that her method restricts the range and power of the novel unnecessarily. As an effort of clear intellectual penetration into life, we could hardly demand anything better than *Middlemarch*. But it is still too much an effort, and not enough an accomplished insight; it remains, as the author has called it, a study, rather than a finished dramatic representation.

Turning from George Eliot to Dickens again, we observe that his faults of undue personal prominence range themselves on a far lower intellectual plane. He is
not troubled by analysis, because he hardly enters upon that function, even in the
deliberations which have preceded his writing; if we are to judge from the character
of that writing, and from what has been made public as to his state of mind during
composition, and the confidences which he imparted in the mid-fervor of creation.
But, on the other hand, he is not truly dramatic. Indeed, this follows from his want
of analysis. Without having analyzed, he could have nothing to unfold by the dramatic method. His imagination was strong in the grotesque, but it never seems to
have taken the direction of clearly outlined truth of character. His characters may
be true to nature, but for all that he does not imagine them for the sake of truth,
but for the sake of their grotesque or other effect. And there is a wide difference
between truth and effect. That it is effect he aims for is proved by the conclusions
of his books, which are never profound or sublime, but unimportant and common-
place. His results are not results in a satisfactory sense, because they consist merely
in a settlement and pensioning for life of the characters, as it were; everything is
"wound up," but we are left at the end without any vital impulse from that winding.
He does not carry our eyes above the level of a very superficial justice. Ah, it was
his wit that charmed us, and not the human nature with which he dealt! This human
nature was to him only a sort of indispensable stage-property; and he was the actor
whom it served to set off. Dickens possessed, in addition to his nimble fancy
(which was often exquisitely graceful), a surprisingly rapid and multifarious observation; but he contented himself with only a flying shot at the truth. He had a fertile
genius, and perhaps he felt that he could afford to take at a discount the riches with
which nature had supplied him; for the rapidity of his labors necessitated constant
advances; but he lost unspeakably by this system. He was confused and carried
away by the idiosyncrasies which took his fancy, and so lost sight of the true artistic
aim; seldom, if ever, taking the pains to abstract himself from himself, and enter
again into the life of others, so that he might faithfully reproduce it,—the good and
the bad alike,—leaving us to draw our conclusions somewhere near the truth. In
Martin Chuzzlewit, he complained that the American people would never tolerate a
satirist. But the essence of good satire lies in the strictest and most sensitive adherence to truth. Irony should be so mingled with an unprejudiced veracity of representation, as to make the reader half uncertain whether that which he is reading be
a mere unwitting record of laughable fact, or a piece of conscious, though guarded,
ridicule. Exaggeration is by no means the chief nor the most powerful element of
satire. If we ridicule a man by calling him worse than he is, we may wound and anger him, but we shall not cut so to the quick, as if we pierce with our ridicule some
really vulnerable point in his constitution. But Dickens seems to have trusted
wholly to first impressions and strong feelings. There is a curious, and, if true, a sad
story extant, as to the unmerited injury which his *Nicholas Nickleby* inflicted upon an
innocent Yorkshire schoolmaster. But, wholly apart from any consideration of
practical injustice of this kind, is it not alarming, to say the least, that the eminent

novelist should take sides, as he does, with the characters in his stories? It is pitiable to see the cases in which those creature of his imagination stand, who have had the misfortune to fall under his displeasure. He has them at his mercy, and he at once abandons them, body and soul; will not even let them be funny; and leaves them standing in the field, as Ralph Nickleby, or Jonas Chuzzlewit, or Merdle, or Chadband, or Heep, mere grinning or frowning or insanely smiling scarecrows, who are to be pelted and maligned on every convenient occasion.[561] This kind of writing merely strengthens prejudice; and however well founded the prejudice may be which it is intended to confirm, it does not aid people in ascertaining subtle truths, or in attaining anything like serenity or justness of view. It is very different from the witty or gentle hitting off of foibles, and the quiet, sympathetic, but inflexibly just penetration of sin and weakness, which always distinguish the genuine, nature-loving truth-seeker and teacher. Taine has rightly defined Dickens as a lyrical-minded genius. Lyrically, we describe people and things by a record of the impressions they leave upon us personally; dramatically, we endeavor to render them both as they exist to their own appreciation and that of others,—using our own impressions, of course, but trying also to imagine the impressions of other observers. Dickens, not being hampered by these endeavors, has no hesitation in labeling his characters "good" or "bad" at the outset. But he is then forced to fall back upon melodramatic incident, which gradually, as his book advances, usurps our attention,—the amusing or grotesque peculiarities of the persons soon losing their novelty,—and carries us to the close in a blinding whirl of excitement; so that we shall not dwell upon the frequently glaring crudity of the work and its deficiency in real character-study. The most bepraised feature of Dickens's genius, and that behind which its artistic short-comings are most frequently sheltered, is but a pyrotechnic sort of humanitarianism, wanting as it does the element of a painstaking and long-suffering charity. If we discuss Dickens's spirit, we must confess him to be altogether too knowing. He goes about picking up characters as curiosities; then holding them up, he makes fun of them, and expects us to laugh in company with him. This does well enough, in a burlesque like *Pickwick*; but as an abiding principle in art it is heartless, and can lead to no real elevation in either writer or reader. If the novel is to advance, we must look for something finer and more earnest than this.

Thackeray, whose books form a sort of irreproachable gossip about life (except for the superfluous sneer), is far more dramatic, in the truest sense, than Dickens. He brings before us a variety of people nearly as great as that which Dickens handles, and all of them more profoundly individual than the persons of the latter, though less strikingly marked on the surface. And his crowds of individuals illustrate and explain each other remarkably. Thackeray has been called by a recent magazine critic eminently subjective, but this dictum will mislead, if accepted without question. His personal utterances are, on the whole, much the weakest portion of his work, and they are often quite unimportant,—the result of a lax habit of garrulity. It is a mistake to suppose, because he made these utterances to satiety, that they indicate the vital and distinguishing quality of his genius. With a style so easy and refined as his, it is not surprising that he could give to his short interspersed dissertations a charm which we sometimes find it difficult to believe was not his chief attraction. And even when we are forced to see that they are often mistimed, we can bear with them, in recognizing that they furnished an escape for the tendency to personal expression, which he so rigorously repressed when his actors had come upon the stage and were fairly about their business. The custom of digression was one which he rather unwisely borrowed from Fielding; but it will not do to let his indulgence in this particular blind us to the masterly exhibitions of his skill in bringing characters before us with the least possible interference, when he chooses to do so. More than one scene might be cited, in which his personages conduct themselves through various complications aided by hardly a word of explanation from the writer to the reader, and yet with such an admirable choice of what should be told of action and gesture and expression, that it is impossible not to receive the detailed and delicate impression of their mutual countermining operations which the author intended to convey. But the most complete and convincing instance of his objective power is supplied by his *History of Henry Esmond*. In this book, he throws himself with entire success into the position of a man living in the reign of Queen Anne, who relates the circumstances of his personal history; and in such a manner, that not only everything takes shape just as it presented itself to the mind of this man (aside from what we are led to see is its intrinsic character), but that the way in which he brings forward the other persons of his tale throws light upon himself, also. Here is no superfluous dissertation; but the author is at the acme of his power. The characterization is nice, completed with a bold and correct hand, masterly; the slow unfolding of their natures in Beatrix and Esmond, and Lady Castlewood and her son, as well as the episodical introduction of other persons, is dramatic in the last degree. It is true, Thackeray did not reach after all attainable sources of sensation, as Dickens did; he confesses, in the preface to *Pendennis*, that he could not successfully draw a rascal such as it had been intended to introduce into that novel. "I found that I failed," he says, "from want of experience of my subject. Never having been intimate with any convict in my life, and the manners of ruffians and jail-birds being quite unfamiliar to me . . . . the idea was abandoned." But this is only saying that he was content to limit his gallery of pictures to subjects which came easily in his way, and which suited his disposition to kindly and wholesome satire. He has done enough to show that, had he chosen, he could have exercised his versatile power upon matters such as that for which he here announced his incapacity. But he preferred to carry his empire only into those regions with which experience had made him familiar. "To describe a real rascal," he continues, "you must make him so horrible that he would be too hideous to show; and unless the painter paints him fairly, I hold he has no right to show him at all." And here he was in great part right. It is a proof of the fineness of his spirit, that he shrank from exhibitions which, like the murder of Nancy in *Oliver Twist*, cannot escape the taint of the merely horrible. Dickens had two ways of dealing with the human dregs which lie at the bottom of most of his intoxicating draughts. One was, to make them objects of fun; and the other was, to treat them with melodramatic appliances, which, in almost every instance, betrayed him into scenes that were baldly horrible, and that sinned against the highest laws of art. In either case, the sort of familiarity he gave us with the lowest and most vicious of human beings was hardly beneficial. Even by the melodramatic treatment, which he no doubt designed to be beneficial, he only succeeds in exciting the reader's instinctive repugnance for uncovered vice and crime to a pitch of unhealthy and ecstatic activity; but he could never arouse in this way a deep, clear, and purifying moral perception. It is possible that Thackeray felt himself so strongly inclined to the literal and unsparing style of representation, as to make it unsafe for him to venture among murders and vagabondage with the same freedom Dickens used. But at least we may be thankful that he saw his limitations in this respect, and that he accordingly avoided falling into the errors which his more popular contemporary so rashly courted.

It will have been observed that, of the three writers just discussed, the strongest praise for dramatic qualities has been given to that one who is most distinguished among them for the personal relation which springs up between him and his readers. But we may venture to believe that if all the interspersed essays were extracted from all his books, this personal relation would remain as strong as ever. And, indeed, this is the case in Thackeray's *Philip*, where the rambling tendency is almost wholly checked.[562] The sensation of personal intercourse arises simply from the unaffected method of narrating, as if all that he tells were matter of personal observation. Though honestly renouncing himself, in the action of his story, he survives personally, as the best novelists should and do survive, in his style. Nothing can be more disastrous than the indifference to style so commonly manifested in the novels of the day. It would be a mistake to suppose that the cultivation of impersonality by the novelist, in his interpretation of character, need in any way lead to the neglect of style. All fine art is the interpretation of nature by the individual, and must, therefore, bear some trace of individual workmanship. We may accept, theoretically, Herbert Spencer's conclusion, that "To have a specific style is to be poor in speech"; but we must observe, nevertheless, that even Shakespeare, with all the variety of utterance which he commands, retains throughout a nameless but abiding quality of style, that unites the components of this variety under the dominion of his sovereign spirit.[563] Style, to be sure, is an outgrowth of the author's personality. But impersonality—the universality of Shakespeare—springs naturally out of personality, also, and can be derived only thence. However impersonal the creative writer may become, he may, as has been said, survive still in his style, this being something of which neither he himself nor any one else can rob him. He sacrifices his own individuality, for the time being, in the creation; but when the work is finished, it has become, through his intervention:

Prime nature with an added artistry.[564]

This retiring attitude of the story-mover does not imply total invisibility, as we have just seen in the case of Thackeray, but only inofficiousness. The stand-point of entire impartiality, by taking nature out of the hands of the man, so to speak, and putting it under the calm, indicative finger of the novelist, necessitates a constantly renewed study of surrounding life, and study of the most sincere and sympathetic kind. When the leading interest lies in the unfolding of incident, or when too much of the book is made up of ruminations aloud on the motives and traits of the actors in it, it becomes dangerously easy for a writer to invent a different succession of incidents, with different scenery, and characters similar to those he had already used, or even precisely the same ones under new names, imagining all the while that he is composing a fresh work. But if an author feels himself compelled constantly to institute the most vigorous investigations into life and character, he is apt always to find himself humbly brought back to nature; and that is the best of all attitudes in which he can find himself. It is, however, only a higher standard of popular taste and of criticism that can make him feel the constant spur to more careful study. We are not, in general, ready to take a hint from our novelist, unless we be told outright what it is intended to convey by that hint; or to enjoy a nice stroke of delineation, unless we be reminded in some way that it is a nice stroke. Let us here compare two passages, one of them taken from a popular living English novelist, the other from Ivan Turgénieff's *Smoke*.[565] This is the first:

> She bowed to the stranger, with studious politeness, but without uttering a word. "*I am obliged to listen to this person," thought the old lady; "but I am not obliged to speak to her.*"[566]

Here the whole italicized statement is absolutely superfluous, and simply blunts the fine point with which the sentence preceding it, had it been allowed to stand alone, might have scored its due effect. Now take the passage from the Russian writer. Ratmirof has been questioning his wife as to her interest in Litvinof, the hero of the book. Without answering him:

> Irene raised her hand, until the light shone full in her husband's face; then she looked him in the eyes attentively and curiously, and began to laugh aloud. "What do you mean?" asked Ratmirof, with a frown. "What do you mean?" he repeated, stamping his foot. He felt that he had been insulted and humiliated, but the beauty of this woman, standing before him with such an easy confidence, dazzled, while it pained him. Not one of her charms escaped his observation; even to the rosy reflection of her finger-tips in the dark bronze of the lamp which she held.... and the insult sank deeper in his breast. Irene continued to laugh. "What! You! You are jealous?" she cried at last, and turning her back on her husband, she left the room. "He is jealous!" he heard her say again, after the door had closed, with a fresh burst of mocking laughter.

Although the emotional crisis in this scene is very great, it will be observed that the writer allows himself only a single reference to Ratmirof's feeling; the effect is chiefly obtained by a studiously simple record of what the two persons said and did. A comparison of detached passages, in this way, is inadequate and unsatisfactory. But it is easy to observe what unnecessary importance the English writer has given to a point which the Russian artist would have passed without wasting a word. And if the reader should carry on comparisons of this kind for himself, he would speed-ily discover that the reckless expenditure of words on the part of novelists of the common stamp, and the consequent loss of time and of vigorous impressions, which falls to their audiences, is enormous.

The excess of subjectivity in the average contemporary novel is not distinctly enough recognized. But it is perhaps not more due to the character of the time than to inheritance. By a curious process of genius, Rousseau, drawing his inspiration from Richardson, transformed the type which the latter had founded, and which was to a great extent dramatic, into a vehicle of personality. In the *Nouvelle Héloïse*, he charged it with his own excess of morbid sentimentality, and in *Émile* converted it into a polemical agent for the dissemination of ideas supporting or connected with his attack upon existing civilization.[567] And it was from Rousseau that Goethe derived *his* style of novel, although the Frenchman was a tyro, and the German a master. Goethe's deep critical insight enabled him to construct with great nicety, even though his objective power was somewhat coldly systematic. Nevertheless, he really followed Rousseau's lead, and was more or less influenced always by the source of this original impulse; although in the short tale entitled simply *Novelle* he seems to have gone to the opposite extreme of depending on an almost invisible *raison d'être*.[568] But *Werther*, published sixteen years after the *Nouvelle Héloïse*, was unmistakably an outgrowth of the latter.[569] Afterwards, in *The Elective Affinities*, he advanced a theory in the form of an illustrative story, conducted with great skill, it must be confessed; and finally, in *Wilhelm Meister*, he embodied the results of life-long meditations, after a fashion which quite diverts the novel from its normal and predisposed direction of growth. This crowning structure he has so enriched, as to make it a treasury of inexhaustible suggestion; and yet, considered as a novel pure and simple, we cannot place the depth and variety of the author's abstract thought altogether to its credit. The peculiar efficacy of a novel, indeed, lies in its gradual, concrete, and insensible instillations of wisdom. Here and there, indeed, the author may give us a few golden grains of formulated wisdom; but in general the abstract truths which he has laboriously eliminated should pass through the substance of his book like some chemic which leaves no trace in the liquid that absorbs it, beyond an increased brilliancy and clearness. But with Goethe the mental discoveries are so wholly the subject of attention, in and for themselves, that he has no warmth of enjoyment left for the reproduction of those surface-appearances, forming a common ground on which the novel may unite readers of the most diverse tendencies and varying calibre. It is true, *Wilhelm Meister* gives evidence of much observation of these appearances, but they have really received the author's attention only as a matter of form; he does not love individualities. What do we care for Jarno, Laertes, Lothario, Mariana, Aurelia, Theresa, and Natalia? Even Wilhelm draws from us but a cold regard; and Mignon is almost the only person in the book calculated to establish anything like a relation founded upon affection, with the reader. On the whole, the figures float before us like the creatures of a phantasm, merely,—resembling colored shapes thrown on the screen before a magic lantern; thin, diaphanous, remote from the sphere of tangible entities within which the novel, as distinguished from allegory, should remain confined. We demand, first of all, that the novelist should preserve a sturdy delight in all visible forms and transient appearances, as well for themselves as for what may underlie them. But Goethe does not take hold of these with real gusto; scenes, persons, and incidents are with him always too exclusively viewed as inferior parts of the great allegorical mosaic he is putting together. Life is here presented as seen from his serene summit of universal culture, without sufficient regard for the stand-point of the ordinary observer. The highest beauties of all poems remain veiled to all but a few, who learn how to detect their presence beneath the drapery; but in *Wilhelm Meister* the veiled beauties are all in all, and he who is slow of appreciation for them must turn from the book hungry. Its external aspect is not only dry beyond endurance to the ordinary reader, but, in addition, a little repulsive, owing to the presence of a slight, contented sensuality which may disgust some and injure others, and which will only become inoperative with the charitable and mature reader, who looks by habit for the best, in preference to the less good. Of course, Goethe addresses himself by design to a limited audience. He has altogether the air of a man discoursing at ease, after dinner; and he has accordingly invited only a chosen circle; he wishes for none but good listeners. No one can dispute the depth of perception and the invigorating wisdom in this novel; but in our present inquiry, we have chiefly to consider the book as related to the development of the novel in its character of poetic form. So considered, it seems an erratic though splendid effort; it stands aside from that line of advance upon which the novel approaches its perfection, as a thing enjoyable for its own artistic perfection, and the solid results of cause and effect in real life which it presents, not less than for its power of imparting the subtlest and most ideal thoughts. But Goethe did not appreciate the inherent dramatic and realistic tendency of the novel; he had purposes of his own to be subserved by it, and even attempted to arrest its progress and fix it where he had left it, by a careful definition of the difference between it and the drama, which he set down to the absolute predominance of subjectivity in the novel.

Traces of the artistic practice of Rousseau and Goethe are to be found in some of the works of George Sand, and certain absurdities which appear in Victor Hugo's novels may perhaps be connected with their principles. But even among writers in our own language, who cannot be so directly associated with those eminent champions of the subjective novel, there is frequently an entirely mistaken notion as to the quality and range of this form of composition, which must be partially attributed to prevailing modes of thought. The scientific motive is the dominant one; our fiction-writers become minute and sectional investigators. They are in search of specimens; and when they have found them, they are very apt to set them before us, connected by some slight story, and laugh or sneer at them a little, as if this were the extent of their obligation, both to the persons of their fiction and to the reader. We need a more reverent view of human nature, for without this nothing constructive can be done in art; nothing great or beautiful. Now and then some one appears who can strike some chord of character with precision, and with harmonious results; but for the most part we are content with cynicism or buffoonery, or melodramatic effect, or argumentative haranguing. It is time that we should draw clear distinctions, and, to begin with, recognize a broad classification of all those novels worthy to be considered at all as works of art; placing in the first division such as more or less partake of the anecdotical style,—familiar narratives,—and those which are finished studies, like *Middlemarch*; while the second division should be reserved to those which achieve a consummate and ideal reproduction of characters and events—"a totality of forms, sounds, and incidents, in short elements and details, so closely united among themselves by inward dependencies, that their organization constitutes a living thing, surpassing in the imaginary world the profound harmony of the actual world."

As yet, the partial and critical, rather than the unifying and creative view, is the most popular. And this, partly owing to confused or mistaken views of the moral obligations of novel-art. Moral truth, however, is not best advanced in works of fiction by direct criticism, or by the opening of a strict debit and credit account, which shall leave the deserving and the undeserving characters at quits, before the finis is written; though a certain moral effect may sometimes appear by these means. Profound moral influence is wholly indirect, in art. When Richardson breaks the bones of one offender by an accidental fall, and makes another sinner swear reform out of hand, he has taught us nothing, added nothing to our wisdom or morality; because, though his intentions are excellent, the device is so clumsy and transparent as to excite our amusement. We smile at his endeavor to impose a mechanical morality upon us. The reformation of rakes in this fashion seems only a change of activity on the same plane with their previous misdeeds: it does not proceed from any deeper source. It is only through clear perceptions into the true quality of our common nature, excited by the artistically recounted history of certain beings possessed of that nature, that the *foundations* of morality are deepened and secured. When the artist succeeds in carrying us sympathetically through the history of these beings, so that we feel points of similarity between ourselves and them, and recognize how great are the possibilities of error and crime in us, as in them, he has quickened our morality by rousing a keener insight into ourselves; and, by questioning indirectly the stability of our virtue, he summons our reserve forces to their support. But in the beginning, he must renounce the purpose of actually reforming anybody for good and all, by what he writes. It is only traits of very limited import that can be changed by this direct effort. Let him look well to his art. If he understands that, and thoroughly, conscientiously possesses himself of his theme, it will be strange indeed if his representation of life, like life itself, should not involve in every fold and turning some real moral enlightenment. Great must be the humility of the worthy novelist; and the greater the genius, often, the greater will be the humility in essential points of art, confessed to himself even though not placarded to the public. He must forget his personal likes and dislikes, in his writings, even cultivating a warm and sensitive charity. Distinctions of high life and low life, as such, should be forgotten by him; distinctions of good men and bad men cautiously used. He must regard each human being as an undetermined quantity, which it is his business to consider in all possible lights. And if he can approximate to a simple, unprejudiced presentation of his persons, he will be fortunate; without taking on himself the vast responsibility of judging them beyond possibility of reprieve. Of course, the degree in which he will exercise this impartiality will vary with varying artistic purposes. But, having imagined an ideal standard for him, we shall be better able to assign to each production its true relative position; and by studying nice distinctions, we shall do him all the more justice, in the end.

The impartiality which is here alluded to, however, must not be confounded with those weak condonations and palliations of error which find a somewhat too ready acceptance in these days. A popular novelist has recently exemplified, in a work to which he has given the forms of both novel and drama, that false and vicious charity which undiscerning readers will be apt to confound with the sincere and unvitiated impartiality of genius which is morally sound. Such performances can only be deplored, and left to the corrective treatment of wise critics, and the gradual growth of a public taste which can be liberal, without becoming tainted by the crime it pities and forgives. Meantime, they should not be allowed to throw discredit upon the endeavors of genuine artistic openness and charity. Those phases of existence which are the less happy, and those characters which are the less eminently good, are the more susceptible of poetical enhancement. The terrors and mistakes and tragedies of life call on the artist to redress them: he alone can give to them the unity of beauty—awe-striking, pity-inspiring beauty. Where passion enters in, there a path has been opened to the poet. He has little to do with people who are perfectly comfortable, who go about their business, and to whom nothing noteworthy happens. Nor are native nobility and self-sacrifice at their purest the most suitable subjects, always; being too good for speech, and rather fit for the completer recognition of heaven than the momentary catch-breath praise of earth. At all events, he cannot rest his chief light on these. The supremest good comes to him in the slenderest rays, falling like starlight upon the tragic life of his mimic humanity. Thus dramatic art deals with the victims of passion, of circumstance, of defeated aspiration, lifting them into a pure and sweet aesthetic atmosphere. To the dramatic artist, the tempests of life seem only to be clearing the air.

Keeping in mind the steady advance of the novel, through many centuries, with its distinct dramatic tendency, and combining with this the ideal standard we are at present able to apprehend, we shall learn how to estimate with some approach to justness the new achievements of new writers. We are proud of the modern love for reading, and flatter ourselves that the average taste in art and literature is advancing. But it can never really advance, unless based on genuine perceptions. People recognize and admire a good book, and are just as ready to admire a bad one, afterward, because they have appreciated only emotionally; it is necessary to have intellectual perceptions, in order to build up a serviceable observatory for the taste. At present, the world swears by Shakespeare; and reads too much trash, because its allegiance to him is mainly perfunctory. Fashions change, and we fancy we have progressed. But this is not enough.

Still, in the lapse of some hundreds of years, the average merit of fiction has been increased. As we have seen, the worst came first,—the egg-shell romances; next, the polished anecdotes of the Italians intervened, followed by all sorts of fabulous adventures, and the affectation of long, simpering pastorals, in France. Then satire came; and the drama emptied its ebbing tide into the novel-form; and now we have seen the days of Jane Austen, Walter Scott, Thackeray, George Eliot, Balzac, and Hawthorne. For something like a century, we have been feeling earnestly after real life. The era of conscientious and artistic novel-writing has been fairly and fully inaugurated. But do not many of the highest summits of possible achievement in this region still remain unscaled? The few dry husks of knowledge here stripped off from that central life of artistic truth, which never will be shown in words, may avail to feed a public interest that is prophetic, in the interval through which we are now passing. But it remains for the masters whom the future may bring us, feeling the press of history behind them, and, within, the inextinguishable impulse to create,—it remains for these still further to expand and ennoble, in their own style, this vital and speaking form which we call the novel.

42

THE NOVEL AND ITS FUTURE

George Parsons Lathrop

Atlantic Monthly (1874).

Originating in the Greek romances of the fourth century, which were themselves the offspring of decline, the novel—this losel of literature and outcast of the wise—finds itself, after a long and adventurous career, at the head of all literary forms for present popularity and power. Called forth as a servant, to amuse some idle intellects, it has at length become the master, the instructor, the educator of vast modern audiences composed of thinking and progressive men. We must confess that, whatever our theoretic reverence for the drama, and whatever the triumphs it still achieves amongst us, the novel is still the more subtle, penetrative, and universal agent for the transmission of thought from poet to people.

Ours is essentially a period of prose. Versification, it is true, is a widespread accomplishment in these days, and there are instances enough of genius making it more than an accomplishment. But, on the whole, its frequency seems not so much to mark a strengthening of its empire, as to emphasize the truth that things most in vogue are most in danger of deterioration. As the quantity of verse increases, the merit has a tendency to subside to a common level. Instead of fountains of song bursting freely from the hillsides, the nineteenth century maintains a large reservoir of liquid verse from which we may draw unlimitedly. The means of rhythmic expression are perhaps more varied and more perfect than at any previous epoch; but they assist lyrical demonstration, for the most part,—dramatic, seldom. It is the dramatic forms, however, which give the most manifold delight. Dramas are the cathedrals of poetry; the lyric verse is their adornment, rising in pinnacles. But we do not build cathedrals nor write great dramas. The novel, therefore, attracts to itself our chief energies. The novel is a portable drama, requiring no stage, no actors, no lights or scenery, and no fixed time of enactment. Moreover, as we shall presently see, it embraces a wide range of subjects not fitted for the salient treatment of the playwright. It is, further, especially adapted to the various and complex inner life of the modern world. The very finest things of which the novel is now capable are rather calculated, in their delicate profundity, for private perusal than public recitation. There is a refined emanation from them which can be appreciated in silence and solitude only, or with but a chosen listener or two at hand to share the influence. But, if the vogue of verse be regarded as an intimation of impending decline, it will be asked why the multiplication of novels is not, in the same manner, to count for a sign of approaching decadence. That there is much danger of disaster to the novel is precisely what I should like to have most clearly understood; but there are reasons favoring its immediate and efficient advance which either cannot be supplied, or are not equally operative in the case of lyric poetry. In the first place it is an organism of a higher type than the lyric, being essentially and substantially dramatic; and in the second place the popular demand supplies it with an immense stimulus, while the lyric is sustained by smaller audiences and less frequent opportunities of devotion from its servants. The drama could alone compete successfully with the novel; but to do so it must undergo reforms more weighty than those which are needful to the perfection of the novel. Let us, however, before attempting to cast the horoscope of the latter form, consider the technical differences of drama and novel more closely, with a view to determining their respective advantages as artistic means.

A convenient starting-point for the discussion is to be found in Goethe's utterance on the subject. In the fifth book of *Wilhelm Meister*, he observes:

> The difference between these sorts of fiction lies not merely in their outward form; not merely in the circumstance that the personages of the one are made to speak, while those of the other commonly have their history narrated for them. . . . But in the novel it is chiefly sentiments and events that are exhibited; in the drama it is characters and deeds. The novel must go slowly forward; and the sentiments of the hero must, by some means or other, restrain the tendency of the whole to conclude. The drama, on the other hand, must hasten, and the character of the hero must press forward to the end: it does not restrain, but is restrained. The novel hero must be passive; at least he must not be active in a high degree: in the dramatic one we look for activity and deeds.

But this definition is certainly inadequate. In reality, it applies to the novel as practiced by Goethe and Rousseau, rather than to the stature of the novel altered and strengthened by recent developments in its history. It is patent that characters and deeds are as requisite in the modern dramatically organized novel, as sentiments and events; and that they bear just the same relation to these as in the drama. We are far enough, also, from demanding that the novel shall "go slowly forward"—a mode of locomotion sustained in *Wilhelm Meister* with almost fatal indefatigableness. Compression and swiftness, on the contrary, are becoming marked characteristics of this species of composition. But it is important to observe Goethe's fundamental distinction,—that of the novel-hero's passivity; for he is still at liberty to retain this attitude whenever it may advantage him. And herein lies a special superiority of the novel over drama, in that it is thus fitted to exhibit the hero as the recipient of impressions only,—concentrating in him the phantasmagoric elaboration of all surrounding life through his individual senses and perceptions; while, at any moment, his position may be reversed, so that his views of things shall no longer predominate, a purely dramatic development being accorded to all alike. In this way a double order of effects lies open to the novelist. And it is from this source that the autobiographical novel derives a chief element of power; the suppression of internal history in every one but the first person leaving the characters of the rest to develop themselves in a wholly dramatic manner. The means to this end, in the drama, are the aside and the soliloquy. But people behind the footlights cannot find an escape for every significant emotion of a moment in asides; nor is facial expression always adequate to the occasion. Although of this latter resource it is only the intellectual effect which the novelist can convey, by those numerous brief, indescribable touches of intimation peculiar to his art; and although he surrenders the inexhaustible charm of actual impersonation, still his mode is the more natural. As for the soliloquy, that is a delicate instrument which must be used with the utmost care,—like the chemist's centigrade-weight, which he dares not lift with the fingers for fear of diminishing its accurate poise by the slight wear and moisture of manual contact.

> And therefore, since I cannot prove a lover,
> To entertain these fair, well-spoken days,
> I am determined to prove a villain.[570]

I confess this jars upon me. This soliloquy of Richard's seems inferior to those of Hamlet and Wolsey, not only in poetical qualities but in its dramatic value. The same sense of inconvenience and unlikelihood attaches to the reverie with which Iago closes the first act of *Othello*. Apparently, when the soliloquy must set forth in direct terms the speaker's motives to impending conduct, instead of dealing with wide-reaching speculations or emotions, it of necessity loses somewhat of its force. It would seem to be the sensitive organ in the constitution of a drama, in which the weaknesses of that order of composition manifest themselves most promptly. But even soliloquy becomes more probable and more acceptable when employed in the novel. For the narrator is an admitted entity from the start, and he enjoys the presumption of having either witnessed, or had faithfully described to him the circumstances of his story which he now gives in reproductive reminiscence. He does not require that we should believe in the instant presence of the persons and their personal responsibility for what they are saying, as the dramatist requires it. However the principles of dramatic development may be involved in his work, the whole affair is professedly drawn from something already past, and is so represented; while in the drama we must relinquish, for the time being, even a subdominant consciousness that the scenes before us have been supplied by an already concluded episode of real life. But not only is the advantage greatly on the novelist's side, when the soliloquy is in question: he is also in great measure relieved from the necessity of using it at all, because licensed to come forward in his own person, when occasion strongly demands direct explanation or enlightenment—an interruption which, for the reasons already mentioned in support of soliloquy, cannot disturb us. The novelist's prerogative of description, too, though unconscionably abused in general, is in many situations, if properly respected by him, a palpable advantage. And in the matter of construction a gain is made over the dramatist's necessary restrictions in this particular, through the novelist's greater liberty of interrupting and rearranging the succession of incidents and events. With these technical advantages on its side, and being addressed to the reader at short range, so that its finest effects need not be lost or slurred over, if delicate and unobtrusive, the novel seems to offer a form in which subjects too little abounding in far-flashing externalities, to find successful embodiment in an acting play, may still be subjected to thoroughly dramatic processes.

Yet the prevalent opinions among too many novel-makers, as well as novel-consumers, in respect of what constitutes the dramatic, make it evident that this species of imaginative literature must clear itself of serious misconceptions, before it can proceed unimpeded in the direction of further improvement. An agitated notion seems generally to have gained ground—always reinforced, doubtless, by a benevolent forethought for those readers who choose their fiction from the book-stall mainly according to the broken and easy aspect of the pages—that the novel should be made above all things "conversational"; and to this mistake, serenity, and the contained and forcible utterance characterizing genuine mastery of the dramatic, are constantly sacrificed. But people have other ways of displaying their characters than by talking, and may be treated objectively by other means than those of conversation. Nor is the determined use of the present tense, by which writers occasionally (but too often) attempt to heighten the "graphic" effect of their scenes, at all essential, or even in any way an enhancement. We must take cognizance of a new modification of the dramatic, exemplified in some of the later achievements in the novel form. The stage necessarily appeals more broadly to the senses, and, in these days of excessive and corruptive mechanical contrivance, the sensuous agency has so far diminished the importance or infected the fineness of the subject-matter, as to charge the term, theatrical, with a certain implication of reproach. Those novels, therefore, which are most completely wrought out in the conversational manner, or in such fashion as to make a transposition to the stage an easy process, are not always the most dramatic, using the word at its best and highest. Dickens, Reade, Wilkie Collins, and Bulwer, have so written. And these possess in common a love of stimulating, melodramatic incident, unfolded in rapid and intricate succession. Collins, in particular, is noted for his ingenious joiner-work, his elaborate and studied mechanism of incidents. The long "narratives" through which he conveys the same history, or different parts of it, by different persons, have, it is true, some faint flavor of the dramatic, being based on that unfailing surprise which arises from the partial and conflicting views taken by different people in regard to one and the same transaction. But all the true glory of dramatic abstemiousness is lost in his execution. His detail is excessive, and his accumulation of small items often redundant. The skill of selection which he exercises never rises above the plane of simple cleverness. He has arrived at a useful formula for methodic enumeration, of which he uniformly avails himself; displaying a surprising distrust of the reader's imaginative ability, or power of apprehending minor points, by a con-

stant wordy explanation of the most trifling matters. A showy familiarity with the
superficial aspects of human nature enables him to dazzle the reader, enough to
conceal the fact that, for himself, he cares much more for his plot than for his persons. The latter are cut out to fit their places in the piece; but their individuality in
this way takes an artificial tone, and their narratives seem little more characteristic
than affidavits in a police-trial—a kind of literature which we may suppose to have
furnished Mr. Collins with a great part of his motif In short, we possess in this
noted sensationalist an inventor, not a discoverer. He is a literary artisan, rather
than an artist. Dickens and Reade, on the other hand, though theatrical in manner,
possess real genius, which might have carried them higher, had they carefully
pruned it and thrown its strength always to the upward. Dickens differs from
Reade, in being far less studied: he is also more crude. Reade is apparently a careful
student of the stage, while Dickens relied on the natural bent of his genius toward
the theatrical. Collins, on the whole, is superior to Reade in the slow worrying and
final decapitation of a mystery—a thing which the latter does not always and especially affect. But, on the other hand, Reade has a swift and sunny sympathy which
Collins lacks; and his comparative openness in the matter of plot, leaves him free to
develop incidents and characters together, by a series of stimulant surprises. His
grand fund of spirits, and his quick sensibility to smiles or tears, are akin to attributes of the finest genius, and carry us on readily through all sorts of incongruities.
But, once pausing or returning, to analyze the structure of his stuff, we find the
conversation (at its liveliest) modeled on the rapid dialogues of brilliant comedy.
Mabel Vane, in *Peg Woffington*, exclaims to Triplet, "And you a poet!" "From an
epitaph to an epic, madam," he answers.[571] Her very next words, "A painter, too!"
he meets with: "From a house front to an historical composition, ma'am." At other
times, as in *Love Me Little, Love Me Long*, and later novels, we find Reade lost in the
mire of multitudinous commonplace, apparently trying to reproduce life beyond all
possibility of mistake, by letting loose upon us a flood of indiscriminate gabble.[572]
Thus he seems to waver between the farcically inclined talk of the stage, and a
deadly literalism. In general, his pictures are not so much drawn from life itself, as
they are spirited transcripts from stage-manners in the guise of real ones, and always strengthened by a considerable observation of real life, besides. But the novel
has, by its history, assumed, and in this essay I have claimed, that it comes closer to
real life than any antecedent form. By dropping into the stage-manner, however,
the writer of a novel not only fails to draw nearer to life than before, but—what is
still worse—separates himself from it by a double remove. As life has first been
shown him under the gas-light of the theatre, so he kindles in his book a still fainter
illumination, the reflection of a reflection. But, with all his brilliancy and energy,
Reade disregards this, and plumes himself too openly upon his cleverness, obtrud-
ing the consciousness of his dexterity in the most ill-timed and annoying paragraphs
of bold allusion to it. It cannot be denied that people relish this knowingness, as
they do the equally omnipresent (though unspoken) knowingness of Dickens.
Dickens's characters enter the arena with a jingling of the clown's cap and bells, as

it were; and the audience sees at once that they are about to perform. There is a suggestion of the End Man's manner, in the way he has of opening a dialogue intended to be laughable.[573] And (to return to our other simile) when the intervals of joking are over, we seem to hear the ring-master cracking his whip, as a signal for the serious and breathless business of riding bareback and jumping through paper hoops to begin again. This is a figure only partially true, yet with a truth worth heeding. The public likes this, I have said: but it likes better things, as well. Yet there is an impartiality of omnivorousness, that it is not altogether desirable to sustain. We like to settle the respective merits of authors by the scale of avoirdupois. But, rather than magnitude, it is quality and radical tendency which we ought here to consider; for on these rests the future of fiction.

The more completely a novel remains a novel, the higher must it be rated, as being the more perfect representative of its class. Bulwer was both playwright and novelist, and he is conspicuous for the production of hybrids uniting the features of these two literary forms. His books are crowded with the stalest stage devices. One has but to look through the conversations in *My Novel*, Bulwer's most careful attempt at a reproduction of real life, to see how unshrinkingly he could dilute the pungent currents of nature with the flattest of liquids from the conventional theatrical tap.[574] Much of the dialogue is given in the same form as if written for the stage. But in attempting, at the same time, to remain true to the aspect of common life, the author has been overcome by a disastrous inclination simply to imitate appearances; and the double desire to do this, and to be effective in the style of the stage, has resulted in something at once deplorably dull and intolerably conventional. Mere transcription of facts, aspects, and phases, actually observed by the writer, is—we find it necessary, notwithstanding its self-evidence, once more to announce—neither artistry, nor anything approaching it. On the other hand, conventionalisms, though they are sometimes very necessary, should never be relied on for mere effect's sake, nor admitted at all unless they are genuine, thoughtful, brilliant, or forcible. Those which Bulwer introduces in *My Novel* and elsewhere are, it is true, pointed after a certain fashion: but they are whittled, rather than diamond-cut—sharp pegs, instead of sparkling gems crystallized by the invisible chemistry of genius. And yet these things would, no doubt, pass off well enough upon the stage. But the little green hedge of the foot-lights separates two territories of fiction in which the qualifications to success are, it would seem, by no means identical. Bulwer ignored this fact. Whether we skim the prattling shallows of *Pelham*, or turn the creaking leaves of *Eugène Aram*,—that heavy piece of melodramatic machinery,—or examine the dialogue of the *Lady of Lyons*, we shall hardly fail to meet everywhere the same prolix paucity, although less prolix, of course, in the plays, than in the novels.[575] A knack of proportioning ingredients enabled Bulwer to give his works a pleasant taste to the public; but the critic, unfortunately, knows too well that they were prepared according to recipe. Lord Lytton may be said to have maintained a flourishing "cheap store" or popular emporium of ready-made romance. His novels, like those of Anthony Trollope, though more pretentious and less neatly finished, bear the marks of the mold, still. The excessive activity of his invalid intellect never led him to a real originality. He searched for it on every side, imitating, in turn, Fielding, Sterne, Walter Scott, and Goethe; but had he possessed it, he would have learned this by simply looking within. Originality, it maybe observed here, has even more of sameness in it than of variety; for this lies in the subject-matter, and that is fundamental. Variety and versatility do not, of course, conflict with originality, any more than sameness is always the ensign of it. But it is the abiding peculiarities of a man's point of view (when these are developed, not derived) which make his writing original; and these continue to give it that character, so long as he abstains from conscious exertion to repeat and renew such peculiarities. From a stable and enduring quality of view, springs style, including not only phraseology, but the character of an author's observation, likewise. Thackeray, George Eliot, Hawthorne, Balzac, Turgénieff, possess distinct points of view, from which to contemplate the revolving world. Pausing at some standpoint of ideal perception, they let the variety of life pass under their eyes, and translate its meanings into the new language of their new genius. Hence comes it that large poetic genius is at once radical and conservative: it can look into the roots of things, but it also highly appreciates the value of calm, unchanging heights, upon which to build securely and live happily. Even when engaged in works of deracination and reform, you can see that, in spite of its intelligence, it loves and clings to what is old.

But Bulwer, and the other novelists of the theatrical group, almost wholly lack the distinction of style. Charles Reade is careless, and hardly more than a mannerist, even at his best. Wilkie Collins is lucid, without being concise; simple, not so much from severity, as because it is easy to be so, in the subjects and within the mental scope he allows himself; and devoid of any deep characteristics. Dickens, it may be urged, occupies an undeniably unique point of view. But his talent was even more accessory to his fame, than his genius. Talent is quick at catching a knack that will please the popular taste; but originality measures the sense of this taste, and guides more than it is guided by it. Shall we say that Dickens did not appreciate what was most genuine in himself; did not know in what proportion to combine with the more precious substance of his genius the common alloy of talent, to make it pass current, without debasing it? At all events, the deficiency in style exists. Who does not recall that droll and at the same time almost pitiable method of lengthening out sentences, to suit the increased suspense of a situation? To so many crowded and hurried emotions, we are allowed a corresponding number of clauses connected by colons, semicolons, and dashes,—like supplemental chairs at a hotel-table, to accommodate a rush of visitors. At other times, we accompany the author through long paragraphs of vague and confused description, at his own verbose leisure; and hardly do we find at any point the enhancement of a really beautiful, resonant, masterly verbal style, organically developed from the originality of his observation. Once let us recognize that this original observation is in great part superficial, taking the tinct rather of a brilliant whimsicality than of a profound and vigorous insight, and we shall see why his style is poor and arid.

Balzac laid down the law, that the modern novelist must possess *des opinions arrêtées*: that, in our phrase, he must have "views." But nothing is more dangerous to the fiction writer than views which are based upon prejudice. It is immaterial whether he supports himself with social tradition or commonsense, religious authority or unfettered theory: none of these will justify prejudice. These "views" should be the results of perfectly impartial observation of character, resembling somewhat the immovable, inclosing heavens of the old astronomy, which contained all the spheres and atmospheres. Yet they cannot be altogether, like this, changeless. It is simply profound and sympathetic penetration into character which is demanded. From positive views otherwise founded than upon patient and placid insight, spring the swarms of pamphleteering tales which are the bane of the fictionist's art in our time; and, in the domain of more genuine creation, they lead to the narrowness and limitations of Jane Austen, Miss Edgeworth, and Anthony Trollope. It is true, we should suffer irreparable loss if obliged to surrender Miss Austen and Miss Edgeworth. The world cannot afford to dispense with their pure and gentle feeling. What should we do, without the well-molded gelatinous "forms" of amiability, the excellent Potted Proprieties with which they have supplied us?— wholesome confections which it is to be hoped may regale many a generation yet to come. And yet, despite their charms, and that slow, sleepy spell which Trollope knows so well how to exercise, we cannot but think that writers treating human nature in this way are like placer-miners, who, it is granted, may extract every grain of gold from their field of operations, but only by working in superficial deposits. And, when all is done, the gold-bearing stratum has been sacrificed, washed away in the process: only the barren bed-rock remains to after-comers. These, truly, are the "novelists of manners," for they never get below the crust of society. A change in manners makes occasion for a new writer of the same stamp; and Anthony Trollope, in his generation, takes up the task of Jane Austen and Maria Edgeworth, in theirs. What is this remark of Dr. Johnson's, about Fielding giving us characters of manners, and Richardson characters of nature?[576] It would be obviously unjust to Fielding, to place him with writers like Austen, Edgeworth, and Trollope, excellent as they are in their way.

Reade and Dickens, predominantly men of impulse, give no evidence in their works of having apprehended the importance of "arrested opinions." Dickens, indeed, went so far as to follow out certain unsettled, impetuous feelings, which he mistook for convictions; and so became a propagator of prejudice (though doubtless effecting a great deal of transient good). Reade, appreciating impartiality, and trying to avoid results of this kind, is content with treating mankind as an opportune and curious plaything for the amusement of himself and his reader. But in Victor Hugo we find an altogether singular writer, capable of genuine *opinions arrêtées*,[577] and yet abounding in vagaries, and indulging an unlimited taste for the sensational-picturesque, which compel us to call him theatrical and a mannerist. Here is an author of undeniable genius, a great romantic dramatist, a delicate lyrist, exceptionally noble in his aims, and comprehending the value of an objective treatment of character; who at times delights us with simple and exquisite observation; yet who, for the most part, strays wholly from the ways of nature in his effects, and is wholly extravagant in style. As far as improbability is concerned, it may be said that objections to it, are too often and easily urged in a way to imply that such a thing were quite inadmissible. But if probability were in all cases an indispensable condition of poetic achievement, we should have to condemn much that is obviously above reproach. Nevertheless, it seems certain that the sentiment of probability should never be violated. If the artist should succeed with his illusion, there would be much to justify his use of the improbable. Still, it can scarcely be defended, if it does not also commend itself to the second thought; as it does in the case of Lady Macbeth, who has no children, but who nevertheless exclaims:

> I have given suck; and know
> How tender 'tis to love the babe that milks me.[578]

The truth seems to be, that improbability is a potent means to effect; but when the effect obtained through it is momentary, rather than inherent in the situation's deepest truth, it becomes meretricious, and in degree as it is unessential. With such meretriciousness Victor Hugo seems fairly chargeable, in cases. The fire-cracker-like dialogues with which he emulates Dumas, and which so needlessly confuse us, at times, as to the succession of speakers; the multiplication of short paragraphs, that are in some danger of becoming no paragraphs at all—being often reduced to a single word; and his curious division of a novel into books and parts, with fresh titles and sub-titles as abundant as newspaper-headings, and chapters of every length, from a single paragraph upwards—all this is the issue of an undue desire to impress. Perhaps it should in some measure be excused, because of its service to the author, in carrying the average reader through much that would otherwise appear to him outrageously wearisome. For it is Hugo's plan to connect everything with infinity, on the shortest notice. To fly from the simplest fact into the far ether of abstract thought is his favorite exercise; and to render the reader capable of sharing in these aerial flights, he is obliged to wrap him in a magic cloak of invisibility, woven of sundry expansive and slightly windy phrases. He indites a chapter on a girl's hand, and reaches the weighty conclusion that "Déruchette smiling was simply Déruchette."[579] In another place, describing the nature of a battle, he proudly convinces us, after a series of the most self-evident statements, that "he who leaves the field, is beaten." In fine, he wrestles with nothing, in these cases, as if it were a labor only to be ventured on by intellectual giants like himself; and he comes out of the fight with an immense appearance of victory. Under its guise of pompous emptiness, however, this method conceals capabilities of vigorous surprise and pathetic brevity. Very majestic, to my thinking, is that conclusion of *Les Travailleurs de la Mer*: "Nothing was now visible but the sea." But the defects of this method are more frequent than its beauties. Hugo's desire to air his enthusiasm and to expand in mystic reverie furnishes another example of philosophy injuring art; in the same way that the inclination of George Eliot and Balzac toward philosophical parentheses and interspersed epigram fastens a clog on the dramatic movement of their stories. The novelist, it is true, may fulfill to some extent the functions of a chorus; but he should be very cautious in the fulfillment. Victor Hugo is guilty of "spouting." He tries to magnify, and often to distort, the proportions of all that comes in his way; but things sometimes refuse to be magnified, and leave him in rather a luckless plight. The elasticity and eccentricity of his form he seeks to defend by a mere hyperbole.

"This book," he says, in Cosette, "is a drama, the first person of which is the Infinite."

"Man is the second."[580]

But it is difficult to reconcile ourselves on these easy terms with his reckless practice of "painting up" each and every separate picture in the series which compose a story, so that it may brave the glare of the combined exhibition. This whole question with which we are engaged, as to the grounds for discrimination between theatrical and dramatic novelist, culminates in Hugo's character as a writer of fiction. To get a fresh view of so important a figure, let us subject him to a contrast. Quitting the atmosphere of his lurid spectacles, let us enter the sad-colored everyday world in which rare Thackeray moves. Hugo and Thackeray both indulge in ample comment; but Thackeray's moralizing only partially impedes dramatic action, while Hugo's declamation is so interwoven with the story as to be almost beyond eluding, and is connected with a coarse and dazzling use of colors that reminds one of the scene-painter's trick. In Thackeray there is no hint of effect for effect's sake; but Victor Hugo's novels may be said almost to reek with it. An equally eloquent contrast is furnished by the romances of Hawthorne. "As the feeling with which we startle at a shooting star, compared with that of watching the sunrise at the preëstablished moment," runs Coleridge's fine phrase, "such and so low is surprise as compared with expectation."[581] Now, it is the determined preference of this lower pleasure that distinguishes novelists of the theatrical class. Observe, as opposed to this, that in *The Scarlet Letter* the identity of the unknown sharer in Hester's sin is clearly intimated in the opening scene, and the mind of the reader thus thrown forward, in an attitude of expectation, which the objective treatment pursued throughout the book is designed to assist. Such a master does not find any Jack-in-the-box surprise needful, to engage his audience. But Hawthorne stands in an atmosphere peculiar to himself. To distinguish him from Thackeray, by calling him an idealist, would entail misapprehension; for no novelist possessing genuine insight can fail to be in some sort an idealist. His personal impressions, and keen, unswerving perceptions must enter into the substance of his creation; idea will insensibly enter into every item of the representation. But thus much may be said, that Hawthorne's idealism is exceptionally free from all turbidness. It might be conceived of as a clear and stainless, rounded and buoyant sphere, and capable of bearing us serenely through the most solemn and awful spaces. So far is this idealism from being opposed to that of the acknowledged realistic writers, as people are often inclined to believe it, that we find Hawthorne's realism to be careful, detailed, perfectly true, and perfectly finished. But so suffused is it with fine spirituality, that it does not yet gain popular recognition. Some quality is perhaps wanting in his realism, which would make it more acceptable to the public; but Hawthorne, being engaged with the operation of spiritual laws, did not enter so industriously into descriptive realism as many others have done; although, with a true delight in appearances, he used those particular realistic means which were apt to his purpose with a complete mastery.

Let us consider the import of realism. It is, without doubt, an essential to the best dramatic novel-writing; though in the hands of different authors its manifestations must, of course, vary greatly. One reason for its value is, that it supplies the visual distinctness which is one great charm of the stage. But the necessity for it is more radical. As the painter will study anatomy, in order to a better structural idea of the human form, so the novelist will investigate the functions of all those complicated impulses, emotions, and impressions which we experience from hour to hour, from day to day, and by which our actions and characters are continually controlled, modified, or explained. With his investigation of psychological phenomena, or insight into the mysteries of spiritual being, he must unite the study of all that accompany these in the individual; as corporeality, with that curious network of appearances, habits, opinions, in which each human person is enveloped. Of all eminently realistic novelists, Turgénieff is, I imagine, the most vigorous, acute, and delicate. A little livelier play of fancy, he might, indeed, allow himself, without injury. That he is capable of it, certain rare touches seem to indicate. Speaking of a dandy, in *Dimitri Roudine*, he says: "He tried to give himself airs, as if he were not a human being, but his own statue, erected by national subscription."[582] For freshness, airiness, and genial sarcasm, this equals the best flights of Dickens's fancy. Balzac, as well as Turgénieff, however, seems sometimes to fall below the level of completely artistic representation, simply from neglect of these more elastic motions of the mind. Balzac, in particular, is often too matter-of-fact, or too statistical in his statement of characters, situations, and appearances. It is important clearly to grasp the difference between realism and that which is merely literalism.

I. Realism sets itself at work to consider characters and events which are apparently the most ordinary and uninteresting, in order to extract from these their full value and true meaning. It would apprehend in all particulars the connection between the familiar and the extraordinary, and the seen and unseen of human nature. Beneath the deceptive cloak of outwardly uneventful days, it detects and endeavors to trace the outlines of the spirits that are hidden there; to measure the changes in their growth, to watch the symptoms of moral decay or regeneration, to fathom their histories of passionate or intellectual problems. In short, realism reveals. Where we thought nothing worthy of notice, it shows everything to be rife with significance. It will easily be seen, therefore, that realism calls upon imagination to exercise its highest function, which is the conception of things in their true relations. But a lucid and accurate statement of these relations, in so many words, does not meet the requirements of art. In certain portions of his work, Balzac seems to overlook this: he depends too much upon exact descriptions both of mental processes and physical appearances. He is too much the classifier. In his anxiety to be absolutely correct, he grafts upon his style whole technical vocabularies which confuse and discourage the reader. He often describes houses with a topographical minuteness that ends by effacing from our minds any picture the imagination had formed for itself, and leaving us without the ability to project a new one; and this, when his object is simply to give us a perfect physical impression. It is plandrawing, rather than the painting of a picture; and this defect extends to his descriptions of persons. All description should be simple, pictorial, and devoid of technicalities. Otherwise, one kind of literalism is entailed upon us.

II. In this matter, Turgénieff completely surpasses Balzac. But there is a subtler truth which no pictorial description and no abstract exposition will suffice to convey; for the intimation of which, in fine, fancy alone is fitted. In apprehending this, Hawthorne is supreme. Dickens abounds in instances of fancy, grotesque, humorous, and pathetic; but he is not so uniformly true as Hawthorne. George Eliot, too, sometimes employs it gracefully. But George Eliot, Dickens, and Scott, all have, again, a somewhat excessive regard for the appearances of realness in and for itself, seen in their labored and frequently tiresome imitations of imperfect articulation. This, though undoubtedly a valuable auxiliary in some cases, is only occasionally essential to artistic representation. When carried too far, it makes the writer a copyist, an imitator,—merely a reporter of life. This sort of literalism is exemplified in another way by the novels of Anthony Trollope, who accumulates irrelevancies with a persistence proving him to be for verisimilitude before all things. He will construct a long story out of atomic particles, making it as densely compact as a honey-comb—with the honey left out. He continually gives us, with the utmost gravity, the exact time to a minute, at which some one of his characters takes a train of cars, although this precision has no result in events. And an entire paragraph is consumed by the simple statement that two gentlemen went from the City to a London suburb, in a cab. First, he says that they went hence, and came hither; next, he repeats the declaration, adding that it was long since they had last done so; after which, he goes back and describes their meeting in the street—giving the precise insignificant words which they exchanged; and finally he crowns all with the triumphant announcement that they came home together (as he at first said)—this time explaining that they came by means of a cab. There is a certain fascination in all this: the natural man meets mediocrity half-way: but at bottom it is vicious. Trollope panders to an intellectual laziness which is, unfortunately, characteristic of novel readers; and his books are pervaded by an unhealthy languor. His observation of character is timid and superficial, though abundantly clever; and his impartiality lapses into indifference, a dullness of sensibility. He has but one method of indicating a man's affection for a woman: that is, by making him put his arm around her waist. In Trollope, then, we see how thoroughly demoralizing literalism of this kind may become. It is impossible to prescribe any rules adequate to the various cases in which literalism may occur. But, in general terms, we may say that it is precipitated so soon as the aesthetic balance between idea and fact is, from whatever cause, at all unsettled. We have also seen that realism is assisted by fancy, and quick, pictorial language.

So much being supplied concerning the nature and requirements of realism, we are in a position to recognize the general community of aims in such masters as Hawthorne, George Eliot, Balzac, Thackeray, and Turgénieff. All these are leaders in the best dramatic novel-writing, and their example opposes itself, by its very nature, to the practices of Hugo, Dickens, Reade, and Bulwer. Among themselves, they of course differ in respect of quality and degree of realism, and as to their feeling for pure beauty. We have seen the positive character of Hawthorne's ideal tendency; that of the rest is more negative. Again, they vary in the degrees of pure dramatic effect achieved; and these particular differences are matters of vital consequence. Hawthorne, though thoroughly objective in his rendering, sustains throughout a resonant undertone of poetic reverie; George Eliot and Balzac mingle analytical discourse and philosophic suggestion with the action—the latter, however, being by far the less diffuse, and having an easy grace in analysis which our great Englishwoman lacks. Thackeray, in his turn, takes the part of a grumbling and evil-predicting chorus; and Turgénieff claims little more than the right to introduce his persons, and tersely to explain the periods "supposed to have elapsed." There is fair room for choice among these several modifications of method. If Balzac and George Eliot make their books too much like treatises on human nature, anecdotically illustrated, it must still he said that their system is admirably adapted to bring men to a true appreciation of character and there is small chance of mistaking the special truths which they wish to enforce in their "modern instances."[583] So that what is lost to art, in their case, is possibly a gain to the direct instruction of the human race, in the problems of character and circumstance it constantly has to encounter. But that there is a loss to art, we cannot allow ourselves to forget. The highest dramatic skill would work upon us less directly: it would educate, instead of instructing us. By a gentle, if also searching satire, by a sunny insistence upon the joy of living (the joy of sadness, no less than that of gladness), and by the wise exercitation in us of noble emulation and noble pity, it would insensibly develop, and strengthen, and heal us. I think we are ready for something less medicinal than these magic potions—these bitter brews from sad experience, and deep, undeluded thought—with which the novelists, in these latter and greater days of their dynasty, have come to treat us.

In regard to form, it seems that Turgénieff's example is likely to have the most general and far-reaching influence. His self-exclusion, however, is almost too rigid. This northern athlete demands a muscularity of apprehension in the reader nearly equal to that of his own style of presentation. It is sometimes too violent an exercise to read his books: they set every nerve quivering, hinting the agonies of a vivisection. Besides, he would seem to do himself injustice, in recounting such woful histories as those he chooses, without allowing a single note of hope or of convincing joy to redeem their horror. He is too keenly responsive to outward beauty, to wish the destruction of our faith in some corresponding and essential beauty per-

vading and including all things. Yet, poet as he is, he finds the world all too unpo-
etical. To him, it is apparently not malleable in the fires of profound faith, but offers only fixed, enormous oppositions of loveliness and hideousness over which he
will permit no veil of illusion to rest. There is truth in his picture; but it seems to
deny beauty, and incites to despair. Does it not, then, verge upon error? In marked
contrast to the great Russian, we find the Norwegian novelist and dramatist, Björnsen, who, while as strictly dramatic in the form and movement of his stories as
Turgénieff, is an enthusiastic apostle of beauty, besides. It would be difficult to
conceive of a more delicately inflected piece of dramatic recital, than his novelette
called *The Fisher Maiden*.[584] He has there given the history of an ingenuous, healthy,
highly imaginative girl whose glowing impulses involve her in a curious inconsistency and faithlessness with a pair of lovers, and bring temporary disgrace upon her
mother. But at last her imagination makes an escape into art, and she becomes an
actress. In the prejudiced community she lives in, she cannot do this without a
struggle; and the climax of the tale is in her ultimate triumph, and her engagement
at a theatre in the capital. We enter the theatre, to witness her performance; but the
book closes with the rising of the curtain. How exquisite is this reticence, this reverence for his subject, that compels the poet to leave his revelation of that fresh
maiden heart unspotted by any of the garish splendors or excitements with which
novelists are wont so copiously to supply us! In general, they are only too willing to
raise the curtain on all imaginable scenes, and to expose matters which should
never be made the subject of spectacular interest (although admissible enough
when handled with morally sensitive art). Fiction has too frequently indulged in
what deserves no better name than downright debauchery. The advances it has
made toward temperance, purity, health, and beauty are indeed surprising; but
Björnsen, with his sweet and simple histories, has suggested the possibility of still
greater refinement.

We already see the dawn of a new epoch. Christ's thought, however slow to
manifest itself firmly in the details of our social, political, and religious organization,
has assuredly taken root in the novel. Pity and charity, love, or admiration for the
poor, the common, the unfortunate, and the unrecognized nobility of the world, are
what it is continually endeavoring to arouse and propagate. Dickens's exaltation of
the cruder or more ignorant classes was perhaps excessive; but there was much
truth in his probably much-needed and opportune exaggeration. Thackeray stimulates inferences, by exposing false pretensions, and dethroning the unduly rever-
enced. The tragic element of frequency which George Eliot points out has, in fact,
been already unconsciously accepted, and the moral value of the familiar seized by
the artist. Our heroes and heroines are taken from the rank and file of the race, and
represent people whom we daily encounter; indeed, we shall easily find our very
selves depicted, if we look frankly for such depicture. There is no escaping the
thoughtful and elevating influence of this. Nor need there be any implication of
littleness or dullness in these aims. The great circle of the horizon may draw its ring
around whatever spot shall be chosen as the groundwork of a fiction, and the exact

zenith hang above the heads of its personages. Far from lessening the force of personality in fictitious characters, this choice of the frequent is most favorable to a true discrimination of qualities in character. When we have once become aware of the great number of points in which human beings are nearly identical; of the real coincidence of great people and little people, in minute traits no less than in fundamental characteristics; when, in fine, we perceive the incredible resemblances of men; then we shall best be able justly to estimate their equally astounding differences. The level of humanity is like that of the ocean; but each constituent particle rejoices in its own atomic being, and all have a chance to crest the highest waves, if wind and moon should conspire favorably. The instantaneous photograph is necessary to depict this ocean and its movements. But we must have more than any photograph can give us; with the accuracy of that, should be combined the aesthetic completeness of a picture and a poem in one,—and always of a picture and a poem.

43

IVAN TURGÉNIEFF

Thomas Sergeant Perry

Atlantic Monthly (1874).

Of the novelists now living, Turgénieff is probably not the one who is most widely known, but in the estimation of those who are familiar with his writings he holds a place above any rivals. There is nothing strange in either his comparative obscurity or the warmth of the admiration which more than outweighs the calmer interest that might be felt in a writer who contented himself with a more superficial view of life and a less profound consideration of the problems which await us all, demanding some solution, or, more truly, some attempt at solution on our part. Of the novelist in general it may be said that he has two parts to play in order thoroughly to succeed: he has to entertain the listless, and at the same time, in order to be a great writer, in order to leave a mark on the history of his time, he has to bring to the treatment of the main questions of our existence a wise comprehension of their meaning, and a sympathetic power of interpreting as well as of narrating the events he imagines and puts before us. In his own way, with somewhat different materials, he works at the same task as did the old dramatists, or as do musicians and artists of any sort. The first essential condition is that we be entertained; no useful information unaided by imagination, no mere statistics, will draw spectators to see a play or get readers for a novel; we might as well set the report of the State Board of Health to music. Entertainment, in its less ignoble sense, is what we demand of all artists, whether they work in marble, in colors, or with pen and ink. And of them all we ask for aid, not in the way of almsgiving, of formal philanthropy, but such as we feel in the sympathy of a friend, or when we are encouraged by the sight of a noble example. The novelist differs from the others in the fact that he is more of a realist in his workmanship. A tragedian can have the aid of poetry; the characters in his play, if it be necessary, need only be affected by a single dominant feeling which may raise them above the petty criticism of those details that are considered requisite in a novel, in which the characters, like people in real life, are under the influence of rules of etiquette forbidding the statuesque posing which is allowable in tragedy. In stories the tension of passion is relieved by the description of external peculiarities such as the eye notices even at times of the greatest solemnity; men's and women's faces are described, the motley sequence of feelings is told us; in a word, our imagination is aided every way in forming a picture complete in all the details. How much the predominance of novel-writing at the present day is due to this curiosity for detail is an important question which this is not the time to discuss. But at any rate it is interesting to notice how much that feeling, whatever may be its origin, is hostile to the broad handling required by tragedy, and favors the mechanical exactness to be found in the novel.

But in spite of this difference in external form, the novel is a work of imagination, although drawn, with lighter and more varied touches. The more serious the nature of the problem it discusses, the higher its position as a work of art. Many novels are written which claim to do no more than help the reader to forget the monotonous routine of his daily life. Some, like *The Initials*, are the classics of this kind; they always amuse and have thereby won warm admiration from old and young.[585] Certainly it would be a harsh and futile sort of criticism that should seek to decry such innocent and agreeable work. But while there is a persistent demand for novels of this sort, which succeed more or less well in their business of entertainment, there are always certain writers of higher and more serious aims who take the same form for their writing, since thereby they reach their readers more easily, and it is a form more congenial to themselves in proportion as they are influenced by that mysterious thing, the spirit of the age. That these writers should choose this mode of expression need not cause us any regret, nor is it in any way necessary to open any discussion of the relative positions of a novel and other forms of artistic work. We should here as elsewhere take what we have set before us, with as much gratitude as possible; and when we have novels to read, we should not weep for epic poems. Nowadays novels are written; the authors sometimes dignify their task by the treatment of human life in a thoughtful way, and it is of a writer of whom this remark is exceptionally true that we wish to speak here.

Ivan Turgénieff was born in the district of Orel, in the centre of Russia, November 9, 1818, and there he passed his boyhood; from 1834 to 1838 he studied at Moscow and St. Petersburg.* Then, in his twentieth year he went to Berlin, and at the university in that city he studied especially history and philosophy for two years. Hegel's philosophy, although it had lost somewhat of its earlier glory, still had a controlling influence in Germany at that time, as indeed it had until 1848; but on Turgénieff's mind it seems to have made, or at any rate to have left, an unsatisfactory impression, for we often find in his writings irreverent mention of the German philosopher.[586] After returning to St. Petersburg he for a short time occupied a position under government in the Ministry of the Interior, but this he soon left in

---

* Vide Glagau's *Die Russiche Literatur und Iwan Turgenjew,* [1872] pp. 43-44, to which we are now indebted for most of our statistics.

order to devote himself to literature. He first tried his hand at poetry, but without success. We have never seen a line of his verse, but if, as we are told, it was written in the style of Pouschkine and Lermontoff, who were themselves imitators of Byron, its failure need not be wondered at.[587] His first success was in the prose sketch "Khor and Kalinitsch," which our readers will remember in his *Récits d'un Chasseur.*[588] This appeared in 1846. Soon afterwards he went to Paris, and there he wrote the greater part of the *Récits*, which appeared from time to time in a Russian magazine. It was in 1852 that they first appeared in book-form, after eluding all opposition from the censors of the press, who, according to Mr. Otto Glagau, did not detect the hidden purpose which lay under what seemed to be merely a collec- tion of pictures of Russian life,—the purpose, namely, of portraying the sufferings and degradation caused in that country by the existence of serfdom. Afterwards, however, when they were collected and published together, the censors avenged themselves in the following way. They took for their pretext an article which Tur- génieff had written on the death of Gogol in the same year, and had him banished to his estate for two years.[589] Nothing but the intercession of the Czarovitch, the present Czar, freed him from this sentence. After that time he lived in Russia, France, and Germany until 1863, when he chose Baden-Baden for his home. In that pleasant little town, which was the resort, at one time or another, of almost all the interesting people of Europe, he has since for the most part lived, having for neighbors his friends Louis Viardot and his wife, the celebrated Pauline García Vi- ardot.[590] At times, too, we hear of his presence in England.

Before discussing their literary merits, it should be said of the *Récits d'un Chasseur* that they were in a great measure the cause of the abolition of serfdom by the pre- sent Czar. In this respect they may be compared with *Uncle Tom's Cabin*, but there is no further likeness between these books. Turgénieff's method, here as everywhere, is so quiet, he is so careful to avoid anything like an expression of his own feelings, that the censor's mistake seems very natural. He writes, not with an avowed pur- pose which is to be read between the lines by the most indifferent, but as if his aim were entirely of another sort, simply to describe certain Russian peculiarities, and the inference about serfdom were almost something which had escaped his own observation.

What we find in the *Récits d'un Chasseur* is a number of sketches by a hunter, who evidently, in fair weather and foul, morning and evening, has wandered about the country with his gun on his shoulder, making the acquaintance of all his neighbors, learning to know all the serfs he meets, spending the night in their huts or camping out with them when they have no roof over their heads. In almost every one of the sketches we find some wonderful description of the beauties of nature, which, too, has the merit of being appropriate and readable. Too often even the best of de- scriptions has an air of having been done under some other inspiration than that by which the story was written, into which it is inserted with more or less cleverness; but Turgénieff's enjoyment of nature, and his keen observation, make him a truth- ful painter, while his sensitive avoidance of anything that might fatigue the reader saves him from the most frequent error of the landscape-painter who works with pen and ink. The sketch "Le Bois et la Steppe" especially deserves mention, for it is all description, and all natural. Among so many that are good it is hard, as well as, perhaps, unnecessary, to say which is the best, but among the most impressive, to our thinking, is the one called in the French translation "La Prairie."

At the end of hot July day which the writer has passed shooting grouse, he loses his way, when seeking to return home. At last he finds himself at the top of a precipice overlooking a wide plain; beneath him he sees two fires, around which are collected some human beings. He makes his way down to them, and on approaching he sees they are peasant boys who are guarding horses; they call back the large dogs who are barking violently and threatening to attack him. By their fire he prepares to pass the night. He watches the spreading darkness, and the ever-increasing brilliancy of the fire; every now and then a horse comes into its light, bites a twig from a small bush, and trots away. There is scarcely a sound to break the silence; occasionally the splash of a fish in the river near by is heard as it springs out of the water, and the little waves it has made break softly against the shore. The boys, five in number, gather about the fire; the oldest is only fourteen, the youngest not more than seven. Soon they begin to talk about all the uncanny beings which still exist in the imagination of uneducated Russians. A vague sound, such as often fills the night, is heard, and all, for their nerves are set on edge by their talk, are frightened except Paul, who laughs at them and bids them sup. They still go on with their anecdotes, with every now and then a little alarm at the cry of some night-bird breaking the deep silence. Paul is seen comforting them, and trying to explain away their terror at their ghostly stories, not with the aid of any superior knowledge, but as if he were anxious to silence his own alarm. Soon he determines to go to the river to draw some water; his companions warn him to be careful, listen to his retreating steps, and are telling stories of boys who were drowned, who were dragged into the river by the water-nymphs, when Paul returns safely. He has been frightened, however, for he has heard some one calling him by name; they are all much impressed by this, but soon they go to sleep. The writer, who had been listening to it all, likewise falls asleep, and early the next morning he is off, nodding good-by to Paul. The sketch ends as follows:

> I ought to add that to my great regret Paul died that same year. He was not drowned, he was killed by a fall from a horse. I am sorry for him; he was a capital fellow.

That is all; it is as simple a study as could be written; there is not an incident in it, but it is a perfectly complete picture. Another, which is drawn with similarly slight materials, is the one called "Lgove." In this, the author merely gives us an account of a trifling accident while duck-shooting, the sinking of the boat in which he is with some peasants, and their wading ashore; but the way in which he describes the conduct of some of the serfs, and his conversation with them, throws a great deal of light on his method. He gets talking, for instance, with an old fisherman whose leaky boat the others are putting in readiness; he asks:

"Have you been a fisherman long?"

"Seven years," answered Soutchok.

"And what were you before that?"

"I was a coachman."

"Why did you give that up?"

"My mistress wanted me to."

"Who is your mistress?"

"The one who bought us lately. Don't you know her? She is Elena Timofeïevna—a stout lady who is no longer young."

"Why did she make you a fisherman?"

"Heaven knows! She arrived one fine day from Tamboff, and bade us all assemble in the courtyard. Then she came out before us; some went forward to kiss her hand; that did not seem to vex her, and all the rest did the same thing. Then she began to ask us questions; she asked each of us his name and occupation. When my turn came, she asked me, 'Well, and what are you?' 'I am the coachman,' said I. 'The coachman!' said she, 'a fine coachman you are; you must be my fisherman. You must always keep the table supplied with fish.' So that's the way I became fisherman."

"To whom did you belong formerly?"

"To Serg Pektereff. We had been left him by will, but he only kept us about ten years. I used to be his coachman in the country, but not in town."

"So you had always been a coachman?"

"Oh, no," and he goes on to tell that he had been cook, valet, and likewise an actor. "Our mistress," he says, "had built a theatre."

"What parts did you take?"

"I don't understand."

"What did you use to do in the theatre? "

"Why, don't you know about it? They took me and gave me some handsome clothes; and then I would walk about or stand or sit down, as it happened. They used to tell me what I had to say, and I would say it. Once I played a blind man; yes, they stuck peas under my eyelids to make me keep them shut."

And then he mentions briefly his other occupations, showing us the absolute control held by masters and mistresses over their serfs, the degradation it caused in the victims of the tyranny, and the brutality of those in authority. This sketch we have chosen for the lightness of touch with which the author performs this task. When the boat fills and sinks, the fisherman is afraid of nothing but the writer's wrath. He is always perfectly uncomplaining and humble, demanding nothing for himself. In some of the *Récits*, again, we are told of crueler sufferings, which it makes one's blood boil to read; and of some of the serfs he says, "They generally keep their eyes cast down, but yet one cannot infer anything from that, for it is almost impossible in our beloved country, as every one knows, to tell whether it is sleepiness or hatred that is prominent in a servant's face."

In short, Turgénieff has drawn here a series of pictures which he has hardly anywhere, if indeed he has at all, excelled. In every one we notice the same keen observation, the same care in setting the scene before us, and the same self-control which distinguish him in all his writings. Nor is it to be said that he notices nothing but serfdom and the many misfortunes it causes; he has a keen eye for the ridiculous pomposity of petty proprietors, the eccentrics, who would naturally make their appearance in a state of society in which respectable social position could be maintained in spite of disgraceful ignorance and utter idleness, and for the young men who fall in love with the peasant girls. In short, he gives us nearly every element of Russian country-life in turn, although it is of the peasants that he prefers to write. On the whole, the impression the book leaves is a sad one, so much suffering is described, so hopeless seems the condition of the wretched people who are put before us; and yet, we do not feel as if the writer had written it as an expression of his pessimism, which might be said of some of his later works, but as if he were merely setting before us, with exquisite skill, what had actually met his eyes. He draws from the life, and he gives us lifelike pictures, in which the art seems like the utmost simplicity. It is of a sort that may perhaps be defined, but it cannot be taught; it depends on what is in the writer, not on what is outside of him. Turgénieff sees what any one of us might see, although we are surer to do it when it is pointed out than of ourselves; and while he is more especially noticeable for the careful attention to detail by which he represents our idealized imagination, he directs it with that perfection of taste which in another form is humor, and in this form is sensitiveness, not only to what is effective, but also to whatever might offend, with regard to which it knows no mercy. It is a clumsy system of classification, which leaves us no chance to call it anything but realism as contrasted with the display of the writer's own feelings, which has acquired the name of idealism; neither term does more than point in the direction of certain qualities; it does not define them. To call Turgénieff a realist is right enough as far as it goes, but the word, as we generally use it, needs to be interpreted. He is a realist in the sense of hiding himself, and in the painstaking accuracy he shows with regard to everything his pen touches. But one may be accurate and likewise confusing, in the same way that a catalogue is not a picture. By what arts a great writer invents characters, and gets a deep insight into his fellowmen, of course no exposition is to be found here; we can merely say that Turgénieff performs this difficult task with wonderful skill. The men and women really seem to live. This praise is by no means due to the shorter *Récits* alone; in his stories and longer novels he is equally admirable in this respect.

The short tales are numerous, and have been written at various periods within the last twenty-five years. Some of the gloomiest of them he wrote during the time of his banishment to his estate;[591] such are "Moumou," "A Correspondence," "The Antchar," and "L'Auberge du grand chemin."[592] We say some of the gloomiest, and yet there are none which do not partake of his deep-seated pessimism. What these characteristics are can be judged from the brief analysis of a few. In "Moumou," for instance, we have nothing but the account of a deaf mute of gigantic size, who leads a lonely, friendless life, and whose vague attempt at love-making has been thwarted by his mistress; in despair he makes friends with a dog. At first all goes well; but after a while the lady of the house, who is delicate and nervous, takes a prejudice against the dog, and orders are given that it be sent away. This command is carried into effect; its master mourns its absence, but the intelligent little beast returns. The mute then tries to secure a longer life to his pet by keeping it in his room safe from observation, and taking it out by night for exercise; but by some unlucky chance the dog's barking is heard, and the enraged mistress of the house orders it to be killed. This is told the mute, who undertakes the sad task himself; he washes the little dog with especial care, gives it one last meal, and then takes it out on the river in a boat. He fastens a stone by a rope to its neck and then throws the poor dog overboard, and rows swiftly back. That night he leaves the city and walks to the place in the country whence he came, and which he never leaves again.

In "A Correspondence" there is even less of a story. Two men had passed the summer in the country with two young girls, sisters, and had both fallen in love with them and become engaged. Neither engagement, however, came to anything; one of the men was already about to marry another girl, when the other wrote to her who had formerly been betrothed to his friend, giving this news and begging permission to correspond with her, which, after some reluctance, she grants. Their letters are only fifteen in number, but they picture wonderfully the state of the writers' minds. He is a man past his first youth, with plenty of idle time and his discontented self on his hands, and he writes to her in great measure out of *ennui*, to disburden his heart, which is wearied with contemplation of itself. He, as it were, makes his confession to her; she, for her part, is at first silent; but at length, moved by his frankness, she writes freely, in order to put before him the condition of a girl whose one romance has turned out ill, and who sees nothing before her but an uneventful life which is all disappointment and miscomprehension. He admires and pities her, and determines to visit her; she is pleased and makes ready to receive him; her letter urging him to come is full of delight; but there is a long silence; he does not appear, and the next letter she receives from him is one written on his deathbed some three or four years later, in which he explains his silence and bids her farewell. He had, it seems, fallen in love with, or rather been infatuated by, a dancer, and had followed in her train for years, all the time conscious of his degradation, and equally unable to break the chain which held him. He writes to his old friend a full confession. It may perhaps be objected that a man of the sensitive and refined nature that we can see in his letters could not make so decisive a step in the contrary direction; but we are told, it is to be remembered, that he is a man accustomed to follow every whim; indeed, that is but a natural result of his excessive idleness; and hence we need feel less surprise at his conduct, although even when this is borne in mind it is to a considerable extent remarkable. But in spite of this flaw, the story is very extraordinary on account of the pathetic interest of the letters. We know hardly so faithful a description of failure and the disappointment it is sure to bring to others. There is not a superfluous word; we are not shown how to grieve; we have given us merely the materials of grief, and no one can read the story unmoved.

"The Antchar," a translation of which appeared in *The Galaxy* rather more than a year ago, is another even gloomier tale.[593] "Faust," which has likewise been translated for the same magazine, is of higher merit, and, like "A Correspondence," is told by means of letters.[594] In it we read of a man who meets, after an interval of years, a woman with whom he had formerly been in love. Her education bad been peculiar, and she had never read any poetry, in fact, no works of imagination, in obedience to the whims of her mother, whom she adored. The hero first makes her acquainted with this part of literature, but with a far more serious result than he had anticipated. They fall in love with one another; they meet, but she imagines she sees the ghost of her mother, and flees from him distracted. That is the beginning of the delirium in which she dies.

We need not give an analysis of any more. First, out of fairness to the author, who gets but feeble justice in this way, and, secondly, because these few examples may suffice to give an accurate impression of certain qualities which especially deserve mention. Still, by telling the story we do less harm than might be done if other authors were treated in the same way, because our appreciation of what is Turgénieff's great merit, the power of setting the scene before us, is not diminished any more than is our delight in a picture by a written description of what is painted on the canvas. In both cases we are left free to enjoy the work of the artist.

What we observe in all is the unfailing melancholy which exists, not only in the turn of the plot, but also in the circumstances of many of the stories. This is natural enough in those which were written about the peasantry, but in all there is a dreary picture of superstition, affectation, pretense, half-civilized polish, and idleness. They give us a very black picture of Russian life, which has, apparently, all the outside forms of civilization, distinctions of caste more marked by observance than by intrinsic difference, with a dreary formality wholly unrelieved by humor. In this respect there is a marked resemblance to the Southern States, and especially to them as they were before the war. Perhaps this lack of humor is to be explained by the necessity of preserving fanciful social distinctions which rest only on conventionality. Humor tends to overthrow any such formalities; it implies a certain equality, and so it is not likely to appear among those who feel uneasy about their position. In this country there is pretense enough, and this without invidious distinction of North and South, but there is also plenty of humor to temper it. Of course, our explanation of its absence in Russia is not intended to cover all cases; it is merely suggested for what it is worth. Fully to explain it, we must take into consideration many other things, such as the repressing and degrading effect of the despotic government, the possible influence of the deep religious feeling of the people, etc. That this lack of humor is not due to any want of it in the author should be borne in mind. He himself has plenty of it, as any one who is familiar with his novels will recall; we need only mention, for instance, Pantaleone in *The Spring Floods*, and Uvar Ivanovitch in *On the Eve*.[595]

Another characteristic, and one which like all of his is equally noticeable in the long novels, is his tragic treatment of love. And with this connects itself the quality just mentioned, the lack of humor in the persons about whom the stories are written. Not one of Turgénieff's women ever laughs; there are plenty who giggle, but there is not one who fairly laughs. All the foibles, and indeed the faults of women, he exposes freely; but those whom he chooses for heroines, widely diverse as they are with regard to most of their qualities, are alike in never laughing even when ludicrous things take place before them. In this way, perhaps, they are more idealized, for there is a decided difference between the charm of good-natured *bonhommie* and the seriousness and mystery of half-poetic reserve; and a writer who knows that his main strength lies in the delineation of exalted passion may well be excused for preferring that to the simpler pathos which Turgénieff disregards. But defense is idle where there is no attack, and no one would blame the author for this curious omission; it is more than outweighed by the skill with which these women are drawn.

Every novelist of modern times gives us more or less profound studies of women in his writings, and the more thoroughly he performs this task, the more sure he is of arousing the reader's interest. He makes a completer picture of life, because to be accurate he has to introduce some man or men; and he has a better opportunity for keen analysis in discussing the feelings of a woman in their unselfishness and freedom from sordid motives, than would be the case in writing of men under similar circumstances, who, to make the representation of their lives complete, need an account of the numerous outside influences which occupy so much of their time and attention. Turgénieff gives us most thorough studies of men, but he is excelled by no one in the drawing of women. He knows them as well as a woman could; but his knowledge, if it be sometimes lacking in such sympathy as a woman writer might show for one of her heroines, is always accompanied by a certain reverence, a poetical half mystery, which women do not have when writing about their own sex, probably from their nearness to it, and which, it is hardly necessary to say, differs widely from the contempt which distinguishes some authors who may have made as thorough study, but with unworthy text-books. Another thing, which more than half follows from what we have just pointed out, is the way in which he gives the reader all the conditions of the problem and yet leaves him to solve it as best he may, just as puzzles are put before us in life without a key. Thus in Turgénieff's *Smoke* we have the baffling character of Irene; and how far she was a flirt and how far a passionate woman it would be hard to say; she is at any rate wholly a riddle. Lisa, in the story of that name, is a less complicated character. Ellen, in *On the Eve*, is puzzling with regard to the way in which she loves Insaroff. We see him with all his peculiarities, and we see her fascinated by his strength of purpose, which is so conspicuous amid the weakness and negligence of his companions; but here, as in all the cases mentioned, Turgénieff never explains; he states the circumstances, and we guess at the cause as well as we can.

All of the novels introduce some complication of love-making, and this is of a tragic character. But the tragedy is of two kinds; in some, such as *Smoke*, *The Spring Floods*, and "A Correspondence," to take the most prominent instances, we have the melancholy spectacle of a man yielding to a passion which he knows is degrading, but which he has not the strength to withstand. The plot is to a certain extent the same in these stories, but the treatment is very different. In *Smoke* we have a man who is engaged to his cousin, and who, while awaiting the arrival of his betrothed at Baden-Baden, meets a woman, now a fashionable belle, whom he had formerly been in love with. This is the Irene mentioned above; and the novel tells us of her wiles, the way in which the web is wound about the wretched Litvinoff, her former lover, and pictures to us his gradual succumbing to the temptations which so fatally attract him, and his final release. *Spring Floods* is even more tragically drawn. We have in it the whole story of a young man's first love for a charming girl, which is beautifully told. Circumstances compel him to leave her for a few days; he departs, sure of his love and his own strength, vowing to return soon—but he meets the wife of an old schoolmate of his, a thoroughly vicious woman, and he forgets everything in his degrading love for her; he hurls every duty and every noble feeling aside in order to make himself her slave. This baleful passion ruins his whole life. As may be seen, these are not stories for every one to read, but they do not err by making sin seem sweet. They contain no luscious descriptions of vice with a sermon tardily following like the "applications" of Aesop's *Fables*. Far from it; they mention crimes which it is well to discuss, especially in public, as little as possible, but the moral goes hand in hand with the fault, the punishment is surer than it sometimes is in life. These books show—and herein is a wisdom that might well be followed by those who openly avow they are merely sugaring a moral lesson—that the wicked man suffers, not by mysterious accidents to life and limb which in fact do not inquire into the victim's moral character, but through agonies of remorse and shame, by making vain regret the inevitable result of folly or wrong-doing.

In others the tragedy is of a different sort. "Lisa," for instance, is gloomy enough in its incidents, but there is in it the description of so much loveliness of life that the sadness is more than outweighed. It is the story of a man who when a boy in heart, although older in years, fell in love with the first pretty face he saw, and this happened to belong to a very frivolous young girl, who, after marrying him, proved false to him. Thereupon he left her and returned to his home, where he made the acquaintance of a young girl, Lisa, the heroine of the story. She, by her dignity and lofty nature, gets great influence over him, and when he hears of his wife's death, he asks her to marry him. She consents, but to their great surprise the news turns out to be false; the wife returns and asks for forgiveness. Lisa bids him to receive her again, and to forgive her; as for herself, she withdraws to a convent, and the unhappy husband has to put the heavy load on his shoulders. The reader's feeling is one of sympathy for those poor people who are defrauded of their happiness; and it is sympathy one need not be ashamed of, that is given them, for they bow to their fate without seeking to break higher laws for their selfish profit; the lofty resignation of Lisa, and her pathetic justice, which the husband of the other woman cannot help hoping will be less rigid, while they leave us sad, do yet console us by showing us how much better and higher it right-doing than happiness. We pity and approve at the same time.

On the Eve, again, is a novel which, though full of beauty, although it contains a love-story told with even more wonderful art than any other we know,—that is to say, even more wonderful in this respect than any of Turgénieff's,—is deeply tragic, but in a way that we cannot help feeling is more the result of the willful determination of the author, than of those conditions of life which inevitably bring misery in their train.

We hope our readers are already familiar with the story: with Ellen's preference for the young Bulgarian, and her impatience with her other lovers; with the way in which with mingled modesty and fearlessness she lets him know of her love for him; and with her sad fate. The very skill with which this is told us, the wonderful revelation of a young girl's heart, the appeal to our sympathy throughout, all combine to give us so tender a love for the heroine that we yield entirely to our feelings, and mourn her story without stopping to consider that the poor girl is more the victim of the gloomy nature of the author, than of any fault of her own. There would seem to be a needlessness about her sufferings; we feel almost as if a girl had been sacrificed for our intellectual entertainment. In life there is misery enough which strikes blindly right and left without bringing a satisfactory explanation for its existence; but in a work of art we have a right to ask, not necessarily for nothing but joyousness, for there may be a higher content to be derived from suffering, but for such an account of suffering as shall seem needful and necessary, and not the invention of mere wantonness; it should be the natural outgrowth of the circumstances of the case. In *On the Eve*, is Ellen punished for falling in love? is it for falling in love with a Bulgarian? No, there is no proportion between the conduct of the girl and her sufferings; they are beautifully told, but this inconsequence mars what in some respects is the best of Turgénieff's novels. Nor is the heroine's affliction made use of as a means of amending her faults: she is not rendered less headstrong; she does not return to her feeble-brained, heartbroken mother; she determines to aid the Bulgarians as much as she can, and the novel ends leaving us to understand, apparently, that Ellen is lost at sea. At any rate, she is never heard of again.

But in spite of this serious drawback how delightfully is the story told! The different characters of Bersieneff and Shoubine, the one serious and timid, the other light-hearted and fascinating, and Ellen's pompous father with his hollow affections,—no novelist equals Turgénieff in setting people before us.

It is especially as a study of character that *Dimitri Roudine* is remarkable. It has for its subject a few incidents in the life of a Russian, a man who began life with attractive talents, but whose nature is poisoned by an insuperable desire to shine by words rather than by deeds. The whole novel is nothing but a study of this man and his effect on other and different characters. His ready tongue and apparent enthusiasm make him win the heart of a young girl, but his feebleness, when their love is discovered and she is ready to fly with him, makes her utterly despise him. Her mother, a self-willed, affected old lady, who is very fond of admiration, is pleased at getting a new man who is ready to listen to her, but she is very unwilling to let her daughter think of marrying him. Then there is his old fellow-student, who is at first ready to condemn Roudine, but who, after his disgrace, takes a more generous view of him; and his modest rival, who at last turns upon him; and the young tutor, with his boyish, enthusiastic admiration. The upshot of the whole book is a sort of rec-ommendation to our mercy of those persons whom it would be the easiest to con-demn, those, namely, who excite general envy by their brilliancy, or who disappoint our confidence by letting fine speeches stand for fine actions; indeed, more fairly, it is a sort of warning to be generous in our estimate of others. Not that it is written to convey that moral lesson; but that is what one learns from it, as one learns from his own experience.

Then, too, we ought to observe the life-like way in which the novel is written; we are never granted any side views of the hero which are denied the people in the story; we are deceived or put on guard just as they are; we have to study him just as they do; hence it is that a novel so barren of incident, and in a way so clumsily put together, succeeds so well in interesting the reader, who finds his curiosity aroused and his sagacity baffled in a way that is not over-common about the heroes of fic-tion. Too often these gentlemen are beings whose characters stand out strongly marked with this or that quality, which we either admire or condemn at sight; but in this novel we are perplexed as we are in real life, and this it is which gives the story its great charm.

Fathers and Sons, which appeared in 1860, besides its particular interest for the ac-count it contains of the wave of materialism which was then at its height in Russia, has a general interest from its representation of the frequent conflict between the older and younger generations, which is never to be felt more acutely than in times of intellectual change. Russia, with its uneasy yearning for civilization, seems to have shown the same eagerness to adopt a theory which was to solve the universe without the necessity of lone preliminary training, that one can observe among the Japanese, for instance; and to have given it the devotion which is found only among those who have not had to blush frequently for misplaced enthusiasm. But with all its wonderful power the novel is yet not perfectly satisfactory; Bazaroff, the young student of advanced opinions, without mercy for the softer graces as represented by the nobleman Kirsanoff, comes to an untimely end, not in a way that is at all connected with his peculiar views, but merely at the will of the author. Still, there is much to outweigh this defect; we need only mention the other student, Arcadi, who models his life on that of his friend, but who is soon brought around to conven-tionalities by his love for Katia. All systems of philosophy are pretty much alike to her. We first see Bazaroff's views clashing with the world at large while he is staying with his friend, but it is later, when he reaches his own home, that the full force of the tragedy is felt. All families know more or less of it, but in this story it is pecu-liarly poignant, and there is little that even Turgénieff has written more touching than the confused efforts of the father to understand his son's new ideas, and the young man's vain efforts to convert his father. This it is which lifts up the novel from being a study of an exceptional phase of Russian society to being an account of something of wider interest through its truth, which rises above geographical distinction.

Such, in brief, are Turgénieff's novels. Of books which go so far towards setting before us pictures of life, it is impossible to give a thorough impression in the narrow limits of a magazine article; the novelist has taken so large a field of human nature for his subject, that only detached points can be touched upon, but we have endeavored to indicate some of the most noteworthy of his qualities, which may tempt more novel-readers to the perusal of his writings. The foregoing analyses may show the serious nature of the problems he discusses, as well as the poetical idealization of everything his pen touches. This quality it was that made the *Récits d'un Chasseur* a book so dangerous to the Russian government; and in everything he has written he has known how to touch the heart, not always, to be sure, with equal success, but in a way that no novelist of the time has excelled. We cannot be too grateful to an author who brings the world "To sympathy with hopes and fears it heeded not."[596]

To his skill in drawing character, in setting the *dramatis personae* before us, it would be impossible to give too much praise. He always makes us acquainted with the people by what in life is the only effectual means, by letting us see them face to face, so to speak, and not by merely telling us about them. In a word, his method is picturesque, not analytical. We see the pictures and analyze them by ourselves. And what more need be asked of a novelist than that he draw men and women as they are, with their faults and virtues ever merging into one another, and that he put these people into such relations as arouse our sympathy for some of the most serious matters of human experience? To do this is the constant aim of all creative writers, who are ever aspiring to represent the infinite emotions of life. Those who touch genuine springs of feeling are few, but among the few of the present day Ivan Turgénieff is prominent.

EXPLANATORY NOTES

These notes supply biographical details, where available, and other information relating, principally, to works cited and discussed, literary and mythological allusions, major historical events, and translations of foreign phrases and quotations. In general, a note is supplied only at the first occurrence of an item. Thereafter, the first reference in each Index entry will indicate the page on which the number of any explanatory note may be found.

1   Charles Scribner (1870-1881), publisher. A "burin" is a kind of chisel used for engraving; hence any style of engraving. Charles Burt (1822-1892), engraver

2   Honoré de Balzac (1799-1850), French novelist; Christopher North (pseudonym of John Wilson), *The Noctes Ambrosianae,* 4 vols. (1843).

3   Long Tom Coffin, *The Pilot: A Tale of the Sea* (1823).

4   Horace (Émile-Jean) Vernet (1789-1863), French painter of sporting subjects and battles; Claude Lorrain (1600-1682), often just "Claude" in English, byname of Claude Gellée, French artist renowned for his landscape painting.

5   William Cooper (1754-1809).

6   John A. Collier (1787-1873), statesman; John Paine Cushman (1784-1848) and Joel Barlow Sutherland (1792-1861), politicians and judges; Clark Bissell (1782-1857), lawyer and statesman; James Gadsden (1788-1858), railroad promoter and diplomat who negotiated the "Gadsden Purchase," the acquisition of land by the United States from Mexico, when he was US minister to Mexico in 1853.

7   John C. Calhoun (1782-1850), congressman, secretary of war, and vice president (in 1824); William Jay (1789-1858), jurist and reformer.

8   James Abraham Hillhouse (1789-1841), author of romantic verse and dramas.

9   Catharine M. Sedgwick, *A New-England Tale; or, Sketches of New England Character and Manners* (1822).

10   Walter Scott, *The Pirate* (1822).

11   *Lionel Lincoln; or, The Leaguer of Boston* (1825).

12   *The Prairie: A Tale* (1827).

13   *The Wept of Wish-ton-Wish. A Tale* (1829).

14   Fitz-Greene Halleck, "Red Jacket. A Chief of the Indian Tribes, The Tuscaroras. On Looking at his Potrait by Weir" (1828). The lines, which are misquoted here, are: "Cooper, whose name is with his country's woven/ First in her files, her Pioneer of mind—/ A wanderer now in other climes, has proven/ His love for the young land he left behind."

15   Marie Joseph Paul Yves Roch Gilbert Motier, Marquis de Lafayette (1757-1834), French reformer who had a division under Washington in the American War of Independence. In France, he went on to sit in the Assembly of Notables (1787), the States-General and National Assembly (1789) and, after Jacobin hatred drove him to Austria and imprisonment, the Chamber of Deputies (1821-24). La Fayette revisted American in 1824 at the invitation of congress: he was voted $200,000 and a township.

16   *The Heidenmauer* (1833).

17   The correct title of the novel is *The Headsman: or, The Abbaye des Vignerons* (1833).
18   *England, by an American* (1836).
19   The Battle of Erie took place on September 10, 1813; nine small ships under the command of Commodore Perry defeated a British squadron of six vessels. Perry took over the command of Jesse D. Elliott's (1782-1845) *Lawrence* after his own ship, the *Niagara*, had become crippled. Hitherto, the *Lawrence* had been more or less inactive for over two hours. After the battle Perry praised Jesse's bravery, but he withdrew that praise in 1818 and instituted court-martial charges, but Perry died before the charges could be examined and prosecuted. Cooper's account (in his *History of the Navy*) included Perry's praise of Elliott but failed to note the later court-martial proceedings. William Duer (*New York Commercial Advertiser*), Tristam Burges (*The Battle of Lake Erie*), and Alexander Mackenzie (*North American Review*) condemned Cooper's version of events in 1839. Cooper successfully sued all three and issued his riposte, *The Battle of Lake Erie; or, Answer to Messrs. Duer, Burges, and Mackenzie* in 1843.
20   *Lives of Distinguished American Naval Officers* (1846). William James, who failed in his attempts to succeed as a veterinary surgeon after arriving in America shortly before the 1812 war with Britain, wrote a splenetic account of the various naval battles of that war: *An Inquiry into the Merits of the Principal Naval Actions, between Great Britain and the United States: Comprising an Account of all British and American Ships of War, Reciprocally Captured and Destroyed, Since the 18th of June 1812* (1816). See "Edinburgh Review on James's Naval Occurrences, and Cooper's Naval History," *United States Democratic Review* , 10 (1842), 411-432, 515-541.
21   *Homeward Bound; or, The Chase* (1838).
22   *The Deerslayer, or, The First Warpath* (1841).
23   *The Two Admirals: A Tale* (1842). See William Gilmore Simms, "Cooper, His Genius and Writing" (1: No. 35).
24   *The Wing-and-Wing, or, Le Feu-Follet* (1842).
25   *Wyandotté; or, The Hutted Knoll* (1843).
26   *Autobiography of a Pocket-Handkerchief* originally appeared as a long short story in *Graham's Magazine* (1843): "Le Mouchoir; or, An Autobiographical Romance."
27   *Ned Myers: A Life Before the Mast* (1843).
28   *Miles Wallingford: A Sea Tale* (1843) is a continuation of, rather than a sequel, to *Afloat and Ashore* [not *Ashore and Afloat*]: *A Sea Tale* (1843).
29   Since the seventeenth century, much of rural New York had been concentrated in the ownership of large estates, tenants being given lifetime leases. Cooper was shocked by the major concessions secured by anti-rent protests, these signalling the end of America's manorial gentry.
30   *The Chainbearer; or, The Littlepage Manuscripts* (1845); *The Redskins; or, Indian and Injun: Being the Conclusion of the Littlepage Manuscripts* (1846).
31   *The Oak Openings; or, The Bee-Hunter* (1848).
32   *The Ways of the Hour: A Tale* (1850).
33   Burton's Theater was opened by the English comic actor William Evans Burton (1804-1860) who came to New York in 1834.
34   George Palmer Putnam (1814-1872), publisher and founder of *Putnam's Magazine* (1853-1857, 1868-1871, and 1906-1910).
35   Byron, "Lines on Hearing that Lady Byron was Ill" (1816).
36   Tacitus: in full, Publius (or Gaius) Cornelius Tacitus (c.55-120), Roman historian.
37   John Canfield Spencer (1788-1855).
38   Alexander Slidell Mackenzie (1803-1848), *The Life of Commander Oliver Hazard Perry* (1821).
39   Alexander Slidell Mackenzie was the commander of the *U.S. Brig Somers* in 1842. He ordered the execution of three officers suspected of planning a mutiny, one of them

being Philip Spencer, the son of John Spencer (1788-1855), secretary of war under President John Tyler (1790-1862; president, 1841-1845). Amidst great controversy, he was acquitted of wrong-doing at a Court Martial in 1843.

40   William Leete Stone (1792-1844), editor of the *Commercial Advertiser*. He was successfully sued by Cooper for libellous criticisms of *History of the Navy* and *Home as Found*.

41   Francis Wayland (1796-1865), clergyman and fourth president of Brown University (1827-1855).

42   Eugène (Marie Joseph) Sue (1804-1857), prolific French novelist; Frederick Marryat (1792-1848), English naval officer and novelist.

43   Joseph Addison and Richard Steele (1672-1729), founded, respectively, the *Spectator* and the *Tatler* [not Tattler].

44   A "raconteur" is a teller of stories and anecdotes.

45   Shakespeare, *Hamlet*, Act 1, Scene 4.

46   Shakespeare, *Hamlet*, Act 3, Scene 2.

47   The Six Nations, or Iroquois Indians, which united c.1570 in the north-eastern region of North America, consisted of five nations, Seneca, Cayuga, Onondaga, Oneida, and Mohawk until the Tuscarora Indians joined the confederacy in 1715. The Cherokee Indians originally occupied the mountains of Georgia, Alabama, Tennessee, and Carolina, the Choctaw Indians, the area of the southern Mississippi, and the Catawbas, the south-eastern region.

48   Deviltry.

49   Gnome, a sprite guarding the inner part of the earth and its treasures; kobold, a spirit of the mines; ondine (or undine), a spirit, according to Paracelsus (a name coined by Theophrastus Bombastus von Hohenheim, 1493-1541, German alchemist and physician), that can obtain a human soul by bearing a child to a human husband; sylph, a spirit of the air; fairy, an imaginary being of human form, usually diminutive, light and graceful, capable of kind or unkindly acts.

50   Milton, "Apology for Smectmnuus" (1642).

51   General effect.

52   James Gates Percival (1795-1856), "Poetry" (1843): "In measured file, and metrical array."

53   A Spenserian stanza (which Edmund Spenser devised for *The Faerie Queene*), consists of eight lines of iambic pentameter followed by a single alexandrine, a twelve-syllable iambic line.

54   Job in the Bible.

55   In the Bible, King David fornicated with Bathsheba and disposed of her husband, Uriah, by placing him in the front battle line (2 Samuel 11).

56   *The House of the Seven Gables* (1851).

57   Hawthorne's grandfather, Captain Daniel Hathorne (1731-1796), a privateer, fought and vanquished a British scow off the coast of Portugal while in command of the "Fair American." The incident gave rise to the ballad "Bold Hathorne" (1777).

58   *Fanshawe: A Tale* appeared anonymously at Hawthorne's own expense in 1828.

59   Samuel Griswold Goodrich (1793-1860), Boston publisher and founder of the annual gift book *The Token* (1827-1842).

60   Horatio Bridge (1806-1893), *The Journal of an African Cruiser* (1845), edited by Nathaniel Hawthorne; *The House of the Seven Gables* was published in 1851.

61   George Bancroft (1800-1891), statesman and historian, author of the ten-volume *History of the United States* (1834-1876).

62   Brook Farm was a cooperative community (1841-1847) established nine miles from Boston, at West Roxbury to apply the theories of the Transcendentalist Club. Hawthorne's *Blithedale Romance* (1852) arose out of his experiences there. (François Marie) Charles Fourier (1772-1837), French social theorist. Henri de Saint-Simon (1760-

1825), French social theorist and one of the founders of Christian Socialism. Robert Owen (1771-1858), Welsh socialist and reformer who sponsored numerous experimental communities.

63 Emerson, *Nature* (1836).
64 Zachary Taylor (1784-1850), 11th president of the United States (1845-1849); *The Scarlet Letter* (1850).
65 *True Stories from History and Biography* (1851); the enlarged edition of *Twice-Told Tales* (1837) appeared in 1842.
66 Omitted in the original.
67 Omitted in the original.
68 "Writings of Aubépine: Rappaccini's Daughter," *United States Democratic Review*, 15 (1844).
69 *Mosses from an Old Manse* (1846); "The Custom-House" is the introductory section of *The Scarlet Letter* (1850).
70 The tales here discussed, and throughout, were collected in *Twice-Told Tales* (1837; enlarged, 1842), and *Mosses from an Old Manse* (1846).
71 In Ovid's *Metamorphoses* the sculptor Pygmalion falls in love with his statue of an ideal woman and successfully applies to the goddess Venus for it to be brought to life.
72 Edmund Kean (c.1789-1833), English actor.
73 John Webster (c.1580-c.1625), English dramatist.
74 Jean François Marmontel (1723-1799), French author; Ernst Theodor Wilhelm Hoffmann (1776-1822), German writer; Hans Christian Andersen (1805-1775), Danish writer renowned for his fairy tales.
75 Ariel and Caliban are characters in Shakespeare's *The Tempest*.
76 Elizabeth Barrett Browning (1806-1861), "A Vision of Poets" (1844).
77 Shakespeare, *A Midsummer Night's Dream*, Act 5, Scene 1.
78 Elizabeth Barrett Browning, "The Cry of the Human" (1844).
79 Wordsworth, "Ode on Intimations of Immortality from Recollections of Early Childhood" (1807).
80 Philarete Chasles (1798-1873).
81 A number of periodicals entitled "Cultivator" existed at the time, including the Boston *American Cultivator*, which started in 1840.
82 François de Salignac de la Mothe Fénelon (1651-1715), French prelate and writer; Thomas Hobbes (1588-1679), English political philosopher; Joseph Priestley (1733-1804), English Presbyterian minister and chemist; René Descartes (1596-1650), French philosopher and mathematician.
83 Matthew Gregory Lewis (1775-1818), English novelist and author of *Ambrosio; or, The Monk* (1796); hence "Monk Lewis."
84 Tone; manner; style; fashion; breeding.
85 John James Audubon (1785-1851), a naturalist, writer, and painter born in Haiti and educated in France. He lived on his father's estate near Philadelphia in 1804. Among his books is *The Birds of America* (1827-1838).
86 Jean (or Jane) Elliott (1727-1805), Scottish lyricist; Thomas Cooper (1805-1892), English poet and novelist.
87 Herman Melville (1819-1891); Anthony Trollope (1815-1882), English novelist.
88 Walter Hooker Colton (1818-1840), poet and founding editor of the *American Whig Review* in January, 1845; John Howard Payne (1792-1852), dramatist; John Pierepont (1785-1866), poet; Alfred Billings Street (1811-1881), lawyer, librarian, and poet.
89 John McDermott Moore, *The Adventures of Tom Stapleton; or, Broadway 202* (1850); Cornelius Matthews, *The Career of Puffer Hopkins* (1842).
90 John Lloyd Stephens (1805-1852), traveller and author; Benjamin Silliman (1779-1864), natural historian.

91 Benedict Arnold and John André.
92 The Lowell Institute in Boston, founded by John Lowell (1799-1836), offered free lectures (then printed) by scholars on a vast range of subjects.
93 *Typee: A Peep at Polynesian Life* (March, 1846) was first published in London, England as *Narrative of a Four Months Residence Among the Natives of a Valley of the Marquesas Islands* (February, 1846).
94 *Omoo: A Narrative of Adventures in the South Seas* (1847); *Mardi: And A Voyage Thither* (1849); *White-Jacket; or, The World in a Man-of-War* (1850); *Redburn, his First Voyage. Being the Sailor-boy Confessions and Reminiscences of the Son of a Gentleman in the Merchant Service* (1849).
95 Cooper, *The Pilot: A Tale of the Sea* (1823).
96 "Doctor Dulcamara" is a character in Gaetono Donizetti's (1797-1848) opera *L'Elsir d'amore* (1832) [*The Elixir of Love*].
97 "Agnus Dei": part of the Catholic mass beginning with these words [the "lamb of God"].
98 "Fantoccini" (from the Italian "fantoccio," for "puppet"): a puppet show. "Aegis": a breastplate, emblematic of majesty, associated with Zeus and Athena.
99 William Lane's (d.1814), "Minerva Press," established in 1763, specialized in the bulk production of novels and, by the end of the eighteenth century, in gothic fiction.
100 *Tutoyer*: to "thee and thou" each other; to be on familiar terms.
101 Romulus and Remus: the legendary founders of Rome. They were suckled and fed by a she-wolf until found by a herdsman, Faustulus.
102 Harlequin: an Italian commedia dell'arte character popular from the 16th century. He wore a multi-coloured costume and a black half mask with tiny eyeholes and arched eyebrows.
103 *Mésalliance*: a bad match.
104 Shelley, *The Cenci: A Tragedy in Five Acts* (1819).
105 Longfellow, *Hyperion: A Romance* (1839).
106 Woollens are scoured and beaten in "fulling mills"; Francis Bacon's commitment to scientific method and logic are seen in these terms here.
107 The Rosetta Stone was discovered by a Frenchman, Bouchard (or Boussard), in August 1799. Its inscription, deciphered largely by Thomas Young (1773-1829) and Jean-François Champollion (1790-1832), provided a key to Egyptian hieroglyphic writings.
108 Jacques Callot (c.1592-1635), a French etcher and engraver celebrated especially for the lugubrious realism of his "Caprices of Various Figures," "Hunchbacks," and "Miseries of War."
109 John Burgoyne (1722-1792), English general (and dramatist) who was sent to Boston after the Battle of Lexington (1775).
110 Andrew Jackson (1767-1845), 7th president of the United States (1829-1837); John Coffee (1772-1833); the Indian attack on Fort Mimms took place on August 30, 1813.
111 In one of a sequence of conflicts over "states rights," the State of South Carolina voted to nullify (November 24, 1832) acts of the United States Congress that imposed duties on foreign imports.
112 *Atalantis: A Story of the Sea* (1832).
113 1812-1815.
114 Early poetry by Simms: *Monody on General Charles Cotesworth of Pinckney* (1825); *Lyrical and other Poems* (1827); *The Vision of Cortes, Cain, and other Poems* (1827); *The Tricolor; or, Three Days of Blood in Paris* (1830).
115 *Castle Dismal; or, The Bachelor's Christmas. A Domestic Legend* (1844); *Confession; or, The Blind Heart* (1841) [not *Confessions*]; *Carl Werner, an Imaginative Story. With Other Tales of the Imagination* (1838).
116 *Helen Halsey: or, The Swamp State of Conelachita. A Tale of the Borders* (1845); republished

in 1869 as *The Island Bride.*

117   *The Damsel of Darien* (1839); *Pelayo: A Story of the Goth* (1838); *Count Julian; or, The Last Days of the Goth* (1845).

118   *The Kinsmen; or, The Black Riders of Congaree: A Tale* (1841); republished in 1854 as *The Scout; or, The Black Riders of Congaree.*

119   *The Life of Francis Marion* (1844); *The Life of John Smith: The Founder of Virginia* (1846); *The History of Carolina, from its First European Discovery to its Erection into a Republic: with a Supplementary Chronicle of Events to the Present Time* (1842); *The Life of Chevalier Bayard* (1847); *The Life of Nathanael Greene: Major-General in the Army of the Revolution* (1849).

120   *Southern Passages and Pictures* (1839); *Donna Florida: A Tale* (1843); *Grouped Thoughts and Scattered Fancies* (1845); *Areytos; or, Songs of the South* (1846); *Lays of the Palmetto: A Tribute to the South Carolina Regiment, in the War with Mexico* (1848); *The Cassique of Accabee: A Tale of Ashley River: With Other Pieces* (1849); *Norman Maurice; or, The Man of the People: An American Drama in Five Acts* (1851); "The City of the Silent" (1850), in *Poems Descriptive, Dramatic, Legendary and Contemplative* (1853).

121   "The True Sources of American Independence" (1844); "Self-Development" (1847).

122   Frances Trollope (1780-1863), infamous for her *Domestic Life of the Americans* (1832).

123   *Views and Reviews in American History, Literature and Fiction* (1845).

124   Albany William Fonblanque (1793-1872), English journalist and editor of the *Examiner.*

125   This catalogue is omitted

126   Juvenal, or Decimus Junius Juvenalis (55-60?-127?), *Satire* (4): "Here's Crispinus again."

127   Stowe.

128   Neoteric: modern; recent.

129   John Dryden, *Absalom and Achitophel: A Poem* (1681).

130   The Sibyl of Greek legend was a prophetess often depicted as a frenzied old woman. During the Roman festival of Saturnalia, slaves were given temporary freedom.

131   "But the goat, on which the lot fell to be the scapegoat, shall be presented alive before the Lord, to make an atonement with him, to let him go for a scapegoat into the wilderness" (Leviticus 16: 10).

132   Stowe, *Uncle Tom's Cabin; or, Life Among the Lowly* (1852).

133   Frances (or Fanny) Wright (1796-1852), Scottish-born American reformer and abolitionist. Elizabeth Stanton, née Cady (1815-1902) and Lucretia Mott, née Coffin (1793-1880) had recently (1848) organized the first women's rights convention at Seneca Falls.

134   "That we be no more children, tossed to and fro, and carried about with every wind of doctrine, by the sleight of men, [and] cunning craftiness, whereby they lie in wait to deceive" (Ephesians 4: 13).

135   A "Catalogue of Testimonies" ("concerning the person and Divine Majesty of the Human Nature of Our Lord Jesus Christ") was appended in 1580 to the *The Augsberg Confession,* which had been originally drafted for Charles V (1500-1558), Holy Roman Emperor, by Philip Melanchthon [Greek for original surname, "Schwarzerd"] (1497-1560), a German Protestant reformer and friend of Martin Luther (1483-1546).

136   On January 21, 1853, the "Stafford House Assembly of Ladies," under the Presidency of the Duchess of Sutherland, sent an address on slavery to their sisters in the United States of America. Karl Marx, writing in *The People's Paper,* No. 45, March 12, 1853, identified the irony: "the history of the wealth of the Sutherland family is the history of the ruin and of the expropriation of the Scotch-Gaelic population from its native soil."

137   Notable trials.

138   John Belton O'Neall (1793-1863), South Carolina judge.

139 *Niaserie*: foolishness; nonsense.

140 The "Astor Palace Riot" (at the Astor Palace Opera House) took place in New York on May 10, 1849 as a result of disputes between Edwin Forrest (1806-1872) and the English actor William Charles Macready (1793-1873), both of whom were appearing in New York; Forrest saw it as a battle between democracy and support for English cultural imperialism. Twenty-two people were killed, and at least thirty-six wounded.

141 George Lippard (1822-1854), sensational novelist, was obsessed with the immorality of city life. His *The Monks of Monk Hall* (1844), reprinted as *The Quaker City; or, The Monks of Monk Hall* (1844) was written as an exposé of Philadelphia and its vice. Lippard founded the "Brotherhood of the Union" (here, the "Lippardists") in 1850 to tackle the problems of urban evil and crime.

142 In the Bible, Ananias and Saphira sold their possessions to help the poor and needy; but they conspired to retain some of the proceeds. Ananias died immediately after lying about the issue (Acts 5: 5), to be followed by his wife a few verses later (Acts 5: 10).

143 "Not every one that saith unto me, Lord, Lord, shall enter into the kingdom of heaven; but he that doeth the will of my Father which is in heaven" (Matthew 7: 21).

144 James 1: 26-27.

145 James 3: 13-17.

146 Samuel Henry Dickson (1798-1822) was a physician active in securing a medical college in Charleston, where he continued to work and teach for much of his life. In 1845, he wrote *Remarks on Certain Topics Connected with the General Subject of Slavery* in which he argued for the essential inferiority of the Negro race.

147 James Hogg (1770-1835), Scottish poet and novelist, known as the "Ettrick Shepherd."

148 Pope, "An Essay on Criticism" (1709).

149 Milton, *Comus: A Masque* (1634); the first line should read "Of some gay creatures of the element."

150 An aberrant "and" has been removed here. Simms wrote: "When I say that our Romance is the substitute of modern times for the epic of drama, I do not mean to say that they are exactly the same things, and yet, examined thoroughly, *and* the differences between them are very slight."

151 George Croly (1780-1860), *Salathiel: A Story of the Past, the Present, and the Future* (1828).

152 Fourier, *Théorie de l'unité universelle* (1822).

153 "Epos" is a name given to early epic poetry in the oral tradition; the Sumerian epic *Gilgamesh* (c.3000 B. C.) is the earliest known work of this kind.

154 In Greek mythology, Achilles was the greatest warrior of the army of Agamemnon in the Trojan War. But when Thetis immersed Achilles in the River Styx as a child to secure his invulnerability, she overlooked the part of the heel by which he was being held.

155 Emerson, "Goethe; or, The Writer," in *Representative Men* (1850).

156 Shakespeare, *A Midsummer Night's Dream*, Act 5, Scene 1.

157 The Sabeans (Saba lies in the Southern Arabian Jôf about 200 miles north-west of Aden) are mentioned in the Bible as a distant people who traded, among other things, in perfumes (Jeremiah 6: 20) and incense (Isaiah 9: 6). The Queen of Saba (Sheba) visited Solomon (1 Kings 10). The *Thousand and One Nights* (also known as *The Arabian Nights' Entertainment*), is of uncertain authorship and date; the first reference to it comes in the ninth century.

158 In passing.

159 Troubadours: lyric poets of southern France, northern Spain, and northern Italy who were preoccupied with elaborate love lyrics, but also wrote satirical and political poems; these lyrics were frequently set to (monophonic, unharmonized) music; Minne-

singers: German poet-musicians of the twelfth and thirteenth centuries.

160   Additional.

161   Sensational novels and trashy magazines often had yellow covers.

162   Calmness.

163   "Exemplastic" should be "esemplastic." Coleridge uses it for the shaping and unifying power of the imagination. Chapter 13 of Book 1 of the *Biographia Literaria; or, Biographical Sketches of My Literary Life and Opinions* (1817) is entitled "On the Imagination or Esemplastic Power."

164   Poe, "The Raven" (1845).

165   Poetry. The word derives from the Greek *poētēs*: "doer," "creator."

166   Belief.

167   Milton, *Paradise Lost: A Poem Written in Ten Books* (1667), Book 2.

168   Shakespeare, *The Tempest* Act 4, Scene 1: "We are such stuff/ as dreams are made on [not "of"], and our little life/ Is rounded with a sleep."

169   Falstaff is a character in Shakespeare's *Henry IV*, Parts I and II, *Henry V*, and *The Merry Wives of Windsor.*

170   Shakespeare, *Hamlet,* Act 1, Scene 5: "There are more things in heaven and earth, Horatio,/ Than are dreamt of in your philosophy."

171   Milton, *Samson Agonistes* (1671).

172   Byron, *Manfred: A Dramatic Poem* (1817).

173   Travel companion.

174   J. K. Ingram, *Pirate's Revenge: or, A Tale of Don Pedro and Miss Lois Maynard* (1845); Calvin Henderson Wiley (1819-1887), *Alamance; or, The Great and Fatal Experiment* (1847); William Makepeace Thackeray (1811-1863), *Vanity Fair: A Novel without a Hero* (1847-1848); Goethe, *Wilhelm Meisters Lehrjahre* [*Wilhelm Meister's Apprenticeship*] (1796), continued as *Wilhelm Meisters Wanderjahre* [*Wilhelm Meister's Travels*] (1821-1829).

175   Johann Ludwig Tieck (1773-1853), German poet and critic.

176   *Gesta Romanorum* (c. 14th century): a collection of anecdotes and stories in Latin about the English deeds of the Romans. Goethe, *Reineke Fuchs* (1794); Reynard the Fox is the hero of several European cycles of animal tales in verse that originated in an area between Flanders and Germany in the 10th and 11th centuries.

177   Imaginary travels.

178   Poe, "Hans Phaal: A Tale" (1835).

179   *Bizarreries*: caprices; extravagances; fantasies. August Friedrich Ferdinand von Kotzebue (1761-1819), German dramatist.

180   Charles James Lever (1806-1872), *Charles O'Malley* (1841); *The Confessions of Harry Lorrequer* (1837); Henry Cockton (1807-1853), *The Life and Adventures of Valentine Vox, the Ventriloquist* (1840), and *Stanley Thorn: A Story of Woman's Constant Love* (1841).

181   Thomas More (1478-1535), *Utopia* (1516 in Latin; translated into English in 1556). [Full title: *The Common-Wealth Of Vtopia : Containing a Learned and Pleasant Discourse of the Best State of a Publike-Weale, as it is Found in the Government of the New Ile Called Vtopia.*]

182   Grace Aguilar (1816-1847), novelist and poet; Elizabeth Oakes Smith (1806-1893), magazine contributor, poet, and novelist; Donald Grant Mitchell ["Ike, or Ik, Marvel" being a pseudonym] (1822-1908), *Reveries of a Bachelor; or, A Book of the Heart* (1850), and *Dream Life: A Fable of the Seasons* (1851); Jacques Henri Bernardin de Saint-Pierre (1737-1814), French author.

183   Susan Edmonstone Ferrier (1782-1854), Scottish novelist; Anna-Maria Hall (1800-1881), Irish novelist.

184   Theodore Edward Hook (1788-1841), English man of letters who founded the Tory journal *John Bull*; Allesandro Manzoni, Italian novelist and poet; (1785-1873), Fredrika Bremer (1801-1865), a Swedish novelist who travelled extensively in the United States; Thoma Hope (1770-1831), *Anastasius; or, Memoirs of a Modern Greek* (1819); Alexander

William Kinglake (1809-1891), *Eōthen; or, Traces of Travel Brought Home from the East* (1844).

185 August Wilhelm von Schlegel (1767-1845) and Karl Wilhelm Friedrich von Schlegel (1772-1829).

186 Poe, "Fancy and Imagination: Drake's *Culprit Fay* and Moore's *Alciphon*" (1849).

187 Friedrich Heinrich Karl Fouqué, Baron de la Motte, *Undine* (1811); Coleridge, "Christabel" (1797); Shelley, "Alastor; or, The Spirit of Solitude" (1816).

188 Niccolo Paganini (1782-1840), Italian violin virtuoso and composer.

189 Poe, "The Gold Bug" (1843), "Ligeia" (1838), and "The Fall of the House of Usher" (1839).

190 William Hamilton (1788-1856), Scottish philosopher; Immanuel Kant (1724-1804) and Johann Gottlieb Fichte (1762-1814), German philosophers; Friedrich Wilhelm Joseph von Schelling (1775-1854), German philosopher; "Novalis," the pseudonym of Friedrich von Hardenberg (1772-1801), German Romantic poet and novelist.

191 Charles Kingsley (1819-1875), English author.

192 *Alton Locke, Tailor and Poet. An Autobiography*, and *Yeast: A Problem* (1851).

193 *The Life and Adventures of Nicholas Nickleby* (1838-1839), *The Personal History of David Copperfield* (1849-1850), and *Hard Times: For these Times* (1854).

194 *History of Pendennis* (1848) and *The Newcomes, Memoirs of a Most Respectable Family* (1853-1855). A *"camera obscura"* is a dark room in which an image of objects from outside is projected onto a screen.

195 A *"piquant sauce"* is stinging and pungent, but pleasant and appetizing.

196 A sugared pill (the useful smuggled in as the sweet).

197 "Caudle": thin gruel mixed with alcohol. *Magnum et venerabile nomen*: large and venerable the name. In Greek mythology, Pluto is the god of the underworld.

198 In Greek mythology, everything Midas (a king of Phrygia) touched turned to gold.

199 Dogberry is a character in Shakespeare's *Much Ado About Nothing*. *"Pons Asinorum"*: "asses bridge."

200 "Feuilleton": the lower section of French journal pages, devoted to literary criticism, reviews, and the like; Charles Louis Napoleon Bonaparte, Napoleon III: emperor of France, 1832-1836; Bourbons: French royal house that ruled for generations.

201 In 1817, James Harper (1795-1869) and John Harper established a small printing firm in New York; their brothers, Joseph and Fletcher Harper joined them in 1825 to form Harper & Brothers, the largest book publishers in the United States. The publishing house J. S. Redfield numbered Poe among its writers.

202 Polonius, on Hamlet: "That he is mad, 'tis true; 'tis true, 'tis pity,/And pity 'tis 'tis true" (Shakespeare, *Hamlet*, Act 2, Scene 2).

203 Professor John White Webster (1793-1850) was convicted and executed for the murder of a colleague at Harvard Medical College, Dr. George Parkman (1790-1849), who had lent money to him; the trial, and a conviction based mostly on circumstantial evidence, was highly controversial.

204 Mary Martha Sherwood, née Butt (1775-1851), English writer of children's fiction.

205 Milton, *Paradise Lost: A Poem Written in Ten Books* (1667), Book 1.

206 Longfellow, "A Psalm of Life" (1839); "Excelsior" (1841); "The Song of Hiawatha" (1855).

207 "And it came about when they were in the field, that Cain rose up against Abel his brother and killed him"(Genesis 4: 8).

208 Bryant, "The African Chief" (1825).

209 "I am a man; I think that nothing human is alien to me": Cicero, *De Officis*, I, 30.

210 Mrs Jellyby [not Jellaby] is a character in Dickens' *Bleak House* (1853).

211 Jacobins: byname of the Jacobin Club and identified with the extreme egalitarianism and violence that dominated the French Revolutionary Government from mid-1793

until mid-1794.

212   Gray, "An Elegy Written in a Country Church Yard" (1751): "Far from the madding
      crowd's ignoble strife/ Their sober wishes never learn'd to stray;/ Along the cool
      sequester'd vale of life/ They kept the noiseless tenor of their way."

213   Milton's defence of the press is in *Areopagitica: A Speech for the Liberty of Unlicensed Print-
      ing* (1644).

214   The Kansas-Nebraska Act (1854) repealed the Missouri Compromise (1820), and the
      question of whether the territory of Kansas should be a slave state was now left to
      what Stephen A. Douglas (1813-1861), chairman of the Senate Committee on Territo-
      ries, called "popular sovereignty." The Emigrant Aid Company was formed in 1854 to
      support antislavery immigration; bitter fighting broke out all over the territory as many
      northern cities sent arms to "bleeding Kansas."

215   The *Southern Literary Messenger* ran from 1839-1864, and 1939-1944.

216   George William Curtis (1824-1892), an editor of *Putnam's Monthly* since its inception in
      1853; he lectured extensively.

217   Sir Roger de Coverley, who represents the country gentry, is a member of the fictional
      "Spectator Club" used by Richard Steele and Joseph Addison in *The Spectator* (1711-
      1712; 1714) to project their views about society.

218   Hamlet, Mercutio, and Imogen are characters, respectively, in Shakespeare's *Hamlet,
      Prince of Denmark, Romeo and Juliet,* and *Cymbeline.*

219   Pickwick, Sam Weller, and the Fat Boy are characters in *The Posthumous Papers of the
      Pickwick Club* (1836-1837); Pecksniff and the Infant Phenomenon figure, respectively,
      in *The Life and Adventures of Martin Chuzzlewit* (1843-1844) and *The Life and Adventures of
      Nicholas Nickleby* (1839).

220   Cuddie Headrigg and Ephraim Macbriar are in *The Tale of Old Mortality* (1816); Jona-
      than Oldbuck and Edie Ochiltree, *The Antiquary* (1816); Dominie Sampson, Pleydell,
      Dandie Dinmont, Dirk Hatteraick, *Guy Mannering* (1815); Bailie Nicol Jarvie, *Rob Roy*
      (1818); Richard Moniplies, *The Fortunes of Nigel* (1822); Brian de Bois Guilbert, Isaac
      the Jew, the Clerk of Copmanhurst, Wamba, *Ivanhoe* (1819).

221   In *The Letters of Malachi Malgrowther* (1826), Scott joined the protest against the proposal
      that Scottish banks be barred from issuing notes below £5.

222   Francis Jeffrey, Lord Jeffrey (1773-1850), Scottish jurist and critic; one of the founders
      of the *Edinburgh Review* (1802-1929), which he edited until 1829.

223   John Marshall (1755-1835), American jurist, born in Virginia; chief-justice of the USA
      from 1801-1835.

224   *Claqueurs*: hired, or sycophantic (applauding) supporters.

225   John Howard (1726-1790), English penal reformer.

226   *Ivanhoe: A Romance* (1819); *The Talisman* (1825).

227   *Waverley* (1814); *Kenilworth* (1820); *The Abbot* (1820); *The Monastery* (1820); *Peveril of the
      Peak* (1823); *Woodstock* (1826); *The Legend of Montrose* (1819); *The Tale of Old Mortality*
      (1816); *The Fortunes of Nigel* (1822).

228   Macaulay, "On History," *Edinburgh Review* (1828).

229   Jeanie Deans and Mrs Saddletree are in *The Heart of Midlothian* (1818); Die Vernon, *Rob
      Roy* (1815); Edith Bellenden and Jenny Dennison, *The Tale of Old Mortality* (1816); Lady
      Peveril, *Peveril of the Peak* (1823); Rebecca, *Ivanhoe* (1820); Green Mantle, *Redgauntlet*
      (1824); Margaret Ramsay, *The Fortunes of Nigel* (1822); Mrs Mary Dodds, *St. Ronan's
      Well* (1824); Bessie Maclure, *Old Mortality* (1816).

230   John Gibson Lockhart, *The Life of Sir Walter Scott* (1837-1838).

231   Omitted here is an anonymous poem eulogizing Scott by one of his contemporaries.

232   James Philemon Holcombe (1820-1873), *An Address Delivered before the Society of Alumni,
      of the University of Virginia, at the Annual Meeting, June 29, 1853.*

233   Homer, *The Iliad*: XXVIIb.

234   Thomas Roderick Dew (1802-1846), *An Essay on Slavery* (1849). William Gilmore
       Simms gathered together more of Dew (and others) in: *The Pro-slavery Argument; as
       Maintained by the Most Distinguished Writers on the Southern States, Containing the Several
       Essays, on the Subject, of Chancellor Harper, Governor Hammond, Dr. Simms, and Professor Dew*
       (1852).
235   Albert Taylor Bledsoe (1809-1877), *Liberty and Slavery* (1856); George Fitzhugh (1806-
       1881), *Slavery Justified; by a Southerner* (1850).
236   William Smith (1756-1835), *A Letter to William Wilberforce, Esq., M.P., on the Proposed
       Abolition of the Slave Trade, at Present under the Consideration of Parliament* (1807).
237   Joshua 9: 23: "Now therefore ye are cursed, and there shall none of you be freed from
       being bondmen, and hewers of wood and drawers of water for the house of my God."
238   *Ex parte*: one-sided; partisan.
239   The "Fugitive Slave Act" (1850) allowed runaway slaves to be pursued and captured
       anywhere in the United States.
240   George Fitzhugh, *Sociology for the South; or, The Failure of Free Society* (1854).
241   1619.
242   Publius Cornelius Scipio Aemilianus Africanus Numantinus (237-129 B.C.), Roman
       statesman and general.
243   Wordsworth, *The Excursion* (1814): "Brooding above the fierce confederate storm/ Of
       sorrow, barricaded evermore/ Within the walls of cities."
244   Akenside, *The Pleasure of the Imagination: A Poem in Three Books* (1844): "Till desolation
       o'er the grass-grown street/ Expands his raven-wings, and up the wall,/ Where sen-
       ates once the price of monarchs doom'd,/ Hisses the gliding snake through hoary
       weeds/ That clasp the mouldering column" (Book 2).
245   Jesuits: members of the Society of Jesus, a religious order of men founded by St. Igna-
       tius of Loyola, or Iñigo López de Recalde (1491-1566), a Spanish soldier; Blaise Pascal
       (1623-62), French mathematician, physicist, and theologian.
246   Milton, "At Solemn Music" (1645): "Where the bright Seraphim in burning row/Their
       loud uplifted angel-trumpets blow;/And the Cherubic host in thousand quires."
247   (Johann Chrysotom) Wolfgang Amadeus Mozart (1756-1791); Ludwig van Beethoven
       (1770-1827).
248   Goethe, *Elective Affinities: A Novel [Die Wahlverwandtschaften]* (1810).
249   Bacon, *Advancement of Learning* (1605), Book 2.
250   The "debtor's prison," Barnacle family, and "Circumlocution Office" are in *Little
       Dorritt* (1855-1857).
251   Eugène Sue, *The Mysteries of Paris* (1845).
252   George Sand, *Consuelo* (1843).
253   Charlotte Brontë (1816-1855), *Jane Eyre* (1847).
254   Ottilie is a character in *Elective Affinities: A Novel [Die Wahlverwandtschaften]* (1810).
255   Elizabeth Cleghorn Gaskell, *née* Stevenson (1810-1865), *North and South* (1855).
256   Dinah Maria Mulock Craik (1826-1887), *John Halifax, Gentleman* (1857).
257   Emanuel Swedenborg (1688-1772), Swedish mystic.
258   Sylvester Judd, *Margaret* (1845).
259   Elizabeth Oakes Prince Smith (1806-1893), *Bertha and Lily; or, The Parsonage of Beech
       Glen* (1854). "Moaning women, hard-eyed husbands, and deluges of Lethe": Emerson,
       "Experience" (1844).
260   *Wilhelm Meisters Lehrjahre [Wilhelm Meister's Apprenticeship]* (1796), continued as *Wilhelm
       Meisters Wanderjahre [Wilhelm Meister's Travels]* (1821-1829).
261   Entertainment; diversion.
262   Snodgrass, Tupman, and Winkle are characters in Dickens' *The Posthumous Papers of the
       Pickwick Club* (1836-1837).
263   James Buchanan had been elected president in 1856. The fifth Southern Convention

met in Richmond on January 30, 1856; it adjourned on February 3 and resumed in Savannah in December, 1856.

264 James Kennedy (1820-1890), *Raising the Wind: A Farce* (1803); Dion Boucicault (1820-1890), *Old Heads and Young Hearts: A Comedy in Five Acts* (1847).

265 In Dickens' *The Posthumous Papers of the Pickwick Club* (1836-1837), the *Eatanswill Gazette* is on the side of the Blue party and the *Eatanswill Independent*, the Buff.

266 John Parry (1776-1851), *My Uncle Gabrieli: An Operatic Farce in Three Acts* (1825).

267 The conclusion of the argument does not follow from its premises; a false deduction or inference.

268 Joseph Grimaldi (1779-1837), English pantomime clown.

269 Founded in 1799, the American Tract Society stemmed from the New York Tract Society (1812), the New England Tract Society (1814), and the Religious Tract Society of London (1799).

270 William Homes McGuffrey (1800-1873); George Edward Badger (1795-1866); David Lowry Swain (1801-1868); Stephen Elliott (1806-1866); James Warley Miles (1818-1875); Thomas Curtis (1780-1858); Ashbel Smith (1805-1886); Augustus Baldwin Longstreet (1790-1870); Charles Gayarre (1805-1895); Richard Fuller (1804-1876); Alonzo Church (1829-1859).

271 Thomas Hart Benton (1782-1858), Missouri senator (1820-1850).

272 James Dunwoody Brownson De Bow (1820-1867): founded *De Bow's Review* (1846-1880) after leaving the *Southern Literary Messenger*.

273 Omitted in the original.

274 Calvin Henderson Wiley (1819-1887).

275 Matthew 22: 39: "Thou shalt love thy neighbour as thyself."

276 "Maga": a common abbreviation for *Blackwood's Magazine*, and for magazines in general.

277 B. S. Hedrick (b.1827), *Are North Carolinians Freemen? Read and Judge* (1856).

278 Raphael (1483-1520), or Raffaello Santi (or Sanzio), "The School of Athens" (1510-1511).

279 William J. Grayson (1788-1863).

280 Theodore Canot (1804-1860), *Captain Canot, or, Twenty Years of an African Slaver: Being an Account of his Career and Adventures on the Coast, in the interior, on Shipboard, and in the West Indies; Written out and Edited from the Captain' Journals, Memoranda and Conversations, by Brantz Mayer.*

281 Gerritt Smith (1797-1974), abolitionist. Lewis Tappan (1778-1873) and Arthur Tappan (1786-1865), founded the New York Anti-Slavery Society in 1831, and several abolitionist journals. Niobe, in Greek mythology, boasted of her superior fertility over Titan Leto; her twelve children were killed because of her pride, and she has become the prototype of the bereaved mother. William Lloyd Garrison (1805-1879) founded *The Liberator* (1831-1865), an anti-slavery newspaper. Joseph Giddings (1795-1864) amd John Parker Hale (1806-1873), leaders of the anti-slavery movement in Congress.

282 Thersites, a truthful but scurrilous Greek in Shakespeare's *Troilus and Cressida*.

283 Horace Greeley (1811-1872), abolitionist; founded the *New-York Tribune* (1841), which he edited until his death.

284 William L. Chaplin, an agent of the New York Anti-Slavery Society was arrested in Rockville, Maryland, in 1850 for helping fugitive slaves to escape.

285 William H. Seward (1801-1872), abolitionist senator.

286 Georges Couthon (1755-1794), French revolutionary associated with the "reign of terror."

287 Frances Trollope.

288 *Facts for the People: A Key to Uncle Tom's Cabin, Presenting the Original Facts and Documents upon which the Story is Founded, Together with Ccorroborative Statements, Verifying the Truth of*

the Work (1853).

289 Omitted in the original (1854).

290 John Charles Frémont (1813-1890), the first Republican presidential candidate in 1856 (and defeated by James Buchanan).

291 Theodore Sedgwick (1747-1813).

292 Henry Dwight Sedgwick (1785-1831) and Theodore Sedgwick.

293 Joseph Dwight (1703-1765).

294 *Tales of Glauber-Spa* (1832) was edited by William Cullen Bryant; he, along with Catharine Maria Sedgwick, James Kirke Paulding, William Leggett (1802-1839), Robert Charles Sands (1799-1832), and Gulian Crommelin Verplanck, contributed stories and poems to the collection.

295 *Means and Ends* (1839); *Love Tokens for Children* (1838); *Stories for Young Persons* (1847).

296 Sedgwick contributed a biography of Lucretia Maria Davidson to the *Poetical Remains of the Late Lucretia Maria Davidson, Collected and Arranged by her Mother* (1841); it was reprinted in *Poems by Lucretia Maria Davidson* (1871) and in the *Library of American Biography*, 7 (1871). "The Boy of Mount Rhigi" (1826).

297 *Facts and Fancies for School-Day Readers* (1840); *Beatitudes and Pleasant Sundays* (1828); *Morals of Manners* (1846); "Wilton Harvey" (1845).

298 Calvin E. Stowe (1802-1886).

299 *Sunny Memories of Foreign Parts* (1854).

300 Convers Francis (1795-1823), Unitarian clergyman, scholar, biographer, and historian.

301 *Hobomok: A Tale of Early Times* (1824).

302 *The Rebels; or, Boston before the Revolution* (1825).

303 *The Frugal Housewife: Dedicated to those who are not Ashamed of Economy* (1832).

304 *The Mother's Book* (1831).

305 *The Little Girl's Own Book* was published in 1834, not 1832.

306 *Lives of Madame de Staël, Madame de Roland, Lady Russell, and Madame Guyon*, 2 vols. (1832); *Good Wives* (1832), reprinted as *Biographies of Good Wives* (1843); *A History of the Condition of Women of all Ages and Nations* (1832).

307 *The Coronal: A Collection of Miscellaneous Pieces, Written at Various Times* (1832).

308 *Philothea: A Romance* (1836).

309 Jean-Jacques Barthélemy (1716-1795), *Voyage du Jeune Anacharsis en Grèce. Dans le Milieu du Quatrième Siècle avant L' Ère Vulgaire* (1788).

310 *Fact and Fiction: A Collection of Stories* (1846).

311 "Charity Bowery" (1839).

312 *Letters from New-York* (1843, 1845).

313 Don Giovanni, for example, in the opera by Mozart of than name (1787).

314 Antinous (c.110-130), favourite of the Roman emperor Hadrian (Publius Aelius Hadrianus, 76-138) and deified after he drowned.

315 Melpomene: one of the nine Greek Muses, patron of the lyre and tragedy.

316 *The Marble Faun: or, The Romance of Mount Beni* (1860).

317 "The Snow Image: A Childish Miracle" (1850), in *The Snow Image and Other Twice-Told Tales* (1852).

318 "Preface," *Twice-Told Tales* (1851).

319 Epicurus (341 B.C-270 B.C.), Greek philosopher who extolled the value of simple, ethical, pleasure.

320 "Shakespeare calls moonlight the sunlight sick": not exactly: "This night methinks is but the daylight sick;/ It looks a little paler: 'tis day,/ Such as the day is when the sun is hid"; *The Merchant of Venice*, Act 5, Scene 1.

321 Hepzibah Pyncheon, *The House of the Seven Gables, a Romance* (1851).

322 James Grahame (1790-1842).

323 George Payne Rainsford James (1799-1860), a soldier in the Napoleonic Wars (1792-

1815), popular historian, and romantic novelist; Thackeray parodied him as the "solitary horseman" in his "Barbazure (or Blue-Beard)," which was published in 1847 and appeared in book form as *Novels by Eminent Hands* (1856), because so many of his novels began with two horsemen.

324 These lines by Wordsworth, here truncated, appear twice in his work: a long narrative poem, *The White Doe of Rylstone; or, The Fate of the Nortons* (written in 1807; published, 1815), and *The Borderers: A Tragedy* (written 1786-1787; published, 1842), Act 3: "Action is transitory—a slap, a blow,/ The Motion of a muscle—this way or that—/ 'Tis done, and in the after-vacancy/ We wonder at ourselves like men betrayed:/ Suffering is permanent, obscure and dark,/ And shares the nature of infinity."

325 "The Seven Vagabonds," *Twice-Told Tales* (1837, 1851).

326 "Preface," *The House of the Seven Gables, A Romance* (1851).

327 *The Blithedale Romance* (1852).

328 Franklin Pierce (1804-1869), fourteenth president of the United States; the correct title of Hawthorne's biography is *Life of Franklin Pierce* (1852).

329 *A Wonder-Book for Girls and Boys* (1852); *Tanglewood Tales for Girls and Boys. Being a Second Wonderbook* (1853).

330 Walter Savage Landor (1775-1864), English writer.

331 Sarah Trimmer (1741-1810), editor and principal writer of the *Guardian of Education* (1802-1806).

332 Hugh Blair (1718-1800), Scottish preacher and rhetorician; Richard Hurd (1720-1808), English prelate and writer; Henry Home, Lord Kames (1696-1782), Scottish philosopher; Richard Whately (1787-1863), English Archbishop of Dublin.

333 Natty Bumppo and Uncas, *The Last of the Mohicans* (1826).

334 John Graham of Claverhouse, 1st Viscount Dundee (c.1649-1689), Scottish soldier who enforced Episcopacy (government of the church by bishops) in Scotland under Charles II.

335 *Hours of Idleness. A Series of Poems Original and Translated* (1807).

336 "To a Mountain Daisy on Turning One Down with the Plough in April" (1786).

337 Jedidiah Morse (1761-1826), *Geography Made Easy. Being a Short, but Comprehensive System of That Very Useful and Agreeable Science* (1784); Hannah Adams (1755-1831, often considered the first professional author in America), *History of the Jews, from the Destruction of Jerusalem to the Present Times* (1812).

338 Richard Henry Dana, Sr., *The Idle Man*, appeared in six numbers (1821-1822).

339 Percival, *Poems* (1821); Halleck, *Fanny* (1819); Bryant, *Poems* (1821).

340 William Davis Ticknor (1810-1864).

341 Oliver Wendell Holmes (1809-1894), prodigious man of letters who named the *Atlantic Monthly* at its foundation in 1857; Edwin Percy Whipple (1819-1886), a critic ranked by some at the time with Lowell; John Lothrop Motley (1814-1877), novelist and historian; Charles Anderson Dana (1819-1897), journalist and editor.

342 Shakespeare, *Hamlet*, Act 5, Scene 2: "There's a divinity that shapes our ends,/ Rough-hew them how we will."

343 Frances Wharton, Cecilia Howard, and Alice Munro are characters, respectively, in *The Spy, a Tale of the Neutral Ground* (1821), *The Pilot: A Tale of the Sea.* (1823), and *The Last of the Mohicans: A Narrative of 1757* (1826).

344 Michelangelo: more specifically, Michelangiolo di Lodovico Buoonarroti (1475-1564), Italian sculptor, painter, and poet.

345 Ursula Malbone, *The Chainbearer; or, The Littlepage Manuscripts* (1845) and *The Redskins; or, Indian and Injun: Being the Conclusion of the Littlepage Manuscripts* (1846); Elizabeth Temple, *The Pioneers: or, The Sources of the Susquehanna* (1823).

346 Johann Nepomuk Maelzel (1770-1838), German who patented the metronome and devised, among other delights, a trumpeter automaton; John Paul Jones (1747-1792),

naval commander and hero of the War of Independence.

347 James Logan, known in English as such (c.1725-1780), chief of the Mingo Indians; he refused to make peace after wars consequent on the massacre of his family in 1774; his speech is "reproduced" in Thomas Jefferson's (1743-1826), *Notes on the State of Virginia* (1781-82). William Pitt, 1st earl of Chatham (1708-1778), was dismissed by Sir Robert Walpole, earl of Oxford (1676-1745), supposedly for making a speech full of sarcasm for close on three hours (1736).

348 Magua, *The Last of the Mohicans: A Narrative of 1757* (1826); Chingachgook, *The Deerslayer; or, The First Warpath* (1841), *The Last of the Mohicans: A Narrative of 1757* (1826), and *The Pioneers: or, The Sources of the Susquehanna* (1823); Susquesus, *Satanstoe, a Tale of the Colony* (1845), *The Chainbearer; or, The Littlepage Manuscripts* (1845), and *The Redskins; or, Indian and Injun: Being the Conclusion of the Littlepage Manuscripts* (1846); Tamenund, *The Last of the Mohicans: A Narrative of 1757* (1826); Canonchet, *The Wept of Wish-ton-Wish: A Tale* (1829).

349 Jane Porter (1776-1850), English novelist, *The Scottish Chiefs: An Historical Novel about William Wallace and Robert the Bruce* (1809), and *Thaddeus of Warsaw* (1803).

350 Captain Munson, *The Pilot: A Tale of the Sea* (1823).

351 Milton, *Paradise Lost: A Poem Written in Ten Books* (1667), Book 2.

352 Joseph Mallord William Turner (1775-1851), English artist whose paintings include *The Shipwreck* (1815) and *The Fighting Téméraire* (1839).

353 Walter Scott (1771-1832), *The Monastery* (1820).

354 Antonio, *The Bravo: A Tale* (1831).

355 Alexis, Comte de Tocqueville (1805-1859), French liberal politican and author of *De la démocracie en Amérique* [*Democracy in America*] (1835).

356 The Thirty Years War: a series of conflicts between 1618 and 1648 over Protestant-Catholic rivalries and German constitutional issues which extended into a European-wide conflict.

357 Martin Opitz (1597-1639), German poet.

358 Mars and Apollo, Roman and Greek deities respectively. Gustavus II, or Gustavus Adolphus (1594-1632), came to the Swedish throne in 1611. Magdeburg was stormed on May 20, 1631, amidst great atrocities, by Jan Tserklaes, Count of Tilly (1559-1632), commander of the Catholic army during the Thirty Years' War. Gustavus Adolphus fell in battle at Lützen, near Leipzig, on November 6, 1632.

359 Lope Félix de Vega Carpio (1562-1635) and Pedro Calderón de La Barca (1600-1681), Spanish dramatists and poets.

360 Milton, *Areopagitica: A Speech for the Liberty of Unlicensed Printing* (1644): "an eagle mewing [not "nursing"] her mighty youth."

361 Philip II, Philip-Augustus (1165-1223), French king.

362 The Seven Years' War (1756-1764) saw France, Austria, Sweden, and Russia aligned against Prussia under Fredrick II, the Great (1712-1786); it arose after Frederick seized Silesia in the War of Austrian Succession (1740-1748). Frederick's "Gallic predilections": Frederick played the flute, corresponded with Voltaire, and had Enlightenment proclivities at the cultural level.

363 *Hermann und Dorothea* (1798), by Goethe.

364 After Napoleon was defeated, a peace congress was held in Vienna (1814-1815); its aims were to prevent future French domination.

365 "Know-Nothing Party": the byname of the anti-immigrant, anti-Catholic American Party, which flourished in the 1850s. When asked for information about the organization, members were instructed to say "I know nothing."

366 The Mexican War (April 1846-February 1848) arose as a consequence of the United States' annexation of Texas and resulted in the acquisition of 1,300,000 square kilometres of Mexican territory.

367   Bacon, *Novum Organum; Historia Naturalis et Experimentalis ad Condendam Philosophiam:*
       Sive Phaenomena Universi (1822) [*The New Organon; or, True Directions Concerning the Interpre-*
       tation of Nature].
368   Gray, "Elegy Written in a Country Churchyard" (1751).
369   From the beginning.
370   Quintus Ennius (c.239-169 B.C.) and Lucius Varius (c.74-14 B.C.), Roman poets.
371   Tennyson, *Idylls of the King* (1859).
372   Dora and David Copperfield are characters in Dickens' *The Personal History of David*
       Copperfield (1849-1850). "From honest nature's rule": "Locksley Hall" (1842), by Ten-
       nyson.
373   Shakespeare, *King Richard III*, Act 1, Scene 2.
374   Equal pace; equal development.
375   "Let do": the principle of non-interference.
376   *Discussions on Philosophy and Literature, Education and University Reform: Chiefly from the Ed-*
       inburgh Review; Corrected, Vindicated, Enlarged, in Notes and Appendices (1852).
377   Gebbard Leberecht von Blucher, Prince of Wahlstadt (1742-1819), Prussian field-
       marshall during the Napoleonic Wars (1793-1815).
378   William II, called Rufus (reigned 1087-1100), third, and second surviving son of Wil-
       liam the Conqueror (William 1, 1027-1087); Canute, or Cnut (c.994-1035), king of the
       English, Danes, and Norwegians.
379   Jane Austen (1775-1817), English novelist.
380   George Austen (1731-1805).
381   *Pride and Prejudice: A Novel* (1813).
382   *Journal* (1890).
383   Samuel Egerton Brydges (1762-1837), biographer and author of genealogical works:
       The Autobiography, Times, Opinions, and Contemporaries of Sir Egerton Brydges (1834).
384   Henry Hallam (1777-1859), English historian renowned for his pallid and meticulous
       work.
385   *Mansfield Park: A Novel* (1814).
386   *Persuasion*, written in 1815, was published posthumously in 1818 with *Northanger Abbey*,
       which was sold to a publisher, but neglected thereafter, in 1803.
387   From Samuel Johnson's (1709-1784) "Preface" to his *Dictionary: A Dictionary of the*
       English Language: In Which the Words are Deduced from Their Originals, and Illustrated in their
       Different Significations by Examples from the Best Writers: To which are Prefixed, a History of the
       Language, and an English Grammar (1755).The "well of English undefiled" is also
       Spenser's description of Chaucer in *The Faerie Queene,* Book 4, Canto 2 (1596).
388   *Emma* (1815).
389   *Sense and Sensibility: A Novel* was begun 1797 and published in 1811.
390   George Howard, Lord Morpeth, earl of Carlisle (1773-1848), "The Lady and the
       Novel" (1835).
391   This line should read: "That scarce allowed thy youth to claim."
392   Misquoted: "And Mr. Woodhouse, whose abstemious lip/ Must thin, but not too thin,
       his gruel sip."
393   Mrs. Bennett, *Pride and Prejudice* (1813); Mrs. Norris, *Mansfield Park* (1814); Mr. Wood-
       house and Miss Bates, *Emma* (1815); Mrs. Elton, *Persuasion* (1818).
394   George Henry Lewes (1817-1878), English man of letters.
395   Edward Ferrars. *Sense and Sensibility* (1811); Henry Tilney, *Northanger Abbey* (1818);
       Edmund Bertram, *Mansfield Park* (1818).
396   Uncle Toby is addicted to his military hobby-horse in Sterne's*The Life and Opinions of*
       Tristram Shandy, Gentleman (1760-1767).
397   Harpagon, a character in Molière's *L'Avare* (*The Miser*); Joseph Surface and Sir Lucius
       O'Trigger are, respectively, in Sheridan's, *The School for Scandal* (1877) and *The Rivals*

(1775).

398   In *Mansfield Park* (1814), Fanny's brother, William Price, is a naval officer on the *Thrush.*

399   Admiral Sir Francis Austen (1779-1852).

400   Jacopo Sannazaro (1458-1530), Italian poet; Lucretius, or Titus Lucretius Carus (c.99-55 B.C.), Roman poet; Gaius Valrius Catullus (c.84-c.54 B.C.), Italian lyric poet.

401   The now proverbial question (in relation to a neighbour) "What will Mrs. Grundy say?" is from Tom Morton's (1764-1838) play *Speed the Plough* (1798).

402   Theodore Parker (1810-1860) was ostracized in Boston's orthodox Unitarian circles after he became a Transcendentalist; once installed as a minister of the new Congregational Society of Boston, he spoke from the pulpit against slavery, and for women's rights and other reforms

403   George Eliot, pseudonym of Mary Ann (or Marian) Evans (1819-1880), English novelist: *Adam Bede* (1859).

404   Thomas Cole (1801-1848), *The Voyage of Life: Childhood* (1842).

405   Upstarts.

406   Jean Louis Rodolphe Agassiz (1807-1873), Swiss-born natural scientist and educator. Four volumes of his projected ten-volume *Contributions to the Natural History of the Unites States* (1857-1862) appeared.

407   Nicholas I (1796-1855), emperor of Russia.

408   Phineas Taylor Barnum (1810-1891), American showman who, among other ventures, sponsored the exhibition of the dwarf "General Tom Thumb" (1842).

409   James Bayard Taylor (1825-1878), *Hannah Thurston: A Story of American Life* (1863).

410   Louisa Jane Park Hall (1802-1892), *Miriam: A Dramatic Poem* (1837); Marion Harland, pseudonym of Mary Virginia Hawes Terhune (1830-1922), *Husks* (1863).

411   This must be *selbstabdichtend:* self-sealing; here, clearly articulated sounds.

412   Lowell (1819-1891), *The Biglow Papers:* two series of satirical verses. The first of the verses appeared in *The Boston Courier* (1846) and in book form in 1848; the second, from the *Atlantic Monthly,* was collected in 1867.

413   Seba Smith's collection of essays and tales, *Down East,* appeared in 1855; Gerald Griffin (1803-1840), Irish novelist.

414   Heinrich Heine (1797-1856), German poet and essayist.

415   Dickens, *Bleak House* (1853). Friedrich Anton (or Franz) Mesmer (1734-1815) took up the idea, around 1772, of "animal magnetism"; in Paris, in 1778, he caused a sensation by "curing" diseases in séances; he was denounced as an impostor in 1785.

416   George Fox (1624-1691), founder of the Quakers, or the Society of Friends; Robert Barclay (1648-1690), Scottish Quaker.

417   In Dante's *The Comedy*, later *The Divine Comedy* (c.1314), the Empyrean is the place on the ascent to the heavens where the glory of God can be momentarily glimpsed.

418   The St. Catherine of Alexandria who was tortured on what became known as a Catherine wheel (in 307); Theresa of Ávila (1515-1582), Spanish saint celebrated for her asceticism and ecstasies; St. Clare of Assisi (1194-1235); St. Jane Frances of Chantal (1572-1641).

419   Aspasia (fifth century B.C.), the mistress of Pericles; Marie de France (c.1160-1190), *Lais*; Thais (late fourth century B.C.): a courtesan who travelled with the army of Alexander the Great; Julia (39 B.C.-A.D. 14), the scandalous only child of the Emperor Augustus (62 B.C.-A.D. 14); Fulvia (d. 40 B.C.), in Roman history the wife of Mark Antony (82/81 B.C.-30 B.C.); Messalina Valeria (10 B.C.-A.D. 54), licentious and murderous wife of the Emperor Claudius I (10 B.C.- A.D. 54); Ninon de Lenclos, byname of Anne de Lenclos (1620-1705), notorious French courtesan.

420   Mary Magdalene (first century A.D.), celebrated as the first of the disciples to see the resurrected Christ; St. Mary of Egypt (344-421), who eventually saw the light after

seventeen years of prostitution.

421   "Gyneceum": that part of a large house, among the Greeks, appropriated for the use of women.

422   John Colin Dunlop (1785-1842), *The History of Fiction: Being a Critical Account of the Most Celebrated Works of Prose Fiction* (1814).

423   Prospero, in Shakespeare's *The Tempest* (Act 5, Scene 1), refers to Ariel as his "tricksy spirit."

424   Shakespeare, *Hamlet*, Act 3, Scene 2: "to hold, as 'twere, the mirror up to nature; to show virtue her own feature, scorn her own image, and the very age and body of the time his form and pressure."

425   It is nature, in every respect, that we love and admire; Boileau, *The Art of Poetry* (1680).

426   Alcinous, king of the Phaeacians and father of Nausicaa in Homer's *The Odyssey*.

427   In Greek mythology, Scylla was a female sea-monster who lived in a cave opposite the whirlpool Charybdis; in seeking to avoid one, sailors ran the risk of encountering the other. "Between Scylla and Charybdis": to be between equally unfortunate situations.

428   Charlotte Mary Yonge (1823-1901), *Kenneth; or, The Rear Guard of the Grand Army* (1850); George Walker (1772-1847), *Three Spaniards: A Romance* (1800); Bulwer-Lytton, *A Strange Story: (An Alchemical Novel)* (1863).

429   "Art is the daughter of liberty": Schiller, *On the Education of Man: In a Series of Letters* [*Briefe über die ästhetische Erziehung des Menschen*] (1794).

430   Milton, *Paradise Lost: A Poem Written in Ten Books* (1667), Book 2.

431   Horace, *Ars Poetica* (as the *Epistles to Pisos* was subsequently known): "Aut famam sequere, aut sibi convenientia finge" (*Epistle* III): conventional models of character must be followed, and new characters should be consistent.

432   The two novels of William Wilkie Collins (1824-1889) to appear just prior to this essay are: *The Woman in White: In Three Volumes* (1860) and *No Name: A Novel* (1862); what was to be Mary Elizabeth Braddon's (1837-1915) most popular novel, *Lady Audley's Secret* was published in 1862; Octave Feuillet (1821-1890), French novelist.

433   Shakespeare, *Hamlet,* Act 1, Scene 5: "There are more things in heaven and earth, Horatio,/ Than are dreamt of in your philosophy."

434   Rousseau, *Profession of Faith of a Savoyard Vicar* (1782).

435   The lines are spoken by Philip Faulconbridge, later Sir Richard Plantagenet, the "Bastard" in Shakespeare's *King John* (Act 2, Scene 1).

436   *Aurora Floyd: A Novel* (1863).

437   *The Captain of the Vulture* (1862) was published in the United States as *Darrell Markham; or, The Captain of the Vulture* (1862).

438   Octave Feuillet (1821-1890), *Roman d'un jeune homme pauvre* (1858).

439   Victor Hugo, *Les Misérables* (1862).

440   *Les Misérables* (1862).

441   Alexandre Dumas, in full Alexandre Dumas Davy de la Pailleterie (1802-1870).

442   John William De Forest (1826-1906).

443   Manassas Junction, Virginia saw the first battle of the Civil War (known as "Bull Run" in the north), on July 21, 1861; after ten hours of fighting, with 900 dead, the Union army was defeated and had to retreat to Washington.

444   A rake; profligate.

445   Lord Dalgarno, Scott, *The Fortunes of Nigel* (1822).

446   Charles Reade (1814-1884), English novelist.

447   George Brinton McClellan (1826-1885) was renowned, as an army commander during the Civil War, for his engineering and organizational skills.

448   Benjamin Franklin Butler (1818-1893) occupied New Orleans in April, 1862.

449   Nathaniel Prentiss Banks (1816-1894).

450   "Cracker": a derogatory name given by plantation owners to upcountry farmers who,

here, fought in the War of Independence.

451   Charles I (1600-1649); Charles II (1630-1685), who took the throne on May 29, 1660.

452   William III (1650-1702), William of Orange, reigned 1689-1702.

453   George 1 (1660-1727) and George II (1683-1760), who ascended the throne, respectively, in 1714 and 1727.

454   John George Lambton, earl of Durham (1792-1840); Abraham Cowley (1618-1667), English poet.

455   Venus: Italian goddess associated with cultivation and later identified by the Romans with Aphrodite, the Greek goddess of love; Juvenal, Decimus Junius Juvenalis (55-60?-127?), Roman satiric poet; Atossa was the daughter of Cyrus the Persian (d.529 B.C.) and figures in Pope's "Epistle to a Lady" (1743) as a satiric treatment of the quarrelsome and eccentric Katherine, Duchess of Buckinghamshire (1682-1743); John Evelyn (1620-1706), English diarist and author; Marcus Terrentius Varro (116-27 B.C.), Roman scholar and author; "Calamella" is Lucius Junius Moderatus Columella (first century A.D.), a Roman soldier and farmer who wrote extensively on agriculture.

456   Walt[er] Whitman (1819-1892), American poet.

457   Diana Maria Mulock, Mrs. Craik (1826-1887), American poet and writer of children's stories.

458   The story of the "wandering Jew" was first recorded in the chronicles of Roger Wendover and Matthew of Paris (13th century).

459   Minstrel shows.

460   Stowe, *Dred: A Tale of the Great Dismal Swamp* (1856).

461   John Henry Newman (1801-1890), *Loss and Gain: The Story of a Convert* (1848).

462   Cleveland Coxe (1818-1896), American bishop and author; Henry Edward Manning (1808-1892), second Archbishop of Westminster.

463   Henrietta Camilla Jackson (1807?-1885), *Cousin Stella; or, Conflict* (1859).

464   Eugene Benson (1839-1908), painter, art critic, and essayist.

465   Alfred Billing Street (1811-1881): lawyer, librarian, and poet.

466   Saint Cecilia (2nd or 3rd century Rome), martyr and patroness of music.

467   Drake, "The American Flag," *The Culprit Fay and Other Poems* (1835).

468   James K. Polk (1795-1849) and Zachary Taylor (1784-1850), 11th (1845-1849) and 12th (1849-1850) presidents of the United States respectively.

469   Sir Lancelot: one of the Knights of the Round Table in the Arthurian legend.

470   George Washington was born on February 22, 1732.

471   "Song of Myself," *Leaves of Grass* (1855).

472   Coleridge, "The Rime of the Ancient Mariner" (1798): "'There was a ship,' quoth he."

473   Poe, "Eleanora" (1842), "The Oblong Box" (1850), "The Murders in the Rue Morgue" (1841), "The Fall of the House of Usher" (1839), and "The Black Cat" (1843); Nathaniel Hawthorne (1804-1864). "The Minister's Black Veil" (1837).

474   Harriett Elizabeth Prescott Spofford (1835-1921); "The Assignation" (1835).

475   *Passages from the American Note-books of Nathaniel Hawthorne* (1868).

476   "The Raven" (1845).

477   Charles Pierre Baudelaire (1821-1867), who translated much of Poe's work into French, wrote numerous critical essays on Poe in 1845 and 1846.

478   "And Brutus is an honourable man," Shakespeare's *Julius Caesar,* Act 3, Scene 2.

479   Denis Diderot (1713-1784), French man of letters.

480   The sculpture Venus de Milo (c.150 B.C.), and now in the Louvre, Paris; Aphrodite of Melos, as it was originally called, was found on the Cycladic island of Melos in 1820.

481   "Lenore" (1831); "Morella" (1850).

482   Torquato Tasso, *Gerusalemme Liberata* (1581); Ariosto, *Orlando Furioso* (1516).

483   Ichabod Crane, a character in Washington Irving's (1783-1859) "The Legend of Sleepy Hollow" (1819).

484   Thomas Carlyle, "The Present Time" (1850): "They [the Americans] have doubled
       their population every twenty years. They have begotten, with a rapidity beyond re-
       corded example, Eighteen Millions of the greatest *bores* ever seen in this world be-
       fore,—that hitherto is their feat in History!"
485   Milton, *Comus: A Masque* (1634).
486   Cathay: the name by which China was known to mediaeval Europe.
487   In the Bible, Dan and Beersheba were, respectively, the most northern and southern
       cities in Israel.
488   Stowe, *The Minister's Wooing* (1859).
489   Stowe, *The Pearl of Orr's Island: A Story of the Coast of Maine* (1862).
490   Robert Traill Spence Lowell (1816-1891), *The New Priest in Conception Bay* (1858).
491   Henry David Thoreau (1817-1862).
492   Fra Angelico (c.1400-1455), Italian painter.
493   Henry Headley (1765-1788); John S. C. Abbott (1805-1877); Josiah Gilbert Holland
       (1819-1881).
494   What a time! What morals/manners!
495   Oliver Wendell Holmes (1809-1894), *The Autocrat of the Breakfast-Table* (1858) and *The
       Professor at the Breakfast-Table* (1872).
496   Hippolyte Adolphe Taine (1828-1893), French critic, historian, and philosopher; Louis
       François Veuillot (1813-1883), editor of the (Paris) *L'Univers*, novelist, and poet; Victor
       Henri Rochefort, Marquis de Rochefort-Luçay (1832-1913), French journalist.
497   John Stevens Cabot Abbott (1805-1877), popular (and highly partisan) American his-
       torian; many American newspapers and magazines took *The Ledger* as a title.
498   *Elsie Venner: A Romance of Destiny* (1861) and *The Guardian-Angel* (1861).
499   Wendell Phillips (1811-1884), a prominent Abolitionist and lyceum lecturer.
500   Byles Gridley, a character in *The Guardian-Angel* (1861).
501   Rebecca [Blaire] Harding Davies (1831-1910), *Waiting for the Verdict* (1868).
502   Susan Bogert Warner (1819-1885), *The Hills of the Shatemuc* (1856).
503   Donald Grant Mitchell (1822-1908); Henry Ward Beecher (1813-1887).
504   Anthony Trollope (1815-1882), *The Small House at Allington* (1864).
505   Anne Isabella Thackeray (1837-1919), *The Village on the Cliff* (1866).
506   Manzoni, *I Promessi Sposi* [*The Betrothed*] (1825-1827).
507   The phrase *coelum, non animum* means "the sky, not the mind."
508   Rahel: Rahel Antonie Fredrike Levin (1771-1833; her house in Berlin was the gather-
       ing place of philosophers and writers.
509   David Atwood Wasson (1823-1887), second-generation Transcendentalist minister,
       essayist, and poet.
510   Emerson, "The Humble-Bee" (1846).
511   Andrew Marvell (1621-1678), English poet.
512   Johann Peter Eckermann (1792-1854), German author who assisted Goethe with the
       final editions of his works.
513   King Richard I, Coeur de Lion (1157-1199) and Saladin (d.1193), Muslim sultan of
       Egypt, Syria, Yemen, and Palestine, were protagonists in the Crusades; Saladin cap-
       tured Jerusalem on October 2, 1187.
514   Where there is no delicacy, there is no literature. In writing where there is only force
       and a certain dullness, there is only character depiction.
515   Robert Browning (1812-1889), English poet.
516   George Chapman (1559-1634), English dramatist.
517   Matthew Arnold (1822-1888), *Civilization in the United States: First and Last Impressions of
       America* (1888).
518   Martha Corey was executed as a witch in Salem on September 22, 1692.
519   "Blue Laws": severe laws relating to the regulation of the Sabbath and public morality,

and purportedly implemented by Puritans in seventeenth-century Connecticut. There were no codified examples of such laws until what might well be their fabrication in *A General History of Connecticut* (1782), by Reverend Samuel Peters (1735-1822). The phrase, which has obscure origins, first appeared in an anonymous pamphlet: *The Real Advantages Which Ministers and People May Enjoy, Especially in the Colonies, by Conforming to the Church of England* (1762).

520   Scott, *Minstrelsy of the Scottish Border: Consisting of Historical and Romantic Ballads, Collected in the Southern Counties of Scotland, With a Few of Modern Date, Founded upon Local Tradition* (1802-1803).

521   "Ossoli": Margaret Fuller married the Marquis Angelo Ossoli in Italy.

522   Joseph Isidore Samson (1793-1871), French actor and dramatist.

523   Metta Victoria Victor (1831-1886), author of the antislavery *Maum Guinea and Her Plantation Children; or, Holiday-week on a Louisiana Estate; a Slave Romance* (1862).

524   Melesina Chenevix St. George Trench (1768-1827), *Journal Kept During a Visit to Germany in 1799, 1800,* edited by the Dean of Westminster (1861).

525   Berthold Auerbach (1812-1882), *Auf der Höhe* (1865); translated as *On the Heights: A Novel* (1867).

526   Harriet [Elizabeth] Prescott Spofford (1835-1921), writer of romantic short stories.

527   *Sine qua non*: indispensable; essential.

528   Frank Lee Benedict (1834-1910), *Miss Van Kortland* (1870).

529   Justin McCarthy (1830-1912), *Lady Judith: A Tale of Two Continents* (1871).

530   De Forest, *Overland: A Novel* (1871) and *Kate Beaumont* (1872).

531   Reade, *"It is Never Too Late to Mend"*: *A Matter-of-Fact Romance* (1856). "Juan Fernandez novel": Alexander Selkirk, who inspired Daniel Defoe's (1660-1731), *The Life and Strange and Surprising Adventures of Robinson Crusoe* (1719), deliberately marooned himself on Mas a Tierra, the Juan Fernandez Islands (now Robinson Crusoe Island).

532   Thackeray, *The History of Henry Esmond, Esq., A Colonel in the Service of Her Majesty Queen Anne* (1852).

533   Stowe, *Pink and White Tyranny: A Society Novel* (1871) and *My Wife and I; or, Harry Henderson's History* (1871).

534   Robert Burton (1577-1640), *The Anatomy of Melancholy, What It Is: With all the Kindes, Causes, Symptomes, Prognostickes, and Severall Cures of It: In Three Maine Partitions with their Seuerall Sections, Members, and Subsections: Philosophically, Medicinally, Historically, Opened and Cut Up* (1621).

535   Henry Ward Beecher, *Norwood; or, Village Life in New England* (1868).

536   Stowe, *Oldtown Folks* (1869).

537   Albert Bierstadt (1830-1902), German-born American artist; "Millet": John Everett Millais (1829-1896), English painter.

538   Maria Jourdan Westmoreland (1815-?), *Heart-Hungry: A Novel.*

539   George Eliot, *Middlemarch: A Study in Provincial Life* (1871-1872) and *Romola* (1863).

540   *Entraînant*: captivating, seductive.

541   *Ménage*: household.

542   *Silas Marner: The Weaver of Ravenhoe* (1861); Charles Robert Darwin (1809-1882), scientist notorious for his theories of evolution and natural selection; Thomas Henry Huxley (1825-1895), propagator of Darwin's ideas.

543   Tawny grisette (*amanita fulva*) is a fungus; the term was also used in Paris for women of uncertain morality.

544   François Rabelais (1494?-1553) published his *Les horribles et épouvantables faits et prouesses du très renommé Pantagruel, roy des Dipsodes* "The Horrible and Terrifying Deeds and Words of the Renowned Pantagruel, King of the Dipsodes," (1532) under an anagram of his name, "Alcofri bas Nasier"; there followed *Pantagrueline prognostication* (1533), *La vie inestimable du grand Gargantua* ("The Inestimable Life of the Great Gargantua,"

probably 1534), and *Tiers livre des faits et dits héroïques du noble Pantagruel* ("Third Book of the Heroic Deeds and Words of the Noble Pantagruel," 1546). He was a novice of the Franciscan order, his patron being the Bishop of Maillezais, until he entered the University of Montpelier in 1530.

545   Mark Twain (meaning "two fathoms deep" from Twain's days on Mississippi riverboats) was the pseudonym of Samuel Langhorne Clemens (1835-1810); [Francis] Bret[t] Harte (1836-1902); John [Milton] Hay (1838-1905). Twain, Harte, and Jay were noted for their fictions of the frontier.

546   "One touch of nature makes the whole world kin [not "akin"]: Shakespeare, *Troilus and Cressida*, Act 3, Scene 3.

547   The means by which the disciples of Christ transmitted the Holy Spirit: "So after they had fasted and prayed, they placed their hands on them and sent them off" (Acts 13: 3).

548   "The Celebrated Jumping Frog of Calaveras" (1865); Clemens gathered these pieces together in *Roughing It* (1872).

549   "Dolce far niente": sweet doing nothing. *The Celebrated Jumping Frog of Calaveras County, and Other Sketches* (1867).

550   *The Innocents Abroad; or, The New Pilgrims Progress* (1869).

551   Mark Twain and Charles Dudley Warner (1829-1900), *The Gilded Aged: A Tale of Today* (1873).

552   Thackeray, *Sketches and Travels in London* (1847); these articles originally appeared in *Punch*.

553   Charles Dudley Warner, *Backlog Studies* (1873) and *Saunterings* (1872).

554   Heliodorus's (3rd century A.D.) *Aethiopica* tells the story of Theagenes and Chariclea.

555   Matteo Bandello (c.1480-1562), Italian writer of tales.

556   Cervantes, *Galatea* (1585); Cervantes referred to his "short stories" as *Novelas exemplares* ("Exemplary Novels").

557   Ben Jonson, *Bartholomew Fair* (1614); a play.

558   Thomas Lodge (c.1558-1625) and Robert Greene (1558-1592), English dramatists and romancers.

559   *Amelia* (1751).

560   *The Mill on the Floss* (1860).

561   Ralph Nickleby, *The Life and Adventures of Nicholas Nickleby* (1838-1839); Jonas Chuzzlewith, *The Life and Adventures of Martin Chuzzlewit* (1843-1844); Merdle, *Little Dorritt* (1855-1857); Chadband, *Bleak House* (1853); Uriah Heep, *The Personal History of David Copperfield* (1849-1850).

562   Thackeray, *The Adventures of Philip on his Way Through the World, Showing Who Robbed Him, Who Helped Him and Who Passed Him By* (1861-1862).

563   Herbert Spencer (1820-1903), English evolutionary philosopher.

564   Robert Browning (1812-1889), *The Ring and the Book* (1869).

565   Ivan Segeyevitch Turgenev (1818-1883), *Smoke* (1867).

566   Wilkie Collins, *The New Magdalen: A Novel* (1873).

567   Rousseau, *Julie; ou, la nouvelle Héloïse* [*Julie: or, The New Eloise*] (1761) and *Émile* (1762).

568   Goethe, *Novelle* (1827).

569   Goethe, *Die Leiden des jungen Werthers* [*The Sorrows of Young Werther*] (1774).

570   Shakespeare, *King Richard III*, Act 1, Scene 1.

571   *Peg Woffington* (1853).

572   *Love Me Little, Love Me Long* (1859).

573   "End Man": one of the two men at the extremities of a line of minstrels.

574   Bulwer-Lytton, *My Novel; or, Varieties in English Life "by Pisistratus Caxton"* (1850-1853).

575   Bulwer-Lytton, *Pelham; or, The Adventures of a Gentleman* (1828), *Eugéne Aram: A Tale* (1822), and *The Lady of Lyons; or, Love and Pride: A Play in Five Acts* (1838).

576 James Boswell (1740-1795), *The Life of Samuel Johnson, LL.D., Comprehending an Account of his Studies and Numerous Works, a Series of his Epistolary Correspondence and Conversations and Various Original Pieces of his Composition Never Before Published* (1791): "Sir, (continued he) there is all the difference in the world between characters of nature and characters of manners; and *there* is the difference between the characters of Fielding and those of Richardson. Characters of manners are very entertaining; but they are to be understood, by a more superficial observer, than characters of nature, where a man must dive into the recesses of the human heart."

577 Firm opinions.

578 Shakespeare, *Macbeth*, Act 1, Scene 7.

579 *Les Travailleurs de la mer* [*Workers of the Sea*] (1866).

580 *Les Misérables* (1862).

581 "Romeo and Juliet," *Lectures on Shakespeare* (1811-1812).

582 *Rudin* (1856); translated in French as *Dimitri Roudine*.

583 Shakespeare, *As You Like It*, Act 2, Scene 7: "And then the justice,/ In fair round belly with good capon lined,/ With eyes severe and beard of formal cut,/ Full of wise saws and modern instances;/ And so he plays his part."

584 Björnstjerne Björnson (1832-1910), Norwegian playwright and novelist: *The Fisher Maiden* (1868).

585 Jemima Montogmery Tautphoeus (1807-1893), *The Initials: A Novel* (1850).

586 Georg Wilhelm Friedrich Hegel (1770-1831), German idealist philosopher.

587 Alexandr Sergeyevitch Pushkin (1799-1837) and Mikhail Yurevitch Lermontov (1814-1841).

588 *Récits d'un chasseur* (Paris, 1870) [*Sportsman's Sketches*, 1852.]

589 Nikolai Vasilievich Gogol (1809-1852), Russian novelist and dramatist.

590 Pauline García-Viardot (1821-1910), Spanish mezzo-soprano (and life-long friend of Turgenev) married Louis Viardot, then director of the Théâtre Italien in Paris, in 1840.

591 Turgenev added various stories to his *Sportsmen's Sketches* into the 1870's.

592 "Moumou": "Mumu" (1852); "A Correspondence" (1856).

593 "The Antchar," *Galaxy*, 15 (1873).

594 "Faust: A Story in Nine Letters" (1859).

595 *The Spring Floods* [or *Spring* Torrents] (1872); On *the Eve* (1860).

596 Shelley, "Ode to a Skylark" (1820).